ANNUAL REVIEW OF IRISH LAW 2007

Annual Review
of Irish Law 2007

Raymond Byrne
B.C.L., LL.M., Barrister-at-Law
Director of Research, Law Reform Commission
Lecturer in Law, Dublin City University

William Binchy
B.A., B.C.L., LL.M., F.T.C.D., Barrister-at-Law
Regius Professor of Laws, Trinity College, Dublin

ROUND HALL

 **THOMSON REUTERS**

Published in 2008 by
Thomson Reuters (Professional) Ireland Limited
(Registered in Ireland, Company No. 80867.
Registered Office and address for service:
43 Fitzwilliam Place, Dublin 2)
trading as Round Hall

Typeset by
Gough Typesetting Services
Dublin

Printed by
MPG Cornwall

ISBN 978-1-85800-496-9
ISSN 0791-1084

A catalogue record for this book
is available from the British Library

Thomson Reuters and the Thomson Reuters Logo are trademarks of
Thomson Reuters. Round Hall is a registered trademark of Thomson
Reuters (Professional) Ireland Limited.

Table of Contents

Preface

This is the twenty-first volume in the Annual Review series, and as with previous volumes, our purpose continues to be to provide a review of legal developments, judicial and statutory, that occurred in 2007.

We are conscious of the many changes that have occurred in the period over two decades since the first Annual Review was published, notably in the increasing volume of legislation enacted by the Oireachtas and the consequent increase in secondary legislation. We are equally aware of the increasing volume of case law that emerges each year from the courts and which we assess in each annual volume. Accessibility to this increasing volume of material has changed beyond recognition in recent years, in particular with the advent of electronic sources for both legislation and case law. We appreciate that this will remain an issue requiring constant attention in the years ahead and we merely note here the importance that legal researchers, practitioners and the general public attach to this. We must also record here our particular thanks to the many specialist contributors who have added their particular insights to the various chapters of the Annual Review volumes in recent years and also to our many colleagues whose assistance in ways too numerous to note, have eased the burden of analysing the legislation and case law discussed here.

Returning to this volume, in terms of legislation, we endeavour to discuss those Acts and statutory instruments enacted and made during the year. In terms of case law, this includes those judgments delivered in 2007, regardless of whether they have been (or will be) reported and which were available to us and our contributors by mid-2008.

Once again it is a pleasure to thank those who made the task of completing this volume less onerous. For this twenty-first volume of the Annual Review series, we are delighted to have had the benefit of specialist contributions on Asylum and Immigration Law, Company and Insolvency Law, Constitutional Law, Contract Law, Employment, Equity, Evidence, Information Law and the Ombudsman, Land Law, Landlord and Tenant Law and Conveyancing, Legislation, Planning Law, Practice and Procedure, Probate and Succession Law, Social Welfare Sports Law and Whistleblower Protection included in this volume. We continue to take final responsibility for the overall text as in the past, but are especially grateful for the contributions of Nuala Egan and Patricia Brazil in Asylum and Immigration Law, Grainne Callanan in Company and Insolvency Law, Oran Doyle and Estelle Feldman in Constitutional Law, Fergus Ryan in Contract Law, Desmond Ryan in Employment Law, Brian Tobin in Equity, Liz Heffernan in Evidence, Estelle Feldman in Information Law and the Ombudsman and Whistleblower Protection, Fiona de Londras in Land Law, Landlord and Tenant Law and Conveyancing, Brian Hunt in Legislation, Garrett Simons in Planning and Development Law, Melody Buckley and Martin Canny in Practice and Procedure, Albert Keating in Probate and Succession Law, Gerry Whyte in Social Welfare and Neville Cox in Sports Law.

Finally, we are very grateful to Round Hall, in particular Frieda Donoghue, Maura Smyth, Terri McDonnell, Stephen Lucek and Nicola Barrett, and to Gough Typesetting Services, whose professionalism ensures the continued production of this series.

Raymond Byrne and William Binchy,
Dublin
November 2008

Table of Cases

IRELAND

EUROPEAN COURT OF JUSTICE

EUROPEAN COURT OF HUMAN RIGHTS

ENGLAND AND WALES

NORTHERN IRELAND

AUSTRALIA

CANADA

NEW ZEALAND

SINGAPORE

UNITED STATES of AMERICA

Table of Legislation

Statutory Instruments

EUROPEAN LEGISLATION

INTERNATIONAL TREATIES AND CONVENTIONS

ENGLAND AND WALES

NORTHERN IRELAND

UNITED STATES of AMERICA

Administrative Law

APPROPRIATION

The Appropriation Act 2007 provided as follows. For the year ended December 31, 2007, the amount of supply grants in accordance with the Central Fund (Permanent Provisions) Act 1965 was €45,148,322,000. Under the Public Accounts and Charges Act 1891, the sum for appropriations-in-aid was €4,154,313,000. The 2007 Act also provided, in accordance with s.91 of the Finance Act 2004, for carrying over into the year ending December 31, 2007 undischarged appropriations for capital supply services totalling €126,119,000. This, in effect, allowed this amount, which had not been spent on, for example, large infrastructure projects in 2007, to be carried over into 2008. The 2007 Act also provided that the financial resolutions passed by Dáil Éireann on December 5, 2007 (after the 2007 Budget) would have legal effect provided that, in accordance with s.4 of the Provisional Collection of Taxes Act 1927, legislation was enacted in 2008 (in the Finance Act 2008) to give full effect to the resolutions. The 2007 Act came into effect on its signature by the President on December 21, 2007.

GOVERNMENT DEPARTMENTS

Department of Community, Rural and Gaeltacht Affairs   The main purpose of the Community, Rural and Gaeltacht Affairs (Miscellaneous Provisions) Act 2007 was to confirm and secure an integrated statutory basis for the broad range of functions and responsibilities of the Minister for Community, Rural and Gaeltacht Affairs. The 2007 Act provided a clearer statutory mandate for functions previously transferred to the Minister by way of Transfer of Functions Orders made under the Ministers and Secretaries Acts, along with new programmes introduced since the establishment of the Department in 2002.

The main elements of the 2007 Act are: to confirm the powers, functions and responsibilities of the Minister; to provide for the inclusion, in the Third Schedule in the Freedom of Information Act 1997, of s.18 of the Western Development Commission Act 1998; to amend s.8(5) of the Western Development Commission Act 1998, raising to €1 million the limit of financial or other material aid to enterprises or projects, which the WDC can provide without the consent of the Minister; to amend s.2(4) of the Minister for

Community, Rural and Gaeltacht Affairs (Powers and Functions) Act 2003 in respect of transport services for islands students and ss.3(1)(b) and 3(1)(c) of the 2003 Act in respect of clarifying the Minister's remit in respect of specified functions in respect of new aerodromes and ancillary facilities connected with the provision of air services between the islands and the mainland; and to repeal the Arramara Teoranta (Acquisition of Shares) Acts 1949 to 2002.

Section 2 of the 2007 Act states that the range of functions set out are, and are deemed always to have been, functions of the Minister for Community, Rural and Gaeltacht Affairs. The range of functions outlined includes: community development; voluntary activity and philanthropy; rural development; co-ordination of the national drugs strategy; the Irish language, including the co-ordination of policy in this regard; the development of the Gaeltacht and the islands; and North–South co-operation within the ambit of these functions, including matters in relation to Ulster Scots heritage, culture and language.

This provision is without prejudice to the generality of any other provision of the 2007 Act or of any other enactment conferring functions on the Minister. In other words, the provisions in the 2007 Act do not affect any other existing statutory provisions in relation to the functions of the Minister. In addition, the 2007 Act provides for powers to develop, implement, maintain, expand or terminate any scheme that, in the Minister's opinion, supports or promotes the functions set out in the 2007 Act. Curiously, the 2007 Act makes no reference to the Ministers and Secretaries Acts, which are the legal foundation stones for all Government Departments.

Ministers of State   The Ministers and Secretaries (Ministers of State) Act 2007 was required to give effect to the decision by the Government to increase the maximum number of Ministers of State (junior Ministers) from 17 to 20 (the maximum number of Ministers is fixed at 15 by Art.28.1 of the Constitution). Prior to the 2007 Act, the number of Ministers of State had remained unchanged since 1995, when s.1 of the Ministers and Secretaries (Amendment) Act 1995 increased the maximum from 15 to 17. The key reasons advanced for the 2007 Act was, as in 1995, that of workload. It was stated that, since 1995, the quantum and quality of ministerial work had increased significantly as a result of the greater complexity of the policy agenda, the management pressures in giving political direction to extensive Government programmes, and the increased engagement with stakeholders at all levels, both domestically and in Europe. In addition, it was noted that a Minister of State may receive delegated legislative powers from a Minister in accordance with the Ministers and Secretaries (Amendment) (No. 2) Act 1977. These arguments were disputed by the opposition parties in the Oireachtas, but the changes effected by the 2007 Act have been implemented in practice. At the time of writing (September 2008), the new Government elected in the wake of the 2007 general election continues to contain 20 Ministers of State.

JUDICIAL REVIEW

Much of the case law under Ord.84 of the Rules of the Superior Courts 1986 that arose in 2007 is discussed in the various chapters in this *Annual Review* where the substantive subjects arising are detailed, notably in the Immigration and Planning Law chapters. Further reference may also be obtained through the Table of Statutory Instruments under the entry for the Rules of the Superior Courts 1986.

Asylum and Immigration Law

PATRICIA BRAZIL B.L., Lecturer in Law, Trinity College Dublin
and
NUALA EGAN B.L.

CASE LAW

Application of principle of family unity in refugee application procedure   The extent to which the principle of family unity can be used in the context of the refugee application procedure was considered by the Supreme Court in *AN v Minister for Justice, Equality and Law Reform* [2007] I.E.S.C. 44, Supreme Court, October 18, 2007. The first named applicant was the mother of the second to sixth named applicants and appellants. The proceedings related to deportation orders made in respect of the appellants by the Minister for Justice on August 2, 2002. There was a single legal point at the centre of the appeal. The deportation orders were explicitly made on the basis that each appellant was "a person in respect of whom a deportation order may be made" pursuant to the provisions of s.3(2)(f) of the Immigration Act 1999. That provision relates to "a person whose application for asylum has been refused by the Minister". The question was whether an application for asylum made by the appellants had been refused by the Minister. The first named applicant had applied for asylum, but no separate applications were made for the children. The Minister had a policy of treating such an application as having been made by the family. None of the communications emanating from the Minister or the Refugee Appeals Tribunal, up to and including the refusal of the first named applicant's application, referred to any application by the appellants. They were, however, given notice of the Minister's intention to make deportation orders in respect of them.

The appellants obtained leave from the High Court (Finlay Geoghegan J.) on November 5, 2003 to seek judicial review of those decisions on the single ground that the deportation orders were invalid in that the second to sixth named applicants were not on that date persons whose applications for asylum had been refused by the Minister within the meaning of s.3(2)(f) of the Immigration Act 1999. Peart J. in a judgment dated May 26, 2004, dismissed the application of the appellants for judicial review and certified pursuant to s.5(3)(a) of the Illegal Immigrants Trafficking Act 2000 that his decision involved points of law of exceptional public importance and granted leave to appeal against his decision to the appellants.

The appellants submitted that there was no investigation into the capacity of the children to apply separately or to be heard and that no efforts were made to interview the children. The Minister pointed to the fact that no complaint was made by or on behalf of the appellants that they were not persons in respect of whom refusal orders had been made. The Minister also submitted that by virtue of the language of the relevant sections of the Refugee Act 1996, only a single individual could make an asylum application. Fennelly J. was not satisfied that this was correct, holding that "a single application could, in principle, be made on behalf of a number of persons, particularly where they are members of one family".

It was held by Fennelly J. that there was no application for asylum made by or on behalf of the appellants, nor was there a record of any decision refusing an asylum application on behalf of any of the appellants. The only conceivably relevant decision made by the Minister was that dated August 23, 2000 which was addressed only to the first named applicant and was not addressed to the appellants. Fennelly J. was satisfied that:

> "[T]hat decision could not be treated as being a decision to refuse an application by the appellants without doing violence to its clear terms. In my view, it is incapable of being read as a decision relating to the appellants."

On that basis alone, it was held that the claim of the appellants was "unanswerable"—it was clear that there was never an application for asylum by or on behalf of the second to sixth named appellants.

Fennelly J. noted that the essence of the Minister's defence was that he applied a policy of family unity in accordance with para.213 of the UNHCR Handbook on Procedures and Criteria for Determining Refugee Status, which provides:

> "If a minor is accompanied by one (or both) of his parents, or another family member on whom he is dependent, who requests refugee status, the minor's own refugee status will be determined according to the principle of family unity".

The Minister relied on this statement to justify treating the application of the first named applicant as being an asylum application on behalf of the family. Fennelly J. accepted that there was no question but that asylum seekers arrive in the State as family groups, and that there was equally no question but that the principle of family unity is central to asylum and immigration practices and policies:

> "The most obvious consequence is that, where an asylum seeker is accompanied by his or her children of tender years and such a person is accorded refugee status, it quite obviously enures to the benefit of the

children. Paragraph 184 of the same Handbook states: 'If the head of the family meets the criteria his dependants are normally granted refugee status according to the principle of family unity.' It would be simply inhuman to permit a person to remain in the State and to expel or deport his children. Clearly, that is the principle underlying the Minister's policy. As described, it is a proper and reasonable policy."

However, Fennelly J. noted that the difficulty was the Minister's assumption that the converse was true:

"[H]e extrapolates from the principle that a favourable asylum decision benefits other family members the further untenable proposition that a decision which is unfavourable to one is unfavourable to all.".

Reference was made to para.185 of the handbook, which states that "the principle of family unity operates in favour of dependents and not against them."

Fennelly J. noted that the Minister's policy was to treat the application of the first named applicant as having been made also on behalf of the appellants, and thus to treat them all as a family unit. It was held that such a policy would be reasonable, but that as a matter of fact the Minister did not act in accordance with such policy, by reason of the fact that at no stage in the asylum process did any document emanating from or required by the Minister advert to the existence of applications on behalf of the appellants. Because there was no decision to refuse the appellants asylum, it was held that the claimed basis for the exercise of the power to make the deportation orders did not exist and that those orders were invalid. The Supreme Court allowed the appeals, set aside the judgment of the High Court and made an order of certiorari quashing each of the deportation orders.

Challenge to refusal of residency application by non-national parents of Irish citizen children pursuant to "IBC/05 scheme" As noted in the *Annual Review of Irish Law 2005* (pp.11–12), on January 14, 2005 the Minister for Justice announced revised arrangements for the processing of claims for permission to remain from the non-national parents of Irish children who were born before January 1, 2005, known as the "IBC/05 scheme". The Minister applied fixed criteria in deciding these applications, primarily (a) continuous residency in the State since the birth of the Irish child; (b) evidence of good character since birth of the Irish child; (c) evidence of involvement in upbringing of child. In practice, failure to satisfy the Minister of any one of these criteria resulted in the application for residency being refused. A total of 17,917 applications were received and processed under the IBC/05 Scheme, and on the basis of the cases completed by January 31, 2006, 16,693 applicants were given leave to remain with refusal decisions given in 1,119 cases. The manner in which the scheme was applied was challenged in a number of test cases, with the lead decision being that of *Bode v Minister for Justice*, unreported, High Court, November 14, 2006. (The related cases were *Adio v Minister for Justice, Equality and Law Reform; Dimbo v Minister for Justice, Equality and Law Reform; Duman v Minister for Justice, Equality and Law Reform; Edet v Minister for Justice, Equality and Law Reform; Fares v Minister for Justice, Equality and Law Reform; Oguekwe v Minister for Justice, Equality and Law Reform;* and *Oviawe v Minister for Justice, Equality and Law Reform.* Supplementary judgments in each of these proceedings were also delivered by Finlay Geoghegan J. on November 14, 2006. The decision of Finlay Geoghegan J. in these proceedings is considered in Byrne & Binchy (eds), *Annual Review of Irish Law 2006* (Dublin: Thomson Round Hall, 2007), pp.11–16).

Finlay Geoghegan J. granted each of the applicants' orders of *certiorari* quashing the decision of the Minister to refuse their applications for residency under the scheme on the basis that the Minister's explicit refusal to consider the best interests of the child when examining an application for residency under IBC/05 was a breach of the constitutional rights of the citizen child and failed to observe the key principles set out by the Supreme Court in *L & O v Minister for Justice, Equality and Law Reform* [2003] 1 I.R. 1. The respondent appealed against this decision to the Supreme Court.

Denham J. delivered the judgment of the Supreme Court, and commenced by reiterating that the power of the State to control the entry, residence and exit of foreign nationals is an aspect of the executive power to protect the integrity of the State, which power is exercised by the Minister for Justice on behalf of the State. It was held that the IBC/05 scheme was introduced by the Minister, exercising the executive power of the State, to address in an administrative and generous manner a unique situation which had occurred in relation to a significant number of foreign nationals within the State. However, it was held that those who did not succeed on their application under this scheme remained in the same situation as they had been prior to their application, and were still entitled to have the Minister consider the constitutional and Convention rights of all relevant persons. Thus, Denham J. held:

> "The scheme enabled a fast, executive decision, giving a benefit to very many people. However, a negative decision in the IBC 05 Scheme did not affect any substantive claim for permission to remain in the State. In other words, an adverse decision to an applicant under the IBC 05 Scheme left the applicant in no worse position than he or she was prior to the application as no decision had been made on any substantive rights."

By reason of such finding, the Supreme Court held that "the basic premise of the applicants, and of the High Court, that the Constitutional and Convention rights of the applicants were in issue in the IBC 05 Scheme, was misconceived." Denham J. held that by reason of the nature of the scheme as an exercise of executive power which did not purport to address constitutional or Convention rights, much of the pleadings, judgment and submissions related to matters not in issue. In particular, it was held that:

> "As the IBC 05 Scheme did not address Constitutional or Convention rights applicants who were not successful were left in exactly the same position as they had been prior to their application. There was no interference with any Constitutional or Convention rights. Consequently, it was an error on behalf of the High Court to consider the application of the scheme as an arena for decision making on Constitutional or Convention rights, whether they be, as considered by the High Court: (1) the rights of the child under Articles 40.3 and 41 of the Constitution; (2) Rights under article 8 of the European Convention on Human Rights; or, (3) Rights under article 14 of the Convention; or other rights."

Thus, in so far as the issue of rights under the Constitution and the Convention were considered and decisions made on these issues by the High Court, it was held by Denham J. to be a premature analysis, as these rights would fall to be considered by the Minister in the context of s.3 of the Immigration Act 1999.

The extent to which this view is correct must be queried. Section 3 of the Immigration Act 1999 sets out the powers of the Minister in relation to deportation. Prior to making a deportation order in respect of certain specified categories of persons, the Minister is required to issue a proposal to deport and to invite representations as to why a deportation order should not be made. The Supreme Court in *Bode* held that this process would address the constitutional and Convention rights of Irish citizen children and their families, and that no free-standing application for residence was required. It is unclear why an Irish citizen child should be required to await a proposal from the Minister to deport his or her parents in order to be permitted to assert his or her rights guaranteed under both the Constitution and the Convention. Furthermore, there is no limitation period specified by s.3 within which the Minister must issue a proposal to deport, which could result in an Irish citizen child and his or her family being left in a state of limbo, unable to assert their rights and/or to have such rights considered by the Minister. This aspect of the s.3 process does not appear to have been considered by the Supreme Court, and the compatibility of such approach with the rights of citizen children under both the Constitution and Convention must surely be questioned.

[**Note:** The Supreme Court reserved its judgment as to whether the Minister was entitled to make deportation orders in respect of the parents of Irish citizen children whose non-national parents were refused residence under the IBC/05 scheme. The court delivered a separate judgment in respect of this issue in *Oguekwe v Minister for Justice, Equality and Law Reform* [2008] I.E.S.C. 25, Supreme Court, May 1, 2005. It was held that the Minister had not properly considered the constitutional and Convention rights of the applicants in making the deportation orders, and had failed to conduct an express consideration of, and a reasoned decision on, the rights of the Irish citizen child. Accordingly, the Minister's appeal against the decision of the High Court to grant certiorari in respect of the deportation orders was refused.]

Correct test to be applied in determining application for permission to make fresh application for asylum pursuant to s.17(7) of the Refugee Act 1996 The High Court addressed the correct test to be applied to an application pursuant to s.17(7) of the Refugee Act 1996 in the substantive application in *COI v Minister for Justice, Equality and Law Reform* [2007] I.E.H.C 180, [2007] 2 I.L.R.M. 471. The applicant arrived in Ireland on September 1, 2003 with his sister-in-law with whom he resided as part of a family unit in Nigeria. They both applied for asylum simultaneously. The Refugee Applications Commissioner recommended that the applicant's application be refused and he was notified accordingly by letter dated September 8, 2004. The applicant appealed to the Refugee Appeals Tribunal but was unsuccessful. By letter dated May 26, 2005 the applicant's legal representatives made an application seeking the permission of the Minister to make a further application for a declaration of refugee status pursuant to s.17(7) of the Refugee Act 1996. The application was made on the basis of fresh evidence directly relevant to the applicant's application for refugee status. The fresh evidence was the fact that the Refugee Appeals Tribunal made a decision in favour of the applicant's sister-in-law subsequent to the decision in the applicant's case. The facts relating to the two applications were almost directly identical. By letter dated July 21, 2005 the Minister refused the applicant's request on the grounds that the new evidence submitted did not significantly add to the likelihood of the applicant qualifying for asylum on the totality of the evidence already available and considered, and that each asylum application is assessed on its own individual merits and, consequently, comparisons cannot be accepted as having relevance.

On May 12, 2006 the applicant was granted leave by the High Court (MacMenamin J.) to challenge the refusal to permit the applicant to make a further application for a declaration of refugee status on the basis of fresh evidence. (The decision of MacMenamin J. granting leave to seek judicial review in *COI v Minister for Justice, Equality and Law Reform*, unreported, High Court, May 5, 2006 is discussed in Byrne & Binchy (eds), *Annual Review of Irish Law 2006* (Dublin: Thomson Round Hall, 2007), pp.18–20). McGovern J. commenced by addressing the correct test to be applied to an application pursuant to s.17(7) of the 1996 Act. It was held that it was clear from the preamble to the Refugee Act 1996 that the State, in seeking to give effect to the Geneva Convention and other Conventions mentioned therein, assumed certain obligations and accepted the application of these Conventions to the treatment of refugees save and in so far as the 1996 Act and subsequent legislation imposed controls on the manner in which the Convention is implemented. McGovern J. also addressed the appropriate standard to be applied when reviewing decisions pursuant to s.17(7), and in particular whether such proceedings should proceed on the traditional "*Wednesbury*" test, or whether a higher level of scrutiny ought to be applied. It was held by McGovern J. that:

> "Since the purpose of the 1996 Act, is, *inter alia*, to give effect to the Geneva Convention and other related conventions on the treatment of refugees I think the test of 'anxious scrutiny' is one which the courts should use as well as the *O'Keeffe* principles when considering matters of this kind. Of course if a decision is made on irrational grounds it will be susceptible to legal challenge. But there may be cases which might not come within the *O'Keeffe* definitions of irrationality but might legitimately fall to be reviewed by the courts."

Turning to the present case, it was held that objectively there was a connection between the experience of the applicant and his sister-in-law whose application was accepted. McGovern J. noted that it could not therefore be said that comparisons between the applicant and his sister-in-law were not relevant. It was accepted that it did not necessarily follow that the decision should be the same in each case, but at the very least the comparison was deemed to be relevant to the determination of the nature of the persecution said to be feared. On that basis, McGovern J. concluded that in the context of this application the Minister was in error in stating that comparisons cannot be accepted as having relevance:

> "How can it confidently be said that the reasoning in the applicant's case was correct when his sister-in-law achieved a different result on the same facts and in circumstances where there were so many common features between the two applicants based on their relationship and family history? It cannot be conducive to the proper conduct of the asylum process if this should occur. How can the applicant in this case not feel a sense of injustice if his application has been refused when that of his sister-in-law on the same facts has been accepted? At the very least it gives rise to a legitimate cause for concern and would warrant a review of the case."

In those circumstances, McGovern J. held that the correct test in relation to an application pursuant to s.17(7) of the 1996 Act "is to show that there is a reasonable prospect of a favourable view being taken of the new claim despite the unfavourable conclusions reached on the earlier claim having regard to the additional information available", endorsing the decision of the Court of Appeal in *R. v Secretary of State for the Home Department, ex p. Onibiyo* [1996] Q.B. 768. In the light of the application of an incorrect test by the Minister to the s.17(7) application, McGovern J. granted an order of certiorari quashing the refusal of the Minister to permit the applicant make a further application for a declaration of refugee status.

Entitlement to make application for subsidiary protection under new Regulations   The effect of the Qualification Directive (Directive 2004/83/EC) and implementing domestic Regulations in respect of subsidiary protection applications was addressed in *NH v Minister for Justice* and *TD v Minister for Justice*, unreported, High Court, July 27, 2007 (Feeney J.). The applicants in their judicial review proceedings sought relief arising out of the coming into effect of Council Directive 2004/83/EC of April 29, 2004. The Directive was implemented into Irish law by the European Communities (Eligibility for Protection) Regulations 2006 (S.I. No. 518 of 2006). In both cases the Minister refused to consider applications for subsidiary protection under the Regulations. Each applicant sought an order of certiorari quashing these decisions of the Minister. Each applicant also sought an order of mandamus directing the Minister to accept and process their application. In both cases the Minister claimed that the Regulations had no application to the particular applicants as both of them were persons in respect of whom a deportation order was issued prior to the coming into force of the Regulations on October 10, 2006 and that there was no obligation on the State under the Directive to re-open or reconsider decisions made prior to October 10, 2006. Further it was contended that, in any event, in considering both the applicants' cases prior to the making of the deportation orders, that the authorities necessarily considered whether there was a risk that such applicant would be exposed to serious harm if returned to their home State.

An issue between the parties in these cases related to whether or not the Directive created a right to apply for subsidiary protection, as contended for by the applicants, rather than doing nothing more than laying down minimum standards to be applied under existing procedures, as contended for by the Minister. It was also the Minister's case that the authorities in the State necessarily considered whether there was a risk to the applicants when the Minister considered each of the applicants' written submissions seeking to remain and also considered the issue of refoulement. It was contended on behalf of the Minister that it was not the purpose of the Directive to impose new protection obligations on Member States and that the Directive was proposed in the interest of harmonisation of the rules of the Member States. The Minister also contended that what were now set down as the grounds entitling a person to subsidiary protection were in practice taken into account prior to the making of the deportation orders.

At the outset of his decision, Feeney J. noted that the concept of complementary protection or subsidiary protection had long been recognised both internationally and in this country, such recognition stemming from the fact that the laws and regulations applicable to the regulation of the movement of refugees "are such that not all persons seeking protection fit neatly within legal definitions". Thus, the concept of complementary protection or subsidiary protection allowed persons who were not technically refugees, but who nevertheless had a real need for protection, to remain within a State. Feeney J. also noted that the extent of such complementary protection varied widely within the EU countries, extending from non-refoulement on the one hand to legal authorisation with access to defined benefits on the other hand. It was noted that the position in Ireland prior to the Directive was that persons who had been refused refugee status could avail of s.3 of the Immigration Act 1999, which entitled persons who had failed in their application for refugee status to make written representations to the Minister seeking leave to remain in the State. Section 3(6) of the Immigration Act 1999 identified the matters to which the Minister should have regard to in determining whether to make a deportation order, and the procedure was also subject to the prohibition of refoulement pursuant to s.5 of the Refugee Act 1996. Such applications were often referred to as humanitarian leave to remain, the nature of which were described by Hardiman J in *P, B & L v Minister for Justice* [2002] 2 I.R. 164 as being "in the nature of an ad misericordiam application", with the focus on the personal circumstances of the applicant and humanitarian considerations. Feeney J. noted that if a person succeeded in his representations and the Minister determined to amend, revoke or delay the deportation order, such person did not obtain any defined benefits. It was held that the "ad hoc" nature of such application was further demonstrated by the fact that a successful application under s.3 merely entitled the applicant to remain within the country and did not result in any defined benefits or status.

Feeney J. described the approach of the Minister in dealing with the coming into force of the Regulations as being somewhat anomalous, by reason of the Minister's practice of accepting applications for subsidiary protection from persons in respect of whom deportation orders had been made prior to October 10, 2006 where notification of such orders had not yet been made. The basis upon which it was claimed that the Minister could accept applications for subsidiary protection in such circumstances was Reg.4(2), which provides:

> "The Minister shall not be obliged to consider an application for subsidiary protection from a person other than a person to whom s.3(2)(f) of the 1999 Act applies or which is in a form other than that mentioned in para.1(b)."

It was claimed on behalf of the Minister that there was an implicit discretion reserved by that section to the Minister to consider other applications and that that discretion was unconditional subject only to due compliance with the requirements of constitutional justice and the requirement of the common good. It was held by Feeney J. that the existence of the discretion claimed by the Minister entitling him to consider applications for subsidiary relief from persons who had not been notified of the making of their deportation order prior to October 10, 2006, was inconsistent with the position adopted on behalf of the Minister in respect of these applicants, namely that he could not consider their application for subsidiary relief and that by implication the discretion contained in Reg.4(2) of the Regulations did not and could not extend to persons such as these applicants. Feeney J. concluded:

"If there is an implicit discretion reserved by the provisions of s.4(2) of the Regulations then there does not appear to be any basis as to why such discretion does not extend to persons such as these Applicants as opposed to the persons who have not been notified of deportation orders until after the 6th October, 2006."

Returning to the impact of Council Directive 2004/83/EC, Feeney J. held that it sought to harmonise domestic complementary protection and shifted complementary protection beyond the realm of ad hoc and discretionary national practices to a written regime. The Directive was described as a codification of existing State practices drawing on elements of the Member States' national systems, and was thus based upon existing practices within the Member States rather than imposing a new regime. However, Feeney J. concluded that the fact that the Directive drew on existing state practice did not lead to the conclusion, contended for by the Minister, that it was not the purpose of the Directive to impose any new protection obligations on individual Member States of the European Union.

In determining whether the Directive imposed any new protection obligations in this State, Feeney J. considered it necessary to look at the pre-existing right to subsidiary protection in this country as compared to the codified criteria contained in the Directive. Reference was made to Chapter 5 of the Directive dealing with qualification for subsidiary protection, and Art.2 of the Directive which identifies that persons eligible for subsidiary protection:

"... means a third country national or a stateless person who does not qualify as a refugee but in respect of whom substantial grounds have been shown for believing that the person concerned, if returned to his or her country of origin, or in the case of a stateless person, to his or her country or former habitual residence, would face a real risk of suffering serious harm as defined in Article 15 of the Directive".

Article 15 identifies the matters deemed to amount to serious harm and is a central provision in the Directive. It was held by Feeney J. that:

> "[W]hat is new about Article 15 as compared to the existing practices in various Member States, such as Ireland, is the provision of a written definition of what amounts to serious harm and the provision of a definitive status for persons identified as qualifying for subsidiary protection."

Article 15 states:

> "Serious harm consists of:
> (a) death penalty or execution; or
> (b) torture or inhuman or degrading treatment of an Applicant in the country of origin; or
> (c) serious and individual threat to a civilian's life or person by reason of indiscriminate violence in situations of international or internal armed conflict."

Feeney J. concluded that the matters to be considered by the Minister under the prohibition of refoulement in s.5 of the Refugee Act 1996 differed to some extent from the matters that would now require to be considered under the serious harm definition within Art.15 of the Directive. This was so by reason of the fact that the limitation contained in s.5(1) of the 1996 Act that the threat be on account of an applicant's race, religion, nationality, membership of a particular social group or political opinion is not present in Art.15 and the obligation that a person be likely to be subject to a serious assault requires a different consideration than the consideration required by Art.15(c) of the Directive of a serious and individual threat to a civilian's life or person by reason of indiscriminate violence in situations of international or internal armed conflict. Thus, it was concluded that:

> "It does not appear to follow that consideration of the statutory matters identified in s.5 of the 1996 Act would necessarily result in the Minister having considered in each and every case matters which he is now obliged to consider under the provisions of article 15 of the Directive dealing with serious harm."

Similarly, Feeney J. held that the obligations of the Minister under Art.15 of the Directive were wider than the obligations imposed by the provisions of the Criminal Justice (United Nations Convention Against Torture) Act 2000, by reason of the definition of torture under the 2000 Act as being:

"… an act or omission done or made, or at the instigation of, or with the consent or acquiescence of a public official, by which severe pain or suffering whether physical or mental, is intentionally inflicted upon a person".

The limitation on the definition of torture to acts or omissions done or made or at the instigation of, or with the consent or acquiescence of a public official was held by Feeney J. to be a limitation which did not apply under Art.15 of the Directive. Feeney J. concluded as follows:

"In the majority if not the vast majority of cases where the Minister considered whether or not to make a deportation order prior to the implementation of the Directive the Minister would have to have considered the same or identical matters as would require to be considered in relation to 'serious harm' as defined in the Directive. However it could not be said that that was the position in all cases."

Feeney J. again referred to the discretion contained in Reg.4(2) to allow the Minister to consider an application for subsidiary protection from a person in respect of whom a deportation order had previously been made. However, Reg.4(3) provides a mechanism to allow discretion to be considered, and noted that there could be instances in which there was a substantial time lapse between the Minister's determination and any attempt to enforce a deportation order. It was held that such time lapse gave rise to the possibility that the circumstances either personal or in the applicant's country of origin would have altered: "[A] long delay increases the possibility of relevant fresh facts or circumstances having arisen from the date of the deportation order."

The High Court judge concluded that a correct reading of the Directive was that it did not place any obligation on the State to review or to reconsider decisions already made in relation to subsidiary protection or humanitarian leave to remain. Furthermore, the Directive did not provide the applicants with an automatic right to apply for subsidiary protection or to have the earlier decisions made in respect of refugee protection and subsidiary protection reviewed or renewed. However, Feeney J. concluded that having regard to the discretion conferred upon the Minister by Reg.4(2), the Minister was not precluded from considering applications from persons such as the applicants who had deportation orders made in respect of them prior to the coming into force of the Regulations. It was held that:

"That discretion must be exercised in accordance with the requirements of constitutional justice and would require the Minister to consider on an individual case by case basis whether or not a person had identified altered facts or circumstances from those which pertained at the time that the Minister determined to make the deportation order."

Thus it was concluded that the Minister had a discretion under Reg.4(2) and that to reject the applicants' applications for subsidiary protection as being invalid without regard to that discretion was a breach of the Minister's obligations pursuant to the Regulations. The test which was formulated for regulating the Minister's discretion was stated as follows:

> "Under the Regulations the Minister is not obliged to consider applications from persons who were subject to a deportation order prior to the 10th October, 2006, but it is open to such persons to seek to have the Minister to consider their application if they can identify facts or circumstances which demonstrate a change or alteration from what was the position at the time that the deportation order was made. Those altered circumstances could include a claim that their personal position is affected by the Directive's definition of serious harm. Altered circumstances might also arise as a result of the passage of a prolonged period of time resulting in altered personal circumstances or alterations in the conditions in the Applicant's country of origin. It is open to the Minister in determining whether or not to exercise his discretion to have regard to any new or altered, circumstances or facts identified by the person seeking to have the Minister exercise his discretion."

This decision is of significance by reason of its consideration of the scope of protection available in Ireland both prior to and after the introduction of the 2006 Regulations. The practice of the Minister for Justice in refusing to consider some applications for subsidiary protections was the subject of further litigation before the High Court in July 2008, with judgment awaited at the time of writing.

Obligations of Refugee Appeals Tribunal in assessing appeal without oral hearing The entitlement of the Refugee Appeals Tribunal to raise new issues in determining an appeal which is conducted without an oral hearing was considered by McGovern J. in *NN v Refugee Appeals Tribunal* [2007] I.E.H.C. 230, unreported, High Court, McGovern J., June 28, 2007. The applicant arrived in the State on March 29, 2005. She presented as a South African national and made an application for asylum. She completed a questionnaire in support of her application on April 6, 2005 in which she claimed to be from Zimbabwe and stated her place of birth as Bulawayo. She claimed that she would be persecuted if she returned to Zimbabwe because she was a member and supporter of a group who were opposed to the ruling Mugabe regime and also that if returned as a failed asylum seeker she would be subject to torture, arrest, detention and violence. The applicant had previously applied for asylum in the United Kingdom in 2002 and her application was rejected. She was deported to Harare on January 10, 2005. When the applicant's application for asylum was heard before the Refugee Applications Commissioner she was deemed to be Zimbabwean. The Commissioner accepted that she was from Zimbabwe but rejected her claim on credibility issues relating to her well-founded fear of persecution. The applicant appealed to the Refugee Appeals Tribunal, which appeal was determined without an oral hearing. The tribunal dealt with the applicant on the basis that she was from South Africa. The tribunal member concluded that there was insufficient evidence for her to make a finding that the applicant was a national of Zimbabwe and accordingly it was held that her claim for asylum must be determined by reference to South Africa.

The applicant was granted leave to challenge the decision of the tribunal in refusing her asylum application and also the decision of the Minister in refusing the applicant a declaration of refugee status. McGovern J. noted that it was of some importance in this case that the appeal to the tribunal was not by way of oral hearing, and that the applicant made her appeal on the basis that she had been accepted as a citizen of Zimbabwe and that her fears of persecution related to being returned to that country. In those circumstances, McGovern J. noted that while the applicant had to address the credibility issues that arose in her application, she had no reason to believe that her nationality was in issue. McGovern J. thus held:

> "It may well be that the first named respondent was entitled to question the nationality of the applicant when the matter came before the Tribunal on appeal. But in my view if this were to occur the applicant would have to be put on notice that the RAT wanted this issue reopened on the appeal. To do otherwise would be to treat the appellant in a manner which was wholly unfair."

It was held that for the tribunal to deal with the applicant's refugee application on the basis that she was not from Zimbabwe and that her fear of persecution must be considered in relation to South Africa, amounted to a fundamental reassessment of the applicant's claim. McGovern J. noted that it was open to the tribunal under s.16(6) of the Refugee Act 1996 to request the Commissioner to make such further enquiries and to furnish the tribunal with such further information as the tribunal considered necessary for the purpose of carrying out its functions under the Act. However, there was no evidence that the tribunal did so, and McGovern J. commented that:

> "[O]ne would have expected that if the RAT was going to take such a fundamentally different position to the RAC on the issue of nationality that there would have been some communication between the RAC and RAT under s.16(6)."

Thus, it was concluded:

"There can be no doubt that the RAT and other organs established under the refugee legislation have to act with fairness towards asylum seekers. Where the RAT (as the appellate body) intends to approach the hearing of an appeal on an entirely different premise from that adopted by the RAC, and where this matter has not been raised as a ground of appeal, basic fairness requires that the appellant in the procedure be informed that he or she will have to deal with this issue. If this requires giving the appellant additional time to formulate his or her arguments in relation to this issue then so be it. It is wholly unjust and unfair to deprive the appellant of the opportunity to make an argument on an issue which is deemed to be fundamental by the Tribunal when this issue has already been resolved in the appellant's favour by the RAC and has not, for this reason, become a ground of appeal."

In the circumstances of this case McGovern J. held that the applicant was unfairly treated by the tribunal in not being given an opportunity to offer arguments as to why her case should not be dealt with on the basis that she was from South Africa. McGovern J. emphasised that, in reaching this conclusion, he was not holding that the tribunal was not entitled to revisit the issue of nationality, but rather that if the tribunal intended to proceed on that basis it was required to do so by means of fair procedures. Accordingly, McGovern J. made an order quashing the decision of the tribunal and remitting the matter back to the Refugee Appeals Tribunal for a rehearing.

Obligation of Refugee Appeals Tribunal to consider evidence of torture and country of origin information in determining refugee appeal   The obligation of the Refugee Appeals Tribunal to consider evidence of torture and country of origin information in determining a refugee appeal was addressed in *DVTS v Minister for Justice, Equality and Law Reform and the Refugee Appeals Tribunal* [2007] I.E.H.C. 305, unreported, High Court, Edwards J., July 4, 2007. The applicant was a national of Cameroon who arrived in Ireland on October 8, 2003 and applied for asylum based upon his fear of persecution on account of his political opinion. He was subsequently interviewed by an investigating officer authorised in that behalf by the Refugee Applications Commissioner and, following the said investigation, the Commissioner recommended to the Minister for Justice that the applicant should not be declared a refugee as he had failed to establish a well-founded fear of persecution as defined under s.2 of the Refugee Act 1996. The applicant appealed the recommendation of the Commissioner to the Refugee Appeals Tribunal pursuant to s.16 of the Refugee Act 1996. The applicant's appeal was heard on March 23, 2005 by way of an oral hearing. The applicant himself gave evidence and was cross-examined by the presenting officer. The tribunal also considered certain documents submitted by the applicant, including a political party membership card with a letter of attestation as to his identity and nationality, a birth certificate and two photographs. The applicant also submitted medical reports, including a report furnished by the Centre for the Care of Survivors of Torture dated March 19, 2005 (hereinafter referred to as the SPIRASI report) and certain country of origin information. The tribunal had also been furnished with copies of the reports, documents and representations in writings submitted to the Commissioner under s. 11 and the tribunal had a copy of the Commissioner's s.13 report. In addition, the tribunal sought clarifications of the SPIRASI report, and the clarifications were provided by letter of April 8, 2005.

On June 30, 2005 the tribunal decided to refuse the applicant's appeal. The applicant sought to challenge the decision of the tribunal by way of application for judicial review in the context of which he sought a number of reliefs including an order of certiorari quashing the said decision. The applicant was granted leave to apply for judicial review by MacMenamin J. on February 14, 2007. The grounds upon which leave was granted related to the failure of the tribunal to take relevant considerations as to torture and country of origin information into account in reaching the decision that the applicant was not entitled to asylum in the State and/or that the tribunal took into account irrelevant considerations when making that decision.

Having reviewed a number of authorities concerning the obligations of the tribunal in assessing a refugee appeal, including *Imafu v Minister for Justice, Equality and Law Reform*, unreported, High Court, Clarke J., May 27, 2005 and *Kramarenko v Refugee Appeals Tribunal* [2004] 2 I.L.R.M. 550, Edwards J. concluded that the decision of the tribunal could be legitimately criticised on three major grounds and therefore could not stand. Edwards J. held that in assessing the credibility of the applicant, the tribunal placed reliance upon a significant error of fact in a manner adverse to the applicant, referring to the failure on the part of the tribunal to take into account that the medical evidence contained in the SPIRASI report of March 19, 2005 indicated that both the marks on the applicant's back, and the features noted on the soles of his feet, were to be characterised as highly consistent with the physical abuse and/or torture alleged. It was noted that the Istanbul Protocol defines "highly consistent" as "the lesion could have been caused by the trauma described, and there are few other possible causes". Edwards J. stated that the tribunal appeared to have erroneously noted that the injuries in question were merely consistent with the physical abuse and/or torture alleged, with the Istanbul Protocol defining the phrase "consistent with" as "the lesion could have been caused by the trauma described, but it is non-specific and there are many other possible causes". Edwards J. accepted the submission of the applicant that "highly consistent" equates with "probable", whereas "consistent with" equates with "possible". Accordingly, the learned High Court judge was satisfied that the tribunal placed reliance upon a significant error of fact in assessing the credibility of the applicant.

The second ground on which it was held that the decision of the tribunal could be criticised was that "there does not seem to have been any meaningful attempt on the part of the second named respondent to assess the applicant's claim of having been tortured in the context of the background information of the country of origin." It was held that the tribunal member only alluded to country of origin information in the context of attempting to address the well-foundedness of the applicant's stated fear of persecution. It was held that there did not seem to have been:

> "... an engagement on the part of the second named respondent with the overwhelming evidence from the country of origin that in recent years the torturing of political dissenters by the police and security services in Cameroon was both endemic and systematic. Moreover, several of the sources confirmed the prevalence of the specific type of torture to which the applicant claims to have been subjected, namely, being beaten or whipped by a rubber truncheon type implement, particularly on the soles of the feet. Further, several of the reports confirm instances of systematic harassment of political protesters and the arbitrary detention and subsequent ill-treatment in custody of political protesters. This important information does not appear to have been taken into account by the second named respondent in assessing the credibility of the applicant."

The third ground on which Edwards J. criticised the decision of the tribunal related to the assessment of the well-foundedness or otherwise of the applicant's stated fear of persecution. Edwards J. agreed with the applicant that the tribunal member appeared to have been selective in the material relied upon in arriving at the conclusion that the objective element for a well-founded fear had not been established by the applicant. Edwards J. rejected the respondent's submission that the tribunal member was entitled to select the information that he did on the basis that that was the most up-to-date country of origin information that was before him at the time of the decision; it was held that:

> "There was a significant body of other information before him, submitted by the applicant, that was neither so old nor so out of date as to justify him in failing to take it into account... The second named respondent asserts in his ruling that he had regard to all of the relevant facts. However, the country of origin information before him contained conflicting information. He gives no indication as to how, or on what basis, he resolved the conflicts in the information before him... While this court accepts that it was entirely up to the Refugee Appeals Tribunal to determine the weight (if any) to be attached to any particular piece of country of origin information it was not up to the Tribunal to arbitrarily prefer one piece of country of origin information over another. In the case of conflicting information it was incumbent on the Tribunal to

engage in a rational analysis of the conflict and to justify its preferment of one view over another on the basis of that analysis."

Edwards J. therefore granted the applicant an order of certiorari of the decision of the tribunal.

[**Note:** On November 30, 2007 Edwards J. refused to grant the respondent a certificate of leave to appeal to the Supreme Court; that decision is considered further below.]

Obligation of Refugee Appeals Tribunal to translate documentation furnished in support of appeal The obligation of the Refugee Appeals Tribunal to translate documentation furnished in support of an appeal was considered in *N v Minister for Justice* [2007] I.E.H.C. 257, unreported, High Court, July 30, 2007 (Finlay Geoghegan J.). The applicant was a Romanian national who came to Ireland in 2002 with his wife and daughter, and made an application for asylum on April 2003. In January 2004 the Refugee Applications Commissioner issued reports pursuant to s.13 of the Refugee Act 1996, recommending in each case that the applicant not be granted a declaration of refugee status. The applicant and his wife appealed to the Refugee Appeal Tribunal. Section 13(5) of the Act of 1996 applied to such appeals and accordingly such appeals were to be determined without an oral hearing. On February 27, 2004 the tribunal affirmed the recommendation of the Commissioner that the applicant should not be declared to be a refugee. A similar decision was issued in respect of the applicant's wife. The applicant and his wife each commenced an application for leave to issue judicial review by a notice of motion dated March 11, 2004. By order of the High Court (White J.) of March 6, 2006, leave was granted in each set of proceedings to seek judicial review of the said decisions.

At the time of completing his application for refugee status, the applicant indicated to the Refugee Applications Commissioner that he wished to submit 29 documents in support of his application. All the documents were in Romanian. The applicant was interviewed on behalf of the Commissioner in accordance with s.11 of the Act of 1996. He was not asked any questions about the documents submitted. The documents had not been translated into English prior to the interview. The applicant's solicitor made submissions to the Commissioner at interview that the said documents were relevant to the applicant's claim for refugee status, and further submitted that the documents should be translated if a decision was negative, as the content of these documents was relevant. Prior to the preparation of the s.13(1) report 10 of the 29 documents submitted were translated into English. The remaining 19 documents were not translated. The choice of documents to be translated was made by an official of the Refugee Applications Commissioner. Upon receipt of the decision of the Commissioner, a notice of appeal was completed on the applicant's behalf by his solicitors. The notice of appeal referred to the 29 documents which had been submitted in support of the applicant's claim, and requested that they be translated prior to the determination of the applicant's appeal. Notwithstanding these submissions, the appeal was determined by the tribunal without a translation of the further 19 documents and without any further communication with the applicant or his solicitors in relation to the documents.

It was noted by Finlay Geoghegan J. that the tribunal, in deciding an appeal under s.16 of the Refugee Act 1996, is expressly required by the provisions of subs.(16)(e) to consider "[a]ny documents, representations in writing or other information furnished to the Commissioner pursuant to s.11". It was accepted that s.16(16)(e) of the 1996 Act "should not be construed literally so as to require a Tribunal Member in all circumstances to consider the content of every document furnished by an applicant to the Commissioner pursuant to section 11." Thus, if an applicant furnished an excessive amount of unscheduled and unidentified documents, Finlay Geoghegan J. held that it would be absurd to construe the obligation of the tribunal member under s.16(16) of the 1996 Act as necessarily requiring him to consider all such documents prior to reaching a decision on the appeal:

> "The obligation might be altered for example by inquiries made by the Commissioner or the Tribunal Member of the applicant seeking to establish what the applicant contended to be the relevance of the documents."

However, in the present case it was noted that of the 29 documents which were submitted as being relevant, no inquiries were made by the Refugee Applications Commissioner at interview or otherwise as to why it was contended that the documents were relevant. Finlay Geoghegan J. accordingly held:

> "Construing s.16(16)(e) of the Act of 1996 in accordance with the statutory scheme and the intent that the Tribunal determine an appeal in accordance with the principles of constitutional justice including fair procedures, I have concluded that on the facts herein the Tribunal Member determined the appeal in breach of s. 16(16)(e) and the applicant's right to fair procedures. The section must mean that the Tribunal may not ignore the content of nineteen documents furnished to the Commissioner pursuant to s.11 in circumstances where the applicant both in his application to the Commissioner and again in his grounds of appeal to the Tribunal has asserted the relevance of the documents and no further inquiries were made of him as to the basis of such assertion."

In so far as the respondent had submitted that the court should not grant the applicant an order of certiorari as the applicant had not established before the court the relevance of some or all of the 19 documents, it was held that the applicant was not obliged to establish the relevance of the documents before the court before being granted an order of certiorari. This was so by reference to the statutory scheme established by the 1996 Act, which envisages that the merits of the application be considered by the Commissioner and the tribunal. Finlay Geoghegan J. accepted that it may be that where an applicant furnishes as many as 29 documents in a language other than English that the Refugee Applications Commissioner is entitled, in the course of the interview of the applicant or elsewhere, to have the applicant establish the prima facie relevance of the individual documents to his application for asylum before being necessarily obliged to incur the expense of translating all the documents for the purpose of their consideration as part of the applicant's claim. Similarly, when the appeal was considered by the tribunal member, it was held that it would have been possible for the tribunal pursuant to s.16(6) to request the Commissioner to make further inquiries for the purpose of determining the appeal. Such inquiries could have included inquiries as to the relevance contended for by the applicant of the untranslated 19 documents.

On the facts of this case, it was noted that the failure of the tribunal to consider the 19 untranslated documents was not by reason of any determination by the tribunal that such documents were not relevant to a consideration of the applicant's claim for a declaration of refugee status. It was further held that if that had been the basis of the failure to consider the documents, and the applicant had been given an opportunity before either the Commissioner or tribunal to explain the relevance of the individual documents, then the position would be factually quite different and there could be considerable merit to this submission the respondent. However, this had not occurred, and accordingly Finlay Geoghegan J. held that the applicant had not been afforded fair procedures in the determination of his appeal and accordingly granted the applicant an order of certiorari and an order remitting the matter to the tribunal for determination by another member in accordance with law.

Right to decision on residency application within a reasonable time   The High Court considered the issue of the acceptable period within which the Minister may process an application for residency on the basis of marriage to an Irish national in *KM & DG v Minister for Justice* [2007] I.E.H.C. 234, unreported, High Court, Edwards J., July 17, 2007. The first named applicant was a non-Irish national and was married to the second named applicant who was an Irish citizen. The first named applicant arrived in the State on January 5, 2004 on a student visa which was renewed on a number of occasions. The first named applicant's permission to remain in the State expired on June 30, 2006 and was not renewed. However, the first named applicant did not leave the State on the expiry of his permission to remain and he remained in the State since that time. According to the affidavit of the first named applicant he met the second named applicant after his arrival in Ireland and they were married on July 17, 2006. The first named applicant, by letter dated September 5, 2006, applied to the first named respondent for permission to remain in the State on the basis of his marriage to an Irish citizen. That application was acknowledged by a letter dated October 3, 2006 which stated that such applications would take approximately 12 to 14 months minimum to process. In the course of a subsequent exchange of correspondence between the applicants' solicitors and the respondent, the Minister was pressed to process the applicants' application for residency as soon as possible and it was urged on the Minister that delay in processing the said application was causing undue and unnecessary hardship to the applicants as the first named applicant was not permitted to work. By a letter of January 10, 2007 the Minister wrote to the solicitor for the first named applicant stating that, at that point, applications were taking 11 months minimum to finalise and that it would be a number of months before the first named applicant's application was examined.

On March 26, 2007 the applicants were granted leave to apply for judicial review to seek an order of mandamus requiring the Minister to determine the first named applicant's application for permission to remain in the State on foot of his marriage to the second named applicant within a reasonable time. The applicants also sought a declaration that they were entitled to have a determination on the first named applicant's application for permission to remain in the State promptly and in any case within six months of the date of the application or within such other reasonable time as may be determined by the court. Furthermore, the applicants sought damages for breach of constitutional rights and/or breach of the European Convention on Human Rights and fundamental freedoms. The grounds upon which such reliefs were sought primarily rested on the principles of constitutional and natural justice which applied to the making of a decision on the first named applicant's application for residency, which principles included a right to have a decision made on the first named applicant's application within a reasonable time. The applicants contended that a period of 12 to 14 months, or even the reduced period of 11 months, was an excessive length of time within which to make such a decision. It was furthermore submitted that a person in the position of the first named applicant who was married to an EU national was entitled under European law to have an application for permission to remain in the State determined within six months.

Edwards J. accepted that:

> "[T]he entitlement to a prompt decision is an aspect of constitutional justice. Moreover, quite aside from constitutional justice it is clear from the authorities that the idea of substantive fairness includes a duty not

to delay in the making of a decision to the prejudice of fundamental rights."

The issues requiring determination were stated to be twofold: first, had there been a delay in rendering the administrative decision at issue in this case? Secondly, if there had been a delay, was the degree of delay so unreasonable or unconscionable as to constitute a breach of the applicants' fundamental rights? In considering these issues, Edwards J. held that the relevant factors included the length of the period in question, the complexity of the issues to be considered, the amount of information to be gathered and the extent of enquiries to be made, the reasons advanced for the time taken and the likely prejudice to the applicant of account of delay.

Edwards J. rejected the assertion on behalf of the applicants that a period of six months would be a reasonable period within which the Minister ought to render his decision and held that the Minister was entitled to a greater period of time to make such decision. However, Edwards J. went on to accept the applicants' suggestion that six months was a reasonable period of time to allow for the gathering of information and the making of enquiries. In relation to the actual decision-making process itself once the information has been gathered, Edwards J. held that the Minister must be afforded a further period of three to six months beyond the information-gathering and enquiries stage. Accordingly, it was held that:

> "[T]aking into account the six month period allowed for the gathering of information and the making of appropriate enquiries we are talking about a total period of between 9 months and 12 months as being a reasonable time for the making of a decision by the first named respondent in the first named applicant's case."

In the present case, where the Minister had indicated that the first named applicant would have to wait a period of 11 months minimum from the date of his application to receive a decision, Edwards J. described such period as "sub optimal and close to the limits of what is reasonable" but held that the degree of delay could not be characterised as being unreasonable or unconscionable, and concluded:

> "If the applicant were kept waiting for a decision longer than 12 months I would have no hesitation in finding the delay to be unreasonable and, being unjustifiable notwithstanding any scarcity of resources, unconscionable. However, it is not necessary for me to make any such finding as I am assured that it is likely that the first named applicant will have his decision shortly.
>
> In conclusion I find that, to date, the first named respondent has not acted in breach of constitutional justice. Neither has the first named

applicant been subjected to degrading treatment under Article 3 of the European Convention on Human Rights and Fundamental Freedoms. Further, I do not consider that the degree of delay in the case to date, such as it is, has so prejudiced the applicants as to breach their rights under Article 41 of the Constitution, and under Article 8 of the aforementioned Convention."

As Edwards J. did not find the Minister guilty of unreasonable and unconscionable delay to date, he concluded that it was not necessary to consider the separation of powers issue or the question as to whether or not mandamus would have been an appropriate remedy in this case.

The decision in *M v Minister for Justice* is of great significance to a wide number of immigration applications which are made to the Department of Justice. At the present time, the Department is advising that applications for family reunification pursuant to s.18 of the Refugee Act 1996 are taking a minimum of 24 months to process, and applications for naturalisation pursuant to the Irish Nationality and Citizenship Act 2004 are taking in excess of 30 months to process. It is anticipated that further litigation will issue in the future challenging such delays, and while the decision of Edwards J. provides strong support for such proceedings, the issues as to the separation of powers and distribution of resources were expressly not considered by Edwards J., and are thus likely to feature strongly in future proceedings.

Threshold for invoking exceptional circumstances under Article 8 sufficient to prevent deportation   The High Court addressed the threshold for successfully invoking Art.8 of the ECHR in challenging a deportation order in the substantive application in *Agbonlahor v Minister for Justice, Equality and Law Reform* [2007] I.E.H.C. 166, unreported, High Court, Feeney J., April 18, 2007. The applicants were a family of Nigerian citizens who had claimed asylum in Ireland. Whilst in the State, the third named applicant, who was four years of age, was diagnosed as suffering from attention deficit hyperactivity disorder and intellectual disability and required specialised education and therapeutic services. The family's asylum application was refused and deportation orders were issued in respect of each of them. The family applied to the Minister for revocation of the deportation orders on the ground that their removal would interfere with their rights under the ECHR because the treatment and support required by the third named applicant would not be available to him in Nigeria. The Minister refused to revoke the deportation orders, and the applicants were subsequently granted leave by way of judicial review to quash that decision on the ground that the applicants had an arguable case that the Minister's refusal to revoke was a violation of the applicants' rights under Art.8(1) of the European Convention on Human Rights (for a discussion of the decision of the High

Court on the leave application, see Byrne & Binchy (eds), *Annual Review of Irish Law 2006* (Dublin: Thomson Round Hall, 2007), pp.48–50).

However, the applicants were ultimately refused in their challenge to the decision of the Minister by decision of the High Court on April 18, 2007. In considering the applicants' claim, Feeney J. had regard to the decisions of the English courts on Art.8 in the immigration context, notably *R. (Mahmood) v Secretary of State for the Home Department* [2001] 1 W.L.R. 840, where he cited with approval the dicta of Lord Phillips in relation to the potential conflict between the respect for family life and the enforcement of immigration controls (at 861), namely:

"(1) A State has a right under international law to control the entry of non-nationals into its territory, subject always to its treaty obligations.

(2) Article 8 does not impose on a state any general obligation to respect the choice of residence of a married couple.

(3) Removal or exclusion of one family member from a State where other members of the family are lawfully resident will not necessarily infringe on Article 8 provided that there are no insurmountable obstacles to the family living together in the country of origin of the family member excluded, even where this involves a degree of hardship for some or all members of the family.

(4) Article 8 is likely to be violated by the expulsion of a member of a family that has been long established in a State if the circumstances are such that it is not reasonable to expect the other members of the family to follow that member expelled.

(5) Knowledge on the part of one spouse at the time of marriage that rights of residence of the other were precarious militates against a finding that an order excluding the latter spouse violates Article 8.

(6) Whether interference with family rights is justified in the interest of controlling immigration will depend on
  (i) the facts of the particular case, and
  (ii) the circumstance prevailing in the State whose action is impugned."

Reference was also made to the decision of the House of Lords in *R. (Razgar) v Home Secretary* [2004] 2 A.C. 368 where Lord Bingham identified five questions which an adjudicator should address where removal was being resisted in reliance on Art.8 as follows (at 389):

"(1) Will the proposed removal be of an interference by a public authority with the exercise of the applicant's right to respect for his private or (as the case may be) family life?

(2) If so, will such interference have consequences of such gravity as potentially to engage the operation of Article 8?

(3) If so, is such interference in accordance with the law?

(4) If so, is such interference necessary in a democratic society in the interests of national security, public safety or the economic well being of the country, for the prevention of disorder or crime, for the protection of health or morals, or for the protection of the rights and freedoms of others?

(5) If so, is such interference proportionate to the legitimate public end sought to be achieved?"

These decisions were regarded as endorsing the general principle that a state has a right under international law to control the entry of non-nationals into its territory, albeit subject always to its treaty obligations. Feeney J. further accepted the principle stated by Lord Phillips in *Mahmood* that Art.8 does not impose on the State a general obligation to respect the choice of residence of any immigrant. Feeney J. reviewed the jurisprudence under the Convention in this context, including *Bensaid v United Kingdom* (2001) 33 E.H.R.R. 205 and *Henao v The Netherlands*, unreported, European Court of Human Rights, June 24, 2003, and concluded that the applicants had not demonstrated the "exceptional circumstances" necessary to engage Art.8. Accordingly, the applicants' challenge to the decision of the Minister was refused and the applicants were subsequently deported from the State.

Lynn has commented that the passage in *Razgar* which was relied upon by Feeney J. needs to be treated with some caution because it relates to immigration policy in the United Kingdom which includes the application of immigration rules that are drafted expressly to comply with Art.8 of the Convention:

> "[T]hus, it should only be in 'exceptional' cases that decisions under those rules will actually breach Article 8—ie the decision in *Razgar* should not be characterised as endorsing a general test of exceptionality in the context of Article 8"(Lynn, "The Use of the ECHR in Asylum and Immigration Law", paper presented to ICEL Conference on 'ECHR Update: The Recent Use of the ECHR in the Courts—Procedure, Remedies and Analysis', November 20, 2007).

This view would seem to be supported by the recent decision of the House of Lords in *Huang v Secretary of State for the Home Department* [2007] 2 W.L.R. 581 where it was held (para.20):

> "In an article 8 case where this question is reached, the ultimate question for the appellate immigration authority is whether the refusal of leave to enter or remain, in circumstances where the life of the family cannot reasonably be expected to be enjoyed elsewhere, taking full account

of all considerations weighing in favour of the refusal, prejudices the family life of the applicant in a manner sufficiently serious to amount to a breach of the fundamental right protected by article 8. If the answer to this question is affirmative, the refusal is unlawful and the authority must so decide. It is not necessary that the appellate immigration authority, directing itself along the lines indicated in this opinion, need ask in addition whether the case meets a test of exceptionality. The suggestion that it should is based on an observation of Lord Bingham in *Razgar* above, para 20. He was there expressing an expectation, shared with the Immigration Appeal Tribunal, that the number of claimants not covered by the Rules and supplementary directions but entitled to succeed under article 8 would be a very small minority. That is still his expectation. But he was not purporting to lay down a legal test.'

Therefore, in so far as the decision of Feeney J. purported to apply a legal test of exceptionality in his determination of the *Agbonlahor* proceedings, it is respectfully submitted that the said decision ought not be followed.

Whether doctrine of merger applies to decisions of Refugee Applications Commissioner where applicant invokes right of appeal to Refugee Appeals Tribunal The issue of whether the doctrine of merger applies to decisions of the Refugee Applications Commissioner when the applicant has invoked his or her right of appeal to the Refugee Appeals Tribunal was considered in *NAA v Minister for Justice, Equality and Law Reform* [2007] I.E.H.C. 54, unreported, High Court, Finlay Geoghegan J., February 23, 2007. The applicant was a Somali who arrived in Ireland and applied for asylum in August, 2004. She gave her date of birth as October 21, 1987 and was treated as a minor and put in the care of the Health Service Executive. She attended for interview at the office of the Refugee Applications Commissioner on February 2, 2005, accompanied by a social worker from the HSE and a case worker from the Refugee Legal Service. The applicant did not disclose that prior to arriving in Ireland she had been in the United Kingdom and had there applied for asylum and been refused. In considering the application, the Commissioner identified this fact from the fingerprint taken from the applicant and the "Eurodac" facilities. The United Kingdom Home Office confirmed on October 7, 2004 to the Commissioner that a person with the applicant's fingerprints had made an application for asylum in the United Kingdom on August 30, 2002, under a different name and date of birth, claiming to be from Somalia. On December 8, 2004, the United Kingdom confirmed that they would accept the transfer of the applicant for further consideration of her asylum application under the terms of Art.16(1)(e) of Council Regulation 343/2003/EC . Notwithstanding this, a determination had been made by or on behalf of the Commissioner that the applicant's pending asylum application would be considered and determined in this jurisdiction.

By report dated February 3, 2005 the Commissioner recommended that the applicant should not be declared to be a refugee, and further made a finding that the provisions of s.13(6) applied such that any appeal against the Commissioner's decision would be held without an oral hearing. A notice of appeal was lodged to Refugee Appeals Tribunal on March 2, 2005. This appears to have been accepted as within the necessary 10-day period. The appeal was lodged on the form ASY 1. Ground 6 stated that "further submissions will be forwarded shortly". The notice of appeal was stated to be without prejudice to the applicant's right to institute judicial review proceedings against the decision of the Commissioner. The applicant's representatives subsequently wrote to the Commissioner calling for the withdrawal of its decision. Upon being notified of the Commissioner's refusal of this request, the applicant's legal representatives took steps preparatory to the institution of judicial review proceedings, namely applications for legal aid certificates and related steps. Prior to the institution of such proceedings, however, the applicant was informed by a letter dated April 22, 2005 of the decision of the tribunal on her appeal to affirm the recommendation of the Commissioner that she should not be declared to be a refugee.

The applicant subsequently instituted judicial review proceedings seeking leave to apply for judicial review, seeking, inter alia, an order of certiorari quashing the decision of the tribunal and an order of certiorari quashing the decision of the Commissioner recommending that the applicant should not be declared to be a refugee. Related declarations were also sought, including a declaration that the applicant was entitled to have her application for asylum remitted to the Commissioner to be considered de novo pursuant to the substantive procedures set out in ss.11 and 13 of the Refugee Act 1996 (as amended). The applicant also sought an order extending the time in which to seek such reliefs. There was a single ground upon which the applicant sought certiorari of the decision of the tribunal, namely that its decision was invalid and ought to be quashed on the basis that it had regard to and affirmed the defective recommendation of the Commissioner.

The primary submission made on behalf of the respondents was that leave could not be granted in respect of the decision of the Commission by reason of the fact that as of the date of commencement of the application there was no subsisting decision of the Commission amenable to judicial review by the High Court. It was submitted that the decision or recommendation of the Commissioner had "merged" with the decision of the tribunal. Finlay Geoghegan J. noted that there was no Supreme Court decision determining the question as to whether or not a decision of the tribunal under s.16(2) of the 1996 Act determining an appeal from a recommendation of the Commissioner made under s.13(1) of the Act has the effect in law of meaning that the recommendation of the Commissioner is "merged" with the decision of the tribunal such that it no longer remains a separate and distinct decision amenable to judicial review by the High Court. It was noted that the term "merger" in relation to the refugee context appeared to have been used by Hardiman J. in *GK v Minister for Justice* [2002] 2 I.R. 418, but Finlay Geoghegan J. held that such comments were obiter in the context of that judgment which concerned different procedures to those at issue in the present case.

The High Court judge held that the question as to whether a decision of first instance may be considered to have merged with the relevant decision taken on appeal must be considered "in the context of the relevant statutory scheme, the nature of each decision, the form of the appeal and any continuing effects of the first decision following the decision on appeal." Finlay Geoghegan J. also reviewed a number of decisions of the High Court, including the decision of Smyth J. in *Savin v Minister for Justice, Equality and Law Reform*, unreported, High Court, May 7, 2002 and the decision of MacMenamin J. in *Okungbowa v Refugee Appeals Tribunal*, unreported, High Court, MacMenamin J., June 8, 2005 and concluded that in both cases the term "merger" was used in the sense that the decision of the Commissioner ceased to have legal effect once the decision of the tribunal on appeal was made. Having considered the existing jurisprudence of the High Court, Finlay Geoghegan J. concluded that, notwithstanding the decision of the tribunal, there remained an extant decision of the Commissioner which as a matter of law could be the subject of an order of certiorari. This finding was reached on the basis that:

> "[A] recommendation of the Commissioner that the applicant not be declared to be a refugee made under s.13(1) and including in the report made under that section is envisaged in the statutory scheme created by s.16 and 17 of the Act of 1996 to continue to subsist after a decision of the Tribunal on appeal affirming the recommendation and continues to have certain effects for the applicant. In particular it is the report of the Commissioner under s.13 including her recommendation which triggers the decision to be taken by the Minister under s.17 as to whether the application for a declaration of refugee status is to be granted or refused."

However, it was held that notwithstanding that there may continue to exist a decision which is capable of being the subject-matter of an order of certiorari, there was a distinct issue as to whether the court should grant leave to challenge by way of judicial review a decision of the Commissioner where, prior to the issue of the motion seeking leave, the tribunal has determined the appeal of the applicant against such decision of the Commissioner. It was held that, as a matter of general principle, where an appeal has been determined an applicant has gone too far and the High Court will not subsequently interfere with the first instance decision by way of judicial review. Finlay Geoghegan J. further noted:

"Whilst the court retains a discretion to do so it should only exercise its discretion to grant certiorari of a decision which has been the subject of a decided appeal where there exist special circumstances which make such late interference necessary to do justice for the parties. Such an approach by way of exception appears required by the principles set out above when considered in the context of the purpose of judicial review and distinction from an appeal process. It also appears consistent with the policy of the courts in relation to the non-duplication of procedures and proceedings."

It was held that such special circumstances might be satisfied by:

"...the nature of the grounds asserted in support of certiorari; whether they could be considered on appeal; when the applicant became aware of such grounds; whether the applicant was prevented from bringing the application for leave to apply for judicial review prior to determination of the appeal; whether the applicant acquiesced in or permitted the determination of the appeal; any relevant statutory scheme; the time which elapsed prior to determination of appeal and fairness of appeal procedure."

In the present case, Finlay Geoghegan J. concluded that the applicant had not established any such circumstances which would permit the court to grant leave on a motion issued after the determination of the appeal lodged with the tribunal. Accordingly, leave to seek judicial review against the Commissioner was refused, as was the application in respect of the decision of the tribunal.

Whether High Court should grant certificate of leave to appeal against decision The question of whether the High Court should grant a certificate of leave to appeal against its decision was addressed in *DVTS v Minister for Justice, Equality and Law Reform* [2007] I.E.H.C. 451, unreported, High Court, Edwards J., November 30, 2007. Edwards J. commenced by noting that in his decision of July 4, 2007 ([2007] I.E.H.C. 305) he had granted an order of certiorari in respect of the decision of the Refugee Appeals Tribunal, inter alia, by reason of the failure properly to consider evidence of torture and country of origin information in the determination of the appeal. An application was subsequently made by the respondents for a certificate of leave to appeal pursuant to s.5(3)(a) of the Illegal Immigrants Trafficking Act 2000, which provides:

"The determination of the High Court of an application for leave to apply for Judicial Review as aforesaid or of an application for such Judicial Review shall be final and no appeal shall lie from the decision of the High Court to the Supreme Court in either case, except with the leave of the High Court, which leave shall only be granted where the High Court certifies that its decision involves a point of law."

The question which Edwards J. was asked to certify for the consideration of the Supreme Court on the basis that the point in question was both exceptional and of public important was as follows:

"Whether a tribunal member is obliged, when he has indicated that he has considered all the documents submitted and perused same, to set out on the face of the decision the reason for preferring certain 'country of origin information' over others."

Edwards J. stated at the outset that regard had been had to the decision in *Raiu v Refugee Appeals Tribunal*, unreported, High Court, Finlay Geoghegan J., February 26, 2003, where it was held (at 4):

"The Oireachtas having exercised its discretion in a constitutionally permissible manner, the restriction enacted should be construed in accordance with the normal rules of statutory interpretation. The general policy of section 5(3)(a) of the Act of 2000 is to exclude all appeals from the High Court decisions referred to and only by way of exception from that general principle to permit an appeal where the High Court grants the certificate specified in the subsection.

...

Requirements that the point of law is of 'exceptional public importance' and that 'it is desirable in the public interest that an appeal should be taken to the Supreme Court' are cumulative requirements, which, whilst they may overlap to some extent, require separate consideration by the High Court. This was the view taken by McKechnie J in *Kenny v. An Bord Pleanála* with which I agree. The Oireachtas has clearly indicated in section 5(3)(a) of the Act of 2000 by the use of the word 'exceptional' that not all points of law of public importance may be certified. Many, if not most points of law which arise in a Judicial Review to which Section 5(3)(a) of the Act of 2005 applies, will be of 'public importance' in the sense that that term has been construed by the courts particularly in the jurisprudence relating to applications for security for costs on appeals to the Supreme Court."

Edwards J. determined that he would not certify an appeal to the Supreme Court, on the basis that:

"[W]hile on one view of it there may be a point of law of public importance involved, I do not believe that it is a point of law of such exceptional public importance that it is desirable in the public interest that an appeal should be taken to the Supreme Court."

The reasons for such view were set out at length by Edwards J., including the statement that his decision on the substantive application for judicial review was based on principles which were not:

> "... particularly new or radical... Rather, I sought to apply well established principles which led me to a particular conclusion and gave rise to a particular result in the case."

Edwards J. went on to consider the nature of those principles, as follows:

> "First of all, there is the principle that a judicial or quasi judicial tribunal must have regard to all of the evidence before it and cannot cherry pick the evidence. If it is to act judicially it must consider all of the evidence put before it. If there is a conflict with respect to the evidence, such that the tribunal cannot resolve that conflict, other than by preferring one piece of evidence over another piece of evidence for good and substantial reasons, then it is incumbent on the tribunal or court, as the case may be, to state clearly its reasons for doing so. It is well established that a court or tribunal may not act arbitrarily, it must act judicially and it must proceed on the basis of what is reasonable and rational. In order that an appellate tribunal might know whether the tribunal at first instance has behaved reasonably and rationally it must know the reasons for, or basis on which, the lower tribunal acted."

Reference was also made to the requirement that justice must not only be done but be seen to be done, and the requirement of transparency in the decision-making process.

In relation to the tribunal's treatment of the country of origin information, Edwards J. noted that he had determined that the Refugee Appeals Tribunal was obliged to consider all country of origin information put before it, and again concluded that there was nothing new or radical in this statement:

> "It is true to say, and I acknowledge that the tribunal member did state that he had considered all of the documents submitted, but he went on to prefer a portion of the 'country of origin information' over other 'country of origin information' relied upon particularly by the Applicant, and he did not give a reason for doing so. This was not a peripheral issue in the case. This was a central issue in the case. In my view, he was obliged to engage in a rational analysis of the 'country of origin information' and justify the preferment of one piece of evidence over

> another. Again, I do not believe there is anything new or radical in that proposition."

Edwards J. noted that the applicable procedures in the refugee context were not of a wholly adversarial nature, but were largely of an inquisitorial nature. It was noted that while country of origin information was evidence, "it is not evidence of the sort that would normally be receivable in the ordinary courts, at least in the form which it is received in cases before the Refugee Appeals Tribunal." This was stated to be for a number of reasons, including the fact that it is generally hearsay evidence and is largely in the nature of opinion evidence which in the ordinary course could only be given by a properly credentialled expert giving an opinion as to a matter within his field of expertise. Furthermore, Edwards J. noted that such evidence is almost invariably not the subject of any kind of testing or cross-examination. Edwards J. concluded that because of these differences:

> "[I]t seems to me that exceptional care must be taken by the tribunal in considering 'country of origin information'. This is particularly so in circumstances where material is easily downloaded these days from the internet, the source and provenance of which might be dubious. On the other hand, it might be entirely authoritative. But there are no restrictions or inhibitions on any party who wishes to put any matter in the nature of 'country of origin information' before the tribunal. The tribunal must consider all of the material put before it. However, it is then entitled, having considered that material, to prefer certain material over certain other material, but it must do so for good and substantial and reasonable and rational reasons."

Examples of such reasons were then given, including a view that the source or provenance of a particular piece of country of origin information is dubious or less than authoritative, or is more up to date than other information. Edwards J. noted that there might also be a view that certain information produced, particularly by an agency which was perhaps pursuing a particular agenda, might not be entirely impartial. The learned High Court judge thus concluded:

> "It is perfectly within the province and jurisdiction of the Refugee Appeals Tribunal, or any other body considering information of that type, to prefer some information over other information. What is critical, however, is that they give a reason for doing so. That doesn't mean that every piece of 'country of origin information' must be alluded to in the judgment, but where there is a major conflict and where the status of one piece of 'country of origin information' versus another piece of 'country of origin information' is an issue of very significant importance

in the case, then the judgment should deal with that, and if there is a preferment of one piece of evidence over another it should be justified so that the tribunal can be seen not to have acted arbitrarily but to have acted reasonably, rationally and impartially."

Edwards J. reiterated that while the question posited did on one view canvass an issue of public importance, it could not be described as being so new as to render it a question of exceptional public importance. For those reasons, Edwards J. declined the certify the question.

Whether Minister entitled to require evidence of lawful residence in another Member State in determining application for residence under EU law The manner in which the State implemented the provisions of Directive 2004/38/EC was addressed by the High Court in *SK & TT v Minister for Justice, Equality and Law Reform* [2007] I.E.H.C. 216, unreported, High Court, Hanna J., May 28, 2007. The applicants sought judicial review of the refusal to grant the first named applicant residence in the State on the basis of marriage to an EU national who was resident and working in the State. The applicants complained that the instrument under which the first named applicant's right of residency was refused, the European Communities (Freedom of Movement of Persons) Regulations 2006 (S.I. No. 226 of 2006), was ultra vires Directive 2004/38/EC which deals with the rights of citizens of the European Union and their family members to move and reside freely within the territory of the Member States. Specifically, the applicants contended that the requirement in the regulations that a spouse or family member who was a national of a non-EU state be lawfully resident in another Member State before entering the State went beyond the provisions of the Directive. Further, it was argued that the refusal of the right of residency and the removal of the first named applicant from the State was contrary both to their respective rights under the Constitution and under Art.8 of the European Convention of Human Rights.

The first named applicant was a citizen of India and the second named applicant was a national of Estonia, a Member State of the European Union. The applicants were married in the State on May 18, 2006, having been in a relationship since 2003. The first named applicant had previously applied for asylum in Belgium and been refused. He then entered the United Kingdom and resided there illegally for a period of approximately three years. The applicants travelled to the State in January 2006 with the intention of the second named applicant finding employment in the State, formalising their marriage and setting up their family home. The first named applicant initially applied for asylum in the State, which application was withdrawn after the applicants married and submitted an application for residence on behalf of the first named applicant pursuant to the Directive. Prior to the withdrawal of the asylum application, the Irish authorities made a take-back request to Belgium on May 2, 2006 which request was acceded to by the Belgian authorities on May 31, 2006. A transfer order was made on June 14, 2006 transferring the first named applicant to Belgium. By letter dated July 7, 2006, the first named applicant was advised that his application for residency on the basis of marriage to an EU citizen working within the State had been unsuccessful. The reason given for this decision was that he had not submitted evidence that he had been lawfully resident with his spouse in another EU Member State before coming to Ireland. The applicants obtained leave to apply for judicial review in respect of the said refusal on July 31, 2006.

At the outset, Hanna J. accepted that the intention of the applicants had at all material times been to avoid or by-pass the provisions of Irish immigration law with a view to obtaining for the first named applicant a right of residency as the spouse of a citizen of a Member State of the European Union. However, it was also noted that no case was made that the marriage entered into between the applicants was other than a valid marriage. Against this factual background, Hanna J. considered the legal framework governing the free movement of workers within the European Union. Hanna J. referred to the recently adopted Directive 2004/38/EC which aimed to simplify the formalities for Union citizens and their family members to exercise and enjoy the right of free movement and residence irrespective of the nationality of the spouse or family member. It was noted that the definition of "family member" in Art.2 of the Directive included a spouse, while Art.3 provided that the provisions of the Directive "shall apply to all Union citizens who move to or reside in a Member State other than that of which they are a national, and to their family members ... who accompany or join them." Hanna J. noted that the Minister for Justice gave effect to the Directive by way of the European Communities (Free Movement of Persons) Regulations 2006 (S.I. No. 226 of 2006). The controversy between the parties related to the provisions of Reg.3(2), which provided:

> "(2) These Regulations shall not apply to a family member unless the family member is lawfully resident in another Member State and is-
> (a) seeking to enter the State in the company of a Union citizen in respect of whom he or she is a family member, or
> (b) seeking to join a Union citizen, in respect of whom he or she is a family member, who is lawfully present in the State."

These provisions formed the basis of the Minister's refusal to grant residency to the first named applicant. The applicants sought to impugn this regulation upon the grounds, inter alia, that it did not properly transpose the Directive into Irish law. It was argued that the Directive contained no provision which would require, inter alia, that the first named applicant should lawfully be resident in another Member State prior to seeking to enter the State in the company of the second named applicant or seeking to join the second named applicant. The respondents contended that the Regulations properly transposed the provisions of the Directive, relying on the decision of the European Court of Justice in *Case C/109/01 Secretary of State for the Home Department v Hacene Akrich* [2004] 2 W.L.R. 871 where it was held that a non-EU national who is the spouse of a citizen of the Union, must be lawfully resident in a Member State when he moves to another Member State to which the citizen of the Union is migrating or has migrated. In contrast, the applicants relied upon the decision of the Court of Justice in *Case C-1/105 Jia v Migrationsverket* [2007] 2 W.L.R. 1005 where it was held that:

> "Community law does not require Member States to make the grant of a residence permit to nationals of a non-Member State, who are members of the family of a Community national who has exercised his or her right of free movement, subject to the condition that those family members have previously been residing lawfully in another Member State."

Hanna J. noted that the court in *Jia* was at pains to distinguish the facts of that case from the facts in *Akrich*, emphasising the lawfulness of Ms Jia's presence in Sweden and the fact that she was not seeking to evade national immigration laws. Hanna J. thus concluded that in the light of the factual background of the case before him, "the *Jia* decision should be left to one side." Hanna J. concluded that the provisions of Reg.3(2) reflected and gave effect to the Directive and the decision of the European Court of Justice in *Akrich*. Having dismissed the applicants' arguments that removal of the first named applicant to Belgium in accordance with the transfer order would breach their rights to family and private life pursuant to both the Constitution and the European Convention on Human Rights, Hanna J. dismissed the application.

[**Note:** On March 14, 2008 Finlay Geoghegan J. made a reference pursuant to Art.234 concerning the validity of the Regulations with Directive 2004/38/EC in *Metock v Minister for Justice, Equality and Law Reform* [2008] I.E.H.C. 77. On July 25, 2008 the European Court of Justice in *Case C-127/08 Metock v Minister for Justice, Equality and Law Reform* held that the lawful residence requirement imposed by the domestic Regulations was ultra vires the Directive].

Whether Minister has discretion not to enforce transfer order pending consideration of application for residence based on marriage The existence and scope of the Minister's discretion in respect of the enforcement of transfer orders was considered by the High Court in *LK & FN v Minister for Justice, Equality and Law Reform* [2007] I.E.H.C. 306, unreported, High Court, Birmingham J., July 20, 2007. The applicants were wife and husband, having married in the State in February 2007. The first named applicant was a foreign national. The second named applicant was also a foreign national who was granted a declaration of refugee status on April 16, 2002 and subsequently applied for a certificate of naturalisation, which application was granted on September 25, 2003 and he was subsequently issued with an Irish passport. At the time of her entry to the State, the first named applicant was a person who had sought and failed to obtain asylum in Britain, where she had made an application quoting a different name and a different date of birth. Following an analysis of fingerprints which established that she had made an earlier unsuccessful application in Britain, the authorities here requested the British authorities to take back the applicant and on August 21, 2006 the British authorities agreed to take back the applicant for further consideration of her asylum application under Art.16(1)(E) of Council Regulation 343/2003. The first named applicant was informed of the determination to transfer her application to the United Kingdom and was told of her entitlement to appeal the decision to the Refugee Appeals Tribunal. On September 14, 2006 the tribunal affirmed the determination of the Refugee Applications Commissioner and dismissed the appeal. On August 31 a transfer order was made and the applicant was informed of this fact by letter dated September 4, 2006. Despite being instructed to report to the Garda National Immigration Bureau, the applicant failed to report on September 11, 2006 as requested and the authorities thereafter regarded her as an evader. In February 2007 the applicants married each other and on April 2, 2007 an application for residency status in the State was made on behalf of the first named applicant based on her marriage to an Irish citizen, by solicitors who were then acting on her behalf.

The applicants sought judicial review of the failure of the Minister to halt the implementation of a transfer order pending the consideration of a claim for residency on the part of the first named applicant. The applicants had been given leave to seek judicial review seeking a declaration that the removal of the first named applicant from the State was unlawful prior to the determination of the application for residency based on marriage and family and domestic circumstances, and injunctive relief restraining the respondent from taking any steps to remove the first named applicant pursuant to a transfer order pending consideration of the outstanding applications made to the respondent seeking residency in the State based on marriage to an Irish citizen.

Birmingham J. began by referring to the provisions of Council Regulation 343/2003/EC, which establishes a mechanism for determining the Member State responsible for assessing an application for asylum. Reference was made to Art.3 of the Regulation, which provides that Member States shall examine the application of any third-country national who applies at the border or in their territory for asylum. The Regulation goes on to establish what is described as a hierarchy of criteria for determining the Member State responsible for examining an application for asylum. In the present case it was not in dispute that, applying these criteria, the United Kingdom was the Member State responsible.

Birmingham J. considered the domestic framework governing the making and implementation of transfer orders in this jurisdiction. Section 22 of the Refugee Act 1996 (as amended) empowers the Minister to make such orders as appear to him necessary or expedient to give effect to Council Regulation 343/2003/EC. The orders contemplated by s.22 are contained in the Refugee Act 1996 (Section 22) Order 2003. Reference was made to Art.4(1), which provides that where an application for asylum is made, the Refugee Applications Commissioner shall determine whether, in accordance with the Regulation, the application shall be examined in the State. Article 4(2) provides that the Commissioner shall, before making a determination, take into consideration all relevant matters known to him or her, including any representations by or on behalf of the applicant.

In arguing that there was a right to remain on the part of the applicant pending a decision on the residency application or as a minimum until there has been a specific consideration of whether the applicant can remain pending a decision, the applicant stressed the fact that fundamental human rights issues arise in immigration cases. In that regard, while not challenging the validity of the transfer order that was made, the applicants sought to challenge its implementation and contended that its implementation was now unlawful having regard to the family and domestic circumstances of the applicants with a particular reference to the fact of their marriage. They contended that they enjoyed rights under Arts and 41 of the Constitution and under Art.8 of the European Convention on Human Rights and submitted that, while accepting that those rights were not absolute, there was, as a minimum, a requirement that they should be the subject of consideration.

The applicants relied on the decision of Finlay Geoghegan J. in *Malsheva v Minister for Justice Equality and Law Reform*, unreported, High Court, July 25, 2003, where the applicants were granted leave and an injunction to restrain an interference with re-entry into the State in circumstances where the applicants had married each other during the time between the making of a deportation order and its execution, in a situation where the respondents were on notice of the fact of the marriage and ought to have considered the marital situation. Birmingham J. distinguished the circumstances of *Malsheva* from those of the present case for a number of reasons, including the fact that at issue in *Malsheva* was a deportation order which was different in its terms and effects to a transfer order. The applicant has also placed reliance on the case of *Makumbi v Minister for Justice, Equality and Law Reform*, unreported, High Court, November 15, 2005 (discussed in Byrne & Binchy, *Annual Review of Irish Law 2005* (Dublin: Thomson Round Hall, 2006) pp.57–60), where Finlay Geoghegan J. granted an injunction restraining the respondent from taking any steps to transfer the applicant to the United Kingdom, as well as the declaration that the respondent had discretion not to implement a transfer order and a declaration that constitutional justice required the respondent to determine the request of the applicant not to implement the transfer order made in respect of her.

The respondent placed reliance on *Margine v Minister for Justice, Equality and Law Reform*, unreported, High Court, Peart J., July 14, 2004. In that case the applicant, when facing imminent deportation, sought to halt the process on the basis of being the father of an Irish-born child. Peart J. pointed out that the child had been born and indeed conceived after the making of the deportation order, and held that the objective of upholding the integrity of the asylum process was of sufficient weight to outweigh the asserted family rights, which were not absolute rights, of the applicant. The applicants accepted that it was difficult to reconcile the approach of Finlay Geoghegan J. in *Malsheva* with the approach of Peart J. in *Margine*, but urged that *Malsheva* should be followed on the grounds that it was the more closely reasoned. The respondent urged the court to distinguish *Malsheva*, and emphasised that the *Makumbi* case turned on its own very specific facts. While Birmingham J. accepted that the facts in *Makumbi* were very dramatic and indeed very distressing, it was held that there was nonetheless force in the argument put forward by the applicants that there is either a discretion to halt implementation or there is not. The applicants argued that if it exists then it must be a general discretion, and cannot be confined to rights of like cases.

It was held by Birmingham J. that there was no doubt that if the transfer order was implemented it would undoubtedly impact significantly on the applicants as a married couple. Nonetheless, it was deemed to be relevant that the effect of the transfer order was not to separate the applicants irreparably—"the second named applicant is the holder of an Irish passport and is perfectly free to join his wife in Britain, should he wish to do so." Equally, it was held that if the first named applicant was obliged to travel onward to her country of origin, the second named applicant was in a position to join her or visit her. Birmingham J. also referred to the fact that case law in Ireland, Britain and the case law of the European Court of Human Rights such as *R. (Mahmood) v Secretary of State for the Home Department* [2001] 1 W.L.R. 840 and *Cirpaci v Minister for Justice* [2005] 4 I.R. 109, [2005] 2 I.L.R.M. 547 (*Annual Review of Irish Law 2005*, pp.41–44) all indicate that where one spouse is aware at the time of entering into a marriage that the other spouse's situation is precarious, that this is a relevant consideration.

The applicants accepted that the rights which were asserted by them were not absolute and that there could be competing considerations that required to be weighed in the balance. The applicants' complaint was that there was no such weighing and Birmingham J. held that in this regard the applicants were correct. However, it was held that the Minister was entitled to take the view that where there was a transfer order in existence, the validity of which was not challenged, that he was not going to set the transfer order to one side while consideration was given to the residency application. Birmingham J. concluded as follows:

"I do not believe it is consistent with the policy and objectives of the

Council Regulation that someone who is an asylum seeker in another Council Regulation state or a *fortiori* a failed asylum seeker in another Member State should be in a position to frustrate the operation of the structures created by the Council Regulations by applying for non implementation of the transfer order. I do not believe that a request for a non implementation serves to suspend the transfer order. While I am prepared to accept that the Minister may, at least in certain situations, have a discretion to suspend the implementation of a transfer order or indeed not to implement a transfer order, I do not believe that it follows, that it carries with it as a corollary, an entitlement on the part of the applicants to seek non implementation and with it an obligation on the Minister to give consideration to every such request, and to defer the implementation while consideration takes place."

In those circumstances, Birmingham J. refused to grant the application for judicial review. A similar conclusion was reached by Birmingham J. in *BOB, DOA (a minor) and PO (a minor) v Minister for Justice* [2007] I.E.H.C. 430, unreported, High Court, July 20, 2007. The extent to which such view is consistent with the decision of Finlay Geoghegan J. in *Makumbi* remains to be explored, and the Supreme Court decision in the appeal in *Makumbi* is eagerly awaited to clarify the extent of the Minister's obligations in this regard.

LEGISLATION

Directive on minimum standards on procedures in Member State for granting and withdrawing refugee status (Directive 2005/85/EC) On December 1, 2007, the vast majority of the provisions of the Directive on minimum standards of procedures in Member States for granting and withdrawing refugee status (Directive 2005/85/EC) became directly effective. Both the Immigration, Protection and Residence Bill 2007 and its 2008 incarnation seek to transpose the terms of that Directive into domestic law and to regulate many other issues pertaining to asylum and immigration in the State. The Directive regulates issues such as access for applicants for asylum to legal representatives and to an interpreter, to the duty upon a decision-maker to provide a reasoned decision, and also sets out the obligation of applicants for asylum to co-operate with the conduct of the application procedure. It notes that its provisions set out minimum standards and that Member States may introduce or maintain more favourable standards on procedures, in so far as those standards are compatible with the Directive. Worryingly, while the Directive also establishes a prima facie right to a personal interview in advance of the making of a decision, it also establishes that such interviews may be dispensed with at the first stage of the application process on various grounds, including grounds which arise where the assessor feels that the applicant has made inconsistent, contradictory, improbable or insufficient representations which make his or her claim clearly unconvincing (Art.23(2)(g)). Thus, it would appear that an applicant who is deemed by an assessor to fall within that category may be denied an oral hearing at any stage, thus denying him or her the opportunity to clarify the apparent inconsistencies, a situation which may not accord with the requirements of natural and constitutional justice in this jurisdiction (see, for example, the judgment of Clarke J. in *Moyosola v Refugee Appeals Tribunal*, unreported, High Court, June 23, 2005 discussed in *Annual Review of Irish Law 2005*, pp.38–41).

The Directive also sets out certain basic requirements to be adhered to in the context of applications for asylum by unaccompanied minors and it is noteworthy that it is envisaged therein that the best interests of the child shall be a primary consideration for Member States when implementing the provisions regarding such applications. Finally, it is stated that it is desirable that first instance applications shall be determined within six months of the commencement of the application, although such a timeframe is a guideline only and does not create an enforceable entitlement on behalf of an applicant.

Employment Permits Act 2006 The Employment Permits Act 2006 also came into force January 1, 2007. This extensive piece of legislation replaced the old regulatory scheme of work permits and work visas, as granted to employers in relation to prospective employees, with a new regime regulating the application, grant, renewal, refusal and revocation of employment permits which shall henceforth be granted to an employee and not to the employer. There are, in essence, three main types of arrangement envisaged and regulated by the Act. First, provision is made for a Work Permit scheme for certain specified occupations in the €30,000 to €60,000 salary per annum range and for a very limited list of occupations at salaries of less than €30,000 per annum, where a labour shortage arises. Secondly, a form of "Green Card" is introduced for another list of occupations in which a skills shortage arises, in the annual salary range from €30,000 to €60,000 and for a more extensive list of occupations above €60,000 per annum. Finally, provision is made for a re-established intra-company transfer scheme for temporary trans-national management transfers.

European Communities (Free Movement of Persons) (No. 2) Regulations 2006 (S.I. No. 656 of 2006) On January 1, 2007, the European Communities (Free Movement of Persons) (No. 2) Regulations 2006 (S.I. No. 656 of 2006) came into force, replacing the European Communities (Free Movement of Persons) Regulations 2006 (S.I. No. 226 of 2006). The Regulations were made for the purpose of giving effect in Irish law to the Directive on the rights of citizens of the Union and their family members to move and reside feely within the territory of the Member States (Directive 2004/38/EC).

Under the Regulations, an EU citizen shall not be required to register his/her presence in the State with the immigration authorities, although he/she does not enjoy an unqualified right to reside herein. Such a person shall be entitled to reside in the State for a period of up to three months if in possession of valid identification documents and provided he/she shall not become an unreasonable burden on the social welfare system of the State. An EU citizen who wishes to stay for longer than three months must show that he/she is working; a student; has enough resources to ensure he/she does not become a burden on the social services; or else they must be a family member of an EU citizen in one of those categories. The Regulation also introduces a new status of permanent residence for European Union citizens and their family members after five years' residence in the State.

The provisions of the Regulation shall also apply to non-EU family members of EU citizens in certain circumstances. The term "family member" is defined to embrace "a partner with whom the EU citizen has a durable relationship", which is duly attested. However, Art.3(2) of the Regulation makes it clear that such rights shall accrue to non-EU citizen family members only if they can establish that they have been lawfully resident in another EU Member State before applying for a residence permit in Ireland. This requirement, which represents a considerable hurdle to many families who wish to live together in this State and who otherwise qualify under the terms of the Regulation, is the subject of ongoing litigation in the superior courts, discussed above (see discussion of the High Court decision in *SK & TT v Minister for Justice, Equality and Law Reform* [2007] I.E.H.C. 216, unreported, High Court, Hanna J., May 28, 2007, and as a result of the decision of the European Court of Justice in *Case C-127/08 Metock v Minister for Justice, Equality and Law Reform* (July 25, 2008) it was held that the requirement of prior residence in an EU Member State which the Regulation (and indeed its predecessor S.I. No. 226 of 2006) impose is ultra vires the Directive as the latter contains no comparable precondition to the exercise by a non-EU national spouse of a right to reside within the territories of the European Union.

On January 1, 2007, on the accession of Bulgaria and Romania to the EU, citizens of these countries became entitled to the benefit of the provisions of Directive 2004/38/EC and thus acquired the same rights of access to the State as a citizen of an existing EU Member State, albeit with limited access to the labour market. For the initial two years of accession (subject to review before the end of that time), Bulgarian and Romanian citizens will continue to require work permits as heretofore. However, this requirement will not apply in the case of persons already exempt by virtue of their existing residence status and persons who have been working legally in the State (i.e. with work permit or work authorisation) for a period of 12 months or more.

In January 2007 the Minister for Justice, Equality and Law Reform announced on the website of the Department of Justice, Equality and Law Reform that, by virtue of the application of the 2004 EU Protocol on Asylum for

Nationals of Member States of the European Union, asylum applications shall not be accepted from nationals of other Member States of the European Union including the recent accession States, Romania and Bulgaria. The said Protocol proceeded upon the basis that, in view of the level of protection of fundamental rights and freedoms by the Member States, applications for asylum made by a national of a Member State could be successful only in very exceptional circumstances ("(a) if the Member State of which the applicant is a national proceeds after the entry into force of the Treaty of Amsterdam, availing itself of the provisions of Article 15 of the Convention for the Protection of Human Rights and Fundamental Freedoms, to take measures derogating in its territory from its obligations under that Convention; (b) if the procedure referred to in Article 7(1) of the Treaty on European Union has been initiated and until the Council takes a decision in respect thereof; (c) if the Council, acting on the basis of Article 7(1) of the Treaty on European Union, has determined, in respect of the Member State of which the applicant is a national, the existence of a serious and persistent breach by that Member State of principles mentioned in Article 6(1); (d) if a Member State should so decide unilaterally in respect of the application of a national of another Member State; in that case the Council shall be immediately informed; the application shall be dealt with on the basis of the presumption that it is manifestly unfounded without affecting in any way, whatever the cases may be, the decision-making power of the Member State"), a situation not entirely in keeping with the stated policy of the Minister of blanket refusal of such applications.

Company and Insolvency Law

GRÁINNE CALLANAN, Lecturer in Company Law,
Waterford Institute of Technology

INSIDER DEALING

In January 2002, Fyffes plc ("Fyffes") initiated the first civil action for insider dealing in Ireland. Fyffes' multi-million euro claim was taken against one of its former directors, Jim Flavin; his company, Development Capital Corporation plc; and two of its subsidiaries, S & L Investments Limited and Lotus Green Limited. Fyffes claimed that the respondents had unlawfully dealt in its shares, because at the time of certain share sales in February 2000, Mr Flavin was in possession of "price-sensitive" information, namely the November and December 1999 Trading Reports (the "trading reports"), by reason of his position as a director of Fyffes. This information, which indicated trading difficulties and adverse profit forecasts for Fyffes, was not generally available to the public.

The plaintiff's claim failed as the High Court (Laffoy J.) concluded that while the defendants had dealt, they had not done so unlawfully as the information in the possession of the defendants was not "price-sensitive" (see *Annual Review of Irish Law 2005*). Fyffes appealed.

Fyffes' insider-dealing claim was based, inter alia, on s.108(1) of Pt V of the Companies Act 1990 (the 1990 Act). Part V of the 1990 Act was introduced in Ireland to transpose Council Directive 89/592/EEC (the Directive) but has since been repealed by s.31 of the Investment Funds, Companies and Miscellaneous Provisions Act 2005 (the "2005 Act"). A new regime now exists by virtue of the 2005 Act and the Market Abuse Regulations (S.I. No. 342 of 2005) which together transpose the more recent Market Abuse Directive 2003/6/EC into Irish law. Despite the legislative changes, aspects of the High Court's decision and Supreme Court's conclusions will remain relevant under the new legal framework.

Fyffes plc v DCC plc **[2007] I.E.S.C. 36 (Denham J., Geoghegan J., Fennelly J., Macken J., and Finnegan J.)** The High Court's findings of primary fact were not challenged. Rather, it was the identification and application of legal principles, which ultimately lead to the High Court's price-sensitivity conclusion, which formed the basis of the appeal. The Supreme Court unanimously allowed the appeal. Its key findings can be summarised under the following headings:

1. The reasonable investor test In assessing whether the information in the possession of the first respondent was "price-sensitive", the High Court accepted that an objective text was applicable. On this basis, Laffoy J. had asked whether as a matter of probability a "reasonable investor" would conclude that the information would impact on Fyffes' share price. The Supreme Court unanimously rejected the "reasonable investor" test as an appropriate or useful legal tool. There was no reference to such a concept in the 1990 Act and nor could one be implied from the Directive. In this regard Denham J. observed:

> "It is a method of interpretation which removes the analysis required one step from the law as stated. It creates a system where the law is being looked at through the eyes of a notional person and it renders the situation opaque. It is not a legal principle appropriate to the section. Indeed, as it is not expressly or impliedly in the section there would be a danger of legislating on the issue if this test were applied. In addition, there are a myriad of factors and investors in a market, and to choose some or either as representative of a reasonable investor appears subjective and arbitrary. The issue is the effect on the share price in the market of the information if the information were generally available."

Despite the Supreme Court's rejection of the "reasonable investor" test, Laffoy J.'s analysis in this regard will remain relevant under the new legal framework. The interpretation section of the Market Abuse Regulations 2005 specifically provides that the information in question is "information that a *reasonable investor* would be likely to use as part of the basis of the investor's investment decisions" (emphasis added).

2. Information offset Having established the "reasonable investor" test, the High Court had considered whether a reasonable investor:

> "...having assessed the negative news about Fyffes' performance in the first quarter in the context of the total mix of information available about Fyffes' prospects, would have concluded that the information indicated a lowering of expectations about Fyffes' earnings in the first half of financial year 2000 and in the full year of an order or magnitude that would probably impact on Fyffes' share price to a substantial or significant degree."

With regard to this "total mix of information", the High Court had taken into account other aspects of Fyffes' business and the sentiment in the market at the time. Having considered these factors and then off-setting them against the information contained in the Trading Reports, the High Court was satisfied that a "reasonable investor" would not have considered that the negative

Trading Reports would have impacted on the share price "to a substantial or significant degree".

The Supreme Court rejected this approach. Denham J. suggested that, even if hypothetically the "reasonable investor" test was adopted, off-set was not provided for in the statutory provisions, it was not in the Directive and there was no legal authority for it. Furthermore, to adopt such an approach would involve the unnecessary task of assessing which of the "myriad of factors at play in the market" would apply. The Supreme Court's findings with regard to "off-set" are consistent with the new legislative provisions. The Market Abuse Regulations specifically provide that the information to be assessed is information which is used as "*part* of the basis of the reasonable investor's investment decisions" (emphasis added). Accordingly, even if there are a number of other factors taken into account by the "reasonable investor" those factors will not be relevant to any analysis of the specific information under scrutiny.

3. Common sense approach to information in Trading Reports   The High Court had been invited by Fyffes to conclude that "intuitively the information appeared on its face to be price-sensitive". The High Court had rejected this approach on the grounds that the statutory test did not warrant drawing any conclusion in relation to the information contained in the Trading Reports standing alone. On appeal, his analysis was rejected. Denham J. was satisfied that the Trading Reports could stand alone and indeed could be considered specifically. Fennelly J. while acknowledging that there could be a danger of looking at Trading Reports in isolation suggested that the correct approach was to consider the trading reports in context. This context, he observed:

> "…is the market in Fyffes share at the relevant time and the market's expectations in respect of those shares. It was observed at the hearing that good results may lead to a fall in the share price; conversely, poor figures may lead to a rise. All depends on expectations. In the first case, the market may have been expecting better figures than the good ones published; in the other, the figures will not have been as bad as had been feared. Having made that important qualification, however, one would look for something to counter the normal expectation that bad news about a company's earnings and prospects will cause a fall in the share price. Other things being equal, the November/December figures were such as to be likely to disappoint the market. There was nothing current that other things were not equal. There was no built-in expectation of bad news. Expectations were to the contrary. Thus, I find the approach of the learned trial judge surprisingly cautious. To my mind, the November/December figures were such as to cast serious doubt on the prospects of the company, not only for the first quarter,

but also, as the learned trial judge herself observed, for the first half and even for the full year."

As to the application of the intuitive approach, Denham J. observed:

"[T]he term 'intuitively' more appropriately may be termed as the 'common sense' approach. This is in keeping with the common law approach to commercial issues...There is nothing in the statute that excludes common sense from the analysis as to whether or not information would be likely materially to affect the price of the shares. Consequently, it was an error to exclude common sense from the analysis."

In a similar vein, Fennelly J. remarked:

"[T]he appeal turns on the assessment of the likely price effects of a limited body of comparatively simple facts. In large measure...they are the sort of facts upon which common-sense judgments and opinions can be formed without the input of an extraordinary degree of expertise."

4. American and international jurisprudence   The Supreme Court unanimously rejected the use of American and international jurisprudence, so heavily relied upon by the High Court, as having no value to an analysis of Irish law. In particular, the Supreme Court was satisfied that the US authorities cited were distinguishable from the facts of the present case and, more importantly, that those authorities related to decisions on specific statutory and regulatory laws which were not relevant in Ireland. However, given that the "reasonable investor" test is now relevant under the new legislative framework, certain international authorities, cited in the High Court (the US decision of *TSC Industries Inc v Northway Inc* 426 US 438 (1976) and the Singapore decision in *Public Proseutor v Allen Ng Meng* [1990] 1 M.L.J), may be of persuasive authority in future market abuse cases.

5. "Likely materially"   Section 108 of the 1990 Act provided, inter alia, that it shall not be lawful for a person to deal in securities of a company if he is in possession of information that is not generally available and which is "likely materially" to affect the price of those securities. The Supreme Court accepted that the test was objective and was not dependent on the views of the first respondent or indeed the views of Fyffes' directors. While the words "likely materially" were not defined in the 1990 Act, the court was satisfied that the words should be interpreted in light of the Directive and thus "likely materially" must have the same meaning as "likely to have a significant effect on the price of securities" as stated in the Directive. Under the new framework "likely materially" is specifically replaced by "likely to have a significant effect on the prices of financial instruments".

6. Conduct of Fyffes' directors/fundamental incongruity   The Supreme Court rejected the evidence, accepted as relevant but not determinative by the High Court, that the opinions, knowledge, actions or inactions of the directors of Fyffes had any relevance to an objective test. Therefore, the "fundamental incongruity" term, developed during the High Court hearing, referring to the difference in the position taken by the directors of Fyffes at the time of the sale (when they did not appear to regard the information as price-sensitive) and their later action in bringing the insider dealing case, was irrelevant on the basis of an objective test. Fennelly J.observed:

> "One can only conclude that the 'fundamental incongruity,' if there is one, is just that. It may arise from the remedy provided by the legislature to the company itself. The Directive does not require Member States to provide a civil remedy to a company against those trading in its shares in breach of s.108(1). The incongruity would not exist if the plaintiff were another party to a share transaction, not in possession of the relevant information, and suing...for loss sustained by him. Part V provides a statutory remedy, which is not defeated by incongruity."

7. The use of the March 20 announcement as "a valid proxy"   On March 20, 2000, Fyffes had made an announcement to the market which was in effect a profit warning. This announcement had an immediate adverse effect on the share price. The High Court had excluded Fyffes' March announcement from having any evidential value on the grounds that evidence of a comparator would require parity of information and parity of market conditions. The Supreme Court did not agree with precise parity. In the words of Fennelly J., to adopt such an approach would be "extraordinarily rigid". Rather the Supreme Court was satisfied that the correct approach was to analyse the degree of similarity of the information in the trading reports and the March 20 Announcement, the markets at the relevant times, and the consequences to the share price of the comparative information becoming generally available. Depending on the degree of similarity of information in the trading reports and the comparator (the March Announcement) and the degree of similarity between the markets at the relevant time, the weight to be accorded to the comparator could be determined.

The Supreme Court considered in detail the information in the March Announcement and compared it to that in the trading report. It was satisfied that the information in the March 20 Announcement was significantly similar to the information in the trading reports of November and December 1999 in that the latter indicated that there was bad news about Fyffes' tradings and earnings performance and the former was a profit warning. The Supreme Court then considered the market itself on the relevant dates and was satisfied that there were no significant differences between the market on the relevant dates. Furthermore, even if there were differences the Supreme Court was satisfied that such would just affect the weight to be given to the evidence but would not exclude it. The March 2000 Announcement illustrated the negative effect on the share price of the release of information very similar to that in the trading reports. Furthermore, having analysed the share price over the relevant period, in particular the significant drop after the March Announcement, the Supreme Court was satisfied that the March Announcement "materially" affected the price of the shares and accordingly it was price-sensitive.

8. Conclusion   Having allowed the March Announcement and its effect as a useful comparator and having assessed the market at the relevant dates, the Supreme Court concluded that the information contained in the trading figures would, if it had been generally available on the dates of the share sales, have been likely materially to affect the price of Fyffes shares and allowed the appeal.

This ruling means that the respondents will be liable to account to Fyffes for profits gained as a result of their dealings. In the absence of a negotiated settlement the matter is likely to revert to the High Court for an assessment of damages. The case raises many issues, which will no doubt remain relevant under the new legal framework for insider dealing. One obvious concern, which remains following the decision, is the matter of the "fundamental incongruity" referred to in both the High Court and Supreme Court decisions. While the Supreme Court was satisfied that the beliefs, representations and actions of Fyffes were of no relevance to an objective application of the legislation, it nonetheless raises the question as to whether the new civil liability provisions should be reviewed to perhaps reflect mitigating factors which should be taken into account in any assessment of damages. While the Market Abuse Directive requires sanctions for market abuse it does not specifically require the imposition of civil liability. On the basis of the Supreme Court's analysis, even if the board of a company (or indeed, however unusual, the general meeting itself) authorised the sale by any of its directors of a company's shares knowing what information they had in their possession, then such an approval would be irrelevant in a later action for civil liability by the company against those directors for insider dealing.

EXCEPTIONS TO RULE IN *FOSS v HARBOTTLE*

Fraud on minority/interests of justice   In *Glynn v Owen* [2007] I.E.H.C. 328 the two plaintiffs and the first, second and third named defendants were each 20 per cent shareholders and directors of the fourth and fifth named defendant companies (the companies). The present application concerned a preliminary ruling as to whether the plaintiffs were entitled to pursue on behalf of the companies a claim against the first, second and third named defendant for wrongs allegedly done to the companies under the exceptions to the rule in *Foss v Harbottle* (1843) 2 Hare 261. In terms of the exceptions to the rule, the court referred to the "classic restatement" of the rule and its exceptions set out by Jenkins L.J. in *Edwards v Halliwell* [1950] 2 All E.R. 1064 at 1066 as follows:

> "The cases falling within the general ambit of the rule are subject to certain exceptions. It has been noted in the course of argument that in cases where the act complained of is wholly *ultra vires* the company or association the rule has no application because there is no question of the transaction being confirmed by any majority. It has been further pointed out that where what has been done amounts to what is generally called in these cases a fraud on the minority and the wrongdoers are themselves in control of the company, the rule is relaxed in favour of the aggrieved minority who are allowed to bring what is known as a minority shareholders' action on behalf of themselves and all others. The reason for this is that, if they were denied that right, their grievance could never reach the court because the wrongdoers themselves, being in control, would not allow the company to sue. Those exceptions are not directly in point in this case but they show, especially the last one, that the rule is not an inflexible rule and it will be relaxed where necessary in the interests of justice."

The plaintiffs relied upon the "fraud on the minority" exception. Referring to the relevant authorities (*Burland v Earle* [1902] A.C. 83, *Crindle v Wymes* [1998] 4 I.R. 567 at 593, *Daniels v Daniels* [1978] Ch. 406 and *Pavlides v Jensen* [1956] 1 Ch. 565) the court considered that in order to invoke this exception, the plaintiff must satisfy two requirements. The first is that some benefit must have accrued to the wrongdoers. The second is that the alleged wrongdoers must be in control of the company.

The court was satisfied that the issue of 'control' must be determined in a common sense way in the context of the relevant facts and company structure (referring with approval to *Russell v Wakefield Waterworks Co.* (1875) L.R. 20 Eq., 474 and *Prudential Assurance Co. Ltd v Newman Industries Ltd. (No.2)* [1982] Ch 204).

On the basis of the facts the court was satisfied that the allegations against the defendants were distinct and that it was necessary to consider them separately. In relation to the third defendant, while allegations of wrongdoing were made against him, the plaintiffs did not allege that he had benefited improperly at the expense of the companies. Furthermore, the facts demonstrated that the third defendant became a director and shareholder of the companies at the behest of the plaintiffs, with whom he had prior business connections. He had no business or other links with the first and second defendants and the court was satisfied on the evidence that on the "normal balance of probabilities" the third defendant did not form part of a controlling majority of either of the companies. On this basis the plaintiffs could not claim the "fraud on the minority" exception in relation to the third defendant.

The plaintiffs did allege that the first defendant had wrongfully benefited personally at the expense of the companies. Most of the plaintiffs' claims were made against the first defendant but there were also some made against the second defendant (the son of the first defendant). The court was satisfied that the nature of the allegations against the first and second defendants, were such that they might come within the "fraud on the minority" exception. The court accepted the assumption (for purposes of convenience rather than evidence) that the first and second defendants should be considered jointly in control of 40 per cent of each of the companies. Despite this assumption, the court was satisfied that the first and second defendants collectively were in fact a minority and accordingly the plaintiffs had failed to establish the necessary requirement of "control" to sustain the "fraud on a minority" claim.

The plaintiffs further sought to pursue the derivative claim as an exception to the rule in *Foss v Harbottle* "in the interests of justice". This ground has been referred to in a number of cases concerning derivative actions but the courts have not to date had to rely solely on this "less solidly based fifth exception". Referring to a number of case and academic authorities on this exception (including Keane J. in *Crindle Investments v Wymes* [1998] 4 I.R. 567, Wigram V.C. and Jenkins L.J. in *Edwards v Halliwell* [1950] 2 All E.R. and *Foss v Harbottle* (1843) 2 Hare 261) the court agreed that the formulation of the rule in *Foss v Harbottle* makes it clear that it should not be applied in such a way as to lead to injustice. Nonetheless, Finlay Geoghegan J. cautioned that:

> "[T]he entitlement of a shareholder to pursue by way of derivative action a claim for and on behalf of a company is an exception to an 'elementary principle' as referred to above. As such it should not be broadly or liberally applied. A very strong case would have to be made out. It would also have to be consistent with the principles underlying the rule in *Foss v. Harbottle* and the exceptions to it. These include the reluctance of the courts to interfere in the internal management of a company."

On the basis of the facts and the company structure, the court did not consider that the plaintiff had established any exceptional circumstances, which would justify permitting the claims to proceed "in the interests of justice" or to avoid an injustice. Having rejected the "fraud on the minority" and the "interests of justice" exceptions the court refused to permit the plaintiffs pursue by way of derivative action the claims pleaded against the first, second or third defendants for alleged wrongs and breach of duty to the companies.

RESTRICTION

Sale of insolvent company to an undischarged bankrupt   In *Re Greenmount Holdings Ltd* [2007] I.E.H.C. 246 the liquidator of the company made an application for an order of restriction against the respondents. The first respondent resigned as director in November 2004, having been "bought out" for €130,000 by the company. The third named respondent, the wife of the second named respondent, was appointed to replace the first respondent as director. The second and third named respondents resigned as directors in July 2005 following the sale by the second named respondent of his interest in the company to the fourth named respondent. As the fourth named respondent was at the time of the sale an undischarged bankrupt. Subsequently, the fifth named respondent became a director of the company. The fourth and fifth named respondents had already submitted to a restriction order so the present application only concerned the first, second and third named respondents.

For some years prior to the winding-up relations between the first and second named respondent had broken down. As a result the company did not prepare audited accounts after 2000. The first and second named respondents blamed each other for this state of affairs. The first named respondent claimed that she had attempted to ensure that books and records were prepared at all times and made every effort to rectify the deficiencies, including employing a firm of accountants at her own expense to bring the books and records up to date prior to her resignation as a director. The first named respondent also made allegations of impropriety against the second named respondent and the auditor of the company. In 2003 the auditor was dismissed and a new firm appointed, but for various reasons the former auditor refused to hand over the books and records to the new auditors which contributed to the lack of audited accounts. The second named respondent claimed that in 2002 he became concerned with a number of issues, which were brought to his attention by the company auditors. These issues included payments by the company to a Polish company in which the first named respondent had an interest, withdrawal of monies by the first named respondent from the company's Visa account and the transfer out of the company's bank account of a sum of money on foot of a bank transfer form which purported to contain his signature but which he did not sign. The second named respondent had commenced minority oppression proceedings under s.205 of the 1963 Act with regard to these matters. The third named respondent was appointed as it was suggested to "make up the numbers". She played no role in the day-to-day management of the affairs of the company, but she did discuss company matters with her husband.

The liquidator raised various issues for the court to consider in determining whether the first, second and third named respondents acted responsibly during their tenure as directors of the company including, inter alia, the following:

a) Whether the respondents ensured that the company maintained proper books of accounts;

b) Whether the directors in general and the first and second named respondents in particular, properly functioned as a board of directors and if not, whether any negative consequences were caused to the company by this;

c) Whether the decision of the first, second and third named respondents to procure the company to purchase the first named respondents' share capital in the company for €130,000.00 was a reasonable decision and a transaction that was in the best interest of the company;

d) Whether the decision of the second and third named respondents to transfer control of the company to the fourth named respondent was a responsible decision;

e) Whether the first named respondent's decision to procure the company to issue invoices to a Polish company was a responsible decision.

The court was referred to the usual authorities regarding the level of responsibility owed by directors (*La Moselle Clothing Limited v Souhali* [1998] 2 I.L.R.M. 345; *Kavanagh v Delaney*; *Re Tralee Beef & Lamb Limited* (unreported, High Court, Finlay Geoghegan J., July 20, 2004), *Re Barings plc (No. 5) Secretary of State for Trade and Industry the Baker* (1991) 9 B.C.L.C. 433). On the basis of these authorities the court was satisfied that the company failed to keep proper books and records so as to enable the financial position of the company to be determined with reasonable accuracy after 2000. The court could not determine which of the respondents was responsible for the failure to ensure that the company produced audited accounts after 2000 and the failure to maintain proper books of account. The court accepted that some attempts to regularise the situation were made but that these attempts were impeded by inter-personal disputes and the s.205 litigation. Accordingly the court did not consider that there were sufficient grounds to make a restriction order with regard to the first and second named respondents on this issue. With regard to the third respondent, despite the fact that she was in breach of her duties the court was satisfied that given the short period of her tenure she was not in a position to alter events in the circumstances that arose and refused to make an order restricting her on this ground.

While the court accepted that the respondents had failed to function as a board of directors given the breakdown of the relationship between the first and second named respondents the court did not consider it appropriate to restrict them on this ground. The liquidator contended that the payment of €130,000 by the company to the first named respondent was irresponsible because the company was insolvent at the time and had insufficient reserves to make the payment. The first and second named respondents had obtained separate legal advices and no question was raised as to the sufficiency of the company's reserves to finance the buy-back of the shares. While the court was not entirely convinced that the purchase of the first named respondent's share capital in the company for €130,000 was a responsible decision given its financial difficulties, it was satisfied that given the long-standing disagreements between the first and second named respondent and given that they had obtained professional advice in the matter, no restriction order should be made in respect of that matter.

In July 2005 the second named respondent sold his interest in the company to the fourth named respondent for €1. The liquidator contended that the second named respondent acted in an irresponsible way in disposing of the company in this manner. The court was satisfied that at the time when the second named respondent took the decision to sell the shares in the company to an undischarged bankrupt the company was insolvent and that such a decision was irresponsible on the part of the second named respondent and militated against an orderly winding down of the company's affairs. This action by the second named respondent amounted to a "lack of commercial probity" and the court concluded that on this basis a restriction order was appropriate. The court observed that although the third named respondent had a responsibility in regard to this decision the evidence suggested that the decision was made by the second named respondent. Accordingly, the court refused to make an order restricting the third named respondent.

The liquidator alleged that the first named respondent had an interest in a business in Poland. It was contended by the liquidator that the company facilitated a client at this Polish enterprise to evade tax, without the knowledge of the second named respondent, by raising false invoices. The first named respondent refuted the allegation and suggested that the liquidator had never produced the alleged false invoices or indeed any evidence to suggest that they had been issued. The court expressed concern about these allegations, but was not satisfied that the evidence was sufficient to enable a restriction order to be made against the first named respondent on this ground.

The final matter relating to the allegations of the false invoicing raises once again the issue of onus in respect of s.150 applications. While the onus in s.150 applications technically rests with the directors (with the obvious exceptions of nominee directors) to demonstrate their honesty and responsibility, the reality is that the liquidator must bring to the attention of the court matters which are considered relevant to a charge of dishonesty or irresponsibility. If a company is without funds, the ability of the liquidator to investigate certain matters may be hampered. In a case such as this where a non-resident company was a party to the allegations of certain improprieties it would no doubt have caused considerable cost to a liquidator to attempt to fully investigate this matter. Such an investigation would have been compounded by the fact, which the court acknowledged, that the directors had failed to keep proper books of accounts. While the allegations may have had no factual basis, the case does raise concerns regarding the ability of liquidators, who are statutorily mandated to bring restriction applications, to fully investigate certain matters, and demonstrates the reality of where the onus really falls in the case of restriction applications.

Trading on revenue liabilities   In *Re Pineroad Distribution Ltd* [2007] I.E.H.C. 55 the liquidator of the company was appointed in 2004 and made an application to have the respondent directors restricted. The principal concern of the liquidator related, inter alia, to the continuous trading of the company despite substantial accrued and ongoing tax liabilities. The statement of affairs prepared by the respondents showed that the total revenue debt amounted to approximately 98 per cent of the unsecured creditors of the company and the liquidator contended that the actual revenue liabilities were far in excess of the amount stated in the statement of affairs.

With regard to the degree of responsibility owed by directors the court referred with approval to the usual line of authorities (*Re Squash Ireland Limited* [2001] 3 I.R. 35; *Re Lo-Line Motors Limited* [1988] Ch. 477; *La Moselle Clothing Limited v Soualhi* [1998] 2 I.L.R.M. 345; *Re Tralee Beef and Lamb*, unreported, High Court, July 20, 2004; *Re Swanpool Limited*, unreported, High Court, Clarke J., November 4, 2005; *Business Communications v Baxter*, unreported, High Court, July 21, 1995; *Re The Computer Learning Centre Limited; O'Ferrall v Gill*, unreported, High Court, February 7, 2005; and *Re Usit World plc*, unreported, High Court, August 10, 2005). With regard to the specific act of trading while insolvent to the detriment of the revenue, the court referred to *Re Digital Channel Partners* [2004] 2 I.L.R.M. 35 where Finlay Geoghegan J., dealing with tax failures for a period of some four to five months, stated:

> "There are, I think, two ways of looking at the failures to make tax returns. The failures to make tax returns are clearly in breach of the relevant Taxes Act. Similarly the failure to make the payments are in breach of the Taxes Acts. The mere fact that a company is in breach for, as in this case, a relatively limited period will not of itself, it seems to me, indicate that the directorate of the Company have acted either dishonestly or irresponsibly in such a way as to preclude my concluding that overall they acted responsibly and honestly in relation to the conduct of the affairs of this Company. Unfortunately and inevitably where companies are under significant financial pressure this may occur.
>
> It appears to me that in relation to tax liabilities there must be something more than a limited failure over a period to indicate that the directors have acted irresponsibly. This has been put in a number of different ways and certainly insofar as there may be evidence that there

either has been selective distribution or selective payment of liabilities of a company or indeed a total disregard of obligations to the Revenue or even a decision to effectively seek to use taxation liabilities for the purpose of financing a company, that of itself will normally be indicative of the fact that the directors have been acting at least irresponsibly."

Turning to the company's position in the present application, Hannah J. accepted the liquidator's submissions that the Revenue debt was in the region of €1.8m as opposed to the lesser sum of €900,000 identified in the statement of affairs. Furthermore, the court accepted that the problems with the Revenue debt had built up since 1994 and despite arrangements being made with the Revenue to deal with the issue these arrangements had not materialised and the problems remained. Accordingly it came to pass that the company had traded for a period of approximately two years during which time the company's taxation liabilities were not meaningfully addressed. In this regard Hanna J. observed:

"It would, therefore, appear to be the case that the seeds of the insolvency were sown back in 1994 and these in turn were nourished over the years by culpable ignorance on the part of the respondents. It is surprising to say the least that the Revenue Commissioners did not themselves become involved over the years given that what was clearly a major concern seemed to be making relatively modest VAT returns and failing to make VAT 3 returns on a continuous basis. In any event, it is clear as of the 2001 accounts that there was a major problem with regard to the amount of Value Added Tax owed. In my view, given the proportions of the problem, what otherwise might have been in far less serious circumstances, an understandable and indeed, laudable attempt to trade out of the difficulty in a short term fashion became an act of irresponsibility. If the dimensions of the tax problems were not clear to the respondents as directors by 2001 then they ought to have been."

The court was satisfied that not only had the company failed to address the Revenue problems but had also traded using revenue monies. Hanna J. referred with approval to the decision in *Duignan v Stephen Arthur Carway* (unreported, High Court, January 23, 2002) where McCracken J. stated:

"Indeed it is clear that at least from the beginning of 1993 this Company was being kept alive by the fact that it was in effect trading on monies due to the Revenue, and allowing huge arrears to build up, together with the attendant interest. Quite astonishingly Dr. Forde SC attempted to justify this situation by arguing that if a company is temporarily short of funds, it may be justified in not paying the Revenue and in effect taking a loan on interest to keep the company going. P.A.Y.E. and P.R.S.I. are monies which a company pays to the Revenue on behalf of its employees, and constitutes its employees tax and its employees' social insurance. To try to justify trading by using what is in effect its employees' money without their knowledge or consent, is to me a quite bizarre and totally irresponsible attitude. This appears to have been a policy of the Board of Directors, and is not something which can be attributable to any one particular director. On this ground alone I have no doubt that the directors must be restricted under s. 150."

On the basis of the authorities cited, Hannah J. concluded that the respondents, being at best culpably ignorant of the company's tax affairs, acted irresponsibly. They had failed to acquaint themselves with the company's tax affairs and they had continued to trade and used Revenue monies in so doing. This was borne out by the fact that in the final analysis no creditor was owed more than €2,000 apart the Revenue Commissioners. In continuing to trade for a period far beyond what could reasonably be excused having regard to the enormous scope of their tax problems, the respondents had acted with gross recklessness and contrary to the interests of the creditors of the company. Accordingly the court was satisfied that the respondents should be restricted under s.150 of the 1990 Act.

LIQUIDATIONS

Compulsory or voluntary winding-up? In *Re Permanent Formwork Systems Ltd* [2007] I.E.H.C. 268 a petition was presented to the court to wind up the company following a notice under s.214 of the Companies Act 1963, which was not complied with. When the petition came for hearing the court was informed that on the same morning the company had passed a resolution to wind up the company as a creditors' voluntary winding-up. Counsel for the company submitted that the petition should be dismissed on the grounds that the debt was disputed and that in accordance with the jurisprudence of the court, the voluntary liquidation, which was cheaper and more expeditious than a court winding-up, should be allowed to proceed. Four creditors supporting the voluntary winding-up appeared before the court and were represented by the same solicitor. Two of these creditors were connected to the company and the petitioner also alleged that the other two creditors were "not independent either, suggesting some form of contrivance in the manner that they came to be represented by the same firm of solicitors."

The court restated the well settled principle of law that if a company in good faith and on substantial grounds disputes liability in respect of the alleged debt on which a petition to wind up a company is founded, the petition will be dismissed. The petitioner, a former director and managing director, claimed that he was owed €157,000 by the company. The company admitted it owed the petitioner the amount claimed but submitted that it was entitled to deduct certain sums from that amount. The first sum related to €98,240.67 which represented an amount owed to the company by a company controlled by the petitioner. The second sum of €51,660.74 represented withdrawals from company accounts which were made by a third party on the authorisation of the petitioner. These two sums were, as the court suggested, transmogrified by the company into an amount due by the petitioner to the company on foot of a claim for alleged breach of the fiduciary duty owed by the petitioner, as a director, to the company. The court observed that proceedings for breach of fiduciary duty against the petitioner had not been initiated by the company. The court was satisfied that there was insufficient evidence to justify dismissing the petition on the ground that the debt was disputed.

Irrespective of this issue the court concluded that the winding up of the company was inevitable and the only real issue was whether the court should make an order for the winding up of the company or whether the creditors' voluntary liquidation should be allowed to proceed. The petitioner submitted that the court should make a winding-up order for a number of reasons including, inter alia:

(a) The manner and timing of the voluntary winding-up suggested that the company was seeking to supplant the process of a court liquidation, which was initiated first.

(b) The petition is based on an undisputed debt of €157,000 and the company's set-off argument was spurious.

(c) Given the company's allegations against the petitioner it was appropriate that an independent liquidator be appointed.

(d) The creditors' likely affirmation of the company's choice of liquidator was a cause for concern given the connection of certain creditors to the company.

The court was referred to the decision of the English Court of Appeal in *Re JD Swain Limited* [1965] 1 W.L.R. 909 where Diplock L.J. observed:

> "It seems to me ... that the guide-line has been laid down in this way: In the case of a petition for compulsory winding up, if the only circumstances which are available are that the petitioner seeks compulsory winding up and the majority of the creditors seek that there should be no winding up at all, then prima facie the petitioning creditor is entitled to a winding up unless there are some additional reasons for deciding to the contrary. If, on the other hand, the petitioner seeks a compulsory winding up and the majority of the creditors seek a voluntary winding up, then for the wishes of the petitioner to overrule those of the majority of the creditors there must be some special reason

why the wishes of the majority should be over-ridden. The difference or the distinction seems to me to be an obvious one, namely, in the former case, what is being resisted is any winding up at all, so that the petitioning creditor, if he fails, will be denied the class remedy which he would otherwise have if the winding up took place; whereas, in the latter case, he will obtain the class remedy anyway under the voluntary winding up, and the matter then turns upon his being able to show some reason why the remedy under the voluntary winding up is not an adequate remedy for him."

The court considered the factors to be taken into account in determining whether to make a winding-up order in a situation in which a creditor's voluntary liquidation has already commenced and the petition is presented after such commencement. In *Re Gilt Construction Limited* [1994] 2 I.L.R.M. 456 (which was followed by McCracken J. in *Re Naiad Ltd*, unreported, High Court, February 13, 1995) these factors were summarised in the case headnote as follows:

"(1) The court must be slow to dislodge a voluntary liquidator appointed to wind up a company with the concurrence of a majority, both numerically and in value, of its creditors.

(2) [The Liquidator's] credentials in terms of his professional qualifications and competence were not impugned in any manner which would justify conversion from a voluntary liquidation into a liquidation under the direction of the court.

(3) The court must have regard to a number of factors before dislodging a voluntary liquidator, in particular, the costs involved in a winding up by the court, the delay which would be incurred, the overall value of the assets to be administered, the level of complexity of the winding up and other factors such as the question of *mala fides* on the part of any person involved in the dispute.

(4) The present case involved assets of a relatively small value and so the winding up should be relatively straightforward and simple. In the event that unexpected problems should arise, an application could be brought pursuant to s. 280 of the Companies Act, 1963."

The court also referred to the English decision of *Re Zirceram Limited* [2000] 1 B.C.L.C. 751 where Lawrence Collins Q.C sitting as deputy judge set out the relevant principles as follows:

"(1) One of the reasons, if not the principal reason, for giving weight to the views of the majority of creditors who wish the voluntary liquidation to continue is that they have the largest stake in the assets of the company and their motives (especially if they are connected with the company) for resisting compulsory liquidation may be questionable if there are no assets or no realistic prospects of recovery for the unsecured creditors.

(2) The court may have regard to the general principles of fairness and commercial morality, and the exercise of discretion should not leave substantial independent creditors with a strong legitimate sense of grievance. Fairness and commercial morality may require that an independent creditor should be able to insist on the company's affairs being scrutinised by the process which follows a compulsory order.

(3) Inter-group transactions may require a special scrutiny if they operate to the prejudice of creditors and the court may take account of the fact that an opposing creditor is not an independent creditor, but an associated company.

(4) A compulsory liquidation may be ordered so that there can be an investigation which is not only independent, but seen to be independent. Even if there is no criticism of the liquidator appointed in the voluntary winding up: (a) the fact that associated supporting creditors have gone to great lengths to install, and maintain, him in office, may disqualify him in the eyes of the creditors; (b) the petitioning creditors may view with cynicism any investigation undertaken by a liquidator chosen by the very person whose conduct is under investigation.

(5) A liquidator appointed in the voluntary winding up must be seen not to be taking sides, but even if there is no attack on the probity or competence of the liquidator, or any other criticism, it may nevertheless be right to protect the creditors by a full investigation into the affairs of the company by a fully independent liquidator appointed in the context of a compulsory winding up."

Counsel for the petitioner relied on the principle set out in point (4) above. It was suggested that given the history between the parties, a perception of a lack of independence, where the company chooses the liquidator, would be justified. This, the petitioner submitted, constituted a special reason for making a winding-up order. While the court acknowledged that there were aspects of the company's actions which gave rise to concern, nonetheless the court should have regard to the views of the majority of the creditors who wished the voluntary liquidation to continue. The requirement that the petitioner establish a special reason for making the winding-up order had not been satisfied. The court noted the safeguard now in place, as the Director of Corporate Enforcement had a supervisory role in relation to a voluntary winding-up. Accordingly the court dismissed the petition.

CREDITORS' REMEDIES

In *Re Powertech Logistics Ltd* [2007] I.E.H.C. 43 the applicant creditor had obtained judgment against the first respondent company for circa €290,000 together with costs, which was not satisfied as the company was insolvent. Subsequently, the applicant had sought and was granted an order under s.371(1) of the 1963 Act requiring the first respondent (the company) and the second and third named respondents (the directors of the company), to submit all outstanding statutory annual returns and audited financial statements to the Companies Registration Office in respect of the years 2002–2006 inclusive, within 12 weeks. The order was not complied with within the required period. Shortly thereafter the applicant sought an order under Ord.42 r.32 of the Rules of the Superior Court enforcing sequestration against the property of the respondents and an order of attachment against the second and third named respondents. Soon after that the s.371 order was complied with and the relevant annual returns were filed in the Companies Registration Office.

Order 42, r.32 provides as follows:

> "Any judgment or order against a company wilfully disobeyed may, by leave of the Court, be enforced by sequestration against the corporate property, or by attachment against the directors or other officers thereof, or by order of sequestration against their property."

The applicant confirmed that it was not seeking sequestration against the company as no corporate property existed, but suggested that the court might order the payment of some appropriate amount by the second and third named respondents which would signal the court's disapproval of non-compliance with the s.371(1) order. Laffoy J. did not consider it appropriate to make an order of sequestration for a number of reasons.

First, she considered that the primary purpose of an order under Ord.42 r.32 is to procure enforcement of a judgment or order of the court and in the circumstances, as the order had been complied with, albeit late, the granting of the order would be punitive rather than coercive (*Re Ross Company Limited (In Receivership); Shortall v Swan* [1981] I.L.R.M. 416 referred to). The second objection was based on a procedural point. Order 41 r.8 of the Rules of the Superior Court provides that:

> Every judgment or order made in any cause or matter requiring any person to do an act thereby ordered, shall state the time, or the time after service of the judgment or order, within which the act is to be done; and upon the copy of the judgment or order which shall be served upon the person required to obey the same … there shall be endorsed a memorandum in the words or to the effect following, *viz.*:
> "If you within named AB neglect to obey this judgment or order by

the time therein limited, you will be liable to process of execution
including imprisonment for the purpose of compelling you to obey
the same judgment or order."

Laffoy J. rejected the submission of counsel for the applicant that as
sequestration and not attachment was being sought then Ord.41 r.8 need not be
complied with. The court observed that as sequestration against the property
of a director of a company is a penal sanction, as a matter of principle such
a distinction was not tenable (*Prior v Johnston* 27 I.L.T.R. 108 referred to).
Thirdly, the court concluded that in order to succeed under Ord.42 r.26 the
applicant would have had to satisfy the court that the second and third named
respondents had wilfully disobeyed the s.371 order (referring with approval
to *National Irish Bank v Graham* [1994] 1 I.R. 215). The court was satisfied
that there was no evidence that the failure to comply was wilful.

The applicant also sought, inter alia, an order to have the provisions of the
s.251(2) of the 1990 Act applied to the first respondent pursuant to s.251(1).
Section 251(1) of the 1990 Act provides inter alia that where a company is
unable to pay its debts and it appears to the court that it is not being wound
up because of insufficiency of assets, then many provisions of the Companies
Acts (including s.245 of the 1963 Act) may apply to such a company. The
applicant further sought an order pursuant to ss.245(1) and 245(2) of the
Principal Act requiring the second respondent and the third respondent,
directors of the first respondent, to attend before the court to give information
in relation to the promotion, formation, trade, dealings, affairs and property
of the respondent. The court was satisfied that as the first respondent was not
being wound up because of an insufficiency of its assets s. 251 was applicable.
It was suggested that the applicant's purpose in having the second and third
respondents summoned for examination was to provide information relating
to the promotion, formation, trade, dealings, affairs and property of the first
respondent. It was not suggested that either respondent was known or suspected
to have in its possession any property of the first respondent nor was it suggested
that either was indebted to the first respondent.

As no authority had been referred to in which the application of s.245 in
consequence of an order under s.251 had been considered, the court was referred
to two cases involving the application of s.245 or an equivalent section in a
liquidation context. In *Re Embassy Art Products Limited* [1988] B.C.L.C. 1
Hoffman J., when considering the appropriate use of the equivalent section,
stated:

> "Any application to use the section, which is *prima facie* an invasion
> of the rights of privacy of the persons whom it is sought to examine,
> is subject to the overriding requirement that the examination must be
> necessary in the interests of the winding up and not oppressive or unfair
> to the respondent. It is clear, however, that in applying these principles

there are significant differences in the court's approach to applications by liquidators, on the one hand, and contributories, on the other. Firstly, the liquidator is an officer of the court entrusted with the fulfilment of the court's duty ... to cause the company's assets to be collected and applied in discharge of its liabilities. He therefore has by virtue of his office *locus standi* to apply for an order. A contributory, on the other hand, or for that matter a creditor, must demonstrate that examination will probably result in some benefit accruing to him as such. ... Unless there is a likelihood of such benefit, the contributory or creditor has no more interest in the outcome of the winding up than anybody else..."

In considering whether the contributories had demonstrated that examination was necessary in the interests of the winding-up and that it was likely to result in some benefit to the applicants, Hoffman J. went on to say:

"Next I think it is relevant that no prior notice has been given to the respondents of any of the matters on which it is sought to examine them. In *Re Rolls Razor Limited (No. 2)* ... Megarry J. said that the court retained a discretion to order an examination notwithstanding that the respondent had been given no notice of the subject of the inquiry. He did, however, add that he could visualise cases in which it would be oppressive to seek to examine without such notice having been given, and this seems to me such a case ... There are no doubt cases in which the object of the inquiry would be defeated if the respondent were given advance notice of what he was going to be asked, but this certainly does not seem to me to be one of them. In my view it is oppressive to seek production of documents in the wide terms which have been ordered against the bank and examination of the other respondents in the most general terms without having made any attempt to obtain information by letter or other means in the first place."

The court also considered the High Court decision in *Re Comet Food Machinery Company Limited (in liquidation)* [1999] 1 I.R. 485. Here the applicant had obtained judgment against the company, but before the judgment a resolution to wind up the company had been passed and a new company was formed with the respondents as shareholders. This new company operated from the same premises as the old company and had the same employees. Furthermore it appeared that the other trade creditors of the old company had been paid and the applicant was concerned that the old company had been put into liquidation and the new company formed to frustrate its claim. Although, the court in *Comet* had observed that an application under s.245 by a creditor was unusual, it granted the order given the apparent evidence of "the phoenix syndrome".

In considering the application in the present case, Laffoy J. observed that there was no clear reason advanced by the applicant to demonstrate that some benefit would accrue to the applicant from the examinations sought. The court concluded that the applicant had failed to discharge that onus and that an examination under s.245 would amount merely to a "fishing expedition". The court further observed that there now existed the Office of the Director of Corporate Enforcement, which is empowered to pursue the *pro bono publico* aspects of any failures of the first respondent. Accordingly, the order under s.245 was refused.

DIRECTOR OF CORPORATE ENFORCEMENT

Delegation of "function" by Director distinguished from delegation of "power" In *Re Bovale Developments Ltd; Director of Corporate Enforcement v Bailey & Bailey* [2007] I.E.H.C. 365 the Director of Corporate Enforcement had instituted disqualification proceedings against the respondents. The originating notice of motion was grounded upon two affidavits, including one by Mr Peter Lacy, a partner in the firm of PricewaterhouseCoopers (PwC). The affidavit of Mr Lacy related principally to investigations carried out by his firm in relation to the affairs of Bovale Developments Ltd at the instigation of the applicant. The respondents sought to curtail the evidence put forward by the applicant in the grounding affadavit of Mr Lacy on the basis that there was an allegedly impermissible and unlawful delegation by the applicant of his functions to PwC pursuant to s.12(6) of the Company Law Enforcement Act 2001 (the 2001 Act). The respondents alleged that the evidence which the applicant sought to put before the court and which is to be found in the reports of PwC, was inadmissible as the material used to prepare the reports was not lawfully in the possession of PwC. The respondents submitted:

1)   One of the functions of the Director is to investigate instances of suspected offences under the Companies Acts, as provided for in s.12(1)(c) of the 2001 Act.

2)   The Director may perform his functions through an officer as provided for in s.12(6) but such delegation must be in writing pursuant to s.13(1) of the 2001 Act.

3)   The exercise of the power delegated must be in accordance with the instrument of delegation (s.13(2) of the 2001 Act).

4)   The contract documentation exchanged between PwC and the Director did not include any instrument of delegation and that therefore there was no lawful basis for the transfer of any documentation to PwC and its reports were therefore inadmissible.

5)   PwC is an unincorporated body which amounts to a "person" who can be an officer of the Director within the meaning of s.3(1) (c) of the 2001 Act.

However, it was contended that it is the partners of the firm who comprise an unincorporated body and as it is likely that PwC engaged a number of the firm's employees in the preparation of its report, that they have acted unlawfully and that the reports are tainted by the illegality.

The court rejected all submissions. The court considered that there was a difference in the role played by the Director when performing one of his "functions" as distinct from the exercise by him of one of the "powers" specifically ascribed to him in legislation. The Director has a wide range of functions, including the right to investigate instances of suspected offences under the Companies Acts. While s.3 of the 2001 Act states that the word "functions" includes "powers and duties", the court was satisfied that the Director might carry out many of his functions without necessarily exercising a power. In exercising his functions the Director is entitled to do through an officer (s.12(6) of the 2001 Act) and PwC, as an unincorporated body, is an officer within the meaning of s.3 of the 2001 Act. The Director had chosen to perform one of his functions, namely his investigation of suspected offences that may have occurred in Bovale by delegating this task to PWC as his officer. The court suggested that the respondents were confusing the right of the Director to delegate a specific power under s.13 (which requires strict formalities as to delegation) with his right to obtain assistance in the carrying out of his function through an officer under s.12(6) which did not. The court considered that it would be:

> "... entirely illogical to suggest that every time the Director carried out one of his functions, which are extraordinarily wide ranging, that he must physically prepare an instrument of delegation as is contended for by the respondents. The Court sees no reason, having regard to the provisions of s.12 and s.3 of the 2001 Act, to believe that the evidence put forward by the Director through the reports of PwC is inadmissible by reason of any want of compliance with s.13 of the 2001 Act."

The court also rejected the respondents allegation that the reports of PwC were tainted with illegality because, as a matter of probability, the conclusions reached in the reports are based upon investigations carried out not only by the partners of PwC but by more junior staff. As the court was satisfied that PwC could be an "officer", it was untenable to suggest that, in appointing an officer, the Director must identify by name not only the firm who he wishes to appoint, but also the name of each employee who may carry out the investigative work on his behalf. The court concluded that PwC was at all times acting as a lawfully appointed officer of the Director for the purposes of assisting him in carrying out his functions.

DISQUALIFICATION/INVESTIGATIONS

National Irish Bank   The fallout from the report of the inspectors appointed to investigate the affairs of National Irish Bank and National Irish Bank Financial Services Limited continued during the year with the disqualification of Mr Barry Seymour, the former Executive Director of National Irish Bank. In *Re National Irish Bank Ltd; Director of Corporate Enforcement v Seymour* [2007] I.E.H.C. 102 Murphy J. disqualified Mr Seymour for a period of nine years following an application by the Director of Corporate Enforcement. The inspectors' report had identified serious and significant defaults of management and legal non-compliance within National Irish Bank. As executive director the respondent was, for a period of 27 months, the single most senior employee in the company. The inspectors found that he knew of certain irregularities, he ought to have known of the tax evasion activities and he was ultimately responsible for the failure to eradicate these practices. The inspectors' report acknowledged the steps taken by the respondent during his short tenure to deal with non-compliance within the bank but concluded that these steps were not sufficient to resolve the problems. Murphy J., in reviewing the leading authorities on disqualification of directors, concluded that:

> "[T]he function of the court in addressing the question of unfitness is to decide whether the conduct of which the complaint was made, viewed cumulatively and taking into account any extenuating circumstances had fallen below the standards of probity and competence appropriate for persons fit to be directors of companies. The respondent's conduct had to be evaluated in context. The burden was on the applicant to satisfy the court that the conduct complained of demonstrated incompetence of a high degree assessed in the context of, and by reference to, the role in the management of the company which was assigned to the respondent and by reference to his duties and responsibilities in that role. While it might be said that there was a universal standard, that standard had to be applied to the facts in each particular case. There was no defence to a charge of unfitness based on incompetence to contend that, in discharging the management role assigned to him or which, in fact, he assumed, he had not been shown to be unfit to be concerned in the management of a company. It was not a prerequisite to a finding of unfitness that a respondent should have been guilty of misfeasance or breach of duty in relation to the company. Unfitness might be demonstrated by conduct which did not involve a breach of any statutory common law duty."

The court acknowledged the respondent's effort during his tenure but concluded that Mr Seymour should have been more decisive and effective in eliminating issues of non-compliance and redressing the consequence of improper practices as his successor had done. In the opinion of the court, the respondent demonstrated a lack of a proper standard of conduct and it was satisfied that an order for disqualification should be made.

The Director was not successful in his application to have a former regional manager and head of retail of National Irish Bank disqualified. In *Re National Irish Bank Ltd; Director of Corporate Enforcement v Curran* [2007] I.E.H.C. 181 the court refused to make a disqualification order against the respondent—a former regional manager and head of retail for the bank—despite the fact that he was considered by the inspectors to be part of a management team that was responsible for the improper practices in National Irish Bank. The court was satisfied that the inspectors' allegations, relied upon by the Director, were primarily based on omission rather than the commission of any wrongdoings. Nonetheless the court had to consider whether, given the respondent's position within the bank, he "should have been more assiduous in detecting the extent of non-compliance and in eliminating the improprieties found" and whether the omissions were such that would justify the order sought.

The court was concerned that the inspectors' classification of the respondent as senior management did not quite fit with the organisational chart within National Irish Bank and that accordingly there was some doubt as to whether the respondent was as a matter of fact a member of the senior management. This status was relevant in terms of the respondent's authority and ability to rectify the ongoing improper practices within the bank. The court was critical of the lack of action on the part of the respondent in particular his "dilatory and ultimately ineffectual intervention" in relation to the problems identified by the inspectors. Nonetheless, he distinguished the position of the respondent from those within National Irish Bank and National Irish Bank Financial Services Ltd who had already been made the subject of disqualification orders. Unlike those who had been disqualified, the respondent's involvement in non-compliance was indirect; he was not in a position to require compliance; he did not appear to have the authority to bring about the cessation of the improper practices; and he was not involved in the direction or governance of the Bank. Accordingly, the court did not consider it appropriate to make a disqualification order.

Ansbacher   In *Re Ansbacher (Cayman) Ltd & Others; Director of Corporate Enforcement v Stakelum* unreported, High Court, McGovern J., July 31, 2007 the applicant sought an order for disqualification against the respondent pursuant to s.160(2)(e) of the 1990 Act following the report of the inspectors appointed by the High Court to investigate the nature and extent of the Irish business of Ansbacher (Caymen) Ltd from 1971–99. The respondent was a chartered accountant who worked with the late Mr Desmond Traynor in the firm of Haughey Boland during the 1960s up until 1975 when he set up his own business, which gave commercial and financial advice its clients.

The inspectors found that Ansbacher's affairs were conducted with intent to defraud the revenue and that Ansbacher may have committed a number of criminal offences. The inspectors' report concluded that the respondent had given assistance to Ansbacher in carrying out its Irish business even though it did not appear that the respondent had knowingly done so. However, the report further concluded that the evidence tended to show that the respondent had, through another business vehicle, carried out business with intent to defraud the revenue and that the evidence tended to show that he may have committed other criminal offences. Referring to the leading case law on disqualification and taking into account the findings of the inspector the court concluded that the respondent had displayed "a lack of commercial probity". Counsel for the respondent argued that the court should exercise its discretion and not make an order as the events took place a long time before, the respondent had retired from business and would not be engaged as a director in the future and that accordingly the order was not necessary for the protection of the public. The court considered that in certain circumstances a deterrent element might be necessary in deciding whether or not to make a disqualification order (referring to *Re Westmid Packaging Services Ltd* [1998] 2 All E.R. 124). The court concluded that the respondent had engaged in activities, which facilitated the evasion of tax and that such activity was done in a calculated way. The court was satisfied that there was sufficient evidence to satisfy the court that the respondent was unfit to be concerned in the management of a company and a disqualification order was made for a period of five years.

In *Re Kentford Securities Ltd (under investigation); Director of Corporate Enforcement v McCann* [2007] I.E.H.C. 1 the applicant sought a disqualification order against the respondent. In 1998 an authorised officer was appointed by the then Tánaiste and Minister for Enterprise, Trade and Employment to examine the books and documents of Kentford Securities Limited (the company). This examination resulted from revelations that the company was used as a vehicle by Mr Desmond Traynor to facilitate tax evasion as part of the Ansbacher deposit scheme. Mr Traynor died in 1994. The respondent was a former director and auditor of the company. In the present application there was no suggestion that the respondent had improperly benefited from his position. However, the applicant claimed that his conduct as an auditor was such as to merit disqualification, including the following:

1) The respondent acted as auditor of the company while still a director in breach of s.163 of the Companies Act 1963. His resignation as a director was deliberately back-dated to mislead persons into believing that when he was acting as auditor of the company he was not doing so in breach of that section.

2) Even if the resignation was proper the respondent held himself out to be a director after his "resignation" from this position.

3) While an auditor of the company, the respondent had issued unqualified reports on the company's accounts when he knew or ought to have known, as auditor, that the impression given by the statements that the company was a dormant company showing assets and share capital of IR£2 each was false and misleading since there were large transactions going through the company's bank accounts, and that there were balances held in those accounts. In issuing these unqualified reports the authorised officer believed that the respondent committed offences under s.22(3) of the Companies (Amendment) Act 1986 and s.242 of the Companies Act 1990, and that by so doing he facilitated the defrauding of the Revenue Commissioners.

4) The respondent's submission that he had no knowledge that the company was being used as a vehicle for tax evasion was not accepted by the authorised officer.

5) The respondent had given a backdated document to the authorised officer to support his assertion that he had been assured by Mr Des Traynor that Kentford was a trust company only with no assets or liabilities.

The respondent qualified as an accountant around 1988 and had been employed in a junior capacity in a company called Chartered Secretarial Company (CSC), which provided company secretarial services to the company. The respondent remained in employment in CSC, even after setting up his own accountancy firm. Persons seeking company secretarial services from CSC were, on occasion, approached by the respondent where there was a need for audit or accountancy services.

The court acknowledged the well-known practice at the time for staff of companies such as CSC to be named as shareholders and directors of "off the shelf" companies which were formed by them. When these companies were sold, the staff members would resign as directors and sign share transfer forms in favour of the purchasers. The court noted that while this practice was customary, it "undoubtedly involved and had to involve a scant regard for strict compliance with the statutory obligations regarding returns and forms generally." The court further accepted the statement by the respondent that it was the practice of CSC to obtain and maintain on file undated signed letters of resignation and share transfer forms for members of staff who were directors/shareholders of these nominee companies. Peart J. referred to these practices because:

> "[T]here is no doubt in my mind that the respondent finds himself facing an application for his disqualification at least partly because of the fact that it was, as he has stated in his evidence, commonplace for staff to be appointed as directors and to resign as required, and I have no doubt that this culture of signing perhaps in advance or perhaps in arrears by

> backdating, whatever forms were required or requested to be signed by their employer so that the business of selling shelf companies could function speedily and conveniently, spread beyond documents such as appointment and resignation of directors and share transfer forms, and included in the case of the respondent such forms as he was asked to sign by ... his employer or indeed Mr Traynor directly."

While the court was critical of the practice of signing blank forms and/or backdating documentation, it acknowledged that the respondent was a relatively junior figure at the time of Mr Traynor's dealings with CSC and the company and that he would no doubt have done what was asked by his employer and Mr Traynor. The court also accepted, having regard to the evidence, that the respondent was never aware that anything illegal was taking place in relation to the company. The practices referred to above were considered to have resulted in the respondent signing auditor's reports for years during which he was also perhaps unwittingly a director of the company even if only "on paper". Although the court considered his resignation to have been contrived, such was in keeping with the practices of the time and the court was satisfied that it was not a deliberate or conscious breach of the law.

However, the court accepted that the respondent failed in his duty as an auditor of the company by signing unqualified reports on the financial statements for the years in question. The respondent's submission that he accepted the assurances from Mr Traynor that the company was a trust company was rejected by the court as an inadequate manner of discharging his duty as an auditor. He was required to do more and to "pro-actively satisfy himself from an examination of the bank accounts and books and records of the company that what he was told was in fact the situation". The court was satisfied that the backdated letter from Mr Traynor which was used to support the respondent's assertion that he was at all times made aware that Kentford was a trust company, was not a fabrication perpetrated by the respondent, but that he did not act bona fide when he handed the letter to the authorised officer as he must have been aware that the letter was backdated given the practices of the time. Nonetheless, the court reiterated that these actions were more in keeping with the practices of the time rather than evidence that the respondent was a party to the illegal activities of the company.

The court ultimately concluded that the matters raised by the applicant had occurred between 1988 and 1994 when the respondent was a junior employee in CSC. Nonetheless, it considered that even if the failures to observe proper standards as auditor of the company facilitated the scheme of tax evasion, the respondent was "a very small and insignificant cog in the larger wheel being turned by Mr Des Traynor." The court further noted that a disqualification would have a "devastating" effect on the respondent's accountancy practice and would compromise his capacity to earn a livelihood. In balancing the consequences of the effect of a disqualification order against the legislative intention underlying the disqualification provisions, viz. that the public should be protected from auditors who have fallen short of the standards expected of such an important profession in the commercial life of the country, the court was satisfied that the applicant had not demonstrated that as a matter of probability the respondent would present a current risk to members of the public. Accordingly, the court exercised its discretion in favour of refusing the disqualification order sought.

EXAMINERSHIP

Lack of candour and modification of scheme of arrangement   In *Re Traffic Group Ltd (in Examination)* Clarke J., December 20, 2007, Traffic Group Ltd (the company) had successfully petitioned the court in August 2007 for the appointment of an examiner. In November the examiner presented his report under s.18 of the Companies (Amendment) Act 1990 (the Act). The report proposed a scheme of arrangement that had been generally approved by the various meetings. However, the Revenue Commissioners, a significant preferential creditor, opposed the scheme. The court was satisfied that all the statutory prerequisites for the exercise of the court's entitlement to approve the scheme were met. It was further satisfied that the implementation of the scheme would give the company a real chance of survival and that most of the jobs of the company's employees would be saved.

The Revenue did not contest these findings. Rather, it opposed the scheme on the grounds that there were inappropriate actions by the petitioner leading up to the presentation of the petition by granting a charge over the company's assets to Bank of Scotland Ireland (BOSI) who had advanced monies to the company on foot of a guarantee by some of the petitioners. The granting of the charge would have the effect of reducing the likelihood of these petitioners being liable under the guarantee. Furthermore, in the run up to the petition the liabilities of the company to BOSI were reduced by a substantial sum. While these payments to BOSI conformed with a long-agreed payment schedule, the court was satisfied that the payments had the potential to significantly benefit the guarantors by reducing the liabilities which they had guaranteed and raised issues of fraudulent preference. The Revenue also submitted that the net financial position of the company, as set out in the petition and the verifying affidavits, was overstated by a small but nonetheless material amount. The court accepted that once accounts presented were relatively accurate, "any falling off from absolute correctness" would not justify refusing to confirm the scheme. Nonetheless, the court emphasised that there remains a significant obligation on those who might wish to petition the court in an examinership to ensure that the financial state of the company is presented to the court in as accurate a way as is practically possible in all the circumstances. The Revenue submitted that this lack of accuracy, while not decisive in its own right, should be viewed together with the aforementioned actions of the petitioners.

The court considered the authorities regarding the lack of candour in the examinership process (*Re Wogans (Drogheda) Ltd*, unreported, High Court, Costello J., May 7, 1992 and *Re Selukwe Ltd*, unreported, High Court, Costello J., December 20, 1991) and was satisfied that the actions of the petitioners in the run up to, and during, an examinership, is a factor to be taken into account in confirming or rejecting a scheme of arrangement. However, any such factor should also be weighed against the objective of the legislation.

With respect to the position of principals or shareholders Clarke J. observed:

> "It is important to note that the Act is not designed to immunise the principals or shareholders of a company from the consequences of the company concerned getting into financial difficulties. The value which shareholders may have in a company (whether they are involved in its management or not) may, in practice, be extinguished or greatly diminished by bad judgment in investing in the company in the first place, by bad management (either on the part of the investors themselves or those whom they trusted to run the company) or, indeed, plain bad luck. Whatever may be the cause, it does not seem to me that it is any part or purpose of the Act to solve the difficulties of such shareholders howsoever those difficulties may have arisen. If the Act were so designed it might well give some truth to the verse penned at the time of the introduction of limited liability companies into our legal scheme, which suggested that such companies amounted to a conspiracy by gentlemen (and at the relevant time it almost always would have been gentlemen or those who claimed to be such) whereby they met together to decide by how much they would not pay their debts. It is clear that the principal focus of the legislation is to enable, in an appropriate case, an enterprise to continue in existence for the benefit of the economy as a whole and, of equal, or indeed greater, importance to enable as many as possible of the jobs which may be at stake in such enterprise to be maintained for the benefit of the community in which the relevant employment is located. It is important both for the court and, indeed, for examiners, to keep in mind that such is the focus of the legislation. It is not designed to help shareholders whose investment has proved to be unsuccessful. It is to seek to save the enterprise and jobs."

On the basis of the authorities reviewed, Clarke J. considered that the court should lean in favour of approving a scheme where the enterprise, or a significant portion of it, and the jobs or a significant portion of them, are likely to be saved. However, he did not consider that the court should disregard any lack of candour or other wrongful actions. Accordingly he was satisfied that the court should consider the extent to which it may be possible to modify the proposed scheme of arrangement to "neutralise" the effects of any wrongful actions to ensure that those who may be guilty of a lack of candour or other wrongful action do not benefit from it.

Under the proposed scheme BOSI was being treated as an unsecured creditor, effectively disregarding the effect of the late charge and any consequential benefits to the guarantors. The court also modified the proposals to the effect that the petitioners should not continue, for at least a period of 18 months, to have any role of control in respect of the company. The court was satisfied that this modification went some way to offsetting the lack of candour on the part of the petitioners.

With regard to the payments made to BOSI the court acknowledged that had the company gone into liquidation and those sums been held to be a fraudulent preference, the Revenue Commissioners, as preferential creditor, would likely have benefited significantly by the repayment of such monies. On this basis one could conclude that the scheme as proposed was unduly prejudicial to the Revenue Commissioners. However, as it was not possible to make a finding as to a fraudulent preference, the court at this stage would not rule that the scheme was unfairly prejudicial to the legitimate interests of the Revenue Commissioners. Furthermore, the court was satisfied that a scheme can be approved even where a creditor can do worse than in a winding-up (*Re Antigen Holdings Ltd* [2001] 4 I.R. 600 approved). Accordingly, the court approved the scheme subject to the modification.

SECTION 204 COMPULSORY PURCHASE

In *Walls v PJ Walls Holdings Limited* [2007] I.E.S.C. 41 the appellant had sought to prevent the respondent from compulsorily acquiring his shares in two companies under s.204 of the Companies Act 1963. Smyth J. refused the appellant the relief sought (see *Annual Review of Irish Law 2004*) and the matter was appealed to the Supreme Court. The Supreme Court accepted the reasoning and decision of Smyth J. on all grounds relied upon by the appellant and the appeal was dismissed.

SECTION 390 ORDER FOR SECURITY FOR COSTS

Section 390 of the Companies Act 1963 provides:

> Where a limited company is plaintiff in any action or other legal proceeding, any judge having jurisdiction in the matter, may, if it appears by credible testimony that there is reason to believe that the company will be unable to pay the costs of the defendant if successful

in his defence, require sufficient security to be given for those costs
and may stay all proceedings until the security is given.

It is clear from the extensive case law on s.390 that the order for security for
costs is usually granted provided the defendant can demonstrate that he has a
prima facie defence, the company will not be able to pay the defendant's costs
if successful in his defence and there are no "special circumstances" which
result in the court not exercising its discretion to make the order sought. A
number of recent decisions by the Supreme Court provide further guidance
on the "special circumstances" that would justify refusal of an order and the
amount of security which the plaintiff must lodge.

In *West Donegal Land League Ltd v Údarás na Gaeltachta* [2007] 1
I.L.R.M. 1 a dispute arose over land which was registered in the name of the
second named defendant. The plaintiff company claimed a beneficial interest in
the land and asserted that the second named defendant held the land as trustee
on behalf of the members of the plaintiff company and adduced evidence to
factually substantiate this claim. Rent from the letting of the land had not
been retained by the second named defendant but had been given over to a
committee representing the members of the company with an admission by
the second named defendant that the rental income was held in trust for the
committee. The second named defendant claimed that this was done to avoid
paying capital gains tax and denied that it constituted evidence of a trusteeship.
The second named defendant sought an order for security for costs. Having
established that there was a prima facie defence, that the plaintiff company
would be unable to pay the second named defendant's costs if unsuccessful and
that there were no special circumstances, the High Court (Smyth J.) granted
the order. The decision was appealed.

Denham J. (dissenting) described the special circumstances accepted by
the courts to justify refusal of the order, including a lack of bona fides by the
applicant (referring to *SEE Co Ltd v Public Lighting Services* [1987] I.L.R.M.
255 and *Irish Press plc v EM Warburg Pincus & Co International Ltd* [1997]
2 I.L.R.M. 263). Denham J. observed that the list was not exhaustive and that
accordingly it was necessary to consider the circumstances of the present case
to determine whether there were special circumstances. She was satisfied that
the defendant's admissions and actions raised fiduciary issues and matters
relating to his bona fides. Given the allegations made, Denham J. considered it
appropriate to consider the justice of the case and the court's duty to "advance
the ends of justice and not hinder them" (per Kingsmill Moore J. in *Thalle v
Soares* [1957] I.R. 182). On the basis of the evidence Denham J. was satisfied
that the appellant had raised "special circumstances" to justify the court's
discretion to refuse the order for security.

Geoghegan J., giving the majority judgment, did not consider that the
company could invoke any special circumstances. He observed:

"The case law under section 390 establishes that notwithstanding the insertion of the word *'may'* the court in the absence of special circumstances and as a matter of appropriate exercise of its discretion will in a given case order security for costs in the circumstances provided for by the section. The 'special circumstances' would seem to be limited …"

With regard to the court's discretion in this regard he stated:

"I am satisfied, however, that this does not mean that a court is wide open in its discretion as to whether to grant or refuse the order. This would defeat a clear and … reasonable aim of the Oireachtas as enacted in s.390."

He considered that the case did not raise any matters which could be regarded as a "special circumstance". Referring to Denham J.'s finding that the bona fides of the second named defendant was a special circumstance, Geoghegan J. observed:

"What the learned judge is referring to there is a proven admission at one stage of trusteeship. That was in the context of avoiding/evading paying tax. While that whole episode may be useful ammunition in favour of the plaintiff at the ultimate hearing of the action, I do not think that it is relevant to the question of whether there should be security for costs."

Accordingly he dismissed the appeal subject to a direction regarding quantum. Although Geoghegan J. did not suggest that the issue of bona fides should be excluded, his comments regarding the limitation of the court's discretion in deciding what is a special circumstance will no doubt be perceived as an obstacle for companies who are faced with s.390 applications.

With regard to quantum, the requirement to provide "sufficient security" for costs in s.390 has been analysed in a number of judicial decisions. In *Lismore Homes Ltd v Bank of Ireland Finance Ltd (No. 3)* [2001] 2 I.R. 536; [2002] 1 I.L.R.M. 541 Murphy J. (for the Supreme Court) stated:

"The word 'sufficient' in its plain meaning, signifies adequate or enough and it is directly related in the section to the defendant's costs. The section does not provide for—as it might have—a sufficient sum 'to meet the justice of the case' or some such phrase as would give a general discretion to the court. Harsh though it may be, I am convinced that 'sufficient security' involves making a reasonable estimate or assessment of the actual costs which it is anticipated that the defendant will have to meet. Much of the section can be avoided by the application of the established principles in granting or withholding the order for security. In so far as the quantum of the security may be oppressive in a case where security is in fact ordered, this must be seen in the context in which it arises. It applied only to limited liability companies who are shown to be insolvent. Legislation has conferred many benefits on limited liability companies including, in particular, that very limitation and it is not surprising to find that some burdens are likewise cast by the legislature on companies which enjoy these advantages."

Referring to this passage, Geoghegan J. suggested that it must be read in the context of an assumption that as a matter of probability the defendant, if successful in the action, would enjoy the benefit of the ordinary rule that costs follow the event. He further suggested that he had little doubt that Murphy J. was referring to commercial litigation and in particular money claims. He observed that the present action was very different in terms of the factual background and the nature of the reliefs sought. Accordingly he suggested that at the stage of the application for security for costs, a court may, on the evidence before it, consider whether, even if the defendant is successful, a full costs order would be made. He referred to title actions in the Circuit Court, which do not necessarily result in a full indemnity order for costs in favour of the successful party. Geoghegan J. was of the opinion that there was no reason why the types of circumstances and motives, which have influenced Circuit Court judges, should not equally influence a judge in the High Court. He concluded that this case would not be a simple one of costs following the events and that it would be legitimate to take that factor into account in determining how 'sufficient' security for costs is to be assessed.

In *Dublin International Arena v Campus and Stadium Ireland* [2007] I.E.S.C. 48 the appellant company had been formed to tender for a public contract and having failed in its bid commenced judicial review proceedings. In the course of those proceedings an order requiring the appellant company to provide security for costs against the first respondent company was made under s.390. An order was made to provide security for a proportion of costs in relation to the other respondents (collectively hereinafter called "the State") pursuant to the Rules of the Superior Courts, Ord.29 r.1. The appellant appealed against the order, arguing that s.390 did not apply in an application for review of the award of public contract pursuant to Council Directive 89/665/EEC (the Remedies Directive) as amended and that there was unnecessary delay.

Denham J. (Kearns J. and Finnegan J concurred) considered that the essential issue for determination was whether the delay alleged by the appellant was a "special circumstance" which justify the refusal of orders for security for costs. She referred to *SEE Co v Public Lighting Services* [1987] I.L.R.M. 255 and *Hidden Ireland Holidays Ltd v Indigo Services Ltd* [2005] 2 I.R. 115.

Denham J. agreed with the High Court that the Remedies Directive did not preclude an application for security of costs. Although Denham J. was satisfied that the trial judge had considered the issue of delay, she considered that the decision was open for review in the context of the Remedies Directive. She observed that the original proceedings were commenced in May 2002 and the Statement of Opposition was filed in September 2002. However, the motions for security for costs were not brought until February and March 2003. Given the circumstances of an application for judicial review, where parties are required to act promptly in seeking a speedy remedy, Denham J. was satisfied that there was a delay. Referring to the rules of the Superior Courts (in particular Ord.84A r.2, r.4 and r.6) concerning a review of the award of a public contract—which implement the requirements of the Remedies Directive—Denham J. was satisfied that these rules required promptness and compliance with strict time limits. On this basis Denham J. concluded that there was delay contrary to the procedures to review public contracts and such delay was contrary to the express and implied terms of the rules—national and European—for the review of such contracts. The consequence of the delay in bringing the application for security for costs and the delay in the determination of this issue (for which she considered the State was responsible) impaired the effective implementation of the Community Directives on the award of public contracts (referring to *Grossman Air Service v Austria Case* C-230/02; *SIAC Construction v Mayo County Council* [2002] 3 I.R. 148 and *Dekra Eireann Teo v Minister for Environment and Local Government* [2003] I.E.S.C. 25). Accordingly the court was satisfied that such delay could be considered a "special circumstance" and the motions for security for costs should be refused. The appeal was allowed.

TRANSPARENCY

The Transparency Directive 2004/109/EC was introduced to enhance transparency in EU capital markets for improving investor protection and market efficiency. Many of the requirements of the Directive replace the provisions of the Consolidated Admissions and Reporting Directive 2001/34/EC. The Transparency Directive was transposed into Irish Law by the following:

a) Part 3 of the Investment Funds, Companies and Miscellaneous Provisions Act 2006 (see *Annual Review of Irish Law 2006*);

b) The Transparency (Directive 2004/109/EC) Regulations (S.I. No. 277 of 2007) (the Transparency Regulations) which came into operation on June 13, 2007; and

c) The Interim Transparency Rules made by the Financial Regulator which also came into operation on June 13, 2007.

THE TRANSPARENCY REGULATIONS

Part 1 of the Regulations provide for preliminary matters including commencement, construction, interpretation and application.

PERIODIC FINANCIAL REPORTING

Part 2 of the Regulations provide for periodic financial reporting for issuers of all securities on a regulated market whose home Member State is Ireland. For the purposes of the Regulation the term securities covers a broad range of financial instruments in addition to shares and debt securities.

Issuers of *securities* must make public its annual financial report at the latest *four* months after the end of each financial year and ensure that it remains publicly available for at least five years (Regulation 4(2). The annual financial report shall include the audited financial information, a management report and responsibility statements (Regulation 4(3)).

Issuers whose *shares or debt securities* are admitted to trading on a regulated market and whose home Member State is Ireland must prepare half-yearly financial reports covering the first six months of the financial year and such reports shall be made public within *two* months after the end of the period to which the report relates. These reports must also be kept available to the public for at least five years. The half-yearly financial report shall include a condensed set of financial statements, an interim management report and responsibility statements (Regulation 6).

The "annual financial report" and "half-yearly financial report" are similar to those already required under company law and the Listing Rules, although the reporting deadlines have been shortened to four months in the case of the annual report. The management report, similar to the directors' report under s.158 of the Principal Act must include an indication of the key events which have occurred during the relevant period and their impact on the financial statements and a description of the principal risks and uncertainties for the next financial period. The responsibility statements are a new requirement and they must confirm that the relevant financial statements, prepared in accordance with the relevant accounting standards (currently IFRS), give a true and fair view of the financial position of the issuer and that the management report includes a fair review of the development and performance of the business and the position of the issuer together with the principal risks and uncertainties the issuer faces. The name and function of the individuals responsible within the issuer must be clearly set out in the relevant reports.

Issuers whose *shares* are admitted to trading on a regulated market and whose home Member State is Ireland must make public a statement by its management (interim management statement) during both the first and second six month period of the financial year. This interim management statement shall provide an explanation of material events and transactions that have taken place during the relevant period and their impact on the financial position of the issuer together with a general description of the financial position and performance of the issuer (Regulation 9). The requirement to produce an interim management statement does not apply if the issuer already produces quarterly financial reports. This requirement is new in that the existing company law provisions and Listing Rules did not require the production of such statements.

EXEMPTIONS

Part 3 of the Regulations provides for exemptions in respect of state, regional or local authority issuers, public international bodies of which at least one Member State is a member, the European Central Bank and other Member States' national central banks, whether or not they issue shares or other securities. Exemptions also apply for issuers that issue debt securities where the denomination per unit is at least €50,000, credit institutions whose shares are not admitted to trading on a regulated market but which have, in a continuous or repeated manner, only issued debt securities subject to certain conditions, and certain state-sponsored issuers (Regulation 10).

The Central Bank and Financial Services Authority of Ireland may grant exemptions to issuers whose registered office is in a third country where the law of the third country lays down equivalent requirements (Regulation 11).

LIABILITY FOR FALSE OR MISLEADING STATEMENTS IN CERTAIN PUBLICATIONS

The common law has traditionally provided limited scope to investors who suffer loss as a result of inaccurate statements or omissions in companies' statutory reports and documents. Part 4 of the Regulations addresses this matter by providing that *issuers* will be liable to pay compensation to a person who has acquired securities and suffered loss as a result of relying on statements in or omissions from the relevant reports and it was reasonable for them to be relied upon. The issuer will only be liable where the statement was knowingly untrue or misleading or such statements were made recklessly. Further liability is specifically excluded, thus limiting the liability of investors who disposed of securities on foot of any statements or omissions and any liability to investors on the part of directors or auditors or other agents involved in preparing the inaccurate statements. However, any existing statutory (whether administrative or otherwise) and contractual sanctions in respect of issuers, directors, auditors or agents in relation to the preparation and approval of accounts and reports remain unchanged. By establishing boundaries to the circumstances in which liability will arise and the class of persons to whom actionable duties are owed. Part 4 eliminates some of the difficulties inherent in the common law.

MAJOR SHAREHOLDINGS

Part 5 of the Regulation sets out the Directive's requirements in respect of disclosure of major holdings of shares by investors. A shareholder, who acquires or disposes of shares to which voting rights are attached and which are admitted to trading on a regulated market, must notify the issuer if the proportion of voting rights they hold (whether directly or indirectly) reaches, exceeds or falls below certain thresholds (5 per cent, 10 per cent, 15 per cent, 20 per cent, 30 per cent, 50 per cent and 75 per cent). This notification requirement also applies in the following situations:

1) Where events occur within the issuer, which change the breakdown of voting rights;

2) Where certain situation arise which result in a person being entitled to acquire dispose or exercise voting rights in relation to shares;

3) Where a person holds—directly or indirectly—financial instruments which result in an entitlement to acquire shares to which voting rights are attached.

A person making a notification to an issuer must also notify the competent authority at the same time. In order to facilitate notifications by investors, issuers are obliged to make public information on acquisitions/disposals of their own shares and the total number of voting rights and capital on a regular basis. Certain market participants, such as custodians and market makers are exempt from the notification requirements. Furthermore, the notification will not apply in repect of voting rights attaching to shares provided to or by members of the European System of Central Banks in carrying out their functions as monetary authorities.

CONTINUING OBLIGATIONS
AND ACCESS TO INFORMATION

Part 6 of the Regulations imposes continuing obligations on issuers including, inter alia, the following:

1) Notification of draft changes to their instruments of incorporation;

2) Providing equal treatment of holders of shares who are in the same position;

3) Ensuring all holders of debt securities are ranked pari passu and given equal treatment;

4) Ensuring that all facilities and information necessary to enable holders of shares or debt securities to exercise their rights are available and the integrity of the data is preserved;

5) Ensuring various requirements regarding proxies are satisfied;

6) Providing information about changes in rights attaching to securities, information about meetings, issues of new shares and payment of dividends.

DISSEMINATION OF INFORMATION

Part 7 of the Regulations sets out the requirements for the dissemination of all "regulated information" which broadly covers information required to be disclosed, communicated or announced to the market under the Transparency Directive, the Market Abuse Directive and any further information which may be required from time to time.

COMPETENT AUTHORITIES

Parts 8 and 9 and 10 of the Regulations designate the competent authorities, confer on them powers to police and enforce the new regime and set out the administrative sanctions for breach of the Regulations. The Financial Regulator is the central competent authority with responsibility for carrying out and ensuring the obligations provided in the Regulation are applied. Pursuant to the provisions of Regulation 37, the Financial Regulator has delegated certain functions to the Irish Stock Exchange Limited (ISE). The Irish Auditing & Accountancy Standards Authority (IAASA) has been designated the relevant competent authority for ensuring that the periodic financial reporting requirements are complied with. Part 11 of the Regulations provides for co-operation between the competent authorities.

RELATED REGULATIONS

The European Communities (Admissions to Listing and Miscellaneous Provisions) Regulations 2007 (S.I. No. 286 of 2007) implemented on June 13, 2007 give effect to the provisions of Directive 2001/34/EC (as amended) on the admission of securities to official stock exchange listing and on information to be published on those securities on the prospectus when securities are offered to the public or admitted to trading.

These Regulations revoke the European Communities (Stock Exchange) Regulations 1984 (S.I. No. 282 of 1984) and the European Communities (Stock Exchange) (Amendment) Regulations 1995 (S.I. No. 311 of 1995). The Regulations also repeal ss.89 to 96 of the Companies Act 1990 (dealing with the information to be published when a major holding in a listed company is acquired or disposed of).

STOCK EXCHANGE

On November 1, 2007 the Markets in Financial Instruments and Miscellaneous Provisions Act, 2007 and the European Communities (Markets in Financial Instruments) Regulations 2007 (the MiFiD Regulations) were introduced in Ireland to implement the Markets in Financial Instruments Directive. Under the MiFID Regulations the Financial Regulator is now the competent regulatory authority for authorising the stock exchange as a market operator and is also responsible for monitoring the activities undertaken by market participants in Ireland. The Stock Exchange Act 1995 has now been replaced in its entirety and the Stock Exchange is now governed by the Regulations. The rules of the Stock Exchange have been amended to reflect the new MiFiD regime.

Conflict of Laws

CHILD ABDUCTION

Rights of custody   In *T v O* [2008] I.E.S.C. 55, affirming [2007] I.E.H.C. 326, the Supreme Court affirmed a finding by McKechnie J. that the District Court had rights of custody sufficient to render wrongful the retention by a mother of her twin sons in England, within the meaning of Art.2 of Brussels II *bis* and Art.3 of the Hague Abduction Convention. The mother had been living with the father, to whom she was not married. Their relationship was "like man and wife" and they had been in "a *de facto* unit". Two months previously, the father had initiated proceedings in the District Court seeking to be appointed guardian of the children and seeking directions in connection with custody and access. These had ultimately been adjourned generally with liberty to re-enter.

It was argued on behalf of the mother that the father's inactivity in pursuing his application in the District Court had deprived that court of custody rights in relation to the boys. Murray C.J. (Denham, Hardiman, Geoghegan and Finnegan JJ.) did not agree. He acknowledged that:

> "Undoubtedly one can consider it to be the law in this country that a spurious application to the District Court for directions regarding the custody of a child or one which was manifestly tainted by a want of bona fides could, in the circumstances of a particular case, be deemed not to vest rights regarding custody in the District Court. A similar approach could be adopted in relation to an applicant who having duly brought such an application was so inactive in pursuing it that his or her bona fides or genuine intent to seek the relief sought was called in question."

In the instant case, however, the father had not been guilty of conduct of this kind. It appeared that the District Judge had had doubts as to his jurisdiction to deal with the matter because the children in question were outside the jurisdiction. Murray C.J. thought that he was mistaken in this regard and "at least could have given some directions, even of an interim nature, pursuant to s.11 without making a final determination as to custody."

However, the fact was that, less than three months later, the father had initiated proceedings in England which in turn had led to the Irish proceedings before the High and Supreme Courts. There was no basis for concluding that he had been guilty of such inactivity as to belie the original intention and purpose for which the applications to the District Court had been brought. Indeed Murray C.J. regarded his conduct are "indicative of a desire to persist with his intended proceedings".

The Supreme Court, in view of the fact that the District Court had custody rights, was not called on to consider whether the father also had such rights. The established position under the Hague Convention, as articulated by the Supreme Court: *Re HI (a minor); HI v MG (Child Abduction: Wrongful Removal)* [2000] 1 I.R. 110, was that an unmarried father with only "inchoate rights" which had not crystallised in a court order of custody or other guardianship character, did not have "rights of custody" for the purposes of the Hague Convention. In the High Court in the instant case, McKechnie J. held that Brussels II *bis*, so far as it had application, changed matters. In interpreting and applying this European Community instrument, McKechnie J. considered that the court was entitled to have regard to the European Convention and its Art.8 jurisprudence on family life. The father, if he had an opportunity of pursuing his District Court application would "most likely" have been declared entitled to "substantial rights" in respect of his children. The father "unquestionably" enjoyed Art.8 rights. The "only possible construction" of Brussels II *bis*, to give full effect to the European Convention jurisprudence, was one that recognized that the father's role within the family unit conferred on him "rights of custody" under Art.2 of the Regulation. Any other interpretation, in McKechnie J.'s view, "would in itself amount to an interference with Article 8".

In *Re BPP and POP; PMP v KTP* [2007] I.E.H.C. 217, a married couple, habitually resident in South Africa, were involved in acrimonious divorce proceedings there, complicated by a claim by the wife that the marriage was invalid on account of bigamy. The court was actively involved in making orders relating to the custody and welfare of their children. The wife obtained an ex parte order from a court permitting her to remove the children to Ireland. Notice had not been given to the husband. The wife in seeking this order was somewhat economical with her narrative of the full facts of the history of the litigation. When her husband was apprised of the situation, he obtained an ex parte order the following day restraining the wife from removing the children, but by then she had already taken them to Ireland. The order granting her permission to travel was rescinded a fortnight later. The husband took proceedings in the Irish High Court seeking the return of the children under the provisions of the Hague Convention.

Feeney J. reviewed the Irish and British jurisprudence on what may constitute rights of custody. He quoted extracts from Keane J.'s judgment in *Re HI (a minor); HI v MG (Child Abduction: Wrongful Removal)* [2000] 1 I.R. 110. He concluded, in the light of the factual history of the litigation between the parties in South Africa, that, at the time of the wife's departure with the children to Ireland, rights to custody vested in the South African court. Therefore, in the absence of excusing circumstances, the removal of the children would be in breach of rights of custody attributed to the court, since the South African court had taken upon itself the right to determine the custody or to prohibit the removal of the children.

Wrongful removal   In *Re BPP and POP; PMP v KTP* [2007] I.E.H.C. 217, the facts of which are set out more extensively immediately above, Feeney J. held that the removal by the mother of her children from South Africa to Ireland following an ex parte order permitting her to do so, where that order was subsequently rescinded, was "wrongful" for the purposes of Art.3 of the Hague Convention. It was clear that the rights of custody were at the time of removal vested in the South African court: see above p.86. The court had clearly reserved to itself the issue as to where the children should reside until the proceedings were finally concluded. The order permitting removal, if it could be relied on at all (and Feeney J. was "of the clear view" that it could not) had not meant that South African court had divested itself of the right to determine where the children would ultimately reside or the issues of custody or access: it "only permitted the release of the passports and the entitlement of the children and mother to travel to Ireland and not any more". Since the order had subsequently been determined to be void ab initio and to have been obtained by fraud, it had no effect and could not be relied on by the mother as an excuse. To permit it to have such effect would be "contrary to policy". Finally, in her affidavit supporting her application for the order subsequently declared void, the mother had given an undertaking that she would travel back to South Africa two months later for the High Court resolution of issues relating to the custody and welfare of her children. It could not reasonably be contended by her that the lack of an express requirement to return in the order diluted or removed such obligation.

Of the several reasons given by Feeney J. for holding that the removal had been wrongful, perhaps the only one of any particular strength was that the order permitting removal had subsequently been held to have been obtained by fraud. If one envisages a case where a parent obtains in all good faith an order permitting removal and that order is later declared void for reasons that in no way compromise that good faith, it would seem particularly unjust and capable of working hardship on some children to deem the removal "wrongful", with all the robust consequences that follow under the Hague Convention. Moreover, the fact that the court retains rights of custody does not mean that a removal by a parent which that court authorises is wrongful, any more than where a parent with rights of custody authorises the other parent or, indeed, someone else to remove a child.

Risk of harm or intolerable situation   In *Re KLP and EEP, Minors; MWP v TKP (also known as TKE)* [2007] I.E.H.C. 145, McGovern J. declined to order the return of two children, born in 1992 and 1995, to their father in

Texas. Their mother, who was divorced from their father, had taken them with her to Ireland in 2005. The court had appointed a clinical psychologist to investigate the degree of maturity of the children, whether they objected to being returned to Texas and if so the grounds for that objection and whether it related specifically to living in Texas or a desire to remain in Ireland or whether it related "to an objection to living in the vicinity of a particular parent and/or wish to live with the other parent" and whether any objections expressed had been independently formed or resulted from the influence of another person including a parent or sibling.

The psychologist produced a report and gave evidence. The report contained accounts by the children of certain acts of violence by their father against their mother and the elder child as well as an incident in which the father's girlfriend (later to become his wife) had stabbed their mother. McGovern J. noted that, in the course of her evidence, the psychologist had:

> "… said that it was very unusual for children of their age who have lived as long as they did in the United States to have such negative feelings towards their father and the United States of America. She accepted that the similarity of their accounts was somewhat worrying. She also made the same observation on the fact that neither had any bad words to say about their mother. When pressed she said they were absolutely determined that they were afraid of their father and they were absolutely consistent. [She] expressed the view that it would amount to an intolerable situation if they were sent back to their father who has been given custody of them because that would involve (a) living with their father who frightens them and (b) with the lady who had assaulted their mother."

McGovern J. had "some concerns" about the matters that had troubled the psychologist: the possibility that their mother had exercised undue influence over the children could not be ruled out. It was clear, however, that the psychologist, who was experienced in her profession, was absolutely sure that the children were greatly in fear of their father; there was objective evidence in the papers to show that there was cause for concern about his behaviour to the point that the courts in the United States had found it necessary to make orders restricting his access to the children and to make a protection order. McGovern concluded:

> "[M]aking allowances for the influence of the [mother] over the children I am satisfied that there would be a grave risk to the children of being exposed to physical or psychological harm if they were returned to the United States of America. I am also satisfied that they would be placed in an intolerable position by being returned there on account of

the fact that [their father] is now married to the lady who is accused of assaulting their mother and causing her serious injury."

A few comments may be appropriate. The factual basis for concern about a grave risk of harm appears to have been made out of the evidence. The father did not impress McGovern J., so far as one can discern from the judgment. When cross-examined on the events leading to his wife being stabbed, he declined to answer any questions, relying on his privilege against self-incrimination and an asserted privilege against incriminating his spouse. "Pleading the Fifth" probably has a less pejorative cultural resonance in an American trial; it would not be likely to enhance a claim in Ireland relating to the care of children.

The holding in relation to an intolerable situation is interesting. It would be rather a broad proposition that children should not be returned to a father whose present partner is accused of having used violence against their mother. If the partner presents no risk of harm to the children, to hold that her continuing presence in the family would create an intolerable situation would not always be justified. The realisation by the children of the unpalatable and insulting memory of what she had previously done to their mother would not in itself normally be sufficient, to judge by precedents on the question.

Finally, it is curious that so much of the case relating to harm and an intolerable situation was based on the report and evidence of the psychologist who could give no direct evidence on these questions and whose mandate when approached had been to report on matters relating to the children's wishes rather than on the earlier events that had occurred in Texas. With respect, that "ultimate issue" was a matter for the court rather than for psychologists or psychiatrists, regardless of their experience and expertise.

In *Re BPP and POP; PMP v KTP* [2007] I.E.H.C. 217, the facts of which are stated in greater detail above, p.87, Feeney J. held that the return of three children taken by their mother from South Africa to Ireland should not be thwarted by the defence under Art.13(b). The mother argued that an intolerable situation would arise if she were denied entry into South Africa. In the Australian decision of *State Central Authority Victoria v Ardito*, Family Court of Australia, October 29, 1995, return of a child alone to the United States of America was refused on this basis where it had been established that the mother was denied entry. Feeney J. considered that, if similar factual circumstances had been established in the instant case, the court would have to address the issue; the "great probability" was, however, that the mother and children would receive three-month visas on arrival which could be renewed as a matter of course. The father had undertaken to fund any travel necessary to permit exit and re-entry required for a further visa if the proceedings were not completed within six months.

The mother sought to rely on a Canadian authority which suggested that an intolerable situation might arise where a mother would be returned to Canada where she had no means of support. Again the father's circumstances in the instant case were distinguishable. The father had given financial undertakings for the support and accommodation of the mother and children during the proceedings. Feeney J. invoked Denham J.'s observations in *RK v JK (Child Abduction: Acquiescence)* [2000] 2 I.R. 416 at 434 as to the power of undertakings to abate concerns about potentially intolerable situations.

Finally the mother argued that the lack of legal aid and funds rendered the situation intolerable. British courts have rejected this argument: *Re K* [1995] 2 F.L.R. 550. Feeney J. did not consider he had to decide the matter as the father had given an undertaking to provide some funding to the mother for legal assistance; the court was obliged also to, "to some extent, ...recognise that the dissipation of funds available to [the mother had] to a degree been caused by her own actions".

In *Re CPC; PL v EC* [2007] I.E.H.C. 440, Dunne J. held that the defence of a grave risk of harm had not been made out by a mother who had taken her son, who was born in 1999, from Australia to Ireland in breach of his father's rights to custody. The Australian courts were at the time investigating an allegation that the father had sexually abused the boy. This investigation had not been concluded. The mother's flight with her son had been precipitated by a tentative indication by a judge that he would award access rights to the father. Dunne J. accepted that the mother had raised "a *prima facie* case of sexual abuse" by the father but, on the authority of *AS v PS* [1998] 2 I.R. 244, was satisfied that the mother would have the assistance of the Australian courts in ensuring protection for her son.

The Supreme Court affirmed: [2008] I.E.S.C. 19. Fennelly J. (Kearns and Finnegan JJ. concurring) was not happy with the description of the evidence of sexual abuse as involving a prima facie case:

> "It is indisputable that a risk of sexual abuse is a grave risk. The learned High Court judge has said that there was *prima facie* evidence of sexual abuse before the Australian court. It is undoubtedly the case that the appellant has made such allegations before the Australian court. However, as the learned judge correctly said, that court has not yet ruled on the allegations. The High Court did not hear any direct evidence on the issue, but was informed of the nature of the evidence before the Australian court. I am not sure that it is right to rule on the quality, even at a *prima facie* level, of the evidence before the court of the other country. It is clear that there was a great deal of oral evidence before the Australian court, but this court has seen none of that. Nonetheless, this court must take note of the fact that such an allegation has been made and that it awaits adjudication before the Australian court. It is also clear that the allegation is strenuously denied. It is not possible to go further."

The real issue concerned the position that the court should adopt in relation to the fact that the identical allegations were the subject of proceedings before the Australian court. The mother submitted that she had produced evidence to satisfy the test that the Australian court was unable or unwilling to protect the interests of her son. Fennelly J. gave a robust rejoinder:

> "It is for the Australian court, not this court, to test the strength and veracity of the allegations of sexual abuse. It has heard oral evidence from both parties, tested by cross-examination, over a period of eight days. It has also heard expert witnesses and received their reports. The Australian courts conduct adversarial proceedings in a manner remarkably similar to our own. They are capable of protecting the interests of [the boy]. If the [mother] is dissatisfied with a decision of the Family court, she will have a right of appeal. For these reasons, I am satisfied that the appellant has not made out the case of grave risk."

Wishes of children   In *Re KLP and EEP, Minors; MWP v TKP (also known as TKE)* [2007] I.E.H.C. 145, the facts of which are set out in greater detail above, p.88, McGovern J. refused to order the return of two children, born in 1992 and 1995, to their father in Texas. The children had expressed their strongest objections to being returned. The children had indicated a fear of their father, based on physical assaults by him on the elder girl. They could remember no positive feature about their relationship with him.

McGovern J. was satisfied that both children had attained an age and degree of maturity at which it was appropriate to take account of their views. He considered it significant that both of them had become extremely distressed and fearful when the possibility of their return had been raised by the clinical psychologist who interviewed them.

In *PM v Judge Mary Devins* [2007] I.E.H.C. 380, in judicial review proceedings considered below, Abbott J. noted that, having read the papers relating to earlier proceedings in the District Court and Circuit Court, an issue arose as to "whether the voice of the child was heard and, if not, why not". He considered that "the parties should be advised by the court, and in the interests of the court in ensuring the free movement of judgments as envisaged by the Brussels II *bis* Regulation, to seek to have this matter addressed in whatever way they are advised". The two children involved in the proceedings were very young—five and three years old, respectively. When the relevant proceedings took place, they were four and two and unusually young to have their views canvassed.

In *R v R* [2007] I.E.H.C. 423, Finlay Geoghegan J. set aside an order she had made 11 months previously for the return of a child to Latvia. The order had been made on an *ex parte* basis; the respondent mother had not appeared, although she had been previously served with the proceedings. The views of the child had not been solicited by the court.

Article 11 (2) of Council Regulation (EC) 2201 of 2003 provides that, when applying Arts 12 and 13 of the Hague Child Abduction Convention of 1980, it is to be ensured that the child is given the opportunity to be heard in the proceedings unless this appears inappropriate having regard to his or her age or degree of maturity. Finlay Geoghegan J. referred with approval to the judgment of the English Court of Appeal in *Re F (a child)* [2007] EWCA Civ 393 where Thorpe L.J. and Munby J. had clearly taken the view that the obligation prescribed by Art.11(2) was a mandatory one, failure to comply with which rendered an order invalid. Finlay Geoghegan J. made three observations on the issues that arose. The first was that she did not wish to be understood as holding that the court, in any case where the application is unopposed, must ensure that the child is given an opportunity to be heard before it may make an order for return under Art.12 of the Hague Convention. In the instant case the child was eight-and-a-half years old at the time the application had been heard and at that age the court was "under an obligation at least to have regard to Article 11(2) and to take steps which may have given the child the opportunity to be heard". Finlay Geoghegan J. regretted the absence of any specific assistance given by an Irish court in complying easily with the obligation under Art.11 (2), particularly having regard to its time limits, though she acknowledged that s.36 of the Child Abduction and Enforcement of Custody Orders Act 1991 allowed the court to make orders which should result in the whereabouts of a child being ascertained or, as a matter of last resort, the child's being brought before the court. She observed that the court "must at least take some steps to try and ensure that the child is given an opportunity to be heard unless, of course, it is *prima facie* inappropriate having regard to its age."

Secondly, Finlay Geoghegan J. considered that, in any rehearing of the proceedings, the mother should not be given an opportunity to raise "matters of herself" which she had not chosen to do in the earlier proceedings; it was, however, a separate question as to how the court during the rehearing should deal with any issue which might arise from hearing the child. Finally, she referred to the procedure where children were interviewed and assessed by appropriately qualified people for the purpose of the court's complying with its obligation under Art.11(2). This was normally done with the cooperation of the solicitors acting for the parties, in particular, Legal Aid Board solicitors, with the cooperation of the Legal Aid Board who funded such assessments and interviews and reports to the courts. While Finlay Geoghegan J. expressed indebtedness to the Legal Aid Board for facilitating this process, she noted that it was "not sufficient to meet the court's obligations in all cases".

Settlement in new environment   Article 12(2) of the Hague Convention requires the court, where proceedings have been commenced after the expiration of one year, to order the return of the child "unless it is demonstrated that the child is now settled in its new environment". Bracewell J. in *Re N (Minors) (Abduction)* [1991] 1 F.L.R. 413 at 417 observed that there was:

"... some force ... in the argument that legal presumptions reflect the norm, and the presumption under the Convention is that children should be returned unless the mother can establish the degree of settlement which is more than mere adjustment to surroundings. I find that word should be given its ordinary natural meaning, and that the word 'settled' in this context has two constituents. First, it involves a physical element of relating to, being established in, a community and an environment. Secondly, I find that it has an emotional constituent to denoting security and stability."

Irish courts have endorsed this approach: see *Re R (A Minor); P v B (No. 2)* [1999] 4 I.R 18; *Re TK v RK (Children); AK v AK* [2006] I.E.H.C. 277.

In *Re KLP and EEP, Minors; MWP v TKP (also known as TKE)* [2007] I.E.H.C. 145, McGovern J. quoted Bracewell J.'s observations in holding that two children, born in 1992 and 1995, were settled in their new environment in Ireland, having been brought to Ireland from Texas by their mother in 2005. McGovern J. accepted that the party raising this exception "must clearly show that the settlement was so well established that it over-rides the otherwise clear duty of the court to order the return of the child". He was satisfied that the children were settled in their new environment, adding:

"Whether they are so settled in a physical sense as to come within the ambit of Article 12 is not completely clear although it does appear that they are well settled. I take the view that their settlement in Ireland also has '...an emotional constituent denoting security and stability' as referred to *Re N*. The evidence establishes that they feel safe here and part of this is bound up in the fact that they feel their mother is safe and secure. Accordingly on that basis I would hold that they are settled in their new environment to such an extent as to come within the ambit of Article 12."

Habitual residence   In *PM v Judge Mary Devins* [2007] I.E.H.C. 380, the interesting questions as to the relevance of an unmarried father's rights on the determination of the habitual residence of his two young children fell for consideration in an application for judicial review. The father and mother had been living together in Ireland from 2002 to 2005. Their children were born in 2002 and 2004 respectively. The applicant mother was Scottish, the respondent father Irish. After the couple had lived apart in close proximity for some months, the applicant took the children with her to live in Scotland in March 2006. In May 2006, the father applied to the District Court in Ireland to be made guardian. The mother, through her lawyers, unsuccessfully challenged jurisdiction, on the basis that the children's habitual residence was not Irish and unsuccessfully appealed this issue to the Circuit Court. The District Court, in the May proceedings, had appointed the father as guardian and the Circuit

Court affirmed. In subsequent proceedings in September, 2006 the District Court awarded custody of the children to the father. In these proceedings, the mother was legally represented but did not attend.

The mother later took proceedings for judicial review. The essence of her claim was that the District Court had lacked jurisdiction under Art.8 of Brussels II *bis*. The mother's application was not successful. In Abbott J.'s view, a decision as to habitual residence involves mixed questions of fact and law. The conclusion reached by the District Court did not call for judicial review under the test set out by Morris J. in *Farrelly v Devally* [1998] 4 I.R. 76. The District Court decision clearly fell within the legal parameters set out by McGuinness J. in *Re CM (a minor); CM and OM v Delegacion Provincial de Malaga Conserjeria de Trabajor y Asuntos Sociales* [1999] 2 I.R. 363.

Counsel for the mother had submitted that, as she was the only person with guardianship rights at the relevant time, only she could lawfully direct where they could reside. Although there was no equivalent of a domicile of dependency of children, there was a recognised association between their habitual residence and that of their lawful guardian. Abbott J. characterised this argument as "a rush to certainty as to jurisdiction" based on the bedrock of the mother's rights under Guardianship of Infants Act 1964. Abbott J. noted that counsel was:

> "… buoyed in his view by the manner in which the Supreme Court have upheld the prior rights of the mother as against the natural father who is not a guardian. However, even in this respect the court has to have regard to the fact that the Supreme Court have in certain instances recognised the rights of the natural father, for instance access rights, not as a rule of law but as a 'rule of prudence'. In the situation where an informal relationship has evolved between father and children, such as in this case, the 'rule of prudence' is a matter to be taken into account by the District Court in determining jurisdiction especially having regard to the general tenor of the Brussels II *bis* Regulation which prioritises the child's interests. It is of some interest to note that the forms provided for District Court applications allow for applications by parents (fathers) who are not legal guardians."

In *T v O* [2007] I.E.S.C. 55, the Supreme Court upheld a finding by McKechnie J. ([2007] I.E.H.C. 326) of an Irish habitual residence where a mother refused to return her twin sons to Ireland from England three months after she had gone to England with them to gain "respite from the relationship with the father", to whom the mother was not married but with whom she had been living "like man and wife and as part of a *de facto* family unit", for over three years. McKechnie J. concluded from the evidence that it was consistent only with the mother's absence from the family home being temporary and, until she refused to return the boys, she had not formed any settled intention to cease to have her habitual residence in Ireland. There was "nothing in the evidence, in the correspondence or in court documents" which gave a contrary impression. Since the mother's habitual residence was Irish, it "therefore follow[ed] that the habitual place of residence of the twin boys was also that of this jurisdiction until [April]".

The Supreme Court reviewed the evidence, including the mother's affidavit, in some detail. Murray C.J. (Denham, Hardiman, Geoghegan and Finnegan JJ. concurring) did not consider that the mother's suggestion that the parties might "meet with a mediator to discuss things" supported the inference that at the time she made this suggestion she had no intention of returning to Ireland.

FINANCIAL RELIEF AFTER FOREIGN DIVORCE

In the *Annual Review of Irish Law 2005*, pp 169–78 we analysed Quirke J.'s decision in *M.R. v P.R.* [2005] IEHC 228, the first to provde judicial guidance on Pt III of the Family Law Act 1995 (the "1995 Act"), which enables an Irish court to grant financial relief after a foreign divorce or separation. In *W.Y. v V.C.* [2007] 1 IEHC 400, Sheehan J. declined to grant leave under s.23(3)(a) to apply for a relief order. The spouses had strong connections with Hong Kong. The wife had been born there; they had married in 1991 and had continued to live there until 2002, when the husband obtained a divorce. The wife had not obtained substantial benefits in the divorce proceedings, which, in essence, left each spouse as owners of what was already, or had originally been, owned by each of them in his or her sole name. Under an earlier separation agreement she had fared no better. The husband was awarded custody of their two children. After the divorce the parties travelled to Ireland with their children. They resided together for some months. The wife sought fiancial relief orders under Pt III of the 1995 Act. The essence of her claim was that her former husband had psychological difficulties and had obtained the separation agreement and divorce by duress or undue influence. A claim by her in earlier proceedings that she would not be entitled to an award of ancilliary relief orders if she were now to apply to the Hong Kong courts proved incorrect and led to Sheehan J.'s setting aside of an order by McKechnie J. granting leave under s.23(3)(a).

Sheehan J. acknowledged that the transcript of the Hong Kong divorce proceedings and the terms of the "unusual" separation agreement did lend *"prima facie ... support* to the allegations of duress and undue influence". Nevertheless, the strong connections of the parties with Hong Kong and the availability there of witnesses who could throw light on relevant issues, coupled with the fact that the husband's house in Ireland was the only relevant asset (where the wife claimed that he was worth over ten million Euro), led Sheehan J. to conclude that "the appropriate venue for the wife's claim" was Hong Kong. Sheehan J.'s approach, strongly influenced by that of Thorpe L.J. in *Moore v Moore* [2007] EWCA Civ 361, goes close to adopting a *forum non conveniens* test. This may not fully capture the elaborate, controversial policies underlying Pt III of the 1995 Act which we sought to unearth in the 2005 Annual Review.

Constitutional Law

ORAN DOYLE, Trinity College Dublin
and
ESTELLE FELDMAN, Trinity College Dublin

ACCESS TO COURTS

Isaac Wunder order   The court found evidence of the habitual or persistent institution of vexatious or frivolous proceedings against the defendants in *McMahon v Law* [2007] I.E.H.C. 184 as a consequence of which MacMenamin J. granted an *Isaac Wunder* order against the first named plaintiff who was prohibited from instituting legal proceedings of whatever nature against any of the named defendants without the leave of the High Court. Reference was made to Ó Caoimh J.'s judgment in *Riordan v Ireland (No.5)* [2001] 4 I.R. 463 analysed in *Annual Review of Irish Law 2006*, pp.165–168.

Representation of plaintiff by lay litigant   Prior to substantive proceedings in a damages action, a preliminary issue was adjudicated in *Coffey v Tara Mines Ltd* [2007] I.E.H.C. 249 as to whether the wife of a plaintiff can represent the plaintiff in all proceedings before the court in respect of his claims against the defendants. O'Neill J. noted that the trial of the action had had to be adjourned arising from a number of factors. These included the very serious illness of the plaintiff, his reliance on his wife to act for him, and a complete breakdown in the professional relationship between him and his wife and his solicitor. As a result of the latter, serious allegations had been made against the solicitor and complaints have been made to the Law Society. These latter were not a matter for the court. However, no other solicitor could be found to act for the plaintiff. Following a direction from O'Neill J., a formal application was made to the Legal Aid Board for legal advice and assistance in relation to these cases but this too was unsuccessful.

Consequently, the court was unavoidably confronted with the issue of whether or not the plaintiff's wife was either entitled as of right, or whether a privilege should be extended to her, to represent the plaintiff. This issue had never previously been unequivocally determined by the courts in this jurisdiction. The defendants in the actions opposed the relief sought by the plaintiff's wife, invoking the well-settled principle that only parties themselves or duly qualified lawyers who under statute or under common law enjoy a right of audience can appear as a representative in litigation. The Attorney-General raised no objection.

O'Neill J. found aid in Keane C.J.'s judgment in *RB v AS* [2002] 2 I.R. 428 in which the Chief Justice had stated:

> "A party [as] to litigation in our courts, whether it is civil or criminal, is entitled as a matter of constitutional right to fair procedures. They are also entitled again as a matter of constitutional right to access to the courts and it is a necessary corollary of that right that they may conduct litigation with or without legal representation as they choose...
>
> The trial of cases involving lay litigants thus requires patience and understanding on the part of trial judges. They have to ensure, as best they can, that justice is not put at risk by the absence of expert legal representation on one side of the case. At the same time they have to bear constantly in mind that the party with legal representation is not to be unfairly penalised because he or she is so represented. It can be difficult to achieve the balance which justice requires".

O'Neill J. also considered the judgment of Budd J. in *PMLB v PHJ and PHJ and Company and the Incorporated Law Society of Ireland* (unreported, High Court, May 5, 1992) in which Budd J. had conducted an extensive review of common law authorities on this topic. In particular, O'Neill J. was attracted to the judgment of Somers J. in the Court of Appeal of New Zealand in the case of *GJ Mannix Limited* [1984] 1 N.Z.L.R. 309 at 316 as quoted by Budd J.:

> "But I consider the superior courts to have a residual discretion in this matter arising from the inherent power to regulate their own proceedings. Cases will arise where the due administration of justice may require some relaxation of the general rule. The occurrence is likely to be rare, their circumstances exceptional or at least unusual and their content modest. Such cases can confidently be left to the good sense of the judges."

O'Neill J. distinguished *Battle v The Irish Art Promotion Centre Limited* [1968] I.R. 252, finding that the Supreme Court judgment is not to be seen as an authority which excludes an inherent jurisdiction in the High Court to manage and control its own proceedings and in rare and exceptional cases to permit an unqualified advocate to represent another litigant. He concluded his judgment as follows:

> "It is quite clear, that unless [the plaintiff's wife] is permitted to represent the plaintiff, his actions will proceed no further, and that is an outcome or consequence that would be destructive of the interests of justice. I am quite satisfied that this court should exercise its discretion to move to prevent that situation arising, by permitting [her] to represent the plaintiff in these proceedings".

ADMINISTRATION OF JUSTICE IN PUBLIC

The chicken and the egg   The judgment of Clarke J. in *Independent Newspapers (Ireland) Ltd v Anderson* [2006] 3 I.R. 341 was considered in *Annual Review 2006*, pp.168–169. In 2007 Clarke J. returned to this issue, delivering judgment on December 12, 2007 in *Doe v Revenue Commissioners* [2008] I.E.H.C. 5. Proceeding to the substantive issue required urgency as the plaintiffs, who had made a large tax settlement, sought to prevent the consequent publication of their names in Iris Oifigiúil by the Revenue Commissioners. The plaintiffs' tax advisers and the Revenue disagreed as to the proper interpretation of tax provisions relating to an imposition of penalties on all defaulting taxpayers and in particular the interpretation of s.1053(5) of the Taxes Consolidation Act 1997 as amended. Clarke J. was not required to consider this matter but the following passage from his judgment makes the plaintiff's dilemma clear:

> "A finding by the court that the construction which the plaintiffs seek to place on the relevant provisions of the Taxes Acts was correct, would mean that the plaintiffs could not properly be included in the periodic list of tax defaulters published by the Revenue. However, the fact that the plaintiffs were tax defaulters who had entered into a settlement of the type which I have described earlier in this judgment would, of course, become public knowledge through the route of the court proceedings which, if not permitted to be brought anonymously would, of course, identify the plaintiffs as the tax defaulters concerned" (para 4.11).

McCracken J. in *Re Ansbacher (Cayman) Limited* [2002] 2 I.R. 517 at 520 pointed out that there is something of the chicken and the egg about such matters. Referring to this judgment, Clarke J. emphasised that the court was not told the names of the actual plaintiffs. Their solicitor placed evidence before the court on their behalf. Clarke J. further emphasised that, in taking that course of action, he was following the practice adopted by McCracken J. in *Re Ansbacher (Cayman)*:

> "In that case a preliminary issue as to whether, on the facts of the relevant case, the court had any power to order a hearing *in camera* or in some other way limit the publication of the applicants' names, was determined by McCracken J. in circumstances where the relevant preliminary application was maintained in the name of the applicants' solicitors."

With regard to the plaintiffs' particular situation Clarke J. commented that whatever the position may be with regard to compliant taxpayers:

"[I]t is difficult to see how any constitutional entitlement could be asserted which would prevent the public generally from being made aware of the manner in which others have failed to meet their tax obligations."

Having given due consideration to the case law surrounding the aspect of Art.34.1 which places a "high value on the administration of justice in public", Clarke J. found against the plaintiffs:

"I was not, therefore, satisfied that the court had any jurisdiction to permit proceedings such as those intended by the plaintiffs to be conducted on an anonymous basis. I was not satisfied that any entitlement to confidentiality concerning their tax affairs which the plaintiffs might assert could be of sufficient weight to countervail, even to a limited extent, the constitutional imperative to the effect that justice be administered in public. Nor was I satisfied that a requirement that the proceedings be brought in the names of the plaintiffs amounted to an infringement of the plaintiffs' undoubted right of access to the courts. The fact that the plaintiffs might be discouraged from bringing proceedings if not permitted to bring them anonymously was not, of itself, in my view, a sufficient reason to give rise to a jurisdiction to permit the proceedings to be brought anonymously. Nor, in my view, was the fact that some of the purpose of the proceedings might be lost, in practice, a sufficient factor to give rise to a constitutional jurisdiction to permit these proceedings to be brought anonymously" (para.5.1).

CABINET CONFIDENTIALITY

Article 8(b) of the Access to Information on the Environment Regulations (S.I. No. 133 of 2007) precludes release of information "to the extent that it would involve the disclosure of discussions at one or more meetings of the Government" as this is prohibited by Art.28 of the Constitution. These Regulations are discussed in the Information Law and the Ombudsman chapter in this *Annual Review*.

CHILDREN'S RIGHTS

Children in care

"The work involved in caring for young persons at risk is challenging. It involves particular dedication. It requires the employment of a substantial number of highly motivated staff; the provision of adequate facilities and clear lines of administrative responsibility. It is necessary to identify and match need, resources and spaces. It requires administrative will and a clear identification of objectives. By no means all of these requisites were applied in the decade between 1995 and 2005.

Against this complex and difficult background it is necessary to place on record recognition of the approach taken by the authorities, including the H.S.E., in this case, and also in two others which should be read in conjunction with this judgment. Those further two judgments are *In the matter of S.S. (a minor)* MacMenamin J., the High Court, delivered 15th June, 2007 and *In the matter of D.K. (a child)* Record No. 2006/1974 P, MacMenamin J., the High Court, Unreported, delivered on the same day as this judgment. These three cases had a number of features in contrast to other previous hearings of this type in the last decade. In each of these cases the H.S.E., rather than relying on constitutional or legal defences, sought actually to address the underlying problems and to outline the approach which would be adopted to create an improved framework and procedure for the care of young persons at risk, such as W.R. The H.S.E. not only consented to the hearings; they took the role of initiators. No question of mandatory orders arose for consideration. In the absence of such consent the court obviously would not have engaged in this process" *Re Articles 40 and 42 of the Constitution, HSE v WR(a minor)* [2007] I.E.H.C. 459 at paras 38 to 39.

The first of the three cases which are interconnected in this quote from MacMenamin J.'s judgment had been delivered a month earlier (*Re Article 40.3, Article 41 and 42 of the Constitution, HSE v SS* [2007] I.E.H.C. 185). *HSE v SS* concerned a minor close to his 16th birthday. He had had a deeply troubled childhood and adolescence which had left ongoing emotional and psychological scars ("Such home or family unit as S. ever had have simply disintegrated" (para.2)). Many involved in his care shared the view consistently expressed by his guardian *ad litem*, and latterly by his mother, that it was necessary for S's welfare and protection that he be detained long-term in some form of secure unit. This concern, felt by many involved in S's care, was enhanced by the fact that when he had previously absconded, he frequently placed himself at serious risk by his own behaviour and at the hands of older and predatory males. MacMenamin J. stated that no one unit presently in existence appeared entirely appropriate to deal with S's many difficulties and he summarised S's situation as follows:

"Throughout his life it seems S.'s other constitutional rights, to liberty, to dignity, to development as a human being, have been almost entirely subsumed by concerns as to the protection of his life and welfare. The unpleasant term 'warehousing' is sometimes used regarding persons placed in institutional care. Even this term imparts too strong a sense of permanence and locale to the constant shifts and transience in S.'s life thus far. This observation is made not in any sense of blame but as a simple statement of fact" (at para.15).

It was against this background that MacMenamin J. had to consider two questions. First, he had to consider whether the High Court, in its exercise of its inherent jurisdiction, can make an order for the long-term detention in secure care of minors, where on the evidence such care is required in the interests of the education and welfare of such minor. If the answer to this question were yes, then he had to consider what procedural safeguards should be put in place for the protection of the rights of such minors and their parents and the needs of the family unit under the Constitution and the European Convention on Human Rights Act 2003.

Inherent jurisdiction of High Court *Contrasting detention for care and detention after conviction* MacMenamin J. acknowledged that two legal issues were in the balance. The first was the requirement that in the exercise of its inherent discretion the High Court must observe the principle that when an order for placement of a young person in secure care is to protect his/her life, health or welfare when seriously at risk, such order can only be made on a short-term basis. By contrast, when a young person is sentenced after conviction for an offence this is for a specified term of detention in a penal institution as opposed to a secure care unit. Whilst the purpose of a detention order for care must be protective, not punitive, the fact that it is so intended does not detract from concerns that what is at stake is nonetheless a restriction of the constitutional right to liberty. However, the capacity of the minor to preserve and protect his or her own life and safety when in the community must be introduced into this balancing exercise:

> "Thus, what is termed 'negative liberty', i.e. absence of constraint, is counter-measured against positive liberty, the ability of S. to take control of his own life in a real way when in the community" (para.22). Moreover, any period of detention, of whatever duration, must have a rationale. '[T]he purpose and objective of such detention must be educational, therapeutic and for the purpose and objective of protecting the life and welfare of such young person. The means adopted must be proportionate to the ends sought to be achieved, both as to duration, education and therapeutic care' [para.22].
>
> **24.** In opting between those various choices (including his right to liberty and none of which it was accepted, could cater fully for S.'s needs) this Court adopted a course of action identified by Costello J. in the case of *D.D. v. The Eastern Health Board* (Unreported, High Court, 1995) in the circumstance that the H.S.E. did not dispute that

it owed a statutory duty to S to provide for his accommodation and welfare and to protect his interests pursuant to sections 3 and 4 of the Child Care Act 1991."

Detention under Article 42.5 for short period only   Reviewing case law relating to the nature and range of the High Court's jurisdiction to make orders for detention, having regard to not one, but all the fundamental rights engaged, MacMenamin J. cited *DG v Eastern Health Board* [1997] 3 I.R. 511, *G v An Bord Uchtála* [1980] I.R. 32, *Attorney-General v. X* [1992] 1 I.R. 1, *FN v Minister for Education* [1995] 1 I.R. 409, *DD v Eastern Health Board*, unreported, High Court, May 3, 1995. He concluded that where the State intervenes pursuant to Art.42.5, it must truly be, as stated in that Article, an "exceptional case" and may be for a short period only (paras 43 to 55).

Balance of rights and rationale   MacMenamin J. also considered the jurisprudence of the European Convention of Human Rights. He summarised his findings as follows:

"[T]he capacity and age of the minor, the nature of the place of detention, the extent, quality, and suitability of the educational and welfare facilities available must have a direct bearing on the duration for which this court may order a minor to be detained. The civil jurisdiction engaged may only be exercised on an interim or interlocutory basis, and only, therefore, with regular review by the court. Such process, to be consistent with the rights of a citizen under the Constitution of Ireland, and to accord with Article 5.4 of the European Convention on Human Rights must guarantee that any deprivation of liberty by arrest or detention imports with it a duty upon the State (including this Court) to provide an integral mechanism whereby proceedings can be initiated for the review of the lawfulness of such detention in a speedy manner (see *Kolanis v. UK* [2005] 1 MHLR 238). It is quite clear that in *D.G. v. Ireland* the Court of Human Rights rejected any use of detention as a preventive measure. Only countervailing rights, or a rationale such as those involving life or welfare, may justify such jurisdiction, and only on the basis that the right to life and welfare of a minor is to be placed temporarily, and only so long as proportionate and justifiable, in a superior position in the constitutional hierarchy to other fundamental values such as liberty, equality, or bodily integrity. While the function of the State in these circumstances may be to act as in a parental role and while such role may allow for a purposive interpretation of statute law, such an approach may never justify the abrogation or negation of fundamental constitutional rights" (para.71).

Why have inherent jurisdiction powers been invoked?   Albeit brief,
MacMenamin J. presents an interesting analysis of the efforts, or lack thereof,
of the legislature to address the lacunae in children's legislation dating back as
far as 1908. The absence of a statutory framework is further complicated by the
frequent simultaneous exercise of jurisdiction by more than one court, in the
instant case the High Court in its civil jurisdiction and the District Court in its
criminal jurisdiction. In other cases the civil jurisdictions of both the High Court
and the District Court have been invoked. *HSE v SS* exemplifies the confusion.
S was a subject of simultaneous civil and criminal proceedings in which he
was represented by two, to some extent non-communicating, sets of lawyers.
With approximately 20 cases of this nature on the weekly High Court lists,
perhaps the inherent jurisdiction of the High Court was felt to provide a more
flexible approach to the issues at stake than a statutory regime. Noting that the
Executive was currently reviewing the matter, MacMenamin J. commented that
the "frequent invocation and exercise of 'exceptional' constitutional powers,
absent principles of application or, any statutory or regulatory framework is
undesirable" (para.76).

Rights of parents   With regard to the role of parents, the judgment notes
that an order to detain a minor in secure care must be seen and interpreted in
accordance with the rights, not only of the minor, but also the rights of parents,
whether or not a family unit, and other family members:

> "In particular it is necessary to ensure that, where possible, parents play
> a full role in ensuring that any period of detention is truly therapeutic
> in effect. The rights of such parents are substantive and should, where
> practicable, extend to all stages of the decision-making process in child
> protection cases where either, or both, parent evinces a willingness to
> play a role and to the extent that is in the best interests of the child"
> (para.85).

How long is short-term care?   The judgment stresses the need for appropriate
safeguards to ensure that the balancing of rights of all relevant stakeholders,
particularly those of the minors' parents, continue to be properly met. As
circumstances change perhaps the priority of rights also changes. Therefore,
the court must give due consideration to the nature, adequacy and frequency
of review procedures. MacMenamin J. considered that as a guide, but not as a
conclusive determinant, in the absence of legislation a court might require a first
review of detention within weeks. Thereafter, regard should be given to the time
periods provided for in s.23(b)(4)(a) of the Childcare Act 1991 relating to the
detention by the District Court of children in secure care, and also by analogy
to the time limits and procedural safeguards outlined in s.25 of the Mental
Health Act 2001 relating to the review of involuntary admission of children in

need of mental treatment and the constitutional requirement of proper respect for the family unit which requires that full account is taken of the views and wishes of parents, the child's guardian and other interested parties.

With regard to the duration of an order he accepted the submissions made on behalf of the Attorney-General that because of the wide scope of the High Court's inherent power it might be theoretically possible that, in a highly exceptional case, a court might make orders of predetermined duration which are in *effect* or *result* longer than those outlined above:

> "It is difficult to envisage any circumstance, however, where any such order might (absent on-going review) remain lawful. In order to vindicate the correlative right to liberty of a young person there must be in place a regular failsafe process of regular consideration of such detention so as to ensure the continued proper harmonising, or prioritising, of constitutional rights which may conflict. The procedure for vindication of rights requires the application of scrutiny in direct relation to the duration of detention. This may necessitate in an appropriate case the application of the full range of procedural rights outlined in *Re. Haughey* [1971] I.R. 217" (para.69).

Minor's voice   Of particular interest to those with a specific interest in children's rights is MacMenamin J.'s opinion on giving due regard to the child's wishes:

> "Finally, but vitally in this context, such power [the inherent jurisdiction of the High Court] may be exercised only upon the basis of regular review of the balance of rights as an integral part of the procedure itself. These rights must include adequate opportunity for the views of the minor to be made known to the court in the fulfilment of his or her "natural and imprescriptible rights" (para.69).

The minor's voice, as expressed by independent legal representation, has been singularly absent from many cases involving an under-18's welfare, among the more recent being *North Western Health Board v HW* [2001] 3 I.R 622, *N v HSE* [2006] I.E.H.C. 278, colloquially known as the *Baby Ann* case; *McK v Information Commissioner* [2006] I.E.S.C. 2 and *Ms D* (unreported, High Court, McKechnie J., May 9, 2007). It may be noted that it is generally only in exceptional circumstances such as those pertaining in *SS* when Art.42.5 is invoked that a child of a constitutionally recognised family unit will be given a legal voice. Thus, minors who are a part of such a family unit are deemed to be represented by their parent(s). This, of course, presumes two things. The first is that the parent is capable of articulating what is in the child's best interests and, secondly, that the parent's and the minor child's wishes coincide. Is this aspect of MacMenamin J.'s ratio a chink in the dark tunnel confronting a minor child who has a valid opinion to express about her own welfare? Probably not, as it is more likely that were a minor to attempt to invoke this part of the judgment, *SS* would be distinguished and Art.41 would be cited. The manner in which Art.41 has been interpreted essentially gives paramountcy to parental rights to the exclusion of the court hearing directly from the minor child.

DELEGATED LEGISLATION

Section 124 of the Garda Síochána Act 2005 provides that the Minister for Justice Equality and Law Reform shall:

> "… after consulting with the Garda Commissioner, the Ombudsman Commission and the Inspectorate, and with the approval of the Government, make regulations providing for the establishment of a charter containing guidelines and mechanisms to enable members of the Garda Síochána or other persons to report in confidence allegations of corruption and malpractice within the Garda Síochána."

The Garda Síochána (Confidential Reporting of Corruption or Malpractice) Regulations 2007 were enacted under this section. The clear legislative purpose of s.124 is for the establishment of a "charter" which is provided for in s.4 of the Regulations. At the time of writing this charter has not yet been published. The Regulations themselves concern the reporting in confidence of allegations of corruption and malpractice, including creating the position of confidential recipient. One might raise the question whether some aspects of the Regulations are a step too far from the delegatory intent of the Oireachtas and whether a challenge under *Cityview* might be effective.

These Regulations are discussed in the Whistleblower Protection chapter in this *Annual Review*.

CONSTITUTIONAL JUSTICE

Medical scapegoats   The case of *Prendiville v The Medical Council* [2007] I.E.H.C. 427 can be summed up in two sentences. The High Court quashed the decisions of the Medical Council's Fitness to Practise Committee and of the Medical Council and refused to remit the cases. This arose, inter alia, from findings of breach of natural and constitutional justice. However, given the great and grave injustice visited on three consultant obstetricians and gynaecologists, Dr Walter Prendiville and Dr John Francis Murphy (and, indeed, on Dr Bernard Stuart who had not contested the decisions), such a curt dismissal of the case would seem to compound that terrible injustice. Moreover, such a single sentence treatment does no justice to the comprehensive and detailed judgment of Kelly J. Further, it would not make clear that the governing statute precluded any appeal on the merits of their case and that the doctors were confined to a "second choice" of judicial review.

The circumstances and causes of these three doctors' disgrace are widely believed to be well-known. It is only in reading Kelly J.'s judgment that it becomes clear the extent to which these three doctors have been scapegoated by the Medical Council and the world at large in punishment for the gross failure of the health professional community to curtail Dr Michael Neary's unacceptable gynaecological and obstetric practices. It is no requirement of this analysis to revisit Michael Neary's case nor to restate the horrific wrong suffered by many of his patients treated in Our Lady of Lourdes Hospital, Drogheda. There are details in the judgment of his practice and the potentially restrictive policies of that institution which may have given rise to unnecessary hysterectomies.

Inquiry report genesis for grievance A starting point for this analysis is the non-statutory private inquiry (the Inquiry) into the events at the hospital and in particular para.1.8 of the introduction of Judge Harding Clark S.C. (now Harding Clark J.). Neither this report nor the procedures followed in its compilation fell for consideration in the judicial review. However, Kelly J. noted that both applicants believed they were unfairly dealt with by the Inquiry and as para.1.8 of the report was the genesis for the matters under consideration, that their sense of injustice had not diminished as events developed. With respect to the Inquiry Kelly J. did note that prior to finalising her report, the judge followed a well established-course which, as a matter of fair procedures, is now common to tribunals of inquiry. She furnished to persons to be criticised in the report a draft of that criticism in advance of its finalisation and publication. This was to enable such persons to make submissions and observations on that criticism before the final report was produced. However, Kelly J. stated that whilst that procedure was apparently followed for everyone else, "it was not followed in the case of either Prof. Prendiville or Dr. Murphy. They are aggrieved that they were so treated."

Fitness to Practise Committee Inquiry As a result of the findings of the Inquiry, Patient Focus, a group representative of women affected by Dr Neary's practice, made a complaint to the Fitness to Practise Committee (FPC) of the Medical Council concerning the three consultants who had prepared interim reports into the conduct of Dr Neary. Professor Prendiville faced 12 allegations of professional misconduct; by a majority the FPC found that six allegations had been proved but that five of those six did not amount to professional misconduct. By a majority, it found that the remaining allegation as proved did amount to:

"… professional misconduct as defined by Keane J. in *O'Laoire v. The Medical Council* [(unreported, January 27, 1995)] being conduct in connection with his profession in which the medical practitioner has seriously fallen short of the standards of conduct expected among medical practitioners and not in a sense of any 'infamous' or 'disgraceful' conduct or any conduct involving any degree of moral turpitude, fraud or dishonesty."

With respect to Dr Murphy, the FPC found by a majority that six allegations were proved, of which three did not amount to professional misconduct: "The FPC used precisely the same formula in describing the professional misconduct on the part of Dr. Murphy as it did in respect of Prof. Prendiville."

The FPC recommended that Prof. Prendiville be advised that should he have any reservations in any future report undertaken, then those reservations should be included in his report. The recommendation in the case of Dr Murphy was that he should be admonished in relation to his professional conduct.

Medical Council Inquiry   By invitation both doctors were present and were represented by counsel at the meeting of the Medical Council at which the FPC report was due for consideration. Twenty-two members of the Council were present. "All five members of the FPC who heard the complaints against the applicants were present and participated in the Council's deliberations." Kelly J. stated that at the very outset of the Council meeting the Council President was clearly of the view that the meeting was confined to the question of sanction and had to accept the findings of the FPC on professional misconduct. This interpretation of the Council's role was contested by the applicants both at the time and in the judicial review proceedings. Having deliberated, the Medical Council announced through its President that it had "decided to accept the verdict (sic) of the Fitness to Practise Committee in each case but to impose no sanction in any case". He also announced that it had decided to publish this decision by way of a press release. Kelly J. described this press release as "extraordinary" and "bizarre" and as "very unfair to the applicants who were entitled to expect better from the Council".

Profound adverse consequences   Commenting that a finding of professional misconduct against any professional person is very serious, Kelly J. found that there have been profound adverse consequences for the applicants in the present case. He quoted from Prof. Prendiville's grounding affidavit:

"I am distressed and embarrassed by the FPC finding and the respondent's decision, which I believe to be unwarranted, and by the extent of the publicity surrounding it. I am distressed not only for myself but also for my family. In particular, my family is upset at the calls made in certain quarters that I should not be permitted to practise as a doctor at all. I have dedicated my professional life to the care of pregnant women for more than three decades now. While I readily acknowledge the deep hurt and trauma experienced by the women represented by, for example, Patient Focus and their families, I nonetheless consider the finding of professional misconduct made against me by the Medical Council to be unfounded and irrational. The effects on my professional reputation and my career of the respondents' action in finding me guilty of professional misconduct will be profound and longstanding. I have been described in the press and in the Oireachtas as a disgrace to the medical profession."

Kelly J. concluded that these forebodings proved to be correct. In his judgment he detailed the eminence at a national and international level which both applicants enjoyed prior to the events outlined and some of the consequences of their disgrace, including a reference in the *Examiner* newspaper to "views expressed in certain quarters that [Prof. Prendiville] should consider whether [both doctors] are fit to continue teaching medical students." Kelly J. also quoted from Dr. Murphy's grounding affidavit:

"[T]he media attention since the first announcement of an inquiry into three un-named obstetricians has been huge and intrusive. I say that I work in a highly personal speciality where reputation is of the utmost importance. As a result of my involvement in this inquiry I believe that I have been the subject of extensive comment by patients, staff and the public in general. The decision of the respondent has had a highly corrosive effect on both myself and my family, and has also affected my relationship with friends and colleagues. In my view, the decision has had the effect of negating much of the effort and work I have been engaged in in my profession over the past four decades."

Kelly J. held that the doctors had sustained considerable damage to their standing, reputation and the practice of their profession. In the circumstances, he was in no way surprised that the applicants sought to appeal the decision of the Council.

No right of appeal under Medical Practitioner's Act   Arising from ss.46, 47 and 48 of the Act, an application may only be made for the cancellation of a decision of the Medical Council in circumstances where it has decided to erase or suspend the name of a medical practitioner from the register or to attach conditions to the retention of that person's name in the register. "In circumstances where it decides to advise, admonish or censure the medical practitioner or to impose no penalty (as in the present case) no appeal on the merits lies to this court." Thus, the applicants were confined to a "second choice" of judicial review with its much narrower remit and the inability of the court to address the substantive merits of their case.

Double construction rule of interpretation   Kelly J. considered the Council's approach that it could not reconsider the recommendation of the FPC in the context of this statutory barrier and the effect of this approach. If the FPC by the narrowest of margins finds a medical practitioner guilty of professional misconduct but no sanction is imposed which attracts recourse to the High Court under ss.45 or 46 of the Act, that medical practitioner can never again have the merits of his case considered in any form either by the Council or by the High Court. This being so, Kelly J. applied the double construction rule of statutory interpretation, citing *McDonald v Bord na gCon (No. 2)* [1965] I.R. 217:

> "A construction of the statutory provisions which renders the solemnly assembled Council impotent to consider and, if appropriate, refuse to confirm, a decision of the FPC on the most important decision affecting a doctors career, in circumstances where no appeal on the merits to this court is provided by the Act, is one which ought not to be preferred to the alternative construction urged by the applicants.
>
> The alternative construction results in a report of the FPC being capable of review by the Council which is the body charged by the Act with the control of persons engaged in the practise of medicine. This alternative construction means that a doctor charged and found guilty of professional misconduct by the FPC is not deprived of having his case and that decision considered by the Council. Given the huge importance to any doctors career of a finding of professional misconduct, the alternative construction is, in my view, much more conducive to enjoyment of the rights conferred under the Constitution and the [European Convention of Human Rights]. A decision of the FPC ought to be capable of independent reconsideration by the Council and, in my view, the Act so ordains."

Medical Council acted ultra vires   It followed that the Council was wrong in law in regarding itself as being bound by the decision of the FPC on the applicants' guilt and confining itself solely to the question of penalty. By so doing the applicants were denied the opportunity of having the arguments addressed on their behalf considered in accordance with due process. The Council acted ultra vires in behaving as it did. It also follows that the advice proffered to the Council by its registrar and in-house adviser was wrong in law. While it was not strictly necessary for the court to consider the procedure that was adopted by the Council which led to that advice being given, issues of some importance were involved which might affect future cases. As a consequence Kelly J considered these.

Medical Council's procedures

Composition ... breach of nemo iudex in causa sua   In the first instance, the composition of the Council breached the *nemo iudex in causa sua* rule:

> "That rule is of fundamental importance in bodies exercising judicial and quasi judicial roles. It was in my view objectionable that members of the FPC should have sat as members of the Council to consider their own report on the conduct of the applicants."

Entitlement to strict adherence to the rules of natural justice   The procedures before the FPC and before the Council were fundamentally different. In the latter proceedings there was no independent legal assessor or adviser. The applicants had argued that the manner in which advice was given was irregular. The advice was provided in circumstances unknown to the applicants and where they had no opportunity of addressing through their legal advisers the correctness or otherwise of the advice tendered. Kelly J. began his consideration of these issues with some general comments on natural justice which bear repeating:

> "There is no fixed standard of natural justice which is applicable in all circumstances. The standard is plastic. It varies in accordance with the circumstances. As was said by Keane J. in *Mooney v. An Post* [1994] E.L.R. 103: '... the concept (of natural justice) is necessarily an imprecise one and what its application requires may differ significantly from case to case. The two great central principles—*audi alteram partem* and *nemo iudex in causa sua*—cannot be applied in a uniform fashion to every set of facts.'
>
> The standard to be applied to a person whose conduct is under investigation therefore varies according to the circumstances. In the present case I am satisfied the high standards of natural justice must apply. The allegations made against the applicants were very serious and their whole professional standing was at stake. The applicants were entitled to expect that there would be strict adherence to the rules of natural justice and that justice would not only be done but be seen to be done in their dealings with the Council."

Denial of audi alteram partem *rule*   He continued:

> "It was inappropriate that legal advice be tendered by the very officer who presented the case against the applicants before the FPC. I cannot see how such advice can be seen to be objective. I am not saying that

the advice was in fact biased but there is the perception of bias arising from the role played by the advice giver when the cases where before the FPC.

Secondly, it was in my view quite wrong that the legal advice such as it was, was tendered only to the President and Vice President of the Council. If there was an entitlement on the part of the Council to legal advice, it should have been furnished to all and at the same time. It was not good enough that the verbal advice furnished to the President and Vice President should be retailed by them to the other members of the Council.

Thirdly, the method of receiving the advice was in my view deficient. It was a form of denial of the *audi alteram* rule because it enabled the Council to rely upon information obtained outside the hearing and not disclosed to the applicants who were adversely affected by it."

The court placed most reliance on *The State (Polymark Limited) v ITGWU* [1987] I.L.R.M. 357 and also referred to the English authorities of *Nwabueze v General Medical Council* [2000] 1 W.L.R. 1760 and *Watson v General Medical Council* [2005] E.W.H.C. 1896.

Professional misconduct: expected standards test Holding that the decision of the Council cannot stand and certiorari will go to quash it, Kelly J. then considered the FPC procedure and, in particular, the standard of professional misconduct applied to the doctors. As stated above, the FPC used the definition of professional misconduct indicated by Keane J. in *O'Laoire v The Medical Council*, unreported, High Court, January 27, 1995. Kelly J. referred to this as a masterly judgment and he considered in detail pp.99 to 108 which dealt with the meaning of professional misconduct. Keane J. identified five principles which he deduced by reference to Irish and English case law:

"'1. Conduct which is "infamous" or "disgraceful" in a professional respect is "professional misconduct" within the meaning of s. 46(1) of the Act.

2. Conduct which would not be "infamous" or "disgraceful" in any other person, if done by a medical practitioner in relation to his profession, that is, with regard to either his patients or to his colleagues, may be considered as "infamous" or "disgraceful" conduct in a professional respect.

3. "Infamous" or "disgraceful" conduct is conduct involving some degree of moral turpitude, fraud or dishonesty.

4. The fact that a person wrongly but honestly forms a particular opinion cannot of itself amount to infamous or disgraceful conduct in a professional sense.

5. Conduct which could not properly be characterised as "infamous" or "disgraceful" and which does not involve any degree of moral turpitude, fraud or dishonesty may still constitute "professional misconduct" if it is conduct connected with his profession in which the medical practitioner concerned has seriously fallen short, by omission or commission, of the standards of conduct expected among medical practitioners.'"

The *O'Laoire* judgment held that the fifth principle fell to be modified by virtue of the definition of professional misconduct as contained in the third edition (1989) of the Council's guide *to Ethical Conduct and Behaviour and to Fitness to Practise*. The fifth edition of the guide post-dated the judgment in *O'Laoire's* case by about three years. Kelly J. noted that whilst the Council's guide is merely a guide it is, nevertheless, published under the provisions of s.69(2) of the Act, which imposes a function on the Council to give guidance to the medical profession generally on all matters relating to ethical conduct and behaviour:

"It is not too much to expect that a doctor on consulting the guide would at least be apprised in general terms of what the Council understands professional misconduct to mean. Of course, one is not entitled to look for absolute precision in a guide. The notion of professional misconduct can change from time to time because of changing circumstances and new eventualities. It would be unreasonable to expect the Council to publish a catalogue of the forms of professional misconduct which may lead to disciplinary action. But if a new test is to be applied or a new species of conduct is to be regarded as amounting to professional misconduct, then one would expect the Council to notify its members of that. Indeed, that is precisely what it did by the publication of the sixth edition of the guide in 2004. There can be no doubt, having regard to the wording of the sixth edition of the guide, that from the time of its publication the 'expected standards' test is applicable in relation to professional misconduct on the part of the members of the medical profession."

Kelly J. concluded that the FPC applied the "expected standards" test by reference to the judgment in the *O'Laoire's* case without any account being taken of the modification Keane J. required by reference to the then current guide of the Council. In Kelly J.'s view, they were not entitled to do so, and he held it unreasonable and unfair to expect medical practitioners to be subjected to a test of professional misconduct which the Council had not promulgated or notified to the profession until years after the event.

Absence of reasons   Since the Medical Council bound itself to affirming the decision of the FPC, Kelly J. confined his analysis to the decision of the FPC. Appendix 6 of the judgment contains the FPC report in full. Only eight pages long, six of the pages are devoted to a recital of the identity of the parties to the enquiry and the dates on which it sat, a recitation that the criminal standard of proof was to be applied by the FPC and a setting out of the allegations made against each of Drs Prendiville, Murphy and Stuart. It is only in the final two pages and "in the tersest form possible" that the FPC deals with its decision. By contrast the FPC report on Dr Neary himself ran to in excess of one hundred pages, and clearly was a reasoned one. The Council's contention that there is no duty on the part of the FPC to give reasons was rejected. Kelly J. commented that the applicants were entitled to at least a general explanation of the basis for the majority decision of the FPC. They had not obtained that, which was an example of the inconsistency in practice on the part of the FPC. He relied on *Rajah v Royal College of Surgeons of Ireland* [1994] 1 I.R. 384 and more recently the Supreme Court decision in *FP v Minister for Justice* [2002] 1 I.R. 164. Finding the decision of the FPC also deficient by reason of the lack of reasons given for its findings, Kelly J. held:

> "In my view, the FPC was obliged to give reasons for coming to the conclusion which it did. It was not obliged to provide a discursive judgment, but I accept the applicants complaint that they were left 'absolutely in the dark' as to the basis for the FPC's findings. That is all the more so in the circumstances where it is clear that, contrary to the requirements of s. 45 (3)(c), the report did not specify the evidence laid before the FPC.
>
> A statement of the reasons for the FPC decision would have been essential so as to enable the Council to hear submissions and decide on whether or not it ought to confirm the FPC's findings. Even if I am wrong in the view which I take concerning the role of the Council, and it is in fact no more than a cypher for the FPC save on the question of sanction, the applicants are entitled to know the basis of the decision in the context of an application for judicial review. As was said [in *Rajah v Royal College of Surgeons of Ireland* [1994] 1 I.R. 384] reasons are necessary in order to ensure that the superior courts may exercise their jurisdiction to enquire into, and if necessary, correct such decisions."

Irrationality   It was not necessary for the High Court to consider this topic having regard to the other findings but had it been necessary the task was rendered very difficult by virtue of the absence of any reasons being given by the FPC for its decision.

Remission inequitable and unfair   Finally the High Court refused to remit, inter alia, having regard to the passage of time since the events complained of, the number of years that disciplinary proceeding have been hanging over the applicants, and the undoubted damage which has been done to them. Kelly J. concluded that it would be quite inequitable and unfair to remit the case.

Redressing the balance   Given that *Prendiville* is a judicial review, the question should be asked whether quashing the Medical Council's decisions, the course of action available to the court, is in any way sufficient redress for the medical practitioners involved. The damage to them and their families both in reputation and otherwise is incalculable. This damage transcends the national arena. These doctors held such eminent positions and were in turn held in such high regard by their peers that it is unlikely that matters can ever be set right. Of course, it might be argued that the women who suffered as a consequence of Dr Neary's surgical practices are in a far worse situation. But that is to confuse two separate issues. Dr Prendiville, Dr Murphy and Dr Stuart did not engage in any form of medical malpractice. On the contrary, they were each highly regarded for their own personal behaviour. They acceded to a request by the Irish Hospital Consultants Association (IHCA) to prepare a confidential report on the medical practice of Dr Michael Neary. They had 72 hours to do so. Kelly J. noted early in his judgment that it was in this atmosphere of urgency that the three consultants undertook their task. He further stated:

> "A number of other important features concerning the task being undertaken by the three consultants must be borne in mind. First, none of them had any experience of being asked to prepare a report in these circumstances and for such purpose. Secondly, there was no template or set of rules to which they could refer. Thirdly, the report was being prepared in an industrial relations context. Finally, it was the view of the three consultants that they were to prepare interim reports solely for the use of the IHCA in its dispute with the health board."

Kelly J. records that on November 3, 1998 the three consultants held a four-hour meeting with Dr Neary who had brought photocopies of some of his patients' records:

> "Over the four hour period [nine] cases were discussed and Dr. Neary was questioned in respect of them. He gave clear, comprehensive and coherent answers and explanations. He took the three consultants through his operating notes in respect of each of the patients. It was not possible in the time available to carry out any analysis of the other medical records, which in any event were not arranged in good order.
>   It was evident to the three consultants that Dr. Neary had a low threshold for carrying out peri partum hysterectomies (pph). The

consultants were aware that no complaint had been made against Dr. Neary by any particular patient. They were *au fait* with the ethical code of the hospital which prohibited sterilisation even in situations where medical opinion was to the effect that further pregnancy would be life threatening. They also knew of the lack of availability of certain drugs, which would be readily to hand in the bigger Dublin maternity hospitals, to deal with severe post-partum haemorrhage.

They brought to Dr. Neary's attention the fact that he had a low threshold for intervention by way of pph. Because of that, the three consultants obtained from him an undertaking not to perform any further pph without a supporting opinion from a second consultant. The purpose of this undertaking was to protect Dr. Neary's patients pending the peer review due to be carried out by the Institute. The need for a peer review was clear and in any event had already been agreed to by Dr. Neary."

The three reports are appended to the judgment:

"They supported the continuation of Dr. Neary in his work at the Drogheda hospital pending the [forthcoming peer] review by the Institute. The purpose of these reports was to assist the IHCA and its legal advisors."

A month later Dr Michael Maresh, consultant obstetrician and gynaecologist at St Mary's Hospital, Manchester, reported on his review of the nine cases considered in the reports. He had been commissioned by the North Eastern Health Board:

"He spent several weeks preparing this report [appended to the judgment]. He did not meet Dr. Neary in the course of its preparation. In evidence, which he gave to the FPC, he said that he had approximately 1200 pages of charts before him and that it took at least an hour to collate each of the 9 sets of notes and another four to six hours to draw his conclusions in respect of each case." He came to a different conclusion than the three doctors and following his report Dr. Michael Neary was suspended and eventually struck off. There followed the Inquiry in which Harding Clark J. (as she now is) stated her belief that the three doctors 'were motivated by compassion and collegiality'."

As has been related above, the applicants were aggrieved and remain aggrieved that they were not afforded the opportunity to comment on these findings, which they dispute.

Since the public, this writer included, seized on the phrase "motivated by compassion and collegiality", the accurate narrative of events was either never disseminated or has been lost in the understandable outrage that erupted when Dr Maresh's report was made known. Hence, it seems important to have quoted Kelly J. in some detail.

Distorting the public perspective   Three things are worthy of note at this stage. It has never been made crystal clear in any public statements that the report produced by the three consultants was not for the Medical Council, nor that the evidence on which the three doctors had to work and that the time available to them was of a far different quality than that available to the UK consultant who condemned Michael Neary's practice. Finally, it was never made clear that the three doctors did place restrictions on Dr Neary's practice. Some seven years later, on March 21, 2006, the President of the Medical Council issued a press statement which announced the application for an inquiry and, inter alia, emphasised the "ethical imperative there is on all Medical Practitioners to deal with underperforming colleagues rapidly and fairly in a way that always keeps the safety of patients as the prime goal". The judgment notes that although that press statement was published on the March 21, 2006, it was not until May 2, 2006 that any official notification was sent to the applicants concerning the decision of the Council.

A further press statement was issued by the President of the Medical Council following the deliberations on what sanction to impose on foot of the FPC's findings. This was categorized by Kelly J. as both extraordinary and bizarre:

> "The press release that was issued through a public relations company was extraordinary. It recorded the decision to 'accept the findings of professional misconduct' against the applicants but did not record the decision of the Council not to impose any sanction against them. It is quite clear that the Council took the view that it could do nothing other than accept the FPC findings on all but penalty. Why the statement should record the decision on which the Council had, according to itself, no discretion and not record the only issue on which it had discretion and which was favourable to the applicants is bizarre. It was very unfair to the applicants who were entitled to expect better from the Council."

One can only wonder what the High Court might comment regarding the Medical Council's statement of January 17, 2008 which is reproduced from the Medical Council's website in its entirety:

> "The Medical Council met on 16 January 2008 and decided that it will not be appealing the decision of Mr. Justice Kelly in the High Court consequent on the proceedings brought by Professor Walter Prendiville and Dr John Murphy.

The Medical Council has adopted new procedures in light of Mr. Justice Kelly's decision.

The Medical Council looks forward to the commencement of the Medical Practitioners Act 2007."

On May 6, 2008 *The Irish Times* reported that the Medical Council had set aside its decision on Dr Bernard Stuart, the third of the three consultants who appear to have been unjustly disgraced.

Publication of Medial Council sanctions limited in effect? The Medical Council is permitted under the Medical Practitioners Act to publicise its decisions on sanctions against medical practitioners. This was famously considered by Finlay P. in *M v The Medical Council* [1984] I.R. 485 at 499:

> "Apart from the right and obligation to hold the enquiry itself, the only powers of the Committee or the Council which could be said to be final and, in a sense, binding are the publication of a finding by the Committee of misconduct or unfitness to practice and the Council's power to advise, admonish or censure a practitioner. Even if it could be said that the publication to the public of a finding by a committee of enquiry of misconduct or unfitness was something affecting the rights of a practitioner within the context of the authorities to which I have referred, or if the same could be said of advising, admonishing or censuring, in my view these would be functions *so clearly limited in their effect* and consequence that they would be within the exception provided by Article 37 of the Constitution even if (contrary to what I believe to be the true legal situation) they constituted the administration of justice" [emphasis added].

What may well have been the situation in 1984 most definitely does not hold true for the 21st century. The genie of public disgrace has been let out of the bottle; how is it to be returned and the bottle recorked?

In the course of the judgment in *Prendiville*, Kelly J. noted that the President of the Council asserted that in circumstances where a decision not to impose a sanction of erasure or suspension or attachment of conditions was arrived at, the right of the applicants to practise medicine has not in any way been infringed. He commented that:

> "It is of course true that there is no legal restriction on them but such an approach is highly artificial and takes no account of the practical consequences of the findings upon them and their professional reputations. There can be no doubt that they have sustained considerable damage to their standing, reputation and the practise of their profession."

The High Court was limited in the actions available to it. There was no possibility that the applicants could legally challenge the decisions taken against them on the merits and so it appears that it is only their colleagues who could restore some semblance of their reputation to them. It would require an immense act of openness and generosity for the members of the Medical Council to acknowledge the wrong done to the three consultants. It would require an act of "compassion and collegiality". After the events outlined here nobody should be surprised if such actions, even when intended, are in short supply.

Medical Practitioners Act 2007 requires amendment   The two applicants were statute-barred from taking an action on the merits of their sanction by the FPC and the Medical Council. It appears as if the same situation would apply under the new Medical Practitioners Act 2007. Appeals to the court are precluded in relation to s.71(a) regarding "advice or admonishment, or a censure, in writing". Moreover, s.85 requires the Council to publish a transcript of all or any part of the proceedings of the FPC at an inquiry following consultation with the Committee if it is deemed to be in the public interest. The 2007 Act was passed in May 2007. The judicial review judgment was delivered in December 2007. Hopefully we may record in the 2008 Annual Review that the statutory deficiencies highlighted by the *Prendiville* case have been rectified by amendments to the 2007 Act.

Disciplinary authority of defence forces   Leave for judicial review was refused in *Muldarry v The Officer Commanding 29th Infantry Group Kosovo* [2007] I.E.H.C. 57. The applicant, inter alia, had sought a declaration that the order made by the military authorities that he be repatriated back to Ireland from duty in Kosovo as an administrative measure prior to affording him an opportunity to invoke his rights pursuant to the Defence Act 1954 and the regulations made thereunder, was unconstitutional and contrary to Art.34 of the Constitution. De Valera J. held that the concept of civil rights and obligations cannot apply to military personnel whilst on active service in circumstances such as those pertaining in Kosovo.

The issue of military discipline and fair procedures impacts on the role of the Ombudsman for the Defence Forces and is considered in the chapter on Information Law and the Ombudsman in this *Annual Review*.

DAMAGES FOR BREACH OF CONSTITUTIONAL RIGHTS

In *Shortt v Commissioner of An Garda Síochána* [2007] I.E.S.C. 9, the Supreme Court assessed the damages due to Mr Shortt for a miscarriage of justice. The miscarriage of justice occurred as a result of a conspiracy on the part of two gardaí to concoct false evidence against the plaintiff which resulted in perjured garda evidence being given at the trial of the applicant. Both Murray C.J. and Hardiman J., with whom the other members of the court agreed, held that the principles applicable to damages for breach of constitutional rights applied to the assessment of Mr Shortt's claim. As Murray C.J. put it, Mr Shortt's core constitutional rights to a fair trial and due process had been set at nought by the gardaí's behaviour. The court proceeded to award general damages (including aggravated damages) of €2,250,000 and exemplary damages of €1,000,000.

THE DWELLING PLACE

In *McDonagh v Kilkenny County Council* [2007] I.E.H.C. 350, the applicants had moved their caravans onto land owned by Kilkenny County Council. The Gardaí served notices on the applicants to move on, pursuant to s.19 of the Criminal Justice (Public Order) Act 1992, as amended. O'Neill J. accepted that the applicants' caravans constituted dwellings for the purposes of Art.40.5 of the Constitution. However, the inviolability of the dwelling guaranteed by Art.40.5 did not provide any protection for the applicants trespassing on the land of others.

In *Sfar v Louth County Council* [2007] I.E.H.C. 344, Ms Sfar sought declarations that the seizure by Louth County Council of dogs from her premises was unlawful. The dogs had been seized from areas around the house. Section 16 of the Control of Dogs Act 1986 allows a warden to seize and detain dogs where a breach of the provisions of the Act is suspected. To this end, a dog warden may enter any premises other than a dwelling. Ms Sfar argued that the curtilage of her dwelling constituted a dwelling for the purposes of the Act and for the purposes of Art.40.5 of the Constitution. Murphy J. noted that "dwelling" was defined quite widely in dictionaries and in landlord and tenant contexts. However, he considered that a narrower definition was more appropriate to the issue of searches and seizures, rejecting Ms Sfar's claim:

> "[T] he word 'dwelling' in s.16 of the Control of Dogs Act, 1986 must be construed in the narrow sense as protecting a house where people live and cannot be deemed to extend to outhouses or boiler houses, particularly where they are not capable of being accessed through the house, nor to the curtilage. It is a contradiction in terms to say that a place where animals, farm or domestic, are housed can be a dwelling where people live, whether permanently or temporarily."

EDUCATION RIGHTS

In *O'C v Minister for Education and Science* [2007] I.E.H.C. 170, the plaintiff
(an autistic minor) sought to compel the Minister to provide him with ABA
tuition. The Minister contended that the eclectic model preferred by the
Department of Education, whereby different types of education were offered
to different children, was an adequate discharge of the State's obligations
under Art.42.4 of the Constitution. The case ran for over seven months in the
High Court, with detailed evidence given on many technical issues. However,
Peart J. ultimately decided that the issue was not whether ABA or the eclectic
model was preferable. The question was simply whether the eclectic model was
adequate. In this regard, he held that the plaintiff had not discharged the onus
of proving that the Minister had failed to meet her constitutional obligations:

> "It must be remembered also that the Minister for Education and Science
> is obliged under the Constitution to *provide for education*, and not to
> *provide education*. The Minister does not run the school. The Board of
> Management has responsibility for the hiring of teachers. The Minister
> will provide the school building and will pay the salaries of teachers
> employed in them, and so long as provision is made by the Minister for
> 'appropriate education' his constitutional duty is discharged. The fact
> that one child or a group of children attend a school where the quality
> of education may be different from another, or less than optimal, or the
> class size is greater than another school or schools elsewhere, does not
> mean that the Minister has failed to *provide for* an appropriate education
> as required by the Constitution.
>
> Given the wide range of differences between all children with
> autism, where no single child will have identical needs, and each
> will need to be considered separately in order to decide exactly what
> intervention is needed and from time to time as progress is made and as
> the child grows, it seems obvious that the model of provision decided
> upon by the Minister must be broad in nature in order to accommodate
> those differing needs in such children.
>
> There is nothing to suggest that the Minister has acted in some
> irrational way by making provision in a way that simply cannot be
> appropriate to meet the needs of children with autism. What has been
> decided upon, and in the light of advice from and consultation with
> experts in this area, and following the Task Force Report 2001 is that
> Model A, as well as other models such as Model B, Model C and so
> on, contain within them the ability to provide an appropriate education
> for such children, depending on need and objectives. It is deliberately
> flexible in order to take account of these differences. The Minister has
> the responsibility under the Constitution to make these decisions, and
> he has done so having taken advice. What those opposing the eclectic

approach to provision wish to establish is that what he has come up with is not appropriate because in their view the only appropriate method of intervention for S, and indeed for all autistic children, is ABA to the exclusion of all others. The Minister, having taken appropriate counsel on the matter is entitled to have a different view."

F v Minister for Education and Science [2007] I.E.H.C. 36 was a similar type of case. Smyth J. refused to order discovery of documents relating to the resources available to fund ABA education, on the basis that funding questions did not bear on the question of whether adequate education was being provided to F such as to discharge the State's constitutional obligation under Art.42.4.

ENUMERATION OF SOCIO-ECONOMIC RIGHTS

In *O'Donnell v South Dublin County Council* [2007] I.E.H.C. 204, Laffoy J. followed the obiter dicta of Keane C.J. and Murphy J. in *TD v Minister for Education* [2001] 4 I.R. 259 in refusing to enumerate a constitutional right to be provided with accommodation. However, in the circumstances of that case, Laffoy J. held that South Dublin County Council had breached the applicants' ECHR right to positive respect for their family life by failing to provide them with adequate accommodation. It thus appears that this is one context in which the Irish courts are prepared to allow a gap to open up between what is required by the Constitution and what is required by the Convention.

EQUALITY

In *M v Ireland* [2007] I.E.H.C. 280, the plaintiff successfully challenged the constitutionality of s.62 of the Offences against the Person Act 1861, which provided that a person convicted of committing an indecent assault upon a male could be sentenced to penal servitude for any term not exceeding 10 years. In contrast, the maximum sentence for the same offence committed on a female is two years—under s.6 of the Criminal Law (Amendment) Act 1935. Laffoy J. held in favour of the plaintiff on the following grounds:

> "Section 62 of the Act of 1861, in mandating a maximum penalty for the offence of indecent assault when committed against a male person which is substantially different from the maximum penalty mandated by law when the same offence is committed against a female, is *prima facie* discriminatory on the ground of gender in contravention of Article 40.1. It is inconsistent with the Constitution unless the differentiation it creates is legitimated by reason of being founded on difference of capacity, whether physical or moral, or difference of social function

of men and women in a manner which is not invidious, arbitrary or capricious.

The core question is whether the classification of persons convicted of indecent assault on male persons for different treatment in sentencing is for a legitimate legislative purpose and is relevant to that purpose. In endeavouring to identify the purpose which the classification serves, there is really nothing to go on other than what may be gleaned from the context of the impugned provision within the legislative scheme of the Act of 1861. The impugned provision is an integral part of provisions … which manifest a societal repugnance to homosexual activity in the terminology used, for instance, the references to 'unnatural' offences and the 'abominable' crime of buggery. The same degree of societal disapproval is not apparent in the terminology used in the Act of 1861 dealing with sexual offences against women…

What else can be extrapolated from the submissions as supporting a legitimate legislative purpose? There are two possibilities in the defendants' submissions. One is that male and female victims require different degrees of protection against sexual offences necessitating different levels of denunciation as reflected in sentencing. The other is that gravity of the sexual offence against a woman is inherently greater than that against a man because of the risk of an unwanted pregnancy. The imposition of a substantially more severe maximum penalty for indecent assault of a male person most certainly would not address the second possibility, nor would it address the first possibility if, as I think it is reasonable to assume for present purposes, women are more vulnerable to sexual assault than men.

I can find nothing in the Act of 1861 or in an objective consideration of the differences of physical capacity, moral capacity and social function of men and women which points to a legitimate legislative purpose for imposing a more severe maximum penalty for indecent assault on a male person than for the same offence against a female person. Therefore, I have come to the conclusion that the relevant provision is inconsistent with Article 40.1.

I have come to that conclusion on the basis of the case as presented without having to reach any conclusion on whether the burden of establishing justification lies with the defendants or with the plaintiff. It is also unnecessary to express any view on whether gender-based discrimination warrants a strict scrutiny approach. In my view, no rational justification for the different maximum penalties which statute law prescribes where the offence of indecent assault is committed, whether by a man or a woman, against a male and a female can be divined even on the basis of the most deferential form of scrutiny. That discrimination is the legacy of Victorian mores and social attitudes. It

is an anomaly which just over a quarter of a century ago the Oireachtas
eliminated prospectively."

While Laffoy J.'s judgment is a welcome and robust application of Art.40.1, it
does not significantly advance equality doctrine. For Laffoy J. found it possible
to reach her conclusion—that the legislation was invalid—even applying the
least exacting standard of review to the legislation. The possibility cannot be
discounted, however, that discussion of standards of review and an emphasis
on how weakly such standards have been applied in the past may have caused
the court to apply the low standards somewhat more rigorously.

FAMILY RIGHTS

In *AF v SF* [2007] I.E.H.C. 196, the parties had cohabited for 26 years before
their relationship broke down. The applicant alleged that they had agreed to get
married prior to the cohabitation commencing. The applicant relied on certain
provisions of the Family Law Acts 1981–1996 to seek court orders in relation
to the distribution of property between the parties. The respondent brought a
preliminary motion seeking to strike out the proceedings as being frivolous or
vexatious. In particular, the respondent relied on the earlier judgment of Kelly
J. in *Ennis v Butterly* [1996] 1 I.R. 226 to the effect that agreements to marry
and cohabitation agreements were not enforceable. However, Abbot J. held
that *Ennis v Butterly* might be distinguishable, partly on the basis that Art.41.2
(the role of women in the home) might not be limited to married women.
Moreover, there was a difference between seeking to enforce a cohabitation
agreement and regularising the property arrangements made while the applicant
was caring for the three non-marital children she had with the respondent. In
those circumstances, Abbot J. held that the high threshold for striking out an
action had not been passed.

In *McD v L* [2007] I.E.S.C. 28, the Supreme Court considered whether to
grant an interlocutory injunction restraining two women from removing their
child from the jurisdiction. The two women underwent a civil union ceremony
in England. One of the women had a child by IVF, the sperm being provided
by McD, a friend of the two women. An agreement was reached between
the parties governing the access of the biological father to the child. It was
envisaged that he would have regular access to the child at mutually convenient
times. After some time, however, the two women felt that there was too much
contact. There were then far fewer visits. Mr McD learned that the women
were considering bringing the child on holidays to Australia with a possible
view to relocating to Australia. He instituted legal proceedings to restrain this
course of action. The High Court ordered that the two women be allowed to
bring the child to Australia on holidays, but that—on return to Ireland—the
child's passport had to be surrendered to the court and the leave of the court

obtained for any subsequent departure from the country. The women appealed this ruling to the Supreme Court.

A majority of the Supreme Court held in favour of the biological father on the issue of the interlocutory injunction. Denham J. noted that it was agreed that there was a fair question to be tried. The only issue was where the balance of convenience lay:

> "In considering the balance of convenience in this case, the factors in favour of the respondents include the following:- the welfare of the infant is best served in the custody of the first named respondent, the mother; the mother has a constitutional right to the custody of her child; the first named respondent is Australian and wishes her child to know her family; the parties have entered into a written agreement; the first named respondent is the primary carer for the child; the respondents propose a temporary relocation to Australia, until June, 2008; this is a reasonable and proportionate plan; the second named respondent is the breadwinner and she has taken leave of absence from her job for a year and a temporary job in Australia until June, 2008; the respondents have let their house in Ireland for the year.
>
> On the other hand the factors in favour of the applicant include that he is the biological father; he entered into a agreement with the respondents as to the infant (which will be an issue in the substantive case); he has a right to apply to court for access and joint custody; the applicant has applied to the High Court and this application has to be determined; even if, as appears to be accepted, the relocation to Australia is only for a year, this is at a formative age of the infant.

21. <u>Welfare of the infant</u>

The critical factor in the balancing required of the Court in this case is the welfare of the infant—on which the Court has had no expert assistance. The Court heard submissions by the parties as to their view of the balance of convenience, but that must be considered as being tinted by their interests.

> The welfare of the infant is of paramount importance. In the vacuum of information as to the welfare of the child the Court must use the fulcrum of justice in seeking the balance of convenience. In the circumstances I am satisfied that the welfare of the child must be a weighty factor. In making this decision I do so with the infant in mind. Consequently, I would affirm the judgment of the High Court."

Fennelly J. dissented. In his view, following *O'R v EH* [1996] 2 I.R. 248, Mr McD only had the right to apply to be appointed a guardian. Given his tenuous connection with the child, this was not the sort of right that would justify the court in intervening to preclude the women from travelling to Australia with the child.

This matter came on for substantive hearing before the High Court. In April 2008, Hedigan J. held in favour of the two women against the biological father. This case will be addressed in next year's *Annual Review*.

In another case decided in 2007, some doubt was cast on whether the Supreme Court's approach to the custody rights of unmarried fathers in *O'R v EH* [1996] 2 I.R. 248 was correct. In *T v O* [2007] I.E.H.C. 326, McKechnie J. was required to assess the custody rights of an unmarried father for the purposes of the Hague Convention on the Civil Aspects of International Child Abduction and Council Regulation 2201/2003 (EC). In relation to the Hague Convention, McKechnie J. was content to hold that there were custody rights vested in the District Court which prohibited the removal of the child from the country. However, in relation to Council Regulation 2201/2003 (EC), McKechnie J. considered it necessary to reconsider the rights of unmarried fathers to the custody of their children.

In considering the constitutional position McKechnie J., although indicating that he was bound by the Supreme Court judgments in *K v W* and *O'R v H*, cast considerable doubt on whether that reasoning was correct:

> "**50.** For my part I am of course bound by the majority judgments of the Supreme Court in both of the above cases. Without in any way questioning that principle, I would like however to make some very brief observations, of my own, on the issue. The vast majority of people might readily agree, that parenthood, by itself and no more, may give very little rights, if any, to an unmarried father. Examples of circumstances at this end of the spectrum are numerous and very definitely include, casual encounters, rape, incest, etc. But what about a person who fathers a child within an established relationship, and who from the moment of birth, nurtures, protects and safeguards his child; sometimes to a standard which all too frequently married fathers fail to live up to. As Murphy J. said in *O.R.* [1996] 2 I.R. 248 at 286:
>
>> 'For better or for worse, it is clearly the fact that long-term relationships having many of the characteristics of a family based on marriage have become commonplace. Relationships which would have been the cause of grave embarrassment a generation ago are now widely accepted.'
>
> Indeed could I say that even in the past decade, such relationships have multiplied and continued to so do. In any event, where the above described circumstances exist, could anyone possibly object to what Finlay C.J. said in *S.W.* where he described such a situation as '... bearing nearly all of the characteristics of a constitutionally protected family, when the rights would be very extensive indeed'? If as I respectfully suggest, that our society, which is governed by a Constitution which

declares the principles of prudence, justice, charity and human dignity, might in its maturity so agree, should there not be a greater recognition of the type of father whom I mention? At a minimum should there not be a means readily available so that such a father, whose children had been removed without forewarning or knowledge, can assert and vindicate his rights? I strongly believe that there should be.

51. Even however within the existing structure, is it altogether accurate to say that a caring and devoted father has only, in respect of his child, a right to apply? Putting it in that way, gives the impression that the court seised, is the creator of whatever rights the father might ultimately obtain on an application under the Act of 1964. That, in my view, is not correct. Any rights which a father may have are founded upon, and evolve and develop by reason of, his relationship with his child, and if it exists, with the child's mother. Such rights are alive and present before any court hearing and do not merely spring into existence on the application date. In my view, what the court does is to declare such rights rather than even confirming them, much less creating them. It declares them essentially, or in substantial part, on evidence which is largely historical with of course a prospective and future element to govern an orderly and beneficial relationship into the future. Admittedly it is the declaration which presently renders such rights lawfully enforceable, but as a matter of fact their existence has been created prior to any court hearing. I therefore feel that a father fulfilling a parenting role of the type which I have described, should be recognised as having rights referable to his child, even if such rights are contingent on a declaratory order. Whether such rights may also be described, as 'inchoate rights' is a matter of choice and is largely inconsequential unless put in context.

Could I add that the institution of marriage may have little, if anything, to fear from this approach. In fact one might strongly argue that Society, as a 'general rule' should encourage non marital fathers to act responsibly towards their children and of course towards their children's mother. To acknowledge only a 'right to apply' could hardly be seen as dynamic in this regard."

Despite indicating an unwillingness to question the Supreme Court's approach in the earlier cases, McKechnie J. does question that approach in two ways. First, he seems to propound a policy argument for the granting of substantive— as distinct from merely procedural—rights to unmarried fathers. In this vein, he effectively invites society to agree to grant a greater recognition to the rights of unmarried fathers, given the references in the Constitution to the dignity of the individual and justice, prudence and charity.

In the latter portion of the extract, he seems to go further even than this. For he questions whether the "right to apply" is really just a procedural right. On what basis, he implicitly asks, do judges when faced with such an application decide to grant rights to a natural father? Addressing this question, McKechnie J. adopts the form of natural law reasoning favoured by the courts 30 years previously for the purposes of recognising the rights of unmarried mothers. In *G v An Bord Uchtála* [1980] I.R. 32 at 55, O'Higgins C.J. had reasoned:

> "[T]he plaintiff is a mother and, as such, she has rights which derive from the fact of motherhood and from nature itself. These rights are among her personal rights as a human being and they are rights which, under Article 40, s.3, sub-s.1, the State is bound to respect, defend and vindicate. As a mother, she has the right to protect and care for, and to have the custody of, her infant child. The existence of this right was recognised in the judgment of this Court in *The State (Nicolaou) v. An Bord Uchtála.* [1966] I.R. 567. This right is clearly based on the natural relationship which exists between a mother and child. In my view, it arises from the infant's total dependency and helplessness and from the mother's natural determination to protect and sustain her child. How far and to what extent it survives as the child grows up is not a matter of concern in the present case. Suffice to say that this plaintiff, as a mother, had a natural right to the custody of her child who was an infant, and that this natural right of hers is recognised and protected by Article 40, s.3, sub-s.1, of the Constitution. Section 6, sub-s.4, and s.10, sub-s.2(*a*), of the Guardianship of Infants Act, 1964, constitute a compliance by the State with its obligation, in relation to the mother of an illegitimate child, to defend and vindicate in its laws this right to custody. These statutory provisions make the mother guardian of her illegitimate child and give the mother statutory rights to sue for custody."

Similarly, in the *T case*, McKechnie J. refers to the rights of the unmarried father that are founded upon and evolve on the basis of his relationship with the child. He views the court order as declaratory of the rights that already exist, accepting that it is the court order that renders the rights enforceable. However, a sentence later he phrases this in a different way that has profoundly different implications. Here he states that the rights are contingent on a declaratory order. If this means that the rights themselves (and not merely their enforceability) are contingent on the court order, then this is a much narrower proposition. Nevertheless, McKechnie J. seems to be advancing the proposition that unmarried fathers—even under the existing constitutional dispensation—have real, substantive rights. Although the law provides a procedural remedy (the right to apply), the courts in considering applications are bound (by the natural law?) to declare the rights of the unmarried father that already exist. If this is the case, the Supreme Court decision in *K v W* was probably wrong.

This raises several important issues. First, and most obviously, it does not appear consistent with the decisions of the majority of the Supreme Court in

S v K and *O'R v H*. Secondly, if the reasoning of McKechnie J. were to be adopted by the Supreme Court, it would mark the return of the natural law method of enumerating rights under Art.40.3.1°. Rights are deemed to exist prior to judicial declaration; judges decide which rights to declare based on an observation of natural relationships. This is generally considered to be a dubious form of natural reasoning (the derivation of an "ought" from an "is"). Finally, even if a better natural law argument could be found to support the identification of these rights, there are still legitimate concerns about natural law rights being turned into positive law rights by judicial declaration. From one perspective, these concerns apply with even more force now than they did with reference to the superior courts' enumeration of rights in the 1970s and 1980s. For in that situation, the potential for inconsistency was reduced by the fact that a right was declared to inhere in all mothers. In contrast, McKechnie J. appears to envisage the enumeration of rights by the District Court on an ad hoc case-by-case basis. As against this criticism, however, the right in question (an unmarried father's right to some level of respect for family life) is clearly analogous to constitutional rights that have already been enumerated (those of unmarried mothers). Accordingly, even on the more limited basis for the recognition of rights suggested by Keane J. in *O'T v B* [1998] 2 I.R. 321, there might be a basis for saying that unmarried fathers' rights should be recognised under Art.40.3.1°. The difficulty with this argument is that the courts have always been aware of the asserted similarities between unmarried mothers and unmarried fathers and yet did not extend the rights of the former in any way to include the latter.

On appeal, the Supreme Court resolved the issues solely on the basis of the Convention without exploring the question of unmarried fathers' rights to the custody of their children.

In *Foy v An tArd Chláraitheoir* [2007] I.E.H.C. 470, McKechnie J. considered the claim of the applicant that the State had acted unconstitutionally in failing to put in place a system whereby the post-operative transgender persons can have their acquired identity recognised. McKechnie J. had already considered the same claim advanced by the applicant in her earlier proceedings in 2002. He considered that there had been no change in the factual or legal position in the interim that would warrant him changing his view on the constitutional issue. However, having previously held against Ms Foy on the European Convention on Human Rights ground, on this occasion he followed *Goodwin v United Kingdom* (2002) 35 E.H.R.R. 447 and granted a declaration of incompatibility in respect of certain provisions of the Civil Registration Act 2004. The judgment in *Goodwin* had been delivered the day after his original High Court decision.

In *L v Judge Haughton* [2007] I.E.H.C. 316, Budd J. considered an application by Mr L to quash certain orders made in relation to his children by District judges under the Guardianship of Children Acts 1964–1997. Budd J. recognised the principle of spousal equality established in *Re Tilson* [1951]

I.R. 1. However, he commented that, where the parents disagreed, a decision had to be made as to the best interests of the child. A view jointly taken by the parents some years previously that a particular form of education might be best would not necessarily hold sway when the child had developed interests of her own. Beyond this brief discussion of the *Tilson* principle, the case was decided on statutory grounds.

As noted in last year's *Annual Review*, in *Bode v Minister for Justice* [2006] I.E.H.C. 341, Finlay Geoghegan J. considered the operation of the IBC/05 Scheme by the Minister for Justice. Following the *Lobe* decision, the citizenship referendum in 2004 and alterations to the patterns of births to non-Irish parents within Ireland, the Minister for Justice had decided that:

> "[R]ather than engaging in a case by case analysis, as a gesture of generosity and solidarity to the persons concerned, a general policy would be adopted of granting those persons (the non-Irish parents of Irish born children) permission to remain in the State provided that they fulfilled certain criteria. For this reason, the Minister established IBC/05."

In *Bode*, Finlay Geoghegan J struck down a number of decisions under the IBC/05 scheme on the basis that no consideration had been given by the Minister to the constitutional rights of the child.

The Supreme Court unanimously allowed the State's appeal [2007] I.E.S.C. 62, taking a very different view of the IBC/05 scheme. Denham J., with whom the other members of the court agreed, characterised the scheme in the following terms:

> "The scheme was introduced by the Minister, exercising the executive power of the State, to address in an administrative and generous manner a unique situation which had occurred in relation to a significant number of foreign nationals within the State. However, those who did not succeed on their application under this scheme remained in the same situation as they had been in prior to their application. They were still entitled to have the Minister consider the Constitutional and Convention rights of all relevant persons.
>
> The scheme enabled a fast, executive decision, giving a benefit to very many people. However, a negative decision in the IBC 05 Scheme did not affect any substantive claim for permission to remain in the State. In other words, an adverse decision to an applicant under the IBC 05 Scheme left the applicant in no worse position than he or she was prior to the application as no decision had been made on any substantive rights."

For this reason, there was no obligation on the Minister to consider the rights of the child when making a decision under the IBC/05 scheme. In other words, as a negative decision under the scheme would not put the child in any worse position than she would have been in had the scheme not existed—and as the scheme was an act of Executive generosity—there was no need to consider the rights of the child at that stage. The rights of the child could be considered at the other statutory stages in the decision-making process, for instance when a deportation order was being made. This left open the possibility that the Minister is under an obligation to consider the Irish child's right to have her welfare taken into account when deportation decisions are made about her non-Irish parents.

In the subsequent case of *Dimbo v Minister for Justice* [2008] I.E.S.C. 26, the Supreme Court quashed a deportation decision on the basis that the Minister had not given adequate consideration to the rights of the child. This case will be discussed in next year's *Annual Review*.

S v Minister for Justice [2007] I.E.H.C. 398 provides some guidance as to what is required by the obligation to consider a person's constitutional rights in an administrative process, Dunne J. commenting:

> "[I]t is not necessary for the Minister to spell out specifically that he has considered the impact of the making of an order in circumstances where on the stated facts it must be abundantly clear that there would be an impact. The parents of the first named applicant reside in this jurisdiction. He has two siblings who were born in this jurisdiction. To paraphrase slightly the words of Ryan J. in the decision of *P.F. v. Minister for Justice,* it seems to me to be an untenable proposition that the family circumstances of the first named applicant and the impact of the deportation on the first named applicant and indeed the second and third named applicants and on his parents were not present to the mind of the respondent in making the decision to deport the first named applicant. The respondent had all the information in relation to the circumstances of the first named applicant. He knew the nature and extent of the family unit. It does not seem to me to be necessary to specifically recite that the Minister considered the impact of the deportation on either the first named applicant or the second and third named applicants or indeed his parents or to state expressly that he considered Article 8 [of the European Convention on Human Rights]."

Dunne J. analysed the rest of the applicants' claim by reference to the European Convention on Human Rights, not the Constitution.

Several other cases addressed the issue of family rights in the immigration context in 2007. These cases did not develop the constitutional principles applicable to this area of law and accordingly will not be considered in this chapter. They are addressed in the Asylum and Immigration Law chapter.

THE IRISH LANGUAGE

In *Ó Gribín v An Comhairle Mhúinteoireachta* [2007] I.E.H.C. 454, the applicant had wished to apply for a vacancy as an education/communication officer with an Comhairle Mhúinteoireachta, the Teaching Council. However, neither the application documents nor the Teaching Council Act 2001 had been translated into Irish. The applicant instituted judicial review proceedings seeking translations of the relevant documents. Murphy J held that Art.8 did not directly grant rights to citizens in relation to the Irish language; however, Art.8 did impose certain duties on the State. Murphy J. held that the applicant did have standing to seek the relief sought, even though he had ultimately not applied for the job; he had a right to conduct his official business with the State in Irish without any obstacle that would not apply to a person conducting her official business in English. This right had been thwarted by the absence of an Irish translation.

The court held that, under s.9 of the Official Languages Act 2003, the applicant had a right to the official documentation in Irish. Furthermore, following *Ó Beoláin v Fahy* [2001] 2 I.R. 79, the applicant had a right to an official translation of the 2001 Act. A delay of four years was not reasonable.

LEGISLATIVE POWER

Section 8 of the Animal Remedies Act 1992 grants to the Minister for Agriculture certain powers to make delegated legislation. Section 8(2)(b)(x) provides that regulations may be made for the purpose of giving effect (or further effect) to acts of the institutions of the European Communities which, broadly speaking, relate to veterinary products. Section 8(3)(b)—by way of reference to s.4 of the European Communities Act 1972, as amended—confers statutory effect on such regulations. In *Quinn v Ireland* [2007] I.E.S.C. 16 an issue arose as to whether these regulations with statutory effect could be amended by way of regulation or could only be amended by a statute of the Oireachtas. Denham J., with whom the other members of the court agreed, held that the power to amend primary legislation by way of secondary legislation contained in s.3 of the European Communities Act 1972 could not be inferred into other statutory provisions:

> "To provide that a law may be amended by statutory instrument as in the European Communities Act, 1972, is an exceptional power given by the Oireachtas, pursuant to the Constitution, to a Minister. It was necessitated by the obligations of membership of the European Communities, which itself gave rise to a high volume of technical regulations based on Community law. Such power would, in general, be

an impermissible delegation of legislative powers, without the specific legislative and constitutional foundation.

I am satisfied that it would be a step too far to infer such a power in an Act which did not expressly provide for such a power. Further, I am satisfied that to make such an inference would be to legislate—a matter for the Oireachtas, not a court of law.

Indeed, it would be an unconstitutional construction of the Act of 1993. There being a constitutional construction to the provisions open, then that is the correct construction. In essence, the power created in s.3(2) of the European Communities Act, 1972 is not in the Animal Remedies Act, 1993, and that is fatal to the argument of the respondents. At its height the drafting is ambiguous.

Consequently, the Animal Remedies Act, 1993 not containing any such constitutionally valid express power to the Minister to amend a regulation having statutory effect, I am satisfied that the Minister does not have such power. Therefore, the Minister does not have the power to make regulations to amend previous regulations which he has made under the Animal Remedies Act, 1993 as the original regulations made by the Minister have 'statutory effect'. The fact that new regulations would have the same status as the previous regulations does not meet the problem that statutes may not be amended by statutory instruments unless expressly and constitutionally so provided, as in the European Communities Act, 1972. Such power is a delegation of legislative power only constitutionally sound because it is necessitated by the obligations of the European Community. The issues raised by the absence of the express power to the Minister are fundamental in a parliamentary democracy. A democratic deficit is an issue to be determined by the Oireachtas. It is only when that body expressly and constitutionally delegates its great power that the power may be exercised by a Minister."

LIBERTY

Were there only one case challenging detention under the Mental Health Act 2001 and the newly introduced scheme of Mental Health Tribunals it might not be a cause for comment. However, there have been several judgments in 2007 and the manner in which the fundamental right to liberty of applicants is treated is a cause of concern. This is best illustrated by the decision of the Supreme Court in *MD v Clinical Director of St Brendan's Hospital* [2007] I.E.S.C. 37. Hardiman J. (Fennelly and Macken JJ. affirming) upheld the High Court's order that the applicant was being detained in accordance with law and in his own interest. Nevertheless, anxiety was expressed about certain aspects of the procedures adopted in this case. The first was the omission of the consultant psychiatrist making the order under s.15 (the renewal order) to inform the patient of the statutory provision under which he was being detained. Hardiman J. stated:

> "The patient had an absolute right to be so informed. If the doctor herself was uncertain as to the power she is considering exercising, that is a matter which would cast doubt on the question of whether she should proceed to make an order at all.
>
> ...
>
> [T]here was an obligation on the doctor to give notice of the making of her order to the patient and to the Mental Health Commission within 24 hours of its making: an amendment made 19 days after the original order was purportedly made can hardly be regarded as meeting such a requirement."

It was stressed in the judgment that the requirement to give notice to the patient is a statutory requirement contained in s.16 of the Act. Thus, the obligation to notify the patient of the statutory basis of his detention is mandatory and not a matter for the discretion of the doctor. Moreover, the information must relate to the detention of the patient at the time he is served with the notice and not at any earlier or later time.

Hardiman J. also expressed concern that the legal representative appointed to consider and attend to the interests of the patient had not been informed of the making of the renewal order. He continued:

> "I am equally concerned that, the doctor having omitted to comply with s.16(2)(a), the tribunal nevertheless certified that s.16 had been complied with. It manifestly had not. The tribunal then went on to certify that, 'if there has been a failure to comply with any such provision, the failure does not affect the substance of the order and does not cause an injustice.'
>
> In my view it was illogical to reach both of these findings. If the first finding was correct, the second was *otiose*. If the proviso contained in s.18(1)(a)(ii) (that there has been a failure it did not affect the substance of the order or cause an injustice) requires to be invoked, as it did, then that situation will arise only if there has in fact been a failure to comply with some section of the Act. Moreover I cannot see how it can be certified, as it was, that if there has been a failure to comply with any such provision then the failure did not affect the substance of the order and did not cause an injustice, unless the precise failure in question is identified and its effect ascertained."

In summary, the applicant had not only been denied an "absolute" right to be informed, his legal representative had not been properly informed and the mental health tribunal certified that s.16(2)(a) had been complied with when it manifestly had not. Nevertheless, the applicant's continued detention has been deemed lawful. How is it that a procedure which manifestly failed to fulfil mandatory statutory requirements can be construed as lawful? Notwithstanding the need to provide appropriate healthcare in a safe environment for those who are mentally ill and additionally notwithstanding public safety, where is the constitutional protection if Art.40.4 can be set at nought? For anyone who has the misfortune to come within the mental health system their legal representatives need to be aware that thereby may lie a danger that the courts will engage in the denial of basic constitutional rights.

MONEY LAUNDERING DIRECTIONS

In *Burns v Bank of Ireland* [2007] I.E.H.C. 318, Mr Burns challenged the constitutionality of s.31(8) of the Criminal Justice Act 1994, as substituted by s.21 of the Criminal Justice (Theft and Fraud Offences) Act 2001. Section 31(8) allows members of the Garda Síochána to issue directions to banks in relation to money which is suspected to be the proceeds of criminal conduct. A garda had issued a direction in relation to monies owned by Mr Burns that had been lodged to an Irish bank account. Mr Burns argued that the lack of any time limit to the directions issued pursuant to s.31(8) rendered the section unconstitutional. Gilligan J. rejected this argument, noting that the absence of a time limit in the section did not, of itself, render the section unconstitutional. However, he held that the garda had acted ultra vires the section in not issuing a subsequent direction to the bank, effectively allowing the bank to release the money to Mr Burns, once it became clear to the garda that no prosecution was going to be instituted against Mr Burns. In coming to this conclusion, Gilligan J. seems to have implicitly held that the absence of a specific time limit in s.31(8) was permissible only because it could not be predicted for how long a direction would have to stay in force. However, he effectively used the double construction rule to hold that s.31(8) must be interpreted in such a way as to require a garda to issue a further direction once the initial reason for restraining the bank from dealing with the money had expired.

PARENTAL RIGHTS

O'Neill J. remarked that "it was 'curious' that there was 'so little mention' in the project material [relating to the Ombudsman for Children's Big Ballot] of the family and the constitutional and legal protections afforded to the family" when refusing leave for judicial review to the applicant parent on the ground that the Big Ballot breached the constitutional rights of the family and parents

(*The Irish Times*, November 10, 2007). See also Information Law and the Ombudsman Chapter, SECTORAL OMBUDSMEN, in this *Annual Review*.

PROPERTY RIGHTS

In *Representatives of Chadwick and Goff v Fingal County Council* [2007] I.E.S.C. 49, some of the claimants' land had been compulsorily acquired for the purposes of building a motorway. The claimants had sought compensation not simply for the injury caused by the use of the motorway on the lands taken from them, but also for injury caused by the use of the motorway on other lands not taken from them. This would amount to a re-interpretation of s.63 of the Land Clauses Consolidation Act 1845 and the claimants asserted their constitutionally protected property rights to support this re-interpretation. The Supreme Court unanimously rejected this argument, Fennelly J reasoning:

> "It is common case that the appellants are entitled under the section to be compensated for the value of the property taken, for the effects (if any) of severance and for injurious affection of their retained lands by anticipated use by the Council of the lands acquired from them. It is also common case that, if no land had been taken, there would have been no right to compensation for the damage, inconvenience or loss of amenity caused by the future operation of the motorway. No neighbour of the appellants has any such right, unless land is taken and used for that purpose. The appellants' claim is premised on the proposition that the acquisition has affected or will adversely affect some property right, which is entitled to constitutional protection. What is at stake is the non-tortious effect of activities on land not taken. The injurious affection here in contemplation is the alleged damaging effects to the retained lands of acts which would not give rise to any cause of action at law, particularly the law of nuisance, and does not entail any injury to any existing property right. I find it impossible to discern any unfairness or injustice in this scheme of compensation which could give rise to any issue as to whether, to use the language of Article 40.3.2° of the Constitution, there was an '*unjust attack*' on property rights. It follows, as a corollary, that the claimants' right to sue the Council or any other user either of the land taken or any other lands is undisturbed" ([2007] I.E.S.C. 49 at [36]).

In *Clinton v An Bord Pleanála* [2007] I.E.S.C. 19, the Supreme Court rejected a challenge by Mr Clinton to a compulsory purchase order (CPO) made against his property on O'Connell Street. Mr Clinton contended that CPOs could only be approved by an Bord Pleanála (the Board) under s.213 of the Planning and Development Act 2000 if they were for a particular purpose.

The Board had concluded that the CPO in this case was necessary for the purposes of implementing the Dublin City development plan. Mr Clinton contended that this was not specific enough to be a "particular purpose" for the Act. Geoghegan J., with whom the other members of the Supreme Court agreed, declined to decide whether a CPO could be justified on the sole basis that it served a basic statutory purpose. However, the CPO in this case could be justified by the fact that it was considered necessary for urban regeneration, a more specific purpose recognised by the Oireachtas in s.212(1)(e) of the Planning and Development Act 2000. It was not necessary for the Council to specify the precise development which would take place on Mr Clinton's site in order to achieve the purpose of urban regeneration:

> "[Finnegan P in the High Court] has given a very wide meaning to the expression *'particular purpose'* for the reason which he gives. Having regard to the obligation, as pointed out by the appellant, to construe compulsory acquisition powers in a manner that does not impinge unnecessarily on the constitutional property rights of the owner, I am not altogether convinced that this approach to the statutory provisions by the learned trial judge is correct. But I do not think it necessary to give any final determination in respect of it in this case because, as I have already been indicating, I am satisfied that there is a much narrower reason why the trial judge was correct. The regeneration purpose, which the council had in mind when deciding to make the Compulsory Purchase Order, was expressly permitted by the Oireachtas. It cannot have been envisaged that the council would have to have a specific plan as to how the regeneration was to be carried out and would have to specify that in the CPO because, as in this case, the whole process would usually involve private developers in some form at least and plans as yet unknown which they would propose and envisage and which would eventually require planning permission. That is quite different from property required for the purposes of council offices or a public swimming pool for instance.
>
> It was at all times perfectly clear that the property was being acquired for regeneration of O'Connell Street. In my view, it was only necessary for the council to demonstrate that a CPO was desirable in the public interest to achieve that purpose. It was not necessary to prove how exactly it would be carried out. Quite apart from the necessity to obtain planning permissions into the future, such a requirement would defeat the purpose of the power conferred by the section."

The court deferred consideration of Mr Clinton's challenge to the constitutionality of ss.212 and 213 of the Act. However, Geoghegan J. did suggest that some form of anxious scrutiny is required where approvals of CPOs are being considered by the courts:

"It is axiomatic that the making and confirming of a compulsory purchase order (CPO) to acquire a person's land entails an invasion of his constitutionally protected property rights. The power conferred on an administrative body such as a local authority or An Bord Pleanála to compulsorily acquire land must be exercised in accordance with the requirements of the Constitution, including respecting the property rights of the affected landowner (*East Donegal Co-Operative v The Attorney General* [1970] IR 317). Any decisions of such bodies are subject to judicial review. It would insufficiently protect constitutional rights if the court, hearing the judicial review application, merely had to be satisfied that the decision was not irrational or was not contrary to fundamental reason and common sense."

Geoghegan J. did not suggest what standard other than irrationality might apply to the decision of An Bord Pleanála to approve a CPO. Moreover, it is unclear whether irrationality is considered inappropriate in any circumstance in which constitutional rights are engaged or only in those circumstances where constitutional rights are axiomatically engaged. For example, the courts have adopted different positions as to whether a grant of planning permission increases property rights (the implication of *Re Article 26 and Part V of the Planning and Development Bill 1999* [2000] 2 I.R. 321) or is a manifestation of an overall system which restricts property rights (the implication of *State (FPH Properties SA) v An Bord Pleanála* [1987] I.R. 698). If a refusal of planning permission is seen as engaging property rights in a manner similar to a CPO, it would seem to follow that irrationality is an inappropriate standard of review for all decisions on planning applications that are adverse to the developer. It is unclear if this is the implication of Geoghegan J.'s judgment. All that can be said with confidence is that the courts will soon have to grapple definitively with the issues of anxious scrutiny.

RIGHT TO PRIVACY

In *Domican v AXA Insurance Ltd* [2007] I.E.H.C. 14, Mr Domican sought to restrain AXA from copying him with all correspondence being sent to his solicitor. Mr Domican was suing a Mr Patrick Doyle in relation to a road traffic accident and had issued a written instruction that AXA, Mr Doyle's insurer, should correspond only with his solicitor. One of the grounds on which Mr Domican relied was his constitutional right to privacy. Clarke J rejected this contention:

"[A]lthough not pressed as the strongest point, it was suggested that the receipt of communications from AXA which Mr. Domican, to the knowledge of AXA did not wish to receive, amounted to a breach of

Mr. Domican's constitutional right to privacy. That such a right exists has been clear since *Magee v. Attorney General* [1974] I.R. 284 and *Kennedy v. Ireland* [1987] I.R. 587. As I observed in *Cogley v. RTE* [2005] 4 I.R. 79:

> 'It is ... clear from *Kennedy v. Ireland* that a right to privacy is one of the personal rights of the citizen guaranteed by, though not specifically mentioned in, the constitution.
>
> However it is also clear from Kennedy that the right to privacy is not an unqualified right but is subject to the constitutional rights of others and to the requirements of public order, public morality and the common good.'

5.3 As against those undoubted rights must also be considered AXA's undoubted constitutional right to communicate. Such a right has also been identified in such cases as *Attorney General v. Paperlink* [1984] ILRM 373 and *Murphy v. Independent Radio and Television Commission* [1999] 1 I.R. 12. Equally such a right is not absolute and is subject to qualification.

5.4 It must also be noted that the background to the relationship between the parties to these proceedings is that they are, inevitably, involved with each other. The plaintiff has a claim which, in commercial substance though not in form, is as against AXA. They are not, therefore, total strangers, and it is necessary that there be some communication between them with appropriate respect for both parties' rights. I am not satisfied that it has been established that Mr. Domican's right to privacy extends to the narrow question of the manner in which communication with him is to be conducted. Indeed most of the decided cases involve obtaining and disclosing information rather than communicating information. Clearly if the manner of such communication were oppressive different considerations might apply. However it can hardly be said that the simple receipt of information by being copied directly with it in circumstances where the person concerned will, necessarily, have to receive the same information indirectly through his solicitors could in any event amount to a breach of the constitutional right to privacy."

Clarke J. proceeded to hold that a party's entitlement to have access to the courts and to have the benefit of legal assistance in so doing, carried with it an entitlement to restrain any action which would amount to a material or significant interference with such parties' relationship between them and their legal advisers in the context of litigation or potential litigation. However, he concluded that the actions of AXA in copying correspondence to Mr Domican could not be characterised as a significant interference in the solicitor–client relationship.

In *Gray v Minister for Justice, Equality and Law Reform* [2007] I.E.H.C.

52, the plaintiffs—all members of the same family—sought damages from the Minister for a breach of their right to privacy and a constitutional right to the peaceful enjoyment of their home. The family had moved to Ballybunion under a rural resettlement scheme and had lived there peacefully for a number of years. They alleged that a garda had wrongfully and unlawfully disclosed to a journalist that a convicted rapist was living with them. As a result, they were subjected to a campaign of harassment and intimidation so severe that they were compelled to leave their home and move back to Dublin. Quirke J. accepted the factual basis of the plaintiffs' claim and held that their right to privacy had been infringed:

> "It is also claimed that since the State, through the agency of members of the Gardaí, violated the plaintiffs' constitutionally protected right to privacy and to the peaceful enjoyment of their home, by unlawfully disclosing confidential and sensitive information to members of the media. This, it is contended, caused the plaintiffs to be subjected to abuse, harassment and intimidation of such a character that they were obliged to leave their home in Ballybunion permanently. [Quirke J quoted from *Kennedy v Ireland* and continued.]
>
> That case concerned deliberate, conscious and unjustifiable electronic eavesdropping by agents of the State upon private telephone lines used by the plaintiffs. The Court found that the plaintiffs' rights had been violated and awarded damages.
>
> The violation of the plaintiffs' rights in *Kennedy* was clear. It was caused by deliberate and reprehensible intrusions, by agents of the State, into the private lives and conversations of the plaintiffs without justification. The intrusions included electronic interference by servants of the State who listened to the plaintiffs' conversations, recorded them, transcribed them and made transcripts of the conversation available to other persons.
>
> The facts of the instant case are different. It is true that the peaceful enjoyment by the plaintiffs of their home was disturbed and their privacy was invaded. It is true that they suffered harassment and intimidation and distress and inconvenience as a result of the wrongful disclosure by members of the Gardaí of confidential information about a guest within their home.
>
> However, it is contended on behalf of the State that the plaintiffs' right to privacy in this case was necessarily restricted by the need to vindicate the constitutional rights of others and by the requirements of the common good...
>
> In the instant case it has been established by way of evidence and on the balance of probabilities a member or members of An Garda Síochána negligently disclosed confidential and sensitive information to an organ of the media arising out of a request from a journalist for

verification of information which was already in the possession of the journalist.

On the evidence it is unlikely that the information would have been published without the verification which was provided. In the light of the evidence of Superintendent Maher, I am satisfied also that the disclosure of the information to Conor Keane cannot be excused by reason of any public policy consideration such as the need to protect the constitutional rights of others or the interests of the common good.

It follows that I am satisfied that the unlawful and negligent disclosure by a member or members of An Garda Síochána of the relevant information to Mr. Keane comprised a violation of the constitutionally protected right enjoyed by each of the plaintiffs to privacy and the peaceful enjoyment of their home."

National Maternity Hospital v Information Commissioner [2007] I.E.H.C. 113, inter alia, concerned the balance between the right to privacy and the public interest. Quirke J. noted that the State has a general obligation to respect the right to privacy of its citizens. Thus, public bodies and other State agencies entrusted with private sensitive information affecting the rights and interests of individual members of the public are, in general, required to keep that information confidential. He continued:

"Circumstances may arise where the disclosure of sensitive information, which is held by a public body and which concerns and affects the interests of individual citizens, may be required in the public interest. The legislature, for instance, has expressly authorised the public disclosure by the Revenue Commissioners of certain private and potentially embarrassing financial information concerning members of the public because that disclosure has been deemed to be in the public interest.

It has, by the terms of the [Freedom of Information] Act, authorised the disclosure of certain private sensitive information entrusted to public bodies and other State agencies by members of the public subject to express exceptions identified within the Act. The State's duty of confidence to members of the public in respect of that private sensitive information has thus been qualified *inter alia* by the terms of the Act."

This case is analysed in the Information Law and the Ombudsman chapter in this *Annual Review.*

STANDING

In *Leonard v Dublin City Council* [2007] I.E.H.C. 404, Peart J. set aside an order granting leave to seek judicial review on the ground that s.62 of the Housing Act 1966, as amended, was unconstitutional. This section requires the District Court to issue a warrant for possession to a housing authority where certain formal proofs have been established. The court is precluded from inquiring into the factual basis for the Housing Authority's decision to issue a notice to quit. However, the constitutionality of that section had already been addressed in a number of cases that had not been drawn to the attention of the court when granting leave. Peart J. also implied that the applicant did not have standing to argue that the District Court breached fair procedures in failing to adjourn the matter to allow her to seek legal representation:

> "I am satisfied that the complaint by the applicant that fair procedures were breached by the District Court proceeding to make the order in circumstances where the applicant sought an adjournment so that she could be legally represented is one that does not surpass the threshold of arguability given the decisions to which I have referred. It has been clearly stated on a number of occasions that the District Judge is required by the legislation to make the order sought as soon as the Court is satisfied that the required proofs are in order. In the present case the applicant has not sought to dispute those necessary proofs. She has admitted the breach of her tenancy agreement which gave the Council the power to decide to serve Notice to Quit. She makes no challenge to that decision or to the service of the Notice to Quit itself. It is true that the summons served upon her commanded her to appear in order to show cause why such an order should not be made, but even now on the present application she has not sought to show that there was any ground she may have put forward if she had had the benefit of being legally represented. That would, in my view, be a pre-requisite to argue before this Court that her rights under the Constitution or the Convention to a fair hearing have been infringed. The right to be legally represented is not an absolute right, and the fact that on this occasion she had no solicitor or Counsel to represent her was not a bar to the District Court receiving proof of the matters required to be proved before this order for possession was made."

This passage may be read as importing into the constitutional principles on standing a strict requirement that a plaintiff be able to demonstrate what advantage she would have gained from a constitutional procedure being followed. It is questionable whether such a strict approach is consistent with the relatively relaxed attitude to standing adopted in cases such as *Norris v Attorney-General* [1984] I.R. 36 and *McKenna v An Taoiseach (No 2)* [1995]

2 I.R. 10. However, it is possible to read Peart J.'s comments in a less exacting fashion: given the limited role accorded to a District judge under s.62, it just could not be the case that a housing authority tenant would be prejudiced by the sort of procedure adopted. It is perhaps worth noting that in *Donegan v Dublin City Council*, High Court, May 8, 2008, Laffoy J. declared s.62 incompatible with Ireland's obligations under the European Convention on Human Rights.

In *Grace v Ireland* [2007] I.E.H.C. 90, the plaintiff challenged the constitutionality of s.85 of the Bankruptcy Act 1988. This section effectively provided that a person could be discharged from bankruptcy after 12 years provided all preferential debts had been paid. The plaintiff objected to this provision primarily on the basis that it breached his ECHR and constitutional right to a reasonably speedy resolution of legal proceedings. Laffoy J. rejected this argument as fundamentally misconceived, relying primarily on ECHR authorities. The non-discharge from bankruptcy did not mean lengthy legal proceedings. Laffoy J. also held that Mr Grace did not have standing to maintain his claim as he had not exhausted other remedies by seeking discharge from bankruptcy in other ways.

TRIBUNALS OF INQUIRY

Mandatory requirement of Oireachtas Denham J. in *Fitzwilton Ltd v Judge Alan Mahon* [2007] I.E.S.C. 27 found a want of jurisdiction by the Mahon Tribunal in its decision to proceed to public hearing of the £30,000 Fitzwilton module. In her judgment she commented that the concept behind the establishment of a tribunal is that there be an inquiry into definite matters as a matter of urgent public importance. The tribunal was established in 1997 and she considered that "[t]he fact that the Tribunal is still inquiring 10 years later is the antithesis of an urgent public inquiry." The Houses of the Oireachtas limited the scope of the tribunal by amending its terms of reference. Paragraph J(2) of these amended terms set a limit on subject-matters and also set a time limit:

> "These were mandatory requirements of the Houses. The Tribunal was required to consider, decide and record what additional matters should go forward to a public hearing, and this was to be done by 1st May, 2005."

The tribunal had failed to meet this time limit.

UNFAIR PROCEDURES

According to details given by Kelly J. in *Prendiville v The Medical Council* [2007] I.E.H.C. 427, fair procedures were not universally followed by the independent inquiry into peripartum hysterectomy at Our Lady of Lourdes Hospital, Drogheda. With regard to the inquiry, Kelly J. stated that Harding Clark J. (as she now is) did not afford either Professor Prendiville or Dr Murphy an opportunity to make submissions and observations on criticisms of them before the final report was produced, a procedure that was apparently followed for everyone else. He then quoted from Professor Prendiville's affidavit:

> "I am afraid that I cannot agree with Ms. Justice Harding Clark that the report was prepared out of compassion or collegiality. It was not. It was prepared on the basis of the information made available to me and I had no reason to doubt the veracity of the account given to me by Dr. Neary. Furthermore, I have no recollection of ever expressing regret for my role in preparing the report. These were not observations that I had an opportunity to make to Ms. Justice Harding Clark, as, unlike other persons criticised in her report, I was not provided with a copy of her draft report. Otherwise, I would certainly have made my position on the contents of para. 1.8 of her report known to Ms. Justice Harding Clark."

A full analysis of *Prendiville* is included under the CONSTITUTIONAL JUSTICE heading of this chapter.

Quirke J. dismissed claims of unfair procedures in *National Maternity Hospital v Information Commissioner* [2007] I.E.H.C. 113. This case is analysed in the Information Law and the Ombudsman chapter in this *Annual Review*.

Contract Law

FERGUS RYAN, Head, Department of Law, Dublin Institute of
Technology

ARBITRATION AGREEMENTS

Common Market Fertilizer SA and Anor. v The Owners of the 'MV Sonata',
High Court, Butler J., March 7, 2007, [2007] I.E.H.C. 109   The plaintiffs
owned a large cargo of compound fertiliser that had been damaged while
being transported on board the merchant ship 'MV Sonata'. The ship had
sailed from St Petersburg, Russia to Waterford. A bill of lading (the document
that the transporter gives to the owner of the goods acknowledging receipt of
the specified items and their intended destination) was issued on January 12,
2007. The plaintiffs claimed breach of the contract of carriage and breach of
duty owing to negligence, claiming damages and interest thereon.

On January 29, 2007 the High Court ordered that the MV Sonata be
"arrested". The International Convention Relating to the Arrest of Sea-Going
Ships 1952 (which was incorporated into Irish law under the Jurisdiction of
Courts (Maritime Conventions) Act 1989) permits the arrest and detention of a
ship in respect of a "maritime claim", as defined. A "maritime claim" includes
a claim relating to damage caused to goods or injury sustained by a person
while on board a ship.

In response, the defendant claimed that on foot of an arbitration clause in the
charterparty (the contract under which the vessel had been leased) the parties
were obliged to submit their dispute to arbitration. It sought an order under
s.5 of the Arbitration Act 1980 (or otherwise) staying the court proceedings
so that the matter could be considered at arbitration. The defendant sought a
further order freeing the ship from arrest or, in the alternative, releasing the
ship on payment of security.

The arbitration clause was contained in the charterparty. While the plaintiffs
were not parties to this charterparty, the bill of lading under which the goods
were transported had, the defendant claimed, referred to the arbitration clause in
that charterparty. The defendant thus asserted that the plaintiffs were bound by
the arbitration clause as it and the charterparty were incorporated by reference
to the latter in the bill of lading.

On the facts, the judge determined that the plaintiffs were not bound by
the arbitration clause. The fatal flaw related to the timing of the creation of the
respective documents. The charterparty was "generated", the judge noted, only
after the bill of lading "… and could not, therefore, form part of it". In other

words, the charterparty could not bind the plaintiffs, as *it had not yet come into existence* when the bill of lading was created. The plaintiffs had no opportunity to review the charterparty in advance of entering into the contract and thus could not be bound by its terms (cf. *Olley v Marlborough Court Hotel* [1949] 1 K.B. 532, where a disclaimer was only notified to the plaintiff after she had entered into a contract for accommodation: as such it could not bind her).

The judge thus refused relief under s.5, declining to refer the matter to arbitration, as the arbitration clause was not validly incorporated into the contract with the plaintiffs. This being the case, he also refused the "consequential" order releasing the ship from arrest.

In a further submission, the defendant claimed that the court had no jurisdiction to arrest the ship, as it sailed under the flag of the Commonwealth of Dominica, a Caribbean nation that was not a party to the 1952 Arrest Convention. The judge dismissed this contention, noting that Art.8(2) of the Convention "plainly conferred jurisdiction to arrest a ship flying the flag of a non-contracting State".

In relation to security, the judge noted that the amount of security was likely to be "hotly contested". He concluded that security should be set by reference to the plaintiffs' "reasonably arguable best case". While they might not receive all that they claimed, the plaintiffs had made a reasonably detailed case for $950,000 including interest. The judge thus deemed this to be an appropriate figure for security.

Uniform Construction Ltd v Cappawhite Contractors Ltd, High Court, Laffoy J., August 29, 2007, [2007] I.E.H.C. 295   This case concerned the role of the courts in supervising arbitration awards. It illustrates the reluctance of judges to interfere with an arbitrator's award unless the award would result in substantial injustice. It also illustrates the general principle that in matters of evidence and procedure, an arbitrator's decisions will generally be respected as the final determination of the relevant dispute.

In 2001 the plaintiff, Uniform Construction Ltd, had been contracted by Limerick County Council in connection with substantial road works. Uniform in turn subcontracted certain drainage work and work relating to water mains to the defendant, Cappawhite. The relevant sub-contract was governed by standard Institute of Engineers in Ireland (IEI) conditions of contract, which included a provision for the reference of any dispute between the parties to an arbitrator. The decision of the arbitrator was to be a "final decision".

In May 2001 Cappawhite commenced work on the site. Nonetheless, some 10 months later it terminated the sub-contract claiming that a variety of factors amounted to repudiatory breach by the plaintiff. In November 2002, the matter was referred to arbitration. In 2006, following detailed and lengthy submissions and hearings lasting 13 days in all, the arbitrator issued a decision which, in essence, determined that the defendant was entitled to terminate the sub-contract. Damages were assessed and awarded at €336,011.37.

The plaintiff challenged the arbitrator's decision, seeking:

- an order under s.36 of the Arbitration Act 1954 remitting the matter to the arbitrator for reconsideration; and

- an order under s.38 of the 1954 Act setting aside the award made.

Cappawhite raised a preliminary objection, alleging that, as neither party had requested that reasons be given for the award, the plaintiff could not challenge the reasons offered by the arbitrator. The IEI Arbitration Procedure stipulates that the arbitrator "shall not provide reasons for the award unless requested to do so by at least one of the parties". Even if so requested, the arbitrator retains a discretion as to whether such reasons should form part of the award or should be listed in a separate document not forming part of the award. In the latter case, these reasons are termed "restricted reasons", denoting that they are not part of the award and that the parties are not permitted to rely on them in relation to the award.

Although this was contested by the plaintiff, Laffoy J. concluded that there was no evidence that either party had requested reasons. Nonetheless, she concluded that even if the parties had not requested that reasons be given, she was:

> "… entitled to look at the reasons to determine whether, in accordance with the jurisprudence of the courts of this jurisdiction, Uniform has established that a ground exists for remitting or setting aside the Award".

In *Mutual Shipping v Bayshore Shipping ("The Montan")* [1985] 1 W.L.R. 625, Donaldson M.R. noted that any agreement to prevent such reasons being considered by a court would be void for public policy reasons as "it purports to oust the jurisdiction of the court". Thus, the courts could have regard to an arbitrator's reasons, even if they were considered to be confidential and expressed not to be part of the award. In doing so, however, the court was limited to considering whether a serious injustice had arisen. The court's jurisiction, Donaldson M.R. added, "… cannot be used merely to enable the arbitrator to correct errors of judgment, whether on fact or law, or to have second thoughts, even if they would be better thoughts". The courts would, he concluded, consider the reasons in any case where there was an allegation that they revealed an irregularity (not confined to fraud or misconduct) which gave rise to a "serious injustice".

Laffoy J. agreed that even where they are restricted and not deemed part of the award, the court may nonetheless consider the reasons given. It may do so, however, only with a view to determining whether there is an error of law so fundamental that it cannot be allowed to stand. While the Irish courts could set aside an award where there is an error of law on the face of the award, or refer the matter back to the arbitrator under s.36, this would only be done where, (per McCarthy J. in *Keenan v Shield Insurance Company Ltd* [1988] I.R. 89) there was an "obvious error" of law "so fundamental that the courts cannot stand aside and allow it to remain unchallenged". In *McStay v Assicurazione Generali SpA* [1991] I.L.R.M. 237 Finlay C.J. suggested that the decision must be "...clearly wrong on its face".

Laffoy J. then turned to the substantive issue, that is whether the defendant was entitled to terminate the sub-contract on grounds of repudiatory breach by the plaintiff. The crux of the defendant's various complaints was the manner in which the work was to be completed. In particular, the arbitrator had concluded that there had been significant difficulties and disagreements regarding the allocation and planning of the project (leading, for instance, to workers being employed where there was insufficient work for them to do). These difficulties placed the defendant at a distinct disadvantage in the performance of the contract. Citing *Hong Kong Fir Shipping Co Ltd v Kawasaki* [1962] 2 Q.B. 23, the arbitrator concluded that because of the difficulties experienced, the contract Cappawhite was performing was fundamantally different from the contract to which it had initially agreed. There was, in short, "a totally different performance of the contract from that intended by the parties". The breach was sufficiently fundamental to undermine the whole contract. Thus:

> "... there was a fundamental breach by Uniform arising from the manner in which the sub-contract and in particular the allocation of work was set up and carried out ..."

In this regard the arbitrator considered the failure to provide programme information as crucial, and that it had "sealed the rupture between the parties".

The plaintiff objected to this particular aspect of the arbitrator's decision. It argued that while the defendant had relied on the cumulative effect of the alleged failures, the arbitrator had based his award primarily on the failure to provide programme information. The plaintiff contended that the arbitrator, in focusing on the lack of programme information, had grounded his decision on an issue which the plaintiff had been given no opportunity to address. This amounted, it alleged, to gross procedural unfairness of such gravity as to require the court to set aside the decision or to remit the matter back to the arbitrator owing to misconduct of the proceedings.

In support, the plaintiff cited *Société Franco-Tunisienne D'Armement-Tunis v Government of Ceylon* [1959] 3 All E.R. 25. In that case, the Court of Appeal set aside an arbitration verdict as it had been based on an entirely new point not argued by the parties before the arbitrator (see also *Limerick County Council v Uniform Construction Limited* [2005] I.E.H.C. 347).

Laffoy J. highlighted the policy of the courts in relation to arbitral decisions, and in particular the courts' general reluctance to intervene therein. The courts should not, as McCarthy J. observed in *Keenan v Shield Insurance Company* [1988] I.R. 89, indulge in a "fine-combing exercise". Noting the "...desirability of making an arbitration award final in every sense of the term", McCarthy J. concluded that the courts should be especially reluctant to interfere in the arbitration process.

According to Fennelly J. in the Supreme Court in *McCarthy v Keane* [2004] 3 I.R. 617, for an arbitral award to be set aside for procedural misconduct "something substantial" was required, "...something which smacks of injustice or unfairness". Subject to the overriding requirements of fairness, the policy of the law, Fennelly J. remarked, is "to uphold the certainty of arbitral awards, once they have been made". It was not sufficient, he added, to show merely that there had been an error of judgment, whether on the facts or on the law.

Applying these principles, Laffoy J. concluded that the plaintiff was effectively asking the court to engage in a fine-combing exercise which she felt was inappropriate. Admittedly, Cappawhite had not suggested that any specific difficulty it had experienced was sufficient in isolation to amount to repudiation. It had relied instead on the cumulative effects of the conduct of the plaintiff to establish its case, and indeed had acknowledged that none of the specific allegations viewed in isolation justified the setting aside of the contract.

The cumulative issue in the instant case was whether the defendant was entitled to terminate the contract on the ground that the alleged breaches indicated an intention on the part of the plaintiff not to be bound by the contract. The plaintiff, the judge observed, had been given ample opportunity to refute this allegation. The arbitrator had concluded that the way in which the sub-contract was operated, in particular the allocation of work and the failure to provide programme information, constituted a fundamental breach permitting termination by the defendant. In so deciding, the arbitrator had implicitly rejected Uniform's contention that none of the alleged breaches, either on their own or collectively, amounted to a fundamental breach of the contract.

This finding of liability was, the judge concluded, not based on any new point. The plaintiff had been given a sufficient opportunity to address all of the relevant matters pertinent to the case. The plaintiff, in effect, was now seeking a "second bite of the cherry", an opportunity to make further submissions in the wake of the arbitrator's decision. Even if this would have resulted in the arbitrator having "second thoughts" or better thoughts, it was not appropriate for the court to intervene so as to permit this facility.

In sum, there was insufficient evidence of unfairness to justify either remitting the matter to the arbitrator under s.36 for reconsideration, or setting aside the award under s.38. The parties had been afforded ample opportunity "... to address all aspects of the arbitration", which they had done quite thoroughly and comprehensively. There was, Laffoy J. concluded, no error of law or misconduct so fundamental or substantial as to demand court intervention.

BREACH OF CONTRACT

See also *Uniform Construction Ltd v Cappawhite Contractors Ltd*, High Court, Laffoy J., August 29, 2007, [2007] I.E.H.C. 295 (discussed above under ARBITRATION AGREEMENTS) and *Kane v Massey Ferguson (Ireland) Ltd, Thomas Flynn and Sons Ltd and Agri Credit Ltd*, High Court, Irvine J., December 20, 2007, [2007] I.E.H.C. 457 (discussed below under SALE OF GOODS).

Rothwell v Arrowdale Limited t/a Sheehy Motors, High Court on Circuit, South-Eastern Circuit, County of Carlow, Peart J., November 29, 2007, [2007] I.E.H.C. 395   This case concerned certain statements made in respect of a car, representations which (though honestly made) turned out to be untrue. The case arose on appeal from a verdict of the Circuit Court in the plaintiff's favour.

In early 2003, the plaintiff purchased a car from the defendant. Prior to its purchase, the plaintiff had specifically stipulated that he wanted a vehicle that would give at least 50 miles to the gallon (mpg). Taking this specification into account, the defendant suggested the Volkswagen Passat, which the plaintiff then purchased for €32,500. While various subsequent tests failed to reveal any fault or defect, Mr. Rothwell nonetheless experienced consistently low mileage rates of between 34 and 38 mpg. As a result, in March 2006, he sold the car for €14,500, by which stage the car had clocked up 56,000 miles.

In a civil bill, the plaintiff sought an order rescinding the contract and claiming repayment of the cost of the car. He also sought damages for negligent misstatement and breach of contract. He claimed that had the car been in full working order, he would have been able to sell it for €22,000 but that he had significant difficulty in doing so. The defendant disputed this, claiming that the car would have been worth no more than €18,000.

Peart J. initially noted that the contract could not be rescinded as the plaintiff had already sold the car to a third party. He observed, moreover, that the plaintiff was not entitled to rescind as there had not been a complete failure of consideration. The plaintiff, after all, had received a functioning car, but one that, he claimed, consumed excessive amounts of petrol.

Peart J. nonetheless accepted without hesitation the plaintiff's evidence as to the high fuel consumption he had experienced, the evidence having been honest and convincing. The plaintiff had kept careful records and but for a short period after the repair of the turbo mechanism by the defendant, had failed to experience anything like the mileage which he was initially assured he would get. The judge further accepted that the various tests carried out by the defendants and others (which had suggested varying levels of performance, some good, some bad) were carried out accurately and could not be dismissed. There was no underlying fault rendering the vehicle likely to consume more fuel than the plaintiff had initially been assured. Nor was there any evidence that the manner in which the plaintiff drove had any untoward effect on fuel consumption.

While the ultimate cause remained a mystery, the judge accepted on balance that:

> "... the car did not perform according to the fuel consumption specified by both the manufacturers and the sales representative of the defendant when the plaintiff purchased the car ..."

Where a statement forms part of a contract, the inaccuracy of that statement amounts to a breach of contract, even where the plaintiff cannot establish fault on the part of the person making the statement. While the defendants were blameless, they had nonetheless sold the car on foot of a representation that was instrumental to the sale and of paramount importance to the plaintiff in making his decision. This statement formed part of the contract and, while not sufficient to justify rescission, there was thus a breach of contract as to a material term.

In calculating the damages to be awarded, Peart J. noted that the plaintiff had used the car from January 2003 to March 2006, whereupon he sold it for €14,500. He had traveled 56,000 miles during this period. As such, Peart J. could not simply award damages representing the cost of the car less the price he sold it for, or the price the defendants maintained he should have received. This was because there had not been, the judge observed, a complete failure of consideration. The plaintiff had enjoyed the use of the car, albeit in circumstances where it had underperformed. He thus had derived some benefit from the use of the car, albeit at a cost higher than he had anticipated. As such, it would have been unfair to award damages amounting to the full cost of the car less the proceeds of its sale.

Instead, the judge concluded that the appropriate quantum of damages should be the actual cost of fuel used less the amount that would have been incurred had the plaintiff experienced the level of fuel efficiency promised to him in 2003. In other words, the plaintiff should be compensated for the excess cost of the actual fuel consumption over that promised (i.e. what he had initially expected to pay), which came to €1,625.

On top of damages for the actual loss, the judge concluded that the aggravation, inconvenience and trouble caused to the plaintiff (in particular in consequence of the frequent testing required) justified a further award of general damages, which he estimated at €5,000. In so ruling, the judge affirmed the earlier order of the Circuit Court, though varying the amount of damages to €6,625.

COLLATERAL CONTRACTS

See *Flynn v Dermot Kelly Ltd and New Holland Finance (Ireland) Ltd*, **High Court, O' Neill J., March 16, 2007, [2007] I.E.H.C. 103 and** *Kane v Massey Ferguson (Ireland) Ltd, Thomas Flynn and Sons Ltd and Agri Credit Ltd,* **High Court, Irvine J., December 20, 2007, [2007] I.E.H.C. 457 (discussed below under SALE OF GOODS).**

CONSUMER PROTECTION ACT 1997
(NO. 19 OF 2007)

The enactment of the Consumer Protection Act 1997 marks a milestone in the advancement of consumer rights. While updating several existing consumer protection measures, and replacing others, the Act is primarily aimed at giving effect to the EU Unfair Commercial Practices Directive 2005/29/EC, s.2 of the Act expressly requiring that the Act be construed in the light of the Directive. It also establishes a new National Consumer Agency in place of the Office of the Director of Consumer Affairs. Notably the Act entirely repeals and supplants several important pieces of legislation, including the Merchandise Mark Acts 1887–1931, the Consumer Information Act 1978, the Pyramid Selling Act 1980, the Restrictive Practices (Amendment) Act 1987 and most of the Prices Act 1958 (as amended).

"Consumer" in this context has its usual meaning, that is, a natural person acting for purposes other than that of the person's trade, business or profession. The range of practices covered by the Act is extensive, as exhibited by the exceptionally wide definitions of "goods" and "services" respectively (collectively termed "products") in s.2. "Goods" are deemed to include both real and personal property of any description, gas, electricity and water, and computer software. The term also embraces tickets for events and for transportation, money-off vouchers and promotional coupons. "Services" comprise a wide range of facilities including services for banking, insurance, credit and financing, amusement, cultural activities, entertainment, instruction, recreation or refreshment, as well as accommodation. Also included within the definition are transport, travel, parking and storage, the care of persons, the care of animals or things, membership of a club or organisation, or any service provided as a result of such membership. Services do not, however, include services provided to an employer by an employee under a contract of employment.

Establishment and general functions of the National Consumer Agency Part 2 of the Act provides for the establishment of a new National

Consumer Agency, replacing the Director of Consumer Affairs. The functions of the Agency include:

— The promotion and protection of the interests of consumers;

— The enforcement of consumer protection laws including by way of summary prosecution of breaches of consumer law;

— Encouraging compliance with consumer law;

— Investigating alleged breaches of consumer legislation and, at its discretion, referring such allegations to the DPP, where the Agency has a reasonable ground for believing that an indictable offence has been committed.

Notably, the Agency has power to prosecute summary offences, a significant innovation given the very limited powers vested previously in the Director of Consumer Affairs. In fact, the Act generally represents a significant advance, the powers conferred on the Agency being significantly more rigorous than those previously enjoyed by the Director.

The Act also confers on the Agency a broad advisory function, while s.9 vests the Agency with specific authority to review consumer legislation and to submit proposals for the amendment thereof. The Agency is further empowered generally to advise on how best to protect consumer welfare. Included in the Agency's remit is a requirement to forge contacts with consumer groups and other consumer representatives, and to co-operate, consult with and share information with such groups. In particular, the Act permits the Agency to support voluntary bodies and to co-operate with other public agencies charged with the promotion of consumer welfare (including, most notably, the Irish Financial Services Regulatory Authority).

The Act places a particular emphasis on the development and promotion by the Agency of alternative dispute resolution mechanisms. The Agency is also charged with promoting the adoption of quality assurance schemes and codes of practice as well as the publication of guidelines to traders. The Agency is empowered to carry out and to publish research and analysis. It is invested, moreover, with an educational and advisory remit, requiring it to promote a public awareness of consumer issues and consumer rights.

The Agency is required, in s.20, to draw up and promulgate three-year strategies specifying key objectives and outputs, and to identify the most cost-effective and efficient means of achieving these objectives. Specific provision is also made in s.21 for co-operation and consultation with other consumer protection agencies (including the IFSRA), and in particular encouraging the most efficient use of resources and the avoidance of duplication of work.

Following in this spirit of co-operation, provision is made in s.31 of the Act for the exchange of information relating to alleged offences between the Agency and various public bodies, including the Competition Authority, An Garda

Síochána, the Director of Corporate Enforcement, the Revenue Commissioners, the Central Bank and the IFSRA. Subject to this, unauthorised disclosure by the Agency is prohibited, though this confidentiality requirement is subject to some exceptions, including protection for whistleblowers reporting alleged offences (not limited to offences under this Act) to An Garda Síochána.

The Act transfers the functions of the Director of Consumer Affairs to the Agency. The Act also stipulates that legislative references to the Director in other enactments shall henceforth be interpreted as referring to the Agency, though s.40 and Sch.3 to the Act make specific consequential amendments to various Acts replacing references to the Director with references to the Agency.

Unfair commercial practices—general prohibition   Part 3 of the Act concerns unfair commercial practices as defined. In addition to a general ban on such practices, this part addresses three particular manifestations of such practices in considerable detail. These are:

— Misleading commercial practices (Ch.2);

— Aggressive commercial practices (Ch.3);

— Prohibited commercial practices (Ch.4).

The overriding concept of an unfair commercial practice is defined in s.41. A commercial practice will be deemed unfair if it infringes what is termed "the requirements of professional diligence". This means that it is contrary to one or both of the following:

— The general principle of good faith in the trader's field of activity;

— The standard of skill and care that the trader may reasonably be expected to exercise in respect of consumers.

In addition, the practice must be likely to cause appreciable impairment of the average consumer's ability to make an informed choice and cause the average consumer to make a transactional decision that he or she otherwise would not have made. Notably, the term "average consumer" includes, in relation to a commercial practice directed at a particular group, an average member of that group. Where, moreover, the practice is likely to materially distort the economic behaviour only of a specific clearly identifiable group of consumers who are considered particularly vulnerable because of their mental or physical infirmity, age or credulity, the term "average consumer" means the average consumer of that vulnerable group. This is particularly pertinent in the case of traders who target children, disabled persons or vulnerable older persons.

Misleading commercial practices   Part 3, Ch.2 of the Act prohibits traders from engaging in what are termed "misleading commercial practices". Section 43 of the Act defines a practice as misleading if it involves the provision of false information regarding a number of stipulated matters in circumstances where the information is likely to deceive or mislead the average consumer, causing him or her to make a transactional decision that the average consumer would not otherwise have made. The clear implication is that the misinformation must have been "causative"; in other words, that it is likely to have been instrumental in effecting a sale.

A number of matters are listed as matters in respect of which the provision of misleading information is proscribed. The list is quite comprehensive and detailed, and space does not permit a full discussion of all of the listed matters. Examples include information that misrepresents the geographical origin of a product, a misleading statement of the product's price, weight or volume and a description of an item as "new" when it is in fact second-hand. A misstatement of the benefits or results to be expected from a product is included, as is a misrepresentation of its composition, ingredients, components or accessories (e.g. that it contains real fruit when it in fact does not). Pricing information must be accurate. Statements may be misleading where they misrepresent the key attributes of a trader, such as his identity, assets or qualifications, while a false statement of affiliation or connections with others or of approval or sponsorship by another (e.g. a celebrity endorsement) will also be misleading. Misstatements as to a consumer's legal rights are also covered.

In determining whether a practice is misleading, the court must have regard to the overall factual context in which the practice is carried out. In particular, s.43(6) makes provision in respect of an intimation that a product was previously offered at a particular price. Where this occurs, the court is entitled to have regard to whether the original price at which the trader purported formerly to sell the goods was in fact one made in good faith for a reasonable period of time. Similar principles apply where a product is being offered at below what is claimed to be the recommended retail price.

Section 44 contains particular provisions on practices that seek to "pass off" the goods of the trader as those of a competitor. Similar principles apply where a trader represents that he abides by or is bound by a code of practice with which the trader does not in fact comply (s.45).

Section 46 of the Act deals with practices that serve to mislead by withholding, omitting or concealing "material information". A commercial practice is deemed misleading if the trader omits or conceals "material information" needed to allow the average consumer to make an informed decision whether or not to enter into a commercial transaction. A practice is also deemed misleading where material information is provided but in a manner that renders it unclear, unintelligible, untimely or ambiguous, or where it fails to identify the commercial intent of the practice, leading the average consumer to make a transactional decision that he or she otherwise would not have made.

For this purpose, "material information" includes information regarding certain aspects of the product, unless such information is already apparent to the consumer in the context of the commercial practice. Such material information includes details of the main characteristics of the product, the identity and geographical address of the trader, the price of the product (including taxes) or the manner in which the price is to be calculated, arrangements for payment, delivery or performance, as well as the legal rights of the consumer to withdraw from or cancel the transaction.

Surcharges   Section 48 creates a new offence aimed at combatting the practice of imposing a surcharge for the use of certain modes of payment in preference to others. This addresses in particular the practice of imposing an extra charge for use of a credit or debit card, though it also relates to the practice of penalising customers who do not avail of a direct debit facility for the payment of bills. Where a trader indicates that it will accept payment for goods or services by any one of two or more payment methods, an additional charge cannot be levied in respect of the use of one payment method as distinct from another. Where only one method of payment is accepted, or where more than one payment is permitted, but all such methods of payment attract the same surcharge, s.49 requires that any applicable surcharge must be included in the overall price stated. Where the full stated price includes the surcharge, however, it is not an offence to state that the surcharge is included or to indicate the value of that surcharge.

Labelling regulations   Section 50 generally allows the Minister for Enterprise, Trade and Employment (subject to certain conditions) to make Regulations requiring that specified goods and services be marked with or accompanied by particular information, including the application of a stamp, tag or label on such products. Similar provisions may be applied to advertisements for specified products. It is an offence to supply or advertise a product in breach of such Regulations.

Aggressive commercial practices   Chapter 3 of Pt 3 targets aggressive commercial practices, where a trader seeks to intimidate or harass a potential consumer. Section 53 of the Act defines a commercial practice as aggressive if:

> ... by harassment, coercion or undue influence it would be likely to
> (a) cause significant impairment of the average consumer's freedom
>   of choice or conduct in relation to the product concerned, and

(b) cause the average consumer to make a transactional decision that the average consumer would not otherwise make.

Undue influence for this purpose is defined as the exploitation of a "position of power in relation to a consumer so as to apply pressure…in a way that significantly limits the consumer's ability to make an informed choice in relation to the trader's product". Such pressure need not involve using or threatening to employ physical force.

In determining whether a practice is aggressive, the court must look to the overall factual context in which the practice arises, but is directed specifically to consider the timing, location, nature, or persistence of the conduct and the use of any threatening or abusive language or behaviour. The court may also look to any onerous or disproportionate non-contractual barriers set as a prerequisite to the exercise of legal or contractual rights, to the termination of the contract or to the consumer switching to another product or trader. The use of threats to take action against the consumer (where the trader has no legal basis for such action) or to do something unlawful may also be deemed aggressive. A trader found to have engaged in an aggressive commercial practice is guilty of an offence under the Act.

Prohibited commercial practices   The Act bans outright a number of commercial practices, prescribing the stipulated practices to be criminal offences under the Act. The list of banned practices is exceptionally extensive. It includes:

— A claim that the trader, a particular product or commercial practice has received approval, authorisation or endorsement which the trader in fact does not have, or making such a representation when the trader or practice is not in compliance with that approval, authorisation or endorsement;

— A false representation that the trader has signed up to a code of practice;

— A false representation that the trader is about to cease trading or move premises (e.g. a fake "closing down sale");

— A representation that a product is able to facilitate winning in a game of chance;

— A representation suggesting that the supply of a product is legal, when it is not;

— A representation that a product can cure an illness, dysfunction or malformation if it cannot;

— A representation that a product is free if a consumer has to pay anything other than the necessary and reasonable cost of responding to the representation or collecting or having the product delivered;

— The display of a quality, standard or trust mark, or other symbol that the product is not entitled to carry.

The Act also bans the practice of "bait advertising", that is, inviting consumers to buy a product when the trader has (and fails to disclose) reasonable grounds for believing that the trader will not be able to supply, or procure the supply of the product at the stated price. Similar principles apply where the trader fails to disclose reasonable grounds for believing that he or she will not be able to secure supply for a reasonable time and in reasonably sufficient quantities to meet demand. "Bait and switch" practices are also addressed, the Act prohibiting conduct inviting a consumer to purchase a particular product and then seeking to frustrate the consumer's attempt to buy the product so as to get the consumer to buy a different product.

Putting pressure on a consumer to make a quick decision to buy a product by telling them it is only available (or only available on specified terms) for a limited time is also deemed to be illegal. The consumer should be afforded, the Act indicates, sufficient time to make a reasonably informed choice. Similar provisions apply where a trader makes a representation that is inaccurate to a material degree regarding market conditions or the prospects of the consumer finding the same product elsewhere so as to induce the consumer to buy the product subject to terms and conditions that are less favourable than normal market conditions. For instance, it would likely be illegal for a trader to claim that he was the sole Irish supplier of a popular product that was in fact widely available in the State.

Several provisions ban misleading advertising practices. These include representations to the effect that a right conferred on the consumer by law is a distinctive feature of the trader's promotion or supply. Paid-for editorial content is also targeted, the Act requiring that where promotional media content has been paid for, this must be clearly stated in the text of the publication. The Act addresses representations made that are materially inaccurate as to the nature and extent of a risk to a consumer's personal security, or to that of members of the consumer's household, if he or she does not buy a particular product. It is also illegal to promote a product in such a manner as deliberately deceives or misleads the consumer into believing that the product has been made by a particular manufacturer, when it has not been.

Specific provisions are directed at promotional competitions and 'prize scams', the Act banning the operation, running or promotion of a competition the prizes for which (or reasonably equivalent items) are not in fact awarded. Similarly, it is an offence to represent that the consumer has won or will win a prize if there is in fact no such prize or if the prize can only be claimed on payment by the consumer, or only can be claimed by means that involve the consumer incurring a loss.

Where a consumer has not yet contracted for the purchase of a product, it is an offence to include with marketing material an invoice requiring payment for the product. Likewise the trader is precluded from representing that he or she is acting as a consumer (when he or she is not) or is otherwise not acting for the purposes of the trader's trade, business or profession (when the trader is in fact acting in that capacity.)

Further practices involving, for instance, assertive and unwanted marketing techniques are prohibited by s.55(3). These include persistently making unwanted calls to a consumer (either in person or by phone, fax or e-mail or other means), having been asked to desist. Where a consumer is claiming on an insurance policy, moreover, it is an offence to require the consumer to produce documents irrelevant to the validity of the claim or persistently to ignore a consumer's communications, with the intention of dissuading the consumer from exercising his or her contractual rights under the policy. Advertising that directly encourages children to buy a product or to persuade an adult to do so for them is also targeted. In relation to a product not solicited by a consumer, it is an offence to demand immediate or deferred payment for the product or to require the consumer to return or keep the product safe. Similarly, the Act bans communications suggesting that if a consumer does not acquire a product, his or her job or livelihood will be placed in jeopardy.

Prices: display, weighing and price-fixing   Section 57 of the Act permits the Minister to make Regulations regarding the display of prices and charges. Such Regulations may apply to specific types or classes of products or traders, and may apply to the whole State or, in the alternative, to specified geographical areas.

Section 59 relates to food sold loose and not pre-packed for sale (most typically, though not exclusively, fruit and vegetables) where the price is based on the weight of the product. Where a retailer offers such food for sale, he or she is required to provide a weighing scale or weighing machine. The scale must be placed in a public and prominent position as near as practicable to the food being sold, so that the purchaser may either weigh the item or observe it being weighed prior to purchase. Section 60, moreover, bans a trader from preventing or obstructing a person from reading displayed prices or preventing a person from entering trading premises with a view to reading displayed prices. A breach of s.59 and/or s.60 constitutes an offence under the Act, albeit one only attracting summary criminal proceedings.

Sections 61 and 62 of the Act allow for the setting of maximum prices in respect of a product where there exists a state of emergency affecting the supply of the product. This may happen where the Government is of the opinion that "abnormal circumstances" relate to the supply of the product. An emergency order ordinarily lasts for a maximum of six months, though that period may be extended, if required. The infringement of a maximum price order in such cases is an indictable as well as a summary offence.

Pyramid promotional schemes   Put at its simplest, a pyramid promotional scheme is a scheme the primary feature of which is that a person pays money or money's worth in exchange for an opportunity to make money by introducing other people to the scheme. The key element is that the person gains their compensation primarily by introducing others to the scheme, rather than from the supply or consumption of a product. In other words, scheme members recoup their initial payment from other people who they have introduced to the scheme, who in turn can only make back their money by introducing further people and so on.

For the purpose of the Act, it is no defence to say that the scheme involves the supply of a product, if the primary means of recouping compensation is by introducing others to the scheme. The crux of the matter is whether the opportunity to make money is primarily derived from introducing other people to the scheme as opposed to supplying or consuming the product. In deciding whether this is the case, the court may have regard to the emphasis placed, in the promotion of the scheme, on the participant's entitlement to the product as compared with the compensation for introducing other people. The court may also have regard to the relationship of the consideration given to the value of the product supplied.

It was already an offence, under the Pyramid Selling Act 1980, to induce persons to enter such a scheme. The offences created by the 2007 Act, which replace those previously in place, are more comprehensive and the penalties more exacting. Section 65 stipulates that a person shall not establish, operate or promote a pyramid promotional scheme, knowingly participate in such a scheme or induce or attempt to induce another person to participate in such a scheme. The penalty for breach is far and away the most severe imposed under the Act, being a fine of up to €150,000 or imprisonment for up to five years, or both. The continued breach of s.65 after conviction under that section will, moreover, attract a further fine of €10,000 for each day on which the breach continues. While summary proceedings are generally not envisaged, s.83 of the Act allows for summary prosecution in lieu of indictment, where the offence is considered to be minor in nature.

Section 66 renders void any agreement under which a participant agrees to pay the scheme promoter, or otherwise provide consideration or a gift, in exchange for the opportunity to participate in the scheme. "Scheme promoter" for this purpose includes the person who has established and operates the scheme, but may also include any person seeking to induce or attempt to induce others to join the scheme.

Civil remedies   Relative to the powers formerly held by the Director of

Consumer Affairs, the Act provides a comprehensive and onerous range of penalties and remedies, both to the Agency and to individual consumers. Of particular general note is that where a trader claims that a representation is true, s.68 of the Act places the onus of proving its truth on the trader. If the trader does not establish its truth on the balance of probabilities, the representation will be presumed to be untrue.

Prohibition orders The civil remedies available under the Act include the power in s.71 to seek a "prohibition order" in respect of an act or practice that is banned by the Act (with the exception of an offence involving the weighing of food or reading of prices under ss.59 and 60). It is open to any person, including the Agency and any other prescribed consumer protection body, to seek such a prohibition order before the Circuit Court or High Court. In making its decision, the court shall have regard to all interests involved, including the public interest. It is not necessary, however, to establish that actual loss or damage has ensued as a result of the impugned practice, or that the practice was the result of intentional or negligent conduct on the part of the trader. Once a prohibition order is made, it is an offence to fail to comply therewith. The court is also empowered, in making an order, to set terms and conditions, including a requirement that the trader publish a corrective statement. Section 72 of the Act allows prohibition orders to be made against "code owners", that is, those who formulate or revise codes of practice adopted by traders or who monitor compliance with such codes. Such an application may be made only by the Agency, and only in respect of acts or practices banned by the 2007 Act, though otherwise the operation of s.72 is equivalent to that of s.71.

Undertakings Section 73 allows the Agency to pre-empt breaches or further breaches by accepting a written undertaking from a trader that it will not or will no longer engage in such practices. The undertaking may be sought if the Agency has reason to believe that a trader is committing or engaging in, or has committed or engaged in or is about to commit or engage in a prohibited act or practice. An undertaking (which the Agency is entitled to publish) may include a promise to abide by the Act and to refrain from engaging in prohibited acts or practices. It may also require compensation of consumers affected by the practice, and the publication of a corrective statement by the trader. Notably an undertaking may be obtained not only in respect of breaches of the Act but also breaches of a variety of consumer measures specified in Sch.4 to the Act.

Consumer compensation Section 74 allows a consumer to seek and obtain compensation in the form of damages (including exemplary damages) where the consumer is affected by the conduct of a trader who commits or engages in a prohibited act or practice. For the purpose of this section a prohibited act or practice does not including a misleading commercial practice as defined by s. 45 or a breach of s. 65, relating to pyramid schemes.

Compliance orders Section 75 entitles the Agency to issue compliance notices. Where the Agency has reason to believe that a specified breach of consumer legislation has occurred or is occurring, it may issue a written "compliance notice", directing the trader involved to remedy the breach by a specified date. The trader may appeal the notice to the District Court but if it fails to do so within 14 days of receipt of the notice, the notice will be treated as having been accepted by the trader. On appeal, the judge may confirm, vary or cancel the notice. Failure to comply with a compliance notice is a summary offence.

Criminal penalties   Criminal liability is dealt with in Pt 5, Ch.4. Such prosecutions may be brought within two years of the alleged breach of the Act. Specific provision is made in s.77, where the offence is committed by a body corporate, for the additional prosecution of a director, manager, secretary or other officer of the body where the offence was committed with the consent, connivance or approval of such persons, or as a result of their neglect. A director or employee will be presumed (until the contrary is established) to have consented to an offence if it can be shown that that person's duties, at the relevant time, permitted him or her to make decisions that could have significantly affected the management of the corporate body. Similarly an employee, officer, director or agent of the company who authorises, permits or acquiesces in the offence may also be criminally liable.

A general defence of "due diligence" is provided by s.78. The accused must, however, establish that he or she exercised due diligence and pursued all reasonable precautions in order to avoid committing the offence. The court is also entitled, in mitigation of sentence, to consider any corrective statement made by the offender.

Main penalties   On a first summary conviction under the Act, the defendant may be fined up to €3,000 or imprisoned for no more than six months, or both. On a second or subsequent summary conviction, a fine of up to €5,000 or a term of imprisonment of no more than 12 months, or both, may be imposed. On conviction of an indictable offence, a first conviction attracts a fine of up to €60,000 or a term of imprisonment of no more than 18 months, or both, while a second or subsequent conviction (other than an offence under certain excluded sections), may result in a fine of up to €100,000 or a term of imprisonment of no more than 24 months, or both. Where the convicted person continues to be in breach of the provision in respect of which he was convicted, continued contravention of the relevant provision will attract a penalty of €500 (on summary conviction) and €10,000 (on indictment) per day of continued breach.

Costs and compensation   The convicted person may, under s.80, be required to pay the Agency's costs in investigating and prosecuting the offence. Likewise, under s.81, the offender may be required to compensate consumers affected by the breach. This compensation order may be in addition to or in place of a fine or term of imprisonment, though the consumer is not entitled to claim "on the double" by invoking s.81 while also collecting damages under s.74. The Act also permits the court in respect of misleading and prohibited (though not aggressive) commercial practices and pyramid schemes to order the offender to issue corrective statements.

Fixed payment notices   Section 85 of the Act allows the Agency to issue fixed payment notices in respect of certain specified offences involving a breach of price display regulations passed under a variety of enactments. Such notice has the effect that a prosecution will not be instituted if within 28 days of the date of the notice the alleged offender pays €300 to the Agency. In default of payment, the alleged offender will be prosecuted in respect of the offence.

Miscellaneous   *Consumer protection list*   The Agency is required to maintain and may publish a list of traders who have been punished under the Act, or who have been made the subject of a compensation order, a prohibition order, a compliance notice or an undertaking or who have made a payment to the Agency following a fixed payment notice. The Agency shall specify, in the list, details as to the matters occasioning the relevant conviction, order, undertaking or notice.

Whistle-blowers   Specific protection is provided for whistle-blowers, acting in good faith, who report suspected infringements to the Agency. Such persons will not be liable for damages in respect of such disclosures unless it can be established that the person has not acted reasonably and in good faith. It is however, an offence knowingly to make a false statement to the Agency, which offence may be tried either summarily or on indictment.

Effect of the Act   With the exception of pyramid schemes banned under s.65, a contract for the supply of goods or the provision of services will not be void by reason only of the fact that it infringes the 2007 Act. Moreover, the Act is deemed to operate without prejudice to any rights which a person may enjoy under any other enactment or rule of law, in other words to offer protection in addition to those measures rather than in their place.

Continuation in force of existing orders   The Act provides for the continued operation of current specified display orders made under the Prices Act 1958 as well as under the Consumer Information Act 1978, notwithstanding the repeal, by the 2007 Act, of those statutes.

Consequential amendments   Finally, certain consequential amendments are made to various Acts. The Act makes certain amendments to the Central Bank Act 1942 (as amended), effectively permitting certain functions to be exercised concurrently by both the Central Bank and the Agency.

The Act also amends s.6 of the Sale of Goods and Supply of Services Act 1980, by adding a clause to the effect that a director or employee of a company will be presumed (until the contrary is established) to have consented to an offence if it can be shown that that person's duties, at the relevant time, permitted him or her to make decisions that could have significantly affected the management of the corporate body. Certain amendments are made to the Industrial Development Act 1993, as well as to the Casual Trading Act 1995, the latter permitting the Minister to issue guidelines to local authorities in respect of their functions under the 1995 Act. Additionally ss.5 and 6 of the Hallmarking Act 1981 are amended, deeming a commercial practice to be misleading under the 2007 Act where a false claim is made that an article, not in fact containing precious metal, is made wholly or partly of gold, silver or platinum.

Provision is also made for the detention by customs officers of goods on foot of a request by the Agency in order to test them for safety purposes. It is an offence under the Act to sell, offer for sale, distribute or supply a product that has been legally withdrawn from the market for reasons of safety.

DAMAGES, QUANTUM OF

See **Rothwell v Arrowdale Limited t/a Sheehy Motors, High Court, Peart J., November 29, 2007, [2007] I.E.H.C. 395 (discussed above under BREACH OF CONTRACT).**

Cosmoline Trading v DH Burke and Son Ltd and DHB Holdings, High Court, Finnegan J., June 14, 2007, [2007] I.E.H.C. 186.

This case follows on from proceedings reported in this section in the *Annual Review of Irish Law 2006* (pp.297–299). In the original proceedings, the plaintiff had sought specific performance of a lease in respect of a supermarket premises which had been vacated for renovations (High Court, Finnegan J. February 8, 2006, [2006] I.E.H.C. 38). The case turned largely on the specific facts, the court ultimately ruling that while the plaintiff had not proved the existence of a binding new lease in respect of the renovated premises, the old lease on the premises remained extant and enforceable. Following this decision, the plaintiff sought an order as to the correct quantum of damages for loss of the capital value of and profits from its business.

The full facts as well as the original judgment are set out in the *Annual Review 2006*. In 1997, the plaintiff acquired from the defendants a 35-year leasehold interest in a unit at a shopping centre known as "Abbey Trinity". The plaintiff operated the unit as a supermarket. In 2003 the defendants commenced renovations on the Abbey Trinity premises, during which time the plaintiff agreed temporarily to move its business to another premises owned by the defendants.

The question that arose was whether the parties had agreed that, on completion of the renovations, the plaintiff could move back into the renovated Abbey Trinity premises. The defendants' understanding was that the plaintiff intended to seek alternative premises and would thus be surrendering its original interest. The plaintiff disputed this, and sought specific performance of what it alleged was an agreement that the plaintiff would be allowed to move back to Abbey Trinity once the renovations were complete.

Finnegan P. ruled that the parties had honestly represented their diverging perspectives, and were hence genuinely not *ad idem* regarding the return to the Abbey Trinity premises. He thus concluded that there had been no agreement for the creation of a new lease in respect of the renovated premises. While an agreement for a lease was, in equity, enforceable as a lease, specific performance would only be granted if there was certainty as to a number of key factors. Here, fundamentally, there was a lack of consensus on material and essential terms and thus no concluded agreement for a new lease upon which specific performance could be based.

The judge concluded, however, that the plaintiff had not surrendered its original interest in the Abbey Trinity premises and that the old lease in respect of the premises remained live and enforceable. The parties having failed to reach agreement on this point, Finnegan P. was subsequently asked to assess compensation to the plaintiff in respect of the loss of the capital value of its business, the loss of profits ensuing and interest on both sums. As against this the defendants claimed that the value of various benefits received by the plaintiff should be set off against the plaintiff's claims.

Compensation for the capital value of the business   Finnegan P. concluded first that the date on which the business was to be valued was January 1, 2005, that being the date on which negotiations between the parties finally broke down.

The judge concluded that the business was to be valued at somewhere between 10 and 20 times its gross weekly turnover (the sale price of goods that the supermarket sold per week before expenses and overheads were subtracted).

While the plaintiff contended that the correct multiple was 16.9, the defendants argued that it was much closer to 10. In deciding where on the scale the Abbey Trinity premises fell, the judge had regard to a number of factors including the relatively outdated nature of the premises, the limited number of convenient car parking spaces and the increased competition from several more modern supermarkets that had recently opened up in the surrounding area. Relative to these more upmarket amenities, the plaintiff's business was unlikely to have performed strongly.

Taking all this into account the judge calculated that the appropriate multiple in valuing the premises was 12.5. The gross weekly turnover in 2002 was €98,500. The judge indicated that given the increase in competition in the intervening period, it was unlikely that the trade would have appreciated by 2005. He thus valued the plaintiff's business as of January 1, 2005 at €1.23 million. Prior to January 1, 2005 the parties had been in negotiations towards an agreement: "All that transpired [up to that date] was considered by the parties to be for their mutual benefit". Thus, the judge concluded, 6 per cent interest would be payable only from January 1, 2005 to the date of payment.

Loss of profits　　The plaintiff had sought compensation for loss of profits, but this was refused. Finnegan J. reasoned that the plaintiff had already recovered in respect of the value of its business, with interest, as of January 2005. To award profits on top of this would unfairly privilege the plaintiff. Implicit in this conclusion is the determination that the profits it would have made were already accounted for in assessing the value of the business. Additionally, when the plaintiff left the Abbey Trinity premises in 2003 it had moved into alternative premises belonging to the defendants, from which it traded and made profits. The parties had agreed that no rent would be payable during this time in respect of either the original premises or the alternative premises from which the plaintiff subsequently traded. Clearly to allow the plaintiff now to claim for lost profits would allow it to reap profits on the double.

The defendants had subsequently made a claim for rent in respect of the alternative premises (the plaintiff having enjoyed use of these premises rent free). The judge nonetheless concluded that in assessing compensation for the plaintiff, the defendants should not be awarded any discount for such unpaid rent. The plaintiff had moved its business at the request of the defendants to facilitate their desire to renovate, and as such no deduction should be made in respect of rent unpaid after January 1, 2003.

Credits for benefits received　　As against the compensation awarded, the defendants claimed credit for several benefits which, they asserted, accrued to the plaintiff during the currency of the lease. As part of the original agreement, the plaintiff had agreed to lease several premises in the west of Ireland, but had subsequently surrendered two such premises in Boyle and Drumshanbo.

The benefit to the plaintiff of so doing was valued at €200,000. Similarly, rent in respect of a property leased by the plaintiff in Roscommon was foregone, representing a benefit of €40,323 to the plaintiff. In exchange for agreeing to move out of Abbey Trinity, the plaintiff had been given €55,000. The plaintiff also had the free use of a liquor off-licence at another premises, and, making allowance for its use, the judge awarded a further deduction of €10,000. The judge was satisfied that all deductions, amounting to €305,323, should be set off against the compensation paid to the plaintiff.

The judge thus awarded compensation in the amount of €1.23 million less a deduction of €305,323.

DURESS

***John K Rogers t/a John Rogers Engineering v Iaralco Ltd*, High Court, O'Neill J., March 16, 2007, [2007] I.E.H.C. 130** The defendant in this case was a German-owned manufacturer of car parts based in Ireland. In 1999, it initiated an arrangement that involved sub-contracting some of its work to the plaintiff, an engineer. The relationship proceeded relatively well for approximately a year and a half before turning sour. The source of the ultimate disintegration of the relationship was an agreement to subcontract further work to the plaintiff involving the polishing of Magne bumpers and the cutting of rubber strips. The case turned, in particular, on a dispute over five invoices issued by the plaintiff in respect of this work, which invoices the defendant disputed.

Invoice 1: The plaintiff claimed that a sum of IR£15,000 was owed to him as the balance on sums due for the polishing of the Magne bumpers. Although the parties had not agreed in advance a fee for this work, the judge was satisfied that the intention was to pay a sum that would cover costs and afford a reasonable profit margin to the plaintiff. While the defendant estimated that the work would cost 87p per unit, the plaintiff asserted that the cost was closer to IR£2.11 per unit and thus claimed (allowing for a profit) IR£2.53 per unit.

In Christmas 2000, the plaintiff (under pressure to pay outstanding wages to employees) accepted a cheque for just over IR£16,000, representing a payment of 87p per unit. The parties agreed, however, to resolve the disagreement over the price after the Christmas break. At a subsequent meeting in January 2001, the plaintiff sought a total sum of IR£45,000 which he claimed represented the cost price of the work. The defendant disputed this, but was concerned that non-payment would result in a breach in supply, and the non-return of materials in the plaintiff's possession. Following negotiations, the defendant offered IR£30,000 which the plaintiff agreed to accept. The defendant subsequently paid this, less the IR£16,000 already rendered to the plaintiff.

Subsequently, however, the plaintiff sought to recover the remainder of the IR£45,000 that he had claimed was owing to him. He asserted that he had accepted IR£30,000 under economic duress and that, as a result, the agreement was voidable. In particular, he stated that the defendant was aware that the plaintiff was under pressure to pay his wage bill, and used this to its advantage. He also claimed that the defendant knew that the plaintiff had undergone surgery during Christmas, and sought to turn his consequent vulnerability to its benefit.

In his support, the plaintiff cited *D & C Builders v Rees* [1965] 2 Q.B. 617. That case establishes that an agreement to accept part-payment of a debt in place of the whole debt could not be enforced where that agreement was extracted through misrepresentation or duress. O'Neill J. nonetheless rejected the application of this case, concluding that the circumstances were distinguishable. First, while *D&C Builders* concerned a certain debt that was not in dispute, the IR£45,000 claimed by the plaintiff had never been agreed by the parties: "…it was at all times disputed by the defendants, and ultimately it was compromised at the figure of IR£30,000."

O'Neill J. further refuted any claim of economic duress. He noted that the kind of pressure that the plaintiff was experiencing was no greater than that experienced by many businesses:

> "[T]he factors put forward by the plaintiff as constituting duress or intimidation could not amount to that. The fact that the plaintiff was under the pressure of having to pay wages could not fairly be viewed as a duress exercised by the defendants. In commercial life the pressure of having to pay wages is universal."

While this pressure might have been more severe in cases where the business was under financial strain, this did not bring the pressure into the category of illegitimate pressure vitiating the settlement in this case. Many commercial decisions are undoubtedly made reluctantly and subject to significant financial pressures and strains. It is not enough, however, to say that more ideal circumstances would have yielded a different decision.

In determining what amounts to duress, the English courts have observed that the pressure imposed must be such that it is regarded as "illegitimate", distinguishing this from commercial pressures that are a normal feature of business life. In *Atlas Express Ltd v Kafco* [1989] 1 All E.R. 641 Tucker J. observed that "[e]conomic duress must be distinguished from commercial pressure which on any view is not sufficient to vitiate consent." Lord Scarman taps a similar vein when he notes, in *The Universe Sentinel* [1983] A.C. 366 at 400–401 how "in life, including the life of commerce and finance, many acts are done under pressure, sometimes overwhelming pressure, but they are not necessarily done under duress."

The parties in this case, O'Neill J. noted, dealt with each other at arm's length, with neither having any fiduciary obligations to the other. Each party was thus well within its rights to seek the best bargain possible. There had been no misrepresentation. Nor had there been, in the judge's view, any attempt to take advantage of the plaintiff's difficulties. The defendant had in fact agreed a price that was twice its genuine estimate of the costs. In doing so, it harboured some genuine reluctance, and even felt "hard done by", but nonetheless proceeded with a view to ensuring that the defendant company would be able to meet current orders for car parts. The plaintiff, moreover, had asserted that the defendant's estimate of 87p overestimated the number of parts that could be prepared in an hour, positing that the likely figure was half that proposed by the defendant. Assuming the plaintiff was correct, this meant that the likely cost was IR£1.70 per part, which was roughly what the plaintiff had received under the agreement.

The judge thus refuted the suggestion that unfair advantage had been gained, or that duress had been exercised. Despite the plaintiff's recent hospitalisation, the judge considered that he was sufficiently competent to conclude the settlement. He was satisfied that a binding agreement for a IR£30,000 settlement had been validly reached and was binding on the parties, with the result that the plaintiff could not now claim a further IR£15,000.

Invoice 2: The plaintiff claimed a sum of IR£18,221.25 in respect of rubber strips cut and packaged by the plaintiff. The parties initially agreed a price of IR£3.62 per unit in respect of this work. Although a draft agreement was presented to the plaintiff, the plaintiff never signed this. Nevertheless he had proceeded with the work as per the specification in the draft agreement (and thus was taken implicitly to have accepted the terms offered). The plaintiff subsequently claimed that the work involved was more substantial than initially represented and that, as such, a higher fee was due per unit.

The judge concluded that the work involved in cutting and packing these rubber strips was as per the specification of the defendant set out in the draft agreement. Notwithstanding his failure to sign the agreement, the plaintiff continued to perform the work as per the defendant's specification and made no complaint regarding the agreed price until February 2001.

In February 2001, the defendant agreed to increase the price paid to IR£7.50 per unit, but with prospective effect only. The plaintiff nonetheless claimed that he was entitled to this new fee with retrospective effect, and thus, that a sum of IR£18,221.25 was owed to him, representing the difference between IR£3.62 per unit and IR£7.50 per unit. O'Neill J. however, rejected this claim. The plaintiff had agreed to IR£3.62 and had not sought to renegotiate this until late February 2001. If he was, the judge added, "… asked to do work between November 2000 and February 2001 that he had not contracted to do he was entitled to refuse to do that work. He did not do that."

The judge concluded, moreover, that the work in question was not "significantly beyond or additional to that which he had agreed to do". The plaintiff had agreed (such agreement being indicated by his actions in performing the work) to accept IR£3.62 and had not disputed this. The work was not significantly different from what had originally been specified. As such, the plaintiff had to take what had been agreed and no more.

Invoices 3 and 4:   The plaintiff claimed IR£13,087, the cost of equipment purchased for the purpose of carrying out work for the defendant. While the plaintiff asserted that the defendant had agreed to pay the full purchase cost, the court concluded that the defendant had only agreed to pay a fair market value for the equipment, namely IR£1,300. The defendant having already paid IR£5,000 was to be reimbursed the difference.

The plaintiff next claimed the reimbursement of IR£3,288.45 which had, it asserted, been retained by the defendant in respect of defective parts supplied by the plaintiff. The judge concluded that "[b]eyond the bald assertion of this claim, there was no evidence as to how and in respect of which invoices or goods this claim arises". In other words, the plaintiff (on whom the onus of proof lay) had failed to evince any evidence as to the goods to which this claim related. As such, the claim was dismissed.

Invoice 5:   Finally, the judge dealt with a claim that the plaintiff was entitled to IR£15,000 as an agreed severance payment, made on the break-up of the parties' commercial relationship. Concluding that the defendant had agreed to pay a severance payment, albeit one of IR£10,000 rather than IR£15,000, the judge nonetheless noted that this payment was contingent on the "smooth transfer back to the defendants of the functions subcontracted to the plaintiff". While this "smooth transfer" required the plaintiff to return all of the defendant's materials, the plaintiff had refused to return the materials, claiming a lien over them, forcing the defendant to take out an injunction to recover its materials. This state of affairs, the judge concluded, was wholly inconsistent with the smooth transfer of operations. As such, the plaintiff was not entitled to the severance payment, having breached a condition precedent to its recovery.

In summary, the plaintiff's action failed on all counts. The defendant was to be reimbursed the euro equivalent of IR£3,865 owing to it as a result of the judgment.

ESTOPPEL

***Courtney v McCarthy*, Supreme Court, Geoghegan J., Kearns J. and Finnegan J., December 4, 2007, [2007] I.E.S.C. 58**   The decision of the High Court in this case was reported in the *Annual Review of Irish Law 2006* (pp.251–253). The case relates to a claim for specific performance of a contract for the sale of land. In turn this claim was based on an estoppel preventing the vendor from relying on her right to regard the contract as having been rescinded because of the purchaser's failure to complete on time. Notably, despite the generally expressed reluctance to do so, the Supreme Court verdict overturns the High Court on the inferences to be drawn from the facts, and possibly on the facts themselves. This is highly unusual and rare, the Supreme Court usually deferring to the court hearing the evidence in relation to such matters (see *Hay v O'Grady* [1992] 1 I.R. 210). The decision also employs the doctrine of estoppel to allow the purchaser to enforce a contract for the sale of land, a conclusion that appears to run counter to the orthodox view that estoppel should be used "only as a shield and not as a sword". The verdict illustrates that even where a contract is validly rescinded, a representation to the effect that it can still be completed will give rise to an estoppel which in turn may allow the court to grant specific performance of a previously rescinded contract.

In March, 2005, the plaintiff (hereinafter the "vendor") and defendant, being the purchaser, entered into a contract for the sale of land belonging to the vendor, the agreed sale price being €1.8 million. A 10 per cent deposit was to be paid on execution of the contract. Furthermore, the closing date for completion of the sale was set as April 8, 2005.

The contract of sale contained a number of pertinent conditions, including the provision of a right of way over lands retained by the vendor to facilitate development on the sold land. The precise location of the right of way was to be agreed between the parties. A further condition stipulated that to facilitate any planned development on the sold land, the purchaser would build roads and services thereon, maintaining these facilities until they were taken over by the local county council. The conditions stated that, in default of a timely closing, the purchaser would be required to pay 12 per cent interest on the balance of purchase monies owed. The contract also entitled the vendor, if the sale did not proceed by April 8, to issue a notice requiring completion within 28 days. In default of completion the vendor would be entitled to retain the deposit paid and regard the contract as having been rescinded and the land free for resale.

In late April, the purchaser having failed to complete on time, the vendor issued a notice to complete. There having been no completion in the interim, on May 30 the vendor wrote to the purchaser informing her that the contract had been rescinded on foot of the failure to comply (within 28 days) with the notice to complete. It was generally accepted that, but for the subsequent events, the contract had been validly rescinded for want of timely completion. The case essentially turned on the effect of subsequent events which, the purchaser claimed, revived her right to complete.

Despite the rescission of the contract, the parties and their legal teams continued to discuss the sale into June and July 2005. The purchaser, while in principle willing to close, contested a number of points. In particular, she claimed that the condition requiring her to build and maintain roads on the sold land was void for uncertainty. She further contested any liability to pay interest, which the vendor maintained was due under the contract.

On July 4 the purchaser was informed that the vendor was willing to close the contract on the original, unaltered terms, with a new deadline being set: 2pm on July 11, 2005. While there was some confusion and conflict as to precisely what was meant to happen by then, on the evidence the vendor had envisaged that the parties' lawyers would meet in the vendor's solicitor's office to close the contract. There having been some miscommunication in the interim between the various parties' solicitors, the parties never met up on that date. The purchaser's solicitor, Mr Gavin, was given mixed signals as to whether that meeting would go ahead. The vendor's solicitor, Mr Hickey, was on holiday at the time and it was suggested that his business partner, Mr Fowler, would take care of the closing. In a phone conversation at 11.30am on July 11, Mr Fowler indicated to Mr Gavin that while he was in court that day, the completion could take place the following day, July 12. Later that morning of July 11, Mr Gavin had transferred to the vendor's solicitors the €1.62 million balance owed in respect of the sale.

Notwithstanding Mr Fowler's assurance, Mr Hickey rang at 12.30 p.m. on July 11 demanding to know why Mr Gavin was not in his office. Despite the latter's indication that he was willing to complete on behalf of the purchaser, and had arranged to transfer the monies owing under the contract, Mr Hickey indicated that it was too late and that the sale was off.

Subsequently, the vendor claimed that as the conditions for reinstatement of the contract had not been met, and the sale had not been closed by the new deadline, the contract was again rescinded and the deposit forfeited. Her solicitors repaid the €1.62 million, notifying the purchaser that the contract was at an end, a sale to a new purchaser having been agreed. The purchaser nonetheless claimed specific performance of the agreement. In response, the vendor sought declarations to the effect that this was not possible as the contract had been validly rescinded on July 11.

The High Court granted the vendor's requested declarations (see the discussion in the *Annual Review of Irish Law 2006* (pp.251–253)), Laffoy J. concluding that the purchaser was not entitled to complete the sale. The judge ruled that the conditions precedent to completion had not been met by the new stipulated deadline of 2pm on July 11. In particular, she concluded, the purchaser had not recognised her liability to interest and would not have paid such interest.

In response to the claim that the vendor was estopped from relying on her right to treat the contract as rescinded, Laffoy J. noted that any such estoppel had been subject to meeting all of the contractual conditions, including the requirement to pay interest and to agree on the precise location of a right of way. The purchaser (Laffoy J. observed) had not in fact met these conditions, and was asserting instead her right to close on her own conditions. Although the vendor had suffered detriment in releasing the €1.62 million (and incurring a week's interest thereon), this detriment had not occurred on foot of the representation, which required full compliance with the terms of the contract. This included a commitment to pay interest, which the purchaser had (Laffoy J. claimed) continued to resist.

The High Court thus concluded that as the purchaser had not, by July 11, met the conditions for reinstatement of the contract, the vendor was entitled to regard her right to rescind as having been restored and the deposit legally forfeited. The purchaser had not proved willing to meet her end of the bargain and, as such, it was not unconscionable to allow the vendor to go back on her representation.

The Supreme Court (Geoghegan and Finnegan JJ.; Kearns J. concurring) disagreed with this conclusion. It observed that Mr Fowler's statement to Mr Gavin, that he would close on July 12, had the effect of extending by one day the time period during which closure could occur. The confusion between the vendor's solicitor and his business partner, Mr Fowler, had led to a situation where Mr Gavin was reasonably led to believe that the sale could be completed on July 12.

The issue of estoppel was central to the decision. The Supreme Court agreed that the contract had been validly rescinded as of May 30, 2005. Nonetheless, the vendor's subsequent representation that she was willing to complete on the original terms had revived the purchaser's right to complete. This representation gave rise to an estoppel such that the vendor was prevented from relying on the rescission, and the purchaser was given a fresh right to complete provided the originally agreed contract was closed by 2pm on July 11. The effect of the miscommunication, and in particular of Mr Fowler's deferral of the closure to July 12, was to extend the deadline for completion by one day. As regards detriment, the court was satisfied that the purchaser's action in transferring payment on July 11 (and incurring interest on that amount) was sufficient to amount to detriment on her part, such that the vendor could not resile from her representation to permit the delayed closure.

The court was satisfied that, despite some initial intimations to the contrary, the purchaser was willing to close based on the agreed terms of the original agreement. Whatever arguments had previously arisen, as of July 11 the purchaser was no longer contesting any aspect of the agreement, but had conceded that she would close on the originally agreed terms. In short, whatever the vendor was offering, the purchaser and her solicitor were willing to take.

Geoghegan J. concluded that the purchaser was reading and willing to close the sale by the extended deadline on the basis of the original agreement, fully intending to perform and comply with the terms of that agreement. He observed that while the purchaser had hoped she might escape liability to pay interest, she had in fact conceded, at the time of closing, that if interest was sought she would have to pay it. Thus, he ruled, the trial judge had erred in concluding that the purchaser had attempted to close "on her own terms", the purchaser having been both willing and able to pay the interest if this was the price of concluding the contract.

The court further observed that an estoppel had arisen based on the vendor's representation that she would accept completion by the extended deadline provided the contract was completed in accordance with the original terms, with no accepted deviations therefrom. The vendor had promised to permit completion in accordance with the contract by the new deadline (as extended). The purchaser had relied on this representation to her detriment by transferring the balance of the purchase monies (and thus incurring interest on those sums borrowed). This being the case, the vendor could not resile from the representation made.

Geoghegan J. observed that whether the estoppel was deemed to be based on common law estoppel by representation (based on a statement of existing fact) or the equitable remedy of promissory estoppel (based on a representation as to future conduct) was largely irrelevant. The two forms of estoppel, he noted, often overlapped. At any rate, he concluded, the common law remedy was no longer confined to representations of existing fact but extended to an "estoppel by convention". An estoppel by convention involved the parties agreeing inter se that they would act as though a particular fact were true (even if it were not). Here, while both parties knew that the contract had been lawfully rescinded, they acted on the artificial assumption that the contract remained alive if completed by the specified date in accordance with the original terms. As such, the vendor was bound to treat the agreement as if it had not been rescinded, and thus to allow completion on the original terms by the extended deadline.

Geoghegan J. moreover, appeared willing to gloss the orthodox view that estoppel can only be used as a "shield" and not a "sword", that it cannot be used to found a cause of action. Modern English case law, he noted:

"… demonstrates that while there may be a technical truth in this adage it is certainly irrelevant as far as having an operative effect. It certainly does not mean any longer, if it ever did mean it, that estoppel can only be used as a defence and never ground a cause of action."

As a result, the purchaser, although technically raising the issue of estoppel as part of her defence in response to the vendor's attempted rescission, was able to claim specific performance of a rescinded contract for the sale of land based on an estoppel. The vendor was estopped from raising the rescission as a bar to specific performance provided the purchaser was ready and willing to complete at the appointed date and time, extended by one day. Geoghegan J. agreed that she was willing and able to complete on all the agreed terms, and thus that the vendor was estopped from relying on the rescission.

Finnegan J. concurred. By virtue of the estoppel, the purchaser had been given an added opportunity to close by the extended deadline. She "was not afforded this opportunity" because the vendor had purported "… to resile at

12.30pm on the 11th July in advance of the time stipulated 2pm and indeed in advance of the altered date the 12th July 2005."

He also agreed that the purchaser had in fact completed on the agreed terms, the purchaser having effectively conceded that the interest was payable. Finnegan J. added that the remaining matters, being the right of way and the condition as to the building of roads and services on the sold lands, were not in fact in contention as "a term of the concession made by the vendor was that there should be completion in accordance with the contract". In other words, the purchaser had completed the sale in an unqualified manner on the terms as agreed and not on any purported terms of her own making.

This being the case, the court awarded specific performance of the contract, awarding interest for the delayed completion up to July 11, 2005.

FRUSTRATION

See *Mount Kennett Investment Company v O'Meara*, High Court, Smyth J., November 21, 2007, [2007] I.E.H.C. 420 (discussed below under SPECIFIC PERFORMANCE).

IMPLIED TERMS

See *Common Market Fertilizer SA v The Owners of the "MV Sonata"*, High Court, Butler J., March 7, 2007, [2007] I.E.H.C. 109 (discussed above under ARBITRATION AGREEMENTS); *Flynn v Dermot Kelly Ltd and New Holland Finance (Ireland) Ltd*, High Court, O' Neill J., March 16, 2007, [2007] I.E.H.C. 103 and *Kane v Massey Ferguson (Ireland) Ltd, Thomas Flynn and Sons Ltd and Agri Credit Ltd*, High Court, Irvine J., December 20, 2007, [2007] I.E.H.C. 457 (discussed below under SALE OF GOODS); and *Scaife v Falcon Leisure Group Ltd*, Supreme Court, December 4, 2007, [2007] I.E.S.C. 57 (discussed below under PACKAGE HOLIDAYS AND TRAVEL TRADE ACT 1995).

INCORPORATION OF TERMS BY REFERENCE

See *Common Market Fertilizer SA v The Owners of the "MV Sonata"*, High Court, Butler J., March 7, 2007, [2007] I.E.H.C. 109 (discussed above under ARBITRATION AGREEMENTS).

INSURANCE CONTRACTS

***Corrigan v Conway, Drumgoole and the Motor Insurers' Bureau of Ireland,
High Court, De Valera J., January 31, 2007, [2007] I.E.H.C. 32*** On August
7, 2000, the plaintiff, Ms Corrigan, was injured in a car accident. At the time,
her partner, Mr Drumgoole, was driving the car in which she was a passenger.
The car belonged to Ms Corrigan and Mr Drumgoole was not insured to drive
the vehicle.

Earlier in the evening, Ms Corrigan, who was five months pregnant, drove
the couple and their daughter to a restaurant in Rathmines. For this purpose
she used her own car. While in the restaurant, Ms. Corrigan started bleeding.
Worried that there might be complications arising from her pregnancy, she
asked to be taken to the Coombe maternity hospital. Mr Drumgoole drove the
car. En route, the vehicle was involved in a serious collision with another car.
The plaintiff having suffered injuries, she was taken by ambulance to St James'
Hospital (the nearest accident and emergency facility).

In an earlier ex tempore judgment, De Valera J. concluded that Mr Drumgoole
was responsible for the accident, awarding total damages of €54,160.57. Joseph
Drumgoole was not insured to drive the vehicle. Nonetheless, by virtue of a
1988 agreement between the Minister for the Environment and the Motor
Insurers' Bureau of Ireland (MIBI), the MIBI agreed to compensate persons
injured as a result of road accidents involving uninsured drivers, stolen vehicles
and unidentified or untraced drivers, to the full range of compulsory insurance
required by the Road Traffic Act 1961.

Paragraph 5(2) of the agreement, however, stipulates that the MIBI will not
accept liability where at the time of the accident the injured party "*knew, or
ought reasonably to have known, that there was not in force an approved policy
of insurance in respect of the use of the vehicle...*" (emphasis added). In other
words, the MIBI would not compensate a person who had been aware that the
driver was uninsured but willingly travelled with him or her regardless. The
question that consequently arose was whether, at the relevant time, Ms Corrigan
knew or ought reasonably to have known that her partner was not insured.

In *Kinsella v The Motor Insurers' Bureau of Ireland* [1992] I.E.S.C. 19,
Finlay C.J. observed that whether a claimant "ought reasonably have known"
that the driver was uninsured had to be determined by reference to the specific
context:

> "The issue is not: would a reasonable person have known, but
> rather: should the particular individual, having regard to all relevant
> circumstances, have known? For example, obviously, a person with
> defective reasoning or mental powers, or a young child, could not
> possibly be defeated by this clause."

Due to the urgent circumstances in which Ms Corrigan found herself, De Valera

J. was satisfied that neither she nor her partner had directed their attention to the issue of insurance. The plaintiff's medical state was, the judge considered, a "relevant circumstance" in determining her state of mind. Given the fact that she was five months pregnant and bleeding, it was reasonable to assume that she was in such a high state of anxiety that she could hardly have had the issue of insurance to "the forefront of her mind". It was "quite reasonable" to conclude, the judge believed, that the situation had fostered "... a degree of anxiety to such an extent that it drove from her, and from her partner's mind all other matters ..." and, in particular, had displaced any thoughts of insurance cover.

The judge thus concluded that the urgent medical circumstances that arose in the restaurant were "... sufficient to drive other matters, such as the insurance situation, from her mind". As a result, the judge concluded that the MIBI could not invoke para.5(2) of the 1988 Agreement, and was thus liable to pay compensation to the plaintiff. It is notable that the court enforced the agreement notwithstanding the fact that the plaintiff was not a party to it. While para.2 of the agreement confirms that a person claiming compensation may seek to enforce its terms, the agreement and its enforcement in this case raise a novel question about the application of the privity of contract doctrine, which (to their credit) neither the MIBI nor the judge saw fit to raise or consider.

James Power v Guardian PMPA Insurance Ltd, High Court, Laffoy J., February 2, 2007, [2007] I.E.H.C. 105   While this case largely turns on matters of statutory interpretation, some interesting points of contract law arise, including issues of privity of contract and the construction of a contract by reference to statutory requirements.

In 1991, the plaintiff (then aged 26) was involved in a car accident, as a result of which he sustained serious injuries. He had been a front seat passenger in a Ford Fiesta van driven by his friend, Mr Wheeler. While the defendant insurance company had insured the vehicle, it claimed that the insurance policy did not cover injuries to passengers travelling in the vehicle. It therefore refused to pay any insurance in respect of injuries to the plaintiff.

In the 1980s and 1990s, in response to high motor insurance premiums, many young male drivers purchased car-derived vans (such as the one involved in this case). While sharing many of the attributes of cars, these vehicles had been design-modified to allow them to be used for commercial purposes. The Ford Fiesta van in this case was, for instance, similar to the car of the same name, the main difference being that, in place of rear seats, it had an enlarged boot for carrying goods. Although this was generally suitable for commercial purposes, it was also popular among young males as it attracted lower taxes and more favourable insurance rates. In particular, there was a practice of insuring such vehicles under commercial policies, which were often cheaper than rates for private cars, a key drawback being the exclusion of cover for passengers.

The crux of the case against the defendant was that regulations made under the Road Traffic Act 1961 required that a vehicle constructed with the primary purpose of carrying passengers be insured in respect of injuries to passengers. Although the plaintiff claimed (based on contract) that the policy in fact covered front seat passengers, he further alleged that statutorily such a requirement arose with the result that the policy had to be read as covering front seat passengers. The plaintiff thus sought a declaration to the effect that Mr Wheeler was insured to carry passengers and that the defendant was required, as a result, to indemnify the driver in respect of the suit taken by the plaintiff.

Laffoy J. first considered the effect of statutory provisions requiring that motor vehicles be insured. Section 56 of the Road Traffic Act 1961 requires that a person shall not use in a public place a mechanically propelled vehicle unless it is:

> "… insured against all sums without limit … which the user … shall become liable to pay against any person (exclusive of the excepted persons) by way of damages or costs on account of injury to person or property caused by the negligent use of the vehicle at the time by the user".

Crucially, the section stipulates that there is no statutory obligation to insure "excepted persons", defined by s.65(1)(a) as meaning any person who is injured while in or on the insured vehicle, essentially either the driver or a passenger in the insured vehicle. In other words, as a general rule there is no statutory requirement to obtain passenger cover. The subsection allows, however, for statutory regulations to identify certain classes of vehicles in respect of which insurance *would* be required, in other words to remove certain persons from the definition of "excepted persons" if they were a driver or passenger in specified vehicles. Under the Road Traffic (Compulsory Insurance) Regulations 1962 (S.I. No. 14 of 1962) such vehicles were deemed to include in Reg.6(1)(b): *"vehicles constructed primarily for the carriage of one or more persons"* (emphasis added). In short, if the vehicle had been constructed principally to carry passengers, passenger cover would be statutorily required. (These measures preceded the implementation by subsequent 1992 Regulations of the Third Directive on Motor Insurance, Council Directive 90/232/EEC, which requires that cover be provided for *all* passengers where the vehicle contains *any* passenger seating. As the Directive did not have to be implemented until the end of 1995, the new provisions did not have the force of either EU or domestic law, until *after* the events arising in this case.)

The net question that thus arose was whether (under the 1962 Regulations) the vehicle had "been constructed primarily for the carriage of one or more passengers". Essentially, the plaintiff argued that regardless of the terms of the actual policy, the statutory obligation to insure against injuries to passengers required that the policy be read as including passenger cover. As the defendant company maintained that this was an approved policy, the plaintiff argued, it inevitably followed that if the vehicle had "been constructed primarily for the carriage of one or more passengers" the policy must necessarily include passenger cover.

Section 76 of the Road Traffic Act 1961 seeks to protect the interests of third parties. Effectively it circumvents the requirements of privity by allowing a person injured in a car accident, who is not the insured car owner, to sue the car owner's insurance company directly, if certain conditions apply. These conditions include the absence of the car owner from the State, the inability to locate the insured party or "…that it is for any reason just and equitable" to do so. However, s.76 only applies where the policy was in respect of insurance that the insured was legally required to have under the Act.

Laffoy J. remarked that in order to satisfy s.76, giving the plaintiff the right to sue the insurer, it was not sufficient that the vehicle was compulsorily insurable by law. The claimant was required first to establish that as *a matter of contract* an indemnity existed in respect of the claim. In other words, it was not enough to show that the indemnity was legally required in respect of passenger cover, but *that it was in fact in place* in the contract entered into by Mr Wheeler.

The judge then turned to consider the meaning of the phrase "vehicles constructed primarily for the carriage of one or more passengers". For this purpose she concluded that a vehicle is constructed "when it is ready to leave the factory capable of functioning as a mechanically propelled vehicle". The phrase thus meant, literally, "…vehicles put together or assembled principally for transporting one or more persons other than the driver." Regardless of whether the specific vehicle had evolved from a prototype intended for a different purpose, or as an embellishment of an older vehicle designed with other uses in mind, it was the state in which the particular vehicle had left the factory that was crucial in determining its primary purpose. Indeed the 1962 Regulations, she observed, also covered station wagons and estate cars adapted by the manufacturer so as to include passenger seats in the rear.

Applying these principles to the vehicle in this case, Laffoy J. concluded that Mr Wheeler's Ford Fiesta van was not a vehicle constructed primarily for the carriage of one or more passengers. Regardless of the use made of it, the vehicle had in fact been designed as a commercial vehicle, the main purpose of which was the transport of goods. Although it had been developed from the Ford Fiesta car (and was thus a "car-derived van"), it was properly to be considered a commercial vehicle, which meant that it attracted lower rates of excise duty and VAT than cars. Being a commercial vehicle, it also attracted a lower rate of road tax as well as a much lower rate of insurance than might otherwise have applied.

The key difference between the original Ford Fiesta model and the Ford Fiesta van was that, while there were two seats in the front, with seat belts, the rear of the van contained no seating, but instead a flat metal floor suitable for carrying goods. The original Fiesta car was indisputably designed to carry passengers. Whether the adapted van was also so designed:

> "... turns on whether, because of its construction, omitting the rear seats
> and thereby reducing its passenger-carrying capacity and correspondingly
> increasing its goods-carrying capacity, it can nonetheless be regarded
> as constructed principally for the carriage of persons."

This was, she ruled, a vehicle designed essentially for commercial, goods-carrying purposes. The fact that the vehicle had been embellished to give it a sportier appearance was not relevant for this purpose. While the various embellishments undoubtedly were calculated to make the vehicle more attractive to young males, this did not detract from the primary carriage function of the vehicle.

Thus, Mr Wheeler's vehicle did not fall within the class of vehicles in respect of which passenger cover was compulsory. As such, a commercial policy excluding passenger cover in respect of such a vehicle was legal. While Mr Wheeler was not in breach of the Road Traffic Act 1961 in carrying passengers, he nonetheless was exposing himself to liability for injury to the passenger, without the benefit of indemnifying insurance.

The judge further dismissed the claim that the policy *in fact* concluded between Mr Wheeler and the defendant only excluded passenger cover in respect of the rear of the vehicle and not the front seat. The policy documentation had expressly excluded cover for passengers. Mr Wheeler had, moreover, signed a waiver form specifically acknowledging that "...the policy does not include insurance cover for passenger risk". Notwithstanding some disagreement on this point, the judge was satisfied that the driver had been informed in advance that the policy excluded any passenger cover. In fact, when this point was again related to him after the accident, Mr Wheeler had not sought to challenge it or to take action to compel the defendant to indemnify him.

The issue of privity of contract was also raised. It was contended that as a matter of contract law, the plaintiff was precluded from reliance upon a contract to which he was not a party. While s.76 provided an exception to the privity rule, this applied only in respect of *insurance that must by law be obtained by the driver.* The plaintiff claimed, however, that an exception to the privity rule arose based on the "principled approach exception". The contract, he had (unsuccessfully) alleged, stipulated that Mr Wheeler would be indemnified in respect of front-seat passengers. As the plaintiff was a person in respect of whom such an indemnity would apply, the plaintiff had a common law right to enforce the insurance policy. In response, the judge remarked that:

> "That proposition, if it were correct, would seriously dent the doctrine
> of privity of contract...Even if there was a sound factual basis to support
> the plaintiff's proposition, I am not satisfied that it is sound in law."

While the Supreme Court of Canada had, she remarked, recognised the rights of "... a defendant third party sued by one contracting party to rely on a contractual term where the contracting parties had intended to extend the benefit of the term to the third party", the plaintiff's contention went "well beyond" this limited exception.

Thus, while sympathising with the plaintiff, Laffoy J. nonetheless concluded that the law "does not provide a remedy for him", at least against the insurance company.

INTERLOCUTORY INJUNCTIONS

***JRM Sports Ltd t/a Limerick Football Club v Football Association of Ireland*, High Court, Clarke J., January 31, 2007, [2007] I.E.H.C. 67**   The crux of this case was whether Limerick Football Club could be prevented from competing in the 2007 FAI League of Ireland. Given the brief timeframe involved, the injunction sought, though interlocutory, was likely to determine the matter of whether Limerick would participate in 2007.

In 2006, the FAI introduced new arrangements for the licensing of soccer clubs playing in the League with a view to "tightening up" processes for the administration of football. These were designed to enhance the professionalism and management of the League, including the manner in which clubs were administered and generally conducted their business. As part of the new régime, a more rigorous licensing procedure was put in place for 2007 participation in the League. Under these new arrangements, Limerick Football Club sought but was refused a licence, effectively excluding them from the League for the 2007 season. An appeal body established for this purpose upheld the exclusion that had been issued originally by the FAI's licensing committee.

In late January 2007, Peart J. granted an ex parte interim order temporarily preventing the FAI from negotiating or contracting with any other club to replace Limerick FC in the League. The club subsequently sought an interlocutory injunction effectively to allow the club to play in the League (starting March 2007) and to preclude any other club from playing in their place pending full trial of the issues.

Clarke J. first observed that the new licensing rules adopted by the FAI were clear, unambiguous and sufficiently intelligible to be understood by the average club official. He was, moreover, satisfied that the club was clearly and properly notified of the new, tighter licensing regime for 2007, including the existence of the appeal process. The purpose of the appeal process was to consider whether the conduct of the original licensing committee (which had refused the licence) had been fair and appropriate, and whether, moreover, the result represented a fair and reasonable outcome. In other words the appeal permitted a review both procedural and substantive in nature. In particular, the appeal body was entitled to take the view that the original outcome was overly severe, despite the fairness of the process adopted.

The judge noted that the arrangements under scrutiny were grounded in a contract between the parties. In signing the contract, the club officials had indicated that they were aware of and understood the relevant rules. Having signed the document, any consequences of failing to so familiarise themselves were, the judge ruled, "entirely their own fault".

Given the adverse effects of a negative finding, Clarke J. concluded that the contract included an implied term that the principles of natural justice would be observed and fair procedures applied in determining a licence application. Nonetheless, the central question that arose was whether the FAI was in breach of its contractual obligations. While it is required to act fairly, the contract clearly states that it is the FAI that decides on applications. The court's role in this case was confined, Clarke J. observed, to determining whether the decision was one that was open to the FAI to make, the judge having "...no role in deciding the merits or otherwise of who would be licensed".

Clarke J. noted that a decision would not be deemed irrational by a court "...unless the decision could not reasonably have been made on the materials that were available" (see *O'Keeffe v An Bord Pleanála* [1993] 1 I.R. 39). He was satisfied, in this regard, that there was "ample material" to justify the refusal to licence the club. In particular, the decision was "well supported by the documented failures of Limerick FC to comply with the process". Thus, the decision taken was one that the FAI was entitled to make.

A complaint regarding the composition of the appeal body was dismissed on the basis that a fully and properly composed body was convened in full compliance with the rules. Additionally, the plaintiff's confusion as to whether new evidence could be put before the appeals body was deemed to be confusion for which the club officials were solely responsible, it being abundantly clear from the rules that this was not permitted.

Likewise, the judge dismissed the claim that the club did not have adequate prior knowledge of the likelihood that their application would be dismissed. There were, he noted, obviously significant difficulties with the Limerick FC application. On any reasonable reading of the correspondence that the club had received from the FAI it would have been manifestly clear that their bid for a licence was in jeopardy. Indeed, having regard to the correspondence, the judge found that the club officials could not have been shocked by the refusal unless they "... had placed their heads so firmly in the sand and had refused to read what was written in clear terms".

The club alleged that it had been turned down on the grounds of financial difficulties that it was experiencing. It noted that other clubs that had been licensed were experiencing similar difficulties, a point accepted in court. The judge ruled, however, that it was not the club's financial weakness per se but rather the financial management of the club that had been a factor in refusing the licence. In particular, the club had failed to submit management accounts or to appoint an "appropriate financial officer". These were, the judge observed, not merely administrative matters, at least one club having dropped out of the previous year's League mid-season due to a lack of financing. As such, the FAI was fully entitled, given the commercial and sporting consequences of such an eventuality, to demand that proper financial management systems be in place. The complaint of prejudice due to their financial position per se was thus misplaced.

The club also complained about the failure of the appeal body to elicit the club officials' opinions on the severity of the decision against the club. The judge observed, however, that having sought the appeal, the onus was on the club to make the case that it had been severely treated. While the board was entitled to ask questions, it was not required to make the club's case for it. There was no evidence either that the board did not consider all relevant matters or that the club was refused an opportunity to put its case.

The judge also expressed some doubt as to accuracy of the evidence used to obtain the initial interim order made by Peart J. Where an interim injunction is sought ex parte there is a duty on the claimant to inform the court of all relevant facts, including those that might not favour its case. As only one side is represented, the claimant has a duty of candour in such circumstances, requiring that it "put[s] all the cards on the table". Manifestly, the judge observed, this had not happened here—indeed some of the facts were, he ruled, "distorted". In the context, the court had discretion to refuse to grant an order (even if otherwise merited):

> "... on the basis that the parties have abused their right of access to the Court by, in substance, misleading the Court by not putting forward all of the relevant facts."

In this case, the misstatements and omissions were "significantly material". There was thus considerable doubt whether Peart J. would have granted the order had he known the full facts. While Clarke J. was prepared to accept that the inaccuracies were accidental rather than deliberate, this conclusion did not favour the plaintiff. It meant, he observed, that the club's only defence to the charge that it had misled the court was that its officials "did not apply their minds" to the rules governing the process. Those rules being clear and intelligible, the plaintiff only had itself to blame if the process did not live up to its expectations.

A final complaint was made about the non-availability to the club of a report on the original conclusion of the licensing committee. While the rules required that a report on the refusal would be sent to the club five days in advance of the appeal, the club received this report only one day before the appeal body sat. The report was, moreover, emailed to the club officers after they had left Limerick to travel to Dublin for the appeal. As such, they did not have the report available to them in advance of the appeal.

Clarke J. dismissed this complaint. The short notice was justified as the FAI and the club had agreed to bring the appeal forward, thus making it impractical to provide the report five days in advance. Furthermore, if the officials had read the rules, they ought to have known that they were entitled to the report. If they had not received an advance copy, they should then have raised this with the appeals body. The fact that they had not seen the report in advance of the appeal was therefore largely their own fault. There was, moreover, nothing in the report which either (a) had not already been related to the plaintiff; or (b) which would not already have been apparent from a reading of the rules. The original FAI decision had been related by letter, which the plaintiff had received. In substance, the letter did not differ materially from the content of the report, the letter having addressed broadly the same issues that would have been apparent on a reading of the report. Having sight of the report, the judge concluded, would not have added anything to the club's ability to make its case on appeal.

The court thus ruled that Limerick FC had not made out its case for an interlocutory injunction. Even if the case had been made out that there was a fair issue to be tried, the judge was nonetheless satisfied that the balance of convenience lay with refusing an injunction.

The judge did concede, given the sporting considerations involved, that damages would not have provided an adequate remedy for either side. There were matters at stake that went beyond the realm of commerce, including club, city and county pride and the passion and commitment of players and supporters. Nevertheless, the judge also had to consider the interests of the FAI in promoting and managing the sport of soccer in Ireland. He was particularly reluctant to interfere in the FAI's governance function. While they were not above the law, sporting organisations should generally be allowed to "get on with the job" with which they were charged. This was "particularly so" when any proposed interference would potentially have significant implications:

> "If every time a party was able to pass the relatively low threshold of suggesting that it had a legal case against a sporting body and was able to interfere with the way in which that sporting body carried out the management of the sport on that basis it is likely that the administration of major sports would grind to a halt".

The overall effect on the management and administration of the sport was thus a factor attracting significant weight. In reality, Limerick FC was seeking a mandatory order, requiring the FAI to give it a licence against the clear view of the FAI that this was not appropriate. If granted, this would require the League to proceed for a full season with a team that the body charged with managing the sport believed, on sustainable grounds, should not be included. Thus, even if he had been satisfied that there was a fair issue to be tried, the judge stated that he would have declined to grant the injunction, the balance of convenience having been against so doing.

Clarke J. thus refused the injunction and vacated the interim order granted by Peart J. He added that it was not necessary for him to conclude whether or not the latter had been misled, as this was superfluous given his decision to refuse the requested injunction.

***Claystone Ltd, Oliver Barry and Noeleen Barry v Eugene Larkin, Twinlite Development and Dallus Developments Ltd*, High Court, Laffoy J., March 14, 2007, [2007] I.E.H.C. 89** This case concerns a dispute regarding the specifications for a house to be constructed in north-west Dublin. Although the plaintiffs had sought specific performance of an alleged contract, the key points at this stage were procedural, the plaintiffs having sought an interlocutory injunction and the defendants having sought a motion to dismiss the claim of the plaintiffs. The case illustrates the reluctance of the courts to dismiss a claim as being wholly without merit unless the case is clearly bound to fail, though the conclusion may usefully be contrasted with *Price v Keenaghan,* discussed below under SPECIFIC PERFORMANCE, where a motion to dismiss was accepted.

In April 2004, the first plaintiff agreed to sell a parcel of land comprising 6 acres to the first defendant for €3.45 million. The defendants intended to use the land to build houses for sale to the public. A special condition in the contract provided that two four-bedroom houses in the development would be sold to the first plaintiff or its nominees for €185,000 each. For this purpose the second and third plaintiffs, Oliver and Noeleen Barry, were nominated as beneficiaries, two sites being subsequently identified by Deed of Covenant.

The dispute centered on one of those sites that backed onto property in which Oliver and Noeleen Barry resided. The Barry family had acquired this site specifically with the intention of building a house (close to their own) for their son Ciarán and his family. The location of the house, backing onto the Barrys' existing home, made it more likely, they believed, that they would acquire planning permission for a larger house than originally envisaged.

With this in mind, in October 2005 Oliver Barry and Eugene Larkin (the first defendant) discussed the possibility that the house on the site closest to the Barrys' family home would be extended to provide a larger house for their son's family. The plaintiffs alleged that the parties agreed that Twinlite (the second defendant) would apply for planning permission for a larger home to be built on this site. They asserted, furthermore, the existence of an agreement that, if planning permission was obtained for a larger house, the price of the house would increase in proportion to the expanded floor space thereof.

In July 2006, the local authority granted planning permission for an extended house, the change in size being approved. The plaintiffs claimed that having obtained the planning permission, Ciarán Barry (the plaintiffs' son) and Michael Larkin (the first defendant's son) had agreed all necessary changes to the specifications for the home.

In October 2006, the defendants commenced building in line with the specifications for the larger house. Subsequently, however, a dispute arose between the parties as a result of which the defendants refused to build the house according to the changed specifications. Instead, they proceeded to build the smaller house, in line with the original plans. The plaintiffs claimed that this was a retaliation prompted by legal proceedings concerning the development of the estate. The defendants denied this, claiming that the reversion to the original plans stemmed from the delay of the Barry family in finalising negotiations for the building of the larger house.

The plaintiffs sought specific performance of the agreement to build the larger house. As an interim measure, they sought an interlocutory injunction preventing the defendants from building a smaller house on the site in line with the original plans. In response, the defendants sought a motion under Ord.19 r.28 of the Rules of the Superior Courts to strike out the plaintiffs' case on the ground that it disclosed no reasonable cause of action.

The court considered, first, the notice to strike out the action. Laffoy J. noted that, in addition to Ord.19, the court had an inherent jurisdiction to stay proceedings if "it is clear that the plaintiffs' claim must fail". She observed, however, that a court should be cautious in exercising this jurisdiction and should be slow to dismiss a case without clearly satisfying itself that the case had no merit. She noted in particular the possibility that facts that might initially appear to be clear might, in the light of oral evidence, "disclose a different picture". In sum, the judge must be satisfied that no matter what might transpire during the full trial of the action, the plaintiff would not succeed.

In support of the motion to dismiss, the defendants claimed that (a) there was no concluded agreement regarding the enlargement of the house; and (b) even if there was, it was not enforceable as there was no memorandum or note in writing, as required by the Statute of Frauds 1695.

The defendants first contended that there was no agreement varying the terms of the original bargain based on the original plans. The original agreement required only that the houses were to be of similar specification to those to be built elsewhere on the site, and there was no concluded agreement varying this commitment. In particular they alleged that as Ciarán Barry and Michael Larkin (the sons of the plaintiffs and first defendant respectively) were not parties to the original agreement, they could not have acted so as to vary that agreement. Laffoy J., however, rejected this particular claim, noting that Ciarán Barry had acted with full authority from his parents and with the full consent of both his father and the second defendant. It was clear also that Michael Larkin acted with full approval from the defendants.

The defendants went on to claim that there had been no agreement as to the revised specifications, and in particular the price of the enlarged house. The plaintiffs countered that while the price may not have been finally agreed, a mechanism for determining the price was in place. They further alleged that the specifications had been made known to the defendants in December 2006 and that there had been no objection to the specifications at that time.

Given the interlocutory nature of this case, it was not necessary to determine whether or not a sufficiently precise agreement had been reached. The key question was "whether it can be predicted with confidence that the plaintiffs will fail to establish a concluded agreement" on the variations proposed. Laffoy J. was satisfied that there was at least an arguable controversy as to the existence of a concluded agreement. As such the case could not be struck out on this ground.

As to the second contention, the defendants alleged that even if an agreement had been reached, it was unenforceable for lack of written evidence of its existence, as required by the Statute of Frauds 1695, s.2. A variation to a contract for the sale of land must also be evidenced in writing (*McQuaid v Lynam* [1965] I.R. 564).

The plaintiffs responded, contending that the agreement was enforceable notwithstanding the lack of written evidence. They first asserted that the contract was a building contract and not a contract for the sale of land. The second contention centred on the presence of acts of part performance. In the absence of a note or memorandum in writing, equity will allow the enforcement of the contract where there is a "concluded oral contract" and the plaintiff has taken steps that indicate an intention to perform the contract (see *Mackey v Wilde* [1998] 2 I.R. 578). In order for this rule to apply, the defendant must have "induced such acts or stood by while they were being performed" such that it would be unconscionable to allow the defendant to plead the Statute of Frauds.

The plaintiffs argued that Ciarán Barry's conduct in seeking and paying for planning permission for the new house and finalising the new specifications constituted acts of part performance. The defendants countered that the acts relied on as part performance did not in fact meet the test set out. First they contended that the acts of the defendants could not be relied upon as part performance by the plaintiffs, a point accepted by the judge as accurate though she added that such activities may be "evidentially significant". She nonetheless rejected the contention that the actions of Ciarán Barry and his wife could not be regarded as amounting to part performance as they were not parties or plaintiffs. This was, she claimed, unmeritorious, Ciarán Barry having acted at all times with the full authority and blessing of the plaintiffs. Nor did she accept that the negotiations and planning for the larger house commenced only after planning permission therefor was obtained in December 2006.

Laffoy J. acknowledged that it was not necessary, in interlocutory proceedings, to determine whether there was or was not an enforceable contract. This conclusion depended on the evidence put forward at trial as to acts of part performance and the judge's assessment of that evidence. It was by no means a foregone conclusion that the plaintiffs would fail to establish the enforceability of the agreement. "[I]t cannot", she concluded, "be confidently predicted that the plaintiffs are bound to fail."

The judge further accepted that the argument could be made that the agreement was a building agreement rather than an agreement for the sale of land, and thus not subject to the Statute of Frauds. Laffoy J. agreed that it was at least possible that such an agreement could legitimately be the subject of specific performance, notwithstanding the courts' traditional reluctance to grant specific performance of building agreements. The plaintiffs thus at least had an "arguable case" that specific performance would be an appropriate remedy.

In short there was a fundamental conflict of fact on several aspects of the case, such that the judge could not conclude with confidence that the plaintiffs were bound to fail. The defendants thus were denied relief either under Ord.19. r.28 or under the inherent jurisdiction of the court.

In relation to the application for an interlocutory injunction, Laffoy J. observed that as the defendants had failed to establish that the plaintiffs' case was without merit, it necessarily followed that there was a bona fide question for determination in the case. As to the adequacy of damages, the house to be built was adjacent to the Barry family home, and was intended specifically as the residence of their immediate family. Given these unique circumstances, the judge was satisfied that damages would not be adequate if they were to succeed in their claim.

Furthermore, if the planned smaller house were allowed to proceed to completion, and the plaintiffs were to win their case, the prospect of its demolition and the reconstruction of a larger house would be slim. Although the defendants had offered to demolish the smaller house if the plaintiffs were successful, Laffoy J. felt that besides being unnecessarily wasteful, this was unlikely to occur. The courts were, she felt, reluctant to order demolition. On the other hand, damages would be an appropriate remedy if the defendants were to succeed, the loss being quantifiable, and there being no suggestion or evidence that the plaintiffs would be unable to pay damages to the defendants, should the remedy of specific performance be refused.

The balance of convenience, the judge concluded, lay in favour of granting the interlocutory injunction, restraining the building of the smaller house pending trial. Laffoy J. reminded the parties that the court is not required in interlocutory proceedings to resolve conflicts of evidence or to determine the facts. Nor is the judge expected to determine the applicable law, which, she added, called for "detailed argument and mature consideration". While difficult issues of law and fact arose for determination, given the interlocutory nature of the proceedings, it was not possible to conclude definitively on these matters. The judge's function in these interlocutory proceedings was simply to determine "whether the plaintiff's case was hopeless" and, if it was not, whether it was appropriate to maintain the status quo pending trial.

INTERPRETATION OF CONTRACTS

See also *James Power v Guardian PMPA Insurance Ltd*, **High Court, Laffoy J., February 2, 2007, [2007] I.E.H.C. 105 (discussed above under INSURANCE CONTRACTS) and** *McCabe Builders (Dublin) Limited v Sagamu Developments Ltd, Laragan Developments Ltd and Hanly Group Ltd*, **High Court, Charleton J. November 23, 2007, [2007] I.E.H.C. 391 (discussed below under OFFER AND ACCEPTANCE).**

Collins v J Ray McDermott SA, **Supreme Court, March 29, 2007, [2007] IESC 14** This case concerned the interpretation of an employment contract, and in particular the application of the *contra proferentum* rule thereto. The net issues in this case are the effect of a binding agreement that an injured employee would be paid compensation until "maximum medical improvement" occurred, and the impact of unrelated intervening injuries on that obligation.

The plaintiff in this case, a professional diver, had been injured while working for the defendant. The accident occurred in Dubai in August 1996 on a ship which had been chartered by the defendant. The plaintiff had been working as a diver laying pipes. While on board the ship he had fallen down a staircase and was consequently hospitalised for nine days. His injuries included cerebral contusion, hearing loss coupled with tinnitus in his right ear, and shoulder injuries. The accident also gave rise to a heightened risk of epilepsy, though it was accepted by all parties that this risk would recede to normal levels within five years of the accident.

Having failed in a negligence claim against the defendant, the plaintiff sought to enforce the terms of an employment contract that he claimed applied in this case. The plaintiff was unable to establish the precise terms of the employment contract. The defendants had, however, in September 1996, issued a letter to the plaintiff after the accident in which they had agreed to pay:

> "...$150 a day in worker's compensation disability pay (maintenance). After two months you will receive pay of $75 per day for up to an additional ten months or until you are at maximum medical improvement".

While agreeing that this letter represented the contract of the parties in relation to disability pay, the parties fell out over the precise meaning of this commitment. Although the defendant had ceased payments in 1998, the plaintiff claimed that he was entitled to continue receiving payments until 2001, when he had been due to reach maximum medical improvement.

There was, however, a complicating factor. In April 1998 the plaintiff contracted meningitis and had an epileptic fit. Counsel for the plaintiff conceded that this could not be attributed to the accident, i.e. that this intervening incident could not be causally linked to the 1996 head injury. The defendant argued that this intervening event effectively relieved it of any obligations towards the plaintiff, the new circumstances having ruled out any chance of the plaintiff returning to work as a diver. The plaintiff countered that notwithstanding the intervening illnesses, the plaintiff was still entitled to payments up to the point of maximum medical improvement. Arguing that the heightened risk of epilepsy continued for five years following the accident, the plaintiff claimed that the payments should continue until August 2001.

In the High Court Murphy J. (December 18, 2003) noted that the defendant had, by paying a sum of $46,200, "acceded to an obligation to compensate for a period up to maximum improvement". The contractual terms, he concluded, "were not limited to the two months' full compensation and ten months' half compensation" but instead required the defendant to maintain payments until Mr Collins had reached a point where he could improve no further. The date of maximum improvement was, he concluded, October 1998. As a result he ordered that a sum of $13,650 be paid, representing the balance due up to the date of maximum improvement.

The High Court judge had, however, dismissed the plaintiff's claim in negligence. On appeal by the plaintiff, the Supreme Court upheld this verdict in relation to negligence. The Supreme Court proceeded, however, to hear a cross-appeal from the defendant in respect of the damages paid on foot of the contractual claim.

The issues on appeal to the Supreme Court boiled down to the following:

— What obligations were owed on foot of the 1996 letter?

— What was the effect of the intervening events? Did these events have the effect of frustrating or nullifying the obligation of support?

Speaking for the Court, Kearns J. observed first that in so far as there was any ambiguity in the letter, the benefit of the doubt would be given to the plaintiff. This was in line, he noted, with the *contra proferentum* rule, requiring that any ambiguity arising in respect of the meaning of a contract should be resolved in favour of the person who did not draft the contract. The rationale behind this rule is compelling: the person who wrote the contract (the *proferens*) has been afforded the opportunity to shape the contract as he or she sees fit. If the *proferens* had, in the process, failed to be clear, it was only fair that he or she suffer the consequences.

The court agreed that the letter was ambiguous. In this case, it was certainly open to suggest that the obligation terminated at the expiry of 12 months. However, the alternative interpretation—that payment would continue until the plaintiff had reached maximum medical improvement—was also open. Given the conflicting interpretations, the one most favourable to the plaintiff was to be preferred.

Maximum medical improvement, the court accepted, related only to improvement in respect of the specific injury caused in 1996, and did not embrace recovery from illnesses unrelated to the accident. The court concluded that the period of maximum medical improvement was five years, being the time within which the risk of epilepsy would subside to normal levels.

The defendant, however, had argued that the intervening events relieved them of this obligation. The court observed, first, that the onus was on the employer to prove that this was the legal effect of the subsequent illnesses. The defendant had cited no authority for this proposition. The 1996 letter had been written after the accident, the defendant having been aware that recovery may have taken some time. The court agreed that the events of 1998 had increased the plaintiff's risk of further epileptic fits. They had *not*, however, *replaced the original risk* attendant on the 1996 accident. The 1998 events, in other words, added "an additional risk" but in no way replaced or reduced the prospect of epilepsy attendant on the 1996 accident.

The defendant had argued that the plaintiff should only be paid while unfit to work as a diver. The court disagreed, interpreting the contract as meaning that the payments were to be made until maximum medical improvement occurred, even if he had been fit to return to work. The court did agree that if the plaintiff had died in 1998 the obligation to make payments would have ceased (further medical improvement being impossible on death), though this did not detract from the obligation to pay in this case. The court distinguished between the termination of the contract of employment and the termination of the obligation to make payments in respect of the accident, noting that the obligation to make payments was not contingent on the continuation of the diver's employment.

The undertaking in this case was to make payments until such time as the plaintiff reached maximum medical improvement in respect of the injuries sustained in 1996. This was undertaken with full knowledge of the extent of the injuries sustained. The defendant had thus bound itself to pay the plaintiff until such time as medical recovery was complete. On the evidence this was after five years, Kearns J. adding that he could:

> "... see no reason in these circumstances why the [defendant] should obtain some windfall bonus because the plaintiff contracted meningitis and epilepsy for unrelated reasons. If anything these matters can, on one view, be seen as pushing further away the point of maximum physical recovery for the occupational injury though that case has not been pursued."

The Supreme Court thus concluded that the plaintiff was entitled to payments under the letter for five years, that is, until August 2001. They thus upheld the verdict that the contractual claim was well-founded, but varied the date on which payments were due to end from October 1998 (as per the High Court decision) to August 2001.

OFFER AND ACCEPTANCE

See *Price and Lynch v Keenaghan Developments Ltd*, **High Court, Clark J., May 1, 2007, [2007] I.E.H.C. 190 (discussed below under SPECIFIC PERFORMANCE).**

McCabe Builders (Dublin) Limited v Sagamu Developments Ltd, Laragan Developments Ltd and Hanly Group Ltd, **High Court, Charleton J. November 23, 2007, [2007] I.E.H.C. 391** This intricate case concerns the issue of contract formation, specifically whether the parties had entered into a concluded building contract in respect of the development of lands in Kilmacanogue, Co. Wicklow. The case is typical of the "battle of the forms" type scenario, a dispute having arisen as to whether a contract had been agreed (if at all) based on the plaintiff's specifications or those proposed by the defendants. The crux of the decision, however, was that the parties had in fact reached no conclusion at all. There had been no meeting of minds on fundamental matters, in particular whether the defendants or plaintiff had accepted certain risks in respect of the development.

The defendants in this case (which were related development companies), wished to build 32 houses and 14 apartments at a site named (quite appropriately, as it turned out) "Rocky Valley". In July 2005, the plaintiff building company successfully tendered for the project, a price of €15.3 million ex VAT subsequently being agreed. In late August of the same year the defendants issued a letter of intent so as to facilitate the commencement of work valued at €1 million. In November 2005 the defendants sent the plaintiff a RIAI-issued standard form contract, which was signed by the plaintiff in January 2006.

The parties nonetheless conflicted as to the nature and terms of the contract. The plaintiff contended that it was entitled to extra payment in respect of unforeseen difficulties with the work, the project having been complicated by a number of unforeseen factors. These included:

•   The amount of rock required to be excavated which, the plaintiff claimed, was approximately 20 times what was originally represented to it;

•   Delays and difficulties involved in carrying out work due to boundary disputes about which the plaintiff had not originally been informed;

•   Alleged changes in the specifications for the building works, which changes were denied by the defendants.

The net result of these and other problems was a 40-week delay in completion of the project.

The defendants argued that it was their understanding that the contract was a fixed-price contract. In essence they contended that money claimed by the plaintiff for "overruns" in the project was not due, as the work carried out was part of the plaintiff's original contractual obligations. The plaintiff, for its part, claimed that they were entitled to be paid extra in respect of aspects of the work that had proved more costly than originally anticipated. The nub of the case was whether the risk of such extra costs had been assigned by the contract to the plaintiff, or alternatively rested with the defendants.

A number of matters were in contention. Chief amongst them was the contractual status of a bill of quantities ("BOQ") issued as part of the tender process. A bill of quantities is a bidding document itemising the materials and labour required for construction work. Typically such a document would also include the quantity of items needed and their unit or cost price. When issued with a request for tenders, a BOQ allows the tenderers to estimate with greater accuracy the likely cost price of the building works. Each tenderer would set out, beside each item, its proposed rate in respect of that item and the tenders would be compared and judged on that basis.

The issue was important for the following reason: if the bill of quantities formed part of the agreement, the parties would be taken to have agreed that the plaintiff accepted all risks (including that of unforeseen costs arising) in respect of the project. Essentially, the plaintiff would be required to carry out the works at the agreed rates and would not be able to claim extra for overruns or unforeseen costs.

Charleton J. concluded that the bill of quantities had not formed part of the contract. The defendants, he observed, had chosen to rely on the "blue form" of the RIAI standard form of building contract, which it had issued to the plaintiff following the conclusion of the tender process. This form expressly *excluded* the bill of quantities from forming part of the contract, the BOQ becoming merely a schedule of rates for the materials and work. Thus, although the plaintiff had signed the BOQ, it had done so in a context where the blue form of contract expressly excluded the BOQ from forming part of the contract. Indeed the standard form document employed by the parties contained an express heading in bold stating that quantities did not form part of the contract. While the parties had every opportunity to amend the contract so as to incorporate the BOQ, they had not done so.

Notably the standard form contract had offered two alternate clauses, the first of which included the BOQ as a contractual document, stating that the contract sum would provide for the quality and quantity of work set out therein. The parties, however, had expressly chosen a second alternate clause, which excluded the BOQ from the contract, with the contractor instead providing a schedule of rates in respect of the work. The parties had specifically crossed out and initialed the crossing out of the first alternative, thereby preferring the second alternative clause.

In determining the true import of the contract, Charleton J. noted that the intention of the parties was crucial, but must be elicited by reference to the words that the parties have chosen to express their meaning, gauged against the surrounding circumstances. Given that the defendants had drafted the contractual documents, the judge added, the onus was on them to establish the assignment of risk to the plaintiff. They "had charge of the form and wording of the documents". If they wished to confer full risk on the plaintiff they could have done so by expressing this intention in clear and suitable language. Yet they had not done so.

Citing *Interfoto Picture Library Limited v Stiletto Visual Programmes Limited* [1989] Q.B. 433, Charleton J. indicated that any ambiguities in the documents would be construed against the defendants. Given the onerous nature of the suggested allocation of risk to the plaintiff, "an unusually high level of notice must be given of it", the judge adding that:

> "[A] clause imposing an unusual obligation, and departing from a standard printed form, should not be so unclear in terms of its wording as to attract two days of evidence from expert witnesses on each side of this case, as to what it means within the context in which it occurs."

In sum, far from providing clearly that the BOQ should be included, the Articles of Agreement expressly negated such inclusion. It thus "... becomes impossible to conclude that the parties have agreed that descriptions in the Bill of Quantities should be part of the contract obligation."

The defendants nonetheless contended that the course of dealings between the parties, comprised of a number of letters, documents and discussions, evidenced an agreement to displace this express provision, thus incorporating into the contract the descriptions in the BOQ. The judge noted that in tender situations not subject to public procurement rules, it is possible for negotiations after tender to yield an agreement different from that envisaged by the successful tender. The question here is whether such an agreement was reached. Charleton J. thus turned to consider the course of the negotiations with a view to determining whether a contract had been concluded and, if so, on what terms.

It was clear that the defendants had a formed a firm intention that the price paid to the plaintiff would be all-inclusive, a fixed-cost price, the risk being placed firmly on the plaintiff. The judge concluded, however, that the parties had failed to define their obligations in respect of this matter. In particular, the judge ruled that negotiations and discussions leading up to the commencement of work had not resulted in any agreement on the key point as to whether the BOQ would form part of the contract.

In short, the matter of who bore the risk had never been contractually agreed. The parties had never confirmed what the contractual obligations were, and what would happen if extra work was to be performed above and beyond these obligations. Given the complex and intricate nature of building contracts, the judge was satisfied that no "prudent contractor" would have concluded a building agreement in the absence of a detailed and specific contract containing carefully outlined obligations. Indeed the issuing of a letter of intent on August 26 confirmed the view that there was no concluded contract. In the judge's view, the letter was sought and given precisely "because of the absence of a contract", the terms still to be agreed being far from minimal. The letter specifically suggests, indeed, that the parties would "sign a contract in the not too distant future, thus expressly acknowledging the "absence of [a] fully signed contract".

Subsequently, relations deteriorated seriously, due in part to the difficulties encountered on site and consequent delays in completion. In November 2005, the contract documentation was sent to the plaintiff. While the plaintiff signed the RIAI standard contract form included with the documentation, it refused to acknowledge as contractually binding any earlier correspondence it had received from the defendant, which correspondence had suggested that the price to be paid was "all-inclusive". While the defendant asserted that the earlier correspondence formed an integral part of the contract, the plaintiff disputed this, claiming that the RIAI blue form applied and declining to sign these letters (thus refusing to acknowledge their contractual status).

Charleton J. noted that it was essential "that the minds of the parties should meet as to their mutual obligations". These obligations must, moreover, be expressed in such a way as to allow them to be ascertained with reasonable certainty. While the law provided various devices to ascertain the true meaning of an ambiguous contract, the court could not imply terms so as to provide clarity where the parties in fact were not *ad idem* as to the fundamental obligations in the contract. Citing *Mackey v Wilde (No. 2)* [1998] 2 I.R. 578, the judge observed that:

> "If parties are at cross purposes as to the meaning of a crucial term, or where an ambiguity in a crucial term cannot be clarified by reference to the dealings between the parties, the business context within which it occurred, commercial efficacy, or plain sense, then there has been a failure to form a contract".

The judge concluded that there had been no concluded contract. Fundamentally "the minds of the parties never met as to central issues that are crucial to their different understandings of what would otherwise be their mutual obligations." The parties had never agreed, in particular, the crucial matter of pricing and responsibility for unforeseen extra costs in completing the works. The parties held two completely opposing views of their mutual obligations, the defendants believing that the contract was an all-in, fixed-price affair with no provision for excess claims, while the plaintiff assumed that it would be recompensed for the extra costs ensuing. There was no agreement on a fundamental matter central to the negotiations, and thus no binding contract.

The final issue related to work completed by the plaintiff. Charleton J. ruled that, in the absence of a concluded contract, the plaintiff was to be remunerated on a *quantum meruit* basis. This allows for compensation to be awarded where the parties erroneously believe that there is a valid contract or that such a contract will soon be finalised. Unless the party doing the work has accepted the risk that a contract may not be finalised, the court will award what it considers reasonable compensation for the work, to prevent unjust enrichment.

The precise amount of compensation was to be fixed in arbitration. For guidance, however, the judge noted that the plaintiff was entitled to reasonable recompense for work already done in respect of the benefits conferred. This work should be valued "…on a basis that allows for reasonable remuneration to the plaintiff" based on 2005 values. In setting such remuneration, the arbitrator should take account of the defendants' right to reasonably competitive value from the plaintiff.

PACKAGE HOLIDAYS AND TRAVEL TRADE ACT 1995

Scaife v Falcon Leisure Group Ltd, **Supreme Court, Hardiman J., Fennelly J., Macken J., December 4, 2007, [2007] I.E.S.C. 57** This case concerns the interpretation of the Package Holidays and Travel Trade Act 1995. In particular, it highlights the potential liability of travel agents for injuries sustained to consumers as a result of the negligence of suppliers of services based in foreign countries.

Ms Scaife, the plaintiff, had booked a package holiday through the defendant, Falcon Leisure Group. The package offered half board (lodgings, breakfast and evening meals) at a hotel in Salou, Spain, the holiday taking place in May 1998. The hotel was, the High Court concluded, generally of a good standard, a point underlined by the fact that this was a return visit for the plaintiff and others in her group.

On May 21, 1998, Ms Scaife was having her evening meal in the hotel. While walking towards the buffet table, she slipped on liquid foodstuff that had previously been spilled on the tiles directly adjacent to the table, sustaining injuries as a result. The High Court accepted that she could not have seen the spillage. There was, moreover, no sign or warning in place to indicate its presence.

The net question that arose for consideration was whether and to what extent the holiday organiser was liable for the plaintiff's injuries. The question turned ultimately on the interpretation of s.20 of the Package Holidays and Travel Trade Act 1995, which had transposed into Irish law EC Council Directive 91/314/EEC of June 13, 1990 on package travel, package holidays and package tours.

Section 20 of the 1995 Act indicates that ordinarily the organiser will be held liable for any damage caused by the failure to perform the contract or the improper performance of the contract. Section 20(1) states that:

> "The organiser shall be liable to the consumer for the proper performance of the obligations under the contract, irrespective of whether such obligations are to be performed by the organiser, the retailer, or other suppliers of services but this shall not affect any remedy or right of action which the organiser may have against the retailer or those other suppliers of services".

Section 20(2) provides a defence where the failure or improper performance is due neither to any fault of the organiser or the retailer nor to that of another supplier of services, but rather:

— are attributable to the consumer;

— are attributable to a third party unconnected with the provision of the services contracted for, and are unforeseeable or unavoidable; or

— are due to force majeure or an event which the organiser, the retailer or the supplier of services, even with all due care, could not foresee or forestall.

It was accepted that, for the purposes of the 1995 Act, the defendant was the "organiser" of a "package holiday", Ms Scaife a "consumer" and the hotel proprietor a "service supplier". The main point of controversy was whether and to what extent a package organiser can be deemed liable for the conduct of service suppliers with which the organiser has contracted.

The High Court (Herbert J.) acknowledged that the organiser was not required to act as an insurer in respect of any injury or damage sustained on the holiday. The court nonetheless concluded that the package organiser could be held responsible for negligent conduct on the part of the supplier. In an ex tempore decision, Herbert J. observed that the hotel proprietor had an implied legal duty "…to take reasonable care to ensure that his hotel was reasonably safe and was maintained in a reasonably safe condition for visitors to the hotel." Although the hotel was generally of a good standard, it had failed in this case to implement an appropriate system to avoid an accident occurring, in particular in failing to put in place a sufficiently clear warning of the risk.

Although the accident was not attributable to any negligence on the part of the organiser per se, Herbert J. had agreed that, on an interpretation of the Directive and of s.20 of the Act, the organiser was liable for the supplier's lack of reasonable care. The intention of the Directive, he noted, was to allow holidaymakers who are injured during a package holiday to sue the organiser of the package rather than the supplier of the service. The purpose of this facility was to avoid the considerable cost and inconvenience that would otherwise have arisen had the consumer been obliged to sue the supplier in a foreign country. The holidaymaker would instead be able to take action in the Irish courts against the organiser with whom it arranged the holiday, obviating the need to take expensive and time-consuming proceedings abroad. The High Court noted that:

> "[A]lthough in this case Falcon Leisure Group (Overseas) Ltd. could be said to have done nothing wrong whatsoever … because of the business which they are in, that is organising and selling package tours, they have to accept as one of the downsides of that, that they will be responsible if somebody providing a [service] does not properly perform the contract".

Herbert J. added that, if sued, it would be open to the organiser to pursue the actual tortfeasor for compensation.

On appeal, the Supreme Court (per Macken J., Hardiman and Fennelly JJ. concurring) upheld this verdict. Speaking for the whole court, Macken J. agreed that the Act did not require the organiser to act as an insurer or guarantor against any injury however sustained on the holiday. Nor was the Act imposing a rule of strict liability. Nonetheless, she observed, s.20 imposed primary liability on the organiser of the package holiday for any failure or improper performance in relation to the contract. While maintaining a right in favour of the organiser to sue the service supplier, the Act clearly permitted the consumer to sue the organiser in respect of the deficiency in performance, irrespective of the fact that the organiser itself was not at fault. The fact that the performance of the contract is delegated to other parties does not detract from the organiser's core obligation. The obligations under the contract remain those of the organiser and "do not become the independent obligations of the service supplier".

Macken J. rejected the proposition that the organiser was merely facilitating a contract between the supplier and consumer, a point that, she observed, had been clarified by the Act. Even if a lower standard applied in Spain (which had not, in any case, been established), the Directive favoured a high level of protection for consumers and thus required the interpretation most favourable to the consumer. Macken J. thus concluded that "…the standard by which the acts in question are to be judged is that of reasonable skill and care" in the performance of the contract. If not expressly contained in the relevant contract, such a standard would, she added, be "readily implied".

Furthermore, the judge agreed that there had been improper performance within the meaning of s.20. The organiser's obligations were not confined to ensuring that the hotel structure itself was physically safe. The plaintiff had contracted for bed and half board, which included the provision of an evening meal. The exercise of reasonable skill and care in the provision of this particular aspect of the service was a necessarily implied condition. The judge concluded that, in the circumstances, the hotel had not exercised reasonable skill and care in relation to the spillage. The plaintiff, moreover, could not reasonably have been expected to see or avoid the spillage, nothing having been done to warn customers or to divert them from the spot. Macken J. thus upheld the High Court verdict that reasonable skill and care had not been applied. The appeal was dismissed, and the appellant deemed liable for the injuries caused.

The case illustrates the potency of the 1995 Act. The Act places the primary responsibility of ensuring due skill and care on the organiser of the package holiday. The merits of this approach are considerable. The consumer makes a contract with the organiser of the holiday. The consumer may not necessarily choose or even know the identity of the supplier of hotel accommodation, meals and flights. The organiser makes all these arrangements, the consumer having no say in or influence over the terms agreed with third parties. The costs, inconvenience and other difficulties involved in requiring a consumer to pursue a claim in a foreign country are easy to appreciate. The issue of privity of contract also arises: the consumer may have difficulty enforcing a supply contract to which he or she was not a direct party. The tour operator, moreover, is clearly in a better position to recoup damages than the consumer, having a better appreciation of doing business in the relevant foreign country. It is furthermore better placed to negotiate with suppliers for just such an eventuality and to secure insurance against injuries arising to customers. Given that the tour operator supplies considerable business to a supplier, it is in a much stronger position than the average consumer to insist on favourable terms.

PRIVITY OF CONTRACT

See *Flynn v Dermot Kelly Ltd and New Holland Finance (Ireland) Ltd,* **High Court, O' Neill J., March 16, 2007, [2007] I.E.H.C. 103 and** *Kane v Massey Ferguson (Ireland) Ltd, Thomas Flynn and Sons Ltd and Agri Credit Ltd,* **High Court, Irvine J., December 20, 2007, [2007] I.E.H.C. 457 (discussed below under SALE OF GOODS);** *Corrigan v Conway, Drumgoole and the Motor Insurers' Bureau of Ireland,* **High Court, De Valera J., January 31, 2007, [2007] I.E.H.C. 32 and** *James Power v Guardian PMPA Insurance Ltd,* **High Court, Laffoy J., February 2, 2007, [2007] I.E.H.C. 105 (discussed above under INSURANCE CONTRACTS); see** *Scaife v Falcon Leisure Group Ltd,* **Supreme Court, December 4, 2007, [2007] I.E.S.C. 57 (discussed above under PACKAGE HOLIDAYS AND TRAVEL TRADE ACT 1995).**

PUBLIC POLICY

Uniform Construction Ltd v Cappawhite Contractors Ltd, **High Court, Laffoy J., August 29, 2007, [2007] I.E.H.C. 295 (discussed above under ARBITRATION AGREEMENTS).**

QUANTUM MERUIT

See *McCabe Builders (Dublin) Limited v Sagamu Developments Ltd, Laragan Developments Ltd and Hanly Group Ltd*, **High Court, Charleton J. November 23, 2007, [2007] I.E.H.C. 391 (discussed above under OFFER AND ACCEPTANCE).**

RESTRAINT OF TRADE

Eamon Finnegan v J & E Davy, **High Court, Smyth J., January 26, 2007, [2007] I.E.H.C. 18** This case concerns a relatively novel manifestation of the rule against restraint of trade in employment contracts. The verdict illustrates that a unilaterally imposed term deferring payment of a portion of yearly bonuses and making its payment contingent on employees not leaving to work for a competitor is a clause in restraint of trade and thus void. Notably, the case illustrates that a contract may be in restraint of trade even if it does not in fact physically prevent the employee from working for a competitor provided that it unfairly and unjustifiably penalises the employee for doing so.

In September 1990 the plaintiff, Mr Finnegan, was offered and accepted a job with the defendant, a stockbroking firm based in Dublin. During his time at the company, a bonus scheme was in operation. Bonuses were awarded based on the company's performance as well as that of the individual employee. In January 1992, he received his first bonus in respect of the year 1991 and this practice continued in subsequent years.

For 1997, the plaintiff was awarded a bonus of IR£100,000. IR£60,000 of this was to be paid upfront but in contrast with previous years' bonuses the remaining IR£40,000 would be retained and paid the following year. The plaintiff was informed that the deferred sum would only be paid if he stayed with the firm. While he objected to this, he had little choice, the judge found, but to accept. It was conceded that the money would be paid to an employee leaving to pursue a career in a different field. If, however, the employee left to work with a competing stockbroking firm, the deferred payment would not be paid. This distinction was, the judge considered, particularly relevant. The money was not being retained to finance the recruitment of replacement staff or to compensate for loss of experienced staff. Thus the condition had not been imposed generally to discourage staff from leaving. The clear purpose of the new scheme was, rather, to prevent staff *taking up employment with a competitor.*

In 1998 the plaintiff earned a IR£200,000 bonus, but this was, he learned, to be split three ways, a third being deferred for payment until 1999 and a third until 2000, conditional again on his remaining with the firm. Again the plaintiff objected, remarking that this delayed his receipt of the full monies by two years, though the deferred sums would attract interest. The judge was satisfied again that he had not acquiesced in the situation.

In September 2000, the plaintiff left to work for NCB Stockbrokers. In response, the defendant refused to pay IR£65,000 retained in respect of the year 1998 and IR£140,000 retained in respect of the year 1999. The plaintiff sued for these sums, totalling, with interest, IR£260,000.

Smyth J. awarded payment of these outstanding bonuses to the plaintiff, ruling that the policy of retention was in restraint of trade and thus void. While agreeing that firms were generally afforded a margin of appreciation in respect of the operation of bonus schemes, the judge concluded that the retention of funds in this case was unfair.

The defendant's claim was that the deferred elements were retained with a view to incentivising staff for future years, the purpose being "to generate loyalty". The judge however disputed this contention. The bonus, he observed, was a right:

> "... already earned, declared and set aside in a specific account as a result of past endeavours which had vested and notwithstanding that vesting became conditional upon future commitment to other endeavours in the future ..."

This point (that the money had already been earned) was underlined by the fact that the retained sum attracted interest. Yet, despite the fact that he had already earned the money, the plaintiff had no control over the deferred funds pending payment. He could not invest the money or use it to make purchases or pay debts.

The judge was satisfied that the real purpose of the deferral scheme was "to create a financial and practical restriction on employees who wished to continue to act as stockbrokers going to another firm of stockbrokers." After all, the payments would be made to staff who left provided they did not do so to work with a competitor. In other words, the fundamental concern of the defendant was not that staff would leave, but that they *would leave to join competing firms.*

Bonus payments were based on profitability and individual performance in the previous calendar year. Although the bonuses were theoretically discretionary, the judge concluded that the practice of the defendant over several years gave rise to a legitimate and reasonable expectation that (subject to the success of the firm and of the relevant employee) a bonus would be conferred.

Smyth J. concluded that the imposition of the deferred bonus scheme represented a unilateral attempt to amend the plaintiff's contract, to which he had not consented and in respect of which he had not acquiesced. In a manner that was arbitrary and irrational, the defendant had sought unilaterally to change the basis for payment from one of past performance to payment for not competing with the firm. This change was, the judge added, ineffective as a matter of law as it was (a) non-consensual; (b) made without notice and in particular without notice in writing; and (c) effectively in restraint of trade. There was no difference, the judge added, between a contract restraining outright a person from carrying on a trade and one that imposes a penalty on or withholds a benefit from a person who leaves an employment to work with a competitor. It was the substance of the restraint rather than its form that was crucial. Smyth J. thus refused to accept that because the plaintiff was physically free to leave at all times, there was no restraint, merely a financial incentive to stay.

In *John Orr Ltd v Orr* [1987] I.L.R.M. 702, Costello J. remarked that all restraints of trade were contrary to public policy and thus void unless they could be justified as reasonable in the parties' interests and that of the public. The onus of proving justification lay with the person seeking to enforce the restraint. A non-compete clause in an employment contract could be enforced if it was necessary to protect the employer's proprietary interest, such as in protecting trade secrets or client relationships. In this case, however, Smyth J. was satisfied that the information available to the plaintiff was relevant only for a matter of months at the most, if not weeks. The restraint was, the judge observed, extensive in its scope, embracing any employment of whatever nature in any location where the business was one of stockbroking. It was thus:

> "... difficult to envisage how the restraint is in any way necessary to protect any proprietary interest of the defendant much less the public and *a fortiori* the Plaintiff".

The judge was also satisfied that future loyalty was not a condition of the contract, and that the deferred sums were designed to prevent competition rather than reward loyalty. In particular the calculation of both the global sum available for bonuses and the particular sums paid to individual staff were based on past performance and not future loyalty.

The judge added that the enforcement of a condition, particularly if unusual or onerous, required that it "fairly and reasonably be brought to the other party's attention". The plaintiff knew nothing of the retention practice (which the judge agreed was indeed onerous and unusual) until 1997, with the full impact not being known until 1998. The defendant thus had sought unilaterally and without timely notice to impose an onerous provision which (in substance if not form) was in restraint of trade. The plaintiff was only informed of this clause six years into his employment. This was, in the judge's view, unreasonable and unjustified. An award was made in the plaintiff's favour.

SALE OF GOODS

See also the discussion above under CONSUMER PROTECTION ACT 2007.

[Note: While the following two cases involve the leasing rather than sale of goods, they involve implied terms to the effect that goods be of "merchantable quality" and thus are dealt with under SALE OF GOODS.]

Flynn v Dermot Kelly Ltd and New Holland Finance (Ireland) Ltd, **High Court, O'Neill J., March 16, 2007, [2007] I.E.H.C. 103** In April 1998 the plaintiff, a farmer, acquired a brand new tractor from the first defendant, a business specialising in the sale of agricultural machinery. In order to effect the acquisition, the plaintiff entered into an agreement whereby the second defendant, a finance company, would purchase the tractor from the first defendant and then lease it to the plaintiff farmer.

In June 1998, at the end of a lengthy day's work, the tractor was destroyed in a fire caused by an electrical fault in its control panel. Fuelled by a moderate wind, the fire then spread to other adjacent tractors causing, in total, €42,387 worth of damage. The plaintiff claimed that the fault resulted from an "inherent defect" in the tractor's electrical system which rendered the tractor unfit for its intended purpose and not of merchantable quality.

While there was some initial dispute as to the cause of the fire, the judge accepted that the most likely cause was a fault in Mr Flynn's new tractor. The most likely scenario, he concluded, was that the fire ignited within Mr Flynn's tractor cab, spreading to the fuel tank and then to the other tractors.

The next question that arose was whether either the first or second defendant could be held liable for this defect. The question was complicated by the fact that, instead of a straightforward sale to the plaintiff, the first defendant had sold the tractor to the finance company, the second defendant, who in turn had leased it to the plaintiff.

The first issue that arose was whether the Consumer Credit Act 1995 applied. Section 76(2) of the 1995 Act stipulates that, subject to certain exceptions that do not apply here:

"... Where the owner lets goods under a hire-purchase agreement in the course of a business, there is an implied condition that the goods

> are of merchantable quality within the meaning of section 14 (3) of the
> Sale of Goods Act, 1893 ..."

By virtue of s.88 of the Act, s.76 also applies to consumer hire agreements.
Nonetheless, because the plaintiff was using the tractor for the purpose of his
business as a farmer he was not a "consumer" for the purpose of that Act. Under
s.2 of the 1995 Act, a consumer is defined as a "natural person acting outside
his trade, business or profession". The judge thus ruled that the agreement for
the lease of the tractor was not a consumer hire agreement, the plaintiff not
being a consumer in this context. Thus s.76 did not apply.

The judge then turned to consider the terms of s.13 of the Sale of Goods
and Supply of Services Act 1980. Section 13(2) implies into every contract for
the sale of a motor vehicle (except a contract in which the buyer is a person
whose business it is to deal in motor vehicles) a condition that:

> "... at the time of delivery of the vehicle under the contract it is free
> from any defect which would render it a danger to the public, including
> persons travelling in the vehicle".

The plaintiff had a contract with the second defendant, from whom the tractor
was leased. As this contract, however, was for the lease of the tractor rather
than its sale, s.13 did not apply. Thus, the conditions as to quality and fitness
did not apply in respect of the lease. There being no express warranties or
conditions as to quality or fitness, the second named defendant (the finance
company) was not liable for the defect.

The critical problem in respect of the first named defendant was an absence
of privity. Technically, the plaintiff had not bought the tractor from the first
defendant, but rather had leased it from the second defendant, who in turn had
bought it from the first defendant. At first glance, this presents a difficulty in
that the plaintiff and first defendant had not strictly speaking contracted with
each other.

Nonetheless O'Neill J. looked behind this technicality to consider the
totality of the arrangement. He noted that the "entire basis of the transaction
is that the plaintiff went to the first defendant to acquire a new tractor". While
the specific mode of acquisition involved leasing from the finance company, "a
necessary and unavoidable part of this transaction" was the sale of the tractor
to the finance company. This would not have occurred, the judge observed, if
the plaintiff had not entered into the leasing agreement.

Thus, in overlooking the technical absence of privity the judge considered
the commercial reality of the situation. The lease by the second defendant to
the plaintiff was intimately linked to the contract of sale between the first and
the second defendants. In other words, *the sale would not have taken place
were it not for the lease agreement.* Realistically, these were not separate and
distinct contractual arrangements. The commercial reality of the situation

viewed globally, the judge concluded:

> "… dictates the existence of a collateral contract between the plaintiff and the first named defendant whereby the first named defendant agreed to sell the tractor to the second defendant in consideration of the plaintiff entering into the leasing agreement with the second named defendant."

This collateral contract was for the supply of a new tractor. Necessarily, the judge concluded, such a contract contained an implied condition that the tractor was "of merchantable quality and free from defects which would render it dangerous or unfit for its intended purpose". (Whether this implication arose by reference to the presumed intention of the parties or otherwise remains unclear.) Given the age of the tractor, it being brand new, the defect in this case was a fundamental breach of the implied term as to quality. There was no doubt that the defect in this case was profound, even fundamental, in that it destroyed the tractor and other farm machinery. This being the case, the court concluded that the first named defendant had breached the collateral contract and was liable for agreed damages of €42,837.

This decision illustrates a willingness to look behind the absence of privity between the first defendant and the plaintiff. Given the circumstances, this appears eminently reasonable. It would have been artificial in the extreme to view the contract between the defendants as entirely distinct and separate from the lease agreement. Secondly, the decision illustrates the utility of the collateral contract in circumventing the harshness of the strict privity rule. By inferring the existence of a collateral contract, the judge was able—quite appropriately it might be said—to place an obligation on the first defendant to supply a tractor free of defects.

***Kane v Massey Ferguson (Ireland) Ltd, Thomas Flynn and Sons Ltd and Agri Credit Ltd,* High Court, Irvine J., December 20, 2007, [2007] I.E.H.C. 457** The facts and conclusion of this case are quite similar to those in *Flynn v Dermot Kelly Ltd*, discussed directly above. The net point again turned on whether a tractor built by the first defendant and supplied by the second defendant under finance received from the third was fit for purpose and thus of merchantable quality.

Mr Kane is a farmer and part-time mechanic. In late 1997, he decided to obtain a new tractor from the second defendant, an authorised supplier of Massey Ferguson farm equipment, for use in his business. Having test-driven a particular tractor he decided, subject to certain modifications being made, to acquire it through a lease agreement. The scenario was similar to *Flynn v Dermot Kelly Ltd* above, the third defendant Agri Credit having purchased the tractor from the supplier (the second defendant) and then leased it to the plaintiff. In part payment, the plaintiff traded in an older tractor, in respect of which he was given a discount.

The plaintiff subsequently complained that the tractor was not fit for purpose and not of merchantable quality. The main plank of his contention was that the tractor tended to lose power when driving up an incline or when pulling a load. Despite persistent efforts on the part of the second defendant to rectify these difficulties, the tractor continued to underperform. As a result, the plaintiff claimed he was unable to use the tractor for the intended purpose. The extent of this failure was, he alleged, such as to amount to a breach of contract permitting rescission of the agreement.

Irvine J. first considered the condition of the tractor. Preferring the evidence of the plaintiff, she concluded that the tractor was in fact unfit for purpose. She was satisfied on the facts that "... the vehicle did not perform as expected for the specifications of this particular model". The defendants' assertion that the vehicle was functioning well was, moreover:

> "... too much in conflict with the extent of the repairs, labour and investigations carried out by them upon this tractor in the two years subsequent to its sale."

Irvine J. further refuted allegations that in so far as problems had been experienced, these were in any way attributable to the plaintiff's own negligence. In particular, she rejected as groundless suggestions that contaminated fuel and inadequate servicing had led to the problems encountered.

The court thus accepted that there were persistent and serious problems with the tractor, which problems had not been rectified by regular repair. Irvine J. further accepted that these difficulties were in no way attributable to either the neglect of the plaintiff in servicing the tractor, or to the use of contaminated fuel. The court thus concluded that the tractor was not fit for purpose. Although the second defendant had done everything in its power to rectify the problem, it persisted.

As in *Flynn v Dermot Kelly Ltd,* the court concluded that the lease agreement with Agri Credit was not a consumer hire agreement for the purpose of the Consumer Credit Act 1995. By his own admission, Mr Kane had acquired the tractor for use in his business and, as such, was not a "consumer" for the purpose of the Act. As a result, Agri Credit could not be held liable for the condition of the product leased.

Nonetheless, the court readily implied that a collateral contract existed between the plaintiff and the second defendant, under which the second defendant agreed to sell the tractor to Agri Credit for lease to Mr Kane. The consideration for this contract was the agreement of the plaintiff to enter into the lease agreement together with the trading in of an older tractor. Given the new tractor's unfitness for purpose, Irvine J. found against the first and second defendants jointly and severally, their being liable for breach of contract (assessment of damages being deferred to a later date).

SET-OFF, RIGHT OF

See *Cosmoline Trading v DH Burke and Son Ltd and DHB Holdings*, **High Court, Finnegan J., June 14 2007, [2007] I.E.H.C. 186 (discussed above under DAMAGES, QUANTUM OF).**

SPECIFIC PERFORMANCE

See also *Claystone Ltd, Oliver Barry and Noeleen Barry v Eugene Larkin, Twinlite Development and Dallus Developments Ltd*, High Court, Laffoy J., March 14, 2007, [2007] I.E.H.C. 89 (discussed above under INTERLOCUTORY INJUNCTIONS); *Courtney v McCarthy*, Supreme Court, Geoghegan J., Kearns J. and Finnegan J., December 4, 2007, [2007] I.E.S.C. 58 (discussed above under ESTOPPEL).

Price and Lynch v Keenaghan Developments Ltd, **High Court, Clark J., May 1, 2007, [2007] I.E.H.C. 190**   This case concerned an alleged contract for the sale of a waterfront property, the net point being whether a claim for specific performance could be struck out for lack of substance. The plaintiffs having claimed specific performance of an agreement, the defendant sought to strike out the proceedings under Ord.19 r.28 of the Rules of the Superior Courts, claiming that there was absolutely no merit to the plaintiffs' legal assertion.

In May 2006, the plaintiffs viewed a Co. Leitrim holiday home development, the defendant being the developer of the property. The plaintiffs were particularly interested in one house under construction, a waterfront property which was being advertised for sale for €499,000. Initially, the plaintiffs enquired as to whether the property could be modified to their personal specifications, which the developer seemed in principle willing to consider. On May 4 the defendant sent the plaintiffs the defendant's detailed plans for the property. On May 8 the first plaintiff returned the plans to the defendant's agent highlighting essential changes that the plaintiffs wished to see effected. The plaintiffs, furthermore, indicated their aspiration to negotiate a price "…and if the modifications and price can be agreed, to move on quickly to sign the contract to enable the work to proceed as quickly as possible." They offered a combined price of €450,000 as a "fair price" for the property, once built to the plaintiffs' proposed specifications. Notably, in a note faxed the following day, the plaintiffs requested a speedy reply, adding that "[i]f the developer does not think the proposed changes are feasible, we would like to move ahead with the purchase of another house we have seen in Cavan."

On May 10, a third party offered the full asking price for the property without requiring any modifications. While the plaintiffs were given the opportunity to match or improve on the offer, they declined to do so. On May

11 the property was sold to the third party. In the intervening period, the second plaintiff had enquired as to whether the proposed changes were acceptable to the defendant, noting that the plaintiffs were "under pressure" to make a final decision in relation to the property in Cavan. Following the sale, on May 13, the first plaintiff wrote to the estate agents asking that they be offered first refusal if the proposed sale fell through for some reason. He also requested that the estate agent let the plaintiffs know if any similar waterfront property became available.

The plaintiffs subsequently claimed that they had an oral agreement for the sale of the land to them. Having issued proceedings for specific performance, they registered a *lis pendens* against the property. The defendant then sought to have the proceedings struck out and the *lis pendens* lifted. The defendant contended that the plaintiffs' proceedings were unsustainable on the facts and an abuse of process, the plaintiffs having, it claimed, no reasonable prospect of success.

In concluding in the defendant's favour, Clark J. ruled that there was no basis on which specific performance could be granted, there having been no agreement with the plaintiffs for the sale of the property. She noted, first, that specific performance is "…an equitable remedy and is thus very much dependent on the particular facts of each case and to the application of long established principles". She remarked further that the "courts do not enforce agreements which are personal in their nature", an apparent reference to the plaintiffs' attempts to enforce inclusion of the bespoke modifications of the property that they had proposed.

Specific performance, she concluded, was only possible on foot of a concluded agreement, which was in this case absent. While the plaintiffs had made various proposals, the parties had never agreed on the essential terms of the contract. The defendant, in particular, had not agreed to withhold the property from sale pending negotiations. Nor had it agreed to the modifications proposed.

The doctrine of part performance, moreover, while softening the "rigours" of the Statute of Frauds 1695, could only be invoked where there was at least a concluded oral agreement. Ordinarily the Statute of Frauds requires that a contract for the sale of land will not be enforced unless it is evidenced by a note or memorandum in writing containing the essential terms of the agreement. An exception arises where there is an oral agreement coupled with behaviour on the part of the person seeking specific performance that is consistent with the existence of a concluded contract. This "part performance" allows the contract to be enforced in the absence of written evidence, the purpose being to prevent inequitable reliance on a statute in order to avoid an agreement. Clark J. observed, however, that at a minimum part performance required the existence of a concluded oral agreement, which was not present here. Part performance was never intended, she concluded, to "aid an incomplete oral agreement".

On the facts, Clark J. had "no difficulty in finding that there was no concluded agreement at all". "The essential elements of a concluded contract", she observed, "are absent on the letters and e-mails generated by the plaintiffs." She was supported in this view by the regular references in the correspondence to the house that the plaintiffs were considering purchasing in Cavan:

> "If the plaintiffs believed themselves bound by a concluded contract to purchase the house in Drumshanbo, they would not have referred to their option to purchase the house in Cavan."

Additionally, several elements of the alleged contract had not been agreed. The price had not been agreed, the plaintiffs having proposed a lower price than that at which the house had been advertised. Similarly, the proposed variations to the house had not been agreed nor had the inclusion of a proposed berth. At best, the plaintiffs had made a series of proposals, but it was clear that the defendant had not accepted them. The parties quite simply were not *ad idem* on the essential elements of the contract, in particular the price, the modifications and the closing date. "Any court faced with the same correspondence would have no difficulty in finding that there was no concluded agreement at all".

Clark J. then turned to consider whether, in the circumstances, the proceedings should be struck out. The courts have an inherent jurisdiction to stay proceedings to prevent an abuse of process of the court. This jurisdiction may be invoked where the proceedings are "frivolous or vexatious" but also "if it is clear that the plaintiff's claim must fail", particularly where the continuation of the case would cause irrevocable damage to a defendant. Such jurisdiction, however, must be exercised with caution, and invoked only where the court is convinced that the case will ultimately fail. In particular, the courts should afford the plaintiff the opportunity to defend the application and stave off being struck out.

The plaintiffs had argued that, provided their pleadings, however weak, invoked some recognised remedy, they should be allowed to proceed. The judge agreed, however, that the plaintiffs' claim was ultimately very unlikely to succeed. The effect of allowing the case to proceed, she added, would probably tie up the lands for a long period (delaying considerably the eventual sale). Such delay (which could last several years) was likely to cause substantial injustice "...both to the owner of the land and to a subsequent innocent purchaser". In this case, Clark J. concluded, the documents before the courts revealed that the plaintiffs had "no chance of success". The court should thus, she concluded, "grasp the nettle and strike down such unmeritorious proceedings". The proceedings were thus struck out and the *lis pendens* lifted.

***Mount Kennett Investment Company v O'Meara,* High Court, Smyth J., November 21, 2007, [2007] I.E.H.C. 420** This case concerned an attempt to obtain specific performance of a contract. The net point was whether a vendor who had experienced difficulties in acquiring title to a property which it had agreed to sell to the purchaser could nonetheless be obliged to sell the property as agreed. The case raises interesting points on the extent to which frustration and impossibility of performance may restrict the remedy of specific performance.

The case concerned the proposed sale of a showground in Clonmel, the freehold in which was held by Clonmel Horse Show and Agricultural Society, a registered charity. In 1988 the Society leased the property to Clonmel Leisure Group Ltd, a private company in respect of whom the three defendants were directors. In essence, the defendants had agreed, by contract, to sell the freehold interest in the property to the plaintiff. This first required them to acquire the fee simple interest from the Society.

While the Society was agreeable to selling the freehold to the defendants, this sale required the consent of the Charitable Commissioners. The Charitable Commissioners, however, had objected to the sale on the ground that the benefit to the Society was inadequate relative to the market price of the land. The net concern of the Commissioners appeared to be that the defendants stood to make a considerable profit from the sale on to the plaintiff, at the expense of the Society.

The plaintiff nonetheless sought specific performance of the contract for sale, under which the defendants had agreed to surrender their outstanding lease and acquire the fee simple interest in the property for sale on to the plaintiff. Notwithstanding these commitments, and repeated requests to complete the contract, the defendants failed to do so. In essence, the defendants asserted that as the Charitable Commissioners had refused to consent to the sale by the Society to the defendants, the contract was incapable of performance and thus had been frustrated.

The court nonetheless granted specific performance of the contract. Smyth J. first noted the discretionary nature of the remedy of specific performance, observing that even where a valid contract is proven and no defence is established, the court may still decline specific performance. However, where a valid contract for the sale of land is involved, the onus lies on the defendant to establish that specific performance should not be awarded.

While the defendants conceded that the contract was not conditional on obtaining the consent of the Charitable Commissioners, they nonetheless pleaded that specific performance should not be granted because the contract had been frustrated by the refusal of the Commissioners to consent to the proposed sale. The Commissioners had expressed concern that the overall arrangements were not to the benefit of the charity as the proposed sale price was not, they believed, for full market value.

The judge nonetheless was satisfied that if the defendants had been willing to accept a lesser profit, the Commissioners' approval would have been forthcoming. The Commissioners more than likely did not "expect a fully philanthropic purchaser to exist". Nevertheless, the Commissioners very reasonably believed that the Society should be the main beneficiary of the sale. They could, Smyth J. concluded, "… scarcely permit with impunity the selling on of the Society's property within short intervals by speculative investors, each making appreciable profits". In short, had the defendants been willing to accept a lower profit margin, the sale would have been approved.

In conclusion, the judge ruled that the absence of the Commissioners' consent did not discharge the contract. Frustration, the judge observed, generally involved some unforeseen supervening event not in contemplation when the contract was entered into. In this case, by contrast, the defendants were fully aware that they would need the Commissioners' consent to give effect to the purchase and sale. Thus there was no frustration of the contract. The defendants had committed themselves to obtaining the freehold and had failed to do so.

Smyth J. further rejected the contention that the contract should not be enforced due to the impossibility of performance. The evidence before the judge clearly demonstrated that the Commissioners' consent would have been forthcoming had the defendants been willing to make a lesser profit than they initially had hoped. If the defendants had offered "a sufficiently adequate price to the Society", the judge concluded, "…the requisite consent would on the balance of probability have been forthcoming".

The defendants were thus responsible for their own predicament in failing to take "any meaningful step to secure the consent". Frustration or impossibility of performance may entitle a defendant to block specific performance. In this case, however, the reason the sale could not go through was because of the defendants' own "neglect and default", their being unwilling to give the Society its full due in respect of the property. Essentially, the judge concluded, the defendants wanted more of the profits than were reasonably due to them. They had agreed to sell the freehold property to the plaintiff. The plaintiff was entitled to hold them to this bargain. The plaintiff was thus awarded a decree of specific performance in respect of the contract.

STATUTE OF FRAUDS 1695

See *Price and Lynch v Keenaghan Developments Ltd*, **High Court, Clark J., May 1, 2007, [2007] I.E.H.C. 190 (discussed above under SPECIFIC PERFORMANCE);** *Claystone Ltd, Oliver Barry and Noeleen Barry v Eugene Larkin, Twinlite Development and Dallus Developments Ltd*, **High Court, Laffoy J., March 14, 2007, [2007] I.E.H.C. 89 (discussed above under INTERLOCUTORY INJUNCTIONS).**

Criminal Law

JOHN P. BYRNE B.C.L., LL.M. (N.U.I.), Barrister-at-Law and
RAYMOND BYRNE

In terms of legislative activity during the year, the most significant enactment was the Criminal Justice Act 2007, which arose in the context of a series of murders in the State towards the end of 2006 and which it was considered required a legislative response. In this respect, it can be considered as the second major legislative initiative within 12 months—the first being the Criminal Justice Act 2006 (*Annual Review of Irish Law 2006*, pp.302–323)—aimed at dealing with organised criminal activity, in particular activity linked to the use of firearms and connected with the importation, supply and sale of drugs. The main elements of the 2007 Act thus concern amendments to the law on the availability of bail, firearms and drugs offences and significant reform of sentencing procedure.

The 2007 Act also implemented some of the recommendations made in the 2007 *Final Report of the Balance in the Criminal Law Review Group* (chaired by Gerard Hogan S.C.). The Review Group, which had been established in November 2006, had considered, for example, the extent to which the circumstances in which adverse inferences could be drawn from silence could be amended and had published an interim report on this issue in early 2007: Pt 4 of the 2007 Act deals with this issue. A number of recommendations in the Final Report of the Review Group were not implemented in the 2007 Act, but it should be noted in this respect that the Review Group's Final Report was published at the same time (March 2007) as the Bill that became the 2007 Act. It remains to be decided whether other aspects of the Review Group's recommendations, which included recommending changes to the exclusionary rule in criminal trials and the introduction of prosecution appeals against acquittals, will be brought before the Oireachtas by the Government.

APPEALS

Point of law of exceptional public importance In *People (DPP) v Ashibougwu* [2007] I.E.C.C.A. 65, Court of Criminal Appeal, July 27, 2007, the Court of Criminal Appeal (Fennelly, Gilligan and Hanna JJ.) indicated that how a trial judge deals with any suggestion of racial prejudice in the trial process may well give rise to a point of law of exceptional public importance under s.29 of the Courts of Justice Act 1924 in a future case. The applicant was a young black man originally from Nigeria who had lived in Ireland for a number of years. He was convicted by a jury in the Central Criminal Court on a charge of rape on a majority verdict. The applicant was sentenced to nine years' imprisonment. On appeal, the applicant argued that the case for an acquittal was so strong that the only basis upon which the jury could have convicted was racial prejudice. The Court of Criminal Appeal dismissed the application as entirely unfounded on the evidence, noting that no suggestion of racial bias had been raised during the trial. However, the court indicated that it was axiomatic and fundamental to law and to the Constitution of Ireland that every human person is entitled to be treated equally before the law and that racial equality is fundamental to Irish law. The court stated:

> "It follows that, of course, if there had been the slightest suggestion of racial prejudice in the jury, the jury composition, the behaviour of an individual juror, revelation of the opinions of an individual juror, the court would have had to take action. The action would have depended on the circumstances of the case but it could have included the discharge of the jury. It might have included a strong and clear direction to the jury on the danger of prejudice on the grounds of race. "

The court noted that the manner in which a trial judge addresses a real risk of racial bias, for instance, by direction to the jury or otherwise, might well give rise to a point of law of exceptional importance. But in the present case, because there had been no suggestion of racial bias at trial, this did not therefore arise and the application under s.29 of the 1924 Act was refused.

It is worth noting that s.59 of the Criminal Justice Act 2007 further amended s.29 of the 1924 Act, which had been significantly amended by s.22 of the Criminal Justice Act 2006 (*Annual Review of Irish Law 2006*, pp.311–312). The purpose of the amendments effected by s.59 of the 2007 Act was to clarify two aspects of s.29, as amended. A new s.29(5A) of the 1924 act was inserted for the purpose of clarifying that points other than the certified point can be argued before and determined by the Supreme Court in an appeal under s.29. A new s.29(9A) was also inserted into the 1924 Act which provides that s.29 of the 1924 Act shall not affect the operation of s.3 of the Criminal Justice Act 1993 (which concerns the Director of Public Prosecution's power to seek a review of unduly lenient sentences).

ARREST AND DETENTION

The Criminal Justice Act 2007 made a number of significant changes to the procedures concerning arrest and detention in Garda custody.

Detention periods and re-arrest: seven-day detention in Garda custody for certain offences   Section 50 of the Criminal Justice Act 2007 introduced a significant new Garda detention powers, permitting up to seven days' detention in Garda custody in respect of four categories of offences:

     (i) murder involving the use of firearms or explosives;
     (ii) murder of a Garda or prison officer (formerly known as "capital murder");
     (iii) possession of a firearm with intent to endanger life;
     (iv) kidnapping or false imprisonment involving the use of a firearm.

Prior to the 2007 Act, the maximum period of detention permitted where a person was detained for such offences was, under s.4 of the Criminal Justice Act 1984, 24 hours. Section 50 of the 2007 Act replicates the phased arrangements for detention for up to seven days in s.2 of the Criminal Justice (Drug Trafficking) Act 1996. Section 50(3) of the 2007 Act sets out the phasing in five stages:

A suspect may be detained:

- initially for a period not exceeding 6 hours;

- for a further period not exceeding 18 hours on the authorisation of a member of an Garda Síochána not below the rank of superintendent;

- for a further period not exceeding 24 hours on the authorisation of a member of an Garda Síochána not below the rank of chief superintendent;

- for a further period not exceeding 72 hours following an application to a District Court or Circuit Court judge by a member of an Garda Síochána not below the rank of chief superintendent; and

- for a further 48 hours following an application to a District or Circuit Court judge by a member of an Garda Síochána not below the rank of chief superintendent.

All periods of detention in s.50 are subject to the condition that the detention is necessary for the proper investigation of the offence in question and that proper custody records are maintained in accordance with the Criminal Justice Act 1984 (Treatment of Persons in Custody in Garda Síochána Stations) Regulations 1987 (*Annual Review of Irish Law 1987*, pp.119–20). In addition, a person must not be detained under s.50 for a period exceeding more than 168 hours.

Section 51 of the 2007 Act specifies the conditions under which a person detained under the provisions of s.50 may or may not be re-arrested. Such persons may only be re-arrested on the authority of a judge of the Circuit Court or District Court following an application by a member of the Garda Síochána not below the rank of superintendent.

Section 52 of the 2007 Act sets out a number of procedural safeguards—and adverse consequences—for persons detained under s.50. In particular, s.52 applies the provisions of ss.4(4), 4(7), 4(8), 4(8A), 4(11), 5, 6(1) to 6(4), 8, 18, 19 and 19A of the Criminal Justice Act 1984 to such detentions. In terms of safeguards, s.5 of the 1984 Act concerns reasonable access to a solicitor. In terms of adverse consequences, ss.18, 19 and 19A of the 1984 Act, as amended in significant respects by Pt 4 of the 2007 Act (ss.28 to 32), discussed below, deal with the inferences that may be drawn from the failure of a detained person to answer certain questions or account for certain things.

Fingerprints and photographs   Section 48 of the Criminal Justice Act 2007 amended s.6 of the Criminal Justice Act 1984 by providing for the photographing and taking of fingerprints and palm prints from a person detained on a second or further occasion if the fingerprints, photographs or palm prints were imperfect. A new s.6A of the 1984 Act was also inserted to provide for the taking of fingerprints and palm prints using reasonable force where the detained person fails to co-operate. This was intended to deal with a concern expressed by the Irish Human Rights Commission concerning the previous changes to the 1984 Act made by ss.12 to 14 of the Criminal Justice Act 2006 that excessive force might have been permitted in this situation: see *Annual Review of Irish Law 2006*, p.309.

Retention and destruction of records   Section 49 of the 2007 Act inserted a new s.8 into the Criminal Justice Act 1984 by replacing the presumption in favour of destruction of fingerprints, palm prints and photographs with a presumption in favour of retention. This is subject to appeal to the Garda Commissioner for destruction cases and, on further appeal, to the District Court. Such an appeal may be brought where: criminal proceedings have not been instituted against the requester within 12 months from the date of the taking of the records, and the failure to institute such proceedings within that period is not due to the fact that he or she has absconded or cannot be found; or if a prosecution was instituted and (i) the requester is acquitted, (ii) the charge against the requester in respect of the offence concerned is dismissed under the Criminal Procedure Act 1967, or (iii) the proceedings are discontinued.

Bodily samples   Section 53 of the 2007 Act amended ss.2 and 4 of the Criminal Justice (Forensic Evidence) Act 1990 to include references to the detention powers under s.50 of the Criminal Justice Act 2007 for the purposes of the taking of bodily samples and the destruction of records and samples under the 1990 Act.

Regulations on cautions to replace the "Judges' Rules"   Section 32 of the
Criminal Justice Act 2007 provides that the Minister for Justice may make
Regulations concerning the administration of cautions by members of the Garda
Síochána to detained persons. These Regulations may include provision for
the forms of caution to be administered to a person in different circumstances
and in different classes of cases, and the procedures that are to apply where a
caution has to be withdrawn and a different caution administered. Regulations
under s.32 of the 2007 Act would replace the form of caution specified in the
"Judges' Rules", the non-statutory rules developed by the judges of the English
Court of Criminal Appeal in 1918 in *R. v Voisin* [1918] 1 K.B. 531 concerning
the conduct of police questioning, including the form of caution:

> "Do you wish to say anything in answer to the charge? You are not
> obliged to say anything unless you wish to do so, but whatever you say
> will be taken down in writing and may be given in evidence."

The Judges' Rules were given judicial recognition in Ireland in cases such as
People (Attorney-General) v Cummins [1972] I.R. 312 and, indeed, the text of
the Judges' Rules were appended to the report in the *Cummins* case and also as
an appendix to vol.2 of Frewen (*Judgments of the Court of Criminal Appeal
1979–1983*). The original 1918 version had been revised by the judges of the
English High Court in 1930 and issued with a British Home Office Circular in
1930: see *Halsbury's Laws of England*, 3rd (Simonds) edition, vol.10 (1955),
pp.470–473.

The Judges' Rules do not, however, have the force of law (see, for example,
People (DPP) v Farrell [1978] I.R. 13) but there is extensive case law on
their interpretation, as to which see generally McGrath, *The Law of Evidence*
(Round Hall, Dublin, 2004). In this respect, Regulations under s.32 of the
2007 Act would have the benefit of providing greater clarity on the effect of a
caution, just as the equivalent Regulations in the United Kingdom (first made
under the UK Police and Criminal Evidence Act 1984 (PACE)) have had in
that jurisdiction. Nonetheless, it is notable that s.32(4) of the 2007 Act states
that a failure on the part of any member of the Garda Síochána to observe
any provision of any Regulations concerning cautions to be made under the
2007 Act "shall not of itself render that member liable to any criminal or civil
proceedings or of itself affect the admissibility in evidence of anything said
by, or the silence of, a person" to whom the caution is given. Section 32(4) is
identical to the terms of s.7(3) of the Criminal Justice Act 1984 which, equally,
provide that non-compliance with Regulations for the treatment of persons in
custody made under s.7 of the 1984 Act (see the 1987 Regulations discussed
below) does not "in itself" affect the admissibility of evidence obtained in
breach of them. The case law on the meaning of s.7(3) of the 1984 Act—and
indeed, the long-established case law on the Judges' Rules—is therefore likely

to be of great importance when Regulations on cautions are made under s.32 of the 2007 Act.

Recording interviews: copies to accused by court order   Section 56 of the 2007 Act sets out the circumstances in which a copy of any recording of the questioning of a person by the Garda Síochána may be given to the person. It provides that a copy of the recording may only be given to the person or his or her legal representative where that person is charged with an offence before a court and then only if the court so directs. The court may make the giving of the copy of the recording subject to conditions. Section 56 also revoked reg.16 of the Criminal Justice Act 1984 (Electronic Recording of Interviews) Regulations 1997 (S.I. No. 74 of 1997). The 1997 Regulations govern generally the giving of copies of recordings and reg.56 had provided for giving a copy of all recordings to the accused on request. The restrictions introduced by the 2007 Act were explained on the basis that accused persons involved in organised crime were requesting tapes of interviews which were then being shown to the person directing the criminal gang of which the accused was a member, thus leading to the accused being potentially open to serious danger, depending on the content of the taped interview.

Recording interviews: admissibility   Section 57 of the 2007 Act provides for the admissibility in evidence at the trial of a person of an electronic recording and/or a transcript of such a recording of the questioning of the person by the Garda Síochána in connection with the offence. The purpose of the section is to dispense with the obligation on the Garda Síochána to make a contemporaneous written record of an interview with a suspect, subject to certain safeguards, now that such interviews are routinely audio-visually recorded.

BAIL

Part 2 of the Criminal Justice Act 2007 (ss.5 to 23) made significant further amendments to the law relating to bail, including the Criminal Procedure Act 1967, the Criminal Justice Act 1984 and the Bail Act 1997. It provides amongst other matters for: additional information to be made available to the court; opinion evidence of a member of the Garda Síochána of chief superintendent rank or higher to be admissible as evidence in certain cases; improvements to the administration of bail; the court to have the option to impose electronic monitoring as a condition of bail in certain cases; additional conditions to be imposed on bail when a person is appealing a sentence of imprisonment from the District Court to the Circuit Court; and for the prosecution to have a right to appeal a decision of the District Court in respect of bail.

Section 6 of the Criminal Justice Act 2007 inserted a new s.1A into the Bail Act 1997 and provides for a person who is charged with a serious offence as specified in the Schedule to the Bail Act 1997 to provide a signed written statement as part of his or her application for bail. The information to be contained in the statement concerns his or her occupations, sources of income, property, criminal record including any offences committed while on bail previously and any previous applications for bail. The requirement for the statement can be dispensed with in certain circumstances. It is an offence to knowingly provide false or misleading information. To avoid prejudice to the applicant's right to a fair trial the court may prohibit publication of information relating to the statement. Publication in breach of such a prohibition is a criminal offence.

Section 7 inserted a new s.2A into the Bail Act 1997 and provides that the opinion of a member of the Garda Síochána not below the rank of chief superintendent that refusal of bail is reasonably necessary to prevent the commission of a serious offence by the applicant for bail is admissible as evidence before a court hearing an application for bail by a person charged with a serious offence (as defined in the Schedule to the Bail Act 1997). To avoid prejudice to the applicant's right to a fair trial the court may prohibit publication of information relating to the opinion evidence. Publication in breach of such a prohibition is a criminal offence.

Section 8 amended s.5 of the Bail Act 1997 to provide for recognisances which need not include monetary conditions: see below the changes to s.22 of the Criminal Procedure Act 1967 made by s.18.

Section 9 amended s.6 of the Bail Act 1997 to remove the requirement that the applicant be of good behaviour as a condition of a recognisance, while retaining the requirement that the applicant not commit an offence while on bail. In addition, the changes provide that a recognisance include notification to the applicant of the possibility of seeking a variation of a condition of the recognisance.

Section 10 inserted a new s.6A into the Bail Act 1997 to allow the court, when admitting a person who is appealing a sentence of imprisonment imposed by the District Court to bail, to make the recognisance subject to a wider range of conditions than was available prior to the 2007 Act. In addition to the conditions that must be imposed (that the appellant prosecute the appeal, attend court as required and not commit an offence while on bail) the court may choose from the conditions set out in s.6(1)(b) of the 1997 Act (as amended by s.9 of the 2007 Act).

Section 11 inserted a new s.6B into the Bail Act 1997 and allows the court to make a recognisance subject to the condition that the person be monitored electronically. This possibility will be available to the court where: (i) a person charged with a serious offence is to be admitted to bail or a person is appealing a sentence of imprisonment imposed by the District Court; and (ii) the court considers that it is appropriate to impose conditions that the person reside or remain in a particular district or place in the state or that the person refrain from attending at certain premises or other places. Where a recognisance is made subject to a condition as to electronic monitoring an "authorised person" will be responsible for monitoring compliance.

Section 12 inserted a new s.6C into the Bail Act 1997 and provides for the admissibility of documentary evidence in proceedings relating to a breach of an electronic monitoring condition.

Section 13 inserted a new s.6D into the Bail Act 1997 and empowers the Minister for Justice, with the consent of the Minister for Finance, to enter into such arrangements including contractual arrangements, as he or she considers appropriate for the operation of electronic monitoring (in effect, the privatisation of electronic monitoring).

Section 14 amended s.8 of the Bail Act 1997. As with s.8, above, this was to provide for recognisances which need not include monetary conditions: see below the changes to s.22 of the Criminal Procedure Act 1967 made by s.18.

Section 15 substituted a new s.9 into the Bail Act 1997 to provide that estreatment of recognisances is at the discretion of the court. In addition, the new s.9 expanded the options available to the court where a condition of a recognisance is breached by allowing, inter alia, for the appointment of a receiver. It also provides for a warrant of committal to issue where a court order as to estreatment or forfeiture etc is not complied with rather than the current enforcement procedure of distress warrants which authorise the Gardaí to seize goods etc.

Section 16 inserted a new s.11A into the Bail Act 1997, empowering the Minister for Justice to make Regulations prescribing any matter or thing which is referred to in the Bail Act 1997 or for the purpose of enabling any provision of the Bail Act 1997 to have full effect.

Section 17 amended the Schedule to the Bail Act 1997. The Schedule lists the offences that are to be regarded as "serious offences" for the purposes of the 1997 Act. The amendments made by s.17 of the 2007 Act updated the Schedule to reflect the amendments to the Firearms Acts 1925 to 2006 made by the Criminal Justice Act 2006 (*Annual Review of Irish Law 2006*, pp.312–313).

Section 18 amended s.22 of the Criminal Procedure Act 1967 to provide that recognisances need not contain a condition as to the payment of moneys into court—this is now a matter for the court to determine having regard to the circumstances of the case, including the means of the person and the nature of the offence in relation to which the person is in custody.

Section 19 amended s.28 of the Criminal Procedure Act 1967 in order to provide that the prosecution may appeal to the High Court against a decision in relation to bail. Prior to the 2007 Act, only the applicant could appeal. In addition, the amendment provides that the High Court may transfer its appeal function in certain circumstances to the Circuit Court (i.e. when the case is triable by the Circuit Court) where the appellant has been remanded in custody by the District Court.

Section 20 amended s.31 of the Criminal Procedure Act 1967 to provide that release on bail in certain cases by a member of the Garda Síochána does not need to be conditioned on payment of moneys. Similarly, s.21 amended s.68 of the Children Act 2001 to provide that release on bail in certain cases by a member of the Garda Síochána does not need to be conditioned on payment of moneys.

Section 22 amended s.11 of the Criminal Justice Act 1984. Section 11 of the 1984 Act provides that a sentence for an offence committed while a person is on bail should be consecutive on the sentence for the original offence. The amendment effected by s.22 of the 2007 Act was to address what was described as an anomaly by which an offence committed by a person who is unlawfully at large following the revocation of bail did not, prior to the 2007 Act, attract the consecutive sentence requirement.

Section 23 amended s.13 of the Criminal Justice Act 1984 in two respects. Section 13 of the 1984 Act created the offence of failure to surrender bail and s.23 of the 2007 Act amended it in order to increase the maximum fine that may be imposed from £1,000 to €5,000. Since this is a summary offence which must, under s.10(4) of the Petty Sessions (Ireland) Act 1851 ordinarily be prosecuted within six months, s.23 also disapplies s.19(4) of the 1851 Act and provides instead that prosecutions may be taken within 12 months.

CODIFICATION OF CRIMINAL LAW

The Criminal Justice Act 2006 (Commencement) Order 2007 (S.I. No. 25 of 2007) brought into force Pt 14 of the Criminal Justice Act 2006, which provides for the establishment of the Criminal Law Codification Advisory Committee (see *Annual Review of Irish Law 2005,* pp.261–262 and *Annual Review of Irish Law 2006*, p.317). The Committee is chaired by Professor Finbarr McAuley, University College Dublin, with membership drawn from centres of criminal law expertise including the policy, advisory, prosecution, drafting, practising profession and universities. The work of the Committee is facilitated by a permanent Secretariat and a Research Support Unit, both of which are based at University College Dublin. For an outline of the content of the proposed first Code instrument, see the Committee's *First Programme of Work 2008–2009*, available at *www.criminalcode.ie.*

DELAY

In *Noonan v Director of Public Prosecutions* [2007] I.E.S.C. 34; Supreme Court, July 27, 2007, the applicant sought to prohibit her trial on 16 charges of offences contrary to s.32(2)(a) of the Larceny Act 1916 (as amended by s.9 of the Larceny Act 1990). It appeared that the offences were alleged to have taken place between January 1, 1990 and May 7, 1992. It had been indicated that the applicant would be pleading not guilty. It appeared that a series of delays ensued due to several factors, including initial delays, systematic delays, and the death of a witness. The High Court (Ó Caoimh J.), in a judgment delivered on July 9, 2004, refused her application. The applicant appealed against that refusal to the Supreme Court (Murray C.J., Denham and Hardiman JJ.) and the court ordered prohibition of her trial.

Giving the leading judgment on the issue, Denham J. said that in all the circumstances of the case, where the alleged offence took place approximately 17 years ago, and where the procedures from complaint to return for trial had taken 10 years, a general overview of the process required to be taken. She indicated that the kernel issue for the court was justice. She said the systemic delay in the District Court was a matter "for grave concern". In light of the "exceptional circumstances of the case" she considered it would be unjust and oppressive for the prosecution to proceed.

Murray C.J. noted that "Ireland has by far the lowest ratio of judges per 100,000 of population in Europe" and that "even by common law standards our number of judges… is very low and there is some evidence to believe that the brunt of the difficulties caused by this are felt in the District Court." In the circumstances of the case, the appeal was allowed.

ENDANGERMENT

Reckless endangerment: advertence required   In *People (DPP) v Cagney and McGrath* [2007] I.E.S.C. 46; [2008] 1 I.L.R.M. 293 the Supreme Court (Murray C.J., Hardiman, Geoghegan, Fennelly and Kearns JJ.) dealt with the mental element of the offence of endangerment in s.13 of the Non-Fatal Offences Against the Person Act 1997 and in particular whether it was a suitable "fall-back" charge to manslaughter. In the case the appellants were charged with manslaughter contrary to common law and with an offence contrary to s.13. They were found not guilty of manslaughter but guilty of an offence under s.13. Section 13(1) states that:

> "A person shall be guilty of an offence who intentionally or recklessly engages in conduct which creates a substantial risk of death or serious harm to another."

The Court of Criminal Appeal dismissed the appellants' application for leave to appeal their conviction but certified that the case involved a point of law of exceptional public importance. The Supreme Court held that the conviction could not stand.

Delivering the leading judgment, Hardiman J. reviewed the origins of s.13, noting in particular that it originated in a recommendation in the Law Reform Commission's 1994 *Report on Non-Fatal Offences Against the Person* (LRC

45–1994). Hardiman J. noted that the Commission itself had been aware that the offence was open to some criticism in that it was wide-ranging in its potential scope. While Hardiman J. did not expressly cast doubt on the offence itself, he concluded that it was not suitable as a fall-back offence to manslaughter, since an acquittal on the manslaughter charge would indicate that the prosecution had failed to establish advertence by the defendants. Hardiman J. noted that the offence under s.13 of the 1997 Act, when committed recklessly as opposed to intentionally, requires advertence. The constituent parts of the offence as applicable may be construed as the accused intentionally or recklessly engaging in conduct which creates a substantial risk of death or serious injury, to which he has adverted, to another. Recklessness, in the context of a s.13 offence, is subjective and not objective and involves not merely the taking of a risk but the advertent taking of a risk; one which the accused knew could cause a substantial risk of death or serious injury.

The Supreme Court thus concluded that it would not be appropriate to use the endangerment offence as a "fall-back" charge to manslaughter. This is because manslaughter can be proved even without the need to prove recklessness creating a substantial risk of death or harm. This means that where, as in the *Cagney and McGrath* case, defendants are found not guilty of manslaughter, they cannot be found guilty of endangerment. The appropriate alternative charge in such a case would be assault.

FIREARMS AND OFFENSIVE WEAPONS

Part 6 of the Criminal Justice Act 2007 (ss.34 to 40) made a number of further amendment to the Firearms Acts 1925 to 2006 (the principal 1925 Act had been amended in significant respects by the Criminal Justice Act 2006: see *Annual Review of Irish Law 2006*, pp.312–313).

Section 34 amended s.2 of the Firearms Act 1925 (which deals with restrictions on the possession, use and carriage of firearms) to provide specifically for a Garda superintendent to authorise employees and agents of airport authorities, in the course of their duties, to carry and use firearms for bird control purposes without having to acquire a firearms certificate. In addition, the amended s.2 of the 1925 Act provides for a Garda superintendent to authorise the National Museum to accept and hold firearms of historical significance without having to obtain a firearms certificate.

Section 35 amended s.15 of the Firearms Act 1925 (as amended by s.42 of the Criminal Justice Act 2006) in a manner similar to the change made in respect of the minimum sentence in drugs offences made by s.33 of the 2007 Act: see above. This also involved the insertion of what was described as a "construction clause" which states that the purpose of the 10-year "mandatory" minimum sentence for certain firearms offences should be imposed in all but the most exceptional cases and that reductions in the minimum sentence should be exceptional and confined to cases where particular or specific circumstances apply. Similar "construction clauses" were inserted: by s.36 of the 2007 Act (into s.26 of the Firearms Act 1964 as amended by s.57 of the Criminal Justice Act 2006); by s.37 (into s.27 of the Firearms Act 1964 as amended by s.58 of the Criminal Justice Act 2006); by s.38 (into s.27A of the Firearms Act 1964 as amended by s.59 of the Criminal Justice Act 2006—s.38 also specifically provided for the extension of the offence in s.27A to the possession of ammunition in suspicious circumstances); and by s.39 (into s.27B of the Firearms Act 1964 as amended by s.60 of the Criminal Justice Act 2006).

Section 40 amended s.12A of the Firearms and Offensive Weapons Act 1990, which deals with shortening the barrel of a shot-gun or rifle, by providing for the inclusion of s.27 of the Firearms Act 1964, which deals with the prohibition of use of firearms to assist or aid escape, in the list of first offences for which a court must impose the prescribed mandatory minimum sentence on persons convicted of a second or subsequent offence of shortening the barrel of a shot-gun or rifle.

INFERENCES TO BE DRAWN IN CERTAIN CIRCUMSTANCES

As already indicated at the beginning of the Chapter, above, Pt 4 of the Criminal Justice Act 2007 (ss.28 to 32) implemented the recommendations made in the 2007 *Report of the Balance in Criminal Law Review Group*. The Hogan Review Group concerned drawing inferences from a failure or refusal to account for circumstances and expanded the circumstances in which inferences may be drawn in proceedings from a failure to mention particular facts. We have discussed above s.32 of the 2007 Act, which provides for the making of ministerial regulations in relation to the administration of cautions by members of the Garda Síochána to detained persons.

Section 28 substituted a new s.18 into the Criminal Justice Act 1984. Prior to the 2007 Act, s.18 of the 1984 Act had provided for the drawing of inferences in criminal proceedings for an arrestable offence (one carrying five years' imprisonment) from the failure or refusal of an accused to account for objects, marks etc when requested to account for them on being questioned or charged by the arresting member of the Garda Síochána. The amended version of s.18 of the 1984 Act allows for the question to be put to the suspect by any garda, not just the arresting garda, and also provides for certain explicit safeguards. First, it will not be possible to convict on an inference alone, without corroboration, or to draw an inference unless the accused was cautioned in clear language and was afforded a reasonable opportunity to consult a solicitor before such failure or refusal occurred. Secondly, the amended version of s.18 of the 1984 Act will not apply to questioning in Garda custody unless the interview is recorded or the person consents in writing to it not being recorded.

Section 29 substituted a new s.19 into the Criminal Justice Act 1984. Prior to the 2007 Act, s.19 of the 1984 Act had provided for drawing inferences in criminal proceedings for an arrestable offence from the failure or refusal of an accused to account for his or her presence at a particular place when requested to account for that on being questioned or charged by the arresting member of the Garda Síochána. As with the changes made to s.18 of the 1984 Act by s.28 of the 2007 Act, the amended s.19 of the 1984 Act allows for the question to be put to the suspect by any garda, not just the arresting garda, and also provides for certain explicit safeguards.

Section 30 inserts a new s.19A into the Criminal Justice Act 1984 and provides for the circumstances in which inferences may be drawn in any subsequent criminal proceedings from a failure by an accused to mention particular facts when questioned by the Garda Síochána or when being charged with an arrestable offence. The safeguards included in ss.18 and 19 of the 1984 Act, as amended by the 2007 Act, are replicated in this section. Since s.19A of the 1984 Act, as inserted by s.30 of the 2007 Act, deals with all arrestable offences, s.5 of the Offences Against the State (Amendment) Act 1998 and s.7 of the Criminal Justice (Drug Trafficking) Act 1996, which deal with particular offences only, were repealed by the 2007 Act (see Sch.1 to the 2007 Act). Consequential changes to s.2 of the Offences against the State (Amendment) Act 1998 were made by s.31 of the 2007 Act.

MANSLAUGHTER

Law reform　In 2007, the Law Reform Commission published a *Consultation Paper on Involuntary Manslaughter* (LRC CP 44–2007) in which the Commission considered the current law of manslaughter in Ireland and made provisional recommendations for reform of the law. As the Consultation Paper pointed out, currently the law of homicide is divided into murder and manslaughter. Murder occurs if a person intended to kill, or cause serious injury to, another person who dies as a result. Murder also carries a mandatory life sentence. Manslaughter is any unlawful killing that is not murder and currently consists of two categories, voluntary manslaughter and involuntary manslaughter. The Commission noted that "voluntary manslaughter" generally describes what would otherwise be murder but where there is some excusing circumstance, such as provocation, which reduces the offence from murder to manslaughter. Involuntary manslaughter currently comprises two sub-categories.

First, manslaughter by an unlawful and dangerous act, where the killing involves an act constituting a criminal offence, carrying with it the risk of bodily harm to the person killed. In *People (DPP) v Horgan* [2007] I.E.C.C.A. 29; Court of Criminal Appeal, May 3, 2007 (Kearns, Murphy and Mac Menamin JJ.), concerning an appeal following a conviction for rape and manslaughter, the Court of Criminal Appeal stated that manslaughter during the course of a rape constituted unlawful and dangerous act manslaughter and, indeed, the court referred with apparent approval to the Law Reform Commission's *Consultation Paper on Involuntary Manslaughter* (which had been published the previous month) by way of a summary of existing law. The court considered that manslaughter which took place during the course of a rape is elevated into this "most serious category of manslaughter". The court was of the view that there were strong public policy considerations which demand that a rape accompanied by violence which carries an appreciable risk of death, must be seen as being in a most serious category of manslaughter and must attract a sentence at the higher range.

The second sub-category is manslaughter by gross negligence, where the death arises from a negligent act or omission by the accused involving a high risk of substantial personal injury. The Commission noted that convictions for this type of manslaughter are extremely rare.

The Law Reform Commission provisionally concluded that, in general, the current law of involuntary manslaughter is satisfactory, but that a number of specific amendments should be considered and it invited submissions on those. For example, the Commission provisionally recommended that low levels of deliberate violence should be removed from the scope of unlawful and dangerous act manslaughter and be prosecuted as assaults instead. This would mean that a person who pushes someone, causing them to fall and fatally hitting their head off the ground would be charged with assault rather than manslaughter. Judges should take the fact that a death occurred into account when imposing sentence.

The Commission also provisionally recommended that the current test for gross negligence manslaughter should be amended so that a person would only be liable for gross negligence if he or she was mentally and physically capable of averting to, and avoiding the risk of substantial personal injury at the time of the fatality. In 2008, the Commission published its *Report on Homicide: Murder and Involuntary Manslaughter* (LRC 87–2008), which contains the Commission's final recommendations on involuntary manslaughter and on the mental element in murder (on which it had published a Consultation Paper in 2001: see *Annual Review of Irish Law 2001*, pp.199–202). We will return to this Report in the *Annual Review of Irish Law 2008*.

MISUSE OF DRUGS

Mens rea: no awareness required that drugs were above a certain value In *People (DPP) v Power* [2007] I.E.S.C. 31; Supreme Court, July 26, 2007 the defendant was convicted of an offence under s.15A of the Misuse of Drugs Act 1977 (as inserted by s.4 of the Criminal Justice Act 1999). Section 15A(1) states that:

"A person shall be guilty of an offence under this section where—

(a) the person has in his possession, whether lawfully or not, one or more controlled drugs for the purpose of selling or otherwise supplying the drug or drugs to another in contravention of regulations under section 5 of this Act, and

(b) at any time while the drug or drugs are in the person's possession the market value of the controlled drug or the aggregate of the market values of the controlled drugs, as the case may be, amounts to €13,000 or more."

The defendant applied to the Court of Criminal Appeal for leave to appeal his conviction on the basis that the trial judge had erred in law in failing to direct the jury that it was a necessary ingredient of the offence in s.15A that the accused was aware that the quantity of the controlled drug alleged to be in his possession exceeded the statutory amount. The matter was certified by the Court of Criminal Appeal as a point of law of exceptional public importance. The Supreme Court (Murray C.J., Denham, Fennelly, Macken and Finnegan JJ.) held that it is settled Irish law that, where a criminal offence is created by statute, and the statute is silent as to mens rea, there is a presumption that mens rea is required in relation to the offence as a whole and in relation to each constituent part of the offence. The presumption can only be displaced by clear words or by necessary implication. As regards s.15A, it is not necessary that the prosecution prove that the accused knew or ought to have known that the market value of the controlled drugs or the aggregate of the market values of the controlled drugs amounts to €13,000 or more.

OFFENCES AGAINST THE STATE

Membership of unlawful organisation: belief evidence   In *People (DPP) v Kelly (V)* [2007] I.E.C.C.A. 110; Court of Criminal Appeal, 6 December 2007 the issue of "belief evidence"—evidence of belief from a Garda superintendent given under the Offences Against the State (Amendment) Act 1972 that the accused is a member of an unlawful organisation—was considered. The applicant was convicted by the Special Criminal Court of the offence of membership of an unlawful organisation (the IRA) under s.21 of the Offences Against the State Act 1939. The applicant's fingerprints were found in a vehicle which contained a handgun, a gas canister, two balaclavas, and black woollen gloves. When arrested he was wearing a tee shirt which carried the inscription "Oglaigh na hEireann" together with an image of a number of men in combat gear discharging weapons and a legend "unbowed and unbroken". He was sentenced to five years' imprisonment.

He applied to the Court of Criminal Appeal for leave to appeal his conviction and sentence on the ground, inter alia, that a Detective Chief Superintendent gave evidence at the trial of his belief that the applicant was a member of the IRA—belief evidence—but was not in a position to disclose the basis of that belief owing to the confidential nature of the information. The Superintendent offered to produce the documentation if such a request was made. The applicant submitted that there was no guide in law to assist the Special Criminal Court in determining the weight to be attributed to "evidence of belief" when no information is available to the court as to the source of the information.

The Court of Criminal Appeal (Finnegan, Herbert and MacMenamin JJ.) considered it was significant that the superintendent had offered to make the documentation available but that the applicant had not availed of that offer. The court cited the judgment of Fennelly J. in the Supreme Court decision *People (DPP) v Kelly* [2006] 3 I.R. 115 where he had stated:

> "It is of crucial importance that there was quite extensive evidence, other than the evidence of the Chief Superintendent, which convinced the Special Criminal Court that the accused was a member of the IRA on the relevant date. The court said that it took into account the fact that the Chief Superintendent had claimed privilege. It did not on the other hand, explain this remark any further. The court, in my view, should have explained the weight, if any which it attached to the evidence of the Chief Superintendent, in view of the claim to privilege."

The Court of Criminal Appeal stated it should consider "the cumulative evidence" against the applicant. It was noted that the "belief evidence" was not the only evidence against the applicant. Another factor considered was that the applicant had not denied under oath the charges against him. The court considered that the Special Criminal Court had been quite correct to consider the following circumstances: (a) that the belief was not associated with any of the events relating to matters which occurred on the date in question; (b) that the belief was not associated with any actions or admissions made by the accused at that time; (c) that the belief was not based on the questioning pursuant to s.2 of the Offences Against the State (Amendment) Act 1998; (d) that the Chief Superintendent had held the belief for some six years; (e) the experience of the chief superintendent; (f) the demeanour of the Chief Superintendent in the witness box; and (g) that there was other evidence against the applicant.

In the result, the court concluded that the court of trial was entitled to accept the evidence of the Chief Superintendent and to weigh and consider it together with the evidence as a whole. The court stated:

> "This court is satisfied that Fennelly J. in his comments quoted above did not intend to require the court of trial to express the weight it attaches to belief evidence in the form of a mathematical notation or other scale

of values but rather that weight should be attributed to the same where there is countervailing evidence such as a denial on oath. It was not necessary, in the circumstances of this case, to attribute weight to any particular ingredient in the evidence the accumulative effect of which led to the applicant's conviction."

The *Kelly* decision follows the earlier Supreme Court *Kelly* decision by emphasising the importance of scrutinising "belief evidence" when such evidence is the "sole plank" in the prosecution case.

POSSESSION OFFENCES

Possession of articles or money in connection with certain offences Section 46 of the Criminal Justice Act 2007 amended s.183 of the Criminal Justice Act 2006 and added a new s.183A into the 2006 Act. The substituted s.183 provides that a person is guilty of an offence if he or she possesses or controls any article, as defined, in circumstances giving rise to the reasonable inference that he or she possesses or controls the article concerned for the purposes of the commission, preparation, facilitation or instigation of specified offences. The offences to which the section applies are false imprisonment under s.15 of the Non-Fatal Offences against the Person Act 1997, a drug trafficking offence under s.3 of the Criminal Justice Act 1994, murder, murder to which s.3 of the Criminal Justice Act 1990 applies (the old offence of capital murder) and the common law offence of kidnapping to which s.2 of, and para.4 of the Schedule to, the Criminal Law (Jurisdiction) Act 1976 applies.

Section 183, as amended, states that it is a defence for a person charged with an offence under the section to prove that at the time of the alleged offence he or she did not possess or control the article concerned. An article is said to mean a substance, document or thing. A "document" includes a map, plan, graph, drawing, photograph or record, or a reproduction in permanent legible form, by a computer or other means (including enlarging), of information in non-legible form. "Information in non-legible form" includes information on microfilm, magnetic tape or disk. A person guilty of an offence under this section is liable on conviction on indictment to a fine or to imprisonment for a term not exceeding five years or both.

Section 183A provides that it shall be an offence for a person to be in possession of or in control of monies, as defined, with a minimum value of €5,000 in circumstances giving rise to a reasonable inference that he or she possesses or controls the assets concerned for the purposes of the commission, preparation, facilitation or instigation of specified offences. The list of offences is slightly more extended than the list which applies to s.183. All of the s.183 offences are included as well as an offence under s.14 of the Criminal Justice (Theft and Fraud Offences) Act 2001, which relates to obstruction of

Garda acting on a warrant, and an offence under s.17 of the Criminal Justice (Public Order) Act 1994, which relates to blackmail, extortion and demanding money with menaces. Section 183A sets out the same defence as applies to s.183. "Monies" is defined as coins and notes in any currency, bank drafts, postal orders, certificates of deposit and any other similar instruments easily convertible into money. The same penalty applies as for s. 183.

Possession of article in connection with robbery   Section 47 of the Criminal Justice Act 2007 amended s.15 of the Criminal Justice (Theft and Fraud Offences) Act 2001, which makes it an offence for a person to be in possession of any article with the intention that it be used in the commission of the offence of robbery. As amended by the 2007 Act, it is a defence for a person to demonstrate that the article was not in his or her possession for the purposes of committing any of the offences specified in subs.15(1) of the 2001 Act. The 2007 Act also increased to €5,000 the maximum fine for the offence of withholding information in relation to stolen property under s.19 of the 2001 Act.

PROCEDURE

Appeals: new evidence in appeal   The criteria for determining whether new evidence can be introduced on appeal were dealt with in *People DPP) v O'Regan* [2007] I.E.S.C. 38; Supreme Court, July 30, 2007. The defendant had been convicted of rape and, on appeal, he attempted to introduce new expert medical evidence to counter the opinion evidence given at trial that the victim had been raped. The Court of Criminal Appeal refused to admit the new evidence, on the basis of the test set out in *People (DPP) v Willoughby* [2005] I.E.C.C.A. 4; Court of Criminal Appeal, February 18, 2005, discussed below. The court subsequently refused the applicant a certificate under s.29 of the Courts of Justice Act 1924 that the case involved a point of law of exceptional public importance, but the Attorney-General later granted a certificate under s.29 of the 1924 Act, thus bringing the matter to the Supreme Court.

In *O'Regan* the Supreme Court (Murray C.J., Geoghegan, Fennelly, Kearns and Macken JJ.) held that the correct approach in cases of this nature had been set out by the Court of Criminal Appeal in *People (DPP) v Willoughby* [2005] I.E.C.C.A. 4; Court of Criminal Appeal, February 18, 2005. In *Willoughby* the court (Kearns, deValera and Clarke JJ.) laid down the following criteria:

> "1. Given that the public interest requires that a defendant bring forward his entire case at trial, exceptional circumstances must be established before the court should allow further evidence to be called. That onus

is particularly heavy in the case of expert testimony, having regard to the availability generally of expertise from multiple sources.

2. The evidence must not have been known at the time of the trial and must be such that it could not reasonably have been known or required at the time of the trial.

3. It must be evidence which is credible and which might have a material and important influence on the result of the case.

4. The assessment of credibility or materiality must be conducted by reference to the other evidence at the trial and not in isolation."

In *O'Regan* the Supreme Court agreed with these criteria and added that in order to comply with the requirements set out in *Willoughby* it is not necessary to assert or establish unreasonable, irrational, illogical or negligent conduct of the defence at the trial. The court noted that, in the present case, no expert medical evidence had been adduced at the applicant's trial to counter the prosecution's expert testimony. The court held that there was no indication that this decision by defence counsel was irrational or negligent. The Supreme Court also decided that the Court of Criminal Appeal had applied the *Willoughby* principles correctly in determining that the expert evidence the applicant sought to adduce did not meet the requirements set out in *Willoughby*, noting in particular that the evidence would not have established to any degree of certainty that a rape had not occurred in this case.

Corroboration   In *People (DPP) v Kelly (V)* [2007] I.E.C.C.A. 110; Court of Criminal Appeal, December 6, 2007 (discussed above under the heading OFFENCES AGAINST THE STATE) the applicant had been convicted of membership of an unlawful organisation (the IRA) under s.21 of the Offences Against the State Act 1939. On appeal, he argued that all of the evidence against him at trial was circumstantial—fingerprints had been found in the same vehicle as a gun and other items but his fingerprints were not found on any of the items. He argued that his mere presence in proximity to the incriminating items was incapable of amounting to corroborative evidence against him.

The Court of Criminal Appeal (Finnegan, Herbert and MacMenamin JJ.) considered that while circumstantial evidence could be explained innocently in each individual instance the court was not "required to be blind to the cumulative implausibility of innocence as an explanation for the evidence". The court noted that in *People (DPP) v Cahill and Costello* [2001] 3 I.R. 494 Keane C.J. cited with approval the view expressed in *R. v Exall* (1866) 4 F & F 922, 929 that:

"There may be a combination of circumstances, no one of which would raise a reasonable conviction or more than a mere suspicion; but ... taken together may create a conclusion of guilt ... with as much certainty as human affairs can require or admit of."

In the *Kelly* case, the court stated:

"The court is satisfied that each of the circumstances surrounding the applicant's arrest considered in isolation, whilst of themselves not capable of leading to a conviction, nonetheless form part of a matrix of facts to which the court was entitled to have regard together with other evidence and all of which taken together would be sufficient for a jury properly directed to convict."

Thus, the court held that individual pieces of evidence, each of which can be innocently explained, may come together to form a "matrix of facts" against the accused and on that basis the court upheld the conviction.

Costs In *People (DPP) Kelly (A)* [2007] I.E.H.C. 450; Central Criminal Court, December 19, 2007, the applicant had been acquitted on a charge of murder after a trial that had lasted 18 days and had applied for costs. The applicant had been a co-accused in the trial; his co-accused had been found guilty. Order 99 of the Rules of the Superior Courts 1986 states:

"1. The costs of and incidental to every proceeding in the superior courts shall be in the discretion of these courts respectively... 3. The costs of every action, question, or issue tried by a jury shall follow the event unless the court, for special cause, to be mentioned in the order, shall otherwise direct. 4. The costs of every issue of fact or law raised upon a claim or counterclaim shall, unless otherwise ordered, follow the event."

In *People (Attorney-General) v Bell* [1969] I.R. 24, the Supreme Court held that this rule applied to criminal proceedings. In that case, Kenny J. decided that costs were in the discretion of the trial judge following on the acquittal of any accused. In *Hewthorn & Co Ltd v Heathcot* 39 I.L.T.R. 248, Kenny J. stated:

"It is well settled law, as is shown by the authorities cited to me, that when costs are in the discretion of a judge he must exercise that discretion upon the special facts and circumstances of the case before him and not be content to apply some hard and fast rule."

In *Dunne v Minister for the Environment* [2007] I.E.S.C. 60, the Supreme Court discussed an issue as to costs in the context of public law issues being raised and determined, as was argued, to the benefit of clarifying for the community the law in an important area. In the course of his judgment, Murray C.J. stated:

"The rule of law that costs normally follow the event, that the successful party to proceedings should not have to pay the costs of those proceedings which should be borne by the unsuccessful party, has an obvious equitable basis. As a counterpoint to that general rule of law the court has a discretionary jurisdiction to vary or depart from that rule of law if, in the special circumstances of a case, the interests of justice require that it should do so. There is no predetermined category of cases which fall outside the full ambit of that jurisdiction. If there were to be a specific category of cases to which the general rule of law on costs did not apply, that would be a matter for legislation since it is not for the courts to establish a cohesive code according to which costs would always be imposed on certain successful defendants for the benefit of certain unsuccessful plaintiffs."

In the *Kelly* case Charleton J. indicated that where a court considers that it should exercise a discretion to depart from the normal rule as to costs it is not completely at large but must do so on a reasoned basis indicating the factors which in the circumstances of the case warrant such a departure. The matter of the identification of the relevant factors, and the application of discretion based on them, was considered peculiarly a matter for the trial judge. Charleton J. considered that the trial judge in a criminal case is not bound only to consider the evidence admitted before the jury. The judge has discretion which allows the trial judge to inquire into the conduct of the prosecution and the defence. Charleton J. considered that in considering the discretion as to costs, the trial judge might usefully ask the following questions:

"(1) Was the prosecution justified in taking the case through it being founded on apparently credible evidence?
(2) Did anything within the investigation by the Gardaí give rise, of itself, to the existence of a serious inherent doubt as to the guilt of the accused? I use this test, in distinction to a matter that might raise a reasonable doubt because, firstly, the trial judge must distance himself or herself from the evidence and, secondly, it is for the jury to judge whether there is any reasonable doubt about the guilt of the accused.
(3) Was there any indication that the case had been taken against the accused through being based on an abuse of his rights through oppressive questioning, which contributed to a confession that was unreliable in law?
(4) Whether the accused was acquitted by direction of the trial judge or acquitted upon consideration by the jury? Then one might go on to consider the reason for such acquittal by the trial judge, whether as to

a failure in technical proofs or if it was one of the rare cases of inherent weakness in evidence that had actually been offered.

(5) If there had been an acquittal by direction of the trial judge, was this one based upon a decision that required the exclusion of evidence, and if so, whether that exclusion was based upon a serious, as opposed to a mistaken, abuse of the accused's rights? This is not a circumstance to apply the rule as to the exclusion of evidence based on a mistake that accidentally infringes some constitutional right of the accused. What might be considered here is deliberate abuse by the servants of the State.

(6) What answer had the accused given to the charge when presented with an opportunity to answer it? The purpose of a Garda investigation is not to provide an opportunity to an accused person to state what his defence is: *McCormack v Judge of the Circuit Court* [2007] I.E.H.C. 123. The purpose of any fair investigation, however, is to seek out the truth; sometimes according with an initial police view as to who is guilty and oftentimes contradicting it. A fair interview upon arrest would naturally bring an accused person to the point that he or she is expected to deal with the preliminary outline of the case inculpating the suspect and allow him or her an opportunity, if he or she wishes, the chance to say what the answer to it is or might be, in a case based on circumstantial evidence.

(7) What was the conduct of the accused in the context of the charge that was brought, specifically in terms of who he was associating with and on what ostensible basis? Sometimes an accused can be partly responsible for attracting suspicion by dealing with and having close relations with those who are closely linked to criminal activity. Such a relationship may be explained in evidence in an apparently reasonable way, but at other times the course of dealings may be left untreated in any reasonable way in the evidence. Suspicion can arise against an accused in other ways, such as by running away or apparently destroying what might be relevant evidence.

(8) What was the conduct of the accused in meeting the case at trial?

(9) Whether any positive case was made by an accused such as might reasonably be consistent with innocence and whether any right was exercised to testify as to that case or whether an opportunity was used under the Prosecution of Offences Act 1974 to communicate with the Director of Public Prosecutions as to the nature of that defence?

(10) Have the prosecution made any serious error of law or fact whereby the case became on presented on a wrong premise? The same question is applicable to the defence."

Applying those criteria in the *Kelly* case Charleton J. ruled that the applicant should not be granted costs. This was principally on the basis that the applicant had drawn suspicion onto himself based on his own conduct. This included his responses to certain questions and his refusal to talk, on his arrest on the murder charge.

Evidence outside book of evidence   In *People (DPP) v Fahy* [2007] I.E.C.C.A. 102; Court of Criminal Appeal, November 28, 2007, the applicant had been convicted of several offences including obtaining by false pretences contrary to s.2 of the Larceny Act 1916, as amended by the Larceny Act 1990, and attempted theft contrary to s.4 of the Criminal Justice (Theft and Fraud Offences) Act 2001 and common law.

The judgment of the court states that one of the grounds of appeal was that the prosecution had been "in breach of the Criminal Justice (Miscellaneous Provisions) Act 1967, sections 4B, 4C and 4D as inserted by the Criminal Justice Act 1999, section 9" in that it had led evidence not contained in the book of evidence or in the statement of further evidence. There is, of course, no such Act as the "Criminal Justice (Miscellaneous Provisions) Act 1967" and the reference is, presumably, to ss.4B, 4C and 4D of the Criminal Procedure Act 1967, as inserted by s.9 of the Criminal Justice Act 1999 (which replaced the preliminary examination procedure in the 1967 Act with a new procedure for sending an accused forward for trial on indictment). It is an unfortunate comment on the poor state of the Statute Book that the leading counsel who prepared the grounds of appeal, and the Court of Criminal Appeal itself, found it difficult to state the correct name of the Act on which the appeal turned. This underlines the importance of the Statute Law Restatement function discussed in the Legislation chapter, below, which would provide, for example, the most recent text of the Criminal Procedure 1967, as amended, in a single text.

Turning to the substance of the actual argument made in the *Fahy* case, the applicant argued that the evidence led by the prosecution at his trial was not probative and was prejudicial to him. It included evidence of a €3.8 million offer for a field which was "blurted out" by a witness unprompted during the course of giving oral evidence. In addition, the applicant was not given sight of a document contained in a list of exhibits after having requested sight of it, which was clearly in breach of s.4B of the 1967 Act, as inserted by the 1999 Act.

In approaching the issues raised, the Court of Criminal Appeal (Finnegan, Feeney and Irvine JJ.) returned to fundamental principles of evidence and cited with approval the comment of Hardiman J. in *People (DPP) v Shortt (No. 1)* [2002] 2 I.R. 686 at 693:

> "All evidence must be relevant to a matter in issue as the first condition of admissibility. There are exceptions to the admissibility of relevant

evidence, but irrelevant evidence is never admissible: see *Cross and Tapper on Evidence* (9th edition) at pp 55 and 56."

The Court in *Fahy* stated that the effect of the introduction of inadmissible evidence will depend upon the circumstances of the particular case. The court noted that in its decision in *People (DPP) v Marley* [1985] I.L.R.M. 17 it had held that, while in the case of a trial by jury it may be possible for the trial judge to cure any prejudice arising by giving appropriate directions to the jury, there may be cases where the evidence is so prejudicial that it creates a real and substantial risk of an unfair trial which cannot be avoided by any directions that might be given to the jury. In those circumstances it is appropriate to discharge the jury.

In this case, the court noted that a "special feature" was the non-compliance with s.4B of the Criminal Procedure Act 1967. In those circumstances, and considering the nature of the prejudicial evidence in the case, the court was satisfied that "the introduction of inadmissible evidence in the manner in which it occurred created a real and substantial risk of an unfair trial." The court therefore allowed the appeal and directed a retrial.

Sending forward for trial: pre-trial application on validity of search warrant The decision of the Supreme Court in *Cruise v O'Donnell* [2007] I.E.S.C. 67; Supreme Court, December 20, 2007 also involved the procedure inserted into the Criminal Procedure Act 1967 by the Criminal Justice Act 1999, which replaced the preliminary examination procedure in the original 1967 Act with a new procedure for sending an accused forward for trial on indictment (the *Fahy* case, above, involved another aspect). The appellant had been charged with a number of serious drugs offences. In advance of his trial he applied to the respondent judge of the Circuit Court to determine whether a search warrant, which was used to obtain evidence against him, was valid and, if found not to be valid, to order that the charges be dismissed. It appeared from the evidence that the warrant failed to include on its face the premises sought to be searched by the Gardaí, or had entered the wrong address.

The respondent judge declined to consider the application, taking the view that this was a matter for the trial judge. The applicant then sought judicial review of that refusal. The *Cruise* case thus involved an opportunity to determine the effect of the provisions on sending forward for trial inserted into the 1967 Act by the 1999 Act. The core issue presented was whether a form of pre-trial application to dismiss was possible, or whether (as the respondent judge had considered) any issue such as the validity of a warrant was a matter for the trial judge.

The case thus turned on the interpretation of s.4E of the Criminal Procedure Act 1967, as inserted by s.9 of the Criminal Justice Act 1999. Section 4E(1), (4) and (5) states:

"(1) At any time after the accused is sent forward for trial, the accused may apply to the trial court to dismiss one or more of the charges against the accused ...

(4) If it appears to the trial court that there is not a sufficient case to put the accused on trial for any charge to which the application relates, the court shall dismiss the charge.

(5) (a) Oral evidence may be given on an application under subsection (1) only if it appears to the trial court that such evidence is required in the interests of justice."

The Supreme Court (Murray C.J., Denham, Hardiman, Geoghegan and Fennelly JJ.) stated that the aim of s.4E of the 1967 Act was, so far as possible, to confer on the trial court a jurisdiction similar to that formerly exercised by the District Court at the conclusion of the (now repealed) preliminary examination. The question for the court was, therefore, the same as it was formerly for the District Court: is there a sufficient case to put the accused on trial? Or put otherwise, is there a prima facie case?

Fennelly J. delivered the leading judgment for the court, with which Murray C.J., Denham and Geoghegan JJ. agreed. Fennelly J. noted that, in determining matters of this type at pre-trial stage, evidence will generally not be admitted. While he accepted that s.4E(5) of the 1967 Act permitted oral evidence to be admitted, this was not to be read as constituting a general power for the judge to admit evidence at that stage. The court considered that the purpose of any such oral evidence must be to cast light on the issue which the court has to determine, namely whether, on the book of evidence, there is a sufficient case to put the accused on trial. The book of evidence is, effectively, the prosecution's case against the accused including charges, affidavits of witnesses, forensic evidence results. Evidence could, therefore, be admitted to explain the identity of persons, places or things referred to in the documents.

Fennelly J. stated it was:

"... necessarily difficult to lay down comprehensive rules about this. The guiding principle is the *interests of justice*, but controlled by the context of the application and the circumstances of the particular case. Always, the issue is whether a sufficient case is disclosed."

Turning to the present case Fennelly J. said the crux of the matter was that the respondent judge had ruled that the validity of search warrants was to be determined at the trial and could not be the subject-matter of an application to dismiss pursuant to s.4E of the 1967 Act. In effect, he had declined jurisdiction to consider the question of validity of the search warrant. His decision did not turn on whether he should admit evidence. Fennelly J. considered that the respondent judge had erred in reaching that conclusion. He stated:

"He should have been prepared to consider arguments on the issue of validity as disclosed in the documents and, possibly, whether evidence should be admitted to explain the circumstances of the search or the identity of the premises though only in the sense that a ruling of invalidity would have the effect of ruling out all the evidence against the accused. I do not think it has been established that there is any overriding rule that the decision on whether there is a sufficient case to put a person on trial precludes the judge hearing such an application to dismiss from ruling that there is no case, where that involves concluding that the only evidence advanced against the accused is plainly inadmissible. An example would be where the only evidence was clearly hearsay."

The outcome of the *Cruise* case was that the Supreme Court therefore remitted the matter to the Circuit Court to resume consideration of the appellant's application for dismissal of the charges against him. In that respect, the court's interpretation of s.4E of the 1967 Act, as outlined in the leading judgment of Fennelly J., allows for an element of pre-trial determinations.

In a concurring judgment in the *Cruise* case, Hardiman J. discussed in more explicit terms the key policy issue posed in the case: whether s.4E of the 1967 Act, inserted by the Criminal Justice Act 1999 with the explicit purpose of abolishing the preliminary examination procedure, had created a form of pre-trial hearing to be held in the trial court and, if so, whether that could encompass matters of law that had previously been at issue in the preliminary examination process. Hardiman J. noted that the Director of Public Prosecutions had submitted that the question of the invalidity or insufficiency of the warrant can be determined only by the trial judge. Hardiman J. responded to this by reference to the wording of s.4E:

"Undoubtedly it would have been open to the Oireachtas to lay down that this should be so but it has not done so, speaking only of the 'trial court'. His Honour Judge O'Donnell is undoubtedly a judge of the Circuit Court. The applicant cannot know in advance who the judge presiding over the trial will be so that, if he wishes to avail of s.4E he must bring his motion in the Circuit Court and await its assignment by the proper authorities to whatever judge they regard as appropriate. He cannot determine the identity of the Judge who will decide the result of his motion. The identity of the trial judge is usually not known (in Dublin) until the morning of the trial."

More tellingly, Hardiman J. expressed the view that, in addition to the apparent textual breadth of s.4E, there were wider policy reasons to support a wide interpretation of its reach. He noted:

"Quite clearly (to speak only of the right to apply to have a charge dismissed) if there is a single point which may avail the defendant to the extent of fatally undermining the charges against him, it is a great advantage to have this determined before the trial itself. Disposal in this way represents a major saving of time and expense to both sides, avoids inconvenience to witnesses and to the often forgotten jury persons, brings a rapid end to the defendant's anxieties (which in this case must be considerable since one of the charges against him carries a mandatory minimum sentence of ten years imprisonment) and brings about a resolution of the action between the prosecutor and the defendant at the earliest possible time, freeing up court time for other cases."

Hardiman J. reinforced this policy reason for an expansive view of s.4E from the accused's perspective with further arguments based on judicial case management:

"We live in an era of case management, when a serious attempt is being made to deal with all litigation, civil or criminal, in an efficient manner. The most superficial consideration of efficiency will lead to the conclusion that it is considerably more efficient to deal with matters, which must by their nature be dealt with without a jury in any event, before the jury is sworn and taken away from their ordinary occasions rather than afterwards. I accord the fullest possible respect to Chief Justice Ó Dálaigh's statement [in *People (Attorney-General) v McGlynn* [1967] I.R. 232 at 239] about the essential unity and continuity of a criminal trial and entirely agree with it. Disposing of evidential issues before the jury is sworn will assist and emphasise, rather from detract from, that unity and continuity. In other jurisdictions where pre-trial motions to suppress evidence and similar procedural devices are well established, the fundamental nature of a jury trial is not considered to be trenched upon."

It is also notable that Hardiman J. accepted that, in 2003, the *Report of the Working Party on the Jurisdiction of the Courts: the Criminal Jurisdiction of the Courts* had recommended the introduction of a new preliminary hearing mechanism for all cases on indictment. One of the purposes of this was "to enable the determination of those types of issues of admissibility of evidence which by their nature are capable of being dealt with prior to trial" (see para.85 of the Report). Indeed, he noted that the Director of Public Prosecutions had argued that, the fact that the Working Party had called for this in 2003 shows that it did not regard the innovations introduced in the 1999 Act as constituting such a mechanism. But Hardiman J. noted that the views of the "very respected Working Party [which, indeed, had been chaired by Fennelly J.] cannot be dispositive of the issue, which is fundamentally one of statutory interpretation. The Working Party, indeed, may not have addressed this issue at all."

It remains to be seen whether the decision of the Supreme Court in the *Cruise* case will lead to a significant number of pre-trial hearings prior to trials on indictment. Although Hardiman J.'s judgment clearly indicates a positive disposition towards them, it may be that some defence counsel may prefer to advise their clients to wait until the trial itself before making applications for dismissal on issues of the admissibility of evidence. While in the *Cruise* case a successful application might be of clear benefit to the applicant, the merits of postponing such applications until after the trial has begun may limit the number of applications. Nonetheless, although the majority judgment of Fennelly J. in no way interpreted s.4E of the 1967 Act as involving a full-blown pre-trial hearing on all issues that may arise at trial, it does indicate that some issues can be considered before the trial begins, which in that respect is consistent with the principles of case management referred to by Hardiman J.

Juror communications In *People (DPP) v Mulder* [2007] I.E.C.C.A. 63; Court of Criminal Appeal, July 20, 2007, inappropriate communication with a juror resulted in the Court of Criminal Appeal ordering a re-trial. It appeared from the evidence that during the course of the trial it was intimated to the judge that communications had been made to one of the jurors by a relative of the deceased victim in the case. The trial judge considered that it was a well-established principle that a court should be slow to discharge a jury once it had embarked on a trial. He ruled that he would question the jury in relation to what had happened rather than decide at that stage to discharge them. The judge questioned the foreman of the jury and then the juror in question. He received conflicting accounts from both. The foreman indicated that the juror who had received the communication felt "intimidated" while the juror himself said that he considered he could continue to carry out his function. The jury was not discharged, the trial continued and the jury found the applicant guilty.

On the facts of the case the Court of Criminal Appeal (Geoghegan, McKechnie and Clark JJ.) considered that the information that the juror felt "intimidated" was important. The court stated:

> "While courts should be reluctant to discharge a jury because of individual incidents involving communication with a juror the nature of this intervention and the cumulative effect of the incidents and the conflict to some extent in the reports given to the judge would have all led an observer to be concerned that there would be a risk of an unfair trial."

The court was also concerned that the trial judge, when assessing the situation, had not applied an objective test on the basis of the following inquiry set out in *Bula Ltd v Tara Mines Ltd (No. 6)* [2000] 4 I.R. 412: "Would a reasonable person have a reasonable apprehension that the appellant would not, in the circumstances receive a fair and impartial trial?"

Having regard to the facts, the Court of Criminal Appeal allowed the appeal and directed a re-trial. The court noted that the matter turned on whether the cumulative effect of the incidents would have led an observer to be concerned that there would be a risk of an unfair trial. The court indicated that there may be cases where the court might be in a position to decide that in actual fact there was a fair trial. However, it appears that in the present case the critical factor was the divergence in views between the foreman of the jury and the juror in question on the issue of the state of being of the juror who had received the communication. This difference of opinion and the use of the word "intimidated" to describe his state of being was of importance. Another relevant factor was that the trial judge had used an incorrect test to assess the situation. In those circumstances the court considered that it had no option but to allow the appeal and order a re-trial.

Video link evidence   The Criminal Evidence Act 1992 (Section 13) (Commencement) Order 2007 (S.I. No. 52 of 2007) and the Criminal Evidence Act 1992 (Section 13) (Commencement) (No. 2) Order 2007 (S.I. No. 572 of 2007) brought into effect s.13 of the Criminal Evidence Act 1992 in the Circuit Court sitting in the South Eastern Circuit and the Midland Circuit, and the District Court sitting in District No. 8 and No. 9. Section 13 of the 1992 Act allows for live television link evidence of persons in cases involving physical or sexual abuse (see *Annual Review of Irish Law 1992*, pp.262–263). Section 13 states that if the person is under 17 years of age, such live link evidence may be given unless the court sees good reason to the contrary, and that, in any other case, it may be given with the leave of the court.

SENTENCING

Adjournments   In *People (DPP) v Drinkwater* [2007] I.E.C.C.A. 84; Court of Criminal Appeal, July 31, 2007 (discussed below), the Court of Criminal Appeal (Murray C.J., Herbert and McGovern JJ.) advised courts adjourning sentencing hearings as follows:

> "Although it should not be strictly necessary, it would be good practice, in order to minimise the risk of any misunderstanding if the sentencing judge, when adjourning the question of sentence, was to state that the actual form or nature of the sentence is not yet decided and will not be so decided until the final hearing on sentence."

Appeal: indictable and summary offence involved   In *People (DPP) v*

Shinnors [2007] I.E.C.C.A. 50; Court of Criminal Appeal, May 24, 2007, the Court of Criminal Appeal (Finnegan, Budd and Clark JJ.) held that, where an appeal against sentence—in this case by the prosecution against leniency—involved an indictable and a summary offence, the leniency of the summary offence could be considered by the court. The respondent had been charged with two offences: dangerous driving causing death, contrary to s.53 of the Road Traffic Act 1961, an indictable offence; and failing to keep a vehicle at the scene of an occurrence, contrary to s.106 of the Road Traffic Act 1961, a summary offence. The summary offence under s.106 of the 1961 Act had been added to the indictment pursuant to s.6 of the Criminal Justice Act 1951, which states:

> "Where a person is sent forward for trial for an indictable offence, the indictment may contain a count for having committed any offence triable summarily (in this section referred to as a summary offence) with which he has been charged and which arises out of the same set of facts and, if found guilty on that count, he may be sentenced to suffer any punishment which could be inflicted on a person summarily convicted of the summary offence."

On the charge of dangerous driving causing death, the Circuit Criminal Court jury acquitted the respondent but convicted her of the lesser offence of careless driving contrary to s.52 of the Road Traffic Act 1961. The respondent had pleaded guilty to the summary offence of failing to keep her vehicle at the scene contrary to s.106 of the Road Traffic Act 1961. In respect of the careless driving offence under s.52 of the 1961 Act, the trial judge imposed a fine of €750. In respect of the offence contrary to s.106 of the Road Traffic Act 1961 he imposed a sentence of three months' imprisonment which he suspended and endorsed the respondent's licence and disqualified her from driving for two years.

As indicated, the prosecution brought an application, pursuant to s.2 of the Criminal Justice Act 1993, to review the sentences on grounds of undue leniency. The respondent argued that the prosecution had no right to make such application in respect of the summary offence. The Court of Criminal Appeal rejected that submission. The respondent had argued that the right of appeal conferred by s.2 of the 1993 Act is defined not by reference to the trial procedure but the nature of the offence in respect of which sentence has been imposed and that s.6 of the 1951 Act relates exclusively to trial procedure. The court was satisfied that this was not so and that the submission fails to take account of the view of the Supreme Court in *State (Harkin) v O'Malley* [1978] I.R. 269 that the summary offence, once included in an indictment under s.6 of the 1951 Act, has the same status for the purpose of criminal procedure as any other count in the indictment. Thus, on conviction, the defendant enjoys a right of appeal to the Court of Criminal Appeal, that being an incident of the procedure in the Circuit Court. Likewise, the court was satisfied it was an incident of procedure in the Circuit Court on a trial on indictment that the Director of Public Prosecutions should have a right to apply to the Court of Criminal Appeal under s.2 of the 1993 Act.

Considering whether the sentence passed was unduly lenient, the court noted that the maximum sentence permissible in respect of the offence under s.106 of the 1961 Act is a term of six months' imprisonment or a fine of €1,500, or both. In addition the court had power to impose an ancillary disqualification order under s.27 of the Road Traffic Act 1961. The court also noted that, in reviewing the sentence, it should first look at the circumstances of the offence and determine where on the range of penalties the offence lies. The sentence should be proportionate to the crime and to the personal circumstances of the applicant. At the sentencing hearing there was evidence that the respondent had expressed remorse at an early stage.

In addition, since the offence the family of the deceased had displayed hostility towards the respondent as a result of which she had been living away from her home, her husband and children and close to her employment in Limerick. The respondent gave evidence and expressed her remorse. She had wished to meet with the deceased's family to express her remorse to them but had been dissuaded from so doing. She had no previous convictions. As to her personal circumstances the respondent was a married woman with two children aged 8 and 13.

The court stated that it should not close its eyes to the fact that a death had resulted. The court also considered that by her own account at the time of the occurrence the respondent was driving at 40 miles per hour in a 30 mile per hour zone. The fact that she panicked was considered understandable but could not excuse the fact that she had left the scene. She had an opportunity to contact the Gardaí but she had not done so. She had also parked her vehicle at the rear of her house and that was seen as indicative of an intention to avoid the consequences of her actions. In mitigation the court took into account her repeated expressions of remorse. She had co-operated with Gardaí after they had first contacted her. She had accepted responsibility and made two cautioned statements. She had pleaded guilty to the offence with which the court was concerned and such a plea was indicated in her cautioned statements.

In conclusion, the court emphasised that the offence at issue was a serious offence that could have serious consequences for the administration of justice. By fleeing the scene of an accident a driver could escape the consequences of his or her driving. In that regard it was appropriate in considering a sentence for this type of offence to have regard to deterrence. The court was satisfied that in the present case the sentencing judge had failed to have sufficient regard to the element of deterrence and for that reason the sentence imposed on the respondent was unduly lenient. The court therefore substituted a term of imprisonment of three months, suspended for two years, the conviction to be endorsed on the respondent's licence and the respondent to be disqualified from driving for five years.

Concurrent sentences   In *People (DPP) v Wallace* [2007] I.E.C.C.A. 4; Court of Criminal Appeal, February 2, 2007, the applicant had pleaded guilty in the Circuit Criminal Court to two counts of robbery. He was sentenced to two consecutive sentences of six years on each charge, making a total of 12 years' imprisonment with three years suspended. On appeal, the applicant contested the appropriateness of consecutive sentences in this case and that the trial judge had not given reasons for so doing.

As to the issue of consecutive sentencing per se, the Court of Criminal Appeal (Denham J., de Valera and McGovern JJ.) was satisfied that there was no error in principle by the trial judge. The court considered that the two offences were "very grave"—indeed the court considered that a sentence of 12 years for each with three years suspended would not have been inappropriate. The individual sentences of six years, in light of the nature of the offences, were considered light, and in the circumstances the giving of consecutive sentences was not an error in principle. Consequently the court refused the application on that basis.

As to the necessity to give reasons for consecutive sentences, the court was referred to the decisions of the European Court of Human Rights (ECtHR) in *Hadjianastassiou v Greece* (1993) 16 E.H.R.R. 219; *Ruiz Torija v Spain* (1994) 19 E.H.R.R. 553; and *Garcia Ruiz v Spain* (2001) 31 E.H.R.R. 22. In *Garcia Ruiz v Spain*, the ECtHR reiterated that according to established case law reflecting a principle linked to the proper administration of justice, judgments of courts and tribunals should adequately state the reasons on which they are based. The ECtHR added:

> "The extent to which this duty to give reasons applies may vary according to the nature of the decision and must be determined in the light of the circumstances of the case" (para.26).

In *Wallace* the court was satisfied that it is desirable for a sentencing court to give reasons when imposing consecutive sentences. However, the court retained its inherent jurisdiction to do justice and in this case the court considered there had been a careful, reserved, judgment by the trial judge. While no express reasons for the consecutive sentences were given, express reasons for the sentences were addressed. Inherent in the judgment are the reasons for the sentences. In this basis, the appeal was dismissed.

Dangerous driving causing death   In the *People (DPP) v O'Reilly* [2007] I.E.C.C.A. 118; Court of Criminal Appeal, December 11, 2007, the Court of Criminal Appeal (Kearns, Murphy and Mac Menamin JJ.) declined the opportunity to lay down sentencing guidelines for cases of dangerous driving causing death. The prosecution applied, under s.2 of the Criminal Justice Act 1993, to review a sentence on grounds of undue leniency, following the conviction of the respondent for dangerous driving and related offences. He was sentenced to five years' imprisonment, suspended on condition that the respondent keep the peace and be of good behaviour for a period of six years.

The prosecution submitted, among other matters, that the trial judge failed to have regard for certain aggravating factors in the case which included the fact that the respondent was driving at a time when the quantity of alcohol in his system was in excess of the legal limit and that fact that he drove while uninsured. The prosecution considered that the judge had given undue weight to factors, which the judge considered were mitigating factors, such as the respondent's expression of remorse. In imposing sentence the trial judge had stated, among other matters, that:

> "[I]n my opinion the sending to jail of this young man would not benefit anyone. He had his own jail sentence and he can never forget that. He does not have to be imprisoned by walls. He has shown genuine remorse and had admitted from the very beginning that he had been drinking."

On appeal, the Court of Criminal Appeal stated that when considering an application to adjust a sentence on the grounds of undue leniency, the court should afford great weight to the trial judge's reasons for imposing sentence and that "nothing but a substantial departure from what would be regarded as the appropriate sentence would justify the intervention of this court". The court was satisfied that the sentencing judge had not committed any error of principle per se simply because she had decided to suspend all of a sentence of imprisonment. However, the court emphasised that, when giving judgment, the sentencing court should meet the requirements of personal deterrence, on the one hand, and the requirements of general deterrence, on the other. While the sentencing court had satisfied the requirements of the former category, the court had failed to satisfy those of the latter.

The court therefore quashed the sentenced imposed by the trial judge and in lieu of the suspended sentences, imposed a community service order to work a total of 240 hours pursuant to s.5 of the Criminal Justice (Community Service) Act 1983.

The court in *O'Reilly* accepted that "particular guidelines" are needed when dealing with cases of dangerous driving causing death. However, the court was of the view that the present case was not the appropriate case to deal with that matter, because a number of aggravating factors, commonly associated with cases of that type, were absent. It will be recalled that in *People (DPP) v Sheedy* [2000] 2 I.R. 184 the court had declined an invitation to set out sentencing guidelines in view of the "particular facts" of that case—although the court had set out, in general terms, the approach which should be adopted.

Since *Sheedy*, at least 13 cases of dangerous driving causing death had been tried. In the course of submissions in *O'Reilly*, the prosecution had presented to the court a list of those cases. Counsel indicated to the court that custodial sentences had been imposed in cases characterised by the presence of at least one aggravating factor such as particularly dangerous driving, multiple death and/or consumption of excess alcohol. Counsel had pointed out that there was a "high level of public concern in Ireland arising out of the ongoing high level of fatalities as a result of road traffic accidents". Further, he stated, the Health Service Executive published a report on the role of alcohol and fatal crashes in Ireland in 2003 and the study showed that 28.2 per cent of fatal accidents involved consumption of alcohol by the driver of a vehicle involved. In the result it would appear desirable in the public interest that proper sentencing guidelines emanating from the courts are needed in cases of this type. It is to be hoped that the Irish Sentencing Information System (ISIS) will deliver such guidance for all trial and appellate courts in the near future.

Guilty plea In *People (DPP) v Horgan* [2007] I.E.C.C.A. 29; Court of Criminal Appeal, May 3, 2007, the Court of Criminal Appeal (Kearns, Murphy and Mac Menamin JJ.) ruled that a plea of guilty to manslaughter, in the circumstances of the case, could not be seen as a factor in mitigation of sentence. The prosecution brought an application, pursuant to s.2 of the Criminal Justice Act 1993, to review a sentence on grounds of undue leniency, following the conviction of the respondent in the Central Criminal Court on charges of rape and manslaughter. At a first trial, the respondent had entered a plea of not guilty and denied any involvement in the rape and death of the victim. At the conclusion of the first trial, the respondent was convicted and was sentenced to a term of imprisonment for life on the count of murder and to a term of imprisonment of 10 years for rape, both sentences to run concurrently. On appeal, both convictions were quashed and a re-trial was ordered. At the re-trial he pleaded not guilty to murder but guilty of manslaughter. The respondent at all times maintained his plea of "not guilty" in relation to the count of rape. As indicated, he was convicted of manslaughter and rape in the second trial. The trial judge imposed two concurrent eight-year sentences in respect of the two offences, but suspended six years of the eight-year sentence in respect of each offence, with the sentenced to operate from March 2006, the date of conviction.

The Court of Criminal Appeal stated that the plea of guilty to manslaughter should be seen as "a relatively small value in the particular circumstances that the respondent gave sworn testimony that he had absolutely nothing to do with this matter when first tried". The court considered that on any version of events, the lateness of the plea, coming as it did some five years after the events, greatly lessened its value. The court was clearly mindful of taking into account the entire circumstances of a "guilty" plea on a particular count and was not content to allow the matter to be treated in isolation from other counts or a previous plea in an earlier trial on the same facts. In considering the conviction for rape, the court considered that it could not ignore the fact that the rape offence was aggravated to the greatest possible degree by the dangerous manner in which it was perpetrated. This involved restraining the victim by her neck in an armlock or headlock. Bearing in mind the aggravating factors connected with the manslaughter in this case, the court substituted concurrent sentences of 12 years on each of the convictions for manslaughter and rape, to be backdated to September 2001, the date of the conviction in the first trial.

Misuse of drugs: mandatory sentence   Part 5 of the Criminal Justice Act 2007 comprises a single section, s.33, which amended s.27A of the Misuse of Drugs Act 1977, as previously inserted into the 1977 Act by the Criminal Justice Act 1999 and amended by the Criminal Justice Act 2006. Section 27A, as originally enacted by the 1999 Act, provides for a 10-year "mandatory" minimum sentence, subject to certain conditions, for certain drug trafficking offences. The changes effected by s.33 of the 2007 Act were, first, to set out the amended text concerning the 10 years sentence in a single place and, secondly, to insert what was described during the Oireachtas debate on s.33 as a "construction clause" to indicate that the "mandatory" minimum sentence should be imposed in all but the most exceptional cases and that reductions in the minimum sentence should be exceptional and confined to cases where particular or specific circumstances apply. The background to these changes (and those made by the 2006 Act) can be understood in the context of the unhappiness expressed in the Oireachtas that the "mandatory" sentence (which, as already mentioned was, and remains, subject to certain conditions) was not being imposed in a sufficiently large number of cases.

For discussion of the case law on s.27A, see *Annual Review of Irish Law 2004*, p.248 and *Annual Review of Irish Law 2005*, pp.291–293. An example in 2007 was *People (DPP) v Lernihan* [2007] I.E.C.C.A. 21; Court of Criminal Appeal, April 18, 2007. The prosecution applied, under s.2 of the Criminal Justice Act 1993, to review a sentence on grounds of undue leniency imposed on the respondent, who had pleaded guilty to possession of cocaine with a market value in excess of €13,000 contrary to s.15A of the Misuse of Drugs Act 1977 and possession of cannabis resin contrary to s.3 of the Misuse of Drugs Act 1977. The sentence imposed was four years' imprisonment on each of the two counts, to run concurrently, with the final two-and-a-half years to be suspended. The Court (Denham, deValera and McGovern JJ.) stated that it was satisfied that both aspects of the sentence—the four-year sentence and the suspended sentence of two and a half years—were unduly lenient. The court examined all the circumstances of the case, which included factors such as possession of cocaine to a street value of over €70,000 by the respondent, who was not an addict, and who was involved in a transaction of the drugs purely for commercial gain. The court also noted the early plea of the respondent, limited assistance he gave to the Gardaí, the absence of any previous convictions, and the remorse of the respondent. Nonetheless, in all the circumstances the court considered that the appropriate sentence was one of seven years' imprisonment.

Rape In *People (DPP) v Keane* [2007] I.E.C.C.A. 119; Court of Criminal Appeal, December 19, 2007 the respondent was convicted of rape and was sentenced to three years' imprisonment, suspended on his being of good behaviour in his own bond for €1,000. The prosecution applied, under s.2 of the Criminal Justice Act 1993, to review the sentence on grounds of undue leniency. The Court of Criminal Appeal (Murray C.J., Charleton and Irvine JJ.) quashed the sentence and imposed a sentence of 10 years with three years suspended on certain conditions. The court set down three principles for sentencing in future cases:

1. There is no formula to be applied to sentencing for the crime of rape but there is a general starting position, as set out in *People (DPP) v Tiernan* [1988] I.R. 250 that rape must attract a substantial custodial sentence.
2. The ambit of a judge's obligation under the law to impose a sentence which meets the particular circumstances of a case and of the accused person, even for an offence as grave as rape, does not in principle exclude the possibility of a non-custodial sentence in wholly exceptional circumstances.
3. In reaching its decision, the sentencing court must look at a range of cases and take into account the wide variety of factors which can influence sentencing in rape cases and accordingly hand down the sentence it deems appropriate in all the circumstances.

Repeat offenders Part 3 of the Criminal Justice Act 2007 (ss.24 to 27) provides for new sentencing arrangements for the offences listed in Sch.2 to the 2007 Act, which are those considered to be linked to organised crime; introduces post-release orders to be known as "monitoring orders" and "protection of persons orders"; and amends the Criminal Justice (Legal Aid) Act 1962.

Section 24 provides that references to the offences specified in Sch.2 to the 2007 Act include references to participation as accomplices and references to inchoate offences (attempts, incitements and conspiracies). Schedule 2 lists the following offences:

*   murder;

- an offence under s.4 (causing serious harm), s.5 (threats to kill or cause serious harm) or s.15 (false imprisonment) of the Non-Fatal Offences Against the Person Act 1997;

- an offence under s.2 (causing explosion likely to endanger life or damage property), s.3 (possession, etc. of explosive substances) or s.4 (making or possessing explosives in suspicious circumstances) of the Explosive Substances Act 1883;

- an offence under s.15 (possession of firearm with intent to endanger life) of the Firearms Act 1925;

- an offence under s.26 (possession of firearms while taking vehicle without authority), s.27 (prohibition of use of firearms to assist or aid escape), s.27A (possession of firearm or ammunition in suspicious circumstances) or s.27B (carrying firearm with criminal intent) of the Firearms Act 1964 (as amended by the Criminal Justice Act 2006);

- an offence under s.12A (shortening barrel of shotgun or rifle) of the Firearms and Offensive Weapons Act 1990;

- an offence under s.13 (aggravated burglary) of the Criminal Justice (Theft and Fraud Offences) Act 2001;

- a drug trafficking offence under s.3(1) of the Criminal Justice Act 1994;

- an offence under s.71 (conspiracy), s.72 (organised crime) or s.73 (commission of offence for criminal organisation) of the Criminal Justice Act 2006;

- an offence under s.17 (blackmail, extortion and demanding money with menaces) of the Criminal Justice (Public Order) Act 1994.

Section 25 of the 2007 Act introduced new sentencing requirements where a person who has been convicted on indictment of an offence in Sch.2 and, within seven years of the first conviction, commits another offence in Sch.2. In such cases the court must impose a sentence for the subsequent offence that is at least three quarters of the maximum sentence stipulated under the law for that offence unless to do so would be disproportionate in all the circumstances of the case. In order for this section to apply a number of criteria must be met:

- the person must be 18 years or more;

- the conviction for which the person is being sentenced must be a conviction on indictment for an offence specified in Sch.2 to the 2007 Act;

- the person must previously have been convicted on indictment of one of the offences specified in the Schedule and been sentenced to five years' or more imprisonment; and

- the offence for which the person is being sentenced must have been committed within seven years from the date of conviction for the previous offence (excluding any period of imprisonment) or committed during the period of imprisonment for the first offence.

Where the maximum sentence is life imprisonment the court must specify a sentence of at least 10 years' imprisonment.

Section 26 of the 2007 Act provided for two new types of post-release orders: a "monitoring order" and a "protection of persons order". The court may make a "monitoring order" requiring the offender to notify in writing the inspector of the Garda Síochána of the district in which the offender's home is located, of the offender's address, change of address, or any proposed absence for a period of more than seven days from his or her home. The court may make a "protection of persons order" in relation to the offender for the purpose of protecting the victim of the offence concerned or any other person named in the order from harassment or intimidation by the offender while the order is in force. Both orders are activated on the release of the offender from prison. The orders may last for a period not exceeding seven years. Provision is made for the variation or revocation of the order.

Section 27 amended the Criminal Justice (Legal Aid) Act 1962 in order to extend its provisions to include applications to vary or revoke an order imposed under s.26 of the 2007 Act.

"Sense of grievance" In *People (DPP) v Drinkwater* [2007] I.E.C.C.A. 84; Court of Criminal Appeal, July 31, 2007, the Court of Criminal Appeal (Murray C.J., Herbert and McGovern JJ.) introduced the concept of the accused's "sense of grievance" concerning intimations of sentencing into Irish law. The applicant had been sentenced to two years' imprisonment for burglary, contrary to s.12 of the Criminal Justice (Theft and Fraud Offences) Act 2001. At the sentencing hearing particular emphasis was placed on the fact that the applicant was attempting to overcome a heroin addiction and was attempting to enrol in a centre for the treatment of those with such an addiction. He submitted that a non-custodial sentence might be appropriate if the applicant enrolled in the centre. The judge indicated that he would like to hear more about the centre before "taking a chance" on the applicant. The hearing was then adjourned. At the resumed hearing the sentencing judge refused to consider any details concerning the centre and, as indicated, sentenced the applicant to a custodial sentence. In the Court of Criminal Appeal, counsel for the applicant relied primarily on the applicant's "sense of grievance" by reason of the failure of the trial judge to impose a non-custodial sentence having regard to the circumstances and purpose of the previous adjournment.

For this proposition counsel relied on a number of United Kingdom authorities and referred to *Blackstone's Criminal Practice* (Oxford: Oxford

University Press, 2006), p.1850, which, under the heading "Sense of Grievance", states:

> "If the sequence of events prior to a sentence being passed, taken in conjunction with the actual sentence, leaves the offender with a justifiable sense of grievance, then the court of appeal would feel obliged to remove that sense of grievance, notwithstanding that the sentence is not in itself too severe. The principle has been applied especially in the context of the lower Court ordering reports and thereby raising in the offender's mind an expectation that, if the reports are satisfactory, he will be dealt with by non-custodial means. If the reports are good but the Court nonetheless passes a custodial sentence, the court of appeal will intervene. However, it is necessary to show that the offender's hopes of a non-custodial sentence were legitimately raised. Thus, if the Court, on adjourning for reports, made it clear that it was making no promises as to the eventual outcome, the eventual sentencer is at liberty to ignore a recommendation in the report for a non-custodial sentence, and the court of appeal will concern itself solely with whether the sentence passed was appropriate in all the circumstances."

The Court of Criminal Appeal stated that the accused's "sense of grievance" could operate as a factor on appeal—though it could not be the sole and determinative factor. In the present case, the court considered that it was "quite clear" that the sentencing process in which the judge was engaged was far from complete when he adjourned it but that the sentencing judge had only left the applicant "in hope" that a non-custodial sentence would be imposed. In that respect, the applicant could have no "sense of grievance" as described above and the court rejected his application.

The decision in *Drinkwater* adopts the policy from English law that the applicant, in a given case, could have a legitimate sense of grievance arising from an expectation that a non-custodial sentence would be passed. However, while such a sense of grievance may be a factor for the court on appeal, it has a limited scope, as the outcome in the case itself indicates.

Suspended sentence   Section 60 of the Criminal Justice Act 2007 made some minor changes to s.99 of the Criminal Justice Act 2006 (*Annual Review of Irish Law 2006,* p.315), which allows a court to wholly or partly suspend a sentence of imprisonment subject to the person entering into a recognisance to comply with certain conditions. The changed were stated to be aimed at improving the operation of s.99 of the 2006 Act.

SEXUAL OFFENCES

The Criminal Law (Sexual Offences) (Amendment) Act 2007 made a number of changes to the law on sexual offences, including correcting some errors in the Criminal Law (Sexual Offences) Act 2006 (whose origins are discussed in the *Annual Review of Irish Law 2006,* pp.352–353). When the Criminal Law (Sexual Offences) Act 2006 was enacted, it had omitted to include the offence of soliciting or importuning for purposes of commission of a sexual offence when it updated the Criminal Law (Sexual Offences) Act 1993. In this context, s.2 of the 2007 Act amended s.6 of the 1993 Act, by setting out the offence of soliciting or importuning. It states that a person who solicits or importunes a child (whether or not for the purposes of prostitution) for the purposes of the commission of an act that would constitute an offence under s.2 or s.3 of the Criminal Law (Sexual Offences) Act 2006, relating to defilement of a child under 15 and 17 years of age respectively, or referred to in s.2 of the Criminal Law (Rape) (Amendment) Act 1990, relating to sexual assault, is guilty of an offence. Section 2 of the 2007 Act also amended s.6 of the 1993 Act by setting out an offence of soliciting or importuning a person who lacks full mental capacity. It is regrettable in this respect that the 2007 Act continues to use the phrase "mentally impaired" in this respect less than one year after the State made significant contributions to finalising the 2006 UN Convention on the Rights of Persons With Disability. The 2007 Act states that where a person who solicits or importunes a person who is mentally impaired (whether or not for the purposes of prostitution) for the purposes of the commission of an act that would constitute an offence under s.5 of the Criminal Law (Sexual Offences) Act 1993, relating to the protection of mentally impaired persons, and s.2 of the Criminal Law (Rape) (Amendment) Act 1990, relating to sexual assault, is guilty of an offence. The penalty laid down for either offence under s.6 on summary conviction is a fine not exceeding €5,000, or imprisonment for a term not exceeding 12 months, or to both, and on conviction on indictment to a fine (in effect, an unlimited fine), or imprisonment for a term not exceeding five years, or to both.

Section 3 of the 2007 Act, mirroring s.6 of the 2006 Act, ensures that provisions in the Criminal Law (Rape) Act 1981 concerning matters such as the exclusion of the public from the court, preliminary examination, restriction of evidence and anonymity apply in cases where a person is tried for soliciting or importuning a child or mentally impaired person for the purpose of the commission of a sexual offence. It also provides for separate legal representation and legal aid and, s.3(4) provides for free legal advice for complainants in prosecution of the offence of soliciting and importuning under s.6 of the 1993 Act. Section 4 of the 2007 Act, similar to s.3, provides for the amendment of certain enactments. The Criminal Evidence Act 1992 is amended to include s.6 of the 1993 Act in the definition of "sexual offence" in the Criminal Evidence Act 1992. This means that the provisions in the 1992

Act under which, for example, children can give evidence in court through a television link or through an intermediary in trials for sexual or violent offences, will apply where a person is charged under s.6 of the 1993 Act.

The 2007 Act also amended the Sexual Offences (Jurisdiction) Act 1996 so that persons who are Irish citizens or persons ordinarily resident here who are alleged to have committed sexual offences against a child in another country can be charged in the State. An offence must be an offence both in this country and in the country in which it is alleged to have taken place. The offences are listed in the Schedule to the 1996 Act. They do not include an offence under s.6 of the 1993 Act and the effect of s.4 is to add it to the Schedule. The Bail Act 1997 is amended to make an offence under s.6 an indictable or serious offence under that Act (see also the section on Bail in Part B, p.217). The 2007 Act also amended the Sex Offenders Act 2001 to include an offence under s.6 in the list of offences which entails an obligation to sign on the sex offenders register.

Section 5 of the 2007 Act increased the penalties in the Criminal Law (Sexual Offences) Act 2006 in so far as they relate to defilement of a child under the age of 17 years. The offence of engaging in a sexual act with a child who is under the age of 17 increases from a maximum term of two years' imprisonment to a maximum term of five years' imprisonment. The offence of attempting to engage in a sexual act with a child who is under the age of 17, and any subsequent such offence, increases from a maximum term of four years' imprisonment to 10 years' imprisonment, and in the case of a person in authority who commits such a subsequent offence the maximum term of imprisonment increases from seven years' imprisonment to 15 years' imprisonment.

Section 6 of the 2007 Act amended s.3 of the Child Trafficking and Pornography Act 1998 to create a new offence of meeting a child for the purpose of sexual exploitation. As amended, s.3 of the 1998 Act states that any person in the State, or any citizen or person ordinarily resident in the State, who intentionally meets, or travels with the intention of meeting, a child, having met or communicated with that child on two or more previous occasions, and does so for the purpose of doing anything that would constitute sexual exploitation of the child, is guilty of an offence. The penalty on conviction on indictment is a term of imprisonment not exceeding 14 years. The section, through two different subsections, catches both offences committed in Ireland, and offences by Irish citizens, or persons ordinarily resident in Ireland, committed outside of Ireland.

Section 6 of the 2007 Act redefined the meaning of the term "sexual exploitation" in the Child Trafficking and Pornography Act 1998 setting out the definition of sexual exploitation as meaning, in relation to a child, inviting, inducing or coercing the child to engage in prostitution or the production of child pornography, using the child for prostitution or the production of child pornography, inviting, inducing or coercing the child to participate in any sexual activity which is an offence under any enactment, the commission of any such offence against the child, or inviting, inducing or coercing the child to participate in or observe any activity of a sexual or indecent nature.

SPENT CONVICTIONS

In 2007, the Law Reform Commission published a *Report on Spent Convictions* (LRC 84–2007) which examines whether some very old convictions might be looked on as being "spent" or no longer relevant for certain purposes. The Commission had made provisional recommendations on spent convictions as part of its *Consultation Paper on the Court Poor Box* (LRC CP 31–2004) and the 2007 Report contained its final recommendations on this area (the Commission had already published a separate *Report on the Court Poor Box: Probation of Offenders* (LRC 75–2005): see *Annual Review of Irish Law 2005*, pp.264–265). The Commission noted that under current law, records of criminal convictions of adults are permanent. The Commission's Report emphasises that even very old convictions should always remain relevant—and therefore be disclosed for vetting purposes—when applying for certain sensitive posts, including the supervision or care of children, vulnerable adults or in the context of sensitive public positions, such as those connected with State security or the legal system.

The Report notes that certain offences committed when a person was under 18 years (but not, for example, murder or rape) are already subject to a spent convictions system in s.258 of the Children Act 2001 and therefore do not, in general, have to be disclosed (though they would be disclosed as part of the vetting for sensitive posts). Similar spent convictions laws exist in most other countries, based on the model introduced in Britain by the Rehabilitation of Offenders Act 1974—later extended to Northern Ireland by the Rehabilitation of Offenders (Northern Ireland) Order 1978. The Commission noted that the British 1974 Act and the Northern Ireland 1978 Order was also used as the model for the under-18 spent convictions system in the Children Act 2001.

The Report sets out in detail the elements of the proposed spent convictions law and it also includes a draft Spent Convictions Bill to implement the Commission's recommendations. The Commission sets down the following elements for inclusion: the types of offences which should be excluded completely from the proposed law— (a) any offence triable by the Central Criminal Court, such as murder; (b) any sexual offence as defined in the Sex Offenders Act 2001; and (c) any other offence where a sentence of more than six months (including a suspended sentence) has been imposed in court; the length of time a person must be conviction-free to qualify for the conviction to be regarded as "spent": seven years from the date of conviction where a custodial sentence of up to six months is imposed; five years from the date of conviction where a non-custodial order is made, such as a fine or disqualification; all convictions, including spent convictions, would still be disclosed at a sentencing hearing and in some non-criminal cases such as involving access to children. The system would be automatic, rather than requiring the person to apply to court to have their conviction declared to be spent, as an application-based system would not be transparent and consistent.

The Report discusses the connection between a spent convictions system and the issue of vetting or disclosure of criminal convictions for certain purposes. The Commission supports the call by other bodies to put the current Garda vetting system on a modern statutory footing. The Report also emphasises that certain sensitive posts would continue to require full disclosure of all criminal convictions, including spent convictions. These include: (a) any post involving the care for, supervision of or teaching of any person under 18 years of age, or of any other person who is a vulnerable person; (b) any post in healthcare; (c) judge, barrister, solicitor, court clerk, court registrar or employee of the Courts Service; (d) civil servant; (e) firearms dealer; (f) member of the Defence Forces, prison officer, member of the probation service, member of An Garda Síochána (including reserve members, or traffic warden; (g) accountant; (h) director, controller or manager of a financial institution or of any financial service provider which is regulated by the Financial Regulator.

We note here that a private member's Bill, the Spent Convictions Bill 2007, published by Barry Andrews TD when he was backbencher (since becoming Minister of State for Children), and based on the Law Reform Commission's draft Bill, appears to have been given informal Government approval but it has not at the time of writing (September 2008) been enacted. It is arguable, as the Law Reform Commission suggested in its Report, that such a Bill could be linked to any associated statutory reform of the law on Garda vetting. We note here that the Government Legislative Programme of April 2008 indicates that a Vetting Bill is to be published at some time. This would implement the recommendations made in the 2002 *Report of the Expert Group on Garda Vetting* and appears also to be connected with the ongoing work of the Oireachtas Committee on Child Protection.

Education

APPEALS SYSTEM FOR SUSPENSIONS AND EXPULSIONS

The key objective of the Education (Miscellaneous Provisions) Act 2007 was to implement a specific recommendation in *School Matters*, the 2006 Report of the Task Force on Student Behaviour. The Task Force had been established by the Minister for Education in 2005 with the following terms of reference:

- to examine the issue of disruptive behaviour in schools, especially at second level;

- to consider effective strategies already employed;

- to advise on best practice in fostering positive behaviour; and

- to make recommendations on how best to promote an improved climate for teaching and learning in our schools.

The Report of the Task Force put forward a number of recommendations to place schools in a stronger position to meet the challenges of motivating and catering for their entire student cohort, including those "whose troubling behaviour is reflective of a wider societal breakdown of acceptable norms of courtesy and civility". The 2007 Act deals with just one aspect of the Report of the Task Force, the need to amend s.29 of the Education Act 1998, which deals with the appeals system for long-term suspensions and expulsions (expulsions are called exclusions in the 1998 Act). The appeal system is to the Secretary General of the Department of Education, who then appoints a schools inspector and two other ministerial appointees to hear the appeal.

The changes made to s.29 of the 1998 Act by the 2007 Act provide for a balancing of rights between the educational interests of the student who is taking an appeal and the educational interests of the school community as a whole. In so doing, the 2007 Act sets out a delicate balance of factors, each of which an appeals committee must take into consideration, and which must be weighed, one against the other, in examining the particular circumstances surrounding the decision under appeal. While the 2007 Act deals with the appeals system only, the factors which the appeals committee must take into account also provide a blueprint for schools in making decisions about long-term suspension and expulsions.

The nine factors which the appeals committee must take into account are:

1. the nature, scale and persistence of any behaviour alleged to have given rise to, or contributed to, the decision made by or on behalf of the school board;

2. the reasonableness of any efforts made by the school to enable the student to whom the appeal relates (the "student concerned") to participate in and benefit from education;

3. the educational interests of the student concerned and the desirability of enabling the student as far as practicable to participate in and benefit from education with his or her peers;

4. the educational interests of, and the effective provision of education for, other students of the school and the maintenance of a classroom and school environment which is supportive of learning among the students of the school and ensures continuity of instruction provided to students in any classroom concerned and the school;

5. the safety, health and welfare of teachers, students and staff of the school;

6. the school's Code of Behaviour under s.23 of the Education (Welfare) Act 2000 (which established the National Education Welfare Board) and other relevant policies of the school;

7. the duties on schools or their boards imposed by or under any Act;

8. guidelines issued by the National Education Welfare Board under s.22(7) of the 2000 Act; and

9. such other matters as the appeals committee considers relevant.

Two comments may be made in connection with the sixth heading. In the case of the Code of Behaviour, the appeals committee must take into account to what extent it is in compliance with s.23 of the 2000 Act and any guidelines issued under s.23(3). As to the other relevant policies of a school, the appeals committee must take into account to what extent each of them is implemented, promotes equality of access to and participation in education and is in compliance with any Act that imposes duties on schools or their boards (for example, the Safety, Health and Welfare at Work Act 2005) and in compliance with any relevant guidelines or policies of the Minister for Education.

In effect, these are a blueprint for schools, because they list the factors on which the appeals committee will judge the reasonableness of the decision of the school.

Employment Law

DES RYAN, Lecturer in Law, Trinity College, Dublin

INTRODUCTION

The focus of this chapter is on developments in Irish employment law in 2007. This chapter should be read in conjunction with the chapter on Health and Safety Law in this edition of the *Annual Review*. The developments selected for analysis here are those concerning: (i) injunctions restraining dismissal; (ii) constructive dismissal; (iii) restraint of trade and discretionary bonus schemes; (iv) employment equality claims; (v) industrial relations and the impact of the Supreme Court's *Ryanair* judgment; (vi) settlement agreements in the context of both the fixed-term workers' legislation and protective legislation generally; (vii) bullying and harassment at work. Taken together, these areas allow us to engage in an analysis of key developments to have taken place across the full range of different fora in Irish employment litigation: the pages that follow contain analysis not only of decisions from the Superior Courts but also of determinations of the Employment Appeals Tribunal, the Labour Court, the Rights Commissioner Service and the Equality Tribunal and include reference to the Health and Safety Authority and the Labour Relations Commission.

INJUNCTIONS RESTRAINING DISMISSAL

Difficulties in identifying authoritative principles from interlocutory applications The steady flow of High Court jurisprudence concerning the employment injunction restraining dismissal continued in 2007, with a number of detailed judgments being delivered by the High Court. Before proceeding to analyse a number of the most significant of these developments, one could not do better than to reflect on the observations made in the course of one such case this year, which provide a salutary reminder of both the complexity of this area of employment litigation and of the difficulties in identifying a coherent set of principles from the decided cases. In *Bergin v Galway Clinic Doughiska Ltd* [2007] I.E.H.C. 386 (High Court, November 2, 2007) Clarke J. observed as follows:

> "I think it is fair to state that this area of the jurisprudence of the courts is in a state of evolution and the precise current state of that jurisprudence is far from clear. This situation is not, in my view, helped by the fact

that a great many of the cases do not proceed to trial so that by far the greater number of the authorities consist of decisions of the court at an interlocutory stage rather than after a full hearing. While such authorities may be of very considerable assistance in defining the jurisprudence in relation to the grant or refusal of interlocutory injunctions, some may do little to advance the cause of clarity in respect of employment law generally, for the court is required to approach issues of general employment law, at the interlocutory stage, on the basis of arguability or, perhaps, where the injunction sought is mandatory in substance, likelihood of success. In either case a definitive decision on the legal issues arising (with the exception of those which are relevant solely to the grant or refusal of interlocutory relief) has to await a full trial. In practice the full trial rarely arises. It is the frequent experience of the court dealing with such matters that a great many of the cases which are the subject of an interlocutory ruling are resolved by agreement between the parties before the matter comes to trial. It would be somewhat naïve not to surmise that a significant feature of the interlocutory hearing is concerned with both parties attempting to establish the most advantageous position from which to approach the frequently expected negotiations designed to lead to an agreed termination of the contract of employment concerned. The employee who has the benefit of an interlocutory injunction can approach such negotiations from a position of strength as can the employer who has successfully resisted an interlocutory application."

With this in mind, three of the most important High Court judgments of 2007 in this context will now be examined.

Special considerations in context of the Universities Act 1997   The first decision requiring analysis is the judgment of Clarke J. in *Cahill v Dublin City University* [2007] E.L.R. 113. The plaintiff commenced his employment with the defendant as a senior lecturer in October 1999 and was promoted in 2001 to the position of associate professor. In early 2006 the plaintiff was engaged in discussions with representatives of the National University of Ireland, Galway with a view to exploring the possibility of the plaintiff's moving to that university with his research team where the plaintiff would take up the Chair of Molecular Medicine. At a meeting in March 2006, the plaintiff informed the president of the defendant university of the high probability of this move. Thereafter the defendant continued to press the plaintiff to indicate formally the date of his departure, but the plaintiff maintained that he was not yet in a position to provide same. Against that background the plaintiff received a letter on June 14, 2006 from the defendant's Director of Human Resources, which purported to give the plaintiff three months' notice of the termination of his employment, which was described as coming to an end on September 10, 2006.

The decision was stated to be that of the president of the defendant university. The plaintiff contested the validity of the termination of his contract in this manner, claiming that the termination was invalid either having regard to certain provisions of the Universities Act 1997 ("the 1997 Act") or, alternatively, that the notice of termination was served in breach of fair procedures.

Clarke J. held that the plaintiff's employment had been invalidly terminated, on a number of alternative grounds. The principal ground was because the putative termination did not involve appropriate procedures specified in an internal university statute so as to comply with s.25(6) of the 1997 Act; in the alternative, Clarke J. held that the case turned upon the meaning of the word "tenure" in that legislation; as a further alternative, the termination was unlawful due to the procedural defects addressed in the court's judgment. For present purposes, what is particularly significant about the High Court judgment in *Cahill* is the approach taken by Clarke J. in considering what was the appropriate order to be made in cases involving academic office-holders within the meaning of the 1997 Act. In a key passage, Clarke J. explained why *Cahill* was the type of case in which relief granted could potentially extend beyond a *Fennelly* order requiring the continuance of the payment of salary pending trial (*Fennelly v Assicurazioni Generali Spa* (1985) 3 I.L.T.R. 73):

> "It seems to me that it follows from the provisions of the 1997 Act, which limit the power to dismiss officers, and which require the court, in construing the statute, to lean in favour of a construction which favours the maintenance of academic freedom, that a court should, in turn, lean in favour, in an academic context, of making an order which preserves the entitlement of the academic office holder concerned to continue to operate as an academic in the university world. To take any other view would be to countenance a situation where, in an appropriate case, a university could exclude an academic from the ability to carry out his or her duties in the academic world in circumstances where the sanction imposed (either dismissal or suspension) was in breach of statute. I am, therefore, of the view that where it is established that a suspension or dismissal of an academic office holder is in breach of the provisions of the 1997 Act, the court should lean in favour of making an order which would restore the academic concerned to their duties. In those circumstances the situation which pertains in the case of those office holders who are governed by the 1997 Act, may well differ from the situation which might ordinarily obtain in relation to an ordinary contract of employment."

In the circumstances of the instant case, however, Clarke J. took the view that it was not appropriate to make any order beyond declaring that the plaintiff remained in office and was entitled to a *Fennelly* order directing the continued payment of his salary.

The approach taken in *Cahill* underlines the strong protection for tenured academics under the 1997 Act, a situation which could be considered as increasingly anomalous in an era in which universities in Ireland are becoming more "professionalised" in terms of both the introduction of new management structures and fundamental university restructuring generally (see Clíona Kimber, editorial preceding the reporting of *Cahill* in the *Employment Law Reports* ([2007] E.L.R. 113)). It is understood that this decision is under appeal to the Supreme Court (appeal lodged March 8, 2007).

The need to establish a strong case in context of mandatory relief   A very significant development in recent years concerning the criteria for granting an interlocutory injunction occurred in the Supreme Court decision in *Maha Lingham v Health Service Executive* [2006] 17 E.L.R. 137. Here the Supreme Court emphasised that where mandatory as opposed to prohibitory relief was being sought, the risk of injustice to the defendant, in the event of the relief being granted, is heightened. Accordingly, in such circumstances the applicant would have to show not merely that there was a fair question to be tried, but instead would have to make out a *strong* case that he or she was likely to succeed at the hearing of the action.

Subsequent application of this distinction delineated in *Maha Lingham* between the different thresholds applicable in the context of prohibitory injunctions, on the one hand, and mandatory injunctions, on the other, is to be witnessed in a number of High Court cases (for detailed treatment see for example the judgment of Laffoy J. in *Naujoks v National Institute of Bioprocessing Research and Training Limited* [2007] 18 E.L.R. 25) and indeed has been a recurring theme in the jurisprudence of the High Court in this area in 2007. An example of its application is the judgment of Edwards J. in *Coffey v Connolly and Sons* [2007] I.E.H.C. 319 (High Court, September 18, 2007), where Edwards J. confirmed that "if the applicant is seeking a mandatory interlocutory injunction the threshold is higher [than that in the context of a prohibitory injunction]". Particularly significant in this regard is the judgment of the High Court in *Bergin v Galway Clinic Doughiska Limited* [2007] I.E.H.C. 386 (High Court, November 2, 2007) where Clarke J. described *all* cases in which an employee seeks to restrain dismissal as coming within the *Maha Lingham* heightened threshold test. As Clarke J. observed:

> "[I]n any case in which an employee seeks to prevent a dismissal or a process leading to a dismissal, as a matter of common law, and in whatever terms the claim is couched, the employee concerned is seeking what is, in substance, a mandatory injunction which has the effect of necessarily continuing his contract of employment even though the employer might otherwise be entitled to terminate it. In those

circumstances it is necessary for the employee concerned to establish a strong case in order to obtain interlocutory relief."

Detailed analysis of the *Maha Lingham* distinction was provided by the High Court (Irvine J.) in *Stoskus v Goode Concrete Ltd* [2007] I.E.H.C. 432 (High Court, December 18, 2007).

In *Stoskus* the plaintiff sought a *Fennelly* order ensuring that he be continued to be paid pending the trial of the action. The plaintiff had been dismissed following an investigation into two separate disciplinary matters. The relevant disciplinary process undertaken by the company had involved a hearing at which the plaintiff had been permitted to be represented by another person but not to have his solicitor present. He claimed that this rendered the disciplinary process unfair and sought an interlocutory injunction restraining his dismissal and requiring that he be paid pending the hearing of the action. The defendant company, on the other hand, argued that the manner in which it conducted its disciplinary proceedings had been made known to employees, stressing that the plaintiff had expressly agreed to the use of such procedures when he signed his contract of employment.

In terms of the *Maha Lingham* distinction, counsel for the plaintiff in *Stoskus* contended that the relief sought was not truly mandatory in nature given that the interlocutory relief sought was confined to an order restraining the defendants from relinquishing the plaintiff's salary pending the hearing of the action. Irvine J. rejected this submission. Citing the passage from the judgment of Clarke J. in *Bergin v Galway Clinic Doughiska Ltd*, quoted above, she held that although the relief sought by the plaintiff was framed as prohibitory in nature, the plaintiff was in effect seeking mandatory relief, since he was "asking the court to require the defendant to perform an obligation i.e. the payment of salary, which obligation only exists in the context of an ongoing contractual relationship between the parties."

Irvine J. concluded both that the relief sought was mandatory in nature and consequently that the onus of proof on the plaintiff at the interlocutory hearing was to establish that he had a "strong" case to make at the hearing of the action.

In terms of assessing just how stringent the heightened threshold may be for an applicant to overcome, it is noteworthy that the plaintiff in *Stoskus* failed to satisfy the court that he had made out a strong case. The court attached particular weight to the fact that the plaintiff had voluntarily agreed to participate in the model of disciplinary procedure envisioned in the employment contract which he had signed. Whilst a stateable argument could be advanced to the effect that principles of natural and constitutional justice would require that a solicitor should be present at disciplinary hearings of this nature, the court concluded that such a claim was no more than merely stateable and had not reached the level of a "strong case" which *Maha Lingham* and subsequent case law analysed above now demands.

Summary of 2007 developments post-*Maha Lingham* A number of observations may be made about these developments since *Maha Lingham*. Now that there is a twin-track threshold system in operation depending on the nature of the relief sought —with the requirement of demonstrating a fair question to be tried being sufficient for prohibitory relief, but with mandatory relief requiring a strong case to be shown—it will become extremely important properly to characterise the nature of the relief being sought. In this regard, the two developments noted above are particularly important: the approach of Clarke J. in *Bergin* classes all injunction applications seeking to restrain dismissal as essentially seeking mandatory relief; and the approach of Irvine J. in *Stoskus* clearly suggests that in the determination of the appropriate threshold the courts will be ready to adopt an approach that favours substance over form. If the relief being sought is regarded as mandatory in nature, attempts to plead same as merely prohibitory will likely, as was ultimately the outcome in *Stoskus*, be in vain. Finally, the approach in *Stoskus* illustrates that the requirement of a strong case is, at least when compared to the fair question test, a stringent one.

CONSTRUCTIVE DISMISSAL

Grievance procedures in the context of constructive dismissal Perhaps the most high-profile case of constructive unfair dismissal in 2007 was that of *Harrold v St Michael's House* [2008] E.L.R. 1. Because the determination of the Employment Appeals Tribunal turns upon the degree of engagement by the claimant with the respondent's grievance procedures, it is necessary to set out the background to the case in some detail.

The claimant commenced employment with the respondent in March 1991 as a psychologist. In 2001, the claimant stated that he experienced difficulties with the respondent. In a letter to the chairperson of the Board he expressed concern about what he claimed was a culture of bullying within the organisation and referred in particular to the bullying of a long-standing staff member who had left the organisation. The chairperson of the Board advised the claimant to engage in the respondent's internal grievance procedure in order to have his concerns addressed. Three individuals were nominated to conduct the internal grievance procedure; however, the claimant maintained that two of these individuals had been involved in the bullying of the staff member to whom the claimant had referred when expressing his concerns about the climate of bullying. The claimant therefore stated that while he would engage in the process he would not do so with those two individuals—the persons hearing his grievances would need to be independent.

The claimant was threatened with disciplinary action by the respondent if he did not co-operate with the internal grievance procedure. The respondent's solicitors then wrote to the claimant outlining a formula for an investigative sub-committee of the Board; however, the claimant objected to the presence of a member of the committee on the grounds of his being a friend of the chief executive officer, contending that an objective investigation could not be guaranteed. In or around December 2002, the Board wrote to the claimant informing him that because he had not co-operated with either of the respondent's procedures the case was now closed. The claimant responded that the case had not been satisfactorily or at all resolved and he would now have to deal with the matter outside the respondent. Accordingly, in June 2003 he wrote to the Minister for Health highlighting his concerns; the Minister in turn organised for the Eastern Regional Health Authority to set up an investigation. In October 2003, the investigation resulted in the investigator telling the claimant that he had not co-operated with the procedure.

In or around July 2003, approximately one month after he had written to the Minister, the claimant received a letter from the respondent informing him of a number of concerns the respondent had in relation to his performance and conduct. The claimant maintained that after he wrote to the Minister a campaign was waged by the respondent to damage his reputation and to place him under pressure that he would not be able to endure. A meeting was held where the claimant outlined how all of the eight allegations concerning the claimant's conduct and performance were entirely spurious and an attempt to undermine his integrity. The claimant did not receive any communication from the respondent as to the status of the investigation or any reply to the outcome of concerns he raised in a letter to the respondent in or around November 2003. The claimant ultimately resigned in March 2004 as he felt he had exhausted all avenues of communication and did not have anywhere left to go with the issues of bullying, yet the issues still remained unaddressed by the respondent and he argued that he was being targeted for having raised these issues. He brought a claim for constructive dismissal before the Employment Appeals Tribunal.

Application of *Liz Allen* test   The tribunal noted that the test for the claimant was whether it was reasonable for him to terminate his contract as applied in the very well-known determination in *Allen v Independent Newspapers* [2002] E.L.R. 84, concluding that their task was to:

> "… [E]valuate the evidence heard by it to ascertain whether the claimant had established a factual situation sufficient to bring him within the aforesaid legal parameters. Furthermore the necessary source of evidence in this matter is that produced by the claimant and his fellow employees supplemented where relevant to this employee/employer dispute by other relevant witnesses outside the employment nexus."

The tribunal then went on to consider the evidence called in the case and concluded that the totality of the evidence did not establish the existence of bullying within the organisation. It also concluded that the claimant did not act reasonably in refusing to engage in the process made available to him by the respondent. Rejecting the claim, the tribunal concluded:

> "… that there ha[d] been a consistent pattern of lack of engagement by the claimant with the respondent's grievance procedures. The Tribunal consequently finds that the claimant acted unreasonably in terminating his employment contract with the respondent."

The determination is thus of key significance in underlining the importance of engaging with internal grievance procedures as a pre-requisite for bringing a constructive dismissal claim. This is, however, subject to the qualification that where a failure to have recourse to grievance procedures is itself inextricably bound up with the treatment of which the claimant complains, such failure may not preclude the claimant from success providing that the tribunal is satisfied that such failure was reasonable. (This qualification was emphasised in another determination of the Tribunal in 2007: see *Porter v Atlantic Homecare Limited* [2008] 19 E.L.R. 95).

RESTRAINT OF TRADE AND DISCRETIONARY BONUS SCHEMES

High Court judgment in *Finnegan v J & E Davy* A very significant development in 2007 was the judgment of the High Court in *Finnegan v J & E Davy* [2007] E.L.R. 234, a decision that is at present under appeal to the Supreme Court (appeal lodged March 15, 2007). This widely discussed ruling has important implications for restraint of trade issues (on which see for example Kiwana Ennis, "An Examination of the Law on Restraint of Trade and Discretionary Bonus Schemes in the Light of *Finnegan v J & E Davy*" (2007) 4(1) I.E.L.J. 9). It also marks the first significant Irish contribution to a growing line of case law, principally from the English courts, concerning the exercise of discretion by employers in awarding, and arriving at the amount of, bonus payments. (For detailed treatment of this line of case law, see Ray Ryan and Des Ryan, "Bonus Points: Employers' Discretion in the Determination of Bonus Payments" (2007) 14(8) C.L.P. 166.)

The plaintiff was a stockbroker who sued his former employer for €260,000 in deferred bonus payments earned in 1998 and 1999. The plaintiff worked for Davy between 1990 and 2000. His bonuses were tied to the firm's profitability and his own performance, with the amounts being decided at a yearly meeting with his superiors, where his performance was assessed. He did not receive a bonus in 1992, but in every other year between 1990 and 1997, he earned bonuses of between £3,000 and £30,000. The entire sum was paid shortly after the annual review.

In 1997, the firm began deferring part of the payments. The timeline of events here is significant. At the beginning of 1998, it was agreed that the plaintiff's bonus for 1997 would be £100,000. He was paid £60,000 immediately, but £40,000 was deferred for a year. Its payment was conditional on his remaining with the firm. The plaintiff objected to this, particularly the condition that he stay with the company, but was told that Davy's biggest shareholder, Bank of Ireland, stipulated that bonuses be paid in this way. It was, however, agreed that he would receive the interest earned on the money. A year later, his bonus for 1998 was set at £200,000, payable in three instalments, the first immediately, the second a year later and the third a year after that. His 1999 bonus was fixed at £210,000, payable in three equal instalments over two years. All deferred payments depended on his remaining with the company. The plaintiff left Davy to join a rival firm in September 2000. As a result, he did not receive one instalment of his 1998 bonus and two-thirds of his 1999 payment, a total equivalent to just over €260,000. He argued that the attempt to change the terms of the bonus payment scheme was:

1. a unilateral attempt by the defendant to alter the terms of the employment contract which was not accepted by the plaintiff and which was ineffective;

2. in breach of the employment contract as being an irrational exercise of the employer's discretion; and

3. an unenforceable term as being in restraint of trade.

On behalf of the defendant employer, it was argued that such a deferred payment scheme was a legitimate means of "incentivising" employees and an attempt to generate loyalty. For present purposes, then, the question of whether the duty of fidelity of the employee could be invoked by the employer to justify its approach to the bonus scheme in this case, is relevant. Smyth J. emphatically rejected the argument that the deferral acted to "incentivise" employees and instead found as a fact that the real reason for the deferral was "to create a financial and practical restriction on employees who wished to continue to act as stockbrokers going to another firm of stockbrokers".

The plaintiff argued that in circumstances where bonus payments were calculated by reference to profitability of the firm in a calendar year and the individual performance of the plaintiff during that year, it was arbitrary and irrational to seek to make the payment of that bonus conditional upon the plaintiff remaining in the employment of the defendant for the following two years. The effect of this stipulation would be to change the criteria for the awarding of the bonus from one of profitability and performance to one of loyalty in the future. Smyth J. accepted this argument and deemed the provision which amounted to a restraint of trade to constitute an improper exercise of discretion. Another significant finding of fact in this regard was that those employees who left the firm when outstanding elements of bonuses were unpaid, but who did not go into competition, were paid the outstanding monies. This finding of fact supported the conclusion that if the deferral provision was part of a contract it was part of a contract in restraint of trade.

The judgment prompts a number of observations. First, in concluding that the discretion had been improperly exercised, Smyth J. had regard to a number of English authorities (among the most significant being *Horkulak v Cantor Fitzgerald International* [2004] E.W.C.A. Civ. 1287; [2005] I.C.R. 402.). A number of recent English cases both prior and subsequent to *Finnegan* illustrate the difficulties facing employees in challenging the exercise of discretion by employers in the context of bonuses: among the most significant of the recent cases is the decision of the Court of Appeal in *Commerzbank v Keen* [2006] E.W.C.A. Civ. 1536, [2007] I.R.L.R. 132 and that of the English High Court in *Ridgway v JP Morgan Chase Bank National Association* [2007] E.W.H.C. 1325. (For discussion, see Ryan and Ryan, above.) It is thus the restraint of trade feature of this bonus dispute that appears to have been determinative of the result in *Finnegan*.

EMPLOYMENT EQUALITY

For a detailed review of employment equality developments in 2007, see the Equality Tribunal's Annual Report (available at *www.equalitytribunal.ie*). In assessing the most significant developments to emerge from the jurisprudence of the Equality Tribunal in 2007, it is submitted that of the nine grounds identified in s.6(2) of the Employment Equality Act 1998 ("the 1998 Act") under which claims may be brought before the Equality Tribunal, it is in the context of the age and the disability ground that the most noteworthy determinations were delivered in 2007. A number of cases will now be analysed under each of these grounds.

Age discrimination   The Equality Tribunal continues to encounter a very significant number of claims for discrimination on the grounds of age. So too does empirical evidence from the Equality Authority indicate that age is now "the single biggest reason for workplace discrimination claims" (see Paul Cullen and Laura Slattery, "Age biggest single reason for workplace discrimination" *The Irish Times*, May 19, 2008). Two recurring themes in this area of the case law are, first, the perils of posing any questions as to age or date of birth at the interview stage and, secondly, the willingness of the Equality Tribunal to invoke its jurisdiction pursuant to s.82 of the 1998 Act to make awards solely addressed at reflecting the effects of the discrimination, notwithstanding what might be termed the lack of either causation or loss in the particular circumstances.

Application forms and inappropriate questions   Both of the above-mentioned themes are reflected in the most significant cases from 2007 to emerge from the Equality Tribunal. One such case is *Cunningham v BMS Sales Limited* (DEC-E2007-006) [2008] 19 E.L.R. 165. There the complainant contended that the defendant company had directly discriminated against him on the age ground when it provided him with a registration form requesting his age and date of birth. Mr Cunningham in purporting to complete the form did not give his date of birth and provided an incorrect age. The company then sought to clarify the matter with him and advised him that, in the absence of his providing the details sought, his application would not be further progressed. The company, which was a sales recruiter, argued that as a responsible recruiter, it had to ensure that it could be confident that the details provided by candidates were correct and accurate in order to build a successful working relationship. In addition, the respondent contended that it maintained a duty of care to both clients and candidates alike and thus information supplied must be correct information.

Rejecting the respondent's argument, the Equality Officer held that the claimant had established prima facie evidence of discrimination on grounds of age where the information was sought on the registration form and subsequently pursued with him. Compensation of €5,000 was awarded which was expressly for distress and breach of rights under the Employment Equality Act 1998–2004: it did not contain any element of lost income.

Interviews: questions and procedures   The perils of posing questions relating to the impugned discriminatory ground (here age) are again reinforced by the Equality Tribunal's determination in *MacGabhainn v Salesforce.com* (DEC–E2007–048). There the Equality Officer held that a job applicant was discriminated against on the grounds of age when asked his age at interview. Significantly, the Equality Officer did accept that she did not believe that the applicant would have been successful in the interview, even if he had not been asked about his age. She ordered that the respondent pay the complainant the relatively small sum of €1,000 in compensation for the effects of the discrimination.

So too is the importance of adhering strictly to protocol at the interview stage reflected in the tribunal's determination in *O'Conghaile v Mercy Mean Scoil Mhuire* (DEC-2007-068) [2008] E.L.R. 107, a claim arising from the claimant's lack of success in a competition for the position of Principal. The successful candidate was younger than the complainant. At interview, the complainant had been asked the following question:

> "Can you offer the selection committee a brief outline as to why you feel, at this stage in your career, that you are the most suitable candidate for the position of principal?"

The complainant contended that this question—which was posed to all candidates interviewed—was an inappropriate question implying that she had to justify her interest with regard to her age, and revealing prejudice by the selection committee on the age ground. The respondent contended that the question was designed to enable each candidate to present a clear account of his or her motivation in applying for the post that was "rooted in the candidate's general assessment of his or her own career path".

Very significantly, this question was listed as one of the factors which led the Equality Officer to uphold the age discrimination claim. In taking this view, the Equality Officer referred to the well-established principle, confirmed in the approach of the European Court of Justice in *Finanzamt Koln-Alstadt v Roland Schumacker* Case C-279/93 [1995] E.C.R. I-225, that discrimination can arise not only through the application of different rules to comparable situations but by the application of the same rule to different situations. The reliance on this judgment is, with respect, somewhat surprising; it may be questioned whether the principle identified and applied by the Court of Justice in *Finanzamt Koln-Alstadt*—a case relating to tax and the different situation of residents as compared to non-residents of a Member State—is one which has any meaningful parallel with the situation in *O'Conghaile* concerning the same question being put to each of the candidates at interview. It is submitted that the respondent's argument concerning the impugned question has considerable force: surely it is legitimate to expect a candidate to be able to locate their application for a promotion in the broader trajectory of their career to date? The inclusion by the Equality Officer of this interview question as one of the bases for upholding the complainant's claim of age discrimination—on the basis of the truism that "the question could have had a different significance for each of the candidates depending on the particular stage of their careers at which they found themselves" —appears unconvincing.

Of greater force and weight in leading to the complaint being upheld was the criticism in *O'Conghaile* of the interview procedures adopted by the respondent. Censuring the employer's failure to take adequate interview notes, the Equality Officer also found a general lack of transparency in allocating marks in the interview process including the failure to determine the amount of marks to be awarded on foot of the reference in advance of the selection process. Upholding the claim of age discrimination, the Equality Officer awarded compensation of €10,000 and directed the respondent to adhere to good practice selection procedure in all future promotions, which would involve adopting and applying a formal marking system agreed prior to any consideration of CVs, ranking candidates by reference to that marking system and retaining all notes from the interviews.

Potential for large awards in age context   A number of other decisions of the tribunal in 2007 demonstrate the potential for large awards to be made in the age context. Amongst the most prominent of such decisions in 2007 was that in *Ruddy v SDS (An Post)* (DEC-2007-020), where the complainant was refused access to an owner-driver scheme which, alongside an alternative offer option of voluntary redundancy, formed part of a restructuring programme. The complainant expressed an interest in the owner-driver scheme as it offered a more generous financial package than the redundancy package and would have allowed him to commence as a self-employed driver. The owner-driver scheme, however, had an upper age limit of 60. The respondent accepted that an age restriction had been placed on the scheme, but argued that without this restriction it would have incurred significant costs, and that accordingly the restriction was permissible under s.34(3) of the 1998 Act. The respondent also argued that as the claimant never formally made an application for the scheme, he lacked locus standi in respect of his claim. The employee in turn contended that he had not formally applied because he considered that the application would have been futile.

On the standing point, the Equality Officer was "satisfied that had the complainant submitted an application it would have been rejected by the respondent on the basis that he was over 60 years of age". She found that the respondent discriminated against the complainant on grounds of age and awarded the complainant €70,316—the difference between the amount the complainant would have been permitted to earn had he been allowed to avail of the owner-driver scheme in 2003 of €92,442 and the amount he received on retirement, €22,126. (For another example of a similarly large award in an age discrimination case, see *Dunne v An Post* (DEC-2007-034), a case involving the same owner-driver scheme as that in *Ruddy* in which the Equality Officer awarded the sum of €80,000 as lost income and €10,000 for the effects of the discrimination).

Discrimination on grounds of disability   Large awards were also in evidence in determinations of the Equality Tribunal in 2007 in the context of disability. A good example of this—as well as of the tribunal's response to the changed landscape in the context of discriminatory dismissals brought about by the extension of the tribunal's jurisdiction to deal with such dismissals under the Equality Act 2004 ("the 2004 Act") —is provided in *Kavanagh v Aviance UK Ltd* (DEC-2007-039). There the complainant was employed as a ramp supervisor. He sustained an elbow injury during the course of his work and during a visit to the company doctor the issue of his cardiac condition was raised, the complainant having undergone a number of cardiac procedures. The company doctor expressed concern at the complainant's fitness to work as he carried out baggage-handling activities. She consulted on various occasions with the complainant's consultant cardiologist. The complainant's doctors certified him as fit to return to work as a supervisor. The doctor employed by the respondent did not certify the complainant as fit to return to work due to his cardiac condition.

The respondent ultimately dismissed the complainant on medical grounds. The complainant argued that he would have been fully capable of performing his duties had reasonable accommodation been provided by the respondent, such as ensuring that he was not required to undertake lifting during the course of his work. The respondent relied on medical evidence that the complainant was not fit to return to work, and claimed that its human resources manager carried out an extensive review of any other roles that might have been vacant but there were no such alternative roles available which could reasonably have been offered to the complainant.

In upholding the complainant's claim, the Equality Officer expressly noted that prior to the 2004 Act the complainant could have sought redress in the Equality Tribunal for the discriminatory treatment and in the Labour Court for the discriminatory dismissal. In a significant comment, she observed that "the potential compensation could not have diminished as a result of the transfer of the jurisdiction for discriminatory dismissal claims", referring to the Framework Directive underpinning the relevant changes brought about by the 2004 Act (Council Directive 2000/78/EC).

Of particular note here is that, over and above the compensation awarded for loss of earnings, the Equality Officer directed that the respondent pay the complainant the sum of €60,000 "by way of compensation for the stress suffered as a result of the discrimination and the failure to provide reasonable accommodation". The amount of this award was expressly said to be in accordance with Art 17 of the Framework Directive, which provides that "sanctions must be effective, proportionate and dissuasive".

This decision also illustrates the onus upon employers to meaningfully engage in consideration of what steps can be taken to reasonably accommodate an employee with a disability. In particular, attempts to rely on broad medical evidence, where that reliance is unaccompanied by either any attempt at considering methods of accommodation or any attempt at consulting with the employee so as to explore the possibilities for such accommodation, may well create an exposure on the grounds of a failure to make reasonable accommodation.

The breadth of the obligation to make reasonable accommodation is well illustrated by the subsequent decision of the Labour Court in December 2007 on an appeal from a determination of the Equality Tribunal in *A Worker (complainant) v A Hotel* [2008] 19 E.L.R. 73. The complainant was employed as a sales executive and commenced work in May 2005. She suffered from a mild form of osteoarthritis. The complainant stated that she informed the respondent of her disability during the three-stage interview process which ensued. The respondent strongly denied this. On her first day of employment the complainant found that she was to work in an office shared by three other people and accessed by a flight of 22 steps. There were no lift facilities to this office. On her second day of employment she complained to the general manager regarding the office facility and also stated that she had suffered pain and discomfort overnight. A meeting was held with the general manager on June 1, 2005 and as he told her he could not find a solution she left the premises that day and her employment ceased. The complainant alleged, inter alia, that she was dismissed on the disability ground. She also claimed that the respondent did not make sufficient efforts to accommodate her disability.

The Equality Officer had determined in favour of the complainant and awarded €15,000 in compensation. When the respondent appealed the decision to the Labour Court, the Labour Court rejected the appeal but varied the order below. The Court agreed with the Equality Officer that no appropriate enquiries were made as to what measures could be taken to enable the complainant to carry out her duties. Owing to this failure, the s.16(1) defence could not be relied on. The Labour Court emphasised that if the protected factor or characteristic is more than a "trivial influence" in the impugned decision, a claim of discrimination will have been made out (referring to the judgment of Peter Gibson L.J. in *Wong v Igen Ltd* [2005] E.W.C.A. Civ. 142, [2005] 3 All E.R. 812).

The nature of the obligation on employers to make reasonable accommodation is well captured by the Labour Court in the following passage:

> "The duty to provide special treatment or facilities is proactive in nature. It includes an obligation to carry out a full assessment of the needs of the person with a disability and of the measures necessary to accommodate that person's disability."

INDUSTRIAL RELATIONS

Impact of Supreme Court judgment in *Ryanair* The single most important development in 2007 in the context of industrial relations is undoubtedly the decision of the Supreme Court in *Ryanair v The Labour Court* [2007] I.E.S.C. 6; [2007] 18 E.L.R. 57. The judgment prompts analysis of the fascinating question of the proper role of the Labour Court and the procedures that the court must adopt.

Background to *Ryanair* judgment The *Ryanair* case centred on the interpretation of the Industrial Relations (Amendment) Act 2001 ("the 2001 Act") which, it will be recalled, was introduced as a result of the social partnership agreement Partnership 2000, following close examination by trade union and employer representatives of the question of trade union recognition.

Pursuant to the 2001 Act, an employer may be compelled to grant union representatives the right to represent unionised employees on workplace issues relating to pay and terms and conditions of employment. The Labour Court can make a determination with regard to these matters, and to dispute resolution and disciplinary procedures, in the employment concerned but cannot provide for arrangements for collective bargaining.

The dispute forming the backdrop to this case began in the summer of 2004 when Ryanair began the conversion of its Dublin fleet. This involved retraining for some 90 pilots, who were told they could either pay €15,000 for the training or alternatively sign a bond abandoning their entitlement to raise matters with the Labour Court. A number of the pilots, members of IALPA (the Irish Airline Pilots' Association and a branch of IMPACT), sought to have the union negotiate with Ryanair about these, and other issues, on their behalf. Ryanair refused to negotiate with the union. Instead, it negotiated with a series of Employee Relation Committees (ERCs) representing each category of employees. Three separate agreements were entered into by Ryanair with each ERC in 1994, 1997 and 2000.

IMPACT then applied to the Labour Court to investigate the trade dispute between the parties under the 2001 Act as amended by the Industrial Relations (Miscellaneous Provisions) Act 2004. The Labour Court held a preliminary hearing pursuant to s.3 of the 2001 Act to determine whether the requirements specified in s.2(1) of the same Act had been met, *viz.* whether a trade dispute existed, whether it was the practice of the employer to engage in collective bargaining negotiations in respect of the grade, group or category of workers who are a party to the trade dispute, if any, and whether the internal dispute resolution procedures had failed to resolve the dispute. The Labour Court decided that it had jurisdiction to hear and determine the substantive issues. It interpreted the definition of "trade dispute" and the reference to a "difference" as permitting the Labour Court to investigate a difference between the pilots and Ryanair concerning the terms of their employment as amounting to a trade dispute for the purposes of the Act. (The Labour Court judgment is reported at [2005] E.L.R. 99).

Ryanair then brought a judicial review application seeking to quash the preliminary decision of the Labour Court on the basis that there was in fact no trade dispute and that in any event the Labour Court had adopted unfair procedures and made an irrational decision. The High Court (Hanna J.) refused the application to quash the decision and stated that "the Labour Court is entitled to manage its own affairs and to conduct proceedings before it as it sees fit provided it so conducts itself within the limits of the statutory provision from which it derives authority". (The High Court judgment is reported at [2006] E.L.R. 1.)

It was against that decision of the High Court that Ryanair appealed to the Supreme Court. The Supreme Court disagreed with the Labour Court's interpretation of the 2001 and 2004 Acts. The Supreme Court judgment has been and is at the time of writing being much discussed, and a full treatment of its implications is beyond the scope of the present chapter. (For detailed treatment see, for example, Michael Doherty, "Union Sundown? The Future of Collective Representation Rights in Irish Law" (2007) 4 (4) I.E.L.J. 96). It is proposed here to reflect briefly on those points on which the Supreme Court differed from the courts below. There are two key points to be considered.

Meaning of "trade dispute"   First, the Supreme Court disagreed with the interpretation given by the Labour Court to the term "trade dispute". While this term is not defined in the 2001 Act, the applicable definition is that set out in s.3 of the Industrial Relations Act 1946 ("the 1946 Act") where a trade dispute is said to include "any dispute or difference between employers and workers or between workers and workers connected with the employment or non-employment, or the terms of employment, or with the conditions of employment of any person". (This definition differs from that contained in the Industrial Relations Act 1990 which defines "trade dispute" in s.8 as being "any dispute between employers and workers which is connected with the employment or non-employment, or the terms or conditions of or affecting the employment, of any person".) The Supreme Court in *Ryanair* agreed that the relevant definition was that contained in the 1946 Act, but disagreed with the Labour Court's construction of that term. The Labour Court had highlighted the use of the word "difference" in the definition in the 1946 Act and had concluded that because of its inclusion in the definition the term must bear a specific meaning not covered by the term "dispute". The Supreme Court disagreed with this construction, Geoghegan J. observing as follows:

> "It is common in statutes to include overlapping nouns or adjectives. For instance, if Ryanair and a particular group of its employees with which it was dealing were in disagreement over the dismissal of some employee, that would incontrovertibly be a *'dispute'*. On the other hand if the disagreement related to interpretation of say a collective agreement, it might at least be argued that that was not a *'dispute'*. The inclusion of the word *'difference'* is intended only to indicate the wider meaning of *'trade dispute'*. In the definition itself both words come within the expression *'trade dispute'*."

The Supreme Court also held that the Labour Court in determining whether there was a trade dispute should have investigated whether there was internal machinery for resolving the perceived problem and whether the machinery had been exhausted.

Collective bargaining   Secondly, the Supreme Court disagreed with the lower courts' approaches to the question of collective bargaining. Ryanair had argued in the Labour Court that the existence of the ERCs and the holding of "town hall" meetings in effect amounted to collective bargaining such that the Labour Court had no right to adjudicate on the dispute. It also argued that no bona fide trade dispute existed between the parties and it submitted that this was part of a strategy on the part of the union to compel trade union recognition.

For the purposes of the Labour Court's preliminary hearing, both sides accepted a definition of collective bargaining adopted by the same court in *SIPTU v Ashford Castle* [2004] E.L.R. 214:

> "Collective bargaining comprehends more than mere negotiation or consultation on individual employment related issues including the processing of individual grievances in relation to pay or conditions of employment. In the industrial relations context in which the term is commonly used it connotes a process by which employers or their representatives negotiate with representatives of a group or body of workers for the purpose of concluding a collective agreement fixing the pay and other conditions of employment applicable to the group or collective of workers on whose behalf the negotiations are conducted.
>
> Normally the process is characterised by the involvement of a trade union representing workers but it may also be conducted by a staff association which is an excepted body within the meaning of the *Trade Union Act 1941*, as amended. However, an essential characteristic of collective bargaining, properly so called, is that it is conducted between parties of equal standing who are independent in the sense that one is not controlled by the other."

The Labour Court had held that Ryanair's communication and consultation processes did not amount to collective bargaining. It analysed the communications issued by the company to employees and it was considered that if it was the practice of the employer to engage in collective bargaining, there would have been some central negotiation on issues such as agreement establishing the ERCs, pension benefits and training arrangements. The Labour Court further emphasised the fact that the pilots had withdrawn from the ERC process so that at the time of the referral to the Labour Court there was no ERC in progress.

The Supreme Court disagreed with this interpretation. It noted, for example, that the unilateral withdrawal by the pilots from machinery put in place by the employer would not of itself entitle the employees to assert that there was no collective bargaining process in place. The Supreme Court further disagreed with the Labour Court's interpretation of whether or not machinery existed for collective bargaining negotiations. While it too cited the *Ashford Castle* definition of collective bargaining, the Supreme Court held that that description of collective bargaining, though appropriate to a unionised workplace, may not always be appropriate to a non-unionised workplace.

Procedural direction from Supreme Court concerning *viva voce* evidence   A separate point of some significance about the approach taken by the Supreme Court in *Ryanair* is that the Labour Court's practice of relying solely on written submissions in the determination of factual matters was criticised. The Supreme Court directed that where factual matters were in dispute, oral evidence should be taken from the employees concerned. In the *Ryanair* case, the employees had not been directly identified in the Labour Court process and were represented throughout by the trade union. The Supreme Court held that without identifying the parties to the dispute (and in particular which pilots were involved in the dispute) the Labour Court did not have before it the evidence on which it could conclude that the internal procedures had failed to resolve the dispute.

FIXED-TERM WORKERS

Severance agreements in full and final settlement of statutory entitlements   A significant ruling in 2007 concerning claims under the Protection of Employees (Fixed-Term Work) Act 2003 (the "2003 Act") was that of the High Court (Smyth J.) in *Sunday Newspapers Limited v Stephen Kinsella and Luke Bradley* [2008] E.L.R. 53. The High Court found that the Labour Court had erred in law in allowing the claimants to consider as void a severance agreement because they mistakenly believed that they had been advised that the severance agreements would not preclude them from bringing claims pursuant to the 2003 Act. More generally, the judgment of Smyth J. helpfully lays out a number of key principles to be followed in the context of severance agreements purporting to compromise protective legislation entitlements.

By way of background, the relevant statutory provisions should be noted. Section 6 of the 2003 Act provides that "… a fixed-term employee shall not, in respect of his or her conditions of employment, be treated in a less favourable manner than a comparable permanent employee." Section 12 of the 2003 Act provides:

> "Save as expressly provided otherwise in this Act, a provision in an agreement (whether a contract of employment or not and whether made before or after the commencement of the provision concerned of this Act) shall be void insofar as it purports to exclude or limit the application of, or is inconsistent with, any provision of the Act."

The respondents ("the employees") were employed by the appellant ("the employer") on fixed-term contracts. They were offered severance packages by the employer, based on the earnings they would have received up to the expiration of their contracts in less than a year. Permanent employees were offered a minimum of one year's salary. A clause in the general conditions of the severance packages provided that no employee was entitled to be paid more than "the normal expected gross amount that otherwise may have been earned to age 65".

Following some discussion and negotiation and appropriate professional advice, the employees signed a severance agreement which was stated to be "in full and final settlement of any and all outstanding entitlements whether statutory or otherwise". The agreement also further stated that it was:

> "… [B]ased on any/all claims in relation to [the employees'] employment with [the employer], stated or as yet un-stated, being fully resolved (including, but not limited to all claims under … the Protection of Employment Acts … and all or any employment legislation)".

The employees brought complaints under the 2003 Act to a Rights Commissioner, claiming, inter alia, that the waiver of their rights under the Act was void. The Rights Commissioner found against the employees on the basis that they had voluntarily, and with the benefit of the representation of their union, accepted a severance package and signed a waiver that confirmed their acceptance of the terms in full and final settlement.

The employees had then successfully appealed to the Labour Court. The Labour Court found, inter alia, that the employees believed, as a result of advice they had received, that they could not contract out of their rights and that any document which they signed would not prevent them from pursuing a claim under the 2003 Act.

Informed consent in context of settlement agreement   The employer successfully appealed to the High Court. Smyth J., in allowing the appeal, clarified a number of key principles which should be followed in all severance agreement situations, not only in the context of the fixed-term workers legislation but in the context of all protective legislation. Starting from the proposition that an employee can lawfully enter into an agreement in relation to his or her statutory rights, Smyth J. emphasised that the question of whether or not such rights have been compromised is a matter for the proper construction of the agreement itself. Informed consent is crucial if the compromise is to be upheld, as the Circuit Court identified in *Hurley v Royal Yacht Club* [1997] E.L.R. 225. Where an employee is being offered a severance package, he or she is entitled to be advised of his entitlements under the employment protection legislation and any agreement or compromise should list the various applicable statutes or at least make it clear that same has been taken into account by the employee. In the absence of such advice, a severance agreement waiving the statutory rights of the employee would be void. In the instant case, Smyth J. held that, given that the employees received appropriate advice and the agreement they signed was expressly stated to be in full and final settlement of any claims or potential claims under several statutes and "all or any employment legislation", their statutory rights had been compromised: s.12 of the 2003 Act is no exception to the principle that a properly informed employee can compromise protective legislation entitlements in this manner.

BULLYING AND HARASSMENT IN THE WORKPLACE

Introduction of new code of practice in 2007   Among the most significant developments in the area of bullying and harassment at work in 2007 was the introduction by the Health and Safety Authority of its *Code of Practice for Employers and Employees on the Prevention and Resolution of Bullying at Work* (available at *www.hsa.ie*), which came into effect on May 1, 2007. The new code of practice is aimed at both employers and employees and refers, in particular, to the duties in the Safety, Health and Welfare at Work Act 2005 ("the 2005 Act"). The new code provides practical guidance for employers on identifying and preventing bullying at work arising from their duties under s.8(2)(b) of the 2005 Act as regards:

> "...managing and conducting work activities in such a way as to prevent, so far as is reasonably practicable, any improper conduct or behaviour likely to put the safety, health and welfare at work of his or her employees at risk".

It also applies to employees in relation to their duties under s.13(1)(e) of the 2005 Act to "not engage in improper conduct or behaviour that is likely to endanger his or her own safety, health and welfare at work or that of any other person". Whilst the code only imposes an obligation to "consider" whether bullying is likely to be a risk when preparing a Safety Statement, it seems difficult to conceive of a workplace where it is not a possible risk.

Definition of bullying   The code recognises (in section 3.1) the established definition of bullying at work as:

> "... repeated inappropriate behaviour, direct or indirect, whether verbal, physical or otherwise, conducted by one or more persons against another or others, at the place of work and/or in the course of employment, which could reasonably be regarded as undermining the individual's

right to dignity at work" (Report of the Task Force on the prevention of workplace bullying, 2001; also used in the 2005 Report of the Expert Advisory Group on Workplace Bullying and in the surveys conducted by the ESRI to determine the incidence of workplace bullying).

It confirms that an isolated incident of the behaviour in this definition may be an affront to dignity but as a once-off incident is not considered to be bullying.

Key procedural changes in new code Although the new code does not differ markedly from its 2002 predecessor, the most significant changes relate to the procedures for resolution of complaints and the proposed involvement of the Labour Relations Commission.

In terms of the procedure for resolution of complaints, a "contact person" remains the first port of call for someone who feels they have been bullied, although the role of this "contact person" has been altered slightly in that, under the new code, the contact person has no involvement in the complaints procedure and does not act as an advocate for either party. He or she is simply required to listen and give guidance to a complainant in relation to the procedures available under internal policies. The complainant may then use an informal procedure and, in the absence of a successful conclusion, proceed to the formal stage.

The code recommends that the employer should first decide if the facts constitute "bullying" and put in place a monitoring system to the satisfaction of the parties. The purpose of this informal procedure is to establish if agreement can be reached between the parties to bring to an end the behaviour complained of. Naturally, the importance of retaining records of the procedure as it progresses is emphasised in the code.

Where the complaint is made against a senior member of the organisation, it may be necessary to have recourse to external services such as the mediation services of the Labour Relations Commission.

The formal procedure requires the complaint to be made in writing and to be signed and dated by the complainant. The person against whom the complaint is made should also be notified, in writing, of the complaint and thereafter a formal investigation will take place pursuant to the employer's internal bullying policy, which should reflect the new code. The code stipulates that there must be an appeals procedure available to the parties following the outcome.

Where internal procedures fail to resolve the complaint, the code provides that the Rights Commissioner Service should be accessible to the persons involved in the complaint. The Rights Commissioner may look at the internal procedures applied and may opt to carry out a new investigation.

Status of code in criminal and civil proceedings Although failure to adhere to the code is not an offence, the code is admissible in evidence in criminal proceedings under s.61 of the 2005 Act. In practice, it is highly likely to be taken into account in civil cases alleging bullying and harassment at work, the most prominent example of which to date is the judgment of the High Court in the case of *Quigley v Complex Tooling and Moulding* [2005] E.L.R. 305, where Lavan J. referred to the definition of bullying as contained in the Code of Practice detailing procedures for addressing bullying in the workplace made under the Industrial Relations Act 1990 (S.I. No. 17 of 2002) and expressly applied it to the plaintiff's evidence. (The recent Supreme Court judgment in the appeal in *Quigley* [2008] I.E.S.C. 44, to be analysed in next year's edition of the *Annual Review of Irish Law*, does not affect this point.)

Equity

BRIAN TOBIN, School of Law, Trinity College Dublin

INTERLOCUTORY INJUNCTIONS

The principles governing the grant of interlocutory injunctions, laid down by the Supreme Court in *Campus Oil Ltd v Minister for Industry and Energy (No.2)* [1983] I.R. 88, have continued to be consistently applied in 2007. It is clear from the decision of Laffoy J. in *Claystone Ltd & Ors v Larkin & Ors* (High Court, Laffoy J., March 14, 2007) that the adequacy of damages was the decisive element in considering where the balance of convenience lies. The parties entered into an agreement whereby the defendants were to purchase land from the plaintiffs and build a dwelling thereon. The defendants were then to sell the completed dwelling to the plaintiffs. The plaintiffs maintained that their agreement with the defendants had subsequently been varied so that a larger dwelling would be constructed on the land. The defendants, having laid the foundations for the larger dwelling, began construction on the smaller dwelling. The plaintiffs sought an interlocutory injunction restraining the defendants from erecting on the land any building or structure other than the larger dwelling, and the defendants applied to have the plaintiffs' case struck out.

Laffoy J. dealt with the defendants' application to strike out first, and having considered both the pleadings and the evidence adduced, she was not satisfied that they had cleared the difficult hurdle of establishing that the plaintiffs' case must fail. Laffoy J. went on to consider the plaintiffs' application for an interlocutory injunction, and applying the traditional *Campus Oil* test she held that:

> "The plaintiffs' application for an interlocutory injunction falls to be determined in accordance with the usual criteria: whether there is a fair *bona fide* question to be tried as between the parties; the adequacy of damages; and where the balance of convenience lies."

Laffoy J. concluded that it was a corollary of the finding that the defendants had not established that the plaintiffs' case must fail that there was a fair bona fide question to be tried.

In considering whether the plaintiffs could be adequately compensated by the granting of damages, Laffoy J. concluded that the plaintiffs had established that, because of the peculiar circumstances of the case damages would not be adequate as a remedy. The peculiar circumstances of the case were the location of the site (it backed onto the plaintiffs' residence) and the family arrangements and circumstances (the plaintiffs wished to acquire the larger dwelling as a suitable residence for their son, his wife and two young children of the marriage). Laffoy J. also felt that if the plaintiffs were eventually successful in the case at trial without an interlocutory injunction having been obtained along the way there was a high degree of probability that the only remedy the court would grant would be an award of damages if construction of the smaller dwelling on the land was completed by the time the matter came to hearing. In Laffoy J.'s view it was highly unlikely that the court would order the demolition of a constructed dwelling.

On the other hand, damages would be an adequate remedy for the defendants. Laffoy J. observed that the defendants had outlined to the court the pecuniary loss which they would incur if, because of the existence of an interlocutory injunction, they were prevented from completing construction work on the site. However she went on to state that it had not been suggested to the court that the plaintiffs could not meet that loss if they were constrained to do so on foot of the undertaking as to damages which they must give the court as a precondition of being granted an interlocutory injunction. Accordingly Laffoy J. held that having considered the question of the adequacy of damages, the balance of convenience lay in favour of granting interlocutory relief to the plaintiffs.

In conclusion, Laffoy J. felt that it was appropriate to apprise the parties of the court's function when dealing with an application for interlocutory relief. She stressed that the purpose of the interlocutory injunction is to maintain the status quo pending the trial of an action and the resolution of the factual conflicts and the determination of the issues of law:

> "As Lord Diplock pointed out in *American Cyanamid Company v. Ethicon Limited* [1975] 1 All ER 504 at p.510, it is no part of the court's function at this stage to try and resolve conflicts of evidence on affidavit as to facts on which the claims of either party may ultimately depend nor to decide difficult questions of law which call for detailed argument and mature consideration. These are matters to be dealt with at the trial."

The outcome for the plaintiff was less favourable in *JRM Sports Ltd. (t/a Limerick Football Club) v Football Association of Ireland* (High Court, Clarke J., January 31, 2007). The plaintiff was refused a licence to play in the League of Ireland for the 2007 football season; first by the defendant's licensing committee and then by its appeal body. The plaintiff brought proceedings to challenge the decision of the defendant's appeal body because it claimed to have been prejudiced in its right to fair procedures. The plaintiff had received, via e-mail, a report relied upon by the defendant's appeal body on the day prior to the hearing of the appeal at a time when its officers had left to travel to Dublin for such hearing. The plaintiff had obtained an interlocutory injunction against the defendant and it now sought the renewal of this so as to enable it to play in the League of Ireland in 2007.

Clarke J. observed that there was ample evidence before the defendant's licensing committee and the appeal board which entitled these bodies to reach the conclusion that it would not be appropriate to licence the plaintiff. He also held that because applications for an interlocutory injunction are ex parte, there is a clear duty on a party who comes before the court without the other party being notified to put before the court all of the facts that might influence its decision. The plaintiff had been factually inaccurate when seeking the initial interlocutory injunction against the defendant and accordingly it was held that:

> "It is clear in those circumstances that the court has a discretion to refuse an order which might otherwise properly be given on the basis that parties have abused their right of access to the court by, in substance, misleading the court by not putting forward all of the relevant facts."

Though he does not explicitly refer to it, here it is indubitable that Clarke J. has in mind the equitable maxim of "he who comes to equity must come with clean hands". This maxim illustrates the discretionary nature of equitable remedies by stipulating that a party must refrain from fraud, misrepresentation, or any other form of dishonest or disreputable conduct if he/she wishes to be granted a form of equitable relief. However Clarke J. refrained from refusing the interlocutory injunction on the basis of this maxim as he felt it unnecessary to reach such a harsh conclusion having regard to the fact that he had come to the view that the relief should not be granted in any event.

As regards the report relied upon at appeal, Clarke J. noted that the plaintiff's officers had not read the defendant's rules even though they had signed up to them. Clarke J. pointed out that if they had done so they would have known of their entitlement to be provided with the report and they could have gone to the hearing requesting from the appeal body an adjournment pending the arrival of the report. Thus the fact that the plaintiff's officers had not seen the report was due to their failure to ask the appeal body at the hearing for an adjournment so as to consider it. In the view of Clarke J.:

> "It does not seem...that in any event having sight of the report could have added anything to the ability of Limerick to present its case at the appeal."

Clarke J. then systematically dealt with each aspect of the traditional *Campus Oil* test. He held that the plaintiff had not established any case that would entitle them to succeed in the proceedings against the defendant "and in those circumstances and on those grounds alone it would be appropriate to refuse an interlocutory injunction." Clarke J. went on to consider the question of whether damages would be an adequate remedy for either side and concluded that they would not be because of important sporting considerations on both sides that could not easily be converted into money. Clarke J. then addressed the issue of the balance of convenience and he asserted that:

> "[I]t seems to me, that the court has to place a significant weight in the balance of convenience on factors such as the overall effect of the giving of the order sought on the proper administration of the sport concerned ... the fact is that by intervening at this stage the court would be imposing on the FAI an obligation to let Limerick in and allow it to play in the current season contrary to what (in the FAI's view and it is, on the evidence, at least a sustainable view) is in accordance with the best interests of the sport. To impose that is not simply a matter of no consequence. It means that the league has to go ahead for an entire season on a basis which those charged with managing the league have decided is not the way in which it should go ahead."

Given this Clarke J. held that even if he had been satisfied that there was a fair bona fide question to be tried he would not have been prepared to grant an interlocutory injunction because the balance of convenience would have been against it. Accordingly Clarke J. refused to continue the interlocutory injunction because the conditions necessary to do so under any of the traditional *Campus Oil* headings did not exist.

THE DOCTRINE OF CONFIDENCE

The equitable doctrine of confidence was recently considered in *Judge Mahon v Post Publications Ltd* (Supreme Court, Fennelly J., March 29, 2007). The plaintiffs, members of the Tribunal of Inquiry into Certain Planning Matters and Payments, were appealing to the Supreme Court against an order of the High Court refusing the Tribunal injunctive relief that would enforce the confidentiality obligation which it had imposed on persons to whom it circulated certain documents. The Tribunal was asking the Supreme Court to hold that it had the power to restrain the publication of the documents until the date of their disclosure at a public hearing. Fennelly J traced the development of the equitable doctrine of confidence from the early English case of *Prince Albert v Strange* (1849) 1 Mac. G. 25 through to the Irish case of *House of Spring Gardens Ltd. v Point Blank* [1984] I.R. 611, and he found that:

> "From all of these cases, the contours of the equitable doctrine of confidence can be described sufficiently for the purposes of this appeal, as follows:

1. The information must in fact be confidential or secret: it must…
    'have the necessary quality of confidence about it';
2. It must have been communicated by the possessor of the information in circumstances which impose an obligation of confidence or trust on the person receiving it;
3. It must be wrongfully communicated by the person receiving it or by another person who is aware of the obligation of confidence."

Fennelly J. noted that in England these principles, which initially applied between private parties, had been extended by case-law to the workings of Government. Fennelly J. observed that:

> "The key principle established in all that litigation was that the government was not in a position to complain of breach of its secrets and publication of confidential information on the same basis as private individuals".

Fennelly J. quoted from the judgment of Mason J. in the High Court of Australia in *Commonwealth of Australia v John Fairfax and Sons Ltd.* (1980) 147 C.L.R. 39, which had previously been cited with approval by Carroll J. in *AG for England and Wales v Brandon Book Publishers Ltd.* [1986] I.R. 597. Mason J. had stated as follows:

> "[T]he court will determine the government's claim to confidentiality by reference to the public interest. Unless disclosure is likely to injure the public interest, it will not be protected".

Fennelly J. felt that this assertion applied to the Tribunal, and he stated that:

> "[T]he question of whether the doctrine of confidence extends to the information of the government or of public authorities has not yet been the subject of judicial determination in this jurisdiction. For what it is worth, I do not see any reason not to follow the line of case-law which has been adopted in England".

However Fennelly J. highlighted the difference between the usual cases involving the equitable doctrine of confidence and the present case in that in the former type of scenario trust or confidence arises from a mutual arrangement of some sort between the person imparting the information and the person receiving the information. Fennelly J. gave the example of information conveyed by the communicator for the purpose of a joint commercial venture where the recipient becomes the repository of such information on an implied basis of trust, firstly in the colloquial sense that the communicator trusts the recipient and, secondly, in the equitable sense of trust. Fennelly J. observed that, regarding the present type of scenario:

> "No such relationship is alleged here. The terms of confidentiality are imposed unilaterally by the Tribunal. They are extremely restrictive. They extend to a person's spouse or other close intimates or associates whether personal or business."

In conclusion Fennelly J. found himself "fully in agreement with the approach adopted by Kelly J" in the High Court and he proceeded to dismiss the plaintiff's appeal for injunctive relief as he could find no authority, statutory or otherwise, express or implied which enabled the Tribunal to impose such far-reaching confidentiality on the recipients of its briefs.

Evidence

LIZ HEFFERNAN, Trinity College Dublin

Affidavit evidence   The nature and timing of challenges to affidavit evidence were considered by Irvine J. in *Director of Corporate Enforcement v Bailey* [2007] I.E.H.C. 365 (November 1, 2007). The applicant Director of Corporate Enforcement served notice of his intention to institute proceedings against the respondents seeking to disqualify them as directors of Bovale Developments Ltd pursuant to s.160(2) of the Companies Act 1990. The respondents moved to strike portions of the applicant's two grounding affidavits, inter alia, on the ground that they contained inadmissible hearsay and opinion evidence. The applicant countered that the respondents' motion was premature and that the evidential issue should not be decided prior to trial. Irvine J. held that the respondents' motion was timely and ought to be dealt with at that juncture. Although delivered in the context of disqualification proceedings, this ruling may bear on other proceedings in which parties rely on affidavit evidence for the final determination of substantive rights and obligations.

Order 40 r.4 of the Rules of the Superior Courts provides that affidavits shall be confined to facts within the deponent's own knowledge, "except on interlocutory motions". Thus, the courts have recognised that affidavits grounding interlocutory applications may contain hearsay provided that the deponent states the grounds for his or her belief relating to the matter (e.g. *Walsh v Harrison*, unreported, High Court, July 31, 2002; *Bridgeman v Kilcock Transport Ltd*, unreported, High Court, January 27, 1995). The issue in *Director of Corporate Enforcement v Bailey* was whether the motion could be classified as interlocutory within the meaning of the rule for the purpose of admitting hearsay.

Irvine J. noted that an application for a disqualification order pursuant to s.160(2) is made by originating notice of motion and heard and determined on affidavit unless the court otherwise directs. The totality of the evidence to be relied upon by the applicant should be contained in the affidavits and, in contrast to criminal proceedings, no new factual material should emerge thereafter. Citing the general requirement in the Rules that affidavits exclude hearsay and the accompanying sanction in relation to costs, the learned judge stated:

> "It is clear that the evidence supporting any alleged wrongdoing at a hearing which is dealt with on affidavit must be just as admissible as evidence which would be given to a court by a witness at an oral hearing".

The rationale for the relaxation of the hearsay rules is that interlocutory applications do not disturb the substantive rights of parties but rather maintain the status quo pending a final determination on the merits. In the view of Irvine J., the affidavits sworn on behalf of the applicant could not be classified as interlocutory in this sense. Although the present proceedings might ultimately be dealt with at an oral hearing, it did not follow that the application was premature. Irvine J. held that the appropriate time to challenge the admissibility of evidence in an affidavit supporting proceedings brought by way of originating notice of motion is the time at which the affidavit is delivered. She continued:

> "Applications such as the present one assist in defining the actual issues which will be pursued by the applicant and thus bring about a reduction in legal costs. In terms of natural justice and fair procedures the Court concludes that it would be unfair to permit an applicant in proceedings which carry a significant potential penalty to swear an affidavit containing a myriad of serious allegations of wrongdoing against a respondent when many of the allegations emanate from the opinion of third parties not under the deponent's control, relate to matters outside the deponent's own personal knowledge and when neither the deponent nor the author of the opinion can reasonably be challenged thereon. It would be unjust to require the respondents to deliver a sworn reply to such assertions thus exposing them to cross-examination thereon when the party responsible for the allegations of wrongdoing is not similarly open to cross-examination. Different considerations apply in proceedings of a plenary nature where it is permissible for a plaintiff in an unsworn document, such as a statement of claim, to make wide-ranging unsworn allegations to which the defendant will respond in a similarly unsworn fashion. In such circumstances, both the parties are subjected to the same rules."

Apart from the spectre of injustice, there would be procedural drawbacks to postponing the application until after the respondents have delivered replying affidavits. For the respondents, for example, it might present the Hobson's choice of responding to matters which are prima facie inadmissible or ignoring them at the risk that they will be deemed accepted at a later point in the proceedings. Moreover, if the inadmissible evidence were included in the affidavits and the respondents obliged to prepare for trial on that basis, the length of the proceedings and the costs of both parties would surely be increased.

Belief evidence   Section 3(2) of the Offences Against the State (Amendment) Act 1972 provides an evidentiary prop to the prosecution of the offence of membership of an unlawful organisation. A statutory exception to the rule against opinion evidence, the subsection allows a garda chief superintendent to give evidence of his or her belief that the accused is a member of an unlawful organisation at the material time. The courts have traditionally allowed the chief superintendent to resist cross-examination as to the basis for his or her belief where responses to questioning would tend to reveal the identity of garda informers. In the landmark case of *People (DPP) v Kelly* [2006] 3 I.R. 115, the Supreme Court upheld the consistency of this restriction on the right to cross-examine with the accused's constitutional guarantee of a trial in due course of law.

The status of belief evidence was raised before the Court of Criminal Appeal in three cases in 2007. In *DPP v Matthews* [2007] I.E.C.C.A. 23 (March 29, 2007) the applicant sought a certificate for leave to appeal to the Supreme Court, his appeal against his conviction for membership having previously been refused. The application rested in essence on the contention that the Supreme Court had left unresolved in *Kelly* a point of law of exceptional public importance, namely, the compatibility of the restricted right to cross-examine with the fair trial guarantee of Art.6 of the European Convention on Human Rights. The Director of Public Prosecutions, as respondent, conceded that the majority judgment in *Kelly* was grounded exclusively in the Constitution and that the Convention featured in the concurring judgment of Fennelly J. alone. Nevertheless, the DPP characterised as "inconceivable" the implication that a divergence between Irish law and the Convention would have escaped the majority or, indeed, that any disagreement with the views of Fennelly J. would not have been voiced. The Court of Criminal Appeal accepted the point and rejected the applicant's "isolated" interpretation of the judgment of the majority in *Kelly*. In the absence of a change in the law or some development undermining the position taken by Fennelly J., there was no basis on which to certify a point of law of exceptional importance.

Some months later, in *DPP v Donohue* [2007] I.E.C.C.A. 97 (October 26, 2007), the Court of Criminal Appeal reiterated this reasoning when refusing a similar application for leave to appeal to the Supreme Court. An interesting twist in *Donohue* was the emphasis placed by the applicant on the procedure adopted by the Special Criminal Court for the viewing and consideration of material over which informer privilege is asserted. It was the applicant's contention that the prosecution must disclose to the defence any documentation forming the basis for the witness's belief, but Macken J. was not persuaded that the Art.6 case law requires as much (e.g. *Rowe v United Kingdom* 30 E.H.R.R. 1 and *Jasper v United Kingdom* 30 E.H.R.R. 441). In the present case, applying the decision in *Ward v Special Criminal Court* [1994] 1 I.R. 60, the Special Criminal Court had determined that it was both entitled to review the documentation and required to do so, irrespective of the wishes of the defence. The Court of Criminal Appeal endorsed this approach as legitimately within the ambit of the Irish and European case law.

Finally, in *People (DPP) v Vincent Kelly* [2007] I.E.C.C.A. 110 (December 6, 2007), alleged error on the part of the Special Criminal Court in accepting belief evidence constituted one of the grounds on which the applicant unsuccessfully sought leave to appeal his conviction for membership of the IRA. The applicant's submission targeted the absence in Irish law of guidance to assist the Special Criminal Court in determining the weight to be attributed to belief evidence where no information is available to the court as to the basis for the belief. In *Kelly*, Fennelly J. had expressed the view that the Special Criminal Court should have explained the weight, if any, which it attached to the belief evidence in that case. Finnegan J. was satisfied that Fennelly J. had not intended to require the trial court to quantify the weight "in the form of a mathematical notation or other scale of values" but rather to express the weight to be attributed to belief evidence "where there is countervailing evidence such as a denial on oath". Here, there had been no denial on oath and the chief superintendent's testimony had been just one ingredient in the prosecution's case. It was not necessary to attribute weight to any particular ingredient in the evidence the cumulative effect of which had led to the applicant's conviction. Finnegan J. also emphasised the significance of the applicant's decision not to avail of the witness's offer to make available to the court documents in his possession which had contributed to his belief.

Best evidence rule   The necessary proofs to sustain a conviction for drunken driving under the Road Traffic Acts were the subject of an appeal by way of case stated in *Fitzpatrick v DPP* [2007] I.E.H.C. 383, November 20, 2007. Following his arrest, the appellant provided two breath specimens which were entered into an intoxyliser machine. Pursuant to s.17 of the Road Traffic Act 1994, two identical statements, indicating the concentration of alcohol in the specimen, were automatically produced by the machine and signed by the appellant; one was furnished to the appellant and the other retained by the respondent garda officer. At the close of the prosecution's case, the appellant moved to dismiss on the basis that a s.17 statement had not been tendered in evidence. The District judge ruled that the statement was not an essential proof and that the appellant had a case to answer. The judge went on to convict the appellant and impose a fine and disqualification from driving but sought the opinion of the High Court on the evidential status of a s.17 statement.

O'Neill J. classified a statement produced pursuant to the section as a document for purposes of proof and, as such, subject to the best evidence rule. He quoted the statement of the rule propounded by O'Flaherty J. in *Primor plc v Stokes* [1996] 2 I.R. 459 at 518:

> "The best evidence rule operates in this sphere to the extent that the party seeking to rely on the contents of a document must adduce primary evidence of those contents, *i.e.* the original document in question. The contents of a document may be proved by secondary evidence if the original has been destroyed or cannot be found after due

> search. Similarly, such contents may be proved by secondary means if
> production of the original is physically or legally impossible ..."

Applying the rule in the context of s.17, O'Neill J. held that where the
prosecution wish to prove the content of the statement but do not produce the
statement itself, the prosecution may not fall back on secondary evidence in
the absence of proof that the original statement was lost or destroyed or cannot
be produced. In the present case, the oral evidence tendered by the prosecution
was inadmissible because no explanation for the absence of the statement had
been given. O'Neill J. pointed to the irony that had the prosecution relied on a
copy of the original, they could have availed of s.30 of the Criminal Evidence
Act 1992 which dispenses with the need to prove that the original has been lost
or destroyed or that its production is otherwise impossible. (For other issues
arising out of the use of intoxilysers and intoximeters, see *DPP v Malone* [2007]
I.E.H.C. 353 (October 15, 2007) and *Kelly v District Judge David Anderson*
[2007] I.E.H.C. 474 (December 19, 2007)).

Corroboration   In criminal proceedings involving an offence of a sexual
nature, the trial judge enjoys a discretion pursuant to s.7(1) of the Criminal
Law (Rape) (Amendment) Act 1990 to caution the jury about the danger of
convicting on the uncorroborated testimony of the complainant. A considerable
body of case law has emerged over the years regarding the nature and exercise
of the trial judge's discretion (see, e.g. *People (DPP) v JEM* [2001] 4 I.R.
385; *People (DPP) v C* [2001] 3 I.R. 345; *People (DPP) v Ferris*, unreported,
Court of Criminal Appeal, June 10, 2002; *People (DPP) v Gentleman* [2003]
4 I.R. 22). In *DPP v Dolan* [2007] I.E.C.C.A. 30 (May 3, 2007), the Court of
Criminal Appeal set aside a conviction for rape and ordered a retrial on ground
that the trial judge had failed to provide a reasoned basis for his decision not
to deliver a corroboration warning. Kearns J. explained:

> "The Court would stress that during the course of a trial it cannot be
> expected that the trial judge will give an elaborate judgment on every
> legal issue which arises for his ruling, but every important ruling must
> at least disclose a decision judicially made, that is to say, one which is
> reasoned and based on legal principle."

In the present case, the ruling failed to meet either requirement. Moreover, it
was a ruling of considerable significance in the overall context of the trial; the
possibility of the warning arose in relation to a charge of anal rape on which the
jury convicted the applicant but not in relation to the other charges on which
the applicant was acquitted. (On the exclusion of rebuttal evidence under the
collateral matter rule in a prosecution for a sexual offence, see *People (DPP)
v Onumwere* [2007] I.E.C.C.A. 48 (May 24, 2007)).

Custodial questioning   Several statutory and case law developments took place in 2007 in relation to the gathering of evidence in custodial detention. Perhaps the most dramatic and controversial of these developments was the inclusion in the Criminal Justice Act 2007 of provisions expanding substantially the circumstances in which inferences may be drawn at trial from an accused's silence in response to questioning. Limited provision for the drawing of inferences from silence had been included in the Criminal Justice Act 1984, the Criminal Justice (Drug Trafficking) Act 1996 and the Offences Against the State (Amendment) Act 1998. Sections 18 and 19 of the 1984 Act enable a trial court to draw inferences from the failure or refusal of a person arrested by the Gardaí to account for the presence of certain objects in his or her possession or for the fact that he or she was found at a particular location. In *Rock v Ireland* [1997] 3 I.R. 484 the Supreme Court upheld the constitutionality of these provisions, relying in part on the existence of statutory safeguards: an inference adverse to the accused may only be drawn where the court deems it proper; an inference may corroborate other items of evidence but cannot support a conviction on its own; and the suspect must be cautioned as to the effect of his or her failure or refusal to answer. In *People (DPP) v Finnerty* [1999] 4 I.R. 364, the court emphasised that in the absence of express statutory inference-drawing provisions such as ss.18 and 19, a suspect is entitled to remain silent during questioning without any negative evidential consequences ensuing at trial.

Part 4 of the 2007 Act develops the law in this area in two salient respects. First, it amends in certain limited respects the existing specific inference-drawing provisions and, secondly, it introduces a more general inference-drawing provision.

As regards the first development, ss.18 and 19 of the 1984 Act originally permitted the drawing of inferences where the accused was arrested without warrant and failed or refused to account for the matters noted above when questioned by the arresting garda officer. The 2007 Act extends the scope of these sections by providing that the questioning that may trigger the drawing of inferences may occur either before or at the time that a suspect is charged with any arrestable offence. The relevant questions may be put to the suspect by any garda and not just the arresting officer (ss.28 & 29 of 2007 Act). The safeguards included in ss.18 and 19 have been refined and strengthened. Whereas these sections previously stated that a person may not be convicted of an offence "solely" on an inference drawn from a failure or refusal to account, the revised language now excludes a conviction based "solely or mainly" on such an inference (ss.18(2) & 19(2)). In addition to the person being cautioned in ordinary language about the effect of a failure or refusal to account, the sections now expressly state that the accused must have been afforded a reasonable opportunity to consult a solicitor before the failure or refusal occurred (ss.18(3)(b) & 19(3)(b)). An inference may not be drawn unless the questioning was electronically recorded or the person waived in writing the entitlement to electronic recording (ss.18(6) & 19(6)). Finally, it is important to recall that these provisions permit rather than require a court to draw an inference from a failure or refusal to account. The original wording (which provides that the court "may draw such inferences … as appear proper") is retained and further language added to the effect that the court "shall, for the purposes of drawing an inference under this section, have regard to whenever, if appropriate, the account of the matter concerned was first given by the accused" (ss.18(5) & 19(5)).

The central plank of Pt 4 of the 2007 Act is a general inference-drawing provision applicable in relation to the full gamut of ordinary arrestable offences. The enactment takes the guise of a new s.19A inserted into the 1984 Act (by s.30 of 2007 Act). It permits the court to draw such inferences "as may appear proper" from the failure of the accused to mention particular facts where that failure is tendered as evidence in any proceedings against the accused for an arrestable offence (s.19A(1)). The predicate questioning may take place at any time before the accused was charged with the offence or when being charged with the offence or when informed by a garda officer that he or she might be prosecuted for it (s.19A(1)(a) & (b)). The basis for the drawing of inferences is that the accused:

> "… failed to mention any fact relied on in his or her defence in [the] proceedings, being a fact which in the circumstances existing at the time clearly called for an explanation from him or her when so questioned, charged or informed, as the case may be".

The court (the judge(s) or the jury, subject to the judge's directions) may draw such inferences when determining whether the accused is guilty of the offence charged or of any other offence of which he or she could lawfully be convicted on that charge (s.19A(1)). However, the power to draw inferences may also be invoked at an earlier juncture in the proceedings when the court determines whether a charge should be dismissed or whether there is a case to answer. In relation to the conditions under which inferences may be drawn, the wording of s.19A mirrors that of amended ss.18 and 19 of the 1984 Act. Thus, an inference may corroborate other evidence (s.19A(1)) but an accused may not be convicted solely or mainly on an inference; the accused must have been cautioned in ordinary language (s19A(1)(a)) and afforded a reasonable opportunity to consult a solicitor before the failure to mention a material fact occurred (s19A(3)(b)); and the questioning must have been electronically recorded or the accused must have consented to it not being so recorded (s19A(6)).

The enactment in s.19A of an inference-drawing provision that applies in relation to all arrestable offences eclipses the pre-existing provision in relation to particular offences contained in s.7 of the Criminal Justice (Drug Trafficking) Act 1996 and s.5 of the Offences Against the State Act 1998. These sections are thus repealed (s.3 and Sch.1 to the 2007 Act). However, the inference-drawing provision in s.2 of the 1998 Act, which applies in relation to the offence of membership of an unlawful organisation, is retained and amended in order to bring it into line with the amended ss.18 and 19 and the new s.19A (s.31 of the 2007 Act).

Taken cumulatively, the inference-drawing provisions of the 2007 Act represent a substantial encroachment on the right to silence under Irish law, rolling back the benchmark set in *People (DPP) v Finnerty*. The provisions raise various interpretative wrinkles which may be ironed out by the courts over time. The general inference-drawing provision contained in the new s.19A is modelled on English legislation which has itself been the subject of controversial discourse (s.34 of the CJPO Act 1994; *R. v Beckles* [2005] 1 All E.R. 705; *R. v Hoare and Pierce* [2005] 1 W.L.R. 1804; *R. v Betts and Hall* [2001] 2 Cr. App. R. 257). A weakness in the Irish measure is its failure to counterbalance the diminution in the right to silence with a strengthened right of access to legal advice. In *Lavery v Member in Charge, Carrickmacross Garda Station* [1999] 2 I.R. 390, the Supreme Court rejected the contention that the right of access to legal advice includes an entitlement to have a lawyer present during questioning. However, the European Court of Human Rights has underscored the complementary protection that these respective rights provide given the implications of inference-drawing provisions (*Condior v United Kingdom* (2001) 21 E.H.R.R. 1). Although s.19A(3)(b) incorporates the requirement, long established in the case law, that a suspect be afforded a reasonable opportunity to consult with a lawyer, arguably the Oireachtas should have gone further and legislated for the presence of the lawyer during questioning now that a suspect's silence, in addition to any admissions, may be used in evidence.

The importance of maintaining a complete and accurate contemporaneous record of the questioning of a suspect is acknowledged in Reg.12 of the Custody Regulations (Criminal Justice Act 1984 (Treatment of Persons in Custody in Garda Síochána Stations) Regulations 1987 (S.I. No. 119 of 1987)) and r.9 of the Judges' Rules. Ireland has lagged behind other countries in reaping the recognised benefits of electronic recording of interviews; the electronic recording regulations (Criminal Justice Act 1984 (Electronic Recording of Interviews) Regulations 1997 (S.I. No. 74 of 1997)), passed as late as 1997, set up a permissive rather than mandatory regime which provides considerable latitude to the Gardaí. The courts have grown increasingly impatient with tardiness in the practical implementation of electronic recording and have made plain that they will not tolerate failures to electronically record interviews other than for very good reasons (*People (DPP) v Connolly* [2003] 2 I.R. 1; *People (DPP) v Michael Murphy* [2005] 4 I.R. 504; *People (DPP) v O'Neill* [2007] I.E.C.C.A. 6 (March 16, 2007)).

Against this backdrop, the decision of the Court of Criminal Appeal in *People (DPP) v Cunningham* [2007] I.E.C.C.A. 49 (May 24, 2007), serves as a reminder that trial judges retain a discretion to admit interviews that have not been video-recorded. The applicant sought leave to appeal his conviction for murder on several grounds including alleged error on the part of the trial judge in refusing to exclude evidence of garda interviews which were not video-recorded. The applicant had been brought to Dundalk garda station which lacked video-recording facilities; the appropriate facilities were in place in Carrickmacross some 13 miles away in a different garda division and also at Drogheda and Kells, but the trial judge accepted that moving the interview to these locations would have disrupted the investigation. The judge also had regard to the fact that the events unfolded on Christmas Eve, "a busy family and social occasion". The Court of Criminal Appeal upheld the decision to admit into evidence the interviews recorded by conventional as opposed to electronic means. Noting that the trial judge had carefully considered all the circumstances and heard detailed submissions, Finnegan J. recalled that s.27(4) of the Criminal Justice Act 1984 expressly provides that a failure to comply with the regulations shall not by itself render evidence inadmissible and that the subsection is "without prejudice to any power of the court to exclude evidence at its discretion". The Court of Criminal Appeal was satisfied that the trial judge's discretion had been exercised properly in this case.

The expectation that the electronic recording of custodial interviews has become the norm is reflected in the Criminal Justice Act 2007. Section 57(1) provides for the admissibility in evidence of an electronic recording and/or the transcript of such a recording. The subsection is limited by its terms to a recording of the questioning of an accused in connection with the investigation of the offence for which he or she is on trial. The effect is to facilitate the use of electronic recordings as proof at trial without displacing the evidential value of statements recorded by traditional means. Subsection 3 expressly preserves the admissibility of a statement recorded in writing, whether or not the statement was signed by the accused and irrespective of whether it was electronically recorded. This is a somewhat curious inclusion given the legislative premise that electronic recording is now routine (explanatory memorandum, p.12). There may be exceptional circumstances in which electronic recording is not feasible and a statement is taken by conventional means. But the section goes further and permits the possibility, however remote, of the admission at trial of both electronic and written recordings, for example where a discrepancy between the two versions is alleged. Where the statement is electronically recorded, subs.2 dispenses with the obligation on the Gardaí to make a contemporaneous written record of an interview with a suspect; the electronically recorded statement may be admissible notwithstanding that it is not in writing and signed by the accused.

Where the questioning of a suspect has been audio- or video-recorded, s.56 states that a copy of the recording shall be given to the person or his or her legal representative only where the person is before a court charged with an offence and then only if the court so directs and subject to such conditions as the court may specify. This measure revoked Reg.16 of the Electronic Recording

Regulations which had obliged the Gardaí to provide a copy in response to a written request unless the Superintendent believed "on reasonable grounds" that to do so would prejudice an ongoing investigation or endanger the safety, security and wellbeing of another person.

The conduct of interviews by the Gardaí was the subject of proceedings for judicial review in *McCormack v DPP* [2008] 1 I.L.R.M. 49. The applicant was arrested on suspicion of snatching a bag from a woman in Dublin city centre and underwent two periods of garda questioning which were electronically recorded. He instituted proceedings in the High Court to restrain his prosecution, arguing that the interviews had been so chaotic and unstructured that he had been deprived of an opportunity to put forward his defence to the charge on the video-recording. Charleton J. refused the relief sought, rejecting the applicant's submission both on the law and the facts.

The learned judge recalled the general rule that an accused is not obliged to make any case in defence of a criminal charge but noted that suspects frequently do so in response to garda questioning. Such statements, though possibly self-serving, may come to light during the course of the prosecution's case at trial. Charleton J. observed that the conduct of investigations, including the manner of questioning, is a matter for the police, subject to certain general guidelines set down in the case law. The purpose of a custodial interview, he opined, is not to enable the accused to make a case on video so that it can be played as part of the defence case in front of a jury; for that purpose, the accused has the option of cross-examining witnesses at trial, calling evidence or taking the stand. Turning to the factual account of the interviews put forward by the applicant, the learned judge concluded that no opportunity had been lost to the accused. With the advent of the tape-recording of interviews:

> "… it has to be expected that interviews recorded on video will be either chaotic, laconic or otherwise reflect the real circumstances of conversations between people who may be under pressure of accusation, of work or of life".

The recordings merely reflected this reality rather than substantiating the objections raised.

In *DPP v O'Neill* [2007] I.E.C.C.A. 8 (March 16, 2007), the Court of Criminal Appeal considered an issue of first impression in this jurisdiction, namely, whether a judge in a criminal trial may sever a memorandum of an interview so as to exclude inculpatory portions, but preserve and admit into evidence exculpatory portions. The applicant sought leave to appeal his conviction for rape on the sole ground that the trial judge had erred in excluding all the contents of a memorandum of interview in circumstances where the defence had objected to the admissibility of only part of the interview. Before the Court of Criminal Appeal, counsel for the applicant contended that whereas the portions of the interview which had been found to be involuntary had been correctly excluded, the jury had been entitled to receive in evidence those portions that had been voluntarily obtained. The distinction had an important practical bearing on the case because, during the interview in question, the applicant had admitted having had sexual intercourse on a consensual basis; counsel argued that this evidence had already been relied upon by the defence to cross-examine the complainant and that its exclusion effectively compelled the defence to call the accused as a witness.

The Court of Criminal Appeal upheld the trial judge's decision to exclude the entirety of the interview. Kearns J. took the view that any other course could lead to undesirable results, such as a trial judge facing the "impossible situation" of having to "dissect the interview on a line by line basis, giving rulings on the admissibility of each line and the voluntariness or otherwise thereof". He conceded that there may be exceptional cases where a voluntary exchange of questions and answers may alter in mid-stream or where statements or interviews may require editing either by agreement between the parties or by ruling of the trial judge so as to exclude material that would be otherwise inadmissible. However, where, as here, "the entire process is found to be tainted", the safer course is to exclude the interview in its entirety.

Disclosure in criminal proceedings   The duty on the part of the Gardaí to seek out and preserve evidence has continued to occupy the courts. *Murphy v DPP* [1989] I.L.R.M. 71 and *Braddish v DPP* [2001] 3 I.R. 127 stand for the principle that the right of an accused to prepare his or her defence encompasses an entitlement to be afforded every reasonable opportunity to inspect evidence relevant to guilt or innocence. The concept of relevant evidence is broadly defined for this purpose and includes any material that appears to have some bearing on an offence or person under investigation or on the surrounding circumstances (*Dunne v DPP* [2002] 2 I.R. 25; *McGrath v DPP* [2003] 2 I.R. 25; but see *McFarlane v DPP* [2006] I.E.S.C. (March 7, 2006)). Delay on the part of the accused in seeking an examination of material in the hands of the Gardaí may undermine a claim that he or she has been deprived of the right to prepare for trial (*Scully v DPP* [2005] 1 I.R. 242). The standard for judicial review restraining a prosecution is that the applicant faces a real risk of an unfair trial. This necessarily connotes a trial in which the unfairness cannot be avoided by appropriate rulings and directions on the part of the trial judge (*Bowes v DPP* [2003] 2 I.R. 25; *Z v DPP* [1994] 2 I.R. 476)).

In *Kelly v DPP* [2007] I.E.S.C. 69 (December 21, 2007), the Supreme Court dismissed an appeal from a refusal to prohibit the applicant's retrial for offences under the Misuse of Drugs Acts. The essence of the applicant's case was that there was a real risk of an unfair trial because the investigating Gardaí had failed to take, retain and preserve fingerprint or palm print evidence from the outer packaging of parcels of cannabis resin recovered at the scene. The Supreme Court held that the applicant had failed to make out a case on the facts.

Evidence had been admitted at the applicant's trial that the parcels had been preserved and examined forensically, and that no fingerprints had been found on the packaging of the parcels. Denham J. noted that the defence had never sought its own forensic examination of the packaging in advance of trial and pointed out that the packaging had been preserved with the consequence that the option still remained open to the applicant. No expert evidence had been adduced to suggest that the passage of time or the handling of the wrappings would have destroyed any prints that might have been left. Hardiman J. agreed that the applicant had not engaged sufficiently with the facts to substantiate his claim for relief by way of judicial review. He observed that "the onus on the applicant is not a high one and evidence in relation to the fingerprinting of various materials is expert evidence of a sort which is readily available".

The rare and exceptional nature of the jurisdiction to intervene in duty to preserve cases was emphasised by Hedigan J. in *Byrne v Judges of the Circuit Court* [2007] I.E.H.C. 366 (October 31, 2007). The applicants sought to restrain their trial for charges relating to the theft of a trailer and a mini-digger valued at €30,000. The offences allegedly took place on July 7, 2004, and on September 27, 2004 the applicants' solicitors wrote the first of a series of letters seeking confirmation that the machinery was being preserved and requesting an opportunity to conduct an independent examination. On March 3, 2005, the applicants' solicitor received a response reporting that the machinery had been returned to the owner having first been photographed by the Gardaí. The trailer remained in the owner's possession and could be made available for inspection, but the mini-digger had since been sold at auction in Scotland. The applicants maintained that the failure of the Gardaí to preserve the mini-digger for purposes of an independent examination placed them at a serious disadvantage in presenting their defence.

Hedigan J. observed that the duty on the Gardaí is to preserve evidence "as far as is necessary and practicable" (quoting Lynch J. in *Murphy v DPP* [1989] I.L.R.M. 71) and that there are circumstances in which preservation must be conducted "with some degree of commonsense and practicality". He remarked that to withhold possession of valuable machinery could have the effect of further victimising the victim of the alleged crime. In this case, the factual relevance of the issue lay in the need to determine the value of the machinery. The mini-digger was of a well-known type and model, its age was known, and its condition could be evinced by inspection of the photographs, the report of the garda inspector, the records of the owner hire company and other independent evidence. Hedigan J. described as speculative the applicants' submission that with the benefit of an independent inspection of the mini-digger they might have been able to convince the District judge that its value was substantially less than the value alleged in the Book of Evidence. He also rejected the first applicant's claim that he was impaired in his ability to defend himself against the specific allegation that he was aware or reckless as to whether the machinery was stolen. The first applicant contended that the absence of an independent inspection deprived him of the opportunity to disprove that the machinery was sold below market value. However, the alternative option of establishing this fact by cross-examination or the production of other evidence remained open to the first applicant. Even if this was not the case, Hedigan J. took the view that the trial judge would be better placed to hear and decide an application in this regard.

The significance of a causative link between a failure to seek out and preserve evidence and the fairness of the pending trial was underscored in a similar fashion by the decision in *Matthews v DPP* [2007] I.E.H.C. 433 (December 14, 2007). The applicants sought prohibition of their trial for assault arising out of an incident which occurred outside two licensed premises in Dundalk. McMenamin J. found that the Gardaí had clearly failed in their duty to seek out video evidence from the licensed premises, but nevertheless refused the relief sought because the applicants had not established a real and substantial risk of an unfair trial by reason of the absence of the video material. The learned judge quoted, inter alia, from the judgment of Kearns J. in *McFarlane v DPP* [2006] I.E.S.C. (March 7, 2006) to the effect that "remote possibilities arising from the loss of evidence should not be allowed to trip up the prosecution or justify stopping the trial from taking place". McMenamin J. considered the key test to be that of reasonableness. Having reviewed the evidential parameters of the present case, he declined the applicants' invitation:

> "... to embark on a series of hypotheses commencing with the proposition that *if* the video cameras were operating on the night in question, *and* they would have captured relevant evidence, unobscured by other people, that such evidence might have exonerated the accused".

The prosecution must disclose any document which could be of assistance to the accused in establishing a defence, in damaging the prosecution case or in providing a lead on evidence that goes to either of these two things (*DPP v Ward* [1999] 1 I.R. 60). In *DPP v Dundon* [2007] I.E.C.C.A. 64 (July 25, 2007), Kearns J., delivering judgment for the Court of Criminal Appeal, stated that a failure on the part of the prosecution to make full pre-trial disclosure "must be shown to have been important, as distinct from technical or trivial if a conviction is to be regarded as unsafe". The court was refusing leave to appeal against the applicants' convictions for the murder of Limerick gangland figure, Kieran Keane. The learned judge went on to explain that the Court of Criminal Appeal must engage with the facts in order to ascertain whether an impugned omission disadvantaged the defence in such a way as to render the trial unfair or the jury verdict unsafe in the particular circumstances of the individual case. The enquiry was analogous to the test for the duty to seek out and preserve evidence discussed above and conditioned by "the commonsense parameters" governing the scope of that duty.

In *Dundon,* the alleged failure to disclose related to certain memos of interviews and statements taken from prosecution witness, Owen Treacy. The applicants argued that the availability of this information might have influenced the defence strategy at trial; specifically, rather than suggest that Treacy was an accomplice, the defence might have mounted an all-out attack on Treacy's character with a view to undermining his credibility as the chief prosecution witness. The Court of Criminal Appeal was satisfied, however, that the failure on the part of the prosecution to make more detailed disclosure "whilst not to be condoned" was not such as to render the conviction "in any way unsafe". On the facts, the failure had not materially affected the ability of the defence to cross-examine the witness as to credit. Thus, as Kearns J. explained, "the omission to furnish every last document which might have referred to Owen Treacy is of a less serious nature than it might otherwise be in another case".

The extent of any right on the part of an accused to production of documents in the possession of third parties presents an interesting question thus far unresolved by the Irish courts. The rules relating to discovery of documents, including third party discovery, do not apply to criminal trials (*People (DPP) v Sweeney* [2001] 4 I.R. 102; *DH v Judge Groarke* [2002] 3 I.R. 522) and whether the obligation to disclose extends to documents outside the prosecution's possession is not settled. In *Judge Michael Reilly v Midland Health Board* [2007] I.E.H.C. 32 (July 26, 2007), the Supreme Court rejected the use of deposition procedure as a possible solution.

The case originated in attempts by the legal advisers of the appellant, who had been charged with sexual offences, to obtain confidential reports in the hands of the Midland Health Board. The latter claimed that the reports were privileged because they referred to interviews of a therapeutic nature. The defence sought to take depositions and/or serve subpoenas *duces tecum* on a number of health board employees and social workers. On a consultative case stated, Macken J. rejected this use of depositions and subpoenas as a means of obtaining third party disclosure and the Supreme Court, in turn, upheld her reasoning and this result. However, Geoghegan J. expressly left over to another day the possible resolution of "undecided issues as to a right to procurement of documentation from a third party which is at least a state or a state funded body". In his view, an issue of this kind would have to be decided in a suitable case by the court of trial and on notice to the Director of Public Prosecutions, the body in question and the Attorney-General.

The right to apply for a dismissal of charges under s.4E of the Criminal Procedure Act 1967 (as inserted by s.9 of the Criminal Justice Act 1999) was discussed by the Supreme Court in *Phipps v Judge Desmond Hogan* [2007] I.E.S.C. 68 (December 20, 2007). The 1999 Act abolished the provisions in the 1967 Act for a preliminary examination of indictable charges in the District Court and replaced them with other measures, including a right on the part of a defendant to apply for the dismissal of the charges before the court of trial pursuant to s.4E. The question raised by this case was whether the defendant is required to give advanced notice of the grounds upon which his or her application for dismissal will be based. The Supreme Court upheld the decision of Quirke J. that s.4E imposes no such requirement by virtue of the presumption of innocence and the burden of proof in criminal proceedings.

Before the Supreme Court, the Director of Public Prosecutions argued that, even in the absence of an express statutory power to oblige a defendant to give notice of the grounds for an application, such a power is implicit in the inherent authority of the trial judge to manage proceedings in his or her court. Hardiman J. rejected this contention, opining that the right to a trial in due course of law precludes the implied interpretation of a power to require disclosure where the statute does not expressly say as much. Given that the prosecution has full access to the facts as the Gardaí see them, as well as their Book of Evidence and proofs advised by senior counsel, he considered it "unlikely in the extreme" that the prosecution would be "embarrassed" by the need to demonstrate the sufficiency of the case against the defendant. If necessary, the prosecution could apply to the trial judge for an adjournment; in addition, the prosecution might appeal the determination of an application under s.4E.

Discovery   The intriguing challenge posed by the need to adapt the rules of court to accommodate technological advances in the keeping of records was placed in sharp relief by the appeal against a High Court order for discovery in *Dome Telecom v Eircom* [2007] I.E.S.C. 59 (December 5, 2007). The plaintiff, a Dublin-based company supplying call card and other freephone telecommunications services, instituted proceedings challenging the imposition of telecommunications interconnection charges by the defendant Eircom. The defendant allegedly failed to impose such charges on international operators, to whom it provided access via its London-based subsidiary, to the detriment of Irish operators such as the plaintiff, who were subject to the charges. A dispute over the parameters of discovery ensued involving lengthy submissions and several hearings before McKechnie J. in the competition court. In particular, the plaintiff sought access to documentation relating to the quantity of "1800" numbers issued by the defendant to licensed operators and/or international carriers per month during a specified period, together with details of the entities to whom they were issued and the volume of minutes trafficked. The purpose of the request was to enable the plaintiff to make out its case of anti-competitive practices and to quantify its claim for damages. The defendant argued that some of this information was already discovered, that further discovery was not necessary to enable the plaintiff to substantiate its case and that the order sought would constitute a disproportionate form of relief. In the latter regard, the defendant relied on key factual concessions it had made on the issue of liability and cited further the cost and burden that would be involved in responding to the order.

McKechnie J. granted the application for discovery on the basis that the documentation sought was relevant and necessary for the purposes of the action.

He had heard evidence that call data records existed within the defendant's computer system but that such records could not now be retrieved without exhuming vast numbers of records from the system. The defendant operated a billing system for operators and customers by reference to call data records, but these bills were generated electronically and held only temporarily. Notwithstanding the burden that retrieval would impose on the defendant, McKechnie J. considered the order necessary to enable the plaintiff to make its case and rejected the suggestion that the defendant's concessions on liability dictated otherwise. The learned judge held that the use of the data in question came within the Rules of the Superior Courts and that the requirement for discovery was not disproportionate.

A majority of a three-judge panel of the Supreme Court allowed the appeal and set aside the order for discovery. Kearns J. emphasised the significance in Ord.31 r.12 of the concept of necessity to the particular stage of the proceedings at which discovery is sought. He pointed out that the special rules in relation to competition proceedings emphasise efficiency and the requirement of minimising costs. Quoting from the judgment of Fennelly J in *Ryanair plc v Aer Rianta cpt* [2003] 4 I.R. 264 at 277 and that of Murray J. in *Framus Ltd v CHR plc* [2004] 2 I.R. 20 at 38, Kearns J. observed that the need for proportionality between the extent or volume of the documents to be discovered and the degree to which the documents are likely to advance the case of the applicant (or damage the case of his or her opponent) assumes particular importance where factual admissions which may permit the resolution of important aspects of the case are made by the party from whom discovery is sought:

> "To put it another way, the assessment of what is necessary or proportionate must take account of any factual admissions or concessions made by either or both parties, notably where liability is totally in dispute and where that issue can conveniently be first determined as a result of admissions or concessions made."

Kearns J. noted that the judgment of the learned High Court judge did not indicate why the concession offered by the defendant was not regarded as sufficient to allow liability to be determined. Nor was a clear indication given as to the cost and burden involved in the gargantuan task which the order for discovery would impose on the defendant. Moreover, while the material sought was undoubtedly relevant, it did not automatically follow that it was necessary at this stage in the proceedings. On the plaintiff's own evidence, only a small proportion of its customers used the 1800 freephone number from mobiles and payphones (the subject of the proceedings) as opposed to fixed-line calling (a subject outside the scope of the proceedings). The issue then was whether cumbersome discovery which related only to a certain aspect of quantum should be regarded as necessary and proportionate at this point in the proceedings. Kearns J. rested his ultimate decision "essentially on pragmatic grounds", opting to defer any decision on discovery of the documentation sought until the issue of liability had been determined. He favoured allowing the appeal on the basis that the High Court order was both unnecessary and disproportionate at the stage of the proceedings at which it was granted. In the event that the plaintiff succeeded on liability, it would then be at liberty to renew the application if it was required for the purpose of assessing damages.

In light of these conclusions, Kearns J. did not consider it necessary to decide whether the discovery sought involved the creation of a document beyond the reach of the Rules of the Superior Courts. Nevertheless, in his dissenting judgment, Geoghegan J. was:

> "... firmly of the opinion that an order of discovery can be made which involves the creation of documents which do not exist made in the kind of context in which it is sought in this case".

Geoghegan J. rejected the idea that the right to discovery should be based on a strict interpretation of the rules of court; where an obvious problem of fair procedures or efficient case management arises, the court has an inherent power to fashion its own procedure or adapt existing rules. The learned judge continued:

> "It is common knowledge that a vast amount of stored information in the business world which formerly would have been in documentary form in the traditional sense is now computerised. As a matter of fairness and common sense the courts must adapt themselves to this situation and fashion appropriate analogous orders of discovery. In order to achieve a reasonable parity with traditional documentary discovery it may well be necessary to direct a party 'to create documents' ...".

Fennelly J. agreed that:

> "... failure by the courts to move with the times by adapting the rules to new technology might encourage unscrupulous businesses to keep their records in a form which would defeat the ends of justice".

In company with Geoghegan J., Fennelly J. rejected this ground of appeal. However, he voted to allow the appeal on the basis that the plaintiff had not established, at this juncture in the litigation, that the likely benefit of obtaining the documentation was sufficient to justify the highly unusual and burdensome form of discovery sought.

Geoghegan J. was of the view that the plaintiff had established that the discovery sought was "necessary" within the meaning of that term in the Irish case law. However, he acknowledged that:

> "[D]iscovery may be 'necessary' and yet so disproportionate as to render it unreasonable for a court to benefit the party seeking discovery by making such an order".

Geoghegan J. indicated that the Supreme Court would be reluctant to interfere with an order made in the course of case management in the competition court. He was satisfied that McKechnie J. had not erred in legal principle and had understood and considered the arguments on both sides. A further consideration was that the time and expense involved in furnishing the discovery in question must be offset against the potential saving in time and cost which might well materialise when discovery was completed. At a minimum, there would be a considerable narrowing of issues either by agreement or as a consequence of case management. Geoghegan J. took the position that some kind of partial hearing would likely add to the litigation and appeals and possibly render more uncertain the ultimate outcome of the action.

Hearsay The absence in civil proceedings of a formal exception to the rule against hearsay for documentary evidence was illustrated in *Director of Corporate Enforcement v Bailey* [2007] I.E.H.C. 365 (November 1, 2007). The rule against hearsay precludes the admission as evidence of an out-of-court statement when offered as proof of the matter stated. The premise is that the finder of fact can better weigh the evidential value of the statement when the declarant testifies in court under oath and is subject to cross-examination (*Eastern Health Board v MK* [1999] 2 I.R. 99; *R. v Blastland* [1986] A.C. 41). However, there are numerous common law and statutory exceptions to the rule which apply in a range of circumstances where courts need to have recourse to hearsay statements and there are grounds for believing that the statements are trustworthy. In the UK, the need for the admission of business records was demonstrated by the landmark decision of the House of Lords in *DPP v Myers* [1965] 1 A.C. 1001 and was subsequently sanctioned by Parliament in relation to criminal and civil proceedings. If a business conducts hundreds or thousands of transactions in any given year, it is doubtful whether any single employee will remember a particular transaction. Nevertheless, habits of precision in the routine gathering and reporting of data by the business's employees suggest that the business's records are probably the most reliable evidence available. The Oireachtas included in the Criminal Evidence Act 1992 a broad exception to the rule against hearsay in relation to business records (ss.5–8) but no equivalent general measure exists in relation to civil proceedings. Documentary hearsay may be admitted in interlocutory applications pursuant to Ord.40 r.4, by consent and occasionally under certain specific and limited statutory provisions (e.g. Bankers' Books Evidence Act 1879 as amended, Companies Act 1963 as amended, and Children Act 1997).

The applicant Director of Corporate Enforcement served notice of his intention to institute proceedings against the respondent directors of Bovale Developments Ltd seeking to disqualify them as directors pursuant to s.160(2) of the Companies Act. The respondents moved to curtail certain evidence put forward by the applicant in two grounding affidavits; that evidence comprised extracts from the second interim report of the Mahon Tribunal of Inquiry into Certain Planning Matters and Payments, documentation from the Revenue Commissioners and material compiled by a firm of chartered accountants. The respondents' objected on the ground, inter alia, that this evidence was inadmissible under the rules against hearsay and opinion evidence respectively. The applicant countered that the respondents' motion to strike out portions of the affidavits was premature and should not be adjudicated on prior to trial. Irvine J. acknowledged the difficulty facing the court in deciding upon the admissibility of the evidence given that it was unclear at that point what role the allegedly offending affidavits would ultimately play in the proceedings. The learned judge distinguished between affidavits tendered as evidence for the final determination of substantive rights and affidavits tendered for interlocutory purposes, noting that the rule against hearsay applies strictly in relation to the former but not the latter category (Ord.40 r.4). The affidavits at issue could not be assumed to be interlocutory in nature with the consequence that the respondents' application was not premature.

Irvine J. held that the evidence constituted hearsay and that only one of the documents in question was admissible under an exception to the rule. This conclusion turned on a preliminary determination that the evidence was being offered to prove the truth of the allegations asserted by the applicant; an out-of-court statement is not caught by the rule if it is offered for an alternative probative purpose such as proving the fact that it was made (*Subramaniam v Public Prosecutor* [1956] 1 W.L.R. 965; *Ratten v R.* [1972] A.C. 378). Here, the affidavits made plain that the court was being invited to consider the documentation "as evidence of wrongdoing" for purposes of deciding whether the respondents should be disqualified as directors and, if so, the appropriate sanction that should be imposed.

Irvine J. emphasised that the admissibility of hearsay evidence is governed by a rule and exceptions thereto and not by a balancing test as suggested by the applicant. She noted that most of the exceptions to the hearsay rule are specifically provided for by enabling legislation and cited as an example s.22 of the Companies Act 1990 which renders admissible the report of an inspector as evidence of fact and opinion for purposes of proceedings to have a person disqualified under s.160(2). The Company Law Enforcement Act 2001 makes no corresponding provision for the Director of Corporate Enforcement to rely on evidence such as the findings of a tribunal of inquiry or a report from a Revenue inspector. In light of the specificity of s.22 of the 1990 Act, the learned judge considered it difficult to infer any departure from the normal rules of evidence for the material at issue in the present proceedings.

As regards the tribunal report, Irvine J. rejected the contention that it was a public document within the scope of the exception to the hearsay rule for public records in civil proceedings (citing *Goodman v Hamilton (No. 1)* [1992] 2 I.R. 542; *Lawlor v Flood* [1999] 3 I.R. 107). Despite almost annual amendment of the Companies Code, the Oireachtas has not seen fit to include a hearsay exception for the findings of tribunals of inquiry. Irvine J. acknowledged that the hearsay rule and its exceptions are not set in stone, but concluded that in the absence of a statutory provision allowing a court to rely on such findings, a departure from the rule should not be inferred. The applicant could use the tribunal report to assist him in finding admissible evidence, but could not present the report to the court as proof of any facts allegedly found therein.

Irvine J. adopted similar reasoning in ruling that documentation from the Revenue Commissioners and the handwritten memoranda of a chartered accountant from auditors of Bovale Developments Ltd constituted inadmissible hearsay outside any statutory exception. However, she refused to order the applicant to remove references to a H4 notice in one of the grounding affidavits. The notice, signed by the same accountant and filed pursuant to s.194 of the Companies Act 1990, stated the auditors' view that Bovale Developments Ltd had failed to keep proper books of account for a specified period. Irvine J. concluded that because the accountant had been acting as an agent of the company when lodging the notice, the issue of hearsay did not arise. In her view, permitting the references to the H4 notice to remain was not likely to prejudice the respondents given that other material supported the suggestion of wrongdoing in the company's record-keeping during the same period.

Hostile witnesses In *People (DPP) v Cunningham* [2007] I.E.C.C.A. 49 (May 24, 2007), the Court of Criminal Appeal emphasised that the determination of whether a witness is hostile for the purpose of permitting counsel to conduct examination-in-chief in the manner of cross-examination is a matter for the discretion of the trial judge. Not having had the opportunity to observe the witness first-hand, the appellate court "should be slow to substitute its view" for that of the trial judge in his or her discretion. The court was rejecting an argument that the trial judge had erred in declaring the applicant's partner a hostile witness so as to enable the prosecution to explore an anticipated conflict between the witness's testimony and pre-trial statements she had given to the Gardaí. Finnegan J. stated:

> "A hostile witness is a witness who at some point after he is sworn appears unwilling, if called by a party who cannot ask him leading questions, to tell the truth and the whole truth. As in this case, the issue tends to arise where the witness's testimony under oath diverges in a material way from an account provided earlier in a pre-trial statement. A trial judge's decision as to whether the witness should be treated as hostile or not is based to a large extent upon a live impression of the

witness's demeanour and credibility and appellate courts in the absence
of clear error are reluctant to substitute their opinion for that of the
trial judge."

The court could find no error in the manner in which the trial judge approached
the issue in the present case. The judge convened a voir dire at which evidence
was received from the witness, her solicitor and three garda witnesses. At
the conclusion of the voir dire, the judge gave a detailed ruling in which he
analysed the evidence, recorded his impression of the witness and explained his
conclusion that the witness was not willing to tell the truth or the whole truth in
her evidence. Above all, the trial judge had the benefit of observing the witness
throughout a protracted examination and cross-examination, a circumstance
characterised by Finnegan J. as "a major factor in the determination of the
issue as to whether a witness is hostile or not".

Misconduct evidence   The admissibility of evidence of an accused's prior
misconduct as background evidence in a case was considered by the Court
of Criminal Appeal in *DPP v McNeill* [2007] I.E.C.C.A. 95 (July 31, 2007).
The applicant was convicted on seven out of eight counts of sexual offences
against a young female neighbour, who was aged between eight and 17 years
at the time of the alleged offences. At trial, the judge allowed the prosecution
to lead evidence of sexual misconduct on the part of the applicant with the
complainant, other than the incidents cited in the indictment, in order to provide
the jury with a background narrative of the nature and development of the
relationship between the two over a period of years. The court refused leave
to appeal against conviction, expressing its satisfaction that the jury acted on
the basis of "an overwhelming volume of proven evidence".

Budd J. engaged in a lengthy review of domestic and comparative case law.
In *R. v Pettman*, unreported, May 2, 1985, the English Court of Appeal set out
the principle that, exceptionally, evidence of background and motive may be
placed before the jury even where such evidence implicates the accused in an
offence other than that with which he or she is charged. Budd J. quoted from the
judgment of Purchas L.J. to the effect that evidence of prior misconduct may be
admitted where it forms part of "a continual background of history relevant to
the offence charged" and where without it "the account placed before the jury
would be incomplete or incomprehensible". Before admitting such evidence,
it is necessary for the trial judge to weigh the probative value of the evidence
against the prejudicial effect likely to flow from its admission (*People (DPP)
v BK* [2000] 2 I.R. 199). In addition, when charging the jury, it is essential that
the trial judge explains that the evidence relates only to background and is not
direct evidence of the offences charged. These principles have been applied in
a number of English and Northern Irish cases outlined in the judgment.

Budd J. concluded that, in the present case, the trial judge had admitted the evidence on the basis that the background of continuous engagement between the complainant and the accused put in context the facts bearing on the vital issue of consent. In his ruling admitting the evidence, the trial judge had emphasised a cautious approach to any exception to the general exclusionary rule and gave clear and cogent reasons for his decision grounded in the specific circumstances of the case. Furthermore, the charge to the jury had taken into account the matters noted above including the prejudicial nature of the evidence.

Photographs and fingerprints and palm prints Section 48 of the Criminal Justice Act 2007 introduced significant changes to the regime governing the taking of photographs, fingerprints and palm prints during custodial detention. The overall effect of these changes is to extend the powers of the Gardaí to record these identifiers and reduce the ability of detained persons to resist the process. First, s.6 of the 1984 Act is amended to allow for the repeated taking of records where the photographs, fingerprints or palm prints originally taken "are lost, damaged or otherwise imperfect". Secondly, whereas the taking of these identifiers previously required the authorisation of a member of the Garda Síochána not below the rank of superintendent, authorisation may now be given at inspector level. Thirdly, under a new s.6A, where a detained person fails or refuses to allow his or her photographs or fingerprints and palm prints to be taken, a member of the Garda Síochána may use "such force as he or she reasonably considers to be necessary to take the photographs or fingerprints and palm prints". The use of such force is subject to several additional safeguards: it must not be exercised without the authority of a garda superintendent, the detained person must be cautioned that the garda intends to use force and has been authorised to do so, the photographs or fingerprints and palm prints must be taken in the presence of an officer not below the rank of inspector, and the taking of the photographs or prints must be video-recorded.

Section 49 of the 2007 Act contains corresponding changes to the power of the Gardaí to retain photographs, fingerprints and palm prints taken during custodial detention. The presumption in favour of destruction enshrined in s.8 of the 1984 Act has been replaced by a presumption in favour of retention. The provision applies to a person who has been arrested and had these identifiers taken but who has subsequently been cleared of wrongdoing in so far as proceedings have not been instituted within 12 months from the date the records were taken or, if they have been so instituted, the person has been acquitted, the charge has been dismissed or the proceedings have been discontinued. As originally drafted, s.8 placed an onus on the Gardaí to destroy such records where any of these eventualities had been met. In the case of a failure to institute proceedings, the original time period of six months was extended to 12 months by s.12 of the Criminal Justice Act 2006. Section 49 of the 2007 Act has now removed the obligation to destroy in s.8 of the 1984 Act and replaced it with an entitlement on the part of the person detained (the requester) to apply in writing to the Garda Commissioner "to have the records destroyed or their use limited" (s.8(1) as substituted by s.49 of 2007 Act). The Commissioner has four weeks from receipt of the request to decide whether to grant or refuse it (s.8(5)) and where he or she refuses the request or grants it only in part, the requester may appeal to the District Court against the decision (s.8(6)). A refusal or grant of an order of destruction by the District Court may be appealed to the Circuit Court (s.8(10)). The Gardaí are free to use the records during the pendency of the procedure in connection with other proceedings or criminal investigations (s.8(13)(b)). Where an order for destruction is made, the Commissioner must notify the requester in writing as soon as the records have been destroyed (s.8(11)). The new regime is prospective and does not apply to records taken before the commencement of the section (s.8(14)).

In *DPP (Walsh) v Cash* [2007] I.E.C.C.A. 108 (March 28, 2007), the application of the exclusionary rule to fingerprint evidence was considered by the High Court on a case stated. The Gardaí had identified the accused as a suspect in a burglary by means of a database which matched prints found at the crime scene with prints previously taken from the accused and stored in garda records. After the accused's arrest, a further set of prints were taken with his consent which also matched crime scene prints. The Gardaí could not establish whether the original set of prints had been lawfully taken and held. The accused submitted that this taint on the suspicion which grounded his arrest necessitated the exclusion of any evidence obtained during his detention. Charleton J. rejected this contention and held that a suspicion which gives rise to a reasonable cause for arrest does not have to be justified on the basis that every element of it arose solely from evidence properly obtained. The decision reflects the view that the rules of evidence do not constrain the Gardaí in each and every aspect of criminal investigation. In particular, there is no onus on the prosecution to prove that information grounding a reasonable suspicion for purposes of arrest was obtained in strict compliance with the law. The point has a particular resonance in the context of criminal identification databases (whether a fingerprint database or potentially a future DNA database). The principal purpose of a database is to generate suspects by matching identifiers found at a crime scene with identifiers previously taken from individuals and held by the Gardaí. The implication of the decision is that this process of generating suspects via the database is not caught by the exclusionary rule. Consequently, the prosecution are not obliged to prove that the identifiers on the database were taken, retained and used in accordance with the various safeguards set down in law.

The case stated also raised the question of whether the Gardaí have the power to take fingerprints from a person on consent rather than under s.6 of the Criminal Justice Act 1984 so as to avoid the requirements of s.8 of the 1984 Act pertaining to the retention and destruction of fingerprints. Section 6 permits the taking of fingerprints on the authorisation of a garda superintendent. In the present case, the accused was invited to consent to the taking of his fingerprints but told that the prints would be taken "one way or another". Charleton J. referred to a line of authority establishing a distinction between a confession which must not have resulted from an illegal inducement and items of objective physical evidence which are not affected by the mood of the suspect (e.g. *People (DPP) v Walsh* [1980] I.R. 294; *People (DPP) v Boyce* [2005] I.E.C.C.A. 143). The learned judge compared the giving of a fingerprint by consent to the voluntary surrender of an item of clothing. A garda is entitled to seek the consent of a citizen, be he or she suspect or not, in relation to the gathering of samples and to take the relevant samples with consent. Charleton J. observed that a failure to produce proof of consent to the taking of a fingerprint would constitute a breach of the Custody Regulations which would render the evidence illegally, as opposed to unconstitutionally, obtained. However, he was reluctant to hold on the existing authorities that a constitutional right to privacy extends to "the map of one's DNA, one's fingerprints or the chemical composition of blood or urine". In the event that the right extends that far, a breach by agents of the State necessitates the exclusion of the evidence.

Prejudicial evidence   The procedural and evidentiary rules that govern legal proceedings are designed to ensure that the only evidence put before a jury is admissible evidence. Occasionally, however, a fact is improperly admitted and a jury becomes privy to some potentially prejudicial matter. The appropriate step to remedy the situation is a matter first and foremost for the trial judge and may depend upon the circumstances of the case. It may be possible for the trial judge to cure any prejudice by means of a direction to the jury. However, if such a direction cannot obviate a real and substantial risk of an unfair trial, it may be necessary for the judge to discharge the jury (*People (DPP) v Marley* [1985] I.L.R.M. 17).

  In *People (DPP) v Cunningham* [2007] I.E.C.C.A. 49 (May 24, 2007), the applicant for leave to appeal argued that the trial judge had erred in refusing to discharge the jury after a prosecution witness included in her testimony recognition evidence which the trial judge had ruled inadmissible on a voir dire. When giving her evidence to the jury, the witness indicated that she had recognised an individual from a previous sighting, although the trial judge had ruled that her testimony be limited to factual descriptions of the two individuals short of recognition. The trial judge refused to discharge the jury and issued a direction to the jury to disregard the impugned aspect of the witness's testimony. The Court of Criminal Appeal quoted from Supreme Court judgments to the effect that discharging a jury should be a remedy of last resort and that a strong and appropriate direction to the jury is generally the appropriate step to be taken (e.g. *D v DPP* [1994] 2 I.R. 465; *Dawson v Irish Brokers Association,* unreported, Supreme Court, November 6, 1998). The present case was on all fours with *DPP v JEM* [2001] 4 I.R. 385, in which the Court of Criminal Appeal held that there was no basis for interfering with a trial judge's refusal to discharge a jury in similar circumstances where the decision was taken after consideration, with reasons given, and having analysed any potential for prejudice. Here, the trial judge had been at great pains in his charge to ensure that the jury excluded from their consideration the evidence improperly admitted.

In *Cunningham*, the Court of Criminal Appeal adopted similar reasoning in rejecting a further ground for appeal, namely, that the trial judge should have discharged the jury having regard to prejudicial comments about the trial that had appeared on an internet website. At trial, counsel for the applicant had argued that it was not known if any juror had accessed the website and that the jury should have been warned at the start of the trial not to access the internet. The trial judge gave a warning to the jury at that stage in the proceedings not to consult any website that might have information or commentary on the case; the judge also asked whether any of the jurors had accessed such a website prior to this warning, to which they collectively answered in the negative. The Court of Criminal Appeal held that in these circumstances there was no real risk of unfairness arising out of the existence of the website. It continued:

> "To hold that such a risk exists would require that at least one juror had visited the website and read the relevant blogs, will be prejudiced against the applicant because of the same, will not comply with his/her oath as a juror and will not comply with the charge of the trial judge."

The spectre of prejudice flowing from the introduction of inadmissible evidence presented a more intractable problem in *DPP v Fahy* [2007] I.E.C.C.A. 102 (November 28, 2007). The applicant, who was a member of Galway County Council, successfully appealed his conviction for various offences relating to theft and false pretences on the ground that the prosecution led prejudicial evidence which it had failed to disclose pursuant to ss.4B, 4C and 4D of the Criminal Justice (Miscellaneous Provisions) Act 1967 as inserted by s.9 of the Criminal Justice Act 1999. The evidence in question constituted notes of a meeting between the applicant and the Director of Services with Galway County Council. When the Director of Services testified at trial, counsel for the prosecution elicited from the witness information contained in the notes but not included in the Book of Evidence.

In the Court of Appeal, Finnegan J. observed that had the material in question been exhibited in a timely manner and furnished to the defence as statutorily required, it would have been possible for the defence to object on grounds of irrelevance. He continued:

> "This is not a case in which the inadmissible evidence was unsolicited by the prosecution but was blurted out by the witness unprompted. Had the *voir dire* taken place in advance of the evidence being given

rather than after it had been given the evidence would not have been given. What occurred is a direct result of the non-compliance by the prosecution with the requirements of the Act."

After the witness had testified, the defence applied unsuccessfully to have the jury discharged. Finnegan J. noted that this eventuality presented a dilemma for defence counsel. Cross-examining the witness or asking the judge to give a direction to the jury ran the risk of compounding the situation. Defence counsel's decision to remain silent in the hope that the jury might not attach any significance to the evidence was an appropriate exercise of his discretion.

The Court of Criminal Appeal was satisfied that the evidence in question was sufficiently prejudicial that the jury ought to have been discharged. In particular, some of the evidence might well have led the jury to infer that the applicant had wealth disproportionate to his income and station in life and dishonestly obtained. In the circumstances, the introduction of inadmissible evidence in the manner in which it occurred had created a real and substantial risk of an unfair trial.

Privilege *(a) Legal Professional Privilege* Legal professional privilege protects from disclosure confidential information communicated between a lawyer and client (*Smurfit Parisbas Bank v AAB Export Finance Ltd* [1990] 1 I.R. 469) or generated by the lawyer in preparation for litigation (*Silver Hill Duckling Ltd v Minister for Agriculture* [1987] I.R. 289. The position of in-house lawyers can be precarious, however, depending on whether they are classified as employees or legal advisers. Although the common law has tended to include communications with in-house lawyers within the cloak of protection (e.g. *Geraghty v Minister for Local Government* [1975] I.R. 300; *Somatra v Sinclair Roche and Temperley* [2001] 1 W.L.R. 2453), the European Court of Justice has expressly excluded them (Case C155/79, *AM & S* [1982] ECR 1575). In *Akzo Nobel Chemicals Ltd v Commission,* Joined cases T-125/03 & T-253/03, the Court of First Instance confirmed this position, holding that legal professional privilege is limited to legal advice tendered "in full independence", i.e. provided by a lawyer "who structurally, hierarchically and functionally, is a third party in relation to the undertaking receiving that advice". Delivered in the specific context of investigations by the Commission into anti-competitive practices, this ruling underscores the significance of the distinction between internal and external legal advice. Although communications with external lawyers are protected, as well as internal notes reporting the content of such communications, the status of preparatory documents drawn up in advance of seeking external legal advice is far less certain.

(b) Journalists' Sources There has been a traditional reluctance on the part of the Irish courts to extend the cloak of informants' privilege to journalists'

sources (*Re Kevin O'Kelly* (1974) 109 I.L.T.R. 97), in the absence of a threat to life or limb (*Burke v Central Independent Television plc* [1994] 2 I.R. 61). The courts have recognised that disclosure of the identity of a journalist's source should be ordered only where necessary and as a last resort (*People (DPP) v Nevin* [2003] 3 I.R. 321) but have stopped short of recognising an affirmative entitlement to confidentiality. In contrast, the European Court of Human Rights has provided more robust protection for journalists' sources as an aspect of press freedom under Art.10 of the European Convention on Human Rights (*Goodwin v United Kingdom* (1996) 22 E.H.R.R. 123).

In *Mahon v Keena and Kennedy* [2007] I.E.H.C. 348 (October 10, 2007), the High Court recognised a privilege for journalists' sources in principle but held that the conditions for the privilege had not been made out in the instant case. The proceedings originated in a confidential letter sent by the Mahon Tribunal of Inquiry into Certain Planning Matters and Payments to Mr David McKenna seeking information in relation to certain payments made to the then Taoiseach, Mr Bertie Ahern. The first defendant, a journalist at the *Irish Times* received, unsolicited and anonymously, a copy of the letter and of the reply from a solicitor for Mr McKenna. The first defendant subsequently wrote, and the second defendant decided to publish, a front-page report in the *Irish Times* on the tribunal's examination of payments to the Taoiseach. The tribunal ordered the defendants to produce the documents comprising the communication received by the *Irish Times*. The second defendant replied indicating that the material in question had been destroyed and that the newspaper disputed the right of the tribunal to issue the order on the grounds that production would run the risk of identifying journalists' sources. The defendants later furnished written statements to the tribunal and appeared before it, but declined to provide information that would lend any assistance in identifying the source of the anonymous communication. The tribunal instituted proceedings in the High Court seeking orders compelling the defendants to comply with the tribunal's order and attend before the tribunal to answer all questions required.

As a threshold matter, the defendants contested the legal power of the tribunal to conduct an inquiry to ascertain the leak of the confidential documents that were furnished to the *Irish Times*. A Divisional High Court held that the tribunal had the necessary legal power and was entitled to have summonsed the defendants before it and produce the documents (*Mahon v Post Publications* [2007] I.E.S.C. 15 (March 29, 2007)). It held further that as a corollary of the tribunal's right to conduct a private investigative stage of an inquiry, it can impose and enforce an obligation of confidentiality in respect of material assembled in its private investigative phase. The court then moved on to consider how the tribunal's right to enforce confidentiality should be balanced against the defendants' entitlements as journalists pursuant to Art.10 of the Convention (freedom of expression) not to have to disclose their sources.

Having briefly summarised some of the leading European cases, the court noted that the availability of sources of information is an essential feature of the operation of a free press. The case law evinced a trend of strictly construing potential interferences with freedom of expression particularly in cases involving publications relating to political matters. The court declared that the exercise of balancing the right of a journalist to resist disclosure against the rights and interests of other persons or institutions is an exercise in a democratic society that is reserved to courts established by law for that purpose. Thus:

> "[T]he deliberate decision taken by the defendants to destroy the documents at issue in this case after they had received a summons to produce these to the Tribunal and after having taken legal advice, is an astounding and flagrant disregard of the rule of law".

Although this "reprehensible conduct" had not been raised as a contempt issue, nevertheless the court viewed the destruction of the documents as "a relevant consideration to which great weight must be given" in striking the appropriate balance between the rights and interests in the case.

The court identified as the starting point in this balancing exercise, "the realisation that in a democratic society the right to freedom of expression is of the highest order of importance". An onus rested on the tribunal to demonstrate that the restrictions on the right by means of the disclosure of sources for which it contended were justified under the conditions set down in Art.10(2). The court was persuaded that the tribunal had discharged this onus and granted the relief sought on the basis that these conditions had been met. The interference was "prescribed by law" in so far as the tribunal had the legal right to seek and impose confidentiality in respect of the material and this right was adequately accessible to the citizenry. The nub of the matter was whether the disclosure was proportionate, i.e. "necessary in a democratic society" in pursuit of the legitimate aim of "preventing the disclosure of information received in confidence" as specified in Art.10(2). The fact that the communication in the case was unsolicited and anonymous weighed heavily in the Court's determination:

> "In respect of anonymous communications, in principle, either the privilege against non-disclosure should not be invoked at all or, if it is to be invoked, only the slightest weight should be attached to it for the plain reason that if a journalist cannot identify the source of his information it is nonsense to say that there is a professional obligation to protect that source from disclosure. If, of course, the questions to be asked could or would lead to the source or give assistance which could result in the identification of the source then we are satisfied that the privilege against disclosure can be invoked."

In all the circumstances of the case, including the destruction of the documents, the court surmised that there was little or no risk that the tribunal's questions would lead to the identification of the source. Consequently, the court attached "very slight weight indeed" to the defendants' privilege against disclosure of their sources while recognising "the potential of a real benefit to the Tribunal" if the defendants' answers to the questions assisting in clarifying whether the tribunal itself had been the source of the leak. In granting the relief sought by the tribunal, the court expressed the view that this was not a case in which the competing interests were finely balanced: the defendants' privilege against non-disclosure was "overwhelming outweighed" by the pressing social need to preserve public confidence in the tribunal and the enquiry undertaken by the tribunal constituted the only means by which this could be achieved.

Notwithstanding the result in this case, the judgment of the High Court reveals how far the Irish courts have travelled in recognising as a matter of legal principle the entitlement on the part of journalists to protect their sources. The positive terms in which the court couches this entitlement underscore the influence that incorporation of the European Convention on Human Rights has exerted over the development of Irish law in this area. The response of the Supreme Court to a likely appeal in this case will be awaited with anticipation and may shed further light on the nature and scope of the privilege.

Standard of proof   In *People (DPP) v Cunningham* [2007] I.E.C.C.A. 49 (May 24, 2007), the Court of Criminal Appeal recalled that when reviewing jury directions on the concept of "reasonable doubt" it must examine the trial judge's charge as a whole and consider whether the judge properly explained the standard of proof (citing *People (DPP) v Kelly*, unreported, Court of Criminal Appeal, March 21, 2001). The applicant for leave to appeal was convicted of murder and appealed, inter alia, on the ground that the jury had been misled on the issue by references in the opening and closing speeches of the prosecution and the judge's charge. The Court of Criminal Appeal rejected this ground and held that the standard of proof had been appropriately explained to the jury by the trial judge. Finnegan J. recognised that the references in question were "perhaps not particularly helpful to a jury" but "taken in the context of the prosecution's opening and closing as a whole and the judge's charge as a whole" the court was satisfied that they were not objectionable.

Unlawfully obtained evidence   The admissibility of evidence in the Irish courts is conditioned by the well-known requirement that the evidence be obtained by exclusively lawful means. The exclusionary rule set down in *People (AG) v O'Brien* [1965] I.R. 142 was revised and strengthened in *People (DPP) v Kenny* [1990] 2 I.R. 110. Finlay C.J. stated that evidence obtained in breach of constitutional rights must be excluded at trial unless the act constituting the breach was committed unintentionally or accidentally or there were extraordinary excusing circumstances. The scope of the exceptions was explored in the subsequent case law. The concept of an unintentional or accidental breach of constitutional rights is objectively defined with the consequence that in practice the prosecution can plead neither that the breach was de minimis nor that the law enforcement authorities acted in good faith. Similarly, the extraordinary excusing circumstances that might justify the admission of the evidence has been narrowly construed. In relation to evidence obtained by illegal, as opposed to unconstitutional means, the trial judge retains a discretion to exclude the evidence on a consideration of all the circumstances (*O'Brien*). The reach of constitutional rights is such, however, that situations in which the admissibility of evidence is challenged by reference to alleged illegal conduct falling short of unconstitutional conduct, are rare.

The absolute tenor of the exclusionary rule has been the subject of controversy in recent years. For example, the far-reaching implications of the rule were demonstrated in *People (DPP) v Laide and Ryan* [2005] 1 I.R. 209, where statements made by an accused in custodial detention were declared inadmissible on appeal because the Gardaí had entered the accused's home on foot of an invalid search warrant and had arrested and cautioned the accused on the premises (*see also Curtin v Dáil Éireann* [2006] 2 I.R. 556; *Competition Authority v Irish Dental Association* [2005] 3 I.R. 208).

The nature and extent of the exclusionary rule was considered by Charleton J. in *DPP (Walsh) v Cash* [2007] I.E.H.C. (March 28, 2007). The matter came before the High Court on a case stated from the District Court where a prosecution for burglary was pending against the accused. The Gardaí identified the accused as a suspect in the burglary by means of a fingerprint database which matched prints found at the crime scene with prints previously taken from the accused and stored in garda records. After the accused's arrest, a further set of prints were taken with his consent, which also matched crime scene prints. An issue arose as to whether the original set of the accused's prints had been lawfully obtained. The accused submitted that any piece of information that might lead to a step in the criminal process—in this instance an arrest—must be proved by the prosecution to have been obtained in strict compliance with law. Charleton J. rejected this contention and held that a suspicion which gives rise to a reasonable cause for arrest does not have to be justified on the basis that every element of it arose solely from evidence properly obtained. Consequently, evidence obtained from a detention is not unlawful by reason of the fact that the detention is based on a suspicion that cannot be proved as being founded exclusively on information lawfully obtained. Charleton J. characterised the accused's argument as an attempt to import the rules of evidence into police procedures where they have no place. The learned judge remarked:

> "If the prosecution was obliged to prove legality in respect of every step leading to an arrest or charge, this would have the result that the prosecution, in presenting a case, would be required not only to show, against objection by the defence, that the evidence which they proposed to lead was lawfully obtained, but to open to the court every facet of

the investigation to ensure that no illegality ever tainted any aspect of
police conduct."

Charleton J. went on to consider in detail the status of the exclusionary rule. He
traced the historical development of the rule, focusing in particular on judicial
analysis of the reference in *O'Brien* to deliberate and conscious violation of
constitutional rights. He discerned three practical consequences to the decision
in *Kenny*: first, every error on the part of law enforcement authorities which
takes their action outside the strict letter of the law leads to the exclusion at
trial of evidence which results directly therefrom; secondly, every breach of an
accused's rights is always pleaded at trial as an a constitutional infringement;
and thirdly, it has become practically impossible to say when a constitutional
right begins and ends.

Later in the judgment, Charleton J. turned to the question of whether
there is any room left for a balancing of rights where a mistaken violation of
the constitutional rights of an accused person has occurred. He observed that
whereas in *O'Brien* the Supreme Court referenced the competing interests
of prosecuting crime and maintaining legal rules in the detection of crime,
in *Kenny*, ensuring proper police conduct was the sole interest identified by
the court. He expressed the view that "this statement of the law may not have
taken into account that more rights than those of the accused are involved in
every criminal prosecution". Charleton J. noted that recognition of the rights
of victims has been very limited in Irish law, but cited cases acknowledging
the balance to be struck between the competing rights of the accused to have
the law observed and the community to have social order maintained. Having
reviewed developments under the European Convention on Human Rights and
in the case law of jurisdictions such as England, New Zealand and Canada,
Charleton J. concluded that Ireland is the only country with a common law
heritage which does not apply a balancing exercise as to the exclusion of
unlawfully obtained evidence. This eventuality is particularly remarkable
given that the exclusionary rule is not expressly provided for in Bunreacht na
hÉireann. Charleton J. concluded:

> "I have difficulty in accepting that the separation of powers doctrine
> allows the courts to invent rules whereby juries, or judges as triers
> of fact in criminal cases, are deprived, on a non-discretionary basis,
> of considering evidence which is inherently reliable. I am bound by
> the decision in *The People (DPP) v Kenny* [1990] 2 IR 110. A rule
> which remorselessly excludes evidence obtained through an illegality
> occurring by mistake does not commend itself to the proper ordering
> of society which is the purpose of the criminal law."

The learned judge opined that whereas the original test as propounded in
O'Brien would have allowed for a balancing of interests (the fundamental

interests of society and the accused and, in addition, the rights of the victim), the rationale of that decision is undermined by *Kenny.*

The decision in *DPP (Walsh) v Cash* was delivered in March 2007, the same month in which the *Final Report of the Balance in the Criminal Law Review Group* was published. In canvassing the arguments for a change in the law, the Group also identified as a central problem the absence of a mechanism whereby the trial judge can weigh competing public interests (p.156). It drew attention to the particular issue of defects in search warrants caused by factors outside the control of the Gardaí and remarked that the US Supreme Court has developed a good faith exception to address this very issue (*United States v Leon* 468 US 897 (1984)). A significant argument in favour of reform referenced in the report is the suggestion gleaned from international experience that a relaxation of the exclusionary rule would not violate human rights norms (p.159). The arguments against change include the traditional justification that the rule provides a mechanism for vindicating the rights of the accused (p.160). The deterrence rationale inherent in the rule would also be undermined: the Group notes the argument that:

> "Any relaxation of the rule would encourage sloppy or substandard police practices, and, indeed, any new provision that evidence would not automatically be inadmissible if the contravention was 'bona fide' would put a premium on ignorance" (p.160).

Finally, the rule ensures that any violation of the Constitution is regarded with the appropriate degree of seriousness and that the courts are not obliged to act upon evidence which they know has been obtained in breach of the accused's rights.

A majority of the Group took the view that the current exclusionary rule is "too strictly calibrated" and should be replaced with a judicial discretion to admit or exclude the evidence having regard to the totality of the circumstances and, in particular, the rights of the victim (p.161). As to the means by which this discretion should be introduced, the majority (p.165) suggested the approach of waiting to see if the appeal provision of the Criminal Justice Act 2006 affords the Supreme Court an opportunity to revisit its jurisprudence and moving towards a discretionary approach. (Section 21 of the 2006 Act inserts a new s.34 into the Criminal Procedure Act 1967 which allows the DPP to refer to the Supreme Court a point of law of exceptional public importance in a case that resulted in an acquittal.) In the event that this does not occur, other options should be considered, such as a constitutional amendment or various legislative models such as the statutory provision of a list of factors which a court may take into account in deciding whether or not to exclude evidence (pp.162–66).

The Chairman of the Group, Dr Gerard Hogan S.C., dissented from these recommendations. Although recognising that the operation of the exclusionary rule may occasionally result in the exclusion of highly probative evidence and, in turn, in an accused's acquittal, he rejected the premise that it ought to be significantly modified by reason of this fact alone (p.287). Dr Hogan argued that the rule is broadly in line with the approach of the US Supreme Court and the German Constitutional Court. In addition to its function of vindicating fundamental rights, it has the salutary effect of ensuring that proper standards are adhered to. Any substantial relaxation of the rule along the lines of the balancing mechanism (which presently applies in respect of mere non-constitutional illegality) would undermine the overall effectiveness of the rule (p.289). Dr Hogan emphasised the constitutional difficulties that would compound any attempt to roll back the exclusionary rule by means of ordinary legislation (pp.291–92) and expressed the view that the anomalies that might result in certain types of cases could not justify a special ad hoc constitutional amendment (p.293).

Family Law

FINANCIAL PROVISION

Previous separation agreement   In *McC v McC*, Circuit Ct, April 17, 2007, McMahon J. gave useful guidance on a number of aspects of the court's functions relating to financial provision on divorce and judicial separation, in particular in regard to situations where the spouses some time previously entered into a separation agreement that purported to represent the final resolution of their respective property and maintenance entitlements. The parties had married in 1982. They had four sons, whose ages ranged from 23 to 12. The spouses separated in 2001 and entered into a deed of separation the following year, in which the wife was given the family home, valued at €1.4 million at the time of the hearing. The husband owned an apartment with a net equitable value of €440,000. Under the agreement he was given a holiday home worth €400,000, The husband, born in 1953, had been obliged to retire from a position as a university biochemist in 1997 on account of a serious visual disability. The wife, born in 1956, continued to work as a teacher.

The wife's net income was €2,800 per month; the husband's disability pension was €2,450. The husband sought variation of the deed of separation, which provided that it was in full and final settlement of all present and future property and financial claims (save for maintenance) that either spouse might have against the other.

The husband in the instant proceedings sought to revisit the property aspect of the agreement. (We consider the wife's attempt to vary its terms relating to access below, p.326)

McMahon J. gave a detailed analysis of the terms of s.20 of the Family Law (Divorce) Act 1996. Section 20(1) requires the court when making orders of financial provision to have regard to the circumstances of the case (which McMahon J. interpreted as all the relevant circumstances). Without prejudice to the generality of this statement, s.20(2) requires the court, when deciding whether to make certain ancillary orders, to take into account and "to have regard to" 12 specific factors. Section 20(3) provides that in considering what ancillary orders should be made, "the court shall have regard to the terms of any separation agreement which has been entered into by the spouses and is still in force". McMahon J. speculated as to why the Oireachtas had decided to make special separate provision for separation agreements, when this could easily have been accommodated with the other 12 factors listed in s.20(2). He concluded that:

"[T]he elevation of the separation agreement into a special dedicated subsection might best be explained as a recognition of the fact that a separation agreement is, first and foremost, a fact based agreement, all the relevant facts being best known to the signatories, and second, purports to be a comprehensive and holistic attempt by the parties themselves to negotiate what is a fair agreement between them. The process which the Court undergoes when 'having regard to' the ages of the parties, one single factor mentioned in Section 20(2), for instance, may be very different from 'having regard to' a separation agreement negotiated between the parties, with a finality clause and with full legal advice, with all its compromises and trade-offs. It is the difference between looking at the individual piece which makes up a mosaic and standing back and viewing the complete picture. It represents the parties' own solution at one time to their marital difficulties and identifies what they consider to be the relevant issues between them and their views, proposals and intentions relating to the breakdown of their marriage. The separation agreement is therefore on a higher scale than the other factors and for this reason justifies separate and discrete mention in the eyes of the legislators".

The use of the phrase "have regard to" meant that such an agreement did not bind the court in deciding what was proper provision in such a case but it did raise the question as to what weight must be given to such agreement when the court was turning its mind to what were the proper orders it should make in divorce proceedings.

McMahon J. noted that the question has been canvassed in several cases in recent years and certain principles were emerging which might now be set down with a degree of confidence as an accurate statement in the law:

"1. The overriding duty of the Court in divorce proceedings is to make proper provision for the spouses and dependants and the relevant time for this assessment is the date of the trial, and it is at that time that the assets are to be valued... Accordingly, any previous separation agreement must be looked at through the present prism of the 'proper provision' clause. The Court cannot avoid this exercise and even where it concludes that the separation agreement should be upheld, it must do so by concluding that at the present time and on present values the separation agreement makes proper provision for the parties in the divorce proceedings.

2. In having regard to the separation agreement, the Courts should show respect for the intention of the parties as expressed in the agreement itself. The agreement is important for two reasons: first it is indicative of what the parties' wishes and intentions were at a particular time and second, it shows what they considered to be fair and reasonable and

acceptable at the time. Undoubtedly, if the agreement was negotiated with the assistance of lawyers on both sides, and was formally reduced to writing and witnessed by the parties, it will carry more weight than agreements informally negotiated without legal advice. Similarly, where the agreement contains a 'full and final settlement clause' it will also be an indicator as to what the parties' intentions were at the time, something which the court should bear in mind.

Although the concept of a clean-break solution is not available in this jurisdiction, the Supreme Court has clearly indicated that the courts should try in appropriate cases to make orders, or respect agreements which strive for stability and certainty in so far as possible in the circumstances of each case. (*DT v. CT* [2002] 3 IR 334; [2003] 1 IRLM 321; *F. v. F* [1995] 2 IR 354; *WA v. MA* [2005] 1 ILRM 517). A properly negotiated separation agreement is very much a factor which seeks finality and certainty and accordingly should be given due recognition in this context. How large such an agreement looms in the Judge's deliberations will vary, of course, with the facts of each case and it is easy to see that it may have greater impact in cases where there are ample resources and where the dependants are not of tender years, or where there are no dependants.

3. A distinction has been drawn between separation agreements which are of recent origin and those which are of older or more ancient vintage (See O'Neill J. in *K v. K* (No.2) [2003] 1 IR 326). The argument is frequently advanced that the court should give more respect to more recent agreements than to older agreements, as there is less likely to be major changes in the relevant circumstances since the recent agreement was entered into, and the parties' intentions having been more recently expressed in a formal fashion should carry more weight with the court. The same may not so easily be said in respect of older agreements. Finally, the more recent the separation agreement the more difficult it will be for one party to argue that circumstances that have occurred in the meantime were not reasonably in their contemplation at the time the agreement was negotiated and signed.

These, however, are mere presumptions and the facts on any individual case may force the Court to a different conclusion in determining whether the separation agreement indeed makes proper provision in the circumstances of the case before it. A recent agreement, of course, where one is available may provide the judge with a convenient starting point in his analysis of what is proper provision. ...

5. It is sometimes argued that the Courts should give more weight to separation agreements where the case is one of ample resources. (See Hardiman J. in *WA v. MA* [200511 ILRM 517, at 530). In such cases it is likely that full legal advice will have been taken at the time of the signing of the agreement and that basic accommodation and

maintenance needs have been adequately provided for between the
parties, the only issue before the divorce Court being the level of luxury
the parties are entitled to. It is easier for a Court in such a case to say
that the desire for certainty and stability in upholding the separation
agreement should take precedence over a detailed recalibrating exercise
involved in revisiting the agreement. Such a tendency can be no more
than that, however, and the facts of any individual case may dictate
a review of the agreement in appropriate cases. Moreover, where the
case is one of meagre resources the court's obligation to make proper
provision will oblige it to have a hard look at the agreement in the light
of the circumstances prevailing at the time of the hearing ..."

Having regard to the fact that the separation agreement in the instant case
had been concluded only four years prior to the proceedings in circumstances
where the parties had been fully legally advised, McMahon J. was loath to
disturb the agreement in any serious fashion. Because of the respondent's visual
disability, however, and the disparity in the property division in the separation
agreement, which favoured the wife substantially, and the fact that the husband
had contributed an inheritance of €240,000 which he had received to the family
assets shortly before the agreement was signed, McMahon J. considered that
a slight property adjustment order was warranted and he ordered that the wife
pay €60,000 to the husband "as a proper adjustment in the circumstances".

Moral claims of third parties   In *ML v SL* [2007] I.E.H.C. 438, Sheehan
J. exercised his discretion in a way that took account, not merely of the
spouses and their children, but of the wider community. The husband was a
very successful builder who, over the years, acquired a substantial property
portfolio of close to €13 million, which included two public houses employing
over 100 people. Sheehan J. observed that this "must have a significant effect
on the local economy". It was clear from the husband's evidence that he was
"committed to the development of his own locality and ha[d] obligations and
responsibilities to those who worked[ed] in these businesses". At the time of
divorce proceedings, the husband was aged 48, the wife 45; there were four
children, ranging in age from 22 to 15. The wife had for a number of years
worked outside the house, though not in recent years. Sheehan J. considered
it "significant" that, "notwithstanding th[is] fact .... the children spent 50% of
the time with the[ir] father". The wife's earnings had played an important role
in the development of the building company up to 1998. The wife continued to
manage several investment properties. Sheehan J. was of the view that she could
well run a business in property management, sales, lettings or interior design,
yielding the income of at least €30,000 in a relatively short space of time.

When exercising his discretion in making ancillary orders, Sheehan J.
concluded that, in the instant case there were "strong reasons" for awarding

property and a lump sum to the wife in lieu of maintenance for her. He declined to make any order affecting the public houses, stating:

> "These premises have been purchased and developed by the husband and are responsible for employing over 100 people locally. It is in the interests of these two businesses and particularly in the interest of the employees that these businesses continue to be owned and run by the husband."

Sheehan J. went on to order the transfer of the family home (worth €800,000) from joint ownership into the wife's sole ownership, as well as an adjoining site (worth €165,000), together with other property with a value approaching €1.8 million, supplemented by maintenance payments for the children during their dependence. He also ordered that 70 per cent of the husband's pension be transferred to the wife.

Sheehan J.'s reference to the interests of employees and the wider community is interesting and, at least at a theoretical level, controversial. It raises questions as to the entitlement or obligation of a court, when seeking to do justice to family members, to have a side agenda of social justice. The employees clearly would have had no direct claim against the husband to have their interests advanced, save only to the extent that employment law and the law of contract supported such a claim. Why should the happenstance of divorce litigation change that fact? Are they to be regarded as persons with "rights" for the purposes of s.20(2)(l) of the Family Law (Divorce) Act 1996?

Fault considerations   In *ML v HL* [2007] I.E.H.C. 438, Sheehan J. held that the court should disregard the conduct of a wife, married in 1984 with four children, who had been involved in an adulterous relationship in 1987 but had become reconciled with her husband and who had recommenced the relationship in 1997, her husband becoming aware of this a year later shortly before the family were to go on holiday together. The following month the wife left her husband but returned several months later. The parties went for counselling but the husband left the family home in 2001. The husband gave evidence that, at times during the period from 1984 to 1987, he "thought he was the happiest man in the country". He was devastated by the revelation that his wife had resumed the affair. Sheehan J., while not wishing to underestimate the suffering of the husband or the children, considered that the wife's misconduct could not be characterised as "obvious and gross", as that term had been interpreted by the Supreme Court in *T v T* [2002] 3 I.R. 334. See the *Annual Review of Irish Law 2002*, pp.279–281.

Although fault has been largely exorcised as a factor to which specific regard should be given, it still can have real, if less overt, effects on how a court makes its orders relating to financial provision. In *LK v MK*, Circuit

Ct, March 13, 2007, McMahon J., granting a decree of divorce, awarded the respondent husband a 7 per cent share of the former family home and ordered that it be transferred from joint ownership to the wife, on the wife's undertaking to maintain their 14-year-old daughter and not to make any future demand on the husband for further maintenance. The respondent had come from Russia in 1991 as a visiting scientist on a temporary contract at a third level institution. He was then aged 26. He became a lodger with the applicant, a teacher then aged 40. They married in 1992; their daughter was born the following year. The respondent's employment ended in 1993 and he sought work in Spain. He returned to Ireland in 1996 and had temporary contracts renewed until 2000. He went back to Spain and thereafter moved to Germany. In all, the partners had lived together for only four-and-a-half years.

The family home was purchased with the wife's money. She succeeded in qualifying as a solicitor in 1995. She went into practice as a sole practitioner in 2000 but was obliged to return to teaching in 2003. During the time he resided in Ireland, the husband made modest contributions to the family income. At the time of the proceedings he was €5,000 in arrears of maintenance in respect of his daughter.

McMahon J. took a stern view of the husband's conduct, though addressing this matter under heads other than that of conduct. He noted that the wife, in abandoning her career as a solicitor, had:

> "... relinquished the opportunity of a more lucrative career because she had to look after the home and care for [her daughter] for many years on her own in the absence of any financial or emotional support from the ... husband."

There was "some justification" in the wife's complaint that the husband had never made any effort to retain or find other employment in Ireland when his temporary contracts expired in 1996: "Instead he doggedly stuck to his narrow specialisation which never developed to a degree of competence which merited a senior position in academic life."

GUARDIANSHIP OF CHILDREN

Parental agreements and the welfare principle   In *L v Judge Haughton* [2001] I.E.H.C. 316, where a lay litigant failed in an application for leave for judicial review arising out of a family law matter in respect of which he misconstrued the effect of certain procedural provisions, Budd J. addressed, obiter, the interesting question as to whether, on the basis of the Supreme Court decision in *Re Tilson, Infants; Tilson v Tilson* [1951] I.R. 1, an agreement between spouses that their children should be educated at home constituted a barrier to a court's addressing that matter in subsequent litigation affecting the welfare of their children. In *Tilson*, the majority (Black J. dissenting) had held that an ante-nuptial agreement in respect of the religious education of children could not be revoked by one party unilaterally. Did this mean that, where such an agreement existed, the court's hands were tied? Budd J., making it clear that he was addressing the context of home-schooling rather than religious education, expressed the view that the court was not prevented from considering the matter in the context of the welfare of the children:

> "On reflection it seems to me that, while parents may at a certain stage agree that a particular type of education or school may be appropriate for one of their children, with the vicissitudes of life and changing circumstances of the family and also the development of the particular child, and the evolving talents and interests and general growth of the personality of the child and his or her interests, then as the child develops different considerations as to what is best for each individual child may arise and these considerations may lead to views which would indicate that a change of regime as to type of schooling is needed. That such a change would be given due consideration and decisions made as to what is genuinely best in the child's interest would appear to be implicit in any such agreement about the education and upbringing of a child. Manifestly it would be wrong to force a child with particular needs and talents into a milieu or type of education which would be inappropriate for the particular child. No doubt if there are conflicting views between the parents then matters may reach a point where the assistance of the court may be required to try to strike the extremely delicate balance which will be required on the basis of reports from teachers and other experts and after hearing the view of each of the parents and after detailed consideration of the relevant circumstances of each child's case and personal development."

This seems a sensible approach. It would be odd if the court's jurisdiction to assess the question of the welfare of a child could, in effect, be ousted by an earlier parental agreement. One should not, however, treat this issue as involving only one obvious answer. A delicate question arises as to the extent to which parental autonomy can be overridden by a court or state agency. We have seen how the Supreme Court adopted a position strongly deferential to parental decision-making in *North Western Health Board v HW* [2001] 3 I.R. 622, analysed in the *Annual Review of Irish Law 2001*, pp.316–38. If one parent, having made an agreement relating to a child which was clearly intended to extend well into the future, perhaps even for the duration of the child's minority, were to be free to have that agreement ignored by a court on application under the Guardianship of Infants Act 1964, such an outcome would undoubtedly impact on the constitutional guarantees under Articles 41 and 42. We have yet to have a developed jurisprudence as to the extent to which a court should exercise restraint in this context so as to ensure the efficacy of these guarantees.

Access   In *LK v MK*, Circuit Court, 13 March 13, 2007, in an access application, McMahon J. took into account the wishes of the 14-year-old daughter of a Russian-born father who had been living abroad since 2000 and whose earlier relationship with her had been broken by periods abroad. McMahon J. observed that the father's attention to his daughter's emotional and educational needs was minimal. Although the father wished to re-establish a relationship with the girl on a phased basis over a period of time, the daughter, whom McMahon J. interviewed in chambers, showed little interest in re-establishing any contact. McMahon J. commented:

> "In view of the fact that that ... father now lives abroad it is difficult to contemplate a gradual regime in the circumstances. Moreover, the strong views expressed by [his daughter] in the case suggest that it would be counterproductive to force access against the child's wishes. It should be noted that [she] is a bright, intelligent and ... articulate child with promising academic potential."

All that McMahon J. was prepared to do in the circumstances was to accept the mother's assurance on the matter that she wanted to facilitate her daughter if and when the child expressed a wish to resume contact with her father. McMahon J. also accepted the mother's evidence that she had no objection to granting access and indeed wished to encourage it when the daughter considered it appropriate. He considered it reasonable, in all the circumstances, that any such access should, in the initial stage at least, be in Ireland only. McMahon J. made no formal order relating to access.

In *McC v McC*, Circuit Court, April 17, 2007, the parents of four boys separated in 2001. They lived close to each other. A separation agreement concluded in 2002 provided for joint custody with a joint parenting schedule by which the children would reside with each parent on an alternate weekly basis. The mother in the instant proceedings sought to have these agreements altered as they were disrupting and unsettling for the children, whose ages ranged from 23 to 12. She claimed that the father had not supervised them properly, that he abused alcohol and that he had taken his younger son to the pub. The father acknowledged that his approach was very relaxed, in contrast to that of his wife, which he characterised as controlling. He pointed out that the youngest son had been declared "student of the week" the week before the hearing. He said that he sometimes took him to have lunch in the pub and to watch football games as he did not have the sports channels at home. He was prepared to desist from this practice if it was a problem for the court.

McMahon J. was not prepared to accede to the wife's request to alter the access provided for in the agreement in respect of the youngest son. He was satisfied from the evidence that the husband had a special bond with the boy. The existing arrangements reflected this bond and accordingly should stand. McMahon J. did, however, take on the board the reasonable concerns of the mother as to the level of supervision exercised by the husband when his son was with him and he required the husband to give sworn undertakings in this regard. These included not taking the boy to public houses for televised sporting events and being stricter about another son's homework.

Unmarried fathers' rights In *Re HL, an infant; J McD v PL* [2007] I.E.S.C. 28, the question of unmarried fathers' constitutional rights came to the court in a factual context that had not previously provoked judicial analysis. The respondents were lesbians, who had been through a civil union ceremony in England. The first respondent had had a son by means of artificial insemination. The applicant, the boy's father, was a homosexual friend of the respondents who had entered into a formal agreement which envisaged that this role would be as a favourite uncle and that he would be welcome to visit the child at times mutually convenient to the parties. The boy was born in May 2006. He was given the applicant's first name as his second name. In the following months there were regular visits between the parties involving dinner in each others' houses. The applicant took the infant for walks in his buggy and "provided items to assist with the new arrival". He offered financial assistance but this was declined. He informed the respondents that he had opened a trust account for the infant, to which he made monthly lodgements.

In September, 2006 the respondents' attitude to the applicant and his role with the infant altered. They informed him that the parties had become too close and that a greater distance and formality was required. After this the applicant had only two further contact visits with the infant, one in October 2006 and one in November 2006.

The respondents formed the intention of spending a year in Australia. The first named respondent, who was Australian, wished to give her son the opportunity to spend time with her family. Her partner secured temporary employment there and they let their house in Ireland.

When he heard of these plans, the applicant obtained an interim injunction against their removing the infant to Australia. He subsequently obtained an interlocutory injunction from Abbott J., which the Supreme Court, by a majority (Denham and Dinnegan JJ., Fennelly J. dissenting) upheld.

Denham J. (Finnegan J. concurring), in seeking to identify where the balance of interest lay, regarded the welfare of the child as "the paramount issue". She did, however, identify certain factors in favour of the respondents and the applicant respectively. In favour of the respondents these included the following:

> "[T]he welfare of the infant is best served in the custody of the first
> named respondent, the mother; the mother has a constitutional right to
> the custody of her child; the first named respondent is Australian and
> wishes her child to know her family; the parties have entered into a
> written agreement; the first named respondent is the primary carer for
> the child; the respondents propose a temporary relocation to Australia,
> until June, 2008; this is a reasonable and proportionate plan ..."

The factors in favour of the applicant included that he was the biological father;
he had entered into a agreement with the respondents as to the infant; he had a
right to apply to court for access and joint custody and had applied to the High
Court for such orders; even if, as appeared to be accepted, the relocation to
Australia was only for a year, this was at a formative age of the infant.

Denham J. went on to observe:

> "The critical factor in the balancing required of the Court in this case
> is the welfare of the infant—on which the Court has had no expert
> assistance. The Court heard submissions by the parties as to their view of
> the balance of convenience, but that must be considered as being tinted
> by their interests. The welfare of the infant is of paramount importance.
> In the vacuum of information as to the welfare of the child the Court
> must use the fulcrum of justice in seeking the balance of convenience.
> In the circumstances I am satisfied that the welfare of the child must be
> a weighty factor. In making this decision I do so with the infant in mind.
> Consequently, I would affirm the judgment of the High Court ...
>
> I am guided by the paramount importance of the welfare of the
> infant, by the young age of the infant, by the fact that a year is a long
> time in the life of a developing infant, and by the injustice that would
> be done to the infant if the applicant is ultimately successful in his
> application."

Denham J. stressed that her holding "should not be inferred as presuming
rights for the applicant."

Fennelly J. dissented sharply. He referred to English jurisprudence—*Payne
v Payne* [2001] 1 F.L.R. 473 and *Poel v Poel* [1970] 1 W.L.R. 1469—which
regarded the welfare of a child as likely to be best served in most cases by
going abroad with the custodial parent when that parent was acting reasonably.
These decisions involved a proposed permanent removal of residence to
another country. A fortiori, where, as in the instant case, the removal was only
temporary. Abbott J. had been influenced predominantly by a law that the
applicant should be allowed to develop a bond with the child, which would
be interrupted by the Australian sojourn. He had stated:

> "I consider that the loss of a critical year, a year when a bond is about

to open up on an objective scale a reciprocal scale between father and son is a period not to be missed if at all possible. I do not see any serious and irreparable loss on the part of the respondents if they miss this year".

In Fennelly J.'s view, by giving that principal reason for granting the interlocutory order, Abbott J. had made it clear that he was predisposed to appoint the applicant as guardian and to grant him rights of access. "Otherwise that reason would not make sense."

Stressing that it was axiomatic that the welfare of the child must be the paramount consideration, Fennelly J. considered that the applicant had not shown, by means of expert or any other evidence, that the welfare of the child would be jeopardised or compromised by his being taken to Australia for the proposed visit of just short of one year:

> "The burden of proof is necessarily on the applicant. The situation is such an extraordinary one that the Court cannot assume any expertise in this very difficult matter. Is the welfare of the child best served by being brought up by a same-sex female couple (one of which is his natural mother) or by those persons with access to a person whose only relationship with him is as sperm donor? Both situations are entirely novel for our courts. I confess that I could not express any, even provisional, view on the matter.
>
> What is clear, however, is that a decision of the Court preventing the appellants from travelling to Australia for the reason given by the learned trial judge is tantamount to deciding that highly complex and difficult issue."

Fennelly J.'s analysis of the legal status and entitlements of the applicant did not purport to be conclusive but it certainly was less than enthusiastic. Having identified the secure constitutional foundations for the first respondent's right as mother of the child, he added:

> "Contrast the position of the applicant. He is not the father of the child by virtue of membership of a family based on marriage to his mother. It may well be that, in the fullness of time, consideration will have to be given to recognition to non-marital relationships of a kind which have become increasingly normal over recent decades. The applicant cannot, however, bring himself even within the scope of any relationship approximating to a family...
>
> [H]is standing in the present proceedings arises only by virtue of section 6A of the Guardianship of Infants Act, 1964, as amended by section 12 of the Status of Children Act, 1987."

In any such application under that provision, s.3 of the Guardianship of Infants Act 1964 required that "the welfare of the infant [be] the first and paramount consideration".

The applicant would need to persuade a court that he was "within the intended scope of that section". His present legal status was no greater than that of an applicant for the status of guardian. He had, as matters stood, no legal or constitutional relationship with the child.

The status of the applicant was "very different from that of an unmarried father who has, or has had, an established relationship with the mother". He was:

> "... far from being in the position of the father of a child 'born as a result of a stable and established relationship,' as envisaged by Hamilton C.J. in [*W. O'R. v E.H.* [1996] 2 I.R. 248]."

The terms of the agreement between the applicant and respondents were, in Fennelly J.'s view, difficult to reconcile with the notion of the applicant's becoming a guardian of the child. It had to be taken into account in considering:

> "... whether the applicant should be permitted, by obtaining an interlocutory injunction, to restrain the first-named respondent from the exercise of the normal right enjoyed by any individual to travel and, by corollary, the normal right of a parent to travel with his or her child or children."

Fennelly J. concluded that the applicant should not succeed, on the basis that a child's welfare normally coincided with reasonable travel decisions of the custodial parent and that, to take account of the possible prejudice to the bond between applicant and child by virtue of the year's absence would, in effect, be presuming that the applicant was entitled to become an appointed guardian.

Let us try to unravel the several issues that this case presented. The first is the general one of the legal position of unmarried fathers. It is scarcely surprising that the Supreme Court should not wish to address this question in a definitive way on such an interlocutory application. The second is the position of sperm donors. As a group, their participation in the parenting process may vary widely, from that of complete anonymity, playing no ongoing parental role whatsoever, to a clearly acknowledged relationship approaching that of a conventional absent father. The applicant in the instant case was closer to the latter model, though his role was complicated by the fact that the mother and her partner were in a lesbian relationship and had gone through a ceremony of civil union in England.

Denham J.'s judgment does not discuss this dimension; Fennelly J.'s judgment does so but he makes no distinction between the different levels of participation that sperm donors can have in the lives of their children. He did, however, acknowledge that there was an empirical dimension to the issue of how the welfare of a child is best served in such circumstances. His description of the applicant as a person "whose only relationship [with the child] is as sperm donor" may be considered to understate the connection, which did envisage his role as a favourite uncle.

There is a further important issue which needs to be addressed generally. If an unmarried father has had an ongoing close relationship with his child and the mother intends to remove that child from the State for a year, what is the father to do? One strategy would be to take the course of action adopted by the applicant in the instant case, of seeking to secure an injunction. In Fennelly J.'s view, a court in such circumstances is not permitted to take into account the fact that the time abroad will damage the father–child relationship as to do this is to prejudge the father's entitlement to be awarded guardianship status. Yet, if the child goes abroad, damage to that relationship will occur. The fact that the father at this point has no rights in relation to his child does not necessarily mean that his prospective rights count as nothing.

We will return to this subject in the 2008 Review when we analyse Hedigan J.'s decision in *Re HL, an Infant; J McD v PL* [2008] I.E.H.C. 96, declining to appoint the applicant guardian of the child.

Cohabitees   In *AF v SF* Abbott J. was called on to consider highly important issues relating to the constitutional protection of marriage, the rights of unnamed cohabitants, especially mothers, the relationship between the law of contract and property entitlements and the current and earlier contours of public policy. The fact that the case involved an application to dismiss proceedings for being vexatious and an abuse of the court meant that his analysis was necessarily tentative; yet the case is important in opening these issues for further reflection.

The parties had lived together from February 1978 until 2004. There were three children of the union, born in 1978, 1980 and 1983. At all material times the parties were married to other people and each had children within their marriage. The applicant claimed that in October 1977 the respondent had proposed to her and had presented her with an engagement ring in December 1977, and that she had accepted the proposal of marriage. She also alleged that, in the course of the relationship, they had purchased a number of properties in their joint names and that they were directors or shareholders in a number of companies. All of these allegations were strongly denied by the respondent.

The applicant sought orders under s.36 of the Family Law Act 1995 and s.44 of the Family law (Divorce) Act 1996 determining the respective interests of the parties in a range of properties, as well as an order under s.5 of the Family Law Act 1981 and a maintenance order for the benefit of their dependent children.

The linchpin of the claims (save for that of maintenance) was that there had been an agreement to marry between the parties. Of course, a formidable apparent obstacle to the claim was that in 1977 people already married were not able to make a legally binding agreement to marry someone other then their spouse during the currency of the marriage. It may be said with some confidence that such an agreement could have no validity, apart altogether from having to address the question of public policy, simply because, being already married, spouses were incapable of entering into what would be a bigamous union which was clearly void.

A somewhat different question is whether a spouse might lawfully make a contract to marry after the marriage to which he or she was then a party terminated, by death, divorce or annulment in the case of a voidable marriage. (It should be noted that, even when there was a constitutional prohibition on divorce, it was possible that a spouse could contemplate divorcing his or her partner. For such a divorce to be capable of legal recognition, it would be necessary for that spouse or his or her partner to have or acquire a domicile outside the State.) At all events, a contract to marry after divorce was considered to offend against public policy in subverting marriage.

Let us look briefly at the relevant statutory provisions. Section 2 of the Family Law Act 1981 provides as follows:

> (1). An agreement between two persons to marry one another whether entered into before or after the passing of this Act, shall not under the law of the State have effect as a contract and no action shall be brought in the State for the breach of such an agreement, whatever the law applicable to the agreement
>
> (2). Subsection (1) shall not have effect in relation to any action that has been commenced before the passing of this Act.

Section 5 of the Family Law Act 1981 deals with the property of engaged couples as follows:

> (1) Where an agreement to marry is terminated, the rules of law relating to the rights of spouses in relation to property in which either or both of them has or have a beneficial interest shall apply in relation to any property in which either or both the parties to the agreement had a beneficial interest while the agreement was in force as they apply in relation to a property in which either or both spouses has or have a beneficial interest.
>
> (2) Where an agreement to marry is terminated, s.12 of the Married Women's Status Act, 1957 (which relates to the determination of questions between husbands and wives as to property) shall apply, as if the parties to the agreement were married, to any dispute between them or claim by one of them, in relation to property in which either

or both had a beneficial interest while the agreement was in force as they apply in relation to property in which either or both spouses has or have a beneficial interest.

Section 44 of the Family Law (Divorce) Act 1996 provides as follows:

Where an agreement to marry is terminated, s.36 of the Act of 1995 shall apply, as if the parties to the agreement were married to each other, to any dispute between them or claim by one of them, in relation to property in which either or both of them had a beneficial interest while the agreement was in force.

The relevant part of s.36 of the 1995 Act provides as follows:

(1) Either spouse may apply to the court in a summary manner to determine any question arising between them as to the title or possession of any property.
   (2) On application to it under subs. (1), the court may—
     (a) make such order with respect to the property in dispute (including an order that it be sold or partitioned) and as to the costs consequent upon the application, and
     (b) direct such inquiries, and give such other directions, in relation to the application
as the court considers proper.

In *Ennis v Butterly* [1996] 1 I.R. 426 Kelly J. held that "agreements, the consideration for which is cohabitation, are incapable of being enforced". He noted that, before the enactment of the Family Law Act 1981, an agreement to marry between two persons who were already married to other people was void for public policy under the common law, and observed that the common law, had, if anything, been reinforced by the guarantees for marriage and the family in the Constitution.

One might have considered that *Ennis v Butterly* represented an insuperable barrier to the applicant's claim. Abbott J. did not, however, think so, for two primary reasons.

The first derived from the English decision of *Shaw v Fitzgerald* [1992] 1 F.L.R. 357, where Scott Baker J., reviewing English legislative provisions similar to those in Ireland, had concluded that it would be "wholly artificial" to interpret [one of them] as:

"... prevent[ing] those couples whose agreement to marry was unenforceable at common law from utilising its provisions, whilst at the

same time permitting its use by those whose agreement is unenforceable
by statute".

Baker J. could see that there might be strong policy reasons why an agreement
to marry should not have effect as a contract giving rise to legal rights, and
that no action should lie for breach of it; but it seemed to him that this was so
whether or not both of the parties to the agreement were married to someone else
when the agreement was made. He drew a clear distinction between "seeking
a legal remedy for breach of such an agreement and utilising a summary
procedure to resolve property disputes which have arisen as a consequence
of it." Those disputes were not, in his view, tainted by any illegality which
might have attached to the agreement, and the legislation seemed to him to
recognise this.

Abbott J. appeared to be impressed by this analysis but surely one should
be cautious about transposing the context of Britain, where divorce had been
continually judicially available for well over a century, to Ireland where
the constitutional prohibition on divorce continued until 1995, nearly two
decades after the alleged engagement and over 14 years after the passage of
the Family Law Act 1981? That Act was designed to address the entitlements
of those whose engagement had terminated (by breach or otherwise); it was
not expressed or arguably designed to provide a judicial framework for the
resolution of property disputes between former unmarried cohabitants. One
should be realistic in acknowledging that, even as long ago as 1981, some
unmarried cohabitation was taking place where the parties had an actual or
a tacit agreement that they would marry in the future, but this was still quite
rare. If the 1981 Act was intended to provide a judicial machinery to deal with
unmarried cohabitation it was guilty of over-breadth and under-inclusiveness
in capturing engaged couples who had not been cohabiting and in excluding
cohabiting couples who had not become engaged. It is noteworthy that, even
in 2008, there is no legislation prescribing proprietary entitlements or other
proprietary consequences following from unmarried cohabitation.

Having noted this, one should also acknowledge that for three decades
the Irish courts have taken a very relaxed attitude towards cohabitation when
making property orders and determinations in the exercise of their equitable
jurisdiction. They have, as it were, turned a blind eye to the sexual component
of cohabitation, treating the parties in broadly the same way as a married couple
without mentioning why they take this course of action.

The second reason why Abbott J. declined to dismiss the proceedings *in
limine* was that he considered there might be some merit in using Art.41.2 as
the foundation for a claim by the applicant. It will be recalled that Art.41.2
comes immediately after the State's undertaking in Art.41.1.2° to protect the
(marital) Family "in its constitution and authority, as the necessary basis of
social order and as indispensable to the welfare of the Nation and the State."
Article 41.2 provides as follows:

1°. In particular, the State recognises that by her life within the home, woman gives to the State a support without which the common good cannot be achieved.

2°. The State shall, therefore, endeavour to ensure that mothers shall not be obliged by economic necessity to engage in labour to the neglect of their duties in the home.

Abbot J. commented:

"There is established authority for the proposition that the family envisaged in Article 41 of the Constitution is the marital family. However in Article 41.2.1° and 2° the role of the woman in the home and the mother is not described with reference to the family and it is arguable that Article 41.2 applies to a woman or mother in the home, whether that child is a marital child or not."

He considered that, if the provisions of Art.41.2 related to the role of women in the home as mothers of children, whether marital or not, it could be said that the "highly principled statement of public policy" in Art.41.1° and 3° should be tempered by "the more pragmatic and utilitarian considerations of Article 41.2.1° and 2°".

He went on to say that he could "find no reason in law or public policy nor in constitutional provisions which may be advanced for the proposition that property or joint property arrangements may not be made to facilitate the nurturing of a non marital child by its mother." The constitutional principles regarding the guarantees for marriage and the marital family were to be "tempered by the need to ensure that non marital children are nurtured without diminishing the guarantees for marriage and the marital family."

There is an argument that Art.41.2 embraces all mothers (though one may doubt that this was the intention of the drafters). It is stretching matters, however, to interpret the Family Law Act 1981 as giving effect to that constitutional guarantee. The problems of over-inclusiveness and under-inclusiveness again rear their head.

In *R v C Deceased; AC v JF* [2007] I.E.H.C. 399 is of interest in raising the question whether a deceased testator may be considered to have had a moral duty to a person with whom he had an unmarried sexual relationship. In this case, there were two children born of two separate mothers, neither of whom had married the deceased. One child was 17 at the date of the deceased's death; the other was three. The mother of the elder child had married and did not feature in Clarke J.'s judgment. The mother of the younger child had not married and was rearing her alone.

Clarke J. held that the deceased had owed a moral duty to the mother of the younger child. He stated:

"It is clear that he owed no equivalent legal duty, for the Succession Act, 1965 does not make any provision for a partner with whom a deceased has had children but who was not married to the deceased. On the other hand it is equally clear from a number of the authorities that the persons in respect of whom a deceased may owe a moral duty are not confined to those persons in respect of whom a legal obligation arises. A parent of a deceased is not someone who has any entitlement to receive assets from a deceased who dies testate. Nonetheless it is clear from the authorities that, in an appropriate case, a deceased may have a moral duty to make some provision for such a parent, which moral duty can be taken into account by the court in assessing what assets might properly be available for claimant children under s.117.

I am, therefore, satisfied that the class of those to whom a moral duty may be owed can go beyond the class of those who might be entitled to make a legal claim on the estate if the deceased did not make provision, or proper provision, for them. It seems to me that that category of persons may include, in an appropriate case, a joint parent of a child or children who remain in need of significant care. The reality is that it must be expected that, for the next significant number of years, the care of [the young girl] will be entrusted to her mother. [The child's] upbringing depends in large part on the fact that her mother will be in a position to care for her until she can be established in her own right.

In those circumstances it does seem to me that, on the facts of this case, it can be said that the deceased did owe a moral duty to [the mother] as … the mother of [the deceased's daughter] and that that is a factor to be taken into account."

The next question Clarke J. had to address was whether it was appropriate to take into account any bequest to his young daughter's mother in considering the daughter's own entitlements. Counsel for the daughter had pointed out that such bequest was not attached with any direct legal obligations to provide for her out of the funds bequested. Clarke J. considered, however, that:

"The practical reality of a case such as this is that the standard of living and care which AC will receive over the next significant number of years is largely dependent on the standard of living that will be available collectively to her and her mother and in those circumstances I am satisfied that it is appropriate to have regard to any bequest to the mother …, which is not abated as a result of these proceedings in order to meet the needs of both [daughter and mother], in assessing the provision that needs to be made for [the daughter]. I say that it is so only in part because I am mindful of the fact that, in making proper provision, the deceased had to have regard to the fact that [the daughter] needs significant sums in her own right in respect of which no other claims can be made other than that they are required to look after [her] needs and interests. … I would not like what I have said to be in any way interpreted as indicating that it is possible to make provision for an infant solely or substantially by making provision for a parent of that infant, save in the case of a married couple whose child might be a claimant under s.117 but whose claim is debarred in respect of diminishing the entitlements of the parent concerned. Assets left to a non marital co-parent are a matter to be taken into account but such bequests are not a means by which the moral obligation of the other parent can be fully or substantially given effect to."

In the instant case, the estate was worth around €1.6 million. The deceased had provided no financial assistance for the elder daughter until 1998 when he began paying a modest sum by way of maintenance. As a result of litigation, he had been paying fairly generous maintenance in favour of his younger daughter. In his will, the testator left his elder daughter €250,000 and his younger daughter €100,000. He left €300,000 to the mother of his younger daughter.

Clarke J. held that the deceased had failed in his moral duty to both daughters. He considered that:

"[s]ome regard, though it be limited, must be had for the fact that provision is being made for the mother of [the younger daughter] which will inure to the benefit of [that daughter] in terms of such provision assisting the general family income that will be available for [her] support …"

He directed that 80 per cent of the available assets of the estate should be made available to the daughters, the elder securing 35 per cent and the younger receiving 45 per cent. In relation to the balance of 20 per cent, he felt that he was obliged to have regard to the fact that the deceased had owed a moral duty to the younger daughter's mother which required that there be a smaller abatement in her case than in respect of the bequests to the deceased's mother and siblings, "in order to respect that moral obligation". This involved directing that 15 per cent of the available assets should be made available to the younger daughter's mother, the remaining 5 per cent of the assets being divided pro rata between the other beneficiaries. This involved a significant reduction in the share the deceased's mother might have received, which was £75,000 and the residue of his estate.

The decision raises a number of wider issues relating to social policy. First, does the assumption of a moral duty on the part of the deceased to the mother of his younger daughter have broader implications for unmarried relationships? In the instant case the person in question was the mother of the deceased's young child, without apparently any other financial source of support. Clarke J. considered that the category of person to whom a testator might owe a moral duty "may include, in an appropriate case, a joint parent of a child or children who remain in need of significant care". This suggests that the moral duty to some extent is child-centred. An unmarried partner who had fallen on very hard times, perhaps on account of illness or even callous treatment by the deceased, would not come within the circumstances canvassed by Clarke J. Nor would a cohabitee who had significant maintenance responsibilities to children of whom the testator was not the parent. This suggests that child-centredness is not the key but rather the cumulation of the blood connection between the deceased, the children and the surviving unmarried parent.

Secondly, one may enquire whether the value judgments underlying Clarke J.'s analysis can be transferred into the context of ancillary orders in proceedings for divorce or judicial separation. Up to now courts have been strikingly circumspect on this question. The new partner tends to be a shadowy figure in the judgments, of whom the less said, in the judges' view, the better. But the question cannot be dodged forever. If, in the instant case, the deceased had been married and was seeking a divorce just before his death, is not the logic of Clarke J.'s analysis that the mother of his younger daughter should have some claim on his assets so as to inhibit the plentitude of what would otherwise be available for his wife?

Finally it is worth noting that the children of a deceased man who left an estate worth €1.6 million were awarded 80 per cent out of his estate. Had they been born within marriage to a mother who was still alive, the court could not have made an order that affected the legal right of their mother to one third of the estate (Succession Act 1965, s.117(3)). The thinking when that Act was passed was that the mother's share should not be disturbed, even in the interests of her children, and that she was likely, in any event, to benefit her children by will when she died. If she did not, they would be entitled in appropriate circumstances to an order under s.117. The result of the instant case is that, where the children's mother is not married to the deceased, the children are entitled to more than children whose mother is married to the deceased. An issue as to the constitutionality of such an outcome surely arises.

PROCEDURE

In *D v D*, Supreme Court, December 5, 2003, McGuinness J. observed that it appeared to be "the policy of the law in the legislation that family law matters should be in the main dealt with by the Circuit Court, certainly family matters such as separation and divorce". Even though the monetary amounts of the property that might be allocated in such litigation were high, the Circuit Court had considerable experience of dealing with property of high value in the exercise of its landlord and tenant jurisdiction.

In *C O'D v WA otherwise known as TH* [2007] I.E.H.C. 197, Abbott J. quoted McGuinness J.'s observations when remitting proceedings to the Circuit

Court. The parties, who were not married to each other, had lived together for 10 years. Two children were born of the relationship. The parties were rich: the applicant's assets were worth €2 million, the respondent's €8 million. The applicant sought, inter alia, several orders for maintenance and a lump sum payment in respect of the children. Abbott J. made an order remitting the proceedings to the Circuit Court. He noted that the instant case involved children, where time was of the essence in resolving matters relating to their welfare. The particular circuit to which the case was being remitted was suitable for proceedings that might run for three days or more. The many witnesses involved would find that venue more suitable. The Circuit Court would be able to dispose of the care far sooner then the High Court, where the availability of a second judge for family matters could not be identified with any certainty. Abbott J.'s earlier doubts about the complexity of the case had been resolved by the applicant's submissions which had indicated that there was "a substantial island of statute law in existence" which enabled the Circuit Court to distinguish *LM v His Honour Judge Liam Devally* [1997] 2 I.L.R.M. 369.

Garda Síochána

COMPLAINTS BOARD

Section 45 of the Criminal Justice Act 2007 provides for amendments to the First and Third Schedules to the Garda Síochána (Complaints) Act 1986 to provide for the terms of office of the Garda Síochána Complaints Board and the Appeals Board respectively to cease upon the repeal of the 1986 Act and its replacement by the Garda Síochána Ombudsman Commission established under the Garda Síochána Act 2005 (*Annual Review of Irish Law 2005*, pp.417–23). The 1986 Act provides for the members of the Complaints Board and the Appeals Board to be appointed for a five-year term. The amendments effected by s.45 of the 2007 Act were necessary to terminate the respective terms of office at an earlier time, when the provisions of the 1986 Act are repealed under the 2005 Act.

MANAGEMENT STRUCTURE

Part 7 of the Criminal Justice Act 2007 (ss.41–43) amended in significant respects the Garda Síochána Act 2005 (*Annual Review of Irish Law 2005*, pp.417–23). The other elements of the 2007 Act are discussed in the Criminal Law chapter, above.

Section 41 inserted a new Chapter 3A into the Garda Síochána Act 2005 (comprising eight sections, ss.33A to 33H of the 2005 Act) to provide for the establishment and functions of the Garda Síochána Executive Management Board. The Board consists of executive members and three non-executive members. The executive members will be comprised of the Garda Commissioner, who will be the chairperson of the Board, the Deputy Garda Commissioners and a member of the civilian staff of the Garda Síochána, at a grade equivalent to that of a Deputy Garda Commissioner. The three non-executive members will be appointed by the Government on the nomination of the Minister. They will be persons with expertise in the strategic and financial management of organisations, the management of their human resources or the planning and review functions relating to them, or persons with other relevant experience. The non-executive members will serve in an advisory capacity only, providing advice in relation to annual policing plans, budgetary matters, allocation of resources, technology and equipment, setting of targets, training, development and leadership and other related matters.

The function of the Board will be to keep under review the performance by the Garda Síochána of its functions and the arrangements and strategies in place to support and enhance the performance of those functions. In particular, the Board will keep under review the arrangements and strategies in place to support and improve the performance of the organisation and the corporate governance arrangements and structures within the Garda Síochána.

Section 42 of the 2007 Act replaced the text of s.42 of the 2005 Act, dealing with inquiries, to the effect that inquiries under s.42, which were prior to the 2007 Act limited to the administration, practice or procedure of the Garda Síochána, can include operations of the force and the conduct of its members. The amended s.42 of the 2005 Act also empowers the person appointed by the Minister for Justice to make an application to the High Court and for contempt of court proceedings, in circumstances where a member of the Garda Síochána or any other person fails to cooperate with the inquiry.

Section 43 provides for a number of amendments to the Garda Síochána Act 2005, some of which arose from suggestions made by the Garda Síochána Ombudsman Commission and others involving minor changes to clarify certain matters which had come to light since the passing of the 2005 Act.

Information Law and the Ombudsman

ESTELLE FELDMAN, Research Associate Trinity College Dublin

INFORMATION COMMISSIONER

All statutory references in this section are to the Freedom of Information Acts 1997 to 2003 unless otherwise stated. The Act has been previously considered in *Annual Review of Irish Law 1997*, pp.2 et seq.; *Annual Review of Irish Law 1999*, pp.1 et seq., pp.350 et seq.; *Annual Review of Irish Law 2000*, pp.273 et seq.; *Annual Review of Irish Law 2001*, pp.391 et seq.; *Annual Review of Irish Law 2002*, pp.306 et seq.; *Annual Review of Irish Law 2003*, pp.373 et seq.; *Annual Review of Irish Law 2004*, pp.319 et seq.; *Annual Review of Irish Law 2005*, pp.430 et seq.; *Annual Review of Irish Law 2006*, pp.430 et seq. In addition to hard copy, documents referred to may be found at the Information Commissioner's website: *http://www.oic.gov.ie*. Since the Freedom of Information Act 1997 came into force there have been two Information Commissioners, Mr Kevin Murphy 1997–2003, and the present incumbent, Ms Emily O'Reilly, since mid-2003; hence references to publications may refer to "he" or "she" depending on the date of publication. It may be noted that in 2007 the separate role of Commissioner for Environmental Information was assigned to the office-holder. A section on this critical area of information available by statutory right is included commencing with this *Annual Review*.

SUPREME AND HIGH COURT APPEALS

Section 42 of the Act governs the right to take an appeal from a decision of the Information Commissioner on a point of law to the High Court. Such decisions issue consequent on a s.34 review (*Annual Review of Irish Law 1999*, pp.351 et seq.). The statutory barrier preventing appeals from the High Court to the Supreme Court was withdrawn by the Freedom of Information (Amendment) Act 2003 (*Annual Review of Irish Law 2003*, p.391). In 2007, the High Court issued judgments in two cases.

Organ retention and *Parents for Justice* *National Maternity Hospital v Information Commissioner and Parents for Justice Ltd, Notice Party* [2007] I.E.H.C. 113 was an appeal against a decision of the Information Commissioner who had varied a refusal by the National Maternity Hospital to provide access to documents pertaining to its relationship with the Post Mortem Inquiry, otherwise know as the Dunne Inquiry, into infant organ retention. In the High Court Quirke J. upheld the Commissioner in every respect, finding, inter alia, that there was "no reason why this Court should interfere with the exercise by the Commissioner of the discretion conferred upon her by the [Freedom of Information] Act." He relied on *Sheedy v Information Commissioner* [2004] I.E.H.C. 192; [2004] 2 I.R. 533; [2005] I.E.S.C. 35 (*Annual Review of Irish Law 2005*, pp.431 et seq.) and Fennelly J.'s affirmation of the principles expounded in McKechnie J. in *Deely v Information Commissioner* [2001] 3 I.R. 439 (*Annual Review of Irish Law 2001*, pp.405 et seq.) relating to judicial review of the Information Commissioner's appeal powers. Quirke J. affirmed that many of the powers conferred upon the Commissioner by the Act are, necessarily, wide:

> "In general, they require the exercise of discretion rather than the application of strict legal standards. The courts will not interfere with the exercise by the Commissioner of her discretion where it has been exercised lawfully."

Locus standi   The first issue in the judgment related to a challenge to the locus standi of the notice party. Whilst this is not a matter of freedom of information law, consideration may provide clarity as to which parties were involved in the initial request to the hospital and in the appeal to the Commissioner. In April 2000 the Minister for Health and Children announced the establishment of a non-statutory Post Mortem Inquiry which included in its terms of reference a review of the post-mortem examination policy, practice and procedure in this State since 1970 and in particular as it relates to organ removal, retention, storage and disposal by reference to prevailing standards both in and outside of the State. Some of the parents of deceased children whose bodily organs may have been retained by hospitals within the State after the conclusion of post-mortem procedures grouped together as *Parents for Justice* (PFJ). This was an unincorporated body which had initiated the freedom of information request and the appeal to the Commissioner.

The court was not entirely clear how or why the notice party (Parents for Justice, Ltd) was joined as a party to the proceedings as it was neither "requester" under s.7 (initial request) of the FOI Act nor a "relevant person" within the meaning of s.14(11) (internal review) and s.34(15) (appeal to the Information Commissioner). Relying on McCracken J.'s judgment for the Supreme Court in *Construction Industry Federation v Dublin City Council* [2005] 2 I.R. 496, Quirke J. was satisfied that the Notice Party did not have *locus standi* in the appeal. Of greater significance, however, he declared himself satisfied that its participation had not affected the outcome of the appeal in any respect:

> "The parties to the appeal have been the Hospital and the Commissioner.

The submissions relied upon by this Court in its determination have been those of the Hospital and the Commissioner."

Exemptions denied   The High Court upheld the Commissioner's decision to grant access to all but a small number of records. Quirke J. held that the hospital had failed to discharge its onus to show that the Commissioner had erred in law in deciding that the balance of the records did not qualify for any of the exemptions claimed by the hospital and should be released. The exemptions claimed were under s.22(1A) (the business or proceedings of a tribunal or inquiry); s.22(1)(a) (legal professional privilege); s.26 (information given in confidence); s.20 (the deliberative process); s.21 (investigations and negotiations); and s.23(1)(a)(iv) (the fairness of civil proceedings in a court or other tribunal).

Section 22(1A) (the business or proceedings of a tribunal or inquiry)   This claim for exemption centred on the discretion of the Commissioner to take account of matters as they stood at the time of her review rather than at the time of the request. The grounds for refusal relied upon by the hospital included the contention that all of the documents sought were documents which related to the inquiry, including documents which were prepared and provided to the inquiry in confidence on the understanding that they would be treated as confidential. The court accepted that the Commissioner was correct in law in finding that the inquiry was a tribunal for the purposes of the Act, and correct in fact in that the tribunal no longer existed at the time of the appeal. The court held that the Commissioner was entitled to consider all of the material before her on the date on which she made her decision and to make her decision having regard to the circumstances that existed at that time.

Section 22(1)(a) (legal professional privilege)   The Commissioner refused access to a number of records accepting that they did come within the provisions of this exemption. In failing to discharge its onus to prove that other records came within the exempted category, the hospital did not identify any relevant record that would be exempt from production in court proceedings on grounds of legal professional privilege. Since the tests outlined and applied by the Commissioner were the correct tests, the court declined to examine the records.

Section 26 (information given in confidence)   The hospital had claimed, inter alia, that the Commissioner's decision in relation to this exemption was irrational and had requested the court to review the records. The court declined to do so, Quirke J. stating that it is not the function of the court to oversee or supervise the discharge by the Commissioner of her functions or the exercise of the discretion vested in her by the provisions of the Act. He noted that s.26(2) had been enacted with the intention of distinguishing between:

(i) records given to or created by public bodies in the course of its functions; and

(ii) records given to or created by staff members (or contractors), of a public body, whilst they were acting in another capacity (e.g. documents written by staff members or contractors in a private or personal capacity).

The application of the exemption provided by s.26(1)(a) is limited to records which either: (1) were given to a public body; or (2) come within (ii) above.

Quirke J. was satisfied that that there had been no mistake of law on the part of the Commissioner in respect of her findings:

(a) that the relevant documents were prepared by persons on behalf of the hospital who were then acting in the course of the performance of their functions;

(b) that the exemption created by s.26(1) of the Act applies only where a duty of confidence is owed by the hospital to a person other than the hospital itself (or its staff or persons providing contractual services for the hospital); and

(c) that s.26(1)(b) was intended to protect the interests of persons to whom a duty of confidence was owed by the hospital.

With regard to s.26(1)(b) the court noted that access to relevant records held or prepared by the hospital must be refused if disclosure of information contained within the documents would constitute a breach of duty of confidence provided for by a provision of an agreement or otherwise by law. It was undeniable that the hospital owed a duty of confidence to the inquiry under the terms of its confidentiality agreement with the inquiry. It also owed a duty of confidence by law to other persons, including parents and next-of-kin of the deceased children who were the subject of the inquiry. The hospital relied on a confidentiality agreement with the inquiry that all documents submitted would remain confidential. The hospital contended that the detailed and scrupulous examination of all of the relevant records conducted on behalf of the Commissioner was inappropriate. It argued that its submission to the inquiry, together with all of the documents appended thereto, should have been dealt with as one "record" by the Commissioner, who should then have adopted a "common sense" approach to the review and sought to establish whether a "reasonable man" would regard the relevant "record" as being confidential in character. Quirke J. did not accept that contention:

"The Act confers upon '… *every person*' a general right of access to relevant records. The right is qualified by precise exceptions identified within the Act. It was appropriate for the Commissioner, when conducting her review, to carefully consider the precise exceptions within the Act which qualified the general right of access which applied to the relevant records. It was within the jurisdiction of the Commissioner to decide whether the documents appended to the Hospital's submission should be dealt with as separate 'records' for the purposes of the Act."

He noted that the Commissioner in her decision, acknowledged, recognised and respected the existence of the duty of confidence owed by the hospital to *"patients and their next of kin"* in the following express terms:

"I accept the Hospital's position that patient confidentiality, and the requirement for patients' consent to release medical records, is important to it both in the context of the Inquiry and in the wider context. I agree that patients and their next of kin would potentially be a class of persons in respect of whom disclosure of information might constitute a breach of a duty of confidence. However, I can only apply the relevant exemptions to actual records and in this case where it would appear that records contain references to potentially identifiable individuals, I intend to direct that such references be removed from any records that I find not to be exempt under the Act." *Case 030830 Parents for Justice and the National Maternity Hospital.*

Quirke J. held that the court:

"… [C]an find no mistake of law or 'irrationality' in that finding. Indeed, it would appear to comprise a 'common sense' approach to the review of the type contended for by the Hospital.
     She gave detailed reasons for that conclusion. I can find no mistake of law in the reasons which she gave. There was sufficient material before her to enable her to reasonably reach the conclusion which she reached."

The Supreme Court considered s.26(1) in *Sheedy v Information Commissioner* [2004] I.E.H.C. 192; [2004] 2 I.R. 533; [2005] I.E.S.C. 35 (*Annual Review of Irish Law 2005*, pp.431 et seq.).

Section 20 (the deliberative process)   The court refused to interfere with the Commissioner's decision that the records relate to positions adopted by the hospital following its deliberations as opposed to material disclosing the internal thinking process within the hospital or the weighing up of options. This decision demonstrated no mistake of law.

Section 21 (investigations and negotiations) Section 21(1)(a) only applies to public bodies prescribed by the Act. It did not apply to the inquiry's own investigations since it was not such a body. The only records relating to the investigations and inquiries that the hospital or any other public body had to conduct were those concerning pharmaceutical companies. Having examined those documents she found that they did not qualify for exemption. Similarly, in relation to s.21(1)(b), with one exception, the Commissioner found the exemption did not apply.

The Supreme Court considered s.21(1)(a) in *Sheedy v Information Commissioner* [2004] I.E.H.C. 192; [2004] 2 I.R. 533; [2005] I.E.S.C. 35 (*Annual Review of Irish Law 2005*, pp.431 et seq.).

Section 43 (non-disclosure of record) The Commissioner did not disclose her grounds for making the exception in accordance with s.43, having regard to the provisions of s.43 of the Act. The court accepted that she was empowered under that section to make that exception and to refuse to disclose her grounds.

The court found that there were no mistakes of law. Further, the court had no reason to conclude that the Commissioner's opinion was not reasonable and was therefore lawful.

Section 23(1)(a)(iv) (the fairness of civil proceedings in a court or other tribunal) The hospital argued that it had advised the Commissioner that civil proceedings were in contemplation or were pending against the hospital arising out of its post-mortem practices. It was contended that disclosure of the relevant records might well impair or prejudice the capacity of the hospital to adequately represent itself in such proceedings and that access to the documents should be refused on that ground. In refusing the exemption the Commissioner commented that no records had been identified in the context of the "harm" envisaged. The court was satisfied that it was within the jurisdiction of the Commissioner, having examined the relevant records, to make that finding.

Fair procedures The hospital contended that the Commissioner failed to provide it with fair procedures because she considered and relied upon submissions made to her by the inquiry and by the Department of Health and Children without first giving the hospital the opportunity to see, consider and comment upon those submissions. The court rejected the hospital's claim that the Commissioner operated in an adversarial context.

Quirke J. commented that the procedures to be adopted by the Commissioner in respect of s.34 reviews are entirely within her discretion provided that they do not offend recognised principles of natural and constitutional justice. He held that the procedures adopted in the review under appeal permitted all of the parties with an interest in the review to make full and detailed written submissions on every relevant aspect which affected their respective interests. He noted that each of the parties who participated in the review was provided with full and equal access to the Commissioner and to her officials. He dismissed the hospital's contention in the following terms:

> "I know of no principle of natural or constitutional law or justice which confers upon parties who make submissions to a decision-making body the right to respond to the submissions made by every other party who participates in the process. The review undertaken by the Commissioner was a statutory process which expressly envisaged and permitted the adoption of informal procedures.
>
> The Commissioner provided the Hospital with extensive opportunities to be heard. It made submissions to the Commissioner on five separate occasions… It is argued that the Hospital should be entitled to respond to any submissions made by any other party. Should those parties then be entitled to respond to the Hospital's response and where would all of this end?"

Prior obstruction by hospital   It seems somewhat ironic that the National Maternity Hospital should claim that the Commissioner behaved in an adversarial manner, unreasonably and inappropriately. During the course of her review, the obstructive behaviour of the hospital in failing to fulfil its statutory obligations in relation to her requests for records in a timely manner was such that the Commissioner drew attention to this in her *2004 Annual Report*. This was reported on in the *Annual Review 2004* and bears repeating:

> "I regard the attitude of the Hospital as falling well short of the standard of reasonableness one is entitled to expect from a publicly funded body engaging in a process with a statutory office such as that of the Information Commissioner. I would go so far as to say that the behaviour of the Hospital in this case amounted to obstruction of my Office in the performance of its functions. This obstruction manifested itself in the following ways: in an unwarranted delay in the provision to my Office of the records at issue in the review; in an attempt to set pre-conditions before the Hospital would agree to co-operate with my review; in the adoption of an adversarial and confrontational approach in its dealings with my Office in relation to the review" (*Annual Report of the Information Commissioner 2004*, p.17).

The extent of the hospital's obstruction was such that for the first time since the establishment of the Office of Information Commissioner she invoked her powers under s.37(2) of the Act which provide for a right of entry to premises occupied by a public body.

The Commissioner was concerned that in its dealings with her Office the hospital engaged counsel in addition to solicitors. She expressed surprise that a public body should need to involve legal advisers in the routine issue of providing her Office with records requested in the course of a review. The detailed account by the Commissioner of the interaction with the hospital and its solicitors concluded as follows:

> "I find it difficult to accept that a public body should involve its solicitors in the quite routine matter of making records available to enable the review to get underway. Indeed, even when minor routine queries arose in the course of the review, in relation to matters such as the numbering of certain records, these matters were dealt with by the solicitors rather than by the Hospital's FOI Officer as is usual. The practice of my Office is that reviews are conducted on an inquisitorial rather than on an adversarial basis. Unfortunately, the Hospital and its solicitors seemed not to appreciate this fact and adopted what I believe was an adversarial approach not only in relation to the original requester but, surprisingly, in relation to the adjudicating authority (my Office). For the future, I believe the Hospital would do well to reflect on the nature of the instructions it gives its solicitors. It would do well, also, to reflect on whether it is justified in incurring what must be substantial legal costs in engaging solicitors to represent it in a way which hinders rather than helps the overall FOI review process" (*Annual Report of the Information Commissioner 2004*, p.19).

Costs for the High Court action were awarded against the hospital. This was in line with the Commissioner's policy of pursuing unsuccessful litigants for costs as outlined in the *Annual Report of the Information Commissioner 2003*; see *Annual Review of Irish Law 2003*, p.383.

Extraordinary concern for confidentiality There can be no criticism of the hospital over its concerns to protect highly confidential and sensitive information, especially if it relates to patients or to their families. However, assuming that no patients or families were identifiable, one might query some of the documentation which the hospital wished to retain as confidential. It is noted in the case that the hospital's written submission to the inquiry:

> "... [C]ontained highly confidential and sensitive information. It provides information on post mortem practices and procedures, the reasons for the carrying out of post mortems and (it) explained the Hospital's approach to its patients (at what is a very difficult time) in

relation to consent, what happened at an autopsy and how burial is
addressed."

It seems most strange that this information would be considered highly
confidential as opposed to being freely disseminated.

Industrial schools not party to "contract for services" The second
case seems to relate more to contract law than interpreting the Freedom of
Information Act. In *O'Grady v Information Commissioner* [2007] I.E.H.C. 152
the appellant, a former industrial school resident, had sought records concerning
himself and his late sister held by four separate religious orders who had run
industrial schools in which they had been detained. The issue was whether the
Commissioner was correct in his view that the religious orders did not have a
"contract for services" with the Department of Education and that, therefore,
records held by the orders could not be deemed as records of the Department
liable for release under the Freedom of Information Act. In dismissing the
appeal, White J. held that the Commissioner did not err in the inferences he
had drawn based on his interpretation of the documentation before him nor did
he err in law in concluding that no contract for services existed.

Since a major reason for requests for records from the Department of
Education and Science relates to records of industrial schools, it may be helpful
to quote the concluding part of White J.'s judgment:

> "Undoubtedly, the Religious Orders by providing such schools were
> providing a service to the State, and, in return, they were being
> remunerated for this service. The provision of a service and the receipt
> of payment in respect thereof, are elements to be found in a contract of
> service. However, it must be borne in mind that the level of remuneration
> was determined solely by the Department and imposed upon the
> management of the school who were statutorily obliged to accept the
> Department's determination without the right of negotiation.
>
> It must also be borne in mind that the source of the funding was
> not the Department alone, but also the Local Authority who could be,
> and indeed were mandated to make payments to the management of
> the schools.
>
> I consider these to be significant features to be taken into consideration
> when determining the relationship between the Department and the
> management of schools, and I consider these elements, together with
> the other statutory regulatory features conferred upon the Department
> to be inconsistent with a contract for services."

ACCESS TO RECORDS OF DECEASED PERSONS

In the *Annual Review of Irish Law 2005*, pp.452 et seq., it was recorded that the Information Commissioner had called for a total review of the Freedom of Information Act 1997 (section 28(6)) Regulations 1999 (S.I. No. 47 of 1999) (the Regulations) as a matter of real urgency (*Annual Report of the Information Commissioner 2005*, pp.23–27. This was with particular reference to the issue of access to the personal records of deceased persons. In her 2006 report the Commissioner renewed her call for immediate review of this highly unsatisfactory situation. In the report under review the Commissioner revisited this matter, welcoming the announcement made by the Department of Finance at a recent FOI Conference, 'Freedom of Information: A 2008 Update', School of Law, TCD, March 2008, that the 1999 Regulations are under review and that new regulations will issue by the end of 2008.

It is to be hoped that the Office of the Information Commissioner will be consulted before the new regulations issue.

SECTION 39 COMMENTARY

The Commissioner has a statutory obligation under s.39 to monitor the operation of the Act and "may prepare and publish commentaries on the practical application and operation of the provisions, or any particular provisions".

Section 29 (interests of third parties) In May 2007 the Commissioner published a commentary on the operation of s.29 of the FOI Act. This section sets out procedures to be followed where a decision to release certain information in a record, in the public interest, could potentially affect the interests of third parties. The Commissioner notes that this is a complex provision which can cause difficulties and confusion for public bodies, requesters, and third parties. Her commentary emphasises the point that s.29 applies only in exceptional cases where specific conditions are met and will have no application in the majority of cases involving third party information. It stresses that s.29 does not provide for a third party to have any kind of veto over the release of records, stating rather that s.29 is a notification requirement and not a mechanism through which consent to the release of records is sought. The Commentary, available at www.oic.ie, is directed primarily at FOI practitioners.

An earlier s.39 commentary is recorded in *Annual Review of Irish Law 2003*, p.388 et seq.

STATUTORY CERTIFICATES AND NOTICES

Certificates of exemption *Section 20* Section 20 Freedom of Information (Amendment) Act 2003 gives discretionary power to Secretaries General of government departments to certify that a record of whatever nature relates to a deliberative process of government and is thus exempt from release. Such a certificate is not amenable to internal review and cannot be appealed to the Information Commissioner. Section 20(1)(c) states, inter alia, that such a certificate shall be final. Effectively this means that the decision is entirely in the hands of the senior civil servant and that *ALL* Ministers, not just the Departmental Minister, are bound by this unreviewable decision. In 2006 the first such certificate was issued by the Secretary General of the Department of Justice, Equality and Law Reform. The constitutional implications of issuing a s.20 certificate were discussed in *Annual Review of Irish Law 2006*, Constitutional Law chapter, pp.236-237. No new certificates were issued under this section in 2007.

Under s.21A(b), if the Secretary General of the Department of State concerned is satisfied that the deliberative processes that led to the issue of the s.20 certificate of exemption have ended, "he or she shall, by certificate in writing, revoke the certificate" and the exemption regarding the record(s) at issue shall cease. The certificate issued by the Secretary General of the Department of Justice, Equality and Law Reform in August 2006 was not revoked in 2007.

Section 25 Under s.25(1) a Government Minister may exempt a record from the application of the Freedom of Information Act (*Annual Review of Irish Law 2000*, p.275 (two certificates issued with expiry dates of February 2, 2002 and March 29, 2002); *Annual Review of Irish Law 2001*, p.409 (one certificate issued); *Annual Review of Irish Law 2002*, p.308 (two certificates issued); *Annual Review of Irish Law 2003*, pp.391–392 (one previously issued certificate renewed for further two years); *Annual Review of Irish Law 2004*, p.326 (two previously issued certificates renewed); *Annual Review of Irish Law 2005*, pp.467–468 (one previously issued certificate renewed); *Annual Review of Irish Law 2006*, pp.410–427 (two previously issued certificates renewed)). The only Minister to have issued certificates is the Minister for Equality, Justice and Law Reform. In 2007 no new certificates were issued; however, the Minister for Justice, Equality and Law Reform renewed one previously issued certificate for a further two years. A copy of the report in respect of this certificate is included in Appendix I of *Annual Report of the Information Commissioner 2007*.

Section 25 review: notice from Department of the Taoiseach Section 25(7)(a) requires that the Taoiseach shall review the operation of s.25(1) at regular, prescribed intervals, first described in *Annual Review of Irish Law 2005*, p.468. The Information Commissioner was informed by the Department of the Taoiseach on February 14, 2008, that on January 30, 2008 the Taoiseach, the Minister for Finance, and the Minister for Enterprise, Trade and Employment reviewed the three existing certificates (the two renewed during 2006 and the third on July 11, 2007) that were in operation for the year ended April 2007, and decided that it was not necessary to request their revocation.

The copy of the notification received by the Commissioner is reproduced in Appendix II of *Annual Report of the Information Commissioner 2007*.

Statutory notices of non-compliance with Information Commissioner requests *Section 37 notice* The Act provides for the issue of a notification under s.37 to the head of the public body requiring the production of information and/or records.

Section 35 notice Section 35 of the Act provides that, where a statement of reasons for refusing a request is inadequate the Commissioner may require the head concerned to furnish a further statement (*Annual Review of Irish Law 2002*, p.275; *Annual Review of Irish Law 2003*, p.393; *Annual Review of Irish Law 2004*, p.326; *Annual Review of Irish Law 2005*, p.468; *Annual Review of Irish Law 2006*, p.421).

No s.35 notices were issued by the Commissioner in 2007, and only one s.37 notice was issued, a considerable improvement on the previous year.

NO NEW BODIES COME WITHIN FOI

The Annual Report 2007 notes that no regulations prescribing public sector bodies for the purposes of the FOI Act were made in 2007. The continuing exclusion of certain major bodies from freedom of information has been a bone of contention with the Commissioner for some years as recorded in her annual reports and reported in *Annual Review of Irish Law 2005*, p.468; *Annual Review of Irish Law 2006*, pp.421–422. Once again the Commissioner names the public bodies which, for want of a regulation issued by the Minister for Finance, remain outside the scope of the Freedom of Information Act:

"An Garda Síochána, the Garda Ombudsman Commission, the Office of the Refugee Applications Commissioner, the Office of the Refugee Appeals Tribunal, and the Judicial Appointments Advisory Board;

The Central Bank and Financial Services Authority of Ireland, the National Treasury Management Agency, the National Pension Reserve Fund Commission, and the State Claims Agency; and

The 33 Vocational Educational Committees, the State Examinations

Commission, the Residential Institutions Redress Board, and the Central Applications Office." (*Annual Report of the Information Commissioner 2007*, p.21).

Statutory right of access withdrawn   To make matters worse, some functions of public bodies previously subject to the FOI Act were removed from its scope because those functions were transferred to new public bodies, e.g. the Road Safety Authority (RSA) which now holds records previously held by the Department of Transport. Another example is the Property Registration Authority, established under the Registration of Deeds and Title Act 2006, which took over the functions of the Land Registry and the Registry of Deeds. Records held by these and similar public bodies are no longer amenable to the public by statutory right although the RSA is operating since its establishment as if it were subject to the Act (*Annual Report of the Information Commissioner 2007*, pp.21–23).

New method of prescription for public bodies urgently required   The Commissioner is very concerned at the numbers of new bodies being created which are not immediately subject to the Freedom of Information Act. The Commissioner reiterates her suggestion that each new public body being created under statute, or each body to which significant public functions are being transferred, should be made subject to the FOI Act, either in its own founding legislation, or by way of a regulation from the Minister for Finance, coinciding with the establishment of the body or the transfer of functions:

> "Compliance with freedom of information legislation is now a well-established part of good administration in Ireland, and there is a high level of awareness among public officials about what is required under the legislation. Whereas it might be argued that new bodies need time to become familiar with, and to train their staff in the FOI Act, before becoming subject to its provisions, I do not accept this argument. I do not accept that new public bodies require a lead-in time in respect of their functions under freedom of information legislation any more than they do in respect of any other legislation with which organisations must be compliant from the date of their establishment (such as health and safety legislation)." (*Annual Report of the Information Commissioner 2007*, p.22).

Unnecessary exclusions in justice, public finance and education sectors   Once again the Commissioner draws attention to the fact that with regard to An Garda Síochána, Ireland is out of step with its counterparts across the developed world in excluding its police force from FOI legislation. The Commissioner is also deeply concerned by the exclusion of the Office of the

Refugee Applications Commissioner and the Office of the Refugee Appeals Tribunal and by the proposed s.130 in the Immigration, Residence and Protection Bill 2008, which would exclude from the FOI Act records relating to an application for protection by the State of a foreign national: in effect, any record relating to a determination of a protection application (any application for refugee status or asylum or any such application). In her view it is "particularly important for bodies which deal with issues so closely related to human rights to operate in a way that is open and accountable". Concerns that sensitive matters will be released under FOI are dismissed by the Commissioner:

> "It is my view that the exemptions in the FOI Act provide adequate protection for any sensitive material related to such processes. Openness and transparency in these matters engender confidence among the population, nationally and internationally, that such important processes are dealt with in an equitable way that is in accordance with best practice and fair procedures." (*Annual Report of the Information Commissioner 2007*, p.23).

Of course, the same principles apply to all public bodies and there is an urgent requirement to extend the Freedom of Information Act and the principles its operation embodies to those responsible for any public expenditure.

COMMISSIONER FOR ENVIRONMENTAL INFORMATION

The role of the Commissioner for Environmental Information is to decide on appeals taken by members of the public who are not satisfied with the outcome of their requests to public authorities for environmental information. The Access to Information on the Environment Regulations (S.I. No. 133 of 2007) (AIE Regulations) assigned this legally separate role of Commissioner for Environmental Information to the holder of the Office of Information Commissioner. The Regulations give effect to Directive 2003/4/EC of the European Parliament and of the Council of January 28, 2003. Chapter 6 of the Information Commissioner's *Annual Report 2007* is devoted to access to information on the environment.

Guidelines Article 14 allows the Minister to publish guidelines which, under art.14(2), a public authority "shall … have regard to", in the performance of its functions under the AIE Regulations. Nevertheless, these Guidelines, published under the title of Guidance Notes, do not purport to be a legal interpretation of the AIE Regulations. This last point requires close attention as the experience of following guidance notes from the Department of Finance in relation to certain aspects of the Freedom of Information Act may have led practitioners into legal error.

The Regulations and the Guidance notes can be found on the Department of the Environment, Heritage and Local Government website: *www.environ.ie/en.*

Two distinct access to information regimes There have been statutory obligations to release environmental information since 1990 under European law and 1993 under domestic law. Since the enactment of the Freedom of Information Act in 1997, both legislative codes have operated in parallel but as fully distinct and separate systems. With these new Regulations this is set to continue and it is important to note that there are significant differences between the two regimes highlighted by the Commissioner for Environmental Information.

What is environmental information? Article 3 of the AIE Regulations defines environmental information as any information in written, visual, aural, electronic or any other material form on the following:

> "(a) the state of the elements of the environment, such as air and atmosphere, water, soil, land, landscape and natural sites including wetlands, coastal and marine areas, biological diversity and its components, including genetically modified organisms and the interaction among these elements,
>
> (b) factors, such as substances, energy, noise, radiation or waste, including radioactive waste, emissions, discharges and other releases into the environment, affecting or likely to affect the elements of the environment,
>
> (c) measures (including administrative measures), such as policies, legislation, plans, programmes, environmental agreements, and activities affecting or likely to affect the elements and factors referred to in paragraphs (a) and (b) as well as measures or activities designed to protect those elements,
>
> (d) reports on the implementation of environmental legislation,
>
> (e) cost-benefit and other economic analyses and assumptions used within the framework of the measures and activities referred to in paragraph (c), and
>
> (f) the state of human health and safety, including the contamination of the food chain, where relevant, conditions of human life, cultural sites and built structures inasmuch as they are, or may be, affected by the state of the elements of the environment referred to in paragraph (a) or, through those elements, by any of the matters referred to in paragraphs (b) and (c)".

Statutory right of access guaranteed   Under art.7(1) of the AIE Regulations:

> "[A] public authority shall, notwithstanding any other statutory provision and subject only to these Regulations, make available to the applicant any environmental information, the subject of the request, held by, or for, the public authority."

It may be noted that, unlike the Freedom of Information Act, no other legislation may counter or trump the requirements under the AIE Regulations so that any attempt to close down or restrict access will fail. Unfortunately this has not been so with the 1997 Act as is evidenced by this and previous chapters on information law in the *Annual Review*.

Exceptions to right   Article 8 to 10 of the AIE Regulations provide for refusal of requests for information in cases where, e.g. personal information, third party interests, commercial secrets or state security are involved. However, exceptions are to be interpreted in a restrictive way and are subject to a public interest test. The one clear exemption is cabinet confidentiality arising from Art.28 of the Constitution.

Promoting access   The Commissioner for Environmental Information notes with interest that:

> "[T]here is also a requirement that public authorities should organise information on the environment which they hold 'with a view to its active and systematic dissemination to the public'. Clearly, this reflects a strong view that public authorities should actively seek to create public interest in, and knowledge of, environmental matters. It sets the tone for the approach public authorities should take when members of the public, or corporate bodies, make specific access requests. The expectation, very clearly, is that access requests will be granted" (*Annual Report of the Information Commissioner 2007*, p.57).

Public authorities   At the outset it should be noted that in the context of the AIE Regulations, a "public authority" encompasses more organisations than "public bodies" subject to the oversight of the Information Commissioner and of the Ombudsman. The Guidance Notes, section 3.2, provide some assistance in establishing what public authorities are included:

> "While it is not practical to list individually all the public authorities to which the AIE Regulations apply, it is sufficient to flag here that such a list would include all authorities exercising 'public administrative

functions and responsibilities, and possessing environmental information'. In particular, and as was the case under the 1998 AIE Regulations, commercial semi-state bodies come within the remit of the AIE Regulations to the extent that they satisfy the above conditions."

In case of dispute as to whether a body is a public authority, within the meaning of the Regulations, the person seeking the information has a right of appeal to the Commissioner for Environmental Information under art.12 of the AIE Regulations.

Fees/charges   Unlike the requirement to pay an upfront fee under the Freedom of Information Act since 2003, a request under the AIE Regulations is free. Should there be refusal at both initial request stage (art.7), and internal review stage (art.11), an appeal to the Commissioner for Environmental Information attracts an upfront payment of €150 (art.15). There may be a charge for processing the information subject to the request; the public authority is obliged to make a list of fees chargeable available to the public (art.15).

Appeals received   Six appeals were received in the period from May 1, 2007 to the end of the year. Of these, two were invalid, and in two cases it was not necessary to proceed to a formal decision as the records were released as a result of the involvement of the Office of the Commissioner for Environmental Information. Decision was awaited on the remaining two at the time of publication of the annual report.

Necessity to promote public awareness on access to information on the environment   The Commissioner for Environmental Information concluded her report on the first year of operation of the AIE Regulations as follows:

"As of now, I think it is fair to say that public awareness in Ireland of the AIE regime is very low. I believe that there is a particular importance in ensuring that public authorities take on the pro-active role, as envisaged in the Directive, of making environmental information available as a matter of course and of encouraging the public to take an interest in environmental matters. For this to happen, it is essential that there be some external body which actually promotes this activity within public authorities and which can report on how well or badly this function is being fulfilled. On the question of good AIE practice, good decision making, and public authorities' own efforts to make environmental information available as a matter of course; as matters stand there is no mechanism available for investigating what is actually happening. One key concern would be whether all public authorities, where a request is refused, actually inform the requester of the grounds for the refusal. Another, and perhaps deeper concern, is whether all public authorities, where a request is refused, inform the requester of his or her rights of appeal, both internally and externally. Both of these are required practices under the Regulations. As regards the level of usage of AIE, it remains to be seen whether reliable data on AIE usage and outcomes will become available. A dedicated website for the Office of the Commissioner for Environmental Information will be launched shortly, and I will publish any of my decisions that have precedent value on that site. To the extent that it is possible, I hope to undertake some promotion of the AIE regime with a view to raising its profile" (*Annual Report of the Information Commissioner 2007*, p.59).

For expert analysis of the Regulations, see Ryall, 'Access to Information on the Environment Regulations 2007' (2007) 14(2) I.P.E.L.J. 57, also presented as a conference paper at 'Freedom of Information: A 2008 Update', School of Law, TCD, March 2008; and for comprehensive analysis of the founding Directive, see Ryall, 'Access to Information on the Environment: The Challenge of Implementing Directive 2003/4/EC' in Feldman (ed.), *Freedom of Information: Law and Practice* (Dublin: First Law, 2006), pp.163–176.

OMBUDSMAN

The Ombudsman is governed by the Ombudsman Act 1980. In addition to hard copy, documents referred to may be found at the Ombudsman's website *http://www.ombudsman.gov.ie/en*. Mr Michael Mills was appointed first Ombudsman in 1984. He was succeeded by Mr Kevin Murphy in 1994, who was succeeded by the present incumbent, Ms Emily O'Reilly, in mid-2003; hence references to publications may refer to "he" or "she" depending on the date of publication.

Information Commissioner and Ombudsman compared Whereas both the Information Commissioner and the Ombudsman deal with matters of administrative accountability, as has been noted previously, there are significant differences in the statutory role and responsibility of each Office (*Annual Review of Irish Law 2000*, pp.276 et seq.; *Annual Review of Irish Law 2001*, pp.409 et seq.; *Annual Review of Irish Law 2002*, pp.310; *Annual Review of Irish Law 2003*, pp.395 et seq.; *Annual Review of Irish Law 2004*, pp.330 et seq.; *Annual Review of Irish Law 2005*, pp.470 et seq.; *Annual Review of Irish Law 2006*, pp.422 et seq.).

OMBUDSMAN (AMENDMENT) BILL

In her *Annual Report 2007* the Ombudsman welcomes the prospect of the Ombudsman (Amendment) Bill being passed in the Dáil summer session in 2008. Assuming this long-awaited Bill is enacted, the Ombudsman notes that it will be an important milestone for her Office and for public administration generally. The failure to legislate for the extension of the Ombudsman's remit has been reported in previous Annual Reviews, e.g. *Annual Review of Irish Law 2006*, p.423.

STATUTORY NOTICES OF NON-COMPLIANCE WITH OMBUDSMAN REQUESTS

Section 7 A s.7 notice is a statutory demand for the provision of information required by the Office of the Ombudsman in examining a complaint and is normally only issued as a last resort when there has been an unacceptable delay on the part of the public body in providing the requested information (*Annual Review of Irish Law 2002*, p.314; *Annual Review of Irish Law 2003*, p.396; *Annual Review of Irish Law 2004*, p.330; *Annual Review of Irish Law 2005*, p.470; *Annual Review of Irish Law 2006*, p.424). Eighteen notices were issued in 2007: seven against local authorities and 11 against government departments. Kildare County Council was in receipt of four s.7 notices, for the third year running the highest number issued against any statutory authority. However, 10 notices were issued against the Department of Justice, Equality and Law Reform. The Ombudsman notes that many of the complaints to her Office against the Department were about delays on the part of the Department in its dealings with its clients; "therefore this makes the further delays in responding to my Office even more unacceptable" (*Annual Report of the Ombudsman 2007*, p.36).

INVESTIGATIVE REPORTS

Section 4 of the Ombudsman Act gives discretion to the Ombudsman to conduct an investigation at her discretion. The vast bulk of complaints to the Ombudsman are dealt with by way of a preliminary examination, whereby it is possible to conclude cases, in a consensual manner, with the co-operation of the public bodies. However, in the *Annual Report 2007*, the Ombudsman notes that there are any number of reasons for opening an investigation but most commonly, one takes place where a case may have some merit but the public body simply does not accept this and no progress towards a resolution is in sight. There is also more likely to be an investigation if it is felt that there are broad systemic issues involved in the case. Moreover, it is only on completion of an investigation that the Ombudsman can make formal recommendations to resolve a complaint to a public body. Should the public body respond in an unsatisfactory manner the Ombudsman may lay a special report on the matter before the Houses of the Oireachtas under s.6(7) (*Annual Review of Irish Law 2000*, p.277 *et seq*; *Annual Review of Irish Law 2001*, p.410 *et seq*; *Annual Review of Irish Law 2002*, p.314 *et seq*.).

In 2007, the Ombudsman published four investigative reports which are available on *www.ombudsman.gov.ie/en/Publications/InvestigationReports*:

Health Service Executive—Fostering *A Summary Report by the Ombudsman involving a complaint about the Health Service Executive's handling of an application to foster three children* (April 2007)

In the Postscript of this investigation report, the Ombudsman expresses the view that while rules and regulations are important in ensuring fairness, they should not be applied so rigidly or inflexibly as to create inequity. By publishing this summary report, she hopes that "lessons can be learnt for the future in terms of how public bodies exercise their onerous responsibilities for dealing with the welfare of vulnerable children in society."

Kildare County Council *Complaint Handling in Kildare County Council - A Report of the Ombudsman's experience of dealing with complaints against Kildare County Council* (June 2007)

This report arose from the "less than adequate service to the Ombudsman" by Kildare County Council over a significant period of time. The Ombudsman advises Kildare County Council that in 2007 and beyond it "needs to demonstrate that it takes notification of complaints from [the Office of the Ombudsman] seriously, as the vast majority of local authorities do, and that it is prepared to provide the Ombudsman with the information requested in an appropriate and timely manner." In the absence of significant improvement, the Ombudsman notes that she may have no alternative but to make a report to the Oireachtas and, if considered appropriate, to the Minister for the Environment, Heritage and Local Government, on the performance of Kildare County Council in providing responses/reports on complaints from the Ombudsman ("Recommendations" section of report).

Planning—Clare County Council *Complaint to the Ombudsman against Clare County Council concerning its handling of planning applications for development at Doonbeg Golf Course* (August 2007)

This is a report of an investigation under preliminary examination procedures and no formal findings or recommendations were involved. Clare County Council's administration of the Planning and Development Regulations 2001 was found deficient in two of eleven complaints by a single complainant.

It was her view that the Council had not followed proper procedure and that the failures involved probably resulted in the loss of an opportunity to exercise a statutory right of appeal for the complainant. For the adverse effect of such loss which could not otherwise be restored, the Ombudsman suggested to the Council that compensation be paid to the complainant, and the Council agreed.

General Register Office *Complaints against the General Register Office* (October 2007)

In dealing with complaints against the General Register Office (GRO), the Ombudsman highlighted a number of cases where she felt that "the actions of the GRO had adversely and seriously affected individuals." The quality of service provided was below the standard which might be expected from a public service organisation. The recommendations she made aimed at improving the quality of service have been accepted by the GRO. "The cases in the report were chosen with a view to assisting those charged with quality customer service improvement within the GRO and the Department of Health and Children to meet the expectations of members of the public using the important service provided by the GRO in the future" (*Annual Report of the Ombudsman 2007*, p.33).

THE OMBUDSMAN AND THE HEALTH SERVICE SECTOR

As noted in last year's Annual Review, under the Health Act 2004 a statutory complaints procedure for the Health Service Executive (HSE) came into effect on January 1, 2007. This new statutory complaints procedure applies to actions of the HSE—and service providers who have contracts with the HSE—to provide health and personal social services. Complaints examined under this procedure, which remain unresolved, can then be referred to the Ombudsman for consideration. (See *Annual Review of Irish Law 2005*, p.470 *et seq*; *Annual Review of Irish Law 2006*, p.425.)

In 2007, 84 hospital-related complaints were received by the Ombudsman. She expects that this number of complaints will increase significantly in the future. The complaints received included issues surrounding an unexpected death in hospital, lack of courtesy in the care and treatment of patients, communication difficulties in respect of the transmission of urgent medical reports between hospitals, lack of dignity and respect surrounding the death of patients in hospitals, inadequate record keeping and failure to apologise for poor service provided (*Annual Report of the Ombudsman 2007* p.34).

SECTORAL OMBUDSMEN

Financial Services Ombudsman The relevant website is *www. financialombudsman.ie*

Restitution confined to actual complainant In *Quinn Direct v Financial Services Ombudsman* [2007] I.E.H.C. 23, Finlay Geoghegan J. found that the Financial Services Ombudsman had exceeded his powers in his direction to Quinn Direct regarding an unpublicised administrative charge. The essence of the original complaint against Quinn Direct was that it had charged an excessive premium at the time the complainant changed his car and subsequently imposed excessive charges when he cancelled his policy. The latter part of the complaint was found not to be substantiated. However, the Financial Services Ombudsman found that an administrative fee of €25 had been imposed on the complainant without notification in his policy documents. Consequent on this finding the Financial Services Ombudsman issued a direction that Quinn Direct return these change-of-vehicle charges of €25 not just to the complainant but to consumers who were charged the same, going back six years from the date of the direction. The essential issue in the case was whether the Financial Services Ombudsman had acted ultra vires in including similar conduct in relation to other consumers who made no complaint.

Interpreting Central Bank Act 1942, Pt VIIB, s.57CI(4)(a), as inserted by s.16 of the Central Bank and Financial Services Authority of Ireland Act 2004, Finlay Geoghegan J. found that it is confined to the conduct to or its consequences for the individual complainant or group of complainants and does not include similar conduct to other consumers.

Garda Síochána Ombudsman Commission (GSOC) All the reports referred to are available on *www.gardaombudsman.ie*

Garda Síochána Ombudsman Commission Annual Report 2007 The GSOC became operational on May 9, 2007. On May 1, 2008, the date on which the Annual Report 2007 was launched, the Chairman of the GSOC, Justice Kevin Haugh commented:

> "[W]e have almost 3,000 (2,905) complaints and almost 300 (294) referrals under section 102 from the Garda Commissioner. We have over 750 investigations into allegations of criminal conduct ongoing. We have sent 9 files to the DPP including one which concerns section 110 of the Act, which makes it an offence to knowingly provide GSOC with false or misleading information in relation to a complaint or investigation" (*GSOC Press Release*, May 1, 2008).

Garda Síochána Act 2005, section 80 Section 80 of the Garda Síochána Act 2005 required the GSOC to publish a two-year report on the effectiveness of the Commission and the adequacy of the functions assigned to it. Section 80(3) states that the report may contain recommendations for improving the effectiveness of the Ombudsman Commission. In the *Report to the Minister for Justice, Equality and Law Reform on (a) the effectiveness of the Ombudsman Commission and (b) the adequacy of the functions assigned to it under the Garda Síochána Act 2005* the GSOC noted its satisfaction that the general objectives and the current design of the organisation are suitable for the purposes set down in the Garda Síochána Act 2005. "There are, however, areas in which the Ombudsman Commission believes that some amendments to the Act are necessary" (para.3.1). The GSOC's recommendations for legislative change are set out in Appendices 2–12 of the report.

Amendments to Garda Síochána Act 2005 Section 43 of the Criminal Justice Act 2007 provides for a number of amendments to the Garda Síochána Act 2005. The Explanatory Memorandum notes that some of these amendments arise from suggestions for amendment made by the Garda Síochána Ombudsman Commission since it took office.

Ombudsman for Children An application for leave for judicial review was denied to a parent who sought to prevent the Ombudsman for Children from conducting the Big Ballot event. The Ballot gave children and young people up to 18 years the opportunity to vote on a number of issues in a referendum-style event in early-November 2007. O'Neill J. held that the applicant did not have locus standi nor had he made an arguable case. The proceedings were reported in *The Irish Times* (November 10, 2007) and referred to in the *Annual Report of the Ombudsman for Children 2007* (p.13). See also *Constitutional Law* in this Annual Review.

Ombudsman for the Defence Forces The relevant website is *www.odf.ie*
In her Annual Report 2007 the Ombudsman for the Defence Forces (ODF) acknowledged her obligation under the Ombudsman (Defence Forces) Act 2004 to have due regard for the operational needs of the defence forces. It is interesting to consider these additional comments of the Ombudsman for the Defence Forces:

> "One of the principles of adjudication is that a wronged person be provided with an appropriate remedy to mitigate the adverse affects of the action giving rise to the grievance that is proportionate and, as far as practicable, puts the person back in the position they were prior to the wrong arising or otherwise compensates for the original unfairness or

maladministration. A number of the referrals to my Office are recorded under the category of 'maladministration' which covers a wide range of alleged errors and impropriety. Some are serious, some may not be so serious, but may have consequences disproportionate to the act itself.

I fully appreciate that finding a suitable remedy to compensate an individual who has, on the balance of probabilities, been adversely affected by unfair procedures or maladministration presents significant challenges to the military command. Of considerable cause of concern to me is that the remedy for one wrong might create a further wrong to another member. There are no simple solutions to this issue" (*Ombudsman for the Defence Forces Annual Report 2007*, p.6).

The difficulties faced by the ODF in meeting her obligations and the impact on complainants will be considered in subsequent Annual Reviews.

STATUTES AND STATUTORY INSTRUMENTS

Citizens Information Act 2007 (No. 2 of 2007) An Act to amend the Comhairle Act 2000 to change the name of Comhairle, so that it shall be known, in the English language, as the Citizens Information Board or, in the Irish language, as An Bord Um Fhaisnéis Do Shaoránaigh; to amend and extend its functions, and, in particular, to confer a function on it to provide, or arrange for the provision of, a personal advocacy service to certain persons with disabilities; to make certain changes to its membership; and to provide for related matters.

Central Bank Act 1942 (Financial Services Ombudsman Council) Levies And Fees Regulations 2007 (S.I. No. 726 of 2007) made by the Financial Services Ombudsman Council in accordance with ss.57BE and 57BF of the Central Bank Act 1942 (as amended) amend the Central Bank Act 1942— Financial Services Ombudsman Council)—Levies and Fees Regulations 2006 (S.I. No. 556 of 2006) and provide for a scheme of levies on regulated entities to fund the operation of the Financial Services Ombudsman's Bureau for the year ended December 31, 2008.

Circuit Court Rules (Pensions Ombudsman) 2007 (S.I. No. 588 of 2007) prescribe Circuit Court procedures in respect of applications brought under s.137 of the Pensions Act 1990 for an order requiring a person to comply with a requirement made of that person by the Pensions Ombudsman, and under s.141 of that Act for an order for the carrying out of determinations of the Pensions Ombudsman.

European Communities (Access to Information on the Environment) Regulations 2007 (S.I. No. 133 of 2007) transpose EU Directive 2003/4/EC on access to environmental information. They revoke the European Communities Act 1972 (Access to Information on the Environment) Regulations 1998 (S.I. No. 125 of 1998), which transposed an earlier EU Directive in relation to the same matter. The Regulations define environmental information and the public authorities from which it may be requested. They also set out the manner in which environmental information is to be sought and provided, and the grounds on which public bodies may decline to provide information in certain circumstances. Provision is made for an appeals mechanism.

The Regulations provide that public authorities may charge a reasonable fee for making environmental information available. The Minister for the Environment, Heritage and Local Government is empowered to publish guidelines to which public authorities must have regard in implementing the Regulations.

For comment see under COMMISSIONER FOR ENVIRONMENTAL INFORMATION above.

European Communities (Information on the Payer accompanying Transfers of Funds) Regulations 2007 (S.I. No. 799 of 2007) provide for appropriate penalties for failure to comply with Regulation (EC) No. 1781/2006 of the European Parliament and of the Council of November 15, 2006 on information on the payer accompanying transfers of funds. This ensures that Special Recommendation VII on wire transfers (SR VII) of the Financial Action Task Force (FATF) established by the Paris G7 Summit of 1989 is transposed in Ireland. The Regulations provide for a penalty of up to €3,000 for any offence, and make the Central Bank and Financial Services Authority of Ireland the appropriate enforcement agency. They also allow for the exclusion of transfers of funds within the State to a payee account permitting payment for the provision of goods and services from the scope of Regulation (EC) No. 1781/2006.

European Communities (Transnational Information and Consultation of Employees Act 1996) (Amendment) Regulations 2007 (S.I. No. 599 of 2007) The purpose of these Regulations is to transpose into Irish law Council Directive 2006/109/EC of November 20, 2006 adapting Directive 94/45/EC on the establishment of a European Works Council or a procedure in Community-scale undertakings or Community-scale groups of undertakings for the purposes of informing and consulting employees, by reason of the accession of Bulgaria and Romania to the European Community.

Non-Life Insurance (Provision of Information) (Renewal of Policy of Insurance) Regulations 2007 (S.I. No. 74 of 2007) require insurers to give clients:

(a) 15 working days' notice in writing of a renewal of the policy and the terms of the renewal; and

(b) a No Claims Bonus Renewal notification.

Pensions Act (Disclosure of Information) (Amendment) Regulations 2007 (S.I. No. 842 of 2007) provide for some technical amendments to the Occupational Pension Schemes (Disclosure of Information) Regulations 2006 (S.I. No. 301 of 2006) as follows:

- to clarify that small schemes operating cross-border are required to produce full annual reports and audited accounts;

- to provide that the information in the annual benefit statement for a DC scheme should relate to a date not being earlier than six months before the date of issue of the statement to allow sufficient time for the collation of the necessary information;

- to defer the entry into operation of the requirement to provide a statement of reasonable projection in respect of occupational pensions until January 1, 2009 to allow for sufficient time for the development of guidance on how the statement should be prepared;

- to provide that the information in the statement of reasonable projection should relate to a date not being earlier than six months before the date of issue of the statement to allow sufficient time for the collation of the necessary information;

- to clarify that deferred members of DB and DC schemes are entitled to the information specified in paras 2 to 6 of Pt 1 of Sch.E, within two months of a request being made;

- to make provision for members to be consulted where the trustees or employer propose in respect of a scheme in wind up to exercise any discretion as to the payment of any of the resources of the scheme to the employer or as to the abatement of assets in the case of insufficiency of resources;

- to provide that DB and DC schemes in their annual benefit statements need only provide details of all contributions, transfers in, etc received by the scheme since the previous annual benefit statement;

- to permit defined benefit schemes to reference information already provided to members specifying how additional benefits on a defined benefits can be acquired and either the amount of the benefits or an explanation of how they will be calculated as an alternative to providing this information in the annual DB benefit statement.

In addition the regulations amend the Trust RACs (Disclosure of Information) Regulations 2007 (S.I. No. 182 of 2007) by:

- providing that the information in the annual benefit statement for a trust RAC scheme should relate to a date not being earlier than six months before the date of issue of the statement to allow sufficient time for the collation of the necessary information;

- providing for the deferral of entry into operation of the requirement to provide a statement of reasonable projection until January 1, 2009 in respect of trust RACs and to provide that the information in the statement of reasonable projection should relate to a date not earlier than six months before it issues;

- clarifying that a trust RAC member who has notified the trust RAC that he no longer proposes to contribute to the trust RAC is entitled to the information specified in Sch.E at any time, within two months of his requesting same;

- providing that a trust RAC in its annual benefit statement to a member need only provide details of all contributions, transfers in, etc received by the trust RAC in respect of that member since the previous annual benefit statement.

Pensions Ombudsman Regulations 2007 (S.I. No. 183 of 2007) The Pensions (Amendment) Act 2002 inserted Pt XI into the Pensions Act 1990. Under Pt XI the Office of the Pensions Ombudsman was established to deal with complaints regarding occupational pension schemes and PRSAs. Section 37 of the Social Welfare and Pensions Act 2007 has extended the jurisdiction of the Pensions Ombudsman to include trust RACs other than trust RACs which invest only in life assurance policies. These Regulations now amend the Pensions Ombudsman Regulations 2003 so as to apply them to trust RACs other that trust RACs which invest in life assurance policies.

Trust RACs (Disclosure of Information) Regulations 2007 (S.I. No. 182 of 2007) Section 54 of the Pensions Act 1990, as amended by s.37 of the Social Welfare and Pensions Act 2007, provides that the trustees of large trust RACs must make prescribed information available to their members. These Regulations prescribe the information to be made available. The information is similar to that which is required to be made available by the trustees of large defined contribution occupational pension schemes.

Land Law, Landlord and Tenant Law, and Conveyancing

FIONA DE LONDRAS, University College Dublin

ADVERSE POSSESSION

Moley v Fee, High Court, Laffoy J., April 27, 2007; [2007] I.E.H.C. 143 concerned the question of whether a constructive trustee could successfully establish a claim of adverse possession against the beneficial owners of land. The land in this case was the subject of an oral agreement for sale in 1975 between the predecessors in title of the plaintiff ("the original purchasers") and the father of the defendant, now deceased ("the landowner"). Pursuant to the 1975 agreement the original purchasers claimed that they had advanced the agreed consideration and begun making use of the land. Consequently they claimed that they had acquired the beneficial ownership in the land, which they then conveyed to the plaintiff. Following complaints from neighbouring landowners and the failure to acquire planning permission, the original purchasers, by their own admission, had lost interest in the land, although they contended that they had continued to use it periodically. The landowner, however, continued to make significant use of the land—he dumped grass cuttings from his nearby caravan park until its closure, used it to store numerous other items, and erected a locked gate which remained there for some time. As a result, the defendant claimed that the landowner had successfully adversely possessed whatever interest the original purchasers might have had in the land and, as a result, the plaintiff had not acquired any ownership from them.

The court accepted the existence of the original oral agreement between the parties and reaffirmed the longstanding principle that a contract for the sale of land, accompanied by consideration, results in beneficial ownership for the purchaser, making the vendor a trustee for the purchasers. That notwithstanding, however, the court held that the landowner could establish a claim for adverse possession by virtue of s.2(2)(a)(i) of the Statute of Limitations 1957, which provides:

> "2(2)(a) In this Act, 'trustee' does not include
>   (i) a person whose fiduciary relationship arises merely by construction or implication of law and whose fiduciary relationship is not deemed by any rule of law to be that of an express trustee..."

The original purchasers in this case had not extinguished the landowner's legal title because of lack of *animus possidendi*. The original landowner, on the other hand, was held to have fulfilled the requirements for adverse possession including demonstration of *animus possidendi* by virtue of his continued and extensive use of the land. As a result, any beneficial ownership of the original purchasers had been extinguished. In the eyes of Laffoy J., the plaintiff in this case had entered into an agreement with the original purchasers with his eyes open and was therefore deserving of no relief.

The case of *Dunne v Iarnroid Eireann*, High Court, Clarke J., September 7, 2007; [2007] I.E.H.C. 314 offered the High Court an opportunity to consider one of the most controversial questions in the law of adverse possession, i.e. whether a landowner's future intended use of the land in question is relevant to a consideration of a claim of adverse possession. This question has mired the law of adverse possession since the case of *Leigh v Jack* (1879) 5 Ex D 264 and, although settled in English law (where future intended use does not affect claims of adverse possession—*Buckingham County Council v Moran* [1990] Ch. 623), has continued to be controversial in Ireland by virtue of the competing *ratione* in the cases of *Lynch v Cork Corporation* [1995] 2 I.L.R.M. 598 (decided 1986) and *Seamus Durack Manufacturing v Considine* [1987] I.R. 677. In *Lynch* the High Court followed the conventional understanding of *Leigh v Jack* and held that where a landowner has a future intended use of the land an adverse possessor must do acts inconsistent with that future intended use in order to establish *animus possidendi*. In *Durack Manufacturing* Barron J. in the High Court held that the primary focus ought to be on the state of mind of the adverse possessor, therefore the future intended use of the land by the owner would be relevant to assessing a claim in adverse possession only where it impacted on the claimant's state of mind to the extent that *animus possidendi* had not been established. In considering the arguments in *Dunne*, Clarke J. laid down a clear summary of the law of adverse possession as it applies in Ireland that ought to finally put an end to speculation around this question in this jurisdiction.

Dunne concerned a piece of land that appeared to have been acquired by the predecessors in title of Iarnróid Éireann by virtue of a Private Act of 1844 for the construction of railways. The claimant in this case argued, first, that the respondent did not in fact have title to this piece of land and, secondly, that even if title was established he had successfully extinguished it by adverse possession. Having established title in the respondent, the court went on to consider whether the claimant had successfully fulfilled the requirements for adverse possession and, if so, whether his claim was barred by the respondent's assertion of title by use of the land. Dunne had used the land to some extent since 1977. Initially the land was used for rearing and grazing a small number of horses and at least some small structures were erected, but Dunne's usage of the land intensified from the early 1990s onwards, around the time that the respondent began to make extensive use of the plot for the renovation of

Clondalkin railway station, including incorporating some of the land into the railway platform and erecting new fencing.

In outlining the principles of adverse possession in Irish law, Clarke J. reaffirmed the long-standing principle that no claim for adverse possession can be established unless the claimant successfully shows *animus possidendi*, i.e. the intention to use the land to the exclusion of all others, including the landowners. *Animus possidendi* is demonstrated by the claimant's acts of user and, in this case, the acts of grazing and rearing horses on the land were held not to be extensive enough to establish the required intention. Rather, *animus possidendi* was first established by the claimant in the 1990s when his user intensified contemporaneously with that of the respondent landowner. Clarke J. usefully outlined a "definition" of acts that are sufficient to establish *animus possidendi*, holding that:

> "[T]he nature of the possession which must be established is one which must be objectively viewed by reference to the lands concerned and the type of use which one might reasonably expect a typical owner to put those lands to" (para. 4.5).

Clarke J. then went on to consider the disputed question of the relevance of a landowner's future intended use for a plot of land and, having reviewed both *Lynch* and *Durack* (considered above), held that *Durack* was to be preferred. The court also summarised the ratio in that case, holding that *Durack* stood for the proposition that where a landowner has a future intended use for a piece of land, it might be inferred that a claimant who knew of this future intended use could be using the land in question with the intention to do so temporarily, in which case *animus possidendi* would not be established (para.4.7).

Lastly the court considered whether, by its acts on the land from the 1990s onwards, the respondent landowner had done enough to negative any adverse possession accrued by the claimant. It is well established that, while the limitation period is being accrued, a landowner can "stop the clock" by assertion of title, which can take the form of acts of ownership and possession of the land. In this case Clarke J. referred favourably to the dicta of Slade L.J. in *Powell v McFarlane* (1977) 38 P&CR 452 (Ch. D.) where he held that "the slightest acts done by or on behalf of an owner in possession will be found to negative discontinuance of possession" (at 427) and therefore stop the claimant's accrual of time. Thus, while a claimant must make extensive use of lands that can be objectively assessed as being of the nature of acts that one might reasonably expect a landowner to do in order to establish *animus possidendi*, a landowner need only make a slight and minimal use of the land to reassert title and stop the limitation period from running. This differentiated standard may seem to be heavily weighed in favour of the landowner; however it is justified by reference to the landowner's superior title to the land and to the fact that, once extinguished, title can not be reinstated by means of any acts of the landowner no matter how extensive.

Dunne thus represents not only a clear and unequivocal response to the long-standing confusion about the role of the landowner's future intended use of disputed land but also a concise and admirable restatement of a number of basic and fundamental principles of the law of adverse possession in Ireland.

COMPULSORY PURCHASE

Although the case of *Edwards v Minister of Transport* [1964] 2 Q.B. 134 has long been followed in Ireland, it has never been considered by the Irish courts. In that case the Court of Appeal held that compensation for injurious affection of land, under s.63 of the Lands Clauses Consolidation Act 1845, was limited to compensation for injurious affection of lands retained by the carrying out of works on lands that were acquired from the claimant by compulsory purchase. In *Representatives of Chadwick (Deceased) v Fingal County Council*, Supreme Court, November 6, 2007; [2007] I.E.S.C. 49 the claimants argued that compensation for injurious affection ought not to be so limited and that it ought to be possible to acquire compensation for injurious affection to lands retained caused by the scheme of construction *in general* and not limited to the carrying out of works on lands actually acquired from the claimants. In this respect the claimants argued that the Supreme Court ought to follow the approach adopted by the High Court of Australia in *Marshall v The Director General, Department of Transport* [2001] H.C.A. 37 (that the effect of acts on land other than those lands actually acquired from the claimant could be taken into account), and that a constitutionally compliant interpretation of s.63 of the 1845 Act required the result for which they advocated. Section 63 of the Land Clauses Consolidation Act 1984 provides:

> "In estimating the purchase money or compensation to be paid by the promoters of the undertaking, in any of the cases aforesaid, regard shall be had by the justices, arbitrators, or surveyors, as the case may be, not only to the value of the land to be purchased or taken by the promoters of the undertaking, but also to the damage, if any, to be sustained by the owners of the land by reason of the severing of the lands taken from the other lands of such owner, or otherwise injuriously affecting such other lands by the exercise of the powers of this or the special act, or any act incorporated therewith."

Fennelly J. in the Supreme Court noted that first, although not binding in Ireland, *Edwards* had been followed in practice for a protracted period of time. Kearns J. made the same point, and noted that the *Edwards* interpretation of s.63 has the effect of ensuring that a claimant:

"...does not obtain some windfall benefit over and above what he is entitled to receive in compensation but is treated in the same way in respect of entitlements in respect of off-site lands as his neighbour from whom nothing is taken".

The rationale for this interpretation of s.63, together with its long-standing acceptance in Ireland, in practice meant that a compelling case would have to be made in order for an alternative interpretation to be accepted. In the court's view neither the argument that *Edwards* was wrongly decided, nor the Australian High Court's decision in *Marshall*, offered such a compelling case; nor did the claimant's arguments as to the alleged constitutional breach resulting from an *Edwards* interpretation.

On reviewing the main authorities underlying *Edwards* (particularly *Re the Stockport, Timperley and Altringham Railway Co* (1864) 33 L.J.Q.B. and *Duke of Buccleuch v Metropolitan Board of Works* (1872) L.R. 5 H.L. 418), Fennelly J. concluded that *Edwards* had been rightly decided. As a result, he restated the principle that compensation for injurious affection under s.63 was limited to claims relating to the injurious affection of lands retained by virtue of the use of lands acquired and could not be based on a claim for compensation on the basis of the scheme of development *in general*. To allow such a result would, in essence, give landowners a veritable "right of veto" over planned development works where no such right would exist had none of their lands been compulsorily acquired. While the court agreed with O'Neill J. in the High Court in this respect, Fennelly J. reversed the High Court's finding that s.63 compensation was limited to compensation for acts that would have been actionable in tort (usually as a nuisance).

Turning to the decision of the Australian High Court in *Marshall*, Fennelly J. noted that the decision itself appeared primarily to be concerned with the meaning of s.63 in the context of the particular Australian legislative scheme and distinguished it from *Edwards* on that basis. While Kearns J. noted that this may offer a basis for distinction, his judgment was concerned primarily with the unconvincing nature of the argumentation in *Marshall* and particularly with the Australian High Court's failure to engage meaningfully with the authorities that underlay *Edwards* (in contrast with Fennelly J.'s thorough consideration there of).

Finally Fennelly J. held that the right to property ownership in the Irish Constitution did not preclude an interpretation of s.63 in line with *Edwards*. In his view, this interpretation of s.63 did not result in a constitutional breach because landowners are entitled to compensation for compulsory acquisition and for injurious affection by virtue thereof to the lands retained. The *Edwards* interpretation of s.63 simply means that landowners from whom some land has been compulsorily acquired are not entitled to compensation relating to acts done on other lands, in the same way as those from whom no land has been compulsorily acquired would not be entitled to compensation for these acts.

As a result, Fennelly J. held that:

> "The injurious affection here in contemplation is the alleged damaging effects to the retained lands of acts which would not give rise to any cause of action at law, particularly the law of nuisance, and does not entail any injury to any existing property right. I find it impossible to discern any unfairness or injustice in this scheme of compensation which could give rise to any issue as to whether, to use the language of Article 40, section 3, sub-section 2 of the Constitution, there was an '*unjust attack*' on property rights. It follows, as a corollary, that the claimants' right to sue the Council or any other user either of the land taken or any other lands is undisturbed".

CONVEYANCING

Courtney v McCarthy, Supreme Court, December 4, 2007; [2007] I.E.S.C. 58 concerned a contract for sale entered into by the plaintiff (the vendor) and the defendant (the purchaser) following a public auction. That contract provided for closing on April 5, 2005 and it was commonly agreed that the sale was not completed on that date, that the contract was rescinded, and that the deposit was thus forfeited by the vendor. Although there were a number of attempts to revive the contract without prejudice to the rescission, the significant events in this case then began on July 4, 2005 when the vendor's daughter telephoned the auctioneer and gave instructions on behalf of the vendor for the sale to be completed at 2 p.m. on July 11. The auctioneer then contacted the purchaser and it was agreed between all that the sale would be completed on July 11 and that, regardless of a number of side issues that had exercised the parties in previous negotiations, the sale to be completed would be the sale contemplated in the original contract. The purchaser was happy to go ahead with this and her solicitor was informed that the completion would be dealt with by a colleague of the vendor's solicitor, a Mr Fowler, as the vendor's solicitor, who was also her son-in-law, Mr Hickey, was then on holidays in Kerry.

Following some difficulty with making contact with one another, the purchaser's solicitor spoke with Mr Fowler on the morning of July 11 when it became clear that Mr Fowler was engaged in court and would not be available to complete on that day. The solicitors agreed that completion would go ahead on the following day, July 12, and the purchaser's solicitor told Mr Fowler that he could transfer the monies on July 11 in any case. Shortly afterwards, Mr Hickey telephoned the purchaser's solicitor to ask why he was not at the office in Dublin to complete the conveyance. The purchaser's solicitor explained that he had not gone to Dublin following his conversation with Mr Fowler but that the monies were available and the sale would be completed on the following day. Mr Hickey, however, told the purchaser's solicitor that it was "too late", that he had wanted the money on that day, and that the sale would not proceed. Following this conversation the purchaser's solicitor contacted Mr Hickey's office by facsimile stating that monies could be released if documents were sent on to him, but received a reply stating that "[a]s previously advised the contract for sale was rescinded and the contract deposit forfeited. Accordingly, this matter is at an end". The respondent purchaser in this case sought specific performance of the contract for sale, claiming that having agreed to complete the sale on July 11 (subsequently postponed to July 12), resulting in the purchaser drawing down monies, the vendor was estopped from insisting upon the original rescission of the contract.

The vendor in this case argued firstly that there was no estoppel and the rescission ought to stand, and secondly that the purchaser ought to be precluded from using estoppel as a "sword" as opposed to as a "shield". The court, however, found that there was a promise that the sale would be closed on July 11 if the terms of the original contract were strictly adhered to, that this was postponed to July 12 by mutual agreement, and that this promise was unequivocally reneged upon by Mr Hickey acting on behalf of the vendor on July 11. In the court's estimation this constituted a case of estoppel by convention—a common law estoppel primarily considered by reference to the case of *Amalgamated Property Company v Texas Bank* [1982] Q.B. 84. In *Amalgamated Property Company* Brandon L.J. referred with approval to the statement of Spencer Bower and Turner in *Estoppel by Representation*, 3rd edn (London: Butterworths, 1977), pp.157–60 to the effect that:

> "This kind of estoppel is founded not on a representation of fact made by a representor and believed by a representee, but on an agreed statement of facts the truth of which has been assumed, by the convention of the parties, as the basis of a transaction into which they are about to enter. When the parties have acted in their transaction upon the agreed assumption that a given state of facts has to be accepted between them as true, then as regards that transaction each will be estopped as against the other from questioning the truth of the statement of facts so assumed."

Geoghegan J. cited Brandon L.J.'s reliance on this assessment from *Amalgamated Property Company* with approval, suggesting that this is the understanding of estoppel by convention that ought to be applied in Irish law. Geoghegan J. also expanded on his view of estoppel and in particular on the relationship between equitable estoppel and estoppel by convention. Although he recognised that they were academically distinct topics, he also held that in this case it would make no difference which of the estoppels was applied because, in reality, they frequently overlap. Although lengthy, Geoghegan J.'s consideration of this is worthy of reproduction here:

"There appears to have been a great deal of argument and submission in the High Court to the effect that counsel for the purchaser had not made it clear whether at the end of the day he was relying on an alleged estoppel by representation or an alleged promissory or equitable estoppel. Even if there was some validity in that criticism it seems to me that it is irrelevant. The two forms of estoppel can frequently overlap, that is to say the common law estoppel by representation on the one hand and an equitable estoppel arising out of a promise on the other. It is clear from some of the modern English case law presented to the court and which I accept, that estoppel by representation need not necessarily be confined to a representation that a particular fact is true. It can be, what has been described as an estoppel by convention, that is to say, the parties agree between themselves artificially to act as though a particular fact was true. Put simply in this case there was a clear promise by the vendor to permit completion of the original contract but without prejudice to the original rescission if the purchaser defaulted. If the purchaser could demonstrate that she suffered detriment as a consequence she could in equity bind the vendor to that promise. The transfer of the monies and consequent liability for interest to the bank constituted such detriment. However, the other form of estoppel to which I referred would also have been operative in this case and would have had the same effect. That can be expressed as being an agreed understanding that provided the closing took place in accordance with the conditions as stipulated as to date and time, the contract would be taken as being alive and not rescinded. I do not think it matters which of these routes one follows. The trial judge herself at one point during the hearing suggested that the true nature of the representation which might give rise to the estoppel could be regarded as being that the agreement would be treated as not rescinded."

Geoghegan J. dealt with the claim that the purchaser ought not to be permitted to rely on the alleged estoppel because she was using it as a sword rather than a shield with equal clarity. In this respect he held that while the distinction between estoppel as a shield and estoppel as a sword may have some technical truth, "it is largely irrelevant as far as having any operative effect" because estoppel can be used as a reply to a defence and therefore ground a counterclaim in practical terms. As a result, this element of the vendor's argument was unsuccessful before the Supreme Court.

In his judgment, Finnegan J. concurred with Geoghegan J.'s conclusion that the purchaser ought to be granted specific performance of the contract, but in spite of the uniformity in result the form of the judgments stand in sharp contrast. While Finnegan J. engages in a very fact-based consideration of the case at hand, Geoghegan J. combines a fact-based consideration with a relatively substantial consideration of the law of estoppel in its practical operation in a laudable attempt to bring some calmness and clarity to this aspect of a complex and sometimes confused area of Irish law.

In *Price v Keenaghan Developments Ltd*, High Court, Clark J., May 1, 2007; [2007] I.E.H.C. 190, the plaintiffs sought specific performance of an alleged contract relating to the sale of land, and the respondents claimed not only that specific performance ought not to be awarded but that the proceedings should be struck out and the lis pendens vacated in order for the sale of the land to a third party to proceed. The facts of the case indicated that although there was no agreement for the plaintiffs to purchase the land in question, the parties had been in correspondence in relation to the land and there was an agreement to discuss potential changes to the planned layout of a house under construction with a view to the plaintiffs considering whether to purchase the property. This was not, however, a contract for sale. As Clark J. held, specific performance does not depend on a written contract but it does depend on a contract for the sale of land and where, as in this case:

> "… the parties are not yet *ad idem* on the essentials of a contract for the sale of land being the price, property parties and other particulars such as the closing date, then there is no concluded agreement and the doctrine of part performance is irrelevant".

As a result specific performance could not be granted on the facts of this case. That notwithstanding, the plaintiffs argued that the case ought not to be struck out and, consequently, that the *lis pendens* ought not to be vacated because specific performance is a recognised remedy and therefore the court's limited jurisdiction to strike out proceedings under Ord.19 r.28 of the Rules of the Superior Court could not be exercised. Clark J., however, reviewed authorities on this power, including in particular the case of *Barry v Buckley* [1981] I.R. 306, in reaching her conclusion that:

> "[W]here as in this case, an examination of the facts contained in the affidavits reveals that the plaintiffs has [sic] no chance of success although the pleadings advance a known and recognised remedy, the court should grasp the nettle and strike down such unmeritorious proceedings".

In this case, as in most contract-related cases, time was of the essence in order to ensure that the subject-matter of the disputed or alleged contract could be made the subject of another contract. As a result of the urgency of the matter and the unlikelihood of success given the absence of a concluded contract, the proceedings were struck out and the lis pendens vacated.

FREEHOLD COVENANTS

The High Court considered the problematic matter of the enforceability of positive covenants between successors in title of the original parties in the case of *Cardiff Meats Ltd v McGrath*, High Court, Murphy J., June 26, 2007; [2007] I.E.H.C. 219. The plaintiffs in this case were lessees of the first defendant, and sought relief for an alleged breach of leasehold covenants to provide maintenance service on behalf of the defendant. The defendant, in turn, was the successor in title of the original purchaser of the demised property and claimed that the third parties (Ringmahon Ltd and Dunnes Stores) were in breach of a freehold covenant to provide maintenance in return for the payment of a service fee. This breach, it was claimed, caused the first defendant to be in breach of the leasehold covenant to the plaintiff and was, therefore, at the root of the proceedings. Ringmahon Ltd and Dunnes Stores Ltd were successors in title of parties to the original conveyance, whereby the positive covenant for provision of maintenance services had been created. They claimed that they were not bound by this covenant either in relation to the plaintiff or in relation to the first defendant. In relation to the plaintiff they claimed unenforceability for lack of privity of estate—an argument that was easily accepted by the court as there was no landlord and tenant relationship between the plaintiff and the third parties. In relation to the first named defendant, the third parties claimed that they were not liable because the burden of a positive covenant does not run with the land.

As Murphy J. noted in his judgment, the enforceability of positive covenants over freehold land has long been problematic in Irish law as a result of the well-established principle that contractual obligations are enforceable only between parties who have privity of contract. As a result, the general rule is that positive covenants do not run with the land. In a limited number of circumstances it is possible to enforce such a covenant against successors in title of the original parties and, in this case, McGrath claimed that the third parties ought to be bound by the covenant under the principle of benefit and burden as classically outlined in this context in the case of *Halsall v Brizell* [1957] 1 Ch. 169. While the court accepted that the principle of benefit and burden can be applied to enforce positive covenants against successors in title of the original parties, Murphy J. held that the principle did not make the covenant enforceable in this context because of the strictly reciprocal nature of the *Halsall* principle. As Murphy J. noted, it was common case that the third parties had not taken any benefit in the form of service charges since 2001–2002, and therefore could not be bound by the burden under *Halsall v Brizell*.

Murphy J. also considered whether the rule in *Tulk v Moxhay* (1848) 2 Ph 774 could be applied in this case to hold the third parties liable for the burden of the positive covenant and concluded that it could not as that rule is limited in its application to restrictive covenants. Having referred to the recent House of Lords decision in *Rhone v Stevens* [1994] 2 A.C. 310, in which the Law

Lords reaffirmed the conventional understandings of both *Halsall* and *Tulk*, Murphy J. concluded that:

> "... the courts would have to enforce a personal obligation against a person who has not covenanted in order to enforce a positive covenant, whereas the court will enforce a negative covenant on the basis that the land is subject to a restriction".

As a result the third parties were not liable for the maintenance obligation to either the first named defendant or to the plaintiff.

EASEMENTS

Dwyer Nolan Developments v Kingscroft Developments Ltd, High Court, Laffoy J., February 9, 2007; [2007] I.E.H.C. 24 concerned the means of calculating quantum of damages for unlawful interference with a right of way. The plaintiff in this case had previously established his entitlement to a right of way accessing lands retained by him when the servient tenement was conveyed to the defendant developers in 1995 (*Dwyer Nolan Developments v Kingscroft Developments Ltd* [1999] 1 I.L.R.M. 141). Although the servient tenement was serviced by numerous public roads, there was no hard-surface access road to the boundary of the retained land; therefore the land was accessible through the servient tenement only by foot or through the use of 4x4 vehicles. In other words, ordinary vehicular access was not possible. The defendant had applied to the local authority for planning permission to construct such a hard surface access way to the retained lands, but this permission was refused on the basis that there was no development plan for the lands to be accessed (which had been zoned for light industrial development but in relation to which no planning permission had been acquired) and the local authority was anxious not to allow the construction of a "road to nowhere". Although the defendant had proposed that both parties make dual applications—the plaintiff for planning permission over the retained lands and the defendant for the construction of the required road way—the plaintiff had not availed of this offer and no such planning permission had been sought or granted. The plaintiff now claimed substantial damages for the failure to construct a vehicular right of way, calculated on the basis of a diminution of value to the land retained.

Laffoy J. in the High Court accepted that damages were payable to the plaintiff but disputed the plaintiff's method of calculating quantum. In submissions the plaintiff had claimed that the court should take into account the value of the land with access for industrial development and the value of the land without such access by virtue of the failure to construct an appropriate hard-surfaced access road. The court, however, held that this calculation failed to take account of what Laffoy J. deemed a number of "imponderables" including whether, when applied for, planning permission would in fact be granted for such development. In her view:

> "[T]he proper approach to measuring the damages to which the plaintiff is entitled cannot countenance an assumption that, but for the defendant's unlawful activity, the retained lands would have a value which reflects the ability, *as opposed to the potential*, to develop them for light industrial purposes" [emphasis added].

In addition, Laffoy J. held that there is an obligation on the plaintiff to mitigate his loss, which the plaintiff in this case failed to fulfil by refusing to accede to the suggestion of dual planning applications by the parties. Although damages were payable, therefore, they were to be calculated by reference to the value of the plot as land that *might be* developed for light industrial purposes, as opposed to land that *would be* developed for light industrial purposes were it not for the defendant developer's unlawful activity.

GARNISHEE ORDERS

Gallagher & Co v McMahon, High Court, Peart J., June 27, 2007; [2007] I.E.H.C. 226 concerned orders of garnishee issued by different courts over the same amount where that amount was insufficient to satisfy both of the judgments to which the debtor was subject. The plaintiff in this case had obtained a judgment against McMahon in the High Court on February 7, 2005 for the sum of €107,075.95. In January of 2006 the Circuit Court had granted judgment against McMahon in favour of Dignam in the amount of €34,589 plus 8 per cent interest. Neither of these judgments had been satisfied in whole or in part by the time that Gallagher was awarded €40,000 damages in a settlement. Following that settlement, Dignam obtained a conditional order of garnishee over the general damages on May 15, 2007, which was made absolute on May 24 of that year. Gallagher obtained a conditional order of garnishee over the same sum in the High Court on May 21, which in turn was made absolute on May 24 *after* the Circuit Court had made its conditional order absolute. The case before the High Court concerned which of these orders for garnishee had priority. Gallagher claimed that as her judgment pre-dated that of Dignam, she had priority over the available monies and that her order for garnishee post-dated that of Dignam by virtue only of the dates for making applications in the respective courts. In addition, the plaintiff argued that the fact that her judgment was registered in the Judgments Office ought to ensure its priority.

Although the court acknowledged that, in hindsight, it would have been better to have made Dignam a notice party on the Gallagher application for an order of garnishee in the High Court, Peart J. could not accept that the fact that the plaintiff's judgment pre-dated that of Dignam, or the fact that it was registered in the Judgments Office, would give her order of garnishee priority. To reach such a conclusion would clearly have forced the court to hold that obtaining a judgment against a debtor created some kind of an interest in a fund that did not even exist at the time of the judgment. In Peart J.'s words:

> "[T]he judgment obtained earliest in time remains simply that—a judgment. It of itself creates no interest, equitable or otherwise, in any fund … or indeed any other asset of the judgment debtor until such time as steps are taken to enforce the judgment".

Thus, because Dignam was the first to obtain an order of garnishee over this particular fund, the first payment to be made from the fund was to be made to her.

JUDGMENT MORTGAGES

In *Dovebid Netherlands BV v William Phelan t/a The Phelan Partnership,* High Court, Dunne J., April 23, 2007; [2007] I.E.H.C. 131 the High Court had an opportunity to consider what is sometimes termed the "technical defence" to a judgment mortgage. This is the claim that where a judgment mortgage affidavit fails to contain all of the information required by s.6 of the Judgment Mortgage (Ireland) Act 1850, or contains a misdescription as to any matter prescribed by s.6, the affidavit and resulting judgment mortgage must fall. Section 6 requires the inclusion of various pieces of information, including the name and description of the parties and the parish of the lands in question, in the affidavit and it was at one time the case that any omission or misdescription, even if not prejudicial to the judgment debtor, would be fatal to the judgment mortgage. Although a number of cases had suggested that there were at least some instances in which the technical defence would not be fatal (*Irish Bank of Commerce v O'Hara,* unreported, High Court, Costello J., May 10, 1989; unreported, Supreme Court, April 7, 1992 and *Ulster Bank v Crawford,* unreported, High Court, Laffoy J., December 20, 1999) and there was some indication that failure to adhere strictly with s.6 would not generally invalidate a judgment mortgage, the question remains somewhat uncertain in Irish law (*AIB v Griffin* [1992] 2 I.R. 70). *Dovebid BV* concerned the failure to include "the County and Barony or the Town or County of a City and Parish or the Town and Parish" in which the lands at issue were situated and the "usual or last known place of abode" of the debtor in the judgment mortgage affidavit.

Rather than apply a strict technical defence to the judgment mortgage in question, Dunne J. held that the appropriate approach is "to consider what was the purpose of the requirement in the legislation as to the description of the property and the place of residence of the judgment debtor". It was her view that these particulars are required by s.6 in order to "adequately and clearly" identify the individual and the land in question and, where the individual and land in question are in fact adequately identified a technical omission or misdescription ought not to invalidate the judgment mortgage. Dunne J. therefore followed the approach adopted in the High Court and Supreme Court in *Irish Bank of Commerce v O'Hara* and in the High Court in *Ulster Bank v Crawford* in assessing whether the affidavit in question fulfils the intended objective of s.6, rather than requiring strict adherence to each of its terms. This "commonsense approach" has long been in operation in England and Wales (*Thorp v Brown* (1867) L.R. 2 H.L. 220) and has recently been advocated by various parties in this jurisdiction (see Law Reform Commission, *Consultation Paper on Judgment Mortgages* (LRC CP 30 – 2004); F. de Londras, "The Technical Defence to the Judgment Mortgage: Time to Say Goodbye?" (2008) 13 (1) C.P.L.J. 5). Such an approach allows for judgment mortgage affidavits to be invalidated where failure to comply fully with s.6 does result in prejudice of some kind or fails to identify the lands and parties adequately while also ensuring that technical but non-prejudicial mistakes in the affidavit are not allowed to cause undue detriment to a judgment creditor.

LANDLORD AND TENANT LAW

In *Moffat v Frisby,* High Court, Laffoy J., March 20, 2007; [2007] I.E.H.C. 140 the High Court considered the effect of a forfeiture notice on a landlord's ability to insist upon and enforce leasehold covenants. In this case, the defendant, who was successor in title to the original landlord, had been in negotiations with the tenant for over a year to appoint an arbitrator by agreement pursuant to a rent review clause in the lease. While these negotiations continued to be ongoing, the landlord had issued a forfeiture notice on the plaintiff tenant and initiated ejectment proceedings against him. Subsequent to the initiation of these proceedings, the landlord's agent wrote to the Society of Chartered Surveyors of Ireland to have an arbitrator appointed for the purpose of carrying out the rent review and an arbitrator was so appointed by the President of the Society some two months after the initiation of the ejectment proceedings. The plaintiff tenant had initiated proceedings for relief from forfeiture, and sought to enjoin the rent review process and have the appointment of an arbitrator set aside on the basis that the forfeiture notice and initiation of ejectment proceedings constituted an election by the landlord for a particular remedy and precluded the landlord from enforcing any entitlements under the lease.

Laffoy J. considered a number of authorities that were opened to her but all of which concerned the effect of a tenant's behaviour on the continuing existence of a lease. While these authorities all confirmed that a tenant can not "have it both ways" (i.e. seek to enjoy entitlements under a lease without fulfilling obligations), she concluded that the same was true of a landlord who elected for forfeiture. In her estimation, relying on Wylie's *Landlord and*

Tenant Law, 2nd edn (Dublin: Butterworths, 1998) "by electing for the remedy of forfeiture, the lessor thereafter deprives himself of remedies based on the continued existence of the lease or tenancy". Laffoy J. went on to state the effect of forfeiture proceedings in admirably concise terms:

> "In my view, the legal position is that when a lessor serves a forfeiture notice and seeks to enforce it by ejectment proceedings or, alternatively, by counterclaiming in the lessee's action seeking relief against forfeiture for a declaration that the lessee is not entitled to such relief, thereafter the lessor is not entitled to treat the terms of the lease as binding the lessee."

As a consequence the landlord's attempt to invoke and enforce the rent review provision in the lease after the issuance of ejectment proceedings was a nullity and, as a result, the arbitator's appointment was null and void.

Údarás na Gaeltachta v Uisce Glan Teoranta, High Court, O'Neill J., March 13, 2007; [2007] I.E.H.C. 95 concerned the extent of a tenant's obligation under a covenant to repair. In this case the defendant tenant was in the business of manufacturing aluminium sulphate (a.k.a. alum), which required the storage of large amounts of sulphuric acid on the premises. In 1993 extensive cracking appeared in the walls of the factory premises, and a portion of the yard which housed the sulphuric acid containers rose dramatically. The parties both engaged engineers and architects who came to different conclusions on the causes of this structural damage. In particular, the plaintiff landlord claimed that the damage arose from the leakage of sulphuric acid into the ground and the resulting formation of gypsum underground. The court, however, was satisfied that the storage facilities and mechanisms of using the sulphuric acid were such that the plaintiff's leakage theory had not been proven on the balance of probabilities. Rather O'Neill J. held that, on the balance on probabilities, there was some leakage of aluminium sulphate into the ground by gradual percolation through the tiled floor in the storage area which, he noted, had been in a bad state of repair since the time of the commencement of the lease and, in particular, had never been grouted. The plaintiff claimed that the defendant tenant was obliged to repair this floor in order to ensure that such percolation was not possible as a result of the covenant to repair contained in the lease itself. The court, however, reaffirmed the long-standing principle that a covenant to repair does not oblige a tenant to carry out any works to improve premises beyond their state of repair at the time that the property was demised to them (see *Lister v Lane and Nesham* [1893] 2 Q.B. 212; *Norah Whelan v Madigan* [1978] I.L.R.M. 136; *Sotheby v Grundy* [1947] 2 All E.R. 761). Consequently there had been no breach of covenant by the tenant. As damages for breach of a covenant to repair flow from the existence of such a breach, the plaintiff landlords were not entitled to any damages in this case.

In *Canty v Private Residential Tenancies Board*, High Court, Laffoy J.,

August 8, 2007; [2007] I.E.H.C. 243 the High Court considered the meaning of numerous provisions of the Residential Tenancies Act 2004 in the context of a complex set of proceedings between Canty, a tenant in a residential tenancy, and the PRTB, which had adjudicated a number of disputes between Canty and his landlord. The court was first required to consider its jurisdiction under s.123(3) of the Residential Tenancies Act 2004, which provides that parties whose disputes have been adjudicated by a Tenancy Tribunal can appeal to the High Court on a point of law. While Laffoy J. referred to the parties' arguments in this relation—and particularly the submissions by counsel for the respondent that s.123(3) appeals ought not to be a substitute for judicial review—and concluded that not all of the points disputed by the claimant could be heard in these proceedings, she did not outline her view of what constitutes a "point of law" under s.123(3). This is regrettable, but it seems possible to read into her treatment of this an assumption that s.123(3) does not allow the High Court to hear matters, such as allegations of bias, that ought to have been disputed by means of a judicial review procedure. Neither, it seems, is the s.123(3) procedure normally to be used to dispute a finding of fact. On this point, Laffoy J. held, referring by analogy to the case stated procedure and the decision of Kenny J. in *Mara (Inspector of Taxes) v Hummingbird Limited* [1982] 2 I.L.R.M. 421, that the High Court ought only to set aside findings of fact by a tribunal where there is no evidence whatever to support them.

Having considered the matter of jurisdiction, Laffoy J. proceeded to consider the procedure for termination of a tenancy agreement by virtue of non-payment of rent. In this respect the terms of the Residential Tenancies Act 2004 are quite clear. Pursuant to s.66 of the Act, the landlord must give the tenant written notice of the amount of rent that is in arrears and then wait for 14 days, during which time the tenant could make good these arrears. On the expiration of this period of time, a 28-day notice of termination is to be provided at the end of which the tenancy agreement can be terminated. Where, as in this case, the tenancy is a Pt 4 tenancy, then the provisions of s.34 must also be complied with. This requires that the tenant would be notified of the alleged breach and given an opportunity to remedy it "within a reasonable time". As s.57(b) of the Act expressly provides that the s.66 requirements are in addition to the requirements for termination stipulated in s.34 both processes must, it seems, be separately engaged in. As Laffoy J. rightly noted:

> "[T]he provisions of the Act of 2004 for the valid termination of a Part 4 tenancy for non-payment of rent are very technical and confusing. It is difficult to understand why, in relation to non-payment of rent, the notification required by para. (a) of ground 1 in s. 34 could not have been made co-terminous with the notification under s. 67(3). As it has not been, it seems to me that prudence dictates that a landlord invoking ground 1 should serve notice in the form required by para. (a) on the tenant allowing at least fourteen days for remedying the breach, that

is to say, discharging the outstanding rent, although, on the facts of a particular case, that period might not constitute a "reasonable time" within the meaning of para. (a)".

In this case the landlord had attempted to terminate the tenancy on two grounds, one being non-payment of rent and the other being that he intended to occupy the premises himself—a valid basis for termination of a Pt 4 tenancy. The tenancy agreement at issue in this case included within it a term that provided that, after November 1, 2005, the landlord could terminate the tenancy agreement by virtue of an intention to occupy the premises himself. In addition to that term, the landlord in fact issued the tenant with a termination notice pursuant to s. 34 Act—he did not merely attempt to terminate on the basis of the terms of the tenancy agreement himself. As a result, the claimant's argument that the inclusion of this term in the tenancy agreement constituted "contracting out of the Part 4 tenancy" as prohibited by s.54 of the Residential Tenancies Act 2004 was unsuccessful. In other words, a term of this nature does not constitute a breach of s.54 of the Act *provided* the normal processes for termination of a Pt 4 tenancy are properly complied with. In addition, Laffoy J. held that the mere service of multiple notices of termination of different grounds, all of which are permitted under the Act, does not call a landlord's bona fides into question.

The tenancy agreement in question in this case included a term allowing for an increase in rent should the tenancy extend beyond a certain date. The applicant claimed that such a rent increase could only be validly imposed if the provisions of s.22 of the Residential Tenancies Act 2004 were complied with. Under s.22(2) a new rate of rent can only be imposed if "at least 28 days before the date from which the new rent is to have effect, a notice in writing is served by the landlord on the tenant stating the amount of the new rent and the date from which it is to have effect". As the new rate of rent in this tenancy agreement was to be imposed on the occurrence of a particular event, Laffoy J. held that it was subject to s.22(b) and required the service of 28 days' written notice on a tenant.

Finally the court considered the meaning and effect of s.86(1)(c) of the Residential Tenancies Act 2004, which provides that, "pending the determination of a dispute that has been referred to the Board", the termination of a tenancy "may not be effected". The claimant argued that this meant that no notice of termination could be served on a tenant until a decision of the Board had become binding on the parties. While Laffoy J. held that "pending the determination of a dispute" should be construed to mean "until a decision of the Board has become binding on the parties", she did not accept that s.86(1)(c) precluded the mere service of a notice of termination by a landlord. Rather, she held, the purpose of s.86 was to maintain the status quo between the parties. The service of a notice of termination does not disturb this status quo and this provision ought to be literally interpreted. In Laffoy J.'s words:

"'[E]ffected' must be given its plain meaning, namely, that the termination of the tenancy was brought about, or accomplished, or consummated. That there is a distinction between the termination of a tenancy being effected and the service of a notice of termination is obvious as a matter of common sense: a notice of termination must specify the termination date, that is to say, the day on which the tenancy will terminate (s. 62(1)(f)), which is fixed by reference to the required notice period. The service of the notice does not effect termination; the expiry of the required notice period does".

While the court's failure to more clearly outline the nature of its jurisdiction under s.123(3) might be regretted, this case demonstrated the enormous complexity involved in the Residential Tenancies Act 2004 and, in her judgment, Laffoy J. both rightly points out some apparently unnecessarily convoluted elements of the termination processes outlined in the Act and indicates the need for the Act's provisions to be given a clear and workable meaning. This approach is entirely in line with the scheme of the Act itself, which was to introduce—to the extent possible—a comprehensible and usable piece of law that both landlords and tenants could generally comprehend and apply. In that respect, Laffoy J.'s approach to the multiple issues raised in the case is to be commended.

REGISTERED LAND

The Land Registration Rules 2007 (S.I. No. 568 of 2007) came into effect on September 1, 2007 and made a number of amendments to the Land Registration Rules 1972. By r.4 (2007) a new provision was substituted for r.44 of the 1972 Rules. Under r.4 (2007) the Property Registration Authority will enter a caution where qualified or possessory title is converted and it appears that there is a lien by means of deposit of title deeds affecting the land on first registration and no subsequent burden is registered. Rule 103 of the 1973 Rules is amended by r.5 (2007), which requires the concurrence of the Property Registration Authority for registration of the following:

(i)   A burden created under a statute or statutory power or under a power registered as a burden or under a trust for securing money registered as a burden;

(ii) A burden created by trustees in exercise of a power under a settlement under which a limited owner is registered;

(iii) Any burden specified in para.(h) or para.(i) of subsection (1) of s.69 of the Registration of Title Act 1964;

(iv) A lien registered as a burden pursuant to s.73 of the Registration of Deeds and Title Act 2006.

The Rules make it clear that any document issued as a certificate prior to September 1, 2007 retains its validity (r.6) and provides that from now on every entry made into a certificate following its first issue is to be authenticated by means of an affixed authentication seal (r.7, amending r.160 (1972)). Rule 164 of the 1972 Rules is replaced by a new r.164 (inserted by r.8 (2007)), which lays down the following procedure regarding orders for production of a certificate:

(1) An application to the Authority under s.105(2) of the Act for an order for the production of a certificate shall be in Form 94 and shall be signed by the applicant or his solicitor.

(2) On receipt of the application, the Authority shall send notice to the person against whom the order is sought, requiring him to state whether he has the custody of the certificate, and, if he has, whether he claims that the dealing for which production is required is one that cannot be registered without his consent and the grounds of his claim.

(3) Where the person having the custody of the certificate claims that the dealing cannot be registered without his consent, the Authority shall, subject to an appeal to the court, determine the question and, for that purpose, may appoint a day and time for the parties to attend before it.

(4) In default of a reply to the notice within the time specified therein, where it appears to the Authority from the statements in the application and the documents lodged for the purpose of the registration for which the certificate is required, that the dealing is one that can be effected without the consent of the person having the custody of the certificate, the Authority shall make the order sought.

A new r.169 is inserted by r.9 (2007) and provides that certificates which are defaced (including erasures), from which parts have been detached, or which were not made in the Registry and properly authenticated will be retained and cancelled. By the new r.170 (inserted by r.10 (2007)) the Authority can dispense with production of a certificate, following the publication (at the applicant's expense) of a suitable notice in local papers and the making of suitable enquiries. Applications to make an entry on the register by persons who have entered into a contract to purchase, lease, or lend money on the security of registered land may be made under s.108 of the Registration of Title Act by the use of the Form 104 (new r.191, as inserted by r.11 (2007)). Where such a priority entry has been made, an application to register the instrument that completes the purchase will take priority under s.108(2) of the Registration of Title Act 1964 provided it is made in compliance with the

Rules (new r.192(1) as inserted by r.12, 2007). If another person makes an application for registration between the priority entry and the registration of the instrument perfecting the purchase, this application for registration will rank after the application of the individual holding the priority entry for the purposes of priority of registration (new r.192(2) as inserted by r.12, 2007). Entries in the register pursuant to s.108 of the Registration of Title Act 1964 are now to be done by using Form 106 (new r.193, as inserted by r.13 (2007)). Where there are two or more priority entries then priority as between them shall be determined by reference to the order in which the applications were received (new r.194, as inserted by r.14 (2007)).

The remainder of the Land Registration Rules 2007 outlines the new Forms and formulae for use under the amended Rules.

Law Reform

In 2007 the Law Reform Commission published two Reports and five Consultation Papers, as well as its Third Programme of Law Reform.

The Commission published a *Consultation Paper on Aspects of Intercountry Adoption* (LRC CP43–2007) and a *Report—Aspects of Intercountry Adoption* (LRC 89 – 2008). We will examine this report in detail in the Annual Review of Irish Law 2008. In the area of criminal law, the Commission published a Consultation Paper on Involuntary Manslaughter (LRC CP44–2007). It held a seminar on the subject in November 2007 and, in January 2008, it published its *Report on Homicide: Murder and Involuntary Manslaughter* (LRC 87–2008), containing its final recommendation on involuntary manslaughter as well as murder (on which latter subject it had in 2001 published provisional recommendations). We will examine the Report in detail in the 2008 Review.

In its *Consultation Paper on Civil Liability of Good Samaritans and Volunteers* (CP47 – 2007), the Law Reform Commission recommends against the imposition of a legal duty to rescue and in favour of immunising good Samaritans and other volunteers from a duty of care in negligence, their liability being limited to cases where they cause injury through their gross negligence. The proposals may come as little surprise, against the background of the Commission's own proposals, 15 years ago, in relation to occupiers' liability and the Supreme Court's radical curtailment of the duty of care in negligence in *Glencar Exploration plc v Mayo County Council* [2002] 1 I.R. 84. Nevertheless, it may be suggested that the normative and policy questions deserve a greater and deeper public debate than they have yet received in Ireland.

Let us consider first the question whether citizens in general, or any particular group of citizens, should be under a duty to intervene for the purpose of assisting someone who has been injured or "who is at risk of such an injury" (para.2.52). The Commission provisionally recommends they should not: It identifies two primary arguments against change. The first is, curiously, based on the principle of altruism:

> "The rationale behind this argument is that the duty to intervene is morally motivated. Thus, it has been asserted that it is inappropriate to set a legal sanction to enforce a moral obligation. Since altruism entails voluntary action in favour of another, it is argued that to transform the

duty of rescue into a legal obligation would deprive it of its altruistic quality [para.2.38]".

The idea that altruism would be damaged by a legal requirement to engage in a minimum degree of altruistic conduct is not self-evidently in harmony with generations of legal experience. Much of family law is designed to encourage altruistic conduct and is backed by legal sanction.

The second argument, based on personal liberty, is that to impose a duty to rescue would be inconsistent with the individualistic spirit of the common law:

> "The common law endeavours to protect the personal liberty of each individual as far as possible and only those restrictions which are necessary to enable peaceful co-existence are permitted. In other words, [the] common law encourages the individual to pursue his or her desires, without requiring him or her to benefit another [para.2.39]."

The only argument adumbrated by the Commission in favour of a change in the law is that advocated by Weinrib, who proposes imposing a positive duty to conduct the rescue of a stranger where this would not unduly inconvenience the rescuer: "The Case for a Duty to Rescue" 90 Yale L. J. 247 (1980). The Commission considers, however, that such a duty to intervene would be of an uncertain nature and that its limited scope would be unlikely to benefit the person at risk to any great extent.

The Commission concludes that the arguments in favour of the status quo are stronger and that the existing relation to professional rescuers, road traffic accidents and employers' duties for the safety of their employees and the public, "are best left to the individual development by the Oireachtas, taking into account the specific settings in which they arise [para.2.51]."

One suspects that the arguments run a little deeper. The truth of the matter is that, while there is no general obligation to assist others, the common law of negligence has developed over the past half century so as to recognise a wide range of relationships that impose affirmative obligations. Apart altogether from the obligations imposed by health and safety legislation over the past couple of decades, employers are under a common law duty to go to the assistance of employees who become ill at work. Parents are not free to ignore the need of their children for help. Occupiers of premises, even before the Occupiers' Liability Act 1995, which imposes an affirmative duty in respect of visitors, were obliged to take steps to assist invitees who had been injured on their property. Carriers are under a similar duty: it is surely inconceivable that an Irish court today, even post-*Glencar*, would follow the Ontario decision in *Van Valkenburg v Northern Navigation Co* 30 Ont. L.R. 142 (1913) in preference to the later decision of the Supreme Court of Canada in *Horsley v Maclaren* [1972] S.C.R. 441.

In deciding whether to impose a duty of care in negligence, following *Donoghue v Stevenson* [1932] A.C. 562, all depends on whether there is sufficient proximity of relationship between the parties and, since *Glencar*, whether it would be just and reasonable to do so. There can be no prior certainty that such a duty will be imposed in a case where the defendant has caused injury to another; conversely, there can be no prior certainty that such a duty will *not* be imposed where the defendant's failure to act has led to the enhancement of injury or to the death of another where intervention would have been perfectly possible and safe to the defendants.

It would be mistaken to read *Donoghue v Stevenson* as biblical authority against the imposition of a duty to intervene. Lord Atkin invoked the parable of the Good Samaritan, not to repudiate its value of human solidarity, but rather to identify it as a core value underlying the duty of care in negligence. He acknowledged that the law's scope of application necessarily would be less than universal but his aim was to encourage courts to recognise the interconnectedness of social life.

The second crucial issue addressed in the Consultation Paper relates to whether a duty of care should be imposed on those who intervene to assist others who have been injured or are at risk of injury. Courts in several common law jurisdictions where this issue has arisen have imposed such a duty taking into account, of course, the emergency character of the situation. Thus, if a rescuer so negligently conducts the rescue attempt as foreseeably to induce a further rescue attempt in which the second rescuer is injured or dies, the first, negligent, rescuer will have to compensate for that wrong: *Horsley v Maclaren* [1972] S.C.R. 441. There does not appear to have been any recorded case at common law where the injured party whose peril induced the intervention has successfully sued the intervenor in negligence.

After *Glencar*, a court, faced with such a claim, might come to the conclusion that it would not be "just and reasonable" to impose a duty of care, on the basis that altruistic interventions should not be discouraged by the fear of litigation. The complete dearth of any successful claim throughout the common law world suggests that such a fear is misplaced.

The Commission provisionally recommends that legislation should provide that no duty of care be imposed but rather that there be a gross negligence threshold in respect of the activities of Good Samaritans, voluntary rescuers and voluntary service-providers. It considers (para.4.53) that this "has the dual benefit of mitigating the potential deterrent effect of imposing liability, while not unduly prejudicing the plaintiff by denying him or her the right to seek redress".

The Commission's Report, *Spent Convictions* (LRC 84 – 2007) recommends the introduction of a limited spent convictions scheme for adult offenders. A similar scheme is already in place for those who offend when under the age of 18: Children Act 2001, s.258. The mode proposed by the Commission is of a hybrid character, which specifically excludes certain offences from its application and applies a sentencing threshold. Excluded are all offences which must be tried in the Central Criminal Court and all sexual offences, as well as convictions which result in a sentence of imprisonment of greater than six months. A conviction-free period of seven years would apply in the case of all sentences of imprisonment of six months or less and a period of five years for all offences attracting a non-custodial sentence.

The Commission goes on to recommend that its proposed spent conviction scheme should not apply in the context of sentencing or in the context of certain civil proceedings relating to the welfare or guardianship of children. It proposes that s.258 of the Children Act 2001 be amended to bring it in line with these recommendations.

The most pressing concern about spent conviction regimes, of course, is that a paedophile or other sexual offender could be enabled to engage in abusive conduct shielded by the law. The exclusion of sexual offences from the proposed scheme goes some way towards allaying this concern. The Commission also recommends that certain jobs, professions and posts should be exempted from the scheme (again proposing a similar modification in relation to s.258).

In several jurisdictions, including Canada, Australia and New Zealand, human rights legislation prohibits discrimination on the basis of prior criminal conviction. The Commission prefers not to make any recommendations on the amendment of equality legislation to include this ground. It explains this choice as follows:

> "The Commission recognises the close connection between the issue of discrimination and spent convictions but the Commission also recognises that the issue of discrimination in terms of an old criminal conviction encompasses a great deal more than discrimination in the context of employment. For a thorough examination of the issue of discrimination in terms of old criminal convictions to take place, there would need to be an analysis of the impact of a criminal conviction on access to services, accommodation, employment, insurance and many other aspects of modern living. While the Commission has touched on the issue of criminal convictions and access to employment in the context of the spent convictions debate, the Commission considers that the issue of discrimination on the basis of an old criminal conviction is separate and distinct from the issue of whether a spent convictions regime should exist for adult offenders in this jurisdiction. The Commission has concluded that the issue of discrimination and, in particular, the amendment of equality legislation to insert a new ground of discrimination, namely, criminal conviction, is one which warrants separate analysis which is inappropriate in the context of this Report. The Commission therefore makes no recommendation

on the amendment of equality legislation to include previous criminal conviction as a prohibited ground of discrimination [para.3.10]."

It is unfortunate that the Commission should not have addressed this issue, for several reasons. It surely fell within the scope of the subject under review. Moreover, it forms an important element in the repertoire of legal strategies to deal justly and humanely with the social integration and economic welfare of those who have been convicted of a criminal offence. It is a far more sophisticated and context-sensitive approach than that of the spent conviction strategy of treating a person convicted of an offence as not having been so convicted. The latter approach involves, if not a "statutory lie", a certain economy with the truth which is at odds with the present era of freedom of information. Of course the right to privacy must also be taken into account. Such a right is not easy to invoke against the public dimension of criminal prosecutions, trials and convictions. A conviction of a criminal offence is a societal response to criminal conduct: for the identity of the offender not to have a public dimension (save in exceptional cases, involving certain sexual offences, for example), the rationale of the criminal justice system would be controverted. There is an argument that, after a reasonably long period of time, a person's right to privacy may be considered to outweigh the entitlement of others to publish the fact of his or her earlier criminal indiscretion; but the very fact that such a time period has to elapse means that the serious social problems facing former prisoners immediately on release from prison cannot be addressed effectively by a spent conviction regime, as the Commission itself acknowledges.

In its Report, *The Law of Landlord and Tenant* (LRC 85 – 2007), the Commission proposes very wide-ranging reform of the law on this subject, backed by a draft Bill which repeals and replaces numerous pre-1922 statutes, including Deasy's Act (the Landlord and Tenant Law Amendment Act Ireland 1860), and restates, with some reforms, the current legislative scheme for business tenancies contained in the Landlord and Tenant (Amendment) Acts 1980, 1984, 1989 and 1994. It does not, however, seek to trespass on the remit of the Residential Tenancies Act 2004. Nor does it deal specifically with agricultural tenancies as a discrete subject, on the basis that their contemporary rarity would not justify such separate treatment. It also avoids the area of ground rents legislation in view of pending litigation in the Supreme Court involving a challenge to its constitutional validity.

In its Consultation Paper, *Consolidation and Reform of the Courts Act* (LRC CP46 – 2007), the Law Reform Commission provisionally recommends the enactment of a consolidated Courts Act with a thematic structure, each Part of the legislation dealing with a particular aspect of the jurisdiction of the courts with each court being separately provided for, where applicable, in a division of the Part. The purpose of such an Act, in its view, is to provide for the allocation of exercise of the judicial power of the State, the administration of justice, the constitution and jurisdiction of the courts, the allocation of jurisdiction between the courts and the management of the courts and judges and officers of the courts.

The structure of the legislation provisionally proposed by the Commission is as follows:

Part 1:   Preliminary and General
Part 2:   Constitution of Courts
Part 3:   Jurisdiction of the Courts
Part 4:   Circuits and Districts (as the jurisdiction of the Circuit and High Court are limited by geographical areas)
Part 5:   Appeals
Part 6:   Judicial Posts
Part 7:   Officers of the Court
Part 8:   Administration of the Courts
Part 9:   Procedure
Part 10:   Savers and Miscellaneous.

The special part of the Act devoted to judges would have provision dealing with precedence between judges, the qualifications of judges of each of the courts, the retirement age, the mode of address of judges, the appointment of temporary judges and the tenure of office of judges. The Commission considers that the issue of the remuneration of judges should not be dealt with in the legislation. It takes the same view regarding the provisions relating to the Judicial Appointments Advisory Board.

The Commission acknowledges that a Courts Act has to have some provisions relating to procedure, but it considers that in order to keep the legislation within manageable bounds, "only matters of the utmost necessity" relating to procedure should be included: para.4.77. The Commission does not consider that the principal provisions of the Courts Service Act 1998 are sufficiently related to the jurisdiction of the courts to merit inclusion in the Courts Act.

In the context of substantive reforms, the Commission provisionally recommends that s.52(2) of the Courts (Supplemental Provisions) Act 1961 be amended to provide for an automatic right of appeal from the High Court to the Supreme Court in cases where the High Court has made a determination on a question of law referred to it from the District Court in the form of a consultative case stated. The Commission also recommends the amendment of the present position whereby a District Court judge may state a consultative case without a prior request from one of the parties to the proceedings, so as to confer a similar power on the judges of the Circuit and High Courts.

The Commission considers that the consultative case stated procedure "is hugely advantageous in providing a mechanism whereby a lower court can obtain an opinion from a higher court" at an interlocutory stage: para.3.57. It does not regard the form of appeal by way of case stated as serving a continuing comparable function and provisionally recommends its repeal.

Legislation

BRIAN HUNT, Mason Hayes+Curran

Table of Acts enacted during 2007

Number	Title	Commencement
1	Health (Nursing Homes) (Amendment) Act 2007	February 19, 2007
2	Citizens Information Act 2007	February 21, 2007; March 30, 2007
3	Health Insurance (Amendment) Act 2007	February 22, 2007
4	Courts and Court Officers (Amendment) Act 2007	March 5, 2007
5	Electricity Regulation (Amendment) (Single Electricity Market) Act 2007	June 18, 2007; November 1, 2007
6	Criminal Law (Sexual Offences) (Amendment) Act 2007	March 7, 2007
7	National Oil Reserves Agency Act 2007	April 16. 2007
8	Social Welfare and Pensions Act 2007	March 30, 2007 and other dates
9	Education (Miscellaneous Provisions) Act 2007	March 21, 2007
10	Prisons Act 2007	May 1, 2007; October 1, 2007
11	Finance Act 2007	April 2, 2007
12	Carbon Fund Act 2007	April 7, 2007
13	Asset Covered Securities (Amendment) Act 2007	April 9, 2007
14	Electoral (Amendment) Act 2007	April 10, 2007
15	Broadcasting (Amendment) Act 2007	April 18, 2007

Number	Title	Commencement
16	National Development Finance Agency (Amendment) Act 2007	April 10, 2007
17	Foyle and Carlingford Fisheries Act 2007	April 10, 2007
18	European Communities Act 2007	April 21, 2007
19	Consumer Protection Act 2007	May 1, 2007
20	Pharmacy Act 2007	April 21, 2007
21	Building Control Act 2007	April 21, 2007
22	Communications Regulation (Amendment) Act 2007	May 15, 2007; July 1, 2007
23	Health Act 2007	March 15, 2007; June 6, 2007; November 5, 2007
24	Defence (Amendment) Act 2007	May 7, 2007; September 24, 2007
25	Medical Practitioners Act 2007	May 7, 2007
26	Child Care (Amendment) Act 2007	May 8, 2007
27	Protection of Employment (Exceptional Collective Redundancies and Related Matters) Act 2007	May 8, 2007
28	Statute Law Revision Act 2007	May 8, 2007
29	Criminal Justice Act 2007	May 9, 2007; May 18, 2007; July 1, 2007;
30	Water Services Act 2007	December 31, 2007
31	Finance (No.2) Act 2007	July 9, 2007
32	Community, Rural and Gaeltacht Affairs (Miscellaneous Provisions) Act 2007	July 9, 2007
33	Ministers and Secretaries (Ministers of State) Act 2007	July 9, 2007
34	Roads Act 2007	July 11, 2007
35	Personal Injuries Assessment Board (Amendment) Act 2007	July 11, 2007

Number	Title	Commencement
36	Criminal Procedure (Amendment) Act 2007	October 25, 2007
37	Markets in Financial Instruments and Miscellaneous Provisions Act 2007	November 1, 2007; January 1, 2007; February 1, 2008
38	Local Government (Roads Functions) Act 2007	November 26, 2007
39	Copyright and Related Rights (Amendment) Act 2007	December 4, 2007
40	Social Welfare Act 2007	December 20, 2007
41	Appropriation Act 2007	December 21, 2007
42	Health (Miscellaneous Provisions) Act 2007	December 21, 2007

FEATURES OF INTEREST IN 2007 ACTS

Speed of enactment The Health Insurance (Amendment) Bill 2007 was noteworthy for a number of reasons. The Bill was drafted in secret, and was enacted within hours of its publication on February 21, 2007.

The Bill was aimed at ensuring that new entrants to the health insurance market could not avoid paying risk equalisation. When the joint issues of new entrants into the health insurance market and risk equalisation were raised in the Dáil in the days prior to the Bill's publication, at no stage did the Taoiseach indicate that the Bill was forthcoming—this is despite the fact that the Bill clearly was in the course of being drafted at that time.

On February 21 the business of the Dáil was interrupted at approximately 7.30 p.m. for the purpose of amending the Order of Business and the Bill was introduced at 10 p.m. and passed all stages in the Dáil at approximately 11 p.m. that evening. The Bill was then introduced into the Seanad at 11.15 p.m., shortly after which it passed all stages.

Consequences of inaccessible legislation The Community, Rural and Gaeltacht Affairs (Miscellaneous Provisions) Act 2007 is most unusual in that the Act was described as being required "to secure a more coherent statutory mandate for functions previously transferred to the Minister by way of statutory instrument and transfer of functions orders …" (637 *Dáil Debates* Col.1245). This would seem to suggest that the glut of statutory instruments concerning the Minister's remit has given rise to confusion, or at the very least, uncertainty, as to the Minister's responsibilities and remit. For that reason, the Act and the reasons behind its introduction do seem to represent, to some degree, an indictment of the state of the Irish Statute Book.

Non-textual amendments   As a result of the better regulation agenda, it is widely recognised that non-textual amendments exacerbate the already inaccessible nature of our statute book. Non-textual amendments are effectively prohibited by the *Drafting Manual to* which parliamentary counsel must adhere. It is of some surprise then to see that section 5 of the Defence (Amendment) Act 2007 directs that "[e]very reference in the Defence Acts 1954 to 2007 or in any instrument made under those Acts to a judge-advocate shall be read as a reference to a military judge". There is no reason, particularly with the aid of an electronic statute book with a search facility, why each of the references in question could not have been identified in a table or schedule in the 2007 Act and a series of textual amendments effected in each instance.

Offences in Regulations   Section 14 of the Communications Regulation (Amendment) Act 2007 contains an interesting provision which inserts a new section 46A into the Communications Regulation Act 2002. The new s.46A provides that if existing, specified regulations give effect to the EC treaties or instruments provide for a summary offence, the Minister may amend those regulations so as to allow for the offences to be triable on indictment. This provision is additional to the terms of the European Communities Act 1972 and the European Communities Act 2007.

Amendment of Bills   On occasion, Ministers initiate Bills in the Houses with the intent of extensively amending the Bill at committee or Report Stage in either House. For example, the Immigration, Residence and Protection Bill 2008 was subjected to 271 Ministerial amendments at Committee Stage in the Dáil. A further example relates to the Criminal Justice Bill which was initiated as a 38-section Bill in 2004. It was the subject of 187 Ministerial amendments at Committee Stage in the Dáil and was enacted in 2006 as a 197-section Act.

The correct approach appears to have been adopted in relation to the Prisons Bill 2005 (containing 13 sections) which the Minister subsequently withdrew and re-published as the Prisons Bill 2006 (containing 42 sections) and which was enacted as the Prisons Act 2007.

Henry VIII   Section 9 of the Carbon Fund Act 2007 is an example of a Henry VIII provision. It empowers the Minister to revoke by order some of the functions conferred on a body under the Act in question. Henry VIII provisions are constitutionally dubious.

Unusual commencement Section 2 of the Foyle and Carlingford Fisheries Act 2007 contains a somewhat unusual commencement provision in that it allows for the commencement of aspects of the Act by reference to specific geographical areas.

Constitutional saving Section 65 of the Pharmacy Act 2007 is clearly a constitutional savings provision relating to property rights. However, it is unusual in the sense that it does not overtly characterised as being a constitutional savings provision.

Drafting errors Section 3 of the Social Welfare and Pensions Act 2007 corrected a drafting error in s.2(1) of the Social Welfare (Consolidation) Act 2005.

The marginal note which accompanies s.1 of the Markets in Financial Instruments and Miscellaneous Provisions Act 2007 contains a drafting error in that the marginal note provides: "Short title and collective citation" when in fact no collective citation is provided in s.1.

STATUTE LAW REVISION

Statute Law Revision Act 2007 The Statute Law Revision Act 2007 is of considerable historical significance in that it effects the repeal of 3,226 Acts and provides, for the first time, a definitive list of 1,364 pre-1922 Acts which continue in force. In effecting the repeal of more Acts than have been enacted in the State since 1922, the Act is the largest single repealing statute in the history of the State.

It can now definitively be said that the Irish Statute Book now consists of 4,584 Acts (1,364 pre-1922 Acts and 3,220 post-1922 Acts (as of end of July 2008)). In addition to this, there are approximately 26,000 statutory instruments which also form part of the Irish Statute Book.

Minister of State Kitt explained that part of the research process which gave rise to the Bill involved the compilation of a detailed database recording the status of more than 26,000 public general statutes. The research team then deduced that more than 4,500 of those statutes were found to either be in force or likely to be in force.

Those 4,500 statutes were then assessed in greater detail to determine which of them had any modern relevance. There then followed detailed rounds of consultation amongst Government departments but also involving the wider public, in response to which over 150 submissions were received.

The Bill, initiated in the Seanad, was positively received in both Houses. The Bill was appreciated as conveying a very good sense of the social and other concerns of a different era. Deputies and Senators availed of the opportunity to recount the subject–matter and detail of some of the Acts involved.

Subject-matter of Acts repealed   Senator Mary O'Rourke observed that:

> "There appear to be many laws from the 13th and 14th centuries which blatantly discriminate against the native Irish and which try to make illegal the Irish language, Irish law and Irish traditions… We think of the Penal Laws and other laws that had very sad consequences for the Irish people. … One 11th century statute provides for 'Frenchmen to pay scot and lot' which was a discriminatory tax applicable only to the French" (185 *Seanad Debates* Cols 1937–1938).

Senator O'Rourke also pointed out that the Assise of Arms Act 1811 forbade Jewish people from owning armour. She also spoke of a 1733 Act whose purpose was to provide for repairing the road leading from Kinnegad to Athlone in the County of Westmeath. She indicated that the Act was required because the road in question had grown "so ruinous and bad that in the winter-season so many parts thereof are impassable to carriages and dangerous to travelers" (185 *Seanad Debates* Col. 1939).

Senator Mary Henry noted that the object of one Act dating from 1154 was to ensure that the sons of "villeins" would not be ordained and she noted that an Act of 1166 directed that vagabonds and strangers were prohibited from staying more than one night in a house unless they became ill or their horse died. Senator Henry observed that many of the Acts in question dealt with the issue of marriage, both in terms of specific marriages but also the issue of marriage generally, such as the recognition of foreign marriages, Odessa marriages and Greek marriages. She also noted that in 1851 an Act was passed to provide for the removal of lunatics from India.

Senator Ryan said that his first impression of the range of legislation being repealed was that much of it related to the consumption of alcohol. He indicated that in the titles of the Acts, he had found references to "beerhouses, spirits, drunkards or inebriates" (185 *Seanad Debates* Col. 1948).

At Committee Stage in the Seanad, Senator Brian Hayes drew the House's attention to the proposal to repeal the Irish Free State Constitution. Minister of State Kitt indicated that the 1922 Constitution is "obsolete following the enactment of the 1937 Constitution" (186 *Seanad Debates* Col. 182).

At both Committee Stage Report and Final Stage in the Dáil, a number of Acts were added to Schs 1 and 2. One such Act added to Sch.2 at Report and Final Stage in the Dáil, for repeal, was Poynings Act 1495. That Act provided that all pre-1495 English statute law applied in Ireland.

Subject-matter of Acts retained   Senator Mary O'Rourke pointed out that the Meath and Counties of Westmeath Act 1543, which is being retained, provided for the division of Meath into two counties. Senator David Norris expressed satisfaction that the Act now entitled St Patrick's Cathedral Act 1474 has been retained as well as the Marsh's Library Act 1707 (185 *Seanad Debates* Col. 1945). He also noted the fact that the Whiteboy Act was being retained, as was the General Post Office Dublin Act and the Dublin Science and Art Museum Act 1884.

Senator Martin Mansergh made known his disappointment at the proposed retention of the Whiteboy Act and he felt that "[i]t is somewhat of a stain on our Statute Book that such legislation should be retained a moment longer than necessary" (185 *Seanad Debates* Col. 1946). By way of response to this, Minister of State Kitt indicated that this Act "may still be relevant to the laws on riots and tumultuous risings" (185 *Seanad Debates* Col. 1951). At Committee Stage in the Seanad, Senator Mansergh returned to the issue. He pointed out that the "Whiteboys were the first evidence of rural resistance to aspects of an entirely unjust system of land tenure, and they were, to a degree, the precursors to the United Irishmen …" (186 *Seanad Debates* Col. 198). He said that he found it "hard to believe we cannot rely on our own legislation to deal with various forms of street disorder" (186 *Seanad Debates* Col. 199).

Senator Lydon was surprised at the proposed retention of the Fairs Act 1204, and he questioned the wisdom of retention of this Act given that its subject-matter was, he said, "the erection of castle and fortifications at Dublin and the establishment of fairs at Donnybrook, Waterford and Limerick" (185 *Seanad Debates* Col. 1947). He was also critical of the retention of the Sheriffs Act 1293 and the Courts Act 1476 which he said provides that "the Lords must wear their robes in Parliament" (185 *Seanad Debates* Col. 1947), as were Senator Ryan (185 *Seanad Debates* Col. 1948) and Deputy Dan Boyle (632 *Dáil Debates* Col. 1198). Senator Lydon questioned what relevance the Marriage (No. 2) Act 1537 could have to the Ireland of today, as that Act he said "concerned the succession between the King and Queen Jane" (185 *Seanad Debates* Col. 1947). He also described the need to retain the Courts Act 1476, which "provides a statutory basis for the wearing of gowns by the Judiciary" as being "absurd" (186 *Seanad Debates* Col. 200).

Senator Paschal Mooney expressed his pleasure at the proposed retention of the Irish Musical Fund Act 1794 as the fund was believed to have been functioning as recently as 1927. The fund was apparently established to support "infirm musicians".

Deputy Dan Boyle questioned the need for the retention of the Parliamentary Privilege Act 1471 which concerns the freedom from arrests of Members of the House of Lords (632 *Dáil Debates* Col. 1198).

Accessibility of pre-1922 legislation   In the Dáil, a number of Deputies remarked about the fact that pre-1922 legislation was not accessible either electronically or in print. On this point, Deputy Emmett Stagg stated:

"[T]he ancient Roman emperor and tyrant Caligula had his laws written in small script and then posted in the Forum upon high pillars 'the better to ensnare the populace'. We go one better than Caligula. We do not bother to post our laws at all" (632 *Dáil Debates* Col. 1193).

Deputy Stagg then went on to recount in detail the practical difficulties which can be faced by a person seeking to obtain a paper copy of a piece of pre-1922 legislation (632 *Dáil Debates* Col. 1194).

Deputy Stagg urged the Attorney-General and his officials to:

"... commit themselves in future, whenever a new Bill involves amendments to legislation that is out of print, to restating in full the law as amended rather than just setting out the amendments" (632 *Dáil Debates* Col. 1195).

Future plans for statute law revision The Office of the Attorney-General has now embarked on a second phase of work which involves the examination of 33,000 local and personal Acts and private Acts, Charters and Letters Patent and Statutory Rules and Orders with the intention of bringing forward a further statute law revision Bill in 2010.

Senator Brian Hayes expressed his support for Minister of State Kitt's plans to commence a review of post-1922 legislation (185 *Seanad Debates* Col. 1936). Senator David Norris also supported the idea of examining post-1922 Acts and statutory instruments (185 *Seanad Debates* Col. 1943). In response, Minister of State Kitt stated that the Office of the Attorney-General has prepared a database of post-Independence legislation and "it is hoped to commence preparation of a new Bill dealing with that in the coming months" (185 *Seanad Debates* Col. 1951).

The Statute Law Revision project in the Office of the Attorney-General has done much to enlighten us as to which pre-1922 Acts remain in place. The historical and social value of an initiative such as this must be recognised. However, in circumstances where the post-1922 statute book is widely accepted to be in a state of considerable disarray, it is difficult to comprehend or justify the current focus of the Office of the Attorney-General's next phase of statute law revision on local, personal and private Acts, which by their very nature are extremely limited in their effect and whose continuance causes little or no difficulties for day-to-day users of the post-1922 statute book.

EUROPEAN COMMUNITIES ACT 2007

The purpose behind the European Communities Act 2007, which effected a number of amendments to the European Communities Act 1972, seems to have been to address the issues which arose following two Supreme Court decisions in *Browne v Att-Gen* [2003] 3 I.R. 305 and *Kennedy v Att-Gen* [2005] 2 I.L.R.M. 401. For an in-depth analysis of the impact of these decisions, see Fahey, "Browne v Attorney General and Kennedy v Attorney General: The Current State of the Ultra Vires Doctrine and the Necessitated Clause" 2005 23 I.L.T. 258.

Section 2(a) of the 2007 Act inserted a new s.3(3) into the 1972 Act. Section 3(3) of the European Communities Act 1972 previously provided: "Regulations under this section shall not create an indictable offence." The newly inserted subs.(3) enables a Minister who is making regulations under s.3(1) of the European Communities Act 1972 to create indictable offences where, in the opinion of the Minister, such an offence is necessary to give effect to the treaties or an instrument of the European institutions. Secondly, it enables a Minister who is making regulations under s.3(1) of the European Communities Act 1972 to provide for a fine of up to €500,000 and a term of imprisonment of up to three years for the purpose of ensuring that the penalties are effective, proportionate, have a deterrent effect and bear some relation to the acts or omissions in question.

Section 3 of the 2007 Act requires that statutory instruments made under s.3(3) of the 1972 Act must be laid before the Houses of the Oireachtas. Section 4(1) of the 2007 Act provides that an existing regulation-making power in any Act may be used to give effect to an EU measure if that EU measure relates in full to the subject-matter to which the existing regulation-making power relates. Section 4(2) of the 2007 Act provides that regulations made under subs.(1) may perhaps go beyond the scope envisaged by the pre-existing regulation-making powers in that they may cover incidental, supplementary and consequential matters. Significantly, it also seems to permit the amendment of primary legislation by secondary legislation.

Section 5(1) purports to confer retrospective validity on an unknown number of statutory instruments which would otherwise fall foul of the decisions of the Supreme Court in *Browne* and also *Kennedy*. It does so by stating that such statutory instruments should be regarded as if they were Acts of the Oireachtas.

STATUTE LAW RESTATEMENTS

Following its conferral with responsibility for the Statute Law Restatements in 2006, the Law Reform Commission published a *Consultation Paper on Statute Law Restatement* (LRC CP45-2007) in July 2007. An Appendix to the Consultation Paper set out, in three different formats, a Restatement of the Freedom of Information Act 1997.

The Consultation Paper set out some options on how the Commission would go about implementing a programme of statute law restatement. It also examined the role which restatement can play in the important task of tidying the statute book, and in doing so it examined comparable projects in other jurisdictions. In view of the increasing role which technology has to play in the dissemination of information, the Consultation Paper also looked at various options regarding the electronic storage and maintenance of the restatements. In addition, the consultation paper also sets out a list of possible candidate Acts for restatement once the programme of restatement gets underway.

Following the conclusion of the consultation process, the Law Reform Commission published its report on this matter in July 2008.

CHRONOLOGICAL TABLES OF THE STATUTES— LEGISLATION DIRECTORY

The Law Reform Commission was conferred with responsibility for the Chronological Tables of the Statutes in 2007; it previously was the responsibility of the Office of the Attorney-General.

Shortly after taking over responsibility for the Chronological Tables, the Law Reform Commission moved to change the title of the Tables to the Legislation Directory.

The Legislation Directory is hosted as part of the Irish Statute Book website. The infrequency with which the Legislation Directory was previously updated has often meant that there were considerable delays between the enactment of a piece of legislation and the tracing and recording of its effect in the Legislation Directory.

With a team of persons dedicated to the task of updating the Legislation Directory already in place at the Law Reform Commission, it is expected that the Legislation Directory will be updated on a far more frequent basis. In July 2008 the Law Reform Commission published a consultation paper on the development and maintenance of the Legislation Directory.

STATUTORY INSTRUMENTS

Electronic Statutory Instruments System (eSIS) Delays in the making available of statutory instruments in hard copy have proven to be problematic for quite some time. On foot of a Government decision taken in June 2007, the electronic Statutory Instrument System (eSIS) was established.

The new system, managed by the Government Supplies Agency, consists of a centralised database to which all new statutory instruments must be uploaded, in a standardised format (pdf), before it is made. The intention is that the statutory instrument will be published in both hard and soft format within four days of being made. An xml version is also made available for the purpose of updating the *irishstatutebook.ie* website. Government Departments are also now required to place an "as made" version of the statutory instrument on their website. A set of step-by-step procedures, entitled *Guidelines on the electronic Statutory Instruments System*, was developed in 2007 and revised in 2008.

Publication of statutory instruments   Section 3(1) of the Statutory Instruments Act 1947 sets out the procedures to be followed on the publication of statutory instruments. Section 2(3) of the Act enables the Attorney-General to exempt a statutory instrument from the requirement to be published, if he is:

> "... of [the] opinion that, by reason of its merely local or personal application or its temporary operation or its limited application or for any other reason, the said statutory instrument, if made, should be exempted".

This matter was raised in the Dáil (630 *Dáil Debates*, February 2, 2007) and it appears that, in the period enquired of, no statutory instruments had been exempted under s.2(3).

Statutory instruments having "statutory effect"   Article 15.2.1° of the Constitution provides:

> "The sole and exclusive power of making laws for the State is hereby vested in the Oireachtas: no other legislative authority has power to make laws for the State."

Consistent with Art.15.2.1° and the case law which has developed around it, legislation has traditionally been categorised as either being primary legislation (Acts) or secondary legislation (statutory instruments).

In recent years there has been a tendency towards the creation of some form of hybrid of legislation which seems to tread dangerously on the line which separates primary legislation from secondary legislation.

The principal example of this is s.4(1)(a) of the European Communities Act 1972 (as amended by s.1 of the European Communities (Amendment) Act 1973) which has had the effect of blurring the line which separate primary legislation from secondary legislation. Section 4(1)(a) (as amended) provides that "[r]egulations under this Act shall have statutory effect".

A similar approach, albeit with far more restrictive application, is contained in s.2 of the Immigration Act 1999 which provides that:

> "Every order made before the passing of this Act under section 5 of the Act of 1935 ... shall have statutory effect as if it were an Act of the Oireachtas."

Similar provisions are also contained in s.6 of the Diplomatic Relations and

Immunities (Amendment) Act 2006) and s.3 of the Stamp Duties Consolidation Act 1999.

Perhaps of most significance is the fact that this approach was utilised in s.5(1) of the European Communities Act 2007 so that an unknown and unidentified body of statutory instruments would have "statutory effect".

This approach was again adopted in the Health (Miscellaneous Provisions) Act 2007, s.5(1) of which provides that:

> "Every order under section 3 of the Act of 1961 made before the passing of this Act shall have statutory effect as if it were an act of the Oireachtas."

This approach has also been replicated in the Local Government Services (Corporate Bodies) (Confirmation of Orders) Act 2008.

Judicial consideration of statutory instruments having "statutory effect" The effect of provisions in primary legislation which seek to imbue statutory instruments with "statutory effect" had not been fully considered until recently. As mentioned earlier, s.2 of the Immigration Act 1999 was one such provision. The meaning and significance of s.2 of the Immigration 1999 Act was considered by Finlay-Geoghegan J. in *Leontjava & Chang v DPP* [2004] 1 I.R. 591, discussed in *Annual Review of Irish Law 2005*, p.526. However, for this purpose it is worth noting one comment made by Finlay-Geoghegan J.:

> "There does not appear to me to be anything in the Constitution which authorises or permits the Oireachtas to determine that a provision which is secondary legislation should henceforth be treated in the legal order of the State as if it were an Act of the Oireachtas".

And she went on to say that:

> "The only provisions which may be treated as a 'law' within the meaning of Article 15 and have the legal status attributable to such a law are laws which have been made by the Oireachtas pursuant to their exclusive law making powers i.e. provisions which are contained in a Bill, passed or deemed to be passed by both Houses, signed by the President and promulgated as a law."

More recently, the effect of s.4(1)(a) of the European Communities Act 1972 Act was considered by the Supreme Court in *Quinn v Ireland* [2007] 2 I.L.R.M. 101. In particular, the Supreme Court had to consider whether regulations which were to be regarded as having "statutory effect" could only be amended by an Act. Denham J. stated (at 107):

> "It has the same status as an Act of the Oireachtas. Therefore the method by which it may be amended requires to be considered from the perspective of this statutory status. As a consequence of having such status, such regulations may only be amended by the Oireachtas. Regulations themselves cannot amend statutes of the Oireachtas— absent express constitutional provisions."

Denham J. considered the relevance of s.15(3) of the Interpretation Act 1937, which provides:

> "Every power conferred by an Act of the Oireachtas to make any regulations, rules, or bye-laws shall, unless the contrary intention appears in such Act, be construed as including a power, exercisable in the like manner and subject to the like consent and conditions (if any), to revoke or amend any regulations, rules, or bye-laws made under such power and (where requisite) to make other regulations, rules, or bye-laws in lieu of those so revoked."

Denham J. found (at 108–109) that s.15(3) cannot be interpreted as covering a regulation which has statutory effect. She went on to hold that:

> "I am satisfied that it would be a step too far to infer such a power [i.e. that a law may be amended by statutory instrument] in an act which did not expressly provide for such a power. Further, I am satisfied that to make such an inference would be to legislate—a matter for the Oireachtas, not a court of law … Therefore, the minister does not have the power to make regulations to amend previous regulations which he has made under the Animal Remedies Act 1993 as the original regulations made by the minister have 'statutory effect'".

Thus, in seeking to resolve a problem, the legislature has, in some instances, conferred "statutory effect" upon some pieces of secondary legislation. As the decision of the Supreme Court in *Quinn* has demonstrated, that approach is a double-edged sword as such statutory instruments can themselves only be amended by an Act. This is something which Ministers will have to bear in mind when they make and then seek to amend statutory instruments made or confirmed under s.50 of the Diplomatic Relations and Immunities Act 2006 (as inserted by s.6 of the Diplomatic Relations and Immunities (Amendment) Act 2006); s.3 of the Stamp Duties Consolidation Act 1999; s.2 of the Immigration Act 1999; s.5 of the Health (Miscellaneous Provisions) Act 2007; s.3 of the Local Government Services (Corporate Bodies) (Confirmation of Orders) Act 2008; and the vast body of statutory instruments which have been made under s.3 of the European Communities Act 1972.

CONSTITUTIONALITY OF LEGISLATION

Section 3 of the Vagrancy Act 1824 made begging in a public place an offence, and provided for a sentence of up to one month's imprisonment. In *Dillon v DPP*, unreported, High Court, March 15, 2007 the plaintiff challenged the constitutionality of s.3 of the Act, principally on the ground that it discriminates between rich and poor. He also claimed that the Act breached his right to freedom of expression. In addition, he claimed that the sentence provided for in the Act was mandatory in nature and therefore constituted an interference with the separation of powers between the legislature and the judiciary.

In the High Court, de Valera J. found that s.3 of the Act is unconstitutional on the grounds that the likely sentence amounted to a disproportionate interference with the constitutional right to freedom of expression (*Irish Times*, March 16, 2007). The court rejected a claim that the sentence provided for in the legislation was mandatory in nature.

Mr Justice de Valera delivered his decision on March 15, 2007 and gave the reasons for his decision on December 4, 2007. A copy of the written judgment has not yet been made available.

INCOMPATABILITY WITH EUROPEAN CONVENTION ON HUMAN RIGHTS

Foy v An tArd Chláraitheoir   In *Foy v An tArd Chláraitheoir*, unreported, High Court, October 19, 2007 McKechnie J. issued the first declaration of incompatibility with the European Convention on Human Rights pursuant to s.5 of the European Convention on Human Rights Act 2003. Whilst born male, the plaintiff, a transsexual, had sought to have her gender recorded as being female. The declaration of incompatibility related to a finding that ss.25, 63 and 64 of the Civil Registration Act 2004 constituted a barrier to the full recognition of the plaintiff's acquired sex.

Section 5(1) of the European Convention on Human Rights Act 2003 provides that:

> In any proceedings, the High Court, or the Supreme Court when exercising its appellate jurisdiction, may, having regard to the provisions of *section 2*, on application to it in that behalf by a party, or of its own motion, and where no other legal remedy is adequate and available, make a declaration (referred to in this Act as 'a declaration of incompatibility') that a statutory provision or rule of law is incompatible with the State's obligations under the Convention provisions.

Whilst the court previously delivered judgment in this matter (July 9, 2002), it was requested to reconsider the matter in light of the European Court of

Human Rights decision in *Goodwin v United Kingdom* [2003] 40 E.H.R.R. 967. McKechnie J. stated that "[t]he decision in *Goodwin,* changed dramatically and irreversibly, the position of transsexuals under the Convention" (at 65). The UK legislature's response to the *Goodwin* case was the enactment of the Gender Recognition Act 2004.

Section 2 of the 2003 Act provides for the interpretation of legislation in a manner which is compatible with the terms of the Convention. McKechnie J. felt that despite the terms of s.2 of the 2003 Act, as s.2 "cannot extend to producing a meaning which is fundamentally at variance with a key or core feature of the statutory provisions or rule of law in question", the only suitable remedy in this case was a declaration of incompatibility (at 48).

He was critical of the State for its failure to respond appropriately to the ECHR decision in *Goodwin* and he questioned "whether the State has deliberately refrained from adopting any such remedial measures to address the ongoing problems" (at 75). Consequently, he felt compelled to:

> "... conclude that by reason of the absence of any provision which would enable the acquired identity of Dr Foy to be legally recognised in this jurisdiction, the respondent State is in breach of its positive obligations under Article 8 of the Convention" (at 77).

He went on later to say that through its failure to enact the required legislation, the State "is every bit as much in breach of its responsibility as if it had enacted a piece of prohibited legislation" (at 81).

McKechnie J. outlined the practical effect of a declaration of incompatibility and pointed out that the Taoiseach is obliged to lay a copy of the court's order before each House of the Oireachtas. He pointed out that the court can have a reasonable expectation that other branches of government would not ignore the importance or significance of making such a declaration. He also indicated that a party in whose favour a declaration of incompatibility has been made can apply to the Government for an ex gratia payment.

It remains to be seen what action, if any, the legislature will take on foot of the declaration of incompatibility issued in this case.

Status of European Convention on Human Rights   The rights contained in the European Convention on Human Rights now form part of the law of the State following the enactment and commencement of the European Convention on Human Rights Act 2003. In *Foy v An tArd Chláraitheoir,* unreported, High Court, October 19, 2007 McKechnie J. availed of the opportunity to clarify the precise status of the Convention in Irish law, stating:

> "It is a misleading metaphor to say that the Convention was incorporated into domestic law. It was not. The rights contained in the Convention

are now part of Irish law. They are so by reason of the Act of 2003. That is their source. Not the Convention" (at 71).

STATUTORY INTERPRETATION

Purposive interpretation   The case of *Cork County Council v Shackleton* [2008] 1 I.L.R.M. 185 concerned the interpretation of s.96 of the Planning and Development Act 2000 (as amended). Clarke J. was clearly frustrated at the legislature's failure to legislate clearly on this matter:

> "Courts are sometimes criticised for adopting interpretations of legislation which critics may regard as going against the *'spirit'* of the legislation concerned. Whatever may, or may not, be the merits of any such criticism, it seems to me that the other side of that coin applies in this case. While the broad drift of the intention of the social and affordable housing provisions of *Part V* of the Act may well be clear ... the reality is that it is very difficult to tell, with even a reasonable degree of certainty, as to how the Oireachtas intended that the legislation should work in practice" (at 198).

In what can be taken to be a criticism of the failure of the Department of Environment to articulate the policy in detail, as well as a criticism of members of the legislature, he went on to say:

> "It has to be said that it is regrettable that the legislation does not appear to have received the level of detailed consideration in advance which it warranted. In such circumstances the courts are left with attempting to do their best with a legislative scheme that gives rise to very significant difficulties of interpretation at almost every turn" (at 199).

In setting out and adopting a particular interpretation of s.96, Clarke J. noted that "it is common case that in more recent times the courts have moved towards a more teleological approach to the interpretation of statutes".

A purposive interpretation was also applied by the Supreme Court in *Ryanair v Labour Court* [2007] E.L.R. 57. Geoghegan J. stated:

> "[I]t is the normal rule that legislation must be interpreted according to the words used but if a literal interpretation would potentially destroy the whole purpose of the legislation ... then it is appropriate that a purposive interpretation be applied."

In Pari Materia and subsequent legislative history   In *DPP v Power* [2008] 1 I.L.R.M. 161 Finnegan J. in the Supreme Court dealt with the question as to whether s.15A of the Misuse of Drugs Act 1977 required the prosecution to establish knowledge on the part of the accused of the market value of the controlled drugs in question.

In seeking to devise the correct interpretation of s.15A of the Misuse of Drugs Act 1977, Finnegan J. stated that "[i]n construing an enactment the court must take into account the state of the law at the time the enactment was passed" (at 170). In relying on the dicta in *R. v Holland Palmer* (1784) 1 Leach 352 at 355, he recited that "Acts *in pari materia* are to be taken together as forming one system and as interpreting and enforcing each other" whether or not the relevant enactment expressly requires this. He rejected the suggestion that the court should be influenced or guided by the terms of s.81 of the Criminal Justice Act 2006 which is *in pari materia*:

> "It is well settled that subsequent legislative history is relevant only as to the view which the legislature took, whether correctly or not, regarding the law with which the enactment deals. There is, however, no question of that history being admissible on a pure question of what the pre-Act law was" (at 171).

Interpretation and the European Convention on Human Rights   Section 2 of the European Convention on Human Rights Act 2003 requires that in interpreting legislation, irrespective of when it was enacted, a court must do so in a way which is compatible with the State's obligations under the European Convention on Human Rights. Section 2 provides as follows:

> 2(1) In interpreting and applying any statutory provision or rule of law, a court shall, in so far as is possible, subject to the rules of law relating to such interpretation and application, do so in a manner compatible with the State's obligations under the Convention provisions.
>
> (2) This section applies to any statutory provision or rule of law in force immediately before the passing of this Act or any such provision coming into force thereafter.

The effect which s.2 of the 2003 Act has on the interpretation of s.13 of the Housing Act 1988 (as amended by Housing (Traveller Accommodation) Act 1998, s.29) was considered by Laffoy J. in *O'Donnell v South Dublin County Council*, unreported, High Court, May 22, 2007. Section 13 of the 1988 Act (as amended) required a housing authority to provide caravan sites for members of the Travelling Community. In reliance upon s.2 of the European Convention on Human Rights Act 2003, the plaintiffs argued that the court should interpret s.13(2) as imposing an obligation on the Council to also provide caravans.

In determining whether s.2 of the European Convention on Human Rights Act 2003 had any application in this instance, Laffoy J. examined the approach taken by the English courts. She explained the approach as follows:

"In the ordinary course of the application of *s.2* of the Act of 2003 one would follow the rubric suggested by Woolf C.J. in [*Poplar Housing v Donoghue* [2001] 3 W.L.R. 183] at p. 204 and one would first ascertain whether, absent *s.2* , there would be any breach of the Convention. If there would, then one would limit the extent of the modified meaning to that which was necessary to achieve compatibility" (at 21–22).

Laffoy J. felt unable to apply that approach to the matter before her as:

"[C]ounsel for the plaintiffs have not pointed to a specific section which, by the application of ordinary canons of construction, would be incompatible with the Convention, nor have they suggested what would have to be read down of the language of such provision or, alternatively, implied into it to render it compatible with the Convention" (at 21–22).

Laffoy J. felt that to read s.13(2) as imposing an obligation on the Council to provide caravans "would cross the boundary between interpretation and amendment" (at 22) and in any event she found that:

"[T]he plaintiffs have not made out a case for the application of *s.2* of the Act of 2003 to the statutory provisions relating to the defendant's duties to the travelling community or persons in the position of the plaintiffs in a manner from which one could conclude that the defendant is infringing its statutory duties to the plaintiffs" (at 22).

The effect of s.2 of the European Convention on Human Rights Act 2003 was also considered by McKechnie J. in *Foy v Ireland*, unreported, High Court, October 18, 2007. With reference to the intent of the legislature as expressed in s.2, McKechnie J. stated:

"… I think it is safe to say that the section cannot extend to producing a meaning which is fundamentally at variance with a key or core feature of the statutory provisions or rule of law in question. It cannot be applied *contra legume* nor can it permit the destruction of a scheme or its replacement with a remodelled one" (at 48).

Effect of a revocation   The case of *Attorney-General v Abimbola* [2007] I.E.S.C. 56 centred around the effects of revocation of statutory instruments on existing situations. At the request of the German authorities, Abimbola had been arrested for the purpose of being extradited to Germany. Part II of the Extradition Act 1965 contained the procedures for surrender of persons to countries in relation to which the Government has made orders applying that Part. By means of the Extradition Act (Application of Part II) Order 2000

(S.I. No. 474 of 2000), the Government applied Pt II of the Act of 1965 to Germany. In 2004, the Government made a further order (S.I. No. 725 of 2004), the effect of which was that Pt II of the Act of 1965 ceased to apply in relation to Germany.

However, a question arose as to consequences which the making of S.I. No. 725 of 2004 had on Pt II of the Act of 1965 and the arrest and detention of Abimbola. Counsel for the State sought to argue that Ireland's obligation to Germany was preserved by s.22 of the Interpretation Act 1937, which is effectively a saving provision applicable in the event of the revocation of a statutory instrument. In rejecting that argument, Fennelly J. stated:

> "The obligation owed, in international law, by this State to Germany does not derive from the revoked statutory instrument but from international agreement or convention. In any event, the sections are concerned with preservation of legal proceedings for the enforcement of obligations *against* the person who has become subject to them. It is not at all concerned with enabling a person or body to enforce an obligation which it owes itself under a distinct legal system."

Limitation of Actions

DISCOVERABILITY OF INJURY

In *Byrne v Hudson* [2007] I.E.S.C. 53, the plaintiff was injured when visiting the home of a young friend whose adult brother allegedly shot a paint gun in his direction, resulting in the loss of sight in one of his eyes. He sued the friend's brother as well as the friend's father. Much later he sued the friend's mother, who raised the Statute of Limitations as a bar. In turn, the plaintiff invoked the 1991 Act, arguing that he had not been aware of the fact that his friend's parents had separated and that the father was living elsewhere, thus making the mother the sole occupier of the house; he also contended that his solicitor had exercised diligence in trying to unravel the position.

Butler J. held that the proceedings against the mother were not barred but the Supreme Court reversed this decision. Macken J. (Kearns and Finnegan JJ. concurring) resolved the case on the basis that the evidence established that the true position had been readily ascertainable by the plaintiff and that thus the limitation clock had not been stopped:

> "It would appear clear from the ... evidence that knowledge that the [mother] was the occupier of the premises ... whether alone or with others, and information that the [father] did not reside at those premises was clearly observable or ascertainable by the plaintiff. Indeed it was known to him. But these facts were undoubtedly also observable and ascertainable by him. Without going further, it seems abundantly clear that the knowledge which the plaintiff might reasonably have been expected to acquire within the meaning of s.2(2)(a) of the Act of 1991 existed and was known to him."

This was enough to resolve the case against the plaintiff, rendering otiose the debate relating to s.2(2)(b), under which, apart from facts which are both observable or ascertainable by a plaintiff, a person's knowledge includes facts "ascertainable by him with the help of medical or other appropriate expert advice, which it is reasonable for him to seek".

Counsel for the mother had invoked *O'Driscoll v Dublin Corporation*, High Court, July 3, 1998, for the purposes of establishing that information or knowledge acquired by a solicitor is not acquired as an expert, but that, where information is acquired as an agent for the plaintiff, this must be imputed to the plaintiff himself. Macken J. did:

"... not consider it necessary for the purposes of this case to determine whether or not, according to the English cases referred to in *O'Driscoll,* a solicitor is not to be considered in any circumstances as being an appropriate expert for the purposes of knowledge ascertainable on the part of the plaintiff within the meaning of s.2(2)(a) of the Act of 1991."

It seemed to her rather that the appropriate position first to be considered was whether the fact that the mother was an occupier of the premises was something ascertainable or observable by the plaintiff. If it was, then the plaintiff was obliged in the usual way to make this information available to the solicitor he employed for the purposes of enabling that solicitor to reach a conclusion as to the correct defendant to be included in any proceedings commenced on his behalf.

Macken J. went on to express the view that:

"... since the provisions of Section 2 are, in reality, an exception to the normal provisions concerning the obligation to commence proceedings for relief in respect of a tort causing personal injuries within a three year period, it is correct to apply the provisions of the section literally and not benignly or by an unduly lax interpretation. There is no suggestion in the Act of 1991 that a plaintiff is in some way to be forgiven for failing to furnish to his solicitor all of the facts which are within his direct knowledge, as here, so as to enable his solicitor commence proceedings against the correct defendant. It seems clear that, had the plaintiff done so in the present case, the information to enable the solicitor to do just that would have been freely and readily available within days of the incident occurring. It may well be that, in certain cases, the ambit or nature of which it is not necessary to speculate upon, it would be appropriate to rely entirely upon a solicitor in respect of matters to be 'ascertainable', whatever about 'observable', when considering Section 2(2)(a) of the Act. But that is not a position which could apply in the present case."

If one goes back to *O'Driscoll v Dublin Corporation*, one finds that the English decisions cited in that case to Geoghegan J.—*Farrell v National Coal Board* (1986) Times L. R. 289 and *Halford v Brooker* [1991] 1 W.L.R. 428—were concerned with a statutory phrase which was crucially different from its Irish equivalent. Whereas the Irish phrase is "other appropriate expert advice", the English phrase is "other appropriate expert evidence". Geoghegan J. observed:

"[T]he view has been expressed in some English cases... which have been opened to me that the reference to 'other appropriate expert evidence' is a reference to the advice of an expert witness rather than to the party's own lawyers and I think that this is correct. But of course the solicitors are agents for their client and therefore knowledge which they might reasonably have been expected to acquire in their capacity as agents must be imputed to the plaintiff himself by virtue of paragraph (a). Indeed this is not seriously disputed."

It appears that a solicitor's knowledge, in Ireland but not in England, may have the effect of activating the limitation clock in either of two ways: where it is knowledge that a solicitor might reasonably have been expected to acquire in his or her capacity as agent of the plaintiff and where it is knowledge that might reasonably have been expected to be conveyed by the solicitor as appropriate expert advice which it is reasonable for the plaintiff to seek.

In *Devlin v National Maternity Hospital* [2007] I.E.S.C. 50, the plaintiffs sought damages in relation to a post-mortem on their stillborn infant, carried out without their prior consent, which involved the removal and retention of organs from the deceased infant. The trial judge held that the Statute of Limitations defeated the claim so far as it was based on the unauthorised character of the post-mortem. The plaintiffs had learned about the post mortem in 1988; this had angered them but nonetheless they had not initiated litigation until 2002. The fact that a nurse had told the father that it was standard practice of the hospital to carry out a post-mortem had not induced him to believe that he would not have had a choice as to whether a post-mortem examination should be carried out and that the plaintiffs had therefore not known they had been wronged. Conversely, the hospital could not invoke s.2(2)(b) of the Statute of Limitations (Amendment) Act 1991 to argue that the knowledge of a consultant pathologist in 1991 of the fact that organs had been removed during the post mortem should be attributed to the plaintiffs. The pathologist learned of these facts when he read the autopsy report. He had not mentioned that dimension in his report to the plaintiffs' solicitor as it had not been a matter which he had been asked to address and he had not thought it relevant. The trial judge did not think that the consultant pathologist's knowledge on this point could be important to the plaintiffs by virtue of s.2(2)(b) because it would not have been reasonable for the plaintiffs to have sought advice from him in that regard.

The trial judge rejected the ingenious argument by the defendants that the claim was barred because, if the plaintiffs had pursued a claim against the hospital for carrying out the post mortem without their consent, they would inevitably have discovered that organs had been retained. They had been under no obligation to pursue such a claim within the statutory period. The trial judge expressed himself as follows:

"[T]hey were under no obligation to pursue such a claim at that time and I do not accept that, because they failed to pursue such a claim and allowed it to become statute barred… thereby depriving themselves of the opportunity to find out that the organs had been retained... by the same default they also allowed the claim in respect of the retention of organs to become statute barred."

Perhaps it might be preferable to avoid the language of "default". A plaintiff whose claim is defeated by a limitation bar is guilty of no necessary default in the sense of legal or moral wrong (although it is of course possible that some cases may happen to involve personal moral failure on the part of a plaintiff or his or her agent). The question under s.2(2) of the 1991 Act is whether an ascertainable knowledge was of a character that the person (the plaintiffs in this instance) "might reasonably have been expected to acquire ..." In the instant case, the plaintiffs had been under no obligation to make a claim in respect of unauthorised autopsy. The fact that, had they happened to do so, they would have discovered facts that would warrant making quite a separate claim is simply irrelevant.

At all events, on appeal to the Supreme Court, Denham J. (Murray C.J. and Finnegan J. concurring) endorsed without further elaboration the trial judge's analysis of the issues relating to the limitation issue.

It is well established that the limitation clock starts ticking once the plaintiff becomes, or ought to become, aware that the injury is significant even though he or she may not realise the full significance of the effect of the injury. The Supreme Court so held in *Bolger v O'Brien* [1999] 2 I.R. 431, which we analysed in the *Annual Review of Irish Law 1999*, 398-401. In *Martin v Irish Express Cargo Ltd* [2007] I.E.H.C. 224, the plaintiff had suffered an injury to his back when lifting a machine over a wall in the course of his work. He required a week's sick leave and complained consistently of lower back pain. He was required to use a TENS machine to alleviate the symptoms but still complained of persistent soreness. His condition was subject to a number of medical reports, in one of which an "undoubted error" was made in relation to the findings of a scan in which it had been indicated that no disc protrusion was disclosed.

Dunne J. held that that the plaintiff's claim, launched many years after the accident, was statute-barred and not saved by the 1991 Act. She observed:

"Even accepting as I do that there was a lack of clarity as to the nature of the plaintiff's injury in that the report of [one of the doctors] as to disc protrusion was wrong, it cannot be gainsaid in my view that the plaintiff was aware of the fact that he suffered a significant injury. He did consult a number of doctors in relation to his injuries. It may well be the case that he was not aware of the fact that a disc protrusion had occurred until much later but as is manifestly clear from the decision of Hamilton C.J. in the *Bolger* case that fact that the plaintiff did not realise the full extent of his injury is irrelevant once it is clear that the plaintiff was aware that he had suffered a significant injury."

SEXUAL ABUSE

In the *Annual Review of Irish Law 2000,* p.315-318, we analysed the Statute of
Limitations (Amendment) Act 2000, which suspends the operation of the State
of Limitations for tort actions for sexual abuse occurring during the victim's
minority for such period as the victim suffers from a disability resulting from
the abuse which substantially impairs his or her will or his or her ability to make
a reasoned decision to bring the action. It may be useful to quote s.2(1):

> A person shall, for the purpose of bringing an action –
>   (a) founded on tort in respect of an act of sexual abuse
>   committed against him or her at a time when he or she had
>   not yet reached full age, or
>   (b) against a person (other than the person who committed that
>   act), claiming damages for negligence or breach of duty
>   where the damages claimed consist of or include damages
>   in respect of personal injuries caused by such act,
> be under a disability while he or she is suffering from any psychological
> injury that –
>   (i) is caused, in whole or in part, by that act, or any other act,
>   of the person who committed the first-mentioned act, and
>   (ii) is of such significance that his or her will, or his or her
>   ability to make a reasoned decision, to bring such action is
>   substantially impaired.

In *RR v PD, The Minister for Defence, Ireland and the Attorney-General* [2007]
I.E.H.C. 252 the plaintiff, who served as a gunner in the Defence Forces for
a period from the late 1980s to the mid-1990s, took tort proceedings against
his employers. It appeared that he had been the victim of sexual assault by his
sergeant major on eight occasions during this period. He had not made any
complaint at the time to his superiors. In court, he explained this by indicating
that there was a culture in the army against making complaints and stating
that he had made a previous complaint of assault against a superior which had
"got nowhere". Johnson J. noted that "[h]is view was quite clearly that no one
would take the word of a gunner over the word of a sergeant major or indeed
a battery sergeant."

The plaintiff first mentioned the abuse to a battery sergeant, after he had left
the army, when the battery sergeant had informed him that two other gunners
had made complaints against the sergeant major and had not been believed.
The plaintiff, having told the battery sergeant of what had happened to him,
swore him to secrecy. In spite of having given an undertaking not to tell anyone,
the battery sergeant disclosed the matter to his superior officers and this led
ultimately to the litigation.

Proceedings in the case were initiated in 2001. The plaintiff invoked s.2

of the 2000 Act. There was a "complete conflict of evidence" between the clinical psychologist who treated the plaintiff and the psychiatrist called by the defendants. In the view of the clinical psychologist, the plaintiff suffered from post-traumatic stress disorder which had substantially impaired his capacity to take the case. The psychiatrist considered that the plaintiff suffered from a personality defect which pre-existed the assaults; she indicated that she had a certain doubt as to whether the assaults had taken place at all.

Johnson J. preferred the evidence of the clinical psychologist. He took into account that, during the hearing, the plaintiff had demonstrated a great deal of distress, in contrast to the experience of the psychiatrist to the effect that the plaintiff had failed to demonstrate any emotional distress. Johnson J. accordingly held that the claim was not statute-barred.

The decision raises a number of interesting issues about the policy of the 2000 Act. The first relates to the fact that the Act applies only to an act of sexual abuse committed against the plaintiff "at a time when he or she had not yet reached full age". Johnson J. does not indicate the plaintiff's age. He does, however note that the plaintiff "was a married soldier at the time of the first incident" in 1989. Manifestly, all of the incidents during the period from 1989 to 1995 must have occurred when the plaintiff had attained full age. Even if he had married below the age of 18, he would have attained full age by marrying, under s.2(1)(b) of the Age of Majority Act 1985.

The problem about disclosure in the context of a gunner in the army is that the hierarchical culture of that institution discouraged those in the lower ranks from making complaints. According to Johnson J.'s judgment, this was the reason given by the plaintiff for his failure to have made a disclosure during his time in the army. It is not easy to equate a well-based prudential assessment as to the probable inefficacy of making a complaint with a psychological injury that substantially impairs a person's will or ability to make a reasoned decision to initiate litigation. There is a strong argument that a claim relating to sexual abuse should not be defeated by the Statute of Limitations where it was not made earlier because institutionalised power hierarchies and prejudice rendered it futile to do so. This is not, however, what the legislation of 2000 purportedly addresses. It is interesting that, under the guise of inhibition of the will, a court is capable of doing justice of a different kind.

CONTRACT

The limitation period for actions "founded on simple contract" is six years: Statute of Limitations 1957, s.11(1)(a). In *Power v Guardian PMPA Insurance Ltd* [2007] I.E.H.C. 105, the plaintiff had been injured when travelling as a passenger in a vehicle driven by his friend, whose insurance policy did not extend cover to passengers. The plaintiff sought to contend to the contrary, arguing that the insurance company was bound to indemnify him under s.76

of the Road Traffic Act 1961. This argument was rejected by Laffoy J. The plaintiff also attempted to establish a separate contractual obligation on the part of the insurance company relative to the driver not to exclude cover for a front-seat passenger. This was rejected on the evidence, but in any event the problem existed of the lack of privity between the plaintiff and the contracting parties. Laffoy J. held that the plaintiff's claim in this context also failed on this basis. Moreover, even if, hypothetically, it had been maintainable, the Statute of Limitations would have defeated it. Had the plaintiff been entitled to invoke s.76(1)(d) of the Road Traffic Act 1961, the limitation period of three years for personal injuries (now two years) would have applied to defeat the claim. The English decision of *Lefevre v White* [1990] 1 Lloyd's Rep. 569 was distinguishable. That case had held that the Statute of Limitations should not run against an insured until he had accepted the unilateral repudiation of contract by the insurance company. In the instant case, the driver had not sued the defendant on the contract of insurance and the plaintiff had not obtained judgment against the driver.

ADVERSE POSSESSION

In *Moley v Fee* [2007] I.E.H.C. 143, Laffoy J. rejected a claim of adverse possession in somewhat unusual factual circumstances. The owner of land in a scenic coastal area agreed in 1975 to sell small portions of it to two would-be purchasers who wished to place mobile homes there. The price was £300 per site. When one of the would-be purchasers sought to place his caravan on his site he was met with local resistance. He succeeded in doing so, but planning permission was refused. Both would-be purchasers lost interest in their sites and did not exercise control over them. In 1999, the plaintiff bought the sites from them, for £500 and £1,200 respectively. The question of ownership thus came into focus. The original owner contested the plaintiff's entitlement to the sites.

Laffoy J. held on the evidence that it had not been established that the purchase price for the sites had been received by the original owner. It was "absolutely clear" on the evidence that neither would-be purchasers had occupied or exercised acts of ownership over the disputed sites of the type that would constitute possession for the purposes of the Statute of Limitations. Moreover, neither had had the necessary *animus possidendi*. In contrast, the original owner had exercised acts of ownership over the disputed sites during this period. Evidence had been given of his dumping grass and other material there on a number of occasions as well as repairing a gate to which he had a key. The fact that he had taken his solicitor to see the disputed area some time in the late 1990s in the context of discussions for a sale to a third party suggested to Laffoy J. that he had considered himself the owner of the land and in possession of it at all material times.

PROCEDURE

In *Allen v Irish Holemasters Ltd* [2007] I.E.S.C. 33, a fatal accident claim was taken under Pt 4 of the Civil Liability Act 1961 by the widow of an employee who had died in a traffic accident in 1997. The claim against the employer alleged that all the equipment in the cargo compartment of the van the employee had been driving had moved forward at the pre-impact speed of the van and struck him; some of the items weighed in excess of 25 kilograms. A fairly standard defence was delivered containing denials of the claim and allegations that the accident had been caused by the deceased's sole negligence or contributory negligence in the manner he had driven the van. The plaintiff did not deliver a reply but in 2005 furnished further and better particulars of negligence adding an additional plea that the defendant had overloaded the van. The defendant objected to this. The plaintiff sought leave to amend the statement of claim by the addition of a paragraph to the effect that the collision had been caused because the van "was grossly overloaded by the defendant rendering it unstable, and incapable of being properly controlled". The High Court judge granted leave to amend and the Supreme Court affirmed.

Finnegan J. (Murray C.J. and Kearns J. concurring) rejected the argument that the new claim sought to be made was barred. He stated:

> "The amendment sought raises a new issue in the action. Moreover, it is not an issue which is raised by the plaintiff but rather one raised by the defendant in its plea of negligence and contributory negligence against the plaintiff. The driving of the vehicle was not an issue raised by the statement of the claim … Here the driving of the vehicle became an issue arising out of the defence and it was open to the plaintiff to respond in a reply attributing the accident to the vehicle being overloaded rather than any negligence on the part of the driver … The cour[t] should extend the time for delivery of a reply which would deal in terms of the overloading of the vehicle with a plea of negligence and contributory negligence against the plaintiff."

One may perhaps hesitate about agreeing with this analysis. The allegation of overloading was not reducible to a refutation of the defence put forward: it involved a new assertion of negligence that was in no way connected with the defence.

One may note briefly an obiter dictum of Smyth J. in *Earl v Cremin* [2007] I.E.H.C. 69 where certain reliefs were sought under the ss.297(a) and 298 of the Companies Act 1963 by way of plenary summons rather than by way of originating notice of motion, which would have been the correct way of proceeding. The motive had been to prevent the Statute of Limitations from defeating the claim; in fact that problem could have been effectively addressed by the correct procedure. Smyth J. forgave the inadvertent error.

He observed:

> "I do not see the plaintiff as having circumvented the statutory protection afforded to potential defendants by the Statute of Limitations when in fact the range of inquiry raised in the statement of claim is less that that which emerged in the summons. There might be some force in this argument if new causes of action or new allegations were introduced at the statement of claim stage."

In *Costello v Commissioner of An Garda Síochána* [2007] I.E.H.C. 330, the plaintiff claimed a range of reliefs, including damages for trespass to the person for harassment, watching and besetting and intimidation, damages for unlawful arrest and "criminal slander'" and a permanent injunction restraining the defendant from watching and besetting the plaintiffs at their home. The claims related to incidents alleged to have occurred over the previous decade. The defendant sought several orders, including one striking out parts of the statement of claim which related to matters pre-dating December 22, 1999, as any possible cause of action arising therefrom was statute-barred by virtue of s.11 of the Statute of Limitations 1957. Laffoy J. declined to make such an order, regarding it as misconceived. She stated:

> "A plea that a claim is statute barred is a matter of defence. It can be dealt with in one of two ways. It can be disposed of by way of the trial of a preliminary issue of law under O. 25, r. 1 of the Rules or under O. 34, r. 2 of the Rules provided the relevant facts are agreed or established. The alternative is that the plea is dealt with in the course of the trial of the action.
>
> Accordingly, insofar as the defendant seeks to strike out in reliance on the Act of 1957, the application is refused."

Laffoy J. did, however, accede to the defendant's application under Ord.19 r.27 of the Rules of the Superior Courts to strike out portions of the statement of claim which failed to identify the date of occurrence of alleged incidents. She expressed the view that, "because of that lack of particularity, the fair trial of the action is likely to be prejudiced".

Local Government

BUILDING CONTROL

The Building Control Act 2007 amended the Building Control Act 1990 both in terms of substantive requirements on building control and also in the method for certifying compliance with the building code. It also provided for a statutory registration system for architects and surveyors for the first time. The 2007 Act came into force fully on May 1, 2008: see Building Control Act 2007 (Commencement) Order 2008 (S.I. No. 50 of 2008).

In terms of the building code, the 2007 Act significantly amended the requirements for fire safety certificates and introduced a new disability access certificate. The key change is that the 1990 Act, as amended by the 2007 Act, prohibits the opening, operation or occupation of a building until a fire safety certificate or disability access certificate (or revised certificates) are granted. The changes made in 2007 on fire safety certificates include the introduction of a seven-day notice or fast-track procedure which must be accompanied by a valid fire safety certificate application and a declaration that the applicant will carry out any modification works required by the fire safety certificate, when granted. This was intended to cater for builders who are anxious to commence work on urgent projects without waiting for up to two months for the application to be processed. In addition, the Building Control Act 2007 states that new applications for a revised fire safety certificate are required where a building design is changed to comply with conditions attached to a planning permission. Another change is to require applications for regularisation certificates where buildings have commenced or have been completed without the necessary fire safety certificate, subject to the necessary documentation and declaration that the works comply with the fire safety requirements of the 1997 Regulations.

The changes made by the 2007 Act to the 1990 Act also provided for the introduction of a disability access certificate. Part M of the Building Regulations 1997 (made under the 1990 Act) sets out the requirements for access to and within non-domestic buildings for people with disabilities. Part M was extended to new (domestic) dwellings from 1 January 1, 2001: see the Building Regulations (Amendment) Regulations 2000 (*Annual Review of Irish Law 2000*, p.328). It was felt that it is often too late to seek to remedy disability access deficiencies once construction is in progress or when a building is finished. For this reason, the changes made by the 2007 Act introduce a disability access certificate system, along the lines of the fire safety certificate system, for new non-domestic dwellings. This also implemented a recommendation of the Commission on the Status of People with Disabilities.

The changes made by the 2007 Act to the 1990 Act also enhanced the enforcement powers of the building control authorities (the large local authorities) in a number of ways. The powers of building control authorities to seek High Court injunctions were extended to remove works or stop work on buildings or projects which do not have fire safety certificates, disability access certificates or regularisation certificates, or where there is non-compliance with enforcement notices served by the authorities. The prosecution process was also simplified by providing building control authorities with the option to institute summary prosecutions for all building code offences in the District Court, as an alternative to prosecution, on indictment, by the Director of Public Prosecutions in the Circuit Criminal Court.

In terms of the registration of titles of certain building professions, the 2007 Act provides for the first time that the use of titles of "Architect", "Quantity Surveyor" and "Building Surveyor" will be confined to persons with recognised qualifications, training and/or experience, whose names are entered on a statutory register. The relevant registers will be administered, in the case of architects, by the Royal Institute of Architects of Ireland (RIAI), and, in the case of Building Surveyors and Quantity Surveyors, by the Society of Chartered Surveyors (SCS).

ROADS

The Local Government (Roads Functions) Act 2007 provided for the transfer of responsibility for non-national roads and the national vehicle driver file, commonly referred to as the NVDF, from the Department of the Environment, Heritage and Local Government to the Department of Transport. Normally, transfer of departmental functions can be proceeded with by way of the making of a transfer of functions order under the Ministers and Secretaries Act 1939. The advice received from the Office of the Attorney-General was that the transfer of functions relating to non-national roads and the national vehicle driver file required the making of some minor amendments to the primary legislation and the enactment of a Transfer of Functions Order. The making of the relevant Order coincided with the commencement of the 2007 Act.

WATER SERVICES

The Water Services Act 2007 (which began its legislative life as the Water Services Bill 2003) was enacted to establish a comprehensive and modern legislative code governing functions, standards, obligations and practice in respect of the planning, management and delivery of water supplies and the collection and treatment of waste water. The 2007 Act, which consolidates and modernises the existing legislative code governing water services, was the first root and branch consolidation and modernisation of water services law for more than 120 years since the Public Health (Ireland) Act 1878. It was pointed out that, while some of the older legislative provisions had stood the test of time, much of the language and many of the concepts were outdated and arcane. Many quaint terms used in the 1878 Act, such as "water-closets" and "water undertakers" are no longer in common usage. Other provisions, such as those referring to "earth closets, water-closets or privy accommodation", have echoes of past centuries and have long since been overtaken.

The term "water services" in the 2007 Act was described during the Oireachtas debate on the 2007 Act by reference to "water in the pipe" from the time following abstraction that it first enters a supply pipe to the point of its subsequent discharge to the environment as treated waste water. It was noted that the 2007 Act does not seek to take a broader environmental view of water resources issues, such as pollution control, water quality in its broadest sense and river basin management. It was therefore intended that the 2007 Act would complement other legislation in this area.

The term "water services" in the 2007 Act encapsulates the provision of water supplies and the subsequent collection and treatment of waste water. Water supply and waste water services were generally provided for separately in the pre-2007 legislation, but such an approach was no longer considered to be appropriate as continued separation could lead to legislative anomalies and would run counter to the ongoing programme of reforming and simplifying the legislative code. Prior to the 2007 Act, water services were provided by county and city councils acting as "sanitary authorities". The 2007 Act provides that, where water services are concerned, county and city councils will cease to be known as sanitary authorities and will become known as "water services authorities".

The 2007 Act establishes the Minister for the Environment, Heritage and Local Government as the national authority for regulating the provision of water services. Section 30 sets out the functions of the Minister for that purpose. It places a duty on the Minister to facilitate the provision of safe and efficient water services and associated infrastructure. The Minister is also required to supervise and monitor the performance by water services authorities of their functions under the Act and is given responsibility for planning and supervision of investment in water services. In this respect, the 2007 Act also provides the Minister with a broad range of powers, including the provision of guidance, the issue of binding directions, and the monitoring of the performance by individual authorities of their functions, including their own supervisory functions as necessary. To assist and advise the Minister in that regard, the 2007 Act also enables the Minister to appoint statutory consultative groups and committees.

The main functions of water services authorities are set out in ss.31 and 32, which provide the basic statutory framework for water services authorities to deliver water services, assist others in providing water services and supervise the delivery of water services by other persons. The Minister may make regulations specifying performance criteria and quality standards which must be achieved regarding those functions. It is envisaged that most of the EC Directives concerning water services, including the drinking water Directive and relevant elements of the urban waste water treatment Directive, will be transposed into national law under those provisions.

Consistent with the EC Directive on Drinking Water, the 2007 Act states that each water services authority is obliged to ensure that water intended for human consumption in its area meets prescribed standards and is provided with powers to prohibit or restrict the use of a water supply, where necessary, to protect public health or the environment. It is envisaged that those powers could be applied either to follow up a water quality incident or at times of drought to protect the integrity of the water supply and related ecosystems.

The 2007 Act also states that each water services authority will carry out its functions in the context of a strategic management framework for the delivery of water services in its area, drawn up in agreement with the Minister. Section 36 provides for the introduction of an operational planning and review cycle across both rural and urban areas in the functional area of each water services authority. Each water services authority will be required to draw up a water services strategic plan for its functional area at intervals of six years, or after such shorter period as the authority may decide, and to submit it to the Department of the Environment for approval. The plan will outline the situation regarding water services in its area of application, both current and projected, and identify appropriate responses with a view to protecting human health and the environment and supporting ongoing sustainable development.

The 2007 Act also puts in place a framework of provisions to protect the integrity of water services distribution and collection networks. Unauthorised connection or discharge to a waterworks or waste water works is prohibited. Section 103 prohibits building over another person's water distribution system or drains without the consent of the relevant water services authority. New powers in ss.55 and 61 enable a water services authority to require a developer to open up water supply pipes and drains for inspection before connection to its services. Water services authorities are given powers to specify technical requirements regarding such connections, and it is an offence under the 2007 Act to make any such connection without the prior approval of the relevant water services authority.

The 2007 Act places a new duty of care on owners and occupiers regarding the sustainable use of water services on their premises and prohibits discharge of anything into a sewer which would block or damage it or adversely affect a waste water treatment process. Water services authorities are provided with powers to direct owners to undertake remedial works, or may themselves carry out any necessary repairs and recover their costs from the owners of the premises. In addition, s.70 specifically obliges occupiers and owners to maintain treatment systems (septic tanks) in such condition as to avoid nuisance or risk to human health or the environment.

Section 56 provides extensive new powers for the purpose of conserving water supplies. An authorised person is enabled to direct the owner or occupier of a premises to take corrective action to prevent water from being wasted or consumed in excessive amounts. Such officers will also have powers of direction regarding the restriction of water use. Exercise of those powers will be subject to appeal to the District Court, except in times of emergency, and the authorised person will have power to cut off or restrict supply pending compliance.

In terms of consumer complaints, s.32(3) enables the Minister to make Regulations on this. In addition, s.51, for example, regulates the temporary interruption of water services and obliges water services providers to give reasonable advance notice of interruptions, except in an emergency. Alternative supplies are required to be provided where domestic drinking water supplies are interrupted for more than 24 hours. To ensure unimpeded access to services, water services authorities will also have powers under s.92 to facilitate the connection of individual premises to water services networks through neighbouring connections.

Section 43 deals with the repair of private connections, linking premises with a sewer or water main. Prior to the 2007 Act, responsibility for such repairs had rested with owners and occupiers, resulting in particular problems and inconvenience where faults or breakage occurs outside the boundary of the premises. In the absence of clear legislative authority, sanitary authorities had experienced difficulty in providing assistance to households, even where it was considered appropriate to do so. It was pointed out during the Oireachtas debate on the 2007 Act that this anomaly had been the subject of much complaint and had attracted adverse criticism from the Office of the Ombudsman. In this context, s.43 enables water services authorities to intervene, to repair or take into their own charge such service connections as they consider appropriate.

Part 5 of the 2007 Act deals with metering and provides for necessary powers of access for installation, reading and maintenance of meters, and investigation of possible offences pertaining to interference with meters or fraudulent use of supplies.

Detailed provisions in relation to rural water services are set out in Pt 6 of the 2007 Act. Chief among these is the proposed introduction of a licensing system to regulate and develop the operations of the group water scheme sector. Each water services authority will be the licensing authority for its functional area, and it will be an offence for any person, other than a water services authority, to provide services other than in accordance with the terms of a water services licence. It was stated that it was intended to apply the licensing requirements of the 2007 Act to the 1,500 or so larger group water schemes serving more than 50 persons (of a total of about 6,000 schemes in total at the time the 2007 Act was enacted). Section 79 of the 2007 Act therefore exempts smaller schemes from licensing. However, there are powers to make regulations to provide for alternative requirements with regard to the registration of smaller schemes and their general compliance with specified standards, as required. Additional administrative powers are also included to enable a water services authority to intervene directly in the operations of a scheme where it considers that its expertise could be applied to the resolution of a particular problem. Section 91 enables a water services authority to take over the operation and management of a waterworks or waste water works on a temporary basis, where it considers that its operation could constitute a risk to public health or the environment, or where a scheme is experiencing operational problems or is consistently in breach of a licence.

Part 7 of the 2007 Act provides for general powers of acquisition for water services purposes and synchronises these functions with local authority powers of acquisition under the Planning and Development Act 2000. The previous powers of acquisition for water services purposes in the Public Health (Ireland) Act 1878 were thus repealed by the 2007 Act.

Part 8 of the 2007 Act includes savers to prevent older, often obscure, pre-1922 statutes from frustrating the application of the 2007 Act. Provision is also included in s.102 to enable An Bord Pleanála to determine fees for appeals to it in relation to licensing of effluent discharges to sewers and waters. This is in line with similar provisions under the Planning and Development Act 2000 and will facilitate the application of similar procedures by An Bord Pleanála in respect of the various appeals processes for which it has responsibility, and further streamline the regulatory process.

While the 2007 Act provides for notable consolidation and reform of water services law, it was also noted during the Oireachtas debate on the 2007 Act that a further consolidation exercise would be required to gather together the relevant legislation on the protection and management of water resources generally, including lakes and rivers. The then Minister for the Environment indicated that this would be considered at some future date (having noted that the Department had already made a significant contribution to consolidation and reform, notably in the planning and local government statutory codes).

Planning and Development Law

GARRETT SIMONS, S.C.

SOCIAL AND AFFORDABLE HOUSING

Dispute resolution mechanism   The correct division of function between An Bord Pleanála and the property arbitrator under Pt V of the Planning and Development Act 2000 (the "PDA 2000") was considered in detail in *Glenkerrin Homes v Dun Laoghaire Rathdown County Council (No. 2)* ([2007] I.E.H.C. 298; unreported, Clarke J., April 26, 2007). The case concerned a dispute as to the terms of an agreement to transfer built units within the application site. The planning authority and the developer could not agree as to which units were to be transferred pursuant to Pt V. The developer argued that this dispute fell within the property arbitrator's jurisdiction, and had referred the matter to him for determination. The planning authority, conversely, argued that only An Bord Pleanála could identify which particular units were to be transferred.

The High Court held that the property arbitrator has an implied jurisdiction to identify, in the case of dispute, which units should be transferred where there is a material difference between individual units, e.g. in terms of size or location. Clarke J. ruled that the identification of the units to be transferred was so inextricably linked to the question of the number and price of the units to be transferred that a jurisdiction on the part of the property arbitrator to determine those matters must necessarily be implied. If the identification of the units could only be the subject of an agreement with the planning authority, or be determined on a reference to An Bord Pleanála, then there would be the potential for stalemate or for a whole series of separate dispute resolution hearings, with a potential for circularity.

In the later judgment of *Cork County Council v Shackleton (No. 1)* ([2007] I.E.H.C. 241; [2008] 1 I.L.R.M. 185), Clarke J. elaborated upon the approach to be adopted by the property arbitrator:

> "Where the sites are not homogenous it seems to me that the property arbitrator must do the best that he can (in the absence of agreement) to identify a set of housing units for transfer where the aggregate of the planning gain attributable to the site on which each of those units has been built approximates to 20% of the total planning gain on the development as a whole, subject only to a balancing payment. In selecting which types of sites and units require to be included in such an arrangement, the property arbitrator should give all due weight to

the reasonable requirements of the planning authority involved as to the type of accommodation which they need to supply for the purposes of social or affordable housing or both."

In *Glenkerrin Homes v Dun Laoghaire Rathdown County Council (No. 2)*, Clarke J. had emphasised that where the dispute between the parties was not confined to the identification of the units to be transferred, but instead went to the question of principle as to by which method a developer was to comply with Pt V, then in the absence of agreement the matter could only be resolved by An Bord Pleanála.

The division of function between the two tribunals thus seems to be as follows: the property arbitrator has jurisdiction over matters which entail valuation, i.e. the number and price of houses to be transferred; the number and price of sites to be transferred; or the amount of any monetary payment to be made. In cases where the method of compliance has been settled on as involving the transfer of built units, the property arbitrator also has an implicit jurisdiction to identify which particular units are to be transferred. An Bord Pleanála has jurisdiction over all other disputes, which will generally require the board to exercise judgment on matters of planning policy.

In at least some cases it will be necessary to make a reference to each of An Bord Pleanála and the property arbitrator in turn. First, it will be necessary to make a reference to An Bord Pleanála in order that the *principle* of the agreement may be determined—for example, whether the developer is to transfer built houses to the planning authority. Thereafter, it may be necessary to make a subsequent reference to the property arbitrator in order that the details—for example, in terms of the number and prices of built houses—can be determined.

Default option: transfer of undeveloped land   Generally, a developer cannot be *compelled* to do other than transfer undeveloped land within the application site. The transfer of undeveloped land thus represents the default option, and the developer must, in effect, volunteer to comply in some other way before any obligation to transfer built units or serviced sites could arise. The judgment in *Glenkerrin Homes v Dun Laoghaire Rathdown County Council (No. 2)* ([2007] I.E.H.C. 298; unreported, Clarke J., April 26, 2007) indicates, however, that the developer may, as a result of his or her conduct, lose the right to insist on the default option, and may, in certain circumstances, be compelled to transfer built units or serviced sites.

This occurs where a developer proceeds to implement a planning permission in circumstances where, first, the planning permission does not leave fallow an area sufficient in size to fulfil the obligation to transfer undeveloped land, and secondly, where the Pt V condition is silent as to the method of compliance. The availability of the default option is predicated on the existence of the possibility of transferring up to 20 per cent of the application site in its undeveloped state to the planning authority. This possibility will not be open where the relevant planning permission allows the whole site to be developed. If a developer proceeds to implement such a planning permission, without first agreeing the method of compliance with the planning authority, that developer might find him or herself backed into a situation whereby the only viable method of compliance which remains open is that of the transfer of built units. Just such a situation came about on the facts of *Glenkerrin Homes v Dun Laoghaire Rathdown County Council (No. 2)*:

> "While it is clear that a developer cannot have an agreement to (say) provide built apartments imposed upon him, I am satisfied that where, without having reached an agreement as to how to meet the social and affordable housing obligations in respect of the planning permission concerned, the developer proceeds to complete the development, the developer, therefore, places itself in a position where the only means of complying with its obligations is to provide either such units or cash. While the developer concerned could not, therefore, have had an agreement in respect of units or cash imposed upon it at the beginning, it has exposed itself to that possibility by rendering any other means of meeting its obligations impossible."

All of this emphasises the desirability from the developer's viewpoint of attempting to nail down the detail of a Pt V agreement at as early a stage as possible.

Equivalent monetary value formula   Part V of the PDA 2000 had been amended by the Planning and Development (Amendment) Act 2002 so as to increase the number of ways in which a developer could discharge his or her obligation. The new methods of compliance included, for example, the provision of land—or, indeed, houses—outside the application site. The option of making a financial contribution was also introduced. Whatever package of measures is put forward, it seems that it must be equivalent in monetary value to the land which would otherwise have been transferred to the planning authority in the event of the default option, i.e. the transfer of undeveloped land. This requirement finds expression in the amended s.96(3)(b), as follows:

> "[…] Subject, in every case, to the provision that is made under this paragraph resulting in the aggregate monetary value of the property or amounts or both, as the case may be, transferred or paid by virtue of the agreement being equivalent to the monetary value of the land that the planning authority would receive if the agreement solely provided for a transfer of land under paragraph (a)."

In its default form, an agreement under Pt V will simply require the transfer to the planning authority of the requisite percentage of the land in an undeveloped state. Presumably, what was intended under s.96(3)(b) was that any alternative package of measures would be equivalent to the planning gain which would have arisen in the event of a straightforward transfer of undeveloped land. This planning gain consists of the notional saving arising from the fact that the planning authority is entitled to acquire land at a discount; the notional saving is the difference between what it would cost to purchase the land on the open market and the actual sum payable by the planning authority under the statutory concept of "existing use" value. Normally the existing use value of the land will be considerably less than the open market value of the land, as the open market value will usually reflect the development potential of the land.

Unhappily, as with much of Pt V, the wording of the legislation in this regard is unsatisfactory. Three particular difficulties arise in practice as follows. First, the phrase "monetary value of the land" seems inapt in that it, arguably, denotes the open market value of the land simpliciter rather than the value of the *planning gain* which accrues to the planning authority in the case of the transfer of undeveloped land.

Secondly, it is not at all clear as to how statutory compensation is to be factored in when reckoning monetary value. In the case of the default option, namely the transfer of undeveloped land, there is a two-way transaction. The developer transfers the requisite percentage of the land: the planning authority makes a payment of compensation, albeit usually discounted by reference to the existing use value of the land. Of course, the transaction is artificial, involving an unequal bargain, in that although consideration (in the form of the payment of statutory compensation) nominally passes from the planning authority, the real benefit of the transaction accrues to the planning authority in that it secures residential land for a payment far less than open market value.

In principle, a similar artificial transaction might be carried out in the case of the transfer of built houses or serviced sites, with the planning authority again making a nominal payment to the developer. It might be more realistic, however, if the planning authority made no payment, and the developer instead simply transferred a *smaller* number of built houses or serviced sites to the planning authority. Smaller, because there will be no payment from the planning authority to set off against the monetary value of the built houses or serviced sites. The *entire* monetary value of each unit will, therefore, be reckoned in calculating the aggregate monetary value of the built houses/serviced sites, and the target (equivalent monetary value) will be reached with a smaller number of units.

Thirdly, the peculiar definition of "existing use" appears to produce a startling result in the case of the transfer of built houses because the valuation date appears to be the date of transfer to the planning authority. In the case of the transfer of built houses, the compensation payable—under s.96(3)(d)—is the site cost, plus the building and attributable development costs. Unlike the position in the case of undeveloped land, however, the site cost may not necessarily be discounted by reference to existing use value. This is because all that the rules require is that *future* development be disregarded. In the case of built houses, the development will, by definition, have already taken place at the date of transfer and—on a literal interpretation of the legislation—this existing development will have to be taken into account in assessing the site cost. Thus, the statutory compensation payable may well be close to market value. This may mean, in effect, that the planning authority achieves no planning gain: the price it pays for the transferred houses is open market value. Under such an analysis, it will always be more attractive for the planning authority either to take a transfer of undeveloped land or to accept a financial contribution.

These three difficulties were addressed in *Cork County Council v Shackleton (No. 1)* ([2007] I.E.H.C. 241; [2008] 1 I.L.R.M. 185). The first issue of principle addressed was as to the interpretation of the terms "monetary value" and "aggregate monetary value". Clarke J. held that the terms should be interpreted as referring to the net benefit to the planning authority of the particular transaction, rather than to the gross or open market value of the land, house or serviced site (as the case may be). Thus, the "monetary value" of the default option of the transfer of undeveloped land consists of the difference between the open market value of the land and the statutory compensation which a planning authority would be required to pay under the existing use formula.

The next issue of principle addressed by Clarke J. was as to how the "existing use" formula operates in the case of the transfer of built houses. As discussed earlier, on one view of the legislation, the existing use of the land in the case of a transfer of a house is a residential use, i.e. its existing use value will coincide with its open market value. On this interpretation, there would be no planning gain to the planning authority in that the existing use formula would not produce any discount on the open market value. Clarke J. rejected an argument that the legislation should be construed in this way, saying that because the planning gain only ever arises on the site cost, an interpretation of existing use value which treated the existing use as residential would be unworkable.

Clarke J. also addressed the question as to whether a planning authority is required to pay statutory compensation in the case of the transfer of houses. Clarke J. interpreted the legislation as requiring such a payment. First, the court accepted the argument made on behalf of the planning authorities that the use of the term "price" in s.96(3)(d) implied that such a sum was, in fact, to be paid by the planning authority, rather than being notionally included in a calculation of the number of units to be transferred. To put the matter another way, the use of the term "price" suggested that a "purchase price" had to be paid by the planning authority. Secondly, Clarke J. held that this interpretation best provided for legal certainty in that it provided a clear formula for calculating the number of houses to be transferred.

JUDICIAL REVIEW

Obligation to raise all issues in earlier litigation The determination of an application for planning permission occurs in two stages: a decision at first instance by the planning authority, with a right of appeal thereafter to An Bord Pleanála. In principle, judicial review is available in respect of either decision. A person dissatisfied with a planning authority's decision thus faces a dilemma: whether to appeal that decision to An Bord Pleanála, or to challenge same before the High Court by way of an application for judicial review. The thrust of the case law is that a person should ordinarily exhaust his rights under the statutory planning process before having recourse to the courts, and thus generally it is appropriate to pursue an appeal to An Bord Pleanála. If necessary, the decision of An Bord Pleanála itself can then be challenged by way of judicial review. It is essential, however, that the legal objection which is subsequently relied upon in the judicial review proceedings has been raised before the board.

The judgment in *Arklow Holidays Ltd v An Bord Pleanála* ([2007] I.E.H.C. 327; unreported, Clarke J., October 5, 2007) indicates that where a challenge to the decision of the planning authority is pursued and is unsuccessful, the applicant for judicial review will not be permitted to raise *new* grounds in any subsequent challenge to the decision of An Bord Pleanála on appeal. Arklow Holidays Ltd opposed the development of a wastewater treatment works and had challenged the decision of the planning authority to grant planning permission for same. An appeal to An Bord Pleanála was stayed pending the determination of the judicial review proceedings. This legal challenge was ultimately unsuccessful, and the appeal before An Bord Pleanála then proceeded. An Bord Pleanála decided to grant planning permission, and this decision was in turn challenged in judicial review proceedings. The grounds advanced in the second judicial review proceedings raised various issues as to the jurisdiction of An Bord Pleanála, and as to the adequacy of the environmental impact statement (EIS). The High Court considered that each of the grounds pursued raised issues which were equally capable of having been raised in respect of the original planning permission process conducted by the planning authority, Wicklow County Council.

The respondents to the second set of judicial review proceedings sought to rely on what was described as the rule in *Henderson v Henderson* ((1843) 3 Hare 100), to the effect that a party to previous litigation is bound not only by matters actually raised in that litigation, but also by matters which ought properly to have been raised but were not. The High Court accepted that the rule—which had originally been formulated in the context of private law proceedings—applied to public law challenges. Clarke J. suggested that if it were permissible for a party to raise some points at the stage of a challenge to a planning decision by a local authority and then raise other points (which could have been raised on the original occasion) at a subsequent challenge to a decision on appeal by An Bord Pleanála, then the rights of all concerned (including the applicant for planning permission, the planning authorities and the board, and the public generally) in the timely determination of planning applications would not be respected.

The High Court rejected an argument that the application of the rule would be inappropriate in a case which involved allegations that the requirements of EC law—specifically the EIA Directive—had been breached. Clarke J. suggested that cases raising EC law issues were to be determined in a manner designated by the procedural law of the Member State concerned, subject always to the principles of equivalence and effectiveness. Neither of these principles were breached: the rule applied equally to proceedings raising national law issues, and the application of the rule would not render any remedy ineffective:

> "There is no practical reason why the points raised in these proceedings could not have been raised at the time of the original challenge to the decision of Wicklow County Council. If they be good points then Arklow Holidays had an effective remedy in relation to them. The way in which that remedy was to be exercised, in accordance with Irish procedural law, was to raise the points at the time of the challenge to the original Wicklow County Council decision. It does not diminish the effectiveness of the remedy to rule that, having omitted to include those points in the original challenge, they can not now be raised in this challenge to the decision of the Board."

Clarke J. concluded, therefore, that the case was an appropriate one in which to apply the rule in *Henderson v Henderson*, and the application for judicial review was accordingly dismissed. There was, in the opinion of the court, no basis for the exercise of its discretion in favour of Arklow Holidays Ltd in circumstances where no real explanation had been given as to why the points now raised were not litigated in the first judicial review proceedings. Finally, it should be noted that Clarke J. expressly left over for consideration to a case where the point directly arises, the question as to the extent to which the rule or, perhaps more accurately, similar considerations, may have any application in a case where no challenge is, in fact, brought to the original planning decision by the local authority, but where the grounds sought to be relied on to challenge a decision of An Bord Pleanála could have been raised had such a challenge been brought.

Leave to appeal to the Supreme Court was subsequently certified: *Arklow Holidays Ltd v An Bord Pleanála* ([2008] I.E.H.C. 2; unreported, Clarke J., January 11, 2008).

Amendment of pleadings   Under ss.50 and 50A of the PDA 2000 (as amended by the Planning and Development (Strategic Infrastructure) Act 2006), judicial review proceedings challenging most types of planning decisions must normally be issued and served within eight weeks of the date of the relevant decision or act. The implications of this time limit for the amendment of pleadings were considered by the High Court in *Sweetman v An Bord Pleanála (No. 1)* ([2007] I.E.H.C. 153; [2007] 2 I.L.R.M. 328). Clarke J. held that where an amendment to the statement of grounds is sought which would amount to the pleading of a new case, and where that amendment is sought outside the statutory time limit, then it can only be granted in circumstances where there is "good and sufficient reason" for allowing the amendment outside time. In substance, the court must be satisfied that there would have been good and sufficient reason for extending the time to bring an application for judicial review based on the new grounds.

Undertaking as to damages   In *Coll v Donegal County Council (No. 2)* ([2007] I.E.H.C. 110; [2008] 1 I.L.R.M. 58), the High Court refused to order an applicant to provide an undertaking as to damages in circumstances where the proceedings raised a public law issue as to the extinguishment of a right of way. Dunne J. refused to order an undertaking as to damages notwithstanding that the applicant openly admitted that she was a "man of straw" and that any undertaking as to damages would be worthless. The judgment goes on to suggest, however, that if a court were satisfied that the use of a particular applicant was a deliberate tactic to frustrate the possibility of an undertaking being obtained—fortified or otherwise—that could amount to an abuse of process such as to merit the requirement of an undertaking as to damages even where matters of public law were at issue.

Costs and public interest litigation   The High Court, in a number of judgments delivered over recent years, suggested that the costs of public interest litigation fall to be dealt with by reference to special principles. The correctness of this approach has since been doubted by the Supreme Court in *Dunne v Minister for the Environment, Heritage and Local Government (No. 3)* ([2007] I.E.S.C. 60; unreported, Supreme Court, December 6, 2007):

> "The rule of law that costs normally follow the event, that the successful party to proceedings should not have to pay the costs of those proceedings which should be borne by the unsuccessful party has an obvious equitable basis. As a counterpoint to that general rule of law the Court has a discretionary jurisdiction to vary or depart from that rule of law if, in the special circumstances of a case, the interests of justice require that it should do so. There is no predetermined category of cases which fall outside the full ambit of that jurisdiction. If there were to be a specific category of cases to which the general rule of law on costs did not apply that would be a matter for legislation since it

> is not for the Courts to establish a cohesive code according to which
> costs would always be imposed on certain successful defendants for
> the benefit of certain unsuccessful plaintiffs."

On the facts of *Dunne (No. 3)*, the Supreme Court, per Murray C.J., held that
there was nothing exceptional in the issues of law raised before the court
which would justify a departure from the general rule that costs should follow
the event. In this regard, Murray C.J. drew a distinction between the subject-
matter of the proceedings, on the one hand, and the legal issues raised in the
proceedings, on the other:

> "Undoubtedly it could be said that issues concerning subject matters
> such as the environment or national monuments have an importance in
> the public mind but a further factor for the Court is whether the legal
> issues raised, rather than the subject matter itself, were of special and
> general public importance. In this case nothing exceptional was raised
> in the issues of law which were before the Court so as to warrant a
> departure from the general rule."

In *Sweetman v An Bord Pleanála (No. 2)* ([2007] I.E.H.C. 361, unreported,
October 25, 2007) the High Court allowed an unsuccessful applicant part of
his costs on the basis that the proceedings had led to a potential evolution in
the jurisprudence in respect of Art.10a of the EIA Directive in at least two
important respects. Clarke J. considered that those matters were of general
public importance.

The fact that a case is a test case, involving the interpretation of obscure
legislation, can justify a departure from the ordinary rule that costs follow the
event. In *Cork County Council v Shackleton (No. 2)* ([2007] I.E.H.C. 334;
unreported, Clarke J, October 12, 2007), the High Court held that the fact
that litigation was necessitated by the introduction of legislation which was
"extremely difficult" to construe, and that one of the parties to the litigation
was a public authority answerable to the very Ministry which introduced the
legislation in the first place, amounted to special circumstances; the justice of
the case would be met by making no order as to costs. Somewhat unusually, the
High Court went on to indicate the view that, whereas the court did not have
any jurisdiction to require the relevant Minister to pay the costs concerned,
the Minister should take whatever steps were appropriate within his remit to
ensure that the local authority was not placed at any financial disadvantage by
reason of not having recovered its costs. Clarke J. stated that the principal reason
why the litigation was necessary was because of the nature of the legislation
introduced and, in those circumstances, the Minister who was responsible for
the legislation should ensure that the local authority suffered no loss by having
played a very necessary role in the clarification of the legislation concerned.

Remittal   Order 84 r.26(4) indicates that where the relief sought in judicial review proceedings is certiorari, and the court is satisfied that there are grounds for quashing the decision, the High Court has a discretion to remit the matter to the decision-maker with a direction to reconsider it and to reach a decision in accordance with the findings of the High Court. The nature of the court's discretion in this regard was considered in detail in *Usk and District Residents Association Ltd v An Bord Pleanála* ([2007] I.E.H.C. 86; [2007] 2 I.L.R.M. 378). The facts of the case were unusual, with An Bord Pleanála conceding that the absence of satisfactory records leading to a decision to grant planning permission meant that it could not establish whether conditions drafted by an inspector were ever approved at a formal board meeting. The inspector had initially recommended that planning permission be refused. The board decided that planning permission should be granted, and requested that the inspector draw up conditions in accordance with the board's determination. There was, however, no record of a subsequent meeting of the board approving the conditions as drafted. In the circumstances, the board conceded that the decision should be quashed.

There was then a dispute between the parties as to whether, on the particular facts of the case, it was appropriate to remit the matter to the board, or whether the planning permission should be quashed simpliciter. This latter course would have required the developer to reapply for planning permission to the planning authority, a course which the court considered would be disproportionate in the circumstances. Kelly J. ruled that the matter should instead be remitted to the board, but went on to make a number of recommendations which he considered would minimise the risk of further judicial review. These included a suggestion that it would be prudent and correct for the board to exercise its jurisdiction to re-open the oral hearing into the appeal, and that the appeal be considered and dealt with by members of the board other than those involved in the impugned decision.

Substantial interest   An applicant for judicial review is required to demonstrate a "substantial interest" in the subject-matter of the application. This requirement has been interpreted as requiring that an applicant have an interest "peculiar or personal" to him or herself. The High Court in *Cumann Thomas Daibhis v South Dublin County Council (No. 1)* ([2007] I.E.H.C. 118; unreported, O'Neill J., March 30, 2007) rejected an argument that a person lacks a "peculiar or personal" interest if some other party has the same or similar interest in the subject-matter of the application. O'Neill J. stated that, in his view, what the phrase "peculiar or personal" imports is that the proposed development the subject-matter of the application is one which affects the applicant personally or individually in a substantial way as distinct from any interest which the wider community, not so personally and individually affected, might have in the proposed development. Thus, as in the case of a housing estate, for example, many people might be affected substantially in this way and all have a "substantial interest".

In *Mulhaire v An Bord Pleanála* (unreported, High Court, Birmingham J., October 31, 2007), it was held that an applicant who had failed to raise a point (as to the timing of the erection of a site notice) before An Bord Pleanála did not have standing to raise that point in judicial review proceedings. This was so notwithstanding the fact that the point had been raised before the board by another objector.

Injunctive relief prior to grant of leave   The High Court has accepted in two related cases that it has jurisdiction to grant injunctive relief—in the form of a stay on proceedings before An Bord Pleanála—prior to the grant of leave to apply for judicial review. In *Harding v Cork County Council (No. 1)* ([2006] I.E.H.C. 80; [2006] 1 I.R. 294; [2006] 2 I.L.R.M. 392), Kelly J. was satisfied that the court did have jurisdiction to grant an injunction, either by reference to the provisions of Ord.84 r.25 or as part of its inherent jurisdiction. Kelly J. rejected the argument put forward on behalf of the notice party developer that the High Court did not have jurisdiction to grant an injunction in advance of the leave application:

> "If the notice party is correct and the court does not have jurisdiction then an absurd result follows. It means that the court is empowered after a grant of leave to seek judicial review has been obtained to make an order to prevent a particular mischief, namely the doing of an act which would alter the status quo in such a way as to make ultimate success by the applicant hollow, but is sterile and impotent to make such an order in advance of hearing the application for leave to apply for judicial review. In my view such a situation would be absurd."

The application for leave to apply for judicial review in *Harding* was subsequently heard by Clarke J., and leave refused: *Harding v Cork County Council (No. 2)* ([2006] I.E.H.C. 295; unreported, Clarke J., October 12, 2006). Clarke J. did, however, grant leave to appeal to the Supreme Court. An application was then made to have the stay on the proceedings before An Bord Pleanála continued. Clarke J. held that just as the High Court has a jurisdiction to grant interim or interlocutory injunctions to preserve the status quo pending a trial, it also had, in an appropriate case, a jurisdiction to continue such injunctions (or to grant new or different injunctions) so as to preserve the *status quo* pending the hearing of the appeal: *Harding v Cork County Council (No. 4)* ([2007] I.E.H.C. 31; [2007] 2 I.L.R.M. 63). Clarke J. extended the stay on the proceedings before An Bord Pleanála for a number of months, and indicated that if the Supreme Court appeal had not been determined within that time, any application to extend the stay further should be made to the Supreme Court directly.

ENFORCEMENT OF PLANNING CONTROL

Seven-year time limit   There is a general time limit of seven years on the taking of enforcement action. An interesting question arises as to whether a developer who engages in *further* unauthorised development can subsequently revert to the baseline level of unauthorised activity. This question typically arises in cases of creeping intensification. The judgment in *Sligo County Council v Martin* ([2007] I.E.H.C. 178; unreported, O'Neill J., May 24, 2007), suggests that such "use rights" as a developer acquires by virtue of the seven-year time limit are fragile and are easily lost. The case concerned the erection and use of a mobile home at a scenic seaside location. The original mobile home had been erected in the early 1970s and was immune from enforcement. The mobile home was replaced by a larger version with a more permanent concrete base. Enforcement proceedings were successfully taken in this regard and the larger mobile home, and concrete base, removed. The developer subsequently sought to "replace" the original mobile home with one identical in size and dimension, leaving the original gravel surface in place. The planning authority brought fresh enforcement proceedings, arguing that the removal of the original mobile home, without the intention of replacing it, was to be regarded as an abandonment of any rights which the developer may have had in relation to the original mobile home. O'Neill J., in granting relief under s.160 of the PDA 2000, indicated that the events should not be analysed solely in terms of the "use" of land, but also in terms of "works". In the opinion of the court, the construction of a new gravel base and the placing thereon of a new mobile home, regardless of its size, constituted "works" within the meaning of s.3(1) of the PDA 2000:

> "I am satisfied therefore that apart from user of this site as a site for a mobile home the process of establishing the mobile home on the site as described in the evidence necessarily involved the carrying out of works and as such it was a development which required planning permission. I am fortified in this conclusion by the fact that at all times since 1974 the placing of a mobile home on this site by the respondent or his father was intended to be and indeed undoubtedly became the placing of a permanent object on this site. There does not appear to have been any question of moving this home and it is plainly obvious it was there as a permanent holiday facility for the respondent and his family. In this context in my view, and having regard to the nature of the work carried out to establish this object on this site, this mobile home is properly to be regarded as a 'structure' as defined in s. 2 of the Act of 2000.

I am satisfied that when the original mobile home was removed in 2000, this was a permanent change and intended to be so, and hence any rights, or more particularly, immunity from action under s.160 of the Act of 2000 which had accrued in relation to that structure were abandoned by the respondent."

Immaterial deviations   In two judgments in 2001 the High Court had suggested that a planning permission covered not only the works specified in the detailed plans, but also any immaterial deviation therefrom: *O'Connell v Dungarvan Energy Ltd* (unreported, High Court, Finnegan J., February 27, 2001) and *Cork County Council v Cliftonhall Ltd* (unreported, High Court, Finnegan J., April 6, 2001). What precisely is involved in this notion of an "immaterial deviation" was considered in some detail recently by the High Court in *Wicklow County Council v Forest Fencing Ltd* ([2007] I.E.H.C. 242; unreported, Charleton J., July 13, 2007). The principal issue in that case was whether the developer was entitled to planning permission by default. Charleton J., having found against the developer on this point, went on to indicate that, in any event, the development as carried out was not in conformity with the planning permission claimed. In a number of instances, buildings had been erected closer to the N11 road than had been indicated in the planning application: the deviation from the plans ranged from between 8 metres to 3.5 metres. The buildings as a whole infringed the planning authority's building line (which required a 100-metre set-back from the national road). There were a number of other differences between the plans and the development as carried out.

Charleton J. indicated that whereas he accepted that planning permissions should be interpreted with some degree of flexibility so as to allow for the practical reality that buildings can sometimes not be built precisely as the plans indicate, this tolerance only extends as far as "immaterial deviations". Charleton J. went on to emphasise that in considering whether a deviation was material, it was necessary to have regard to the importance which the planning legislation attaches to the rights of the owners and occupiers of neighbouring property:

"In general, what is material in relation to a densely occupied suburban area, or a block of flats, may not be material where one is dealing with an extensive site. What is material where neighbours are affected due to the proximity of a development, may become immaterial where they are unaffected. It is difficult to see variations which materially affect neighbours to a development, which trespass outside a site boundary, which exercise rights of easement without permission by supporting structures on a third party property, or which materially affect existing rights of easement, as being minimal. Nor could it be regarded as necessarily immaterial where a letter in support of a planning application promises to obtain agreement as to the way a building proposed may be joined to a neighbouring property, but in fact agreement is absent. This is not to attempt to cut down in any way the court's discretion in approaching its equitable jurisdiction to grant injunctive relief. Each case must be looked at carefully because orders of this kind are very serious."

The High Court also emphasised that the development plan should not be disregarded through deviations from approved plans which are material to it. In all the circumstances of the case before him, Charleton J. concluded that the development as carried out deviated in a material way from the plans as originally submitted to Wicklow County Council.

A related point was addressed by McGovern J. in his judgment in *Dooner v Longford County Council* ([2007] I.E.H.C. 356; unreported, McGovern J., October 25, 2007). The planning authority had—in the context of agreeing a compliance submission—purported to authorise the relocation of a building by a distance of 14.5 metres. McGovern J. held that this constituted a substantial movement having regard to the nature of the site and did not come within the limited degree of flexibility allowed under *Boland v An Bord Pleanála* ([1996] 3 I.R. 435).

Discretion in section 160 proceedings   The nature of the courts' discretion to withhold relief in s.160 proceedings was considered in *Wicklow County Council v Forest Fencing Ltd* ([2007] I.E.H.C. 242; unreported, Charleton J., July 13, 2007). The facts of that case were unusual in that the principal defence asserted on behalf of the developer was that it had the benefit of a default planning permission. The developer's claim in this regard was rejected by Charleton J. In considering whether relief should be refused as a matter of discretion, Charleton J. suggested that just as the court would have had little discretion to refuse to allow the developer the benefit of a default planning permission had his case in that regard been made out, similarly it should have little discretion to withhold relief in circumstances where:

"… [T]he Court has found that there is no default permission: where the developer has, on the contrary, developed the site entirely in accordance with his own wishes and with little or no reference even to the plans in respect of which he once sought permission. The discretion of the Court, in this context, is very limited. The balancing of that discretion must start with the duty of the court to uphold the principle of proper planning for developments under clear statutory rules. Then, the Court should ask what might allow the consideration of the exercise of its discretion in favour of not granting injunctive relief.
To fail to grant injunctive relief in these circumstances, on these

facts, would be to cause a situation to occur where the Court is effectively taking the place of the planning authority. The Court should not do that. This is a major development, for which there is no planning permission. It is in material contravention of the County Wicklow Development Plan. It is built entirely to suit the developer and with almost no reference to legal constraint. I am obliged to decide in favour of the injunctive relief sought."

The importance of public participation in the planning process was emphasised by the High Court in *Sligo County Council v Martin* ([2007] I.E.H.C. 178; unreported, O'Neill J., May 24, 2007) when granting an injunction against an unauthorised mobile home in a scenic area:

"If the court were to not grant relief that would have the effect of granting planning permission for this structure in circumstances where the various procedures set out in the Act of 2000 for the purposes of protecting the public in regard to development would be ignored with the inevitable defeat of a variety of public interests. Firstly there is the interest of the public in general to participate in the planning process by making objection or observation in relation to any particular proposed development. Secondly the expert supervisory role of the local authority as planning authority would be set at nought as it would be entirely excluded."

Second or subsequent enforcement notice   In *Clare County Council v Floyd* ([2007] I.E.H.C. 48; unreported, High Court, Charleton J., January 19, 2007), the District Court stated a case to the High Court as to whether it was open to a planning authority to serve, and prosecute a breach of, a second enforcement notice in circumstances where a prosecution in respect of an alleged breach of an earlier enforcement notice had resulted in an acquittal. Charleton J. held that it was not the law that a person was entitled to maintain an unauthorised development merely by reason of his acquittal in respect of a summons issued for an offence on one particular day (or a continuation thereafter) on one particular occasion. Once the dates as between the two enforcement notices were different, then two separate offences were alleged and the principle of *autrefois acquit* had no application.

Quarries   The judgment in *Callan v Boyle Quarries Ltd* ([2007] I.E.H.C. 91; [2007] 2 I.L.R.M. 546) illustrates the difficulties which a developer seeking to rely on the historic use of land as a quarry will face in resisting enforcement proceedings. The applicant brought proceedings under s.160 of the PDA 2000 alleging that there had been unauthorised development by way of intensification. The High Court drew attention to the fact that much of the evidence tendered on both sides lacked corroboration. Murphy J. also suggested that whereas the onus of proof is on the applicant to advance satisfactory evidence before the court regarding his complaints, where objective, credible evidence of intensification is adduced, the court may have regard to the absence of available evidence of extraction either from the respondent, the operator or the licensor.

ENVIRONMENTAL IMPACT ASSESSMENT DIRECTIVE

Division of function between EPA and An Bord Pleanála Where a development project is subject to licensing by the Environmental Protection Agency (the "EPA"), then both the planning authorities/An Bord Pleanála and the EPA have a function in carrying out the environmental impact assessment ("EIA"). Prior to the PDA 2000, there was a strict division of function, with the EPA confined to considering "environmental pollution", and the planning authorities/An Bord Pleanála prohibited from considering such matters. A more flexible approach was adopted under the PDA 2000, and the present position is that planning permission may be refused where a planning authority or An Bord Pleanála considers the development, notwithstanding the licensing of the activity under either the Environmental Protection Agency Act 1992, or the Waste Management Acts 1996 to 2001, is unacceptable on environmental grounds, having regard to the proper planning and sustainable development of the area in which the development is or will be situate. Where planning permission is granted, however, restrictions apply to the types of planning conditions which may be imposed. Specifically, there are prohibitions on the attachment of conditions for the purposes of (a) controlling emissions from the operation of the activity, including the prevention, limitation, elimination, abatement or reduction of those emissions; or (b) controlling emissions related to or following the cessation of the operation of the activity.

Opponents of development projects have criticised this statutory division of function between the planning authorities/An Bord Pleanála and the EPA, especially as it stood prior to the PDA 2000. The principal objection advanced is that neither body is in a position to carry out an "integrated assessment" of the effects of the project on the environment. This argument was roundly rejected by the Supreme Court in *Martin v An Bord Pleanála* ([2007] I.E.S.C. 23; [2007] 2 I.L.R.M. 401). Murray C.J., in a unanimous judgment, drew attention to the fact that the EIA Directive specifically envisaged that more than one competent authority might be responsible at different stages for carrying out the assessment:

> "It seems to me that it would be absurd to interpret the Directive so as to suggest that in permitting two or more competent bodies to carry out an EIA of the factors referred to in Article 3, including the interaction

between them, by each body at the relevant stage of the process with which it was concerned, that nonetheless it was intended that there must be one body only that carries out an assessment of all the factors as if there was only one stage in the process and it was the only body making the assessment. This would run contrary to the plain meaning of the provisions and scheme of the Directive."

The Supreme Court ruled that the meaning of the EIA Directive in this regard was acte clair, and that there was, therefore, no necessity to make a reference to the ECJ pursuant to Art.234 of the Treaty.

Subsequent to the judgment of the Supreme Court in *Martin*, the European Commission indicated publicly that it intends to pursue infringement proceedings against Ireland pursuant to Art.226 of the Treaty. In a Press Release of October 17, 2007, the Commission stated that it considers that, because of (alleged) weaknesses in Irish legislation splitting decision-making between the planning authorities and the EPA, there are risks that outcomes required by the EIA Directive will not always be achieved. This threat of infringement proceedings was relied upon by objectors to two waste incineration projects in an (unsuccessful) attempt to defer their judicial review proceedings pending the outcome of any proceedings ultimately instituted by the Commission before the ECJ. The grounds relied upon in those judicial review proceedings included, inter alia, an argument that the division of function between the planning authorities/An Bord Pleanála and the EPA was in breach of the requirements of the EIA Directive ("the improper transposition argument"). The objectors accepted that if their judicial review proceedings were to be heard now, in advance of any ruling by the ECJ, the proceedings would have to fail because the argument that the EIA Directive has not been properly transposed has been rejected definitively by the Supreme Court in *Martin*. McCarthy J. refused to adjourn the judicial review proceedings, saying that the High Court was bound by the judgment of the Supreme Court: *O'Leary v An Bord Pleanála* (unreported, High Court, McCarthy J., February 18, 2008).

Review procedure under Article 10a   Member States are required under Art.10a of the amended EIA Directive to provide a "review procedure" before a court of law, or another independent and impartial body established by law, to challenge the substantive or procedural legality of decisions, acts or omissions subject to the public participation provisions of the Directive. The nature of the review procedure required under Art.10a was considered in detail by the High Court in *Sweetman v An Bord Pleanála (No. 1)* ([2007] I.E.H.C. 153; [2007] 2 I.L.R.M. 328). The case concerned a challenge to An Bord Pleanála's assessment of proposed road development under s.51 of the Roads Act 1993 (as amended). The proposed development was below threshold, but was nevertheless subject to EIA on account of its proximity to a candidate Special

Area of Conservation ("cSAC"). The applicant for judicial review argued that Ireland had failed to provide for a review procedure consistent with Art.10a. Under national law, challenges to decisions of An Bord Pleanála are subject to statutory judicial review under s.50 of the PDA 2000; the applicant asserted that such judicial review met neither the procedural, nor the substantive, requirements of the EIA Directive. The principal aspects of the statutory judicial review procedure which were criticised included the following. First, it was said that the requirement that an applicant demonstrate a "substantial interest" was inconsistent with Art.10a, which only required an applicant to establish a "sufficient interest". Secondly, the necessity that an applicant obtain the leave of the High Court before pursuing his or her substantive application for judicial review was said to amount to a barrier to the entitlement to the judicial review. Thirdly, it was argued that the exposure of applicants to the possibility of a costs order made in favour not only of respondents but also of notice parties amounts to a prohibitive cost in breach of the Directive. The High Court dealt with these issues as follows.

The High Court rejected the argument that the requirement to demonstrate a "substantial interest" was inconsistent with Art.10a. Clarke J. suggested that the meaning to be given to particular terms in EC Directives, on the one hand, and in the national legislation of Member States, on the other, need not necessarily be the same:

> "The terms 'substantial interest' and 'sufficient interest' have a particular meaning in Irish judicial review law. It could not be the case that the directive intended to use the term 'sufficient interest' by reference to the judicial review law of Ireland or, indeed, of the United Kingdom which operates a similar regime. Rather it is clear from the text of Article 10a itself that 'sufficient interest' is merely taken to mean the interest which the member state itself determines subject only to the requirement that it give wide access to justice. This latter limitation needs to be seen in the context that the directive itself permits the confining of a right to challenge to those being able to show an impairment of a right."

Clarke J. went on to hold that if it should prove to be necessary, on the facts of any individual case, to give a more generous interpretation of the requirement of "substantial interest" so as to meet the "wide access to justice" criteria set out in Art.10a, then there would be no difficulty in construing the term "substantial interest" in an appropriate manner. In summary, the High Court was suggesting that any alleged inconsistency between the standing requirement under Art.10a and the standing requirement under s.50 of the PDA 2000 could be resolved by adopting an interpretation of national law which was "sympathetic" to the requirements of the EIA Directive. On the particular facts of the case—which concerned a development project within proximity to a cSAC—Clarke J. held that, having regard to the obligation under the Directive to allow wide access to justice and the application of that principle to the necessity to afford a reasonably wide range of people with an opportunity to have their concerns dealt with in relation to sensitive areas, he was satisfied that the applicant had a "substantial interest".

In so far as the requirement to obtain the leave of the High Court in advance of any substantive application for judicial review was concerned, Clarke J. rejected the argument that this requirement was in breach of Art.10a:

> "[...] The fact that, as a matter of Irish procedural law, we speak of a substantive judicial review as referring to a full hearing which occurs after leave has been granted, does not mean that the leave application itself does not amount to a judicial review in the sense in which that term is used in the Directive. It is a review by a court. The applicant, provided that the application is brought in time, can raise whatever issues he, she or it wishes. The court has to give due consideration to all of those issues. Where facts are in issue the court must, at that stage, give the applicant the benefit of the doubt. The hearing of leave applications under s.50 of the 2000 Act frequently takes a number of days. It does not seem to me that there could be any basis for suggesting that a party who is given access to a court to agitate whatever arguments they wish in support of a leave application has not been given a judicial review in the sense in which that term is used in the Directive.
>
> The fact that, if the court thinks that the grounds put forward are insubstantial, it follows that the case does not go any further, does not mean that the applicant concerned has not had a judicial review. It simply means that the case was of insufficient merit to warrant further consideration. The person concerned has had their judicial review and has failed to persuade the court that there is a weighty basis for it. On the other hand if facts need to be gone into or complex and difficult issues of law arise upon which there are weighty arguments on either side then the court will, as a matter of Irish procedural law, require a further hearing before reaching a final decision. However the process taken as a whole affords the applicant access to a court. The mere fact that leave has to be obtained and that, as part of that process in order to obtain leave, substantial grounds need to be established, does not in any way diminish the entitlement of that party to access to a court and a review that it is (within the parameters of Irish judicial review) conducted by a judge of the issues raised. I am not, therefore, satisfied that there is any basis for the contention that the requirement for leave based on substantial grounds infringes the obligation to provide a judicial review as required by the Directive."

The third criticism of the statutory judicial review procedure made by the applicant involved an allegation that the costs of judicial review proceedings under Irish law offended against the requirement under Art.10a that the review procedure not be "prohibitively expensive". This issue had previously been considered by the High Court in *Friends of the Curragh Environment Ltd v An Bord Pleanála (No. 1)* ([2006] I.E.H.C. 243; unreported, Kelly J., July 14, 2006, see *Annual Review of Irish Law 2006*, 470). As pointed out by Clarke J. in *Sweetman*, the legislative background to those earlier proceedings was very different in that *Friends of the Curragh Environment Ltd* concerned a decision of An Bord Pleanála on appeal, and there was some suggestion that the appeal itself, rather than the subsequent judicial review proceedings, constituted the "review procedure" for the purposes of Art.10a. In any case, Kelly J. in *Friends of the Curragh Environment Ltd* held that the provisions of Art.10a were not sufficiently precise, clear or unconditional to render it of direct effect. Clarke J. adopted a somewhat different approach to this issue in *Sweetman*, and sought to rely on the provisions of the Aarhus Convention in interpreting Art.10a of the EIA Directive. The Aarhus Convention provides, at Art.3(8), that each Contracting Party shall ensure that persons exercising their rights in conformity with the provisions of the Convention shall not be penalised, persecuted or harassed in any way for their involvement. Article 3(8) then goes on to state that this provision shall not affect the powers of national courts to award reasonable costs in judicial review proceedings. Notwithstanding the fact that there is no similar provision in the EIA Directive, Clarke J. considered that it was permissible to rely on the provisions of Art.3(8) of the Aarhus Convention in interpreting the phrase "prohibitively expensive" in Art.10a of the EIA Directive. With respect, it is submitted that such an approach to interpretation is inappropriate. First, even in the context of the Aarhus Convention itself, the existence of a connection between the saver—in the specific context of the prohibition under Art.3(8) on the penalisation, persecution and harassment of a person exercising his or rights under the Convention—for the reasonable costs of judicial review proceedings, on the one hand, and the requirement that the "review procedure" in the context of the distinct provisions concerning "access to justice", on the other, is questionable. There is no requirement that the "review procedure" be by way of judicial review—it is expressly provided that the procedure may be before a court of law and/or another independent and impartial body established by law. The most that Art.3(8) does, therefore, is to suggest that where a State opts to provide a review procedure *other* than before a court of law, the jurisdiction to impose costs in judicial review proceedings, in other contexts, survives, subject to the requirement that the costs be reasonable. Where, conversely, a State opts to provide the "review procedure" before a court of law—as Ireland has done under the EIA Directive—then it is required to ensure that the costs of judicial review are not prohibitively expensive.

There is a second, more fundamental, objection to the approach adopted by Clarke J. in *Sweetman*, as follows. The ECJ has emphasised—in the specific context of the EIA Directive—that the terms of a provision of Community law which makes no express reference to the law of the Member States for the purpose of determining its meaning and scope is normally to be given throughout the Community an autonomous and uniform interpretation which must take into account the context of the provision and the purpose of the legislation in question: see *R. (on the application of Wells) v Secretary of State for Transport, Local Government and the Regions* (Case C-201/02), para.37. It follows therefore that the term "prohibitively expensive" must be given an autonomous and uniform interpretation. The fact that Clarke J. felt it necessary to resort to an extrinsic aid to interpretation, i.e. the text of the Aarhus Convention, indicates that the High Court considered that the meaning of the EIA Directive was not clear. In the circumstances, the appropriate response would have been to refer the matter to the ECJ pursuant to Art.234 of the Treaty. Instead, the High Court attempted its own interpretation of Art.10a based on a questionable reference to the text of the Aarhus Convention. The failure to refer this matter to the ECJ presents a real risk of an inconsistent application of Art.10a throughout the Community. Indeed, as a matter of Irish law, we now have two conflicting decisions of the High Court on the interpretation of Art.10a. Kelly J. in *Friends of the Curragh Environment Ltd* considered that the term "prohibitively expensive" was imprecise and, in particular, that it was not clear whether the term referred to court fees, which are chargeable by the State, or to legal costs, which are not. In *Sweetman v An Bord Pleanála (No. 1)*, conversely, Clarke J. was satisfied, by reference to the Aarhus Convention, that the absence of excessive cost requirement of the EIA Directive was not intended to cover the exposure of a party to reasonable costs in judicial review proceedings.

Standard of judicial review   As discussed above, the applicant in *Sweetman v An Bord Pleanála (No. 1)* ([2007] I.E.H.C. 153; [2007] 2 I.L.R.M. 328) had sought to argue that the statutory judicial review procedure provided for under s.50 of the PDA 2000 did not meet the requirements of Art.10 of the EIA Directive. In addition, the applicant also sought to argue, more generally, that the limited grounds upon which judicial review is available under Irish law fall short of what is required under the EIA Directive. In particular, it was suggested—by reference to *O'Keeffe v An Bord Pleanála* ([1993] 1 I.R. 39)—that Irish law does not allow for the "substantive" legality of a decision or act to be challenged.

The High Court addressed this argument on a number of levels. First, Clarke J. suggested that if and in so far as it might be necessary to do so in order to comply with the EIA Directive, the standard of judicial review could be adjusted so as to apply a greater level of scrutiny in relation to environmental judicial review applications. In this regard, an analogy was drawn with the position adopted in respect of immigration judicial review fundamental human rights cases, and the emerging test of "anxious scrutiny":

> "[I]t again seems to me that it is possible to accommodate any requirements which may be found to exist within Article 10a, in the existing judicial review regime. It may mean that the court will have to consider, initially on a substantial grounds basis, and subsequently on a substantive basis, what level of scrutiny is required to meet the Directive's requirements. In turn, in determining whether there are substantive grounds on the facts of an individual case for giving leave to challenge, the court will need to consider whether (at the high water mark of the level of scrutiny for which the court is satisfied substantial grounds exist) there are substantial grounds for the challenge itself. In turn at a substantive hearing the court can apply whatever level of scrutiny it considers is mandated by the Directive."

Clarke J. went on to consider next what precisely was required under the Art.10a review procedure. Clarke J. did not accept that the EIA Directive required that there be a full appeal on the merits, but considered instead that a test such as "manifest error" which still allowed a margin of appreciation to the decision-maker would be sufficient:

> "It is important to note that what the Directive allows persons to challenge is 'the substantive or procedural legality of decisions'. While it is clear that Irish judicial review law allows an extensive review of the procedural legality of decisions, it is important to note that the Directive does not require that there be a judicial review of the substance of the decision itself but rather the 'substantive legality' of the decision. It seems clear therefore (and indeed it was not otherwise argued on behalf of Mr. Sweetman) that the Directive does not require a complete appeal on the merits. In addition to a review of the procedures followed, to determine whether they were in accordance with law, it is also necessary that there be a review of the 'substantive legality' of the decision. It seems to me that current Irish judicial review law goes a long way towards (and indeed may well meet) that requirement. Judicial review proceedings can review whether it was, as a matter of law, open to the decision-maker to come to the decision taken. It can review whether all proper matters were taken into account and no improper matters taken into account. The limitation on the review is that the court is not permitted to 'second guess' a judgment made by the decision-maker on the basis of materials which could allow such a judgment to be reached."

With respect, the High Court's analysis of the grounds of judicial review available under Irish law is somewhat optimistic. In particular, the fact that the courts have to date absolved decision-makers from a duty to give other than the most perfunctory of reasons makes it difficult to prove that a decision was based on irrelevant considerations or on an error of law.

In any event, it must be doubted whether the High Court was correct in characterising the *Sweetman* case as one involving a reasonableness challenge. An Bord Pleanála had imposed—in the context of a decision approving road development—a condition requiring groundwater monitoring along the route of the permitted road "to establish groundwater levels and quality in groundwater flow patterns". The condition required that the monitoring continue for a period of three years following the completion of the proposed road. The stated reason for the condition was to ensure adequate monitoring of potential impacts on a cSAC. The applicant for judicial review made the legitimate point that such a monitoring requirement would be inadequate without some additional measure to provide for further mitigation in the event that the monitoring demonstrated some unforeseen consequence. The EIA Directive requires not only that the decision-maker be informed as to the likely significant effects of a project on the environment before reaching a decision to grant development consent, but also that the public be consulted in relation to the mitigation measures to be taken. The challenge in *Sweetman* therefore raised issues of vires. To suggest that the challenge could be resolved on the basis that An Bord Pleanála had not acted "unreasonably" is unfortunate.

EIA Directive and prison development   The High Court in *Kavanagh v Ireland* ([2007] I.E.H.C. 296; unreported, Smyth J., July 31, 2007) rejected an argument that the development of a prison constituted an urban regeneration project for the purposes of the EIA Directive, holding that the proposed prison constituted a stand-alone institutional use. The High Court also rejected an argument that the provision of a car park brought the project within the EIA Directive. Smyth J. ruled that any car park to be provided in the prison project would be ancillary and incidental to the institutional use; and, in any event, would not be in an urban area, nor form part of an urban development.

In the same case, the High Court ruled that the National Development Plan ("NDP") did not constitute a plan or programme for the purposes of the Strategic Environmental Assessment Directive (Directive 2001/42/EC). Smyth J. held that the NDP was not required by legislative, regulatory or administrative provisions, and that it did not set the framework for future development consents. Rather, it was a financial or budgetary plan and thus not subject to the requirements of the SEA Directive.

COMPULSORY ACQUISITION OF LAND

Particular purpose for which land required   As a result of amendments introduced under Pt XIV of the PDA 2000, planning authorities enjoy extensive powers in respect of what might be described as "proactive planning". In particular, planning authorities are empowered to develop or secure or facilitate the development of land. A planning authority may also secure, facilitate or carry out the development and renewal of areas in need of physical, social or economic regeneration and provide open spaces and other public amenities. To these ends, a planning authority is entitled to use its powers of compulsory acquisition.

A clear distinction is drawn under s.213 of the PDA 2000 between acquisition by agreement and acquisition compulsorily. Land may only be acquired compulsorily where it is required for a "particular purpose". Moreover, if the land is not immediately required for a particular purpose, the planning authority must be of the opinion that the land will be required for that purpose in the future. Conversely, acquisition may be effected by *agreement* in respect of any land which, in the opinion of the planning authority, it will require in the future for the purposes of any of its functions, notwithstanding that the planning authority has not yet determined the manner in which or the purpose for which it will use the land. It seems, therefore, that the concept of a "particular purpose" is crucial in identifying and restricting the power of compulsory acquisition.

In *Clinton v An Bord Pleanála (No. 2)* ([2007] I.E.S.C. 19; [2007] 2 I.L.R.M. 81), it was argued on behalf of one of the landowners affected by a compulsory purchase order that the failure of the acquiring authority to identify the "particular purpose" for which the lands were required invalidated the order. The acquiring authority had indicated to An Bord Pleanála, at the time of the oral hearing into the compulsory purchase order, that it (the acquiring authority) had not made a decision as to the exact type of development which was to be carried out on the lands sought to be acquired, nor had it made a decision as to whether the development would be carried out by a private developer in partnership with the acquiring authority, or by the acquiring authority alone. An Bord Pleanála, in its decision confirming the compulsory purchase order, had stated that the acquisition of the lands was necessary for "the purposes of facilitating the implementation of" the local authority's development plan. The development plan, in turn, referred to the O'Connell Street integrated area plan which designated the site as suitable for urban renewal.

The Supreme Court held that the regeneration purpose which the local authority had in mind when deciding to make the compulsory purchase order constituted a "particular purpose" within the meaning of s.213(3) of the PDA 2000:

"The regeneration purpose, which the council had in mind when deciding to make the Compulsory Purchase Order, was expressly permitted by the Oireachtas. It cannot have been envisaged that the council would have to have a specific plan as to how the regeneration was to be carried out and would have to specify that in the CPO because, as in this case, the whole process would usually involve private developers in some form at least and plans as yet unknown which they would propose and envisage and which would eventually require planning permission. That is quite different from property required for the purposes of council offices or a public swimming pool for instance.

It was at all times perfectly clear that the property was being acquired for regeneration of O'Connell Street. In my view, it was only necessary for the council to demonstrate that a CPO was desirable in the public interest to achieve that purpose. It was not necessary to prove how exactly it would be carried out. Quite apart from the necessity to obtain planning permissions into the future, such a requirement would defeat the purpose of the power conferred by the section."

Statutory compensation: injurious affection   Where a person has had part only of his lands taken by compulsory acquisition, he or she is entitled to claim compensation in respect of both the taken lands and the injury to the retained lands ("injurious affection"). The Supreme Court in *Chadwick (Deceased) v Fingal County Council* ([2007] I.E.S.C. 49; unreported, November 6, 2007) confirmed that the statutory right of compensation only extended to injurious affection caused by development on the lands taken. On the facts, therefore, the landowner was not entitled to claim statutory compensation in respect of a reduction in value of his retained lands (caused by the construction and subsequent use of a motorway) in circumstances where no part of the motorway lay on the lands taken from him. In his judgment, Fennelly J. suggested that compensation for injurious affection was intended to reflect the fact that, but for the compulsory acquisition of his or her land, a landowner would have been entitled to prevent the taken land being used for road development. This rationale did not apply where no road development was to be carried out on the land taken from the particular landowner. The continued existence of a cause of action in nuisance was sufficient protection for a landowner's rights where that person either (i) had no land taken, or (ii) had land taken, but that land did not ultimately comprise part of the road development.

DERELICT SITES ACT

Definition of "derelict site"   Extensive powers—including a power of compulsory acquisition—are conferred on local authorities under the Derelict Sites Act 1990. The exercise of these powers is contingent on the relevant land constituting a "derelict site". A "derelict site" is defined as meaning any land which detracts, or is likely to detract, to a material degree from the amenity, character or appearance of land in the neighbourhood of the land in question because of—(a) the existence on the land in question of structures which are in a ruinous, derelict or dangerous condition, or (b) the neglected, unsightly or objectionable condition of the land or any structures on the land in question, or (c) the presence, deposit or collection on the land in question of any litter, rubbish, debris or waste, except where the presence, deposit or collection of such litter, rubbish, debris or waste results from the exercise of a right conferred under statute or by common law.

The definition of "derelict site" was considered by the High Court in *Hussey v Dublin City Council* ([2007] I.E.H.C. 425; unreported, O'Higgins J., December 14, 2007). The applicant sought an order of mandamus directing the local authority to take steps to ensure that neighbouring land did not continue to be a derelict site. O'Higgins J. rejected a preliminary objection on the part of the local authority to the effect that the duties under s.10 of the Derelict Sites Act 1990 were not enforceable by way of mandamus, holding that the duties were expressed in "clear and unambiguous terms". The court went on to find, on the facts, that the neighbouring premises did not constitute a "derelict site". O'Higgins J. held that in order to constitute a "derelict site" it was not sufficient for a structure on the land to be "derelict" within the meaning of s.3(b) of the Derelict Sites Act 1990, i.e. that the structure be in a "neglected, unsightly or objectionable" condition. Rather, it was necessary to meet the *additional* requirement that such condition detract to a material degree from the amenity, character or appearance of land in the neighbourhood. The words "amenity, character or appearance" were, in the view of the court, directed towards the neighbourhood and surroundings in general, and not the internal condition of specific premises, such as the property next door. It would be unduly strained and artificial to describe the presence of damp and ingress of water, and future danger of spread of rot, as matters detracting or likely to detract from the amenity, character or appearance of land in the neighbourhood. The Derelict Sites Act 1990 was directed towards the effect which a derelict site had on the external amenities of the neighbourhood in general, rather than directed towards the effect on the internal condition of any given house.

APPEAL TO AN BORD PLEANÁLA

Notification of appeal   Under art.69 of the Planning and Development Regulations 2001, a planning authority is required to give notice of the fact that an appeal has been made to An Bord Pleanála to any person who had made a submission at the planning authority stage ("an observer"). The notice must (a) specify the reference number of the board in respect of the appeal; (b) specify the date on which the appeal was received by the board; (c) state that a copy of the appeal is available for inspection or purchase, for a fee not exceeding the reasonable cost of making a copy, during office hours at the offices of the planning authority; and (d) state that submissions or observations in relation to the appeal may be made in writing to the board within the appropriate period and on payment of the appropriate fee. In *Rowan v An Bord Pleanála* ([2006] I.E.H.C. 180; unreported, Feeney J., May 26, 2006) the High Court held that the requirements of art.69 were mandatory, and that failure to comply with same invalidated the appeal to An Bord Pleanála. In reaching this conclusion, Feeney J. rejected the suggestion that the furnishing of other material subsequently to the observer rectified the failure to comply with art.69. Feeney J. also ruled that the failure to institute judicial review proceedings prior to the making of a decision by An Bord Pleanála did not disentitle the applicant to relief.

Material contravention of development plan   The High Court in *Mulhaire v An Bord Pleanála* (unreported, High Court, Birmingham J., October 31, 2007) held that the requirements of s.37(2)(b) of the PDA 2000 are not cumulative, and it is not necessary, therefore, that each of the four criteria specified therein be met before An Bord Pleanála can decide to grant planning permission in material contravention of the development plan.

LOCAL AUTHORITY OWN DEVELOPMENT

Resolution by elected members   Development by a local authority in its own functional area is exempted from the requirement to obtain planning permission. Certain types of local authority development are, however, subject to a form of public consultation under s.179 of the PDA 2000, and Pt 8 of the Planning and Development Regulations 2001. Following public consultation, the manager prepares a written report for submission to the elected members. The report should contain, inter alia, a recommendation as to whether the development should be proceeded with as proposed, or be proceeded with in a varied or modified form (as recommended in the report). The development is to be carried out as recommended in the manager's report unless the elected members by resolution direct otherwise. Any such resolution must be passed within six weeks of the date of receipt of the manager's report. In *Cumann Tomas Daibhis v South Dublin County Council (No. 2)* ([2007] I.E.H.C. 426; unreported, Murphy J., December 14, 2007), the High Court had to consider the circumstances, if any, in which the elected members can revisit an earlier resolution varying development proposals. The proposed development involved the construction of a sports stadium. The elected members had initially resolved to vary the design of the proposed development from that recommended by the manager, with a view to facilitating the playing of sports other than soccer. Subsequently, on being informed that the Minister for Arts,

Sports and Tourism would not agree to make funding available on the basis of the new development proposals, the elected members sought to revert to the development proposals recommended in the manager's report. This decision was challenged by a local GAA club on the basis, inter alia, that the subsequent resolution was contrary to the members' earlier decision which had been made following consideration of submissions and observations by the public and consideration of proper planning and sustainable development. It was further argued that the subsequent resolution would negate the entire process laid down in s.179, by reverting to the original proposal as if no public consultation, no submissions and no consideration to modify had taken place. The High Court rejected these arguments:

> "It seems to the court that the overarching purpose of s. 179, to oblige a local authority to give notice to the public and prescribed bodies of certain classes of development proposed to be carried out and to afford them an opportunity to make submissions and observations in respect of the proposed development, has been complied with. The deputy manager reported: the Council sought initially to vary the recommendation in the hope of getting additional funds and, where those funds were not available, took a pragmatic decision. There was no requirement for further consultation or submission and observations in respect of the proposed development. The applicant was not prejudiced by the failure to make the resolution [within six weeks of receipt of the manager's report]."

In reaching this conclusion the High Court seems to have taken the pragmatic view that the elected members should not be held to their earlier resolution in circumstances where the form of development then proposed could not now be proceeded with in the absence of departmental funding.

PROTECTED STRUCTURES

Places of public worship One consequence of a structure being designated as a protected structure or a proposed protected structure is that the benefit of exempted development is lost in certain circumstances. In particular, the general exemption in respect of works affecting only the interior of a structure is disapplied where such works would affect the character of (a) the structure; or (b) any element of the structure which contributes to its special architectural, historical, archaeological, artistic, cultural, scientific, social or technical interest.

Special provision is made under s.57 of PDA 2000 for cases where a protected structure is regularly used as a place of public worship. Planning authorities and An Bord Pleanála are required to "respect liturgical requirements" in the context of (i) making a declaration as to the type of works which would or would not materially affect the character of the protected structure, and (ii) considering an application for planning permission which relates to the interior of the protected structure. It has to be said that the effect of the first of these two provisions is unclear. The question as to whether particular works materially affect the structure or an element of the structure is an objective one, and it is difficult to understand how the determination of this issue could be informed by regard to liturgical requirements. This is in contrast with the second circumstance identified in s.57, namely the consideration of an application for planning permission. The question of whether particular development constitutes "proper planning" is a subjective one, and the provisions of s.57(6) make it clear that "liturgical requirements" are to be respected in this context. Thus, for example, works which might not otherwise be acceptable might nevertheless be granted planning permission where same are necessary for liturgical requirements.

The statutory obligation to respect liturgical requirements in the context of making a declaration as to the type of works which would or would not materially affect the character of the protected structure was considered by the High Court in *Sherwin v An Bord Pleanála* ([2007] I.E.H.C. 227; [2008] 1 I.L.R.M. 31). An Bord Pleanála, in its declaration, having found that changes in the internal layout of a church materially affected the character of the sanctuary and the structure as a whole, went on to declare that, having regard to the nature of the changes involved and the need to respect liturgical requirements, the works were nevertheless exempted development. This declaration was challenged in judicial review proceedings on the basis that An Bord Pleanála, having found that the works would materially affect the structure, were not entitled to imply an additional exemption, not provided for in the legislation, on the grounds that the works in question were necessitated by the liturgical requirements of worship. The High Court found in favour of the applicant, and set aside the declaration and remitted the matter to An Bord Pleanála. In the course of his judgment, Edwards J. drew attention to the fact that the statutory guidelines misstated the law in so far as they suggested that some works which were necessitated by liturgical requirements and which have a material effect on the character of the structure might not require planning permission.

APPLICATION FOR PLANNING PERMISSION

Site notice   A site notice must be erected within the period of two weeks before the making of an application for planning permission. The High Court in *Mulhaire v An Bord Pleanála* (unreported, High Court, Birmingham J., October 31, 2007) ruled that the erection of a site notice on the same day as that on which the application is made complies with this requirement.

Default planning permission   A planning authority is ordinarily required to make a decision on an application for planning permission within a period of eight weeks beginning on the date of the receipt of the application. This period can, however, be extended in a number of circumstances. One instance where the period will be extended is where the planning authority serves a request for additional information: save in the case of EIA development, the decision is then to be made within four weeks of the request being complied with. An issue arose in *Maye v Sligo Borough Council* ([2007] I.E.H.C. 146; unreported, Clarke J., April 27, 2007) as to how this four-week period was to be calculated in cases where the response contained significant additional data and the planning authority had, accordingly, requested the applicant for planning permission to give further public notice of the application. The High Court held that the time ran from the date of the receipt of the response, not from the date of the publication of the further public notice. As it happens, the legal position had been amended under the Planning and Development Regulations 2006, and time does not now run until the planning authority has received copies of the further public notices. The planning application in *Maye* predated the coming into force of the new regulations, and thus the case fell to be determined under the Planning and Development Regulations 2001. In an aside, Clarke J. queried whether it was open to the Minister to alter the effect of s.34(8) by way of secondary legislation.

On the particular facts of *Maye*, the High Court ultimately concluded that a default planning permission had not arisen, on the basis that the proposed development would represent a material contravention of the development plan.

Practice and Procedure

MELODY BUCKLEY, B.S., J.D.
MARTIN CANNY, B.L.

ABUSE OF PROCESS

The rule in *Henderson v Henderson* The rule in *Henderson v Henderson* (the "*Henderson* rule") ((1843) 3 Hare 100) has recently started to feature with more regularity before the courts in this jurisdiction. Its effect has been summarised as being that "a litigant may not make a case in legal proceedings which might have been but was not brought forward in previous litigation": per Kearns J. in *SM v Ireland* [2007] I.E.S.C. 11; [2007] 3 I.R. 283 at 294. Although sharing some common features with the doctrine of res judicata, it is more commonly seen as forming part of the inherent jurisdiction of the courts to prevent an abuse of their processes.

In *Porterridge Trading Ltd v First Active plc* [2006] I.E.H.C. 285; High Court, Clarke J., October 4, 2006, the plaintiff company claimed that it had a valid lease of property owned by a company which had been placed in receivership by the defendant, from which it had subsequently been excluded. It had been a notice party to a receiver's (s.316) application for directions in the receivership (*Re Salthill Properties Ltd* [2004] I.E.H.C. 145; High Court, Laffoy J., July 30, 2004, aff'd [2006] I.E.H.C. 35; Supreme Court, May 29, 2006). The s.316 motion for directions made certain determinations in relation to arguments advanced by the plaintiff and held against it on some of those points. In subsequent plenary proceedings, the plaintiff sought to argue a number of different points against the defendant bank. The bank argued that this was an abuse of process. Clarke J. held that these latter proceedings were an abuse of process in so far as they sought to re-litigate matters which should more properly have been determined in the receiver's motion for directions. He also struck out large parts of the plaintiff's claim, although leaving intact a portion which was neither ruled on nor properly litigated in the s.316 application.

In *Arklow Holidays Ltd v An Bord Pleanála* [2007] I.E.H.C. 327; High Court, Clarke J., October 5, 2007, the applicant had brought its first judicial review challenging a decision to grant planning permission for a sewage treatment plant in September 1999. These proceedings were ultimately dismissed in February 2004. Undeterred, the applicant brought fresh judicial review proceedings challenging the same decision in 2005, which raised new grounds to those it had previously relied upon. The respondents sought to dismiss these proceedings as an abuse of process relying on the *Henderson* rule, saying that all the grounds of challenge both could and should have been raised in the first proceedings. Clarke J. held in favour of the respondents and dismissed the proceedings. However, readers should note that he subsequently granted leave to appeal to the Supreme Court on the question of whether the *Henderson* rule should apply at all in judicial reviews of planning decisions, and to the instant case before him in light of the conduct of the other parties to the litigation: see [2008] I.E.H.C. 2; High Court, Clarke J., January 11, 2008.

In *SM v Ireland* [2007] I.E.S.C. 11; [2007] 3 I.R. 283 the plaintiff brought judicial review proceedings in 1998 seeking to restrain his criminal prosecution on grounds of delay. The High Court refused these reliefs. In 2003 he issued plenary proceedings claiming, inter alia, a declaration that s.62 of the Offences Against the Person Act 1861 was unconstitutional. The defendants applied to strike out his plenary action on grounds that the earlier proceedings should have raised all of the same issues, and the High Court dismissed the proceedings. On appeal to the Supreme Court the plaintiff's appeal was allowed, with the court noting that a two-year delay by the defendants in raising abuse of process as a defence was a factor which weighed against the court exercising its discretion to dismiss the proceedings and also was evidence that they did not initially see the proceedings as abusive, but only later came to that decision.

Frivilous and vexatious proceedings; *Isaac Wunder* orders The jurisdiction to restrain a party from issuing proceedings without leave of court has been clarified in a number of judgments handed down in several of the proceedings brought by serial litigator Denis Riordan in *Riordan v Ireland (No 4)* [2001] 3 I.R. 365; *Riordan v Ireland (No 5)* [2001] 4 I.R. 463 and now, more recently, *Riordan v Ireland* [2006] I.E.H.C. 312; High Court, Smyth J., October 6, 2006, where Smyth J. displayed a level of exasperation rarely seen in a reserved High Court judgment.

A more mundane application of the *Isaac Wunder* jurisdiction occurred in *McMahon v WJ Law & Co LLP* [2007] I.E.H.C. 51 and 194; High Court, MacMenamin J., March 2 and June 15, 2007. In the first of his two judgments, MacMenamin J. held that the instant proceedings were frivolous and vexatious and disclosed no cause of action against the defendants. In his second judgment, he proceeded to make an order prohibiting the plaintiffs from instituting fresh proceedings against any of the defendants to that action without leave of court. This order was granted in circumstances where he found to be present the following six criteria derived from the *Riordan* cases, namely: (i) persistent institution of vexatious claims; (ii) repetition of earlier grievances; (iii) bringing proceedings which were bound to fail; (iv) bringing proceedings for an improper purpose rather than to assert legitimate rights; (v) rolling forward issues into subsequent cases and adding legal advisers as defendants to the new actions; and (vi) failure to pay costs orders.

In *Talbot v Hibernian Group plc and Amicus* [2007] I.E.H.C. 385; High Court, Irvine J., November 14, 2007, the plaintiff was a former employee of the first defendant and former member of the second defendant (a trade union) who brought proceedings claiming damages against the defendants. The defendants alleged that the plaintiff's claim against them was frivolous and vexatious and bound to fail, both under Rules of the Superior Courts (RSC) Ord.19 r.28 and as set out in *Sun Fat Chan v Osseous Ltd* [1992] I.R. 425. They relied on the facts that previous proceedings in similar terms against the same parties had been dismissed by order of the High Court (Dunne J.) in January 2007 on grounds that they disclosed no reasonable cause of action, and that most of the plaintiff's complaints were statute-barred. Ultimately the court dismissed the proceedings against the plaintiff's former trade union as being bound to fail, but allowed the case against his employer to proceed notwithstanding the infirmities which had been alluded to, as it was accepted that the plaintiff had identified some issues which required determination by the court.

DISCOVERY

Master's Court Before discussing a number of High Court judgments on discovery, it is worth referring to three decisions of the Master from 2007. In *Corscadden v BJN Construction Ltd* [2007] I.E.H.C. 42; Master Honohan, February 9, 2007, the Master discussed when "non-party discovery" (sometimes referred to as "third-party discovery") will be ordered in the Master's Court. This issue is closely related to when "public interest privilege" may be claimed in relation to discovery. In this regard, the Master stated as follows:

> "I propose to follow this logic and refuse applications for non-party discovery of the files of law enforcement agencies save in all cases where the evidence concerning the other (due process) public interest is weighty.
> How weighty? The importance of the integrity of the workings of the various law enforcement bodies is such that only with the very clearest and compelling evidence will an applicant's evidential deficit be adjudged even more compelling."

In the case before him he refused discovery of a Health and Safety Authority (HSA) file into the investigation of a fatal accident, where the applicant was seeking to show that there had been an unsafe system of work in operation. However, in this area perhaps more than in other areas the Master's approach is currently out of step with the majority of the High Court judges, where similar applications are usually granted and claims to public interest privilege more closely examined.

In *Russell v Danann Clean Air Systems Ltd* [2007] I.E.H.C. 16; Master Honohan, January 19, 2007 and *Keane v Aer Rianta* [2007] I.E.H.C. 141; Master Honohan, April 27, 2007, the law as applied by Master Honohan for standard discovery applications was set out. He noted in both decisions that "relevance" and "necessity" have to be approached by looking at the facts of the case, as set out in the pleadings and the affidavits. Blanket discovery is no longer permissible, and it is only if there is an "evidential deficit" that discovery will normally be both relevant and necessary.

Proportionality   Although the Master's view that a party who has alternative means of proving a fact will ordinarily not *need* discovery of related documents may be controversial, this principle finds expression in the judgments of the Superior Courts under the guise of a requirement that there should be some proportionality between the volume of documents to be discovered and the degree to which they are likely to advance the applicant's case or damage his opponent's case: see *Framus Ltd v CRH plc* [2004] 2 I.R. 20 and *PJ Carroll & Co v Minister for Health and Children* [2006] I.E.S.C. 36; [2006] 3 I.R. 431, where Geoghegan J. characterised the discovery sought as being in aid of a "Rolls Royce" preparation for trial, and accordingly had no hesitation in refusing the orders sought.

Proportionality; definition of document   In *Dome Telecom Ltd v Eircom Ltd* [2007] I.E.S.C. 59; Supreme Court, December 5, 2007, the defendant appealed from an order that it discover all documents relating to the quantity of "1800 numbers" issued by it and the volume of 1800 number minutes trafficked during a particular period of time. This discovery had been ordered against the background of the plaintiff alleging that the defendant had engaged in anti-competitive practices relating to the imposition of discriminatory connection charges. Several grounds of objection were raised by the defendant, principal among which were that the discovery sought was disproportionately burdensome relative to its probative value and, secondly, that it would require the defendant to create documents so as to satisfy the order, as all it had at present was electronic data. In relation to the issue of whether this information was discoverable, Fennelly J. stated at para.5 of his judgment:

> "The rules of court have not been adapted so as to make their objectives conformable to modern technology. The courts have, nonetheless, been astute to ensure that genuine discovery can be ordered even when advances in technology have the effect that discovery takes a very different form from that of documents as traditionally understood. In former times, there would have been a written record of every commercial transaction … I accept that failure by the courts to move with the times by adapting the rules to new technology might encourage unscrupulous businesses to keep their records in a form which would defeat the ends of justice."

Geoghegan J. (dissenting, but not on this point) saw no difficulty in the court ordering a party to "create" a document, so that electronic data could be discovered, and expressly refrained from embarking on a consideration of whether it was a "document" at the outset in any event. However, it should be noted that Kearns J. expressly reserved his position on this point.

In relation to the merits of the application, the defendant submitted that the costs of complying would be in excess of €150,000 in light of the volume of data at issue; it also pointed to certain concessions it had made, and said that the relevance went more towards the quantum of loss rather than liability in the case. For all of these reasons, the court reversed the High Court judgment, with Fennelly J. stating at para.21 of his judgment that:

> "[T]he very unusual burden and heavy cost of the discovery in this case requires the court to have a clear view of the litigious benefit to the plaintiff from obtaining the extremely detailed breakdown of information".

However, the plaintiff was given leave to renew its application if it succeeded in establishing liability in the case.

Discovery in patent infringement/revocation cases   In *Schneider (Europe) GmbH v Conor Medsystems Ireland Ltd* [2007] I.E.H.C. 63; High Court, Finlay Geoghegan J., February 2, 2007 and *Medtronic Inc v Guidant Corp* [2007] I.E.H.C. 37; High Court, Kelly J., February 23, 2007, the Commercial Court handed down two judgments on discovery in patent cases. While it is probably accurate to say that the same principles apply to a discovery application in patent cases as in other cases, as the question of relevance of the documents is closely related to the admissibility of the information referred to or contained in the document (e.g. as to subjective intention), this similitude is more illusory than real.

Implied undertakings and discovered documents   It is a settled rule of Irish law that documents obtained in the discovery process may not be used for a purpose other than for that litigation—they are subject to an "implied undertaking" in those terms. In *Cork Plastics (Manufacturing) Ltd v Ineos Compounds UK Ltd* [2007] I.E.H.C. 247; High Court, Clarke J., July 26, 2007 an issue arose as to when that implied undertaking could be lifted, in circumstances where documents obtained by way of discovery in English proceedings were relevant to proceedings with a different opposing party in Ireland. Although the court did not have to make a final decision (as it instead directed the respondent to make bona fide efforts to obtain a release from the implied undertaking, and awaited the result of that exercise), it suggested that "doing justice between the parties" had an important role to play and that such an implied undertaking could be overridden by order of court. A similar issue arose in the linked cases of *Porterridge Trading Ltd v First Active plc* and *Moorview Developments Ltd v First Active plc* [2007] I.E.H.C. 313; High Court, September 7, 2007, where related companies had obtained documents which they sought to use in the linked proceedings. Here, the court encountered less difficulty in absolving them of allegations that use of the documents was in breach of the implied undertaking.

Privilege; waiver of privilege In *Byrne v Shannon Foynes Port Company* [2007] I.E.H.C. 315; High Court, Clarke J., September 7, 2007, the plaintiffs delivered an affidavit of discovery which listed a number of documents in Part 1 of the First Schedule (i.e. over which privilege was not being claimed), but subsequently sought permission to assert a claim of privilege over these documents. Clarke J.'s judgment followed the judgment in *Shell E & P Ireland Ltd v McGrath* [2006] I.E.H.C. 409; High Court, Smyth J., December 5, 2006, which had addressed similar issues in circumstances where privileged documents had been inadvertently exhibited in an interlocutory application.

He expressed the applicable rules in the following terms: (i) if privilege is not claimed over a document when it is listed in the schedule of documents discovered, a party will ordinarily be allowed to amend the schedule prior to inspection of the documents taking place; but (ii) if the other party has inspected the document or otherwise lawfully received a copy, ordinarily the party will be found to have waived privilege over that document. An exception to the latter point was discussed at para.5.1 of his judgment, where he stated that a two-stage test should apply:

> "Firstly, the court must consider whether the solicitor seeing the document or documents concerned realised that a mistake had been made. Secondly, and perhaps most importantly on the basis of the authorities, the court must put itself in the position of a reasonable solicitor and consider whether, on the balance of probabilities, such solicitor would have taken the disclosure to have been as a result of a mistake."

In applying this test to the facts before him, Clarke J. noted that the solicitor for the plaintiff stated on affidavit that he thought that the defendants had chosen not to claim privilege. In relation to how the "hypothetical solicitor" would have reacted to the disclosure, Clarke J. held that while mistakes sometimes do occur in the discovery process, the documents here were so clearly privileged and numerous that it would not be apparent that a mistake had been made; rather, that the defendants had made a deliberate choice in the matter. Thus, the court refused the application to allow the defendants to claim privilege over the disclosed documents.

AMENDMENT OF PLEADINGS

Test to be applied Following the decision of the Supreme Court in *Croke v Waterford Crystal Ltd* [2004] I.E.S.C. 97; [2005] 2 I.R. 383, three judgments of the High Court have gone some way to further clarifying the test to be applied in applications to amend pleadings. In *Woori Bank v KDB Ireland Ltd* [2006] I.E.H.C. 156; High Court, Clarke J., May 17, 2006, the linked cases of *Porterridge* and *Moorview Developments* Clarke J. expressed the test to be applied as follows, at para.3.1 of the judgment in *Moorview*:

> "[A]n amendment should, ordinarily, be allowed unless it would cause prejudice to the other side, subject to the limitation that an amendment ought not to be allowed if the aspect of the case which would then proceed by virtue of the amendment was bound to fail... [T]he reasoning behind that view stems from the fact that, subject to the proceedings being frivolous or vexatious or being bound to fail, a party has, in most cases, an entitlement to plead the proceedings in whatever way it wishes."

The prejudice referred to is "real prejudice" which could not be remedied by an appropriate order in costs or directions as to the progress of the proceedings. The test in effect applies a reverse burden of proof to an application to strike out proceedings as being frivolous or vexatious pursuant to RSC Ord.19 r.28 or the inherent jurisdiction of the courts. If the amendments may in fact be statute-barred, a middle ground was suggested by Clarke J. in his judgment in *Mangan v Murphy* [2006] I.E.H.C. 317; High Court, Clarke J., June 30, 2006 where leave to amend was refused but the applicant was given liberty to bring new proceedings and at a later date to apply to have them heard with the proceedings which were before the court on the amendment application.

SECURITY FOR COSTS

European issues and security for costs In *Dublin International Arena Ltd v Campus and Stadium Ireland Dev Ltd* [2007] I.E.S.C. 48; Supreme Court, October 25, 2007, the Supreme Court reversed an order of the High Court ordering that security for costs be furnished pursuant to s.390 of the Companies Act 1963 and RSC Ord.29 r.1, in circumstances where the applicant was alleging breaches of the Public Procurement Directives. It was conceded that the applicant had no monies to meet an order for costs if it lost the action; the issue before the court was whether "special circumstances" weighed against security for costs being ordered. This judgment shows clearly that a different approach to security for costs will apply if rights conferred under a European Directive are at issue which require that an "effective remedy" be available under national law. In particular, the court examined much more rigorously delays by the respondent in bringing its application for security for costs. The delay was between May 2002 when the proceedings commenced; September 2002 when a statement of opposition was filed; and February 2003 when the application was brought. This amounted to a special circumstance justifying the refusal of an order that security for costs be furnished (although the court noted ruefully that these delays were far shorter than the delay of over two years which the parties experienced in having their appeal heard by the Supreme Court).

COSTS

Measuring costs   In *Mitsubishi Electric v Design Air Ltd (and linked cases)* [2007] I.E.H.C. 303; Master Honohan, May 22, 2007 Master Honohan signalled that RSC, Ord.63 r.6 would in future have a greater role in relation to the costs of applications determined before him. This rule states that:

> "In any case in which the Master may make an order the costs of the application shall be in the discretion of the Master, who may direct payment of a sum in gross in lieu of payment of costs to be taxed."

The *Mitsubishi Electric* decision is in fact a reserved judgment solely on the issue of the costs to be awarded for applications in 13 different cases. In each case Master Honohan had previously ruled on which party was entitled to the costs of the motion; he then invited the parties to address him as to how much work had been involved, so as to allow him to measure the quantum of costs they would be entitled to. While not relied on previously, RSC Ord.63 r.6 clearly gives the Master jurisdiction to proceed in this manner, and in fact the District Court regularly measures costs in civil cases before it. It is difficult to adequately summarise the breadth of the judgment, as it ranges widely over issues of legal costs reform, and the structure of the legal profession. However, in relation to the level of the costs which would be ordered for future applications before him, Master Honohan stated at p.41 of his judgment that costs would be assessed objectively and would relate to the number of hours' work involved (including preparation), and that the hourly rate to be applied would be that of a lawyer with the appropriate level of seniority for the application. For Master's Court applications a barrister would not in every case be needed (and thus would not be a recoverable cost in all cases) but, conversely, contested adjournment applications could lead to a full day's costs (including costs of counsel) being incurred. An uplift on the standard fee (which could amount to 100 per cent of the standard fee) would be possible depending on, e.g. the complexity of the work involved. (He proposed that a fees uplift would likewise be used to differentiate fees between the Circuit Court, High Court, Master's Court etc.) It is to be anticipated that this approach will become more widespread in relation to Master's Court costs applications in future, as many of the same issues are canvassed in the Report of the Legal Costs Implementation Advisory Group ("The Miller Report") of November 2006.

Exceptions to costs following the event In *Cork County Council v Shackleton* [2007] I.E.H.C. 334; High Court, Clarke J., October 12, 2007, the High Court was asked to deviate from the usual rule that costs follow the event. In this case the applicant had successfully applied to set aside a decision of the respondent arbitrator, and had then applied for the costs of the proceedings against the notice party (who had opposed the proceedings and in whose favour the arbitrator had ruled). While recognising that costs ordinarily follow the event, the court noted that a different approach was warranted where the proceedings were a test case involving the interpretation of ambiguous legislation and where the other party was a local authority. The court ordered that each side should bear its own costs, and added an invitation to the Minister for the Environment to reimburse Cork County Council its legal costs.

DELAY AND DISMISSAL OF ACTIONS FOR WANT OF PROSECUTION

Plaintiffs' proceedings dismissed The increasing importance of conducting litigation as expeditiously as possible was evident in several cases decided in 2007 where the plaintiffs' claims were dismissed for want of prosecution due to inordinate and inexcusable delay. In both *Shanahan v PJ Carroll and Co Ltd* [2007] I.E.H.C. 229; High Court, Gilligan, J., April 24, 2007 and *Comcast International Holdings Inc v Minister for Public Enterprise* [2007] I.E.H.C. 274; High Court Gilligan, J. June 13, 2007, Gilligan J. had to consider the following issues: (1) whether the delay by the plaintiff in the commencement and the prosecution of the proceedings was inordinate and inexcusable, and if the delay was inordinate and inexcusable, whether on the balance of justice, the claim should be dismissed; and (2) whether the court should exercise its inherent jurisdiction to dismiss the plaintiff's claim, if the lapse of time since the cause of action arose would cause the defendant to suffer prejudice and be denied a fair trial.

In *Shanahan*, the plaintiffs sued the defendants for personal injuries sustained from smoking and cigarette addiction, and on other grounds. This judgment relates to the defendants' motion to dismiss which was made against McCormack, the second-named plaintiff, who commenced smoking in 1960/61. His cause of action arose approximately 36 years after he started smoking, in September 1996, when he was diagnosed with a smoking-related illness. Gilligan J. concluded that the delay by the plaintiff in prosecuting the proceedings was inordinate and inexcusable. In considering whether the balance of justice favoured the defendants, he followed the reasoning in *Stephens v Paul Flynn Ltd* [2005] I.E.H.C. 148; High Court (Clarke J.) April 28, 2005, where Clarke J. determined that where there was an inordinate delay prior to the issuance of the summons, the plaintiff was obligated to proceed expeditiously. In the instant matter, Gilligan J. found that the plaintiff's solicitors failed to move expeditiously (which they were required to do) to avoid delay. They issued the summons in January 2000, four years after the cause of action accrued and at the very end of the statutory period. Although not a determinative factor, the plaintiff's vicarious liability for his solicitors' actions was considered in deciding where the balance of justice lay. As an actual trial date was unlikely until late 2009, which would be 13 years after accrual of the cause of action, Gilligan J. held that this delay gave rise to a substantial risk that it would not be possible to have a fair trial and that the defendants would suffer serious prejudice.

Gilligan J. also relied on the inherent jurisdiction of the court to consider the effect of the lapse of time on the fairness of a trial. He applied the six criteria discussed by Finlay Geoghegan J. in another tobacco case, *Manning v Benson and Hedges* [2004] 3 I.R. 556; [2004] 2 I.L.R.M. 231, where she said that the court should consider:

"1. Has the defendant contributed to the lapse of time
2. The nature of the claims
3. The probable issues to be determined by the court; in particular whether there will be factual issues to be determined or only legal issues
4. The nature of the principal evidence; in particular whether there will be oral evidence
5. The availability of relevant witnesses
6. The length of lapse of time and in particular the length of time between the acts or omissions in relation to which the court will be asked to make factual determinations and probable trial date".

In reaching his decision, Gilligan J. took into account the court's obligation to comply with the requirement for a speedy trial under Art.6 of the European Convention on Human Rights, and the lack of culpable delay on the plaintiff's part. Despite there being no suggestion of culpable delay on the plaintiff's part, in the circumstances of the case, which required examination of documents and/or testimony extending as far back as 1942, the defendants would suffer a real and serious risk of an unfair trial and accordingly an order was made dismissing the proceedings.

Comcast International Holdings Inc v Minister for Public Enterprise [2007] I.E.H.C. 274; High Court (Gilligan, J.) June 13, 2007 consisted of three consolidated cases. After unsuccessfully tendering for the second GSM mobile telephone licence, the plaintiffs (Comcast) instituted proceedings against the State alleging corruption, misfeasance in public office, fraud and deceit. In all three matters, the causes of action had arisen approximately 12 years prior to the motions to dismiss being heard, and Gilligan J. determined that the cases would most likely be heard approximately 14 years after the causes of action arose. As in *Shanahan*, Gilligan J. followed the reasoning of Clarke J. in *Stephens v Paul Flynn Ltd* [2005] I.E.H.C. 148; High Court, Clarke J., April 28, 2005, and as in *Shanahan* he found that the balance of justice favoured the dismissal of the proceedings. In dealing with the lapse of time since the cause of action arose and the likelihood of a fair trial, he applied the six criteria set out by Finley Geoghegan J. in *Manning v Benson and Hedges* [2004] 3 I.R. 556; [2004] 2 I.L.R.M. 231. He also considered the plaintiffs' claim in light of the European Convention on Human Rights Act 2003 as an important additional factor and found that the 12-year lapse from the date of accrual of the causes of action, and thereafter up to the 14 years post-accrual it would most likely take for the matter to be heard, was unacceptable. As against these factors it remains somewhat unsettling that the courts will allow a tribunal of inquiry to investigate the same issues which had been found in these proceedings to be so historic as to be unacceptable to the interests of justice, and yet a party in whose favour findings of the tribunal may yet be made has no effective remedy or vindication of its rights. Furthermore, such a party is not permitted to point to the slow progress at the tribunal as a sufficient reason for not progressing its civil proceedings. However, this issue was not addressed by Gilligan J.

Plaintiff's proceedings dismissed In *Halpin v Smith* [2007] I.E.H.C. 279; High Court, July 31, 2007 Dunne J. granted the application by the defendant to dismiss the plaintiff's claim for want of prosecution. As she found the delay by the plaintiff was clearly inordinate and inexcusable, the only point she had to give detailed consideration to was the balance of justice. She found that the inordinate and inexcusable delay in the instant matter lasted for five years, during which time neither the plaintiff nor his solicitor gave any reason for the delay. She also found that there was confusion as to the specifics of the claim in the plaintiff's pleadings. She distinguished the instant case from *Rogers v Michelin Tyre plc and Pensioners Trust (No 2) Ltd* [2005] I.E.H.C. 294; High Court, Clarke J., June 28, 2005. In *Rogers,* although the plaintiff's solicitor was responsible for the inordinate and inexcusable delay, at an early date the defendant in that case had been made aware with some precision of the nature of the plaintiff's case. In dealing only with the balance of justice, Dunne J. followed *Stephens v Paul Flynn Ltd* [2005] I.E.H.C. 148; High Court, Clarke J., April 28, 2005 and found against the plaintiff on this issue and dismissed the proceedings.

Defendants' application to dismiss refused   In *McBrearty v North Western Health Board*, High Court, MacMenamin, J., December 14, 2007, three of the defendants, Dr Singh, Dr Glynn and the North Western Health Board (NWHB), unsuccessfully applied to dismiss the plaintiff's claims against them on grounds of delay. The plaintiff's action had been discontinued against the fourth defendant, Dr MacFarlane, prior to the instant applications. Dr Singh also applied to dismiss the plaintiff's claim on the procedural ground of non-compliance with RSC Ord.28 r.7. Dr Glynn entered a conditional appearance and applied to set aside the renewal of the summons arguing that it was not in the interests of justice to do so. The plaintiff's claims against the defendants included medical negligence arising during his birth in 1981. As of the date of these motions, it was not disputed that the plaintiff was severely disabled and would never be in the position to institute proceedings independently. The relevant time periods were as follows:

- January 1, 1981:   The plaintiff's birth and cause of action arose.

- 1991:   The plaintiff's mother first became aware of possible claim.

- July 11, 2000:   The plaintiff's mother consults solicitors.

- November 27, 2001:   Summons served on NWHB and Dr MacFarlane.

- April 25, 2005:   Drs Singh and Glynn joined as co-defendants.

- December 16, 2005:   Drs Singh and Glynn added to the summons.

- May 29, 2006:   Peart J. renewed summons for 6 months.

Dr Singh's application   Dr Singh argued that the plaintiff failed to move to amend the summons within 14 days of the order granting the joinder under RSC Ord.28 r.7. However, MacMenamin J. held that the applicable rule, RSC Ord.15 r.13, is not time-limited. Even if the order for joinder was defective, the defect could be cured by the subsequent order granting a renewal of the summons.

Dr Singh also argued for the dismissal of the plaintiff's claim on the basis of inordinate and inexcusable delay. MacMenamin J. had no difficulty finding that the delay was inordinate as the plaintiff's cause of action arose at the plaintiff's birth 19 years earlier. However, the plaintiff argued that the delay was not inexcusable for a variety of reasons including the fact that he acted as expeditiously as possible in effectuating service on Dr Singh. MacMenamin J. calculated that it took approximately five years for Dr Singh to be served with the notice of summons from the date of the issuance of the summons (November 27, 2001) until approximately four years later, when Dr Singh was joined as a defendant (April 25, 2005) and extending more than one year thereafter, when Dr Singh was finally served with the notice of summons (July 17, 2006). The plaintiff argued that he could not have joined Dr Singh any earlier than he did. He only learned that Dr Singh was the locum during the birth after the NWHB filed its defence on March 7, 2005. However, MacMenamin J., citing *Stephens v Paul Flynn Ltd* [2005] I.E.H.C. 148; High Court, Clarke J., April 28, 2005 as authority for the proposition that a plaintiff must proceed expeditiously where there has already been an inordinate delay in the case prior to the issuance of the summons, concluded that the plaintiff was already guilty of inexcusable delay even before the NWHB filed its defence. The plaintiff could have ascertained the relevant information about Dr Singh if he had taken steps to expedite proceedings against the NWHB and Dr MacFarlane. He found that the plaintiff also took too long (two years) to identify expert consultants and obtain reports, given the need to proceed expeditiously under the circumstances. Although the plaintiff also argued that the court should have considered his personal blamelessness in determining whether the delay was inexcusable, MacMenamin J. followed *Gilroy v Flynn* [2004] I.E.S.C. 98; [2005] 1 I.L.R.M. 290 and *Rogers v Michelin Tyres plc and Pensioners Trust (No. 2) Ltd* [2005] I.E.H.C. 294; High Court, Clarke J., June 28, 2005, where it had been held that the plaintiff's personal blamelessness was only one factor to be taken into account by the court in determining the balance of justice.

In determining that the balance of justice favoured the plaintiff, MacMenamin J. considered various factors, including the need to proceed expeditiously under the European Convention on Human Rights Act 2003, the lack of prejudice to the defendant and the personal blamelessness of the plaintiff. On the issue of prejudice, he found that the matter was essentially a documents case. Sufficient contemporaneous documentation existed, including: nursing records containing a narrative of events; the midwives' records in sequence over the period in question; the labour record as to the facts and circumstances of the plaintiff's birth; and the paediatric records. Furthermore, the witnesses were still available; all but one of the nursing staff involved in the birth were still working at the hospital where the plaintiff was born and Dr Singh and Dr Glynn were still alive. He rejected the claims by Dr Singh and Dr Glynn that neither physician independently recollected the incident. Finally, MacMenamin J. gave sufficient weight to the personal blamelessness of the plaintiff (he was clearly and permanently incompetent) and the fact that he could not be held liable for delay by his solicitors.

Dr Singh (and also Dr Glynn and the NWHB) then unsuccessfully argued that even though the plaintiff instituted suit within the statutory period, the court should exercise its inherent jurisdiction to dismiss the plaintiff's claim due to the lapse of time since the cause of action arose. Two cases were relied on in support of this approach: *Manning v Benson & Hedges* [2004] 3 I.R. 556; [2004] 2 I.L.R.M. 231 and *Shanahan v PJ Carroll and Co Ltd* [2007] I.E.H.C. 229; High Court, Gilligan J., April 24, 2007. However, McMenamin J. distinguished these cases on the basis that the factual issues in *McBrearty* were sufficiently documented to allow a detailed assessment to be made of what was said to have occurred. The records were not inadequate and all of the relevant witnesses to the fundamental claims were available. Furthermore, the time range in the instant case was much more limited than those in the tobacco cases where some of the evidence stretched back over a century. Thus, the alleged detriment suffered by the defendants in the form of the absence of memory and lapse of time did not outweigh the other factors.

Dr Glynn's application Dr Glynn applied to set aside the summons on the grounds that it was not in the interests of justice to grant the order renewing the summons. MacMenamin J. applied a three-part test from *Chambers v Kennefick*, High Court, Finlay Geoghegan J., November 11, 2005, which asked: (1) whether there was a good reason to renew the summons; (2) if there was a good reason to renew, whether it was then in the interests of justice between the parties to grant an order renewing the summons; and (3) where it was found that there was a good reason to renew in the interests of justice, whether the order of renewal should be made on the balance of justice. MacMenamin J. in applying the above test balanced the "good reason for renewal" as the one unavoidable element of detriment to the plaintiff—that his claim would be statute-barred if it were dismissed—as against Dr Glynn's claims of specific or generalised prejudice; in balancing these claims he found in favour of the plaintiff.

Application of the NWHB On the issue of the inordinate and inexcusable delay as to this defendant, MacMenamin J. found the delay of the plaintiff to still be inordinate and inexcusable, but inexcusable to a lesser degree, due to the difference in the conduct of the NWHB from the conduct of the other two defendants. He held that the acquiescence of the NWHB in the plaintiff's delay resulted in the establishment of an estoppel for the following reasons: the NWHB took almost four years to raise the issue of delay; it contributed to the delay in service on Dr Singh by the plaintiff's solicitor (the plaintiff did not find out about Dr Singh's involvement until the NWHB filed its defence on March 7, 2005); and also, by its actions it had caused the plaintiff's legal advisers to incur substantial expenditure. Furthermore, unlike its co-defendants, the NWHB possessed medical and nursing records and traces, and had interviewed the midwives. In determining that the balance of justice favoured the plaintiff, MacMenamin J. held that while the evidence was sufficient to demonstrate that the delay was inexcusable, though to a lesser degree than the other applicants, in light of the totality of issues he was satisfied that the NWHB failed to discharge the onus of proof with regard to the balance of justice.

Renewal of summons granted In *O'Grady v Southern Health Board* [2007] I.E.H.C. 38; High Court, O'Neill J., February 2, 2007 the plaintiff's ex parte application to renew the summons was granted. The defendants moved to set aside the order on the basis that under RSC Ord.8 r.1 the plaintiff had failed to renew the summons in a timely fashion "for other good reason" and that "reasonable efforts were not made to serve such defendant" and that this inordinate and inexcusable delay was prejudicial to their defence. They alleged that the first clear intimation to them of the plaintiff's personal injuries claim occurred six years after the events forming the subject-matter of the claim. O'Neill J., in finding that the balance of justice favoured the plaintiff, weighed the following factors: the consequences to the plaintiff if the summons was not renewed (with any new proceedings being statute-barred); the plaintiff's explanation for his inordinate and inexcusable delay; that he deliberately failed to make reasonable efforts to serve the defendants as he needed the time to obtain medical evidence; and the prejudice which the defendants claimed to have suffered. He found that even though the plaintiff was guilty of inordinate and inexcusable delay in failing to make reasonable efforts to serve the defendant, that his dereliction was outweighed by the threat of the matter being time-barred and the defendants' failure to demonstrate that they suffered severe prejudice by substantial impairment of their defence. He further noted that upon delivery of the plaintiff's statement of claim, the defendants would be in a position to argue that the claim should be dismissed for want of prosecution. He stated as follows:

> "I am of opinion that the time barring of the plaintiff's claim by the non-renewal of the plenary summons, in the absence at this stage of evidence of actual substantial prejudice to the defence of the defendants, is a result which would be in the nature of a pure penalty imposed on the plaintiff, and at this stage of the proceedings is not warranted in the overall interest of achieving a just outcome to the dispute between these parties."

LEGISLATION

Personal Injuries Assessment Board Act 2003 In proceedings brought while an application was being dealt with by the Personal Injuries Assessment Board, Clarke J. in *Domican v AXA Insurance* [2007] I.E.H.C. 14; High Court, Clarke J., January 14, 2007, refused to restrain the defendant (AXA) from corresponding directly with the plaintiff's solicitors despite the client's written instructions stating that all correspondence should be sent directly to his solicitor and not to him. He found that AXA's actions did not amount to a material or significant interference with the solicitor–client relationship in the context of either litigation or potential litigation. He distinguished the approach by the PIAB in the present case from what he characterised as an acrimonious situation where the copying of such correspondence might give rise to an inference by the client that he was not being properly looked after by his solicitor. He also distinguished the instant matter from *O'Brien v PIAB* [2005] I.E.H.C. 100; High Court, MacMenamin J., January 25, 2005, where the practice adopted by the PIAB in declining to accept or act upon client authorisation and by corresponding directly with the client excluded a client from direct contact with his solicitor.

Civil Liability and Courts Act 2004   In *Carmello v Casey* [2007] I.E.H.C. 362; High Court, Peart J. October 26, 2007, Peart J. dismissed the plaintiff's personal injuries claim pursuant to two sections of the Civil Liability and Courts Act 2004: (s.26) knowingly giving false and/or misleading evidence in a personal injuries action; and (s.14) swearing an affidavit that that was in a material aspect false or misleading; and also as the proceedings were held to be an abuse of process. The plaintiff had been injured in a car owned and driven by the defendants. Liability was admitted and the trial proceeded as an assessment of damages only. The defendants' insurance company submitted that the plaintiff deliberately gave false and misleading evidence of numbness on his face to exaggerate his claim. It alleged that the numbness was sustained in an earlier accident involving the branch of a tree which the plaintiff failed to disclose in his replies to particulars. Peart J., in discussing the plaintiff's credibility at trial, stated that "he did not believe in the slightest that the young man would not have remembered the earlier accident". Despite what he characterised as the "draconian nature of s.26", Peart J. was satisfied that the section was in the public interest and mandatory in its terms and that no injustice would result from the dismissal of the plaintiff's action.

INJUNCTIONS

Ex parte applications and non-disclosure   In *JRM Sports Ltd T/A Limerick Football Club v Football Association of Ireland* [2007] I.E.H.C. 67; High Court, Clarke J., January 31, 2007 the plaintiff unsuccessfully sought interlocutory relief restraining the defendant Football Association of Ireland (FAI) from either replacing the plaintiff football club with another, or alternatively, an order enabling them to play in the League of Ireland. The refusal to grant this application for interlocutory relief was based in part on the plaintiff's failure to comply with its obligation of candour (the failure to give full and clear facts of both sides) in disclosing material information during the earlier hearing for the ex parte interim order, which application was heard by Peart J. In passing judgment after the interlocutory hearing, Clarke J. followed the reasoning in *F McK v DC* [2006] I.E.H.C. 185; High Court, Clarke J., May 26, 2006, and *Bambrick v Cobley* [2005] I.E.H.C. 143; [2006] 1 I.L.R.M 81. In determining how the court should deal with the effect of this lack of "candour", Clarke

J. applied the following principles which he had previously enunciated in *Bambrick*:

"(1) the extent or materiality of the matters misstated or omitted; (2) whether the omissions were deliberate or accidental and, (3) whether an order should in any event be given having regard to all the circumstances of the case."

He held that the matters misstated or omitted were material, and although he was unable to determine whether in actual fact they were deliberate or not, he still accepted that they were not deliberate. He then considered this lack of candour along with all of the circumstances of the case, and in examining the balance of convenience he refused the application for the interlocutory injunction.

Enforcement of an undertaking as to damages In *Estuary Logistics and Distribution Co Ltd t/a LS Sales v Lowenergy Solutions Ltd and James Tagney* [2007] I.E.H.C. 410; High Court, Clarke J., December 6, 2007, the High Court had discharged an injunction granted in favour of the plaintiff, due to an abuse of process by the plaintiff in acting in a manner inconsistent with the court order granting the injunction. The defendant applied to enforce its undertaking as to damages and claimed the sum of €109,500 as damages. Rather than immediately enforcing the obligation of the undertaking, after the discharge of an interlocutory order Clarke J. postponed the obligation to be dealt with at trial. He cited *Cheltenham & Gloucester Building Society v Ricketts* [1993] 1 W.L.R. 1545 as authority for the principles concerning the enforcement of an undertaking as to damages on the basis that in both England and Ireland, the process by which interim and interlocutory injunctions are granted must be supported by an undertaking as to damages. He added that the principles enunciated in *Cheltenham* comply with the justice and equity of the situation where an injunction is granted but is ultimately discharged. Clarke J. thus balanced all material factors which included the application of the following principles by Neill L.J. in *Cheltenham* at 1551–1552, to the circumstances of the case, and asked:

"… (a) whether there is a significant possibility that the trial judge may be in a better position to assess all relevant factors (b) whether the nature of the damage alleged is such that it will fall to be considered at the trial in any event and (c) whether the immediate payment of any damages might give rise, in the circumstances of the case under consideration to a risk of injustice."

In the instant matter it was considered highly material that the defendant was insolvent and in liquidation, and in those circumstances the court preferred to await the outcome of the full proceedings before ordering interim payments in favour of one party which may subsequently prove irrecoverable if exceeded by sums awarded to the other party following the full hearing.

THIRD PARTY PROCEDURE

Third party notice struck out   In *Murnaghan v Markland Holdings Ltd* [2007] I.E.H.C. 255; High Court, Laffoy J., August 10, 2007, Laffoy J. set aside third-party proceedings on the basis that the defendant (Markland) failed to serve the third-party notice on a person (McElroy) not a party to the proceeding "as soon as is reasonably possible" pursuant to s.27(1)(b) of the Civil Liability Act 1961. RSC Ord.16 r.1(3) stipulates that a party must obtain leave of the court to issue a third-party notice, and that the application should be brought within a period of 28 days from the date of delivery of the defence. In this case the 28-day time period had expired, and thus the court was asked to exercise its discretion pursuant to s.27(1)(b) of the Civil Liability Act 1961. Two related actions were before the court: *Action 1* consisted of the substantive claim by the plaintiff property-owner for damage to his residence arising out of building work carried out on the adjoining property by the two co-defendants—the adjoining property owner and developer (Markland), and Markland's building contractor, (Cantier). These proceedings were issued on June 5, 2003. On December 1, 2004 the plaintiff obtained a substantial judgment against the two defendants in *Action 1*. *Action 2* consisted of the claim for contribution and indemnification between the co- defendants, with Markland as claimant and Cantier as the respondent. In *Action 2* Markland delivered its points of claim to Cantier on February 17, 2005. Approximately one year later, on January 25, 2006, Markland moved to join McElroy as the third-party defendant. The order for joinder was granted on March 31, 2006, and on April 28, 2006, Markland delivered amended points of claim against McElroy, based on allegations of breach of duty and contract, including the failure to ensure the separation of the two buildings at foundation level, to adequately supervise the works and to take steps to adequately separate the buildings.

Markland argued that it had not joined McElroy at an earlier date because it lacked sufficient information to formulate its claim with clarity. On receipt of Cantier's defence and counterclaim delivered on May 10, 2004, it argued that the lack of clarity in Cantier's pleading necessitated further investigation, which it believed itself required to undertake to avoid a multiplicity of actions. Markland argued that the court should consider its situation analogous to that in *Connolly v Casey* [2001] 1 I.R. 345, where Denham J. held that the joinder of a professional defendant for professional negligence should only be effectuated after the third-party plaintiff had sufficient information to bring the action. Laffoy J. rejected this interpretation of *Connolly* on the basis that the benefits to the system of administration of justice and to the third party, envisaged by Denham J., could not be achieved in the instant matter. Laffoy J. found that Markland could have joined McElroy approximately six months after the issuance of the plaintiff's summons—as early as December 2003—and clearly at an earlier date than the trial of the substantive action, in which judgment was delivered on December 1, 2004. McElroy's involvement in the project began in September 2003, when it was hired to inspect the foundation and continued through the end of 2003. In the opinion of Laffoy J., Markland's approach to the joinder did not obviate a multiplicity of actions, but gave rise to them. She also noted that the result of her decision would open up the possibility of a third trial of a substantive action by Markland against McElroy but refused to speculate as to whether the court hearing that matter would use its discretion and refuse to make an order for contribution pursuant to s.27(1)(b):

> "... If such third-party notice is not served as aforesaid [as soon as is reasonably possible] the court may in its discretion refuse to make an order for contribution against the person from whom contribution is claimed".

LEGISLATION

Personal Injuries Assessment Board Act (No. 35) of 2007   This Act passed into law on July 11, 2007. It amends the 2003 Act by inserting new ss.51A and 51B into the primary Act. These sections provide that if a plaintiff rejects a PIAB assessment which a defendant has consented to, but subsequently fails to recover a sum in excess of that figure in the civil courts, that no order of costs shall be made in his favour, and that the court may order him to pay the costs of the defendant. Secondly, it provides that the costs incurred by a solicitor in processing a claim before the Personal Injuries Assessment Board shall not be allowed at taxation of costs should the plaintiff subsequently receive an award of damages from the civil courts. These provisions are of very significant practical effect, and while there have been difficulties in determining the date from which the two provisions are applicable, their effect is to place a significant costs risk on parties who reject a PIAB assessment but choose instead to bring civil proceedings.

Courts and Court Officers (Amendment) Act No. 4 of 2007   This Act increases the number of ordinary judges in the High Court to not more than 35, the number of judges in the Circuit Court to not more than 37, and the number of justices in the District Court to not more than 60 in addition to the President of the District Court.

RULES OF COURT

The following Rules of Court were made in 2007:

Rules of the Superior Courts

Rules of the Superior Courts (Evidence) 2007 (S.I. No. 13 of 2007)

Rules of the Superior Courts (Statutory Applications and Appeals) 2007 (S.I. No. 14 of 2007)

Rules of the Superior Courts (Jurisdiction, Recognition, Enforcement and Service of Proceedings) 2007 (S.I. No. 407 of 2007)

Rules of the Superior Courts (Criminal Law (Insanity) Act 2006) 2007 (S.I. No. 597 of 2007)

Rules of the Superior Courts (Order 85) 2007 (S.I. No. 767 of 2004)

Rules of the Circuit Court

Circuit Court Rules (General) 2007 (S.I. No. 312 of 2007)

Circuit Court Rules (Industrial Relations Acts) (S.I. No. 12 of 2007)

Rules of the District Court

District Court (Mental Health Appeals) Rules 2007 (S.I. No. 19 of 2007)

District Court (Bench Warrants) Rules 2007 (S.I. No. 73 of 2007)

District Court (Mental Health) Rules 2007 (S.I. No. 97 of 2007)

District Court (Children Summonses) Rules 2007 (S.I. No. 152 of 2007)

District Court (Criminal Justice Act 2006) Rules 2007 (S.I. No. 203 of 2007)

District Court (Community Service) Rules 2007 (S.I. No. 313 of 2007)

District Court (Criminal Justice Act 2006, Part 11) Rules 2007 (S.I. No. 314 of 2007)

District Court (Children) Rules 2007 (S.I. No. 408 of 2007)

District Court (Summonses) Rules 2007 (S.I. No. 418 of 2007)

District Court (Road Traffic) Rules 2007 (S.I. No. 564 of 2007)

District Court (Insanity) Rules 2007 (S.I. No. 726 of 2007)

Prisons

PRISONS ACT 2007

The Prisons Act 2007 provides a statutory basis for (i) the possibility of certain prisoner escort services to be contracted out by the Minister for Justice; (ii) revised prisoner disciplinary procedures, including the establishment of Appeal Tribunals; (iii) planning provisions for the construction of new prisons and extensions to existing prisons; (iv) the appointment on a statutory basis of an Inspector of Prisons; (v) prisoners to participate from prison in certain applications to court by means of a live television link; (vi) charging prisoners for certain optional services; and (vii) the prohibition of unauthorised possession or use of mobile telecommunications devices by prisoners. Provision is also made for the closure of Mountjoy Prison in Dublin (on the basis of the proposed building of a new prison complex at Thornton Hall in County Meath). The 2007 Act also provided that non-commercial work within a prison is excluded from the terms of the National Minimum Wage Act 2000 and the position in relation to the lawful custody of prisoners while absent from prison has also been clarified.

PRISON RULES 2007

Section 35 of the 2007 Act also provided an entirely new statutory basis for the making of Prison Rules. This facilitated the making of the Prison Rules 2007 (S.I. No. 252 of 2007), which replaced with considerable amendments the Rules for the Government of Prisons 1947 (S.I. No. 320 of 1947), as amended. The 1947 Rules had long ago been described as being in need of reform: see the comments of O'Higgins C.J. in *State (Walsh and McGowan) v Governor of Mountjoy Prison*, Supreme Court, December 12, 1975 at 7 of his judgment. In this respect, the 2007 Rules broadly reflect the UN international minimum standards for the treatment of prisoners.

Probate and Succession Law

DR ALBERT KEATING, B.L.
Senior Lecturer, Waterford Institute of Technology

Representative capacity of an administrator   As an administrator derives his title to represent an estate from a grant of administration, he will not have the necessary representative capacity to institute proceedings on behalf of the estate, or indeed, defend proceedings, before a grant is issued to him. As a result of *Ingall v Moran* ([1944] 1 K.B. 160), a plaintiff or defendant will not be able to maintain an action before a grant of administration is issued to him, and a grant subsequently obtained "will not cure the fundamental defect" (see also *Creed v Creed* [1913] 1 I.R. 48). In *Gaffney v Faughan* ([2006] I.L.R.M. 481 at 485), Laffoy J. stated that:

> "It is a fundamental principle of law that the authority of an administrator of the estate of a deceased person derives from the grant of letters of administration and that, until he obtains the grant, the estate of the deceased does not vest in him."

Applying the rule in *Ingall v Moran* she stated that:

> "When a summons is issued the person named as defendant must be competent at that time to answer the alleged wrongdoing and meet the remedy sought. If he is not the action is not maintainable. If he subsequently obtains a grant of administration, that will not cure the fundamental defect and render the action maintainable" (at 485).

Neither can an administrator rely on the doctrine of relation back because in order to maintain an action "he must have a cause of action vested in him at the date of the writ" (*Ingall v Moran* at 167, per Luxmore L.J.).

In *Finnegan v Richards* ([2007] I.E.H.C. 134), the testatrix died on May 13, 2004. Her husband, who was executor of the will, predeceased her. There was no issue of the marriage. Her niece became the next person entitled to apply for a grant of letters of administration with the will annexed. The niece, however, appointed two attorneys, who were the defendants in the proceedings, to act in respect of all matters concerning the administration of the estate and obtained on her behalf a grant of letters of administration with the will annexed on June 26, 2006. A plenary summons was issued on May 9, 2006 in which the plaintiff claimed beneficial ownership of the deceased testatrix's dwelling house. The statement of claim was delivered on September 27, 2006. The plaintiff was faced with a time bar in s.9(2) of the Civil Liability Act 1961 which provides that no proceedings are maintainable against a deceased's estate unless, inter alia, the proceedings are commenced within the period of two years after his death. Accordingly, the plaintiff had to have his proceedings instituted within two years from the death of the testatrix's death, viz. May 13, 2004. The defendants issued a notice of motion on November 17, 2006 in which they sought an order striking out the proceedings on the grounds, inter alia, that at the date of the institution of proceedings by the plaintiff no grant had issued to the defendants and consequently the defendants lacked both the competence and capacity to be sued in a representative capacity, and accordingly the proceedings were a nullity and could not be maintained. McKechnie J. found that the defendants' solicitors were "fully alive to the twin difficulties arising by virtue of s.9 of the Civil Liability Act 1961 and the potential application of what I might call the rule in *Ingall v Moran*." This was clearly evident from correspondence passing between the parties.

McKechnie J. was highly critical of the rule in *Ingall v Moran*, especially in its application to defendants and stated that Singleton J. in *Finnegan v Cementation Company* ([1953] Q.B. 688 at 699) was "perfectly" correct in suggesting that this technicality was "a blot in the administration of the law" and that Lord Templeman in *Austin v Hart* ([1983] 2 W.L.R. 866 at 871) was correct in saying that there should be no extension of the rule's application. He preferred an approach based on justice and where there were no compelling reasons he would refuse to uphold a rule capable of inflicting an injustice. He offered the view that if *Austin v Hart* had been opened to Laffoy J. in *Gaffney v Faughan* ([2006] I.L.R.M. 481), in all probability she:

> "… [W]ould have been impressed with the opinion of Lord Templeman and would at least have paused before extending the rule, by applying it, apparently without precedent, to a situation where the representative person was not seeking to maintain an action, but rather was being named as a defendant in such action."

It seemed to him that any rule of law, such as espoused in *Ingall v Moran*, which had such a "rejectionist label" attached to it by the English Court of Appeal and Privy Council, should only be followed and applied where either the court is bound to so do, or alternatively where the underlying reasons of justification so demand. He went on to state:

> "I cannot identify any particular reason, consistent with the existence of this rule, which persuades me that in the circumstances of this case it is a good rule."

Under the doctrine of relation back, the title of an administrator relates back to the date of the deceased's death, thus allowing the administrator to institute proceedings for any wrongdoing to the assets of the estate during the period between the date of death of the deceased and the issuing of the grant, though it must be emphasised that the doctrine does not become applicable until the grant of administration is issued (*Foster v Bates* (1843) 12 M. & W. 226, 233, per Parke B.; see also *Thorpe v Stallwood* (1843) 5 M. & Gr. 760). The doctrine of relation back was also referred to in *Ingall v Moran* where it was stated by Luxmoore L.J. that although when a grant of administration is made the estate vests in the person to whom the grant is made and the title thereto then relates back to the deceased's date of death, "there is no doubt that both at common law and in equity, in order to maintain an action the plaintiff must have a cause of action vested in him at the date of the issue of the writ" (at 167). McKechnie J. in *Finnegan v Richards* remarked that actions commenced prior to the obtaining of a grant will not benefit from the doctrine even though the plaintiff subsequently obtains a grant, although he went on to state: "I see no reason why the circumstances like the present would not comfortably fall within the reasons which underline the doctrine of 'relation back'."

The Role of the President of the High Court under section 13 of the Succession Act 1965   While a testator's estate devolves and vests in his executors on his death, an intestate's estate or a testator's estate where there is no surviving executor vests, by virtue of s.13 of the Succession Act 1965, in the President of the High Court, until a grant of letters of administration has issued to the person entitled under the Rules of the Superior Courts. The statutory nomination of the President was described in one case as being as one of "convenience" only and subsisted until a grant issued to the person entitled under the Rules of the Superior Courts (*Flack v President of the High Court*, unreported, High Court, Costello J., November 29, 1983). The Supreme Court in *Gleeson v Feehan and Purcell* ([1997] I.L.R.M. 522), however, went so far as to treat the President of the High Court as the "true owner" of an intestate's estate before a grant is issued. Once a grant of letters of administration is made, the President's role under s.13 will come to an end and the estate will then become vested in the person to whom the grant is made, viz. the administrator. McKechnie J. in *Finnegan v Richards* stated that s.13 ensured that "the estate of an intestate person or a person dying without a surviving executor, always vested in some person even in the interval between death and the issuing of a grant." But he found that s.13 was not designed to overcome the difficulty of the representative capacity of a defendant where no grant had issued at the time of instituting proceedings against an estate.

Both Laffoy J. in *Gaffney v Faughan* and McKechnie J. in *Finnegan v Richards* referred with apparent approval to the decision of Costello J. in *Flack v President of the High Court* for the statement that a plaintiff:

"… [C]ould apply for and obtain the appointment of an administrator *ad litem* and join him as a defendant in this suit. The court has a similar power under s.27 of the Succession Act 1965 to make a grant limited to the defence of these proceedings."

The plaintiffs in *Gaffney* and *Finnegan* did not seek the appointment of an administrator *ad litem* (although they could have done) before instituting proceedings, and thereby avoid the consequences of the rule in *Ingall v Moran*.

Conditions attaching to testamentary gifts   Where a testator makes a gift subject to a condition, and there is some doubt regarding the validity of the condition, a construction of it by the courts may become necessary, first, for the purposes of classifying the condition, and secondly, for determining the effect of the condition on the gift. Such a condition attaching to a gift may be classified as either a condition precedent or a condition subsequent. A gift made subject to a condition precedent will fail if the condition is deemed void; a gift made subject to a condition subsequent will not fail even if the condition is void as the efficacy of a gift is not dependent on the success or failure of such a condition (*Re Burke* [1951] I.R. 216 at 224). If there is any doubt as to the nature of the condition the courts will construe it as a condition subsequent because the courts lean in favour of the early vesting of estates (*Re McDonnell* [1965] I.R. 354 at 357; *Mackessy v Fitzgibbon* [1993] 1 I.R. 520; *McGowan v Kelly* [2007] I.E.H.C. 228).

The practical effect of the distinction between a condition precedent and a condition subsequent is that:

"[A] gift made subject to a condition precedent fails altogether, as a rule, if the condition is found to be void or inapplicable, but, if a gift is made subject to a condition subsequent which is found to be void or inapplicable, the condition disappears and the gift takes effect independently of the condition" (*Re Burke* [1951] I.R. 216 at 224, per Gavan Duffy J.).

In the case of a condition precedent, futurity is annexed to the substance of the gift and the vesting is suspended until the event occurs (*Re Farrelly* [1941] I.R. 261 at 268, per Gavan Duffy J.). Where, however, there is any doubt as to the nature of the condition, the court will lean "towards a construction which will hold it to be a condition subsequent, for that construction will lead to an early vesting of the gift, and there is a presumption in favour of early vesting" (*Re Porter* [1975] N.I. 157 at 160, per Lowry L.C.J.; see also *Re McDonnell* [1965] I.R. 354 at 357). The court prima facie treats the condition as subsequent (*Mackessy v Fitzgibbon* [1993] 1 I.R. 520 at 522).

The test for a valid condition subsequent had never been:

> "... [M]ore tersely and more simply formulated than it was in the words of that master of Equity, the late Lord Parker, in *In Re Sandbrook, Noel v. Sandbrook* 75 [1912] 2 Ch. 471 at 477 'conditions subsequent,' he said, 'in order to defeat vested estates, or cause forfeiture, must be such that from the moment of their creation the court can say with reasonable certainty in what events the forfeiture will occur'; the fatal event or events must be described in clear language; so much the law exacts, but it lays down no requirements as to facility of proof, if forfeiture is alleged to have been incurred" (*Re McKenna* [1947] I.R. 277 at 284–285, per Gavan Duffy J.; see also *Clavering v Ellison* (1859) 7 H.L.C. 707 at 725).

Conditions of this kind will also be construed "with strictness and before an interest which has become vested will be defeated it is essential that it be proved that the condition upon which defeasance is to occur has come into operation" (*Re McDonnell* [1965] I.R. 354 at 358). As there is a presumption in favour of early vesting, and where doubt persists as to whether a condition is a condition precedent or subsequent, the court will, prima facie, treat it as a condition subsequent (*Mackessy v Fitzgibbon* [1993] 1 I.R. 520).

Once a condition is classified as subsequent, the next task is to determine the effect of the condition. For a condition subsequent to be effective the courts must see from the beginning, "precisely and distinctly, upon the happening of what event it was that the preceding vested estate was to determine" (*Clavering v Ellison* (1859) 7 H.L.C. 707 at 725). If the event, the happening of which determines the vested estate, is not "precisely and distinctly" stated, the condition may be deemed void for uncertainty, and in the case of a void condition subsequent, the gift will take effect independently of the condition (see *Re McDonnell* [1965] I.R. 354; *Mackessy v Fitzgibbon* [1993] 1 I.R. 520; *McGowan v Kelly* [2007] I.E.H.C. 228; *Sifton v Sifton* [1938] A.C. 656; *Moffat v M'Cleary* [1923] 1 I.R. 16).

Extrinsic evidence may also be adduced and admitted under s.90 of the Succession Act 1965 "to show the intention of the testator and to assist in the construction of, or to explain any contradiction in the will." However, extrinsic evidence showing the testator's intention only will not be admitted as the conjunctive "and" in s.90 connotes "a duality of purpose as a condition for the admission under the section of extrinsic evidence" (*Rowe v Law* [1978] I.R. 55; see also *O'Connell v Bank of Ireland* [1998] 2 I.R. 596). Extrinsic evidence under s.90 may be admissible to show the intention of the testator *and* where it assists the court in the construction of a gift subject to a condition.

In *McGowan v Kelly* ([2007] I.E.H.C. 228), the proceedings concerned the construction of the following provision in the testator's will:

"I give devise and bequeath my house and farm at Carraghs, Ballinlough, County Roscommon to my sister Hilda McGowan of Carraghs, Ballinlough, County Roscommon in trust and on condition that she (Hilda McGowan) transfers, conveys the said house and farm at Carraghs to my nephew Brian Kelly, Birmingham, England son of my late brother William Kelly provided he returns to live there but if he does not wish to take it on that condition then otherwise I give devise and bequeath my house and farm above to my sister Hilda absolutely."

The plaintiff was the executor of the will to whom probate of the will was granted. Brian Kelly named in the provision was the defendant. The testator also devised the residue of his estate to the plaintiff in trust for his three nephews to be divided equally in three shares.

The plaintiff contended that the condition in the provision requiring the defendant to return to live on the farm at Carraghs was a condition precedent, and that that condition was void for uncertainty, and that consequently the gift over in favour of the plaintiff took effect. The defendant argued that the condition was a condition subsequent, and because it was void for uncertainty, the gift to the defendant took effect independently of the condition.

Laffoy J., in the course of her judgment, thought that the fact that the testator devised the house and farm to the plaintiff in trust for and to transfer it to the plaintiff was immaterial to the determination of the issue of whether the condition that the defendant return to live there was a condition precedent or a condition subsequent. It was a limitation of the beneficial interest, including the gift over, not the limitation of the legal estate, which required construction. She found that there was "a welter of authority" for the proposition that such a condition was a condition subsequent (*Moffat v M'Cleary* [1923] 1 I.R. 16; *Sifton v Sifton* [1938] A.C. 656; *Re Coghlan, Motherway v Coghlan and Attorney General* [1963] I.R. 246; *Re Hennessy* (1963) 98 I.L.T.R. 39; *Mackessy v Fitzgibbon* [1993] 1 I.R. 520). Referring in particular to *Mackessy v Fitzgibbon*, she found that there was no difference in substance between the condition under consideration in that case and the condition imposed by the testator in his will. In *Mackessy v Fitzgibbon*, Carroll J. stated that there is a presumption in favour of early vesting, so that, if there is a doubt about whether a condition is precedent or subsequent, the court prima facie treats it as subsequent. Adopting the view of Carroll J., Laffoy J. went on to find that the condition imposed by the testator was a condition subsequent (see also *Re Hennessy* (1963) 98 I.L.T.R. 39 at 45, per Budd J.).

Regarding the question of uncertainty, Laffoy J. thought that the authorities cited in support of the finding that the condition in the will of the testator was a condition subsequent also supported the proposition that the condition was void for uncertainty. She referred in particular to the speech of Lord Cranworth in *Clavering v Ellison* (1859) 7 H.L.C. 707 at 725 where he said:

"I consider that, from the earliest times, one of the cardinal rules on the subject has been this: that where a vested estate is to be defeated by a condition on a contingency that is to happen afterwards, that condition must be such that the courts can see from the beginning, precisely and distinctly, upon the happening of what event it was the preceding vested estate was to determine."

Laffoy J. also referred to *Moffat v M'Cleary* [1923] 1 I.R. 16; *Sifton v Sifton* [1938] A.C. 656; *Re Coghlan, Motherway v Coghlan and Attorney General* [1963] I.R. 246; *Re Hennessy* (1963) 98 I.L.T.R. 39; *Mackessy v Fitzgibbon* [1993] 1 I.R. 520, and concluded that: "By parity of reasoning, it seems to me that the condition imposed by the testator on the defendant is too vague, imprecise and uncertain. So the condition is void for uncertainty."

She found that the condition imposed by the testator on the defendant was a condition subsequent and was void for uncertainty. The practical effect of that was that the defendant took the farm at Carraghs free of the condition.

The construction of wills In *Corrigan v Corrigan* ([2007] I.E.H.C. 367), the plaintiff as executor sought a construction of a provision in the deceased's will. The relevant provision stated as follows:

> "1. I have 21 acres of land in Folio 13658 Co. Westmeath and I have been advised that said land or part thereof is rezoned for residential and/or industrial development. I direct my executors to hold the said lands upon the following trusts:
>
> (a) To allow my son Sean to hold and enjoy the profits of the land for his own benefit until there is acquisition of my lands for the purposes mentioned above. In such event the net proceeds of the sale of my land shall be divided equally amongst all my children and any section of the farm not so acquired shall become the absolute property of my son Sean."

At the time of the execution of the will the land referred to in the bequest was zoned for agricultural use only. Later however certain parts of the land were rezoned for use as a special district for business and enterprise development.

McGovern J. thought that the bequest only made sense in the light of the first part of the clause and seemed predicated on it: This can clearly be seen from the words "… until there is acquisition of my lands for the *purposes mentioned above*" [emphasis added]. On the face of it, it appears that the intention of the testator was that the first named defendant should hold and enjoy the profits of the lands until they were acquired for the development purposes which are stated to be residential and/or industrial. This would appear from the use of the words "to *allow* my son Sean to hold and enjoy the profits of the lands for his

own benefit *until* …" [emphasis added]. In other words, the testator expected the lands or part of them to be acquired for a value that would reflect the fact that they were zoned for residential and/or industrial development. In that event the proceeds of sale would be divided equally among his children and the first named defendant would hold any part of the lands not so acquired.

It was clear from the evidence that the testator acted under a mistake of fact when he declared that "the said land or parts thereof is zoned for residential and/or industrial development." McGovern J. went on to state that he "may well have been advised that that was the case but the advice was wrong and he was therefore acting under a mistake of fact."

McGovern J. stated that when interpreting a will the court may have regard to s.90 of the Succession Act 1965. Section 90 provides that "extrinsic evidence shall be admissible to show the intention of the testator and to assist in the construction of, or to explain any contradiction in, a will." He went on to refer to *Rowe v Law* ([1978] I.R. 55) and *O'Connell v Bank of Ireland* ([1998] 2 I.R. 596) where the Supreme Court held that s.90 must be strictly interpreted. In *Rowe v Law*, Henchy J. stated:

> "I read s.90 as allowing extrinsic evidence to be received if it meets the double requirement of (a) showing the intention of the testator, and (b) assisting in the construction of, or explaining any contradiction in, a will" (at 72).

He went on to state that:

> "[Section] 90 allows extrinsic evidence of the testator's intention to be used by a court of construction only where there is a legitimate dispute as to the meaning or effect of the language used in the will. In such a case … it allows the extrinsic evidence to be drawn on so as to give the unclear or contradictory words in the will a meaning which accords with the testator's intention as thus ascertained. The section does not empower the court to rewrite the will in whole or in part."

McGovern J. found that, owing to the lack of clarity and ambiguity of cl.1 of the bequest, the extrinsic evidence found in the notes taken by the testator's solicitor on taking instructions for the drafting of the will was admissible.

McGovern J. also reviewed the general principles governing the construction of wills:

> "In considering the authorities on this subject it seems that the following principles apply:
> (i) The court will strive as far as it can to give effect to the intention of the testator insofar as this can be ascertained from the will. In limited circumstances the court is permitted to rectify a will

to save it from bad drafting. See *Curtin v O'Mahony* [1991] 2
I.R. 566.
(ii) The court considers the will by placing itself in the position of
the testator sitting in his armchair shortly before his death to see
what he was setting out to achieve.
(iii) As a general rule the court will give legal or technical words
used in a will their legal or technical meaning.
(iv) The guidelines suggested by Lowry L.C.J. in *Heron v Ulster
Bank Limited* [1992] 44 at 52 were approved and adopted by
Carroll J. in *Howell v Howell* [1992] 1 I.R. 290. These are as
follows:
1. Read the immediate relevant portion of the will as a piece
of English and decide, if possible, what it means.
2. Look at the other material parts of the will and see whether
they tend to confirm the apparently plain meaning of the
immediately relevant portion or whether they suggest the
need for modification in order to make harmonious sense
of the whole or, alternatively, whether an ambiguity in the
immediately relevant portion can be resolved.
3. If ambiguity persists, have regard to the scheme of the will
and consider what the testator was trying to do.
4. One at this stage has resort to rules of construction, where
applicable, and aids, such as the presumption of early vesting
and the presumptions against intestacy and in favour of
equality.
5. Then see whether any rule of law prevents a particular
interpretation from being adopted.
6. Finally, and, I suggest, not until the disputed passage has
been exhaustively studied, one may get help from the
opinions of other courts and judges on similar words, rarely
as binding precedents, since it has been well said that 'no
will has a twin brother' (per Werner J. in *Matter of King*
200 N.Y. 189, 192 (1910)), but more often as examples
(sometimes of the highest authority) of how judicial minds
nurtured in the same discipline have interpreted words in
similar contexts."

McGovern J. then had to decide whether the provision in cl.1 of the bequest
was a declaration of the testator's belief, or whether it constituted a condition
attaching to the bequest. He went on to hypothesize that, if it was a condition,
it had to be a condition subsequent. There was a presumption of early vesting
and it was clear that, if the words at the beginning of the bequest constituted
a condition, the first named defendant was to hold and enjoy the profits of the

lands until such time as the condition was fulfilled, namely, the lands were acquired for the purposes of residential and/or industrial development. He referred to the authorities for the proposition that where a condition is attached to a bequest the court should approach the condition prima facie as a condition subsequent unless its construction as a condition precedent was unavoidable (see *McGowan v Kelly* [2007] I.E.C.H. 228; *Mackessy v Fitzgibbon* [1993] I.R. 520; and *Re Porter* [1995] N.I. 157). He went on to say:

> "If a condition subsequent is found to be void the beneficiary takes the bequest freed from the condition. So in this case if the clause 1 of the bequest is a condition subsequent and is found to be void for uncertainty or incapable of taking effect, the first named defendant would take the bequest free from the condition (see judgment of Laffoy J. in *McGowan v Kelly* [2007] IEHC 228 and judgment of Gavan Duffy P. in *Burke and O'Reilly v Burke and Quayle* [1951] I.R. 216 at 223)."

However, McGovern J., in the concluding part of his judgment, found that the bequest to the first-named defendant in cl.1 did not contain a condition.

As regards the effect of a factual error in the belief of the testator, he found that a gift made upon a mistake of fact cannot be cut down or altered to suit the supposed facts. Correction of mistakes by the court can only arise where the words used do not accurately reflect what the testator intended. A court can only supply or omit words in exceptional circumstances and with the greatest caution. If the gift to the first-named defendant was made upon a mistake of fact, then the entire bequest would fail and fall into the residuary estate by virtue of s.91 of the Succession Act 1965.

The plaintiff and the first-named defendant both raised the possibility that the estate intended to be created by the bequest to the first-named defendant could be regarded as a conditional or determinable freehold. It was argued that where the word "until" was used in the grant of a fee simple, the general rule of construction prescribed that it might be construed as giving rise to a determinable fee simple (see Lyall, *Land Law in Ireland*, 2nd edn, (Dublin: Thomson Round Hall, 2000), p.179). McGovern J. was of the view that "[i]f it is a determinable fee simple then it gives rise to a 'possibility of a reverter' in the grant or settlor, in this case, the estate of the deceased." The rule against perpetuities also did not apply to the possibility of a reverter in such a situation (see *Attorney General v Cummins* [1906] I.R. 406). As a result, if the bequest to the first named defendant was a determinable fee simple, then it followed that if the determining events were void for uncertainty or otherwise the entire limitation failed. He turned to Lyall's *Land Law in Ireland*, 2nd edn, p.180 for the statement:

> "At common law, if the determining event occurs, the land reverts automatically to the grantor. The grantor has the possibility of a reverter.

Indeed, this is the only interest that can exist after the determinable fee simple at common law. At common law the grantor cannot, in the same deed create a determinable fee and then provide that if the event occurs, the land is to pass to someone else. The grantor cannot create a gift over to a third party after a determinable fee."

McGovern J., in the concluding parts of his judgment, found that the use of the words "allow" and "until" caused him to take the view that the bequest to the first-named defendant was in the nature of a determinable fee simple. He was satisfied that at common law:

"[T]he testator cannot, in his will, create a determinable fee simple to the first named defendant and then provide that, in the event that a determining event occurs, the land is to pass to someone else. A testator cannot create a gift over to third parties after a determinable fee. On that ground, the entire limitation and entire bequest fails."

He was also satisfied that the determining event specified in cl.1 of the bequest was void for uncertainty and it followed, therefore, that on this basis the entire limitation failed. It followed that the subject-matter of the bequest in cl.1 fell into the residuary estate of the testator.

The moral duty of a testator to make proper provision   Section 117(1) of the Succession Act 1965 provides that:

Where, on application by or on behalf of a child of a testator, the court is of opinion that the testator has failed in his moral duty to make proper provision for the child in accordance with his means, whether by his will or otherwise, the court may order that such provision shall be made for the child out of the estate as the court thinks just.

Section 117(2) provides that:

The court shall consider the application from the point of view of a prudent and just parent, taking into account the position of each of the children of the testator and any other circumstances which the court may consider of assistance in arriving at a decision that will be as fair as possible to the child to whom the application relates and to the other children.

Kenny J. in *In the Goods of GM: FM v TAM* ((1970) 106 I.L.T.R. 82 at 87) thought that the moral duty of a testator was one based on the relationship between testator and child and arises out of such a relationship though "does not of itself and without regard to other circumstances create a moral duty to leave anything to a child", and he went on to state that the existence of the moral duty to make proper provision for his children will be determined by the facts existing at the date of death of the testator and:

> "... [M]ust depend upon: (a) the amount left to the surviving spouse or the value of the legal right if the survivor elects to take this, (b) the number of the testator's children, their ages and their positions in life at the date of the testator's death, (c) the means of the testator, (d) the age of the child whose case is being considered and his or her financial position and prospects in life, (e) whether the testator has already in his lifetime made proper provision for the child. The court must decide whether the duty exists and the view of the testator that he did not owe any is not decisive" (at 87).

Regarding the onus of proof resting on the applicant, Finlay C.J. in *CF v WC* ([1989] I.L.R.M. 815) thought that the phrase "failed in his moral duty to make proper provision for the child in accordance with his means" placed a relatively high onus of proof on an applicant seeking relief under s.117. Having adopted and approved of the general guidelines applied by Kenny J. in *In the Goods of GM: FM v TAM* "as being a correct statement of the law", he went on to add that it was not sufficient:

> "... [T]o establish that the provision made for a child was not as great as it might have been, or that compared with generous bequests to other children or beneficiaries in the will, it appears ungenerous. The court should not, I consider, make an order under the section merely because it would on the facts proved have formed different testamentary dispositions" (at 819).

He emphasized that a "positive failure in moral duty must be established".

Keane J. for the Supreme Court in *EB v SS* ([1998] 2 I.L.R.M. 141) stated that the Oireachtas had transposed the moral duty into a legal duty owed by parents to their children and enforceable in the terms laid down in s.117, thereby suggesting that the relationship of parent and child creates the legal duty and that that relationship activates the provisions of s.117 for the purposes of deciding whether a testator had failed to fulfil this duty by will or otherwise to make proper provision for his children in accordance with his means. McCracken J. in *McDonald v Norris* ([1999] 1 I.L.R.M. 270), apparently following the reasoning of Keane J., said that there is an assumption in the Succession Act that a moral duty exists in general for a testator to make provision for his children and that the provisions of s.117(2) must be considered when deciding whether there has been a failure of such duty.

Kearns J. in *In the Estate of ABC* ([2003] 2 I.R. 250) summarized the principles derived from previous cases on the matter. Kearns J. stated that the following legal principles can, as a result of the authorities, be said to derive under s.117:

(a) The social policy underlying s.117 is primarily directed to protecting those children who are still of an age and situation in life where they might reasonably expect support from their parents against the failure of parents who are unmindful of their duties in that area.

(b) What has to be determined is whether the testator, at the time of his death, owes any moral obligation to the applicants and, if so, whether he has failed in that obligation.

(c) There is a high onus of proof placed on an applicant for relief under s.117 that requires the establishment of a positive failure in moral duty.

(d) Before a court can interfere there must be clear circumstances and a positive failure in moral duty must be established.

(e) The duty created by s.117 is not absolute.

(f) The relationship of parent and child does not itself and without regard to other circumstances create a moral duty to leave anything by will to the child.

(g) Section 117 does not create an obligation to leave something to each child.

(h) The provision of an expensive education for a child may discharge the moral duty, as may other gifts or settlements during the lifetime of the testator.

(i) Financing a good education so as to give a child the best start in life possible, and providing money, which if properly managed, should afford a degree of financial security for the rest of one's life, does amount to making proper provision.

(j) The duty under s.117 is not to make adequate provision but to provide proper provision in accordance with the testator's means.

(k) A just parent must take into account not just his moral obligations to his children and to his wife, but all his moral obligations, for instance, to aged and infirm parents.

(l) In dealing with a s.117 application, the position of an applicant child is not to be taken in isolation. The court's duty is to consider the entirety of the testator's affairs and to decide upon the application in the overall context. In other words, while the moral claim of a child may require a testator to make a particular provision for him, the moral claims of others may require such provision to be reduced or omitted altogether.

(m) Special circumstances giving rise to a moral duty arise if a child is induced to believe that by, for example, working a farm he will ultimately become the owner of it, thereby causing him to shape his upbringing, training and life accordingly.

(n) Another example of special circumstances might be a child who had a long illness or an exceptional talent that it would be morally wrong not to foster.

(o) Special needs would also include physical or mental disability.

(p) Although the court has very wide powers both as to when to make provisions for an applicant child and as to the nature of such provision, such powers must not be construed as giving the court a power to make a new will for the testator.

(q) The test to be applied is not which of the alternative courses open to the testator the court itself would have adopted if confronted with the same situation, but rather whether the decision of the testator to opt for the course he did, of itself and without more, constituted a breach of moral duty to the plaintiff.

(r) The court must not disregard the fact that parents must be presumed to know their children better than anyone else.

The application of these principles may also involve the courts in balancing the circumstances and needs of a testator's children. In *CW v LW* (unreported, High Court, O'Sullivan J., February 23, 2005), when considering the issue of law, O'Sullivan J. asked:

> "[I]n deciding whether the testator discharged his moral obligation to the applicant, do I credit him with the prescient foreknowledge that the applicant will in due course inherit a large sum from her mother?"

He answered by saying that the testator must "be credited with the foreknowledge that she would be taken into wardship and that her committee would, on her behalf, elect to take her legal right, one-third share of his estate." He also referred to s.117(3) of the Succession Act and concluded that the subsection "does appear to contemplate in certain circumstances the treatment of common parents as having what amounts to a shared obligation." When considering the question of whether the testator had discharged his moral obligation to the applicant, he took the testator as having been aware that the applicant would inherit not only the bequest to her under his own will but that she would also inherit a substantial sum from her mother. It was on this basis that he went on to consider whether the testator had discharged his moral duty to the applicant. He would, however, be guided "by the jurisprudence which has been extensively opened during the hearing and not least by the comprehensive list of principles set out by Kearns J. in *In the Estate of ABC* [2003] 2 I.R. 250."

In *A v C* ([2007] I.E.H.C. 120), Laffoy J., when reviewing the law in an application under s.117, referred to the judgment of Kenny J. in *In the Goods of G M: FM v TAM* ((1970) 106 I.L.T.R. 82) and the guidelines laid down by him in relation to an application under s.117, and the judgment of Kearns J. in *In the Estate of ABC* ([2003] 2 I.R. 250) who set down 18 relevant legal principles derived from the authorities in former cases involving s.117, bearing in mind that the "moral duty" is to make "proper provision" for the applicant in accordance with the testator's means, not to make adequate provision.

She stated that "the court's function in adjudicating on an application under s.117 is a two-stage process. The first stage is that the court must decide whether the testator has failed in his moral duty to make proper provision for the applicant child and that decision is made by reference to the circumstances which prevailed at the date of death of the testator. It is only when the applicant child overcomes what the Supreme Court has described as the "relatively high onus" of proof that there has been a positive failure in the moral duty" (*Re IAC* [1990] 2 I.R. 143) that the court proceeds to the second stage, which is to decide what provision is to be ordered for the applicant child. She also referred to the judgment of Carroll J. in *MPD v MD* ([1981] I.L.R.M. 179 at 188) for the statement that "when the court moves to the second stage, the provision must be just at the time the court makes its order, so that the court must have regard to the value of the entire estate at the date of the hearing."

She added that:

> "[T]he requirement that the provision be just may, having regard to the particular circumstances of a case, require the court to take account of changed economic circumstances, any variation in the value of assets, and any variation in the capacity of assets which are or form part of an enterprise which has passed on death as a going concern to yield income, including any regulatory changes which affect the profitability of the enterprise (e.g. changes in European Union law in relation to subsidisation of agricultural enterprises) between the date of the testator's death and the date of the hearing."

Statutory wills The Law Reform Commission, having considered the question of statutory wills in its Report dealing with Vulnerable Adults and the Law (LRC 83-2006), recommended that:

> "[I]n exceptional circumstances, the High Court should be given the discretionary power to order the alteration of a will of an adult who lacks testamentary capacity. The court, acting on its initiative or on an application being made to it by any third party including the proposed

Guardianship Board, would exercise these powers in exceptional circumstances where the justice of the case demands."

It will be noted that the Law Reform Commission recommended that the High Court should be given the discretionary power to order the alteration of an existing will but not "to intervene where no will is in existence". Chapter 3(4), para.3.61 et seq. of the same report deals with the application of the doctrine of ademption, where property forming the subject-matter of a specific devise is sold to fund care arrangements for the testator and recommends that:

> "[I]f land owned by a person who is the subject of a guardianship order is sold to fund their long-term care, the persons who would otherwise have been entitled to the land on the death of the original owner will be deemed to have the same proportionate interest in any surplus monies from the proceeds of sale which remain after the relevant care needs have been provided for."

The Commission also recommends that the discretion afforded to the courts under the proposed statutory will procedure should be capable of accommodating ademption in appropriate circumstances.

The provisions of the Mental Capacity and Guardianship Bill 2007 appear to have adopted certain of the recommendations of the Law Reform Commission's Report dealing with Vulnerable Adults and the Law. It provides at s.11(1) that the law concerning the capacity of a person to make a will shall continue to apply. It provides at s.11(2) that:

> "[W]here a person who has made a valid will loses testamentary capacity, the High Court, acting on its own initiative or on an application to it from the Guardianship Board, may, in the exercise of its discretion, after a will in exceptional circumstances where the justice of the case demands it."

Section 11(3) goes on to provide that:

> "Where land owned by a deceased person, who is the subject of a guardianship order, is sold, the persons who would otherwise have been entitled under the terms of a valid testamentary disposition in a will on the death of the original owner to a share in the proceeds shall be deemed to have the same proportionate interest in any surplus monies from the proceeds of sale which remain."

Safety and Health

MANUFACTURING STANDARDS

Electromagnetic compatibility (EMC)   The European Communities (Electromagnetic Compatibility) Regulations 2007 (S.I. No. 109 of 2007) implemented the 2004 Directive on the Electromagnetic Compatibility (EMC) of products (Directive 2004/108/EC). The 2007 Regulations replaced the European Communities (Electromagnetic Compatibility) Regulations 1998, which had implemented the 1989 Directive on Electromagnetic Compatibility (EMC) (Directive 89/336/EEC) as amended.

OCCUPATIONAL SAFETY AND HEALTH

General Application Regulations 2007   The Safety, Health and Welfare at Work (General Application) Regulations 2007 (S.I. No. 299 of 2007) are a highly significant set of Regulations made under the Safety, Health and Welfare at Work Act 2005 (*Annual Review of Irish Law 2005*, pp.604–618). Like the 2005 Act, the 2007 Regulations apply to virtually all places of work, whether industrial or services, and both public sector and private sector. Since, as we discuss, below, they impose detailed requirements across 15 broad headings in all places of work, they are of general interest to legal practitioners (as well as occupational safety and health practitioners) because they may be used as the basis for a claim of breach of statutory duty (as well as forming the basis for a criminal prosecution).

The 2007 Regulations came into force generally on November 1, 2007. Between the time they were signed and came into force, a relatively small number of problems with the Regulations were identified. These were sufficiently important to be corrected by the Safety, Health and Welfare at Work (General Application) (Amendment) Regulations 2007 (S.I. No.732 of 2007), which came into force on November 12, 2007.

The 2007 Regulations replace—with significant amendments—most of the Safety, Health and Welfare at Work (General Application) Regulations 2003 (*Annual Review of Irish Law 1993*, pp.483–504) (Part 10 of the 1993 Regulations, which deals with Notification of Accidents and Dangerous

Occurrences, is being retained for the time being until agreement can be reached on their replacement. It seems that this is because there is no agreement yet on how to deal with reporting provisions on ill-health, at least in the sense of going further than what used to be called occupational diseases) as well as a number of other Regulations made since 1993 which applied to virtually all places of work (These are: Safety, Health and Welfare at Work (Signs) Regulations 1995 (S.I. No. 132 of 1995); Safety, Health and Welfare at Work (Miscellaneous Welfare Provisions) Regulations 1995 (S.I. No. 358 of 1995); Safety, Health and Welfare at Work (Children and Young Persons) Regulations 1998 (S.I. No. 504 of 1998); Safety, Health and Welfare at Work (Night Work and Shift Work) Regulations 2000 (S.I. No. 11 of 2000); Safety, Health and Welfare at Work (Pregnant Employees etc.) Regulations 2000 (S.I. No. 218 of 2000); Safety, Health and Welfare at Work (General Application) (Amendment) Regulations 2001 (S.I. No. 188 of 2001); Regulations 80 to 123 of the Safety, Health and Welfare at Work (Construction) Regulations 2001 (S.I. No. 481 of 2001); Safety, Health and Welfare at Work (Explosive Atmospheres) Regulations 2003 (S.I. No. 258 of 2003); Safety, Health and Welfare at Work (Work at Height) Regulations 2006 (S.I. No. 318 of 2006); Safety, Health and Welfare at Work (Control of Vibration at Work) Regulations 2006 (S.I. No. 370 of 2006); and Safety, Health and Welfare at Work (Control of Noise at Work) Regulations 2006 (S.I. No. 371 of 2006). The contents of these Regulations have been discussed in the relevant *Annual Review of Irish Law* for the years in question). The 2007 Regulations have also replaced a significant number of sectoral statutory provisions (The Safety, Health and Welfare at Work Act 2005 (Repeals) (Commencement) Order 2007 (S.I. No. 300 of 2007), which was signed on the same day as the 2007 Regulations, repealed (as of November 1, 2007) ss.33, 34, 35, 115 and 116 of the Factories Act 1955 and ss.28 and 29 of the Safety in Industry Act 1980, all of which dealt with lifting equipment. The 2007 Regulations also revoked the following: Factories (Report of Examination of Hoists and Lifts) Regulations 1956 (S.I. No. 182 of 1956); Factories Act 1955 (Hoists and Lifts) (Exemption) Order 1957 (S.I. No. 80 of 1957); Factories Act 1955 (Lifts) (Exemption) Order 1960 (S.I. No. 129 of 1960); Regulations 22 to 35 and 37 and 38 and the Schedule to the Docks (Safety, Health and Welfare) Regulations 1960 (S.I. No. 279 of 1960); Factories Act 1955 (Hoistways) (Exemption) Order 1962 (S.I. No. 211 of 1962); Quarries (Electricity) Regulations 1972 (S.I. No. 50 of 1972); Mines (Electricity) Regulations 1972 (S.I. No. 51 of 1972); Quarries (General) Regulations 1974 (S.I. No. 146 of 1974) to the extent of in Regulation 3, the definitions of "lifting appliance" and "safe working load", Regulations 40 and 41, in the First Schedule "FORM No. 3" and "FORM No. 5" and the Second Schedule; Shipbuilding and Ship-Repairing (Safety, Health and Welfare) Regulations 1975 (S.I. No. 322 of 1975) to the extent of in Regulation 3(1), the definitions of "lifting equipment" and "lifting gear" and Regulations 32 to 48; Factories Act 1955 (Hoistways) (Exemption) Order 1976 (S.I. No. 236 of 1976);

Factories Act 1955 (Hoists) (Exemption) Order 1977 (S.I. No. 13 of 1977); Mines (Electricity) (Amendment) Regulations 1979 (S.I. No. 125 of 1979); Quarries (Electricity) (Amendment) Regulations 1979 (S.I. No. 126 of 1979); and Safety in Industry Acts 1955 and 1980 (Hoists and Hoistways) (Exemption) Order 1985 (S.I. No. 100 of 1985)) dealing with lifting equipment and electrical safety. The 2007 Regulations contain 15 separate major headings.

The 15 headings in the 2007 Regulations and their predecessors   This table sets out the 15 major headings in the 2007 Regulations, what they replaced and any EC Directive they implemented.

General Application Regulations 2007	Previously	EC Directive
Part 2: Workplace and Work Equipment		
Workplace Regulations 2007: Part 2, Chapter 1 of the General Application Regulations 2007	Workplace Regulations 1993: Part 3 of the General Application Regulations 1993	1989 Workplace Directive 89/654/EEC
Work Equipment Regulations 2007: Part 2, Chapter 2 of the General Application Regulations 2007	Work Equipment Regulations 1993: Part 4 of the General Application Regulations 1993 (as amended by General Application (Amendment) Regulations 2001)	1989 Work Equipment Directive, 89/655/EEC (as amended by Directive 95/63/EC, first Amending Directive)
Personal Protective Equipment Regulations 2007: Part 2, Chapter 3 of the General Application Regulations 2007	Personal Protective Equipment Regulations 1993: Part 5 of the General Application Regulations 1993	1989 Personal Protective Equipment Directive 89/656/EEC
Manual Handling of Loads Regulations 2007: Part 2, Chapter 4 of the General Application Regulations 2007	Manual Handling of Loads Regulations 1993: Part 6 of the General Application Regulations 1993	1990 Manual Handling of Loads Directive 90/269/EEC
Display Screen Equipment (VDUs) Regulations 2007: Part 2, Chapter 5 of the General Application Regulations 2007	Display Screen Equipment (VDUs) Regulations 1993: Part 7 of the General Application Regulations 1993	1990 Display Screen Equipment Directive 90/270/EEC
Part 3: Electricity		
Electricity Regulations 2007: Part 3 of the General Application Regulations 2007	Electricity Regulations 1993: Part 8 of the General Application Regulations 1993	1989 Workplace Directive 89/654/EEC

General Application Regulations 2007	Previously	EC Directive
Part 4: Work at Height		
Work at Height Regulations 2007, Part 4 of the General Application Regulations 2007	Work at Height Regulations 2006	2001 Work Equipment at Height Directive 2001/45/EC (2nd Amending Directive to 1989 Work Equipment Directive, 89/655/EEC)
Part 5: Physical Agents		
Control of Noise at Work Regulations 2007: Part 5, Chapter 1 of the General Application Regulations 2007	Control of Noise at Work Regulations 2006 (replacing Exposure to Noise at Work Regulations 1990)	2003 Physical Agents (Noise) Directive 2003/10/EC (replacing 1986 Noise Directive 86/118/EEC, implemented by 1990 Regulations)
Control of Vibration at Work Regulations 2007: Part 5, Chapter 2 of the General Application Regulations 2007	Exposure to Vibration at Work Regulations 2006	2002 Physical Agents (Vibration) Directive 2002/44/EC
Part 6: Sensitive Risk Groups		
Protection of Children and Young Persons Regulations 2007: Part 6, Chapter 1 of the General Application Regulations 2007	Protection of Children and Young Persons Regulations 1998	1994 Young People at Work Directive 94/33/EC [in part: see also Protection of Young Persons (Employment) Act 1996]
Protection of Pregnant, Post Natal and Breastfeeding Employees Regulations 2007: Part 6, Chapter 2 of the General Application Regulations 2007	Pregnant Employees etc Regulations 1994	1992 Maternity Protection Directive 92/85/EEC [in part: see also Maternity Protection Acts 1994 and 2004]
Night Work and Shift Work Regulations 2007: Part 6, Chapter 3 of the General Application Regulations 2007	Night Work and Shift Work Regulations 2000	1993 Working Time Directive, 93/104/EC [in part: see also Organisation of Working Time Act 1997]
Part 7: Safety Signs and First Aid		
Safety Signs at Places of Work Regulations 2007: Part 7, Chapter 1 of the General Application Regulations 2007	Safety Signs at Places of Work Regulations 1995	1992 Safety Signs Directive 92/58/EEC

General Application Regulations 2007	Previously	EC Directive
First Aid Regulations 2007: Part 7, Chapter 2 of the General Application Regulations 2007	First Aid Regulations 1993, Part 9 of the General Application Regulations 1993	1989 Workplace Directive 89/654/EEC
Part 8: Explosive Atmospheres at Places of Work		
Explosive Atmospheres at Places of Work Regulations 2007: Part 8 of the General Application Regulations 2007	Explosive Atmospheres at Places of Work Regulations 2003	1999 Explosives Atmospheres Directive 99/92/EC

Overview of the changes made in the 2007 Regulations   The 2007 Regulations involve more than just a consolidation of existing Regulations under the 15 separate headings already listed. They also involve significant changes in a number of respects, either by introducing completely new obligations or by adding more detail to existing duties. Some of these have been identified by the HSA in their detailed *Guidelines* which have been published since the Regulations came into effect. In December 2007, the HSA published a consolidated version of their *Guidelines* on the 15 headings in the 2007 Regulations. These are available free to download from the HSA website, *www.hsa.ie*. These *Guidelines* provide commentary on most of the detailed provisions of the 2007 Regulations. Given the breadth of topics covered in the 2007 Regulations, it is possible to discuss in this Annual Review a selection only of the significant changes. For a more comprehensive treatment of the 2007 Regulations and the 2005 Act under which they were made, see Byrne, *Safety, Health and Welfare at Work Law in Ireland*, 2nd edn (Douglas, Cork: Nifast, 2008).

The use of reasonably practicable and practicable in the 2007 Regulations   The phrase "reasonably practicable" is used about 25 times in the 2007 Regulations, while "practicable" appears about 22 times. There had been virtually no reference to either phrase in the General Application Regulations 1993, although it is worth noting that "reasonably practicable" had begun to be used again in the Chemical Agents Regulations 2001 and it was used in both the Control of Noise at Work Regulations 2006 and the Exposure to Vibration at Work Regulations 2006 (both of the 2006 Regulations have been incorporated into the 2007 Regulations). For example, the Workplace Regulations 1993 (Pt 3 of the General Application Regulations 1993) stated:

> The floors of rooms shall have no dangerous bumps, holes or slopes and shall be fixed, stable and not slippery.

By contrast, the Workplace Regulations 2007 (reg.9(1)(a) in Pt 2, c.1 of the General Application Regulations 2007) state:

> An employer shall ensure that—
>   (a) the floors of rooms have no dangerous bumps, holes or slopes and are fixed, stable and, *so far as is reasonably practicable*, not slippery.

It is worth noting the effect of such a change. The 2005 Act (and the 1989 Act which it replaced) imposes duties on employers and others to the legal standard of "reasonably practicable". The phrases "practicable" and "reasonably practicable" have been used in occupational safety and health legislation dating back over 100 years. As a result, there have been some useful judicial comments on their meaning. "Practicable" has been interpreted to mean, in effect, technologically possible, without any account being taken of whether it is reasonable that this should be so: if it is technically possible, it is mandatory. "Reasonably practicable" has been interpreted to mean a level of precaution which takes account of the balance between the risk involved in a particular hazard and the cost involved in remedying it. In effect, therefore, an obligation to do something "so far as is reasonably practicable" means that a precaution must be taken if the cost is relatively low by comparison with the risk involved in the work practice or machinery in the workplace. On the other hand, if the cost is quite high and the risk involved can be measured as extremely low, then a duty-holder will have committed no wrong by failing to take the relevant precaution even though it is technically feasible ("practicable").

In *Boyle v Marathon Petroleum (Irl) Ltd*, ([1999] 2 I.R. 460: see *Annual Review of Irish Law 1999*, pp.508–509) the Supreme Court decided that "reasonably practicable" precautions had been taken where certain actions had been taken that had reduced a high risk but had left a residual low risk. The Supreme Court also said that its approach involves three elements:

*   The onus of proving that the precautions were "reasonably practicable" is shifted to the duty holder (this was a civil case, but the same applies in criminal prosecutions: see s.81 of the 2005 Act).

*   The duty is higher than the common law (judge-made) duty of reasonable care (the rule that you are not to be negligent in a way that caused injury or ill-health).

*   Cost is not always to be a factor in determining whether "reasonably practicable" precautions have been taken, but equally a balance has to be struck between the high risk removed by a particular precaution and the remaining low risk that may cause injury or ill-health.

The changes indicated from the 1993 Regulations to the 2007 Regulations arguably mean that floors need only be "reasonably non-slippery" from November 1, 2007, whereas until then any slipping meant that all employers in the State faced up to €3 million fines and/or two years' imprisonment (the maximum penalties under the 2005 Act).

Safety of work equipment in the 1993 Regulations and the 2007 Regulations It is also important to note that, in a number of instances, there has been no change in the text between the 1993 Regulations and the 2007 Regulations.

For example, the Work Equipment Regulations 1993 (reg.19 in Pt 4 of the General Application Regulations 1993) stated:

> It shall be the duty of every employer to ensure that:
> (a) the necessary measures are taken so that the work equipment is suitable for the work to be carried out or is properly adapted for that purpose and may be used by employees without risk to their safety and health.

Similarly, the Work Equipment Regulations 2007 (reg.28 in Pt 2, c.2 of the General Application Regulations 2007) states:

> An employer shall ensure that …
> (c) the necessary measures are taken so that the work equipment is installed and located and is suitable for the work to be carried out, or is properly adapted for that purpose, and may be used by employees without risk to their safety and health.

In *Everitt v Thorsman (Ireland) Ltd and Jumbo Bins and Sludge Disposal Ltd*, ([2000] 1 I.R. 256: see *Annual Review of Irish Law 2000*, pp.423–424) Kearns J. stated that reg.19 of the 1993 Regulations "imposes virtually an absolute duty on employers in respect of the safety of equipment." On this basis, Kearns J. commented:

> "[W]hile there is no blameworthiness in any meaningful sense of the word on the part of the employers in this case, these Regulations do exist for sound policy reasons at least, namely, to ensure that an employee who suffers an injury at work through no fault of his own by using defective equipment should not be left without remedy."

In that case, Kearns J. awarded compensation to the plaintiff, even though his accident and injury had occurred due to a hidden defect in the equipment he was working with and which he employer could not, the judge decided, have in any way reasonably foreseen. In that case, even where the employer had taken "reasonably practicable" precautions, they were still in breach of their statutory duty under the 1993 Regulations. The only consolation for the employer in that case was, as Kearns J noted:

> "[A]n employer in such a situation may usually, though not always, be in a position to seek indemnity from the third party who supplied the work equipment."

For the employer in the *Everitt* case, that was the situation (they were given a 100 per cent indemnity in that case), but as Kearns J. noted this will not always be the case. The work equipment may be old, so that the supplier may not be required to provide an indemnity; the equipment may have been modified (this was argued in the *Everitt* case, but the judge concluded that there was no proof that this had happened); or finally, the supplier may not have the resources to meet a claim or may have gone out of business.

It may be that the *Everitt* case would be decided differently today if, for example, it was argued that the wording of reg.19 of the 1993 Regulations—and now reg.28 of the 2007 Regulations—are taken directly from the 1989 Work Equipment Directive. It could be argued that, since Art.1.1 of the 1989 Directive states that it sets down "minimum safety and health requirements for the use of work equipment", it is difficult to see how the 1993 or 2007 Regulations could impose "virtually an absolute duty on employers in respect of the safety of equipment". But this would be a difficult argument to sustain, especially because in other parts of the 2007 Regulations "reasonably practicable" has been included in text that originated in a Directive that did not contain that phrase.

Lone working and working at remote locations   Regulation 2(3) of the 2007 Regulations states:

> "Without prejudice to the generality of section 19 of the [2005] Act, an employer shall, in identifying hazards and assessing risks under that section, take account of particular risks, if any, affecting employees working alone at the place of work or working in isolation at remote locations."

This is the first specific reference in safety and health legislation to lone working and working in isolation at remote locations. It is important to note the connection between s.19 of the 2005, which deals with risk assessment, and s.20 of the 2005 Act, which deals with Safety Statements. The effect of reg.2(3) is that any lone working and working at remote locations must now be incorporated into Safety Statements.

Regulation 2(3) covers not just late working in an office, laboratory or production facility/factory. It also covers activities such as employees engaged in travelling to distant areas (whether at home or abroad), school outings and the type of work activities engaged in by, for example, pest control workers, drivers, engineers, architects and estate agents who arrange to meet clients away from offices. Indeed, many lone working policies are named after the English estate agent Suzy Lamplugh, who disappeared on her way to what was presumed to be an appointment. It has been pointed out that, when she went missing, the biggest problem the police had was that they did not know where she had gone, who she had gone to see and her colleagues did not know when she should have been back. Lone working policies are intended to reduce this knowledge gap and the relevant risks. The HSA website contains useful guidance on the development of lone working policies, based on the British Health and Safety Executive's publication *Working Alone in Safety; Controlling the risks of solitary work* (There is no specific guidance on lone working in the HSA's *Guidelines* on the 2007 Regulations, presumably because reg.2 falls outside the 15 specific headings already listed (it appears in the "Interpretation and General" part of the 2007 Regulations)).

Workplace Regulations 2007 The main focus of the Workplace Regulations 2007 (Pt 2, c.1 of the General Application Regulations 2007) is to set down standards for workplace design, layout and welfare for indoor workplaces under a large number of headings. These headings include matters such as:

- access to places of work;

- heating;

- lighting;

- preventing slips, trips and falls;

- rest rooms and rest areas;

- room dimensions;

- sanitary facilities;

- traffic movement; and

- ventilation.

Similar detailed requirements were included in previous legislation, such as the Factories Act 1955 and the Office Premises Act 1958 (and in Regulations made under both Acts). But as with most other Regulations made under the 2005 Act (and the 1989 Act before that), the Workplace Regulations 2007 have replaced these older provisions with requirements which apply to virtually all indoor workplaces, whether public sector or private sector. Regulation 4 of the 2007 Regulations states that they apply to any workplace:

> "intended to house workstations on the premises of an undertaking and any other place within the area of the undertaking to which an employee has access in the course of his or her employment."

The effect of this definition is that the 2007 Regulations apply to a large range of places which "house workstations on the premises", including:

- hospitals;
- manufacturing premises,;
- offices;
- schools; and
- shops.

Fire safety and emergencies   Regulations 12 and 13 of the 2007 Regulations implement the relevant fire safety and emergency provisions of the 1989 Workplace Directive 89/654/EEC, which should have been implemented by December 31, 1992. Regulations 12 and 13 state that they are without prejudice to the Fire Services Act 1981 (as amended by the Licensing of Indoor Events Act 2003: see *Annual Review of Irish Law 2004*, pp.441–442), the main legislative framework on fire safety. They also refer to s.11 of the 2005 Act, which provides for the measures to be taken in emergencies and in the case of serious and imminent danger, and it supplements the general duties on employers in s.8 of the 2005 Act to have plans and procedures for emergencies. In general, it could be said that the 2007 Regulations, and s.11 of the 2005 Act, reflect good practice in many organisations. However, the 2007 Regulations have added specific provisions on emergency routes, exit doors and fire-fighting equipment.

Seating and ergonomics   Regulation 18(c) of the 2007 Regulations deals with seating and requires employers to ensure that:

> "[W]here any employees have in the course of their employment reasonable opportunities for sitting without detriment to their work or, where a substantial proportion of any work done by employees can properly be done sitting,
> (i) suitable facilities for sitting are provided and maintained for their use, or

(ii) if this is not practical, they are otherwise ergonomically supported."

Most of reg.18(c) repeats the terms of reg.5 of the Safety, Health and Welfare at Work (Miscellaneous Welfare Provisions) Regulations 1995 (*Annual Review of Irish Law 1995*, pp.449–450) on seating. What is new is the alternative ("or") that "if this is not practical, they are otherwise ergonomically supported". For those standing for long periods, reg.18(c) indicates the need for appropriate seating support. Regulation 18(c)(ii) points to another issue, that seating may not provide appropriate ergonomic support to prevent ill-health. A number of solutions may be available in this respect: for those seated for long periods, the ability to move and stand up from time to time; for those standing for long periods, the ability to sit down from time to time; in both cases, the availability of a "standing or ergonomic chair"; the availability of higher, or variable height, benches (appropriately supported) for production workers, to avoid excessive bending; and the availability of higher benches (appropriately supported) for stand-up (rather than sit-down) office meetings (it has been noted that such meetings tend to be shorter in length).

Persons at work with disabilities Regulation 25 of the 2007 Regulations states:

"Employees with disabilities.
25. An employer shall ensure that places of work, where necessary, are organised to take account of *persons at work with disabilities*, in particular as regards doors, passageways, staircases, showers, washbasins, lavatories and workstations used or occupied directly by those persons."

Regulation 25 is headed "Employees with disabilities", but as can be seen, the actual regulation refers to "persons at work with disabilities". This is not limited to the employees of the employer and seems to include any person at work in a workplace, including self-employed persons and employees of another employer.

Regulation 25 of the 2007 Regulations appears to go much further than the provisions on accessibility in the Employment Equality Acts 1998 and 2004. Section 16(3) of the Employment Equality Act 1998, as amended by s.9 of the Equality Act 2004 (see *Annual Review of Irish Law 2004*, p.259), implemented the 2000 EC Framework Employment Directive 2000/78/EC (The 1998 and 2004 Acts also implemented the EC Equality Directives, Directive 2000/43/EC (the race and ethnic origin Directive) and Directive 2002/73/EC (the gender equal treatment in employment Directive). The 2004 Act also amended the Equal Status Act 2000), which provides a general framework for the prohibition of discrimination in regard to employment and occupation on the grounds of religion or belief, disability, age or sexual orientation. Section 16(3) of the 1998 Act, as amended by the 2004 Act, deals with the duty of employers and persons engaged in vocational training to accommodate the needs of persons with disabilities to enable them to access and participate in employment or training. The original s.16(3) of the 1998 Act had limited the duty on employers to make "reasonable accommodation" or take "appropriate measures" where this gave rise to no more than "a nominal cost". This phrase was used because of the Supreme Court decision in *Re the Employment Equality Bill 1996* [1997] 2 I.R. 321, which had found unconstitutional the provisions on this issue in the Employment Equality Bill 1996, which the court interpreted as imposing virtually all costs associated with this matter on employers (rather than the State, which the court felt was more appropriate, as this was a societal issue). Since s.9 of the 2004 Act implemented Art.5 of the 2000 EC Framework Employment Directive, this would appear to provide sufficient protection against any constitutional challenge. As amended, s.16 of the 1998 Act now requires the employer to take "appropriate measures" (which are not specified) "unless the measures would impose a disproportionate burden on the employer". Section 16(3)(c) of the 1998 Act, as amended by the 2004 Act, provides for three factors to be taken into account in determining what constitutes a "disproportionate burden" on the employer: "(i) the financial and other costs entailed, (ii) the scale and financial resources of the employer's business, and (iii) the possibility of obtaining public funding or other assistance." These factors are precisely those listed in Art.5 of the 2000 Framework Employment Directive.

However, s.16 of the 1998 Act, even as amended by the 2004 Act, imposes a much lower burden on employers than reg.25 of the 2007 Regulations. It is notable that reg.25 states that the employer "shall ensure" that places of work are organised to take account of persons at work with disabilities, and there is no limit to this duty, such as "reasonably practicable" or the "disproportionate burden" test in the 1998 Act, as amended by the 2004 Act. The only limiting words are "where necessary", which appears to concern only the issue as to whether any persons with disabilities are actually, or likely to be, in a workplace. In view of the increasing employment of persons with disability, this seems an increasing likelihood.

Work Equipment Regulations 2007 The Work Equipment Regulations 2007, Pt 2, c.2 of the General Application Regulations 2007, apply to the "use of work equipment" in places of work. This might seem to apply only when equipment is actually operating, but Regulation 27 of the 2007 Regulations defines "selection, installation and use of work equipment" as "any activity involving work equipment, including starting or stopping the equipment, its use, transport, repair, modification, maintenance and servicing and cleaning".

This wide definition means that the Regulations therefore apply to the following stages or "use" of work equipment (though not all will apply to all the work equipment covered by the Regulations, such as a ladder): cleaning, commissioning, dismantling, erecting, installing, maintaining, modifying, operating, planning, programming, removing, selecting, servicing, setting, starting, stopping and transporting.

It might be argued that the general definition in reg.27 does not explicitly cover dismantling and removal of equipment, though it seems to follow from the general definition. In any event, reg.28(o) of the 2007 Regulations explicitly deals with this (this reference was first included in the Work Equipment Regulations 2001, the Safety, Health and Welfare at Work General Application (Amendment) Regulations 2001 (S.I. No. 188 of 2001), which had amended the 1993 Regulations) by stating that work equipment shall be erected or dismantled under safe conditions in particular observing any instructions which may have been provided by the manufacturer. The reference to dismantling is significant. In previous legislation on work equipment, such as the Factories Act 1955, the absence of such a reference was sometimes held by the courts to exclude dismantling activities from the scope of the legislation. The reference to manufacturers' instructions also provides a further link to the EC Directives on product safety, though the 2007 Regulations make specific reference to this issue, discussed below.

The term "work equipment" is not limited to machinery with moving parts, although such equipment poses some of the most obvious risks to people at work. Some of the key risks with machinery arise from poor physical and technological guarding. The term "work equipment" also includes any tool used at work. This includes, in an office environment, chairs, filing cabinets and guillotines; in an assembly line, the conveyor itself and the bench at which a person works; in a warehouse, a forklift truck and the racking; in transport, the car or truck being driven.

Compliance with EC Directives on product safety   Regulation 28(a) requires employers to ensure that:

> ... any work equipment provided for use by employees at a place of work complies, as appropriate, with the provisions of any relevant enactment implementing any relevant Directive of the European Communities relating to work equipment with respect to safety and health.

This means that employers must ensure that work equipment complies with any relevant EC Directive on product safety. A large number of these EC Directives on product safety have been agreed and implemented in Irish law, primarily by Ministerial Regulations. These Directives specify "essential safety and health requirements" criteria with which producers (that is, manufacturers and importers of products) must comply and require them to mark such equipment with the "CE" marking. One of the most significant Directives for the Work Equipment Regulations 2007 is the 1998 EC Directive on Machinery Product Safety 98/37/EC, which was implemented by the European Communities (Machinery) Regulations 2001 (S.I. No. 518 of 2001). The 1998 Directive on Machinery covers many of the most significant pieces of work equipment in terms of high risk, although it is important to note, of course, that "machinery" is not as wide in scope as "work equipment".

Lifting operations and lifting equipment   Regulations 42 to 61 of the 2007 Regulations are the equivalent of the British Lifting Operations and Lifting Equipment Regulations 1998 (the LOLER Regulations). The 2007 Regulations introduce extremely detailed provisions on the "thorough examination" of lifting equipment and replace in a modern form the relevant provisions in the Factories Act 1955 and other statutory Rules and Orders (the majority of the repeals and revocations listed in fn.3, above, arise from the introduction of the new LOLER Regulations in the 2007 Regulations). As well as updating the old provisions, the 2007 Regulations apply to all places of work, not just industrial premises. The 2007 Regulations therefore apply, for example, to hospitals and hotels as well as industrial premises. Like the LOLER, the main elements of the 2007 Regulations require that:

•   lifting operations are properly planned, supervised and carried out by competent persons;

•   lifting equipment is strong and stable enough for the particular use;

•   safe working loads (SWL) or Working Load Limits (WLL) are marked (WLL appears to be the favoured term internationally in recent years);

•   lifting equipment is positioned and installed to minimise any risks;

•   lifting equipment is subject to ongoing thorough examination and, where appropriate, inspection by competent persons.

RADIOLOGICAL (NUCLEAR) SAFETY

Licensing system   The Radiological Protection Act 1991 (Ionising Radiation) Order 2000 (*Annual Review of Irish Law 2000,* pp.397–401), which contains the key requirements concerning the licensing of radiation sources and the relevant standards to which licensees must comply, was amended by the Radiological Protection Act 1991 (Licence Application and Fees) Regulations 2007 (S.I. No. 654 of 2007) (the Radiological Protection Act 1991 (Ionising Radiation) Order 2000 (Revocation) Order 2007 (S.I. No. 653 of 2007) revoked Article 6 of the 2000 Order (which set out the original licensing regime) in order to replace it with the new regime in S.I. No. 654 of 2007). Under the changes made by the 2007 Regulations, the information required by the Radiological Protection Institute of Ireland (RPII) is:

(1) The name and address of the undertaking and a telephone number, fax number or electronic mail address at which it can be contacted at that address.

(2) The address of the premises where or from where the practice is to be carried on and a telephone number, fax number or electronic mail address at which the undertaking can be contacted at that address.

(3) The nature and business of the undertaking.

(4) Into which of the following categories the source or sources of ionizing radiation concerned fall—

   (a) nuclear device/sealed source,

   (b) unsealed radioactive substance,

   (c) irradiating apparatus.

(5) The addresses of any premises, other than the address stated under paragraph 2, at which the source or each source of ionising radiation is to be used.

(6) The proposed date of commencement of the practice.

(7) The following additional information if the Institute requires it:

   (a) a description of the work with ionising radiation,

   (b) particulars of the sources of ionising radiation,

   (c) the quantities of any radioactive substances involved,

   (d) the identity of any person engaged in the practice, and

   (e) the name of the radiation protection adviser.

The changes made by the 2007 Regulations include making mandatory what was only on request under the original 2000 Order. The 2007 Regulations came into force generally on October 1, 2007. Licences granted before that date under the 2000 Order continued in force until their renewal date, from when the 2007 Regulations come into effect for such licensed radiation sources.

Medical radiation   The European Communities (Medical Ionising Radiation Protection) (Amendment) Regulations 2007 (S.I. No. 303 of 2007) amended the European Communities (Medical Ionising Radiation Protection) Regulations 2002 (*Annual Review of Irish Law 2002*, pp.431–433) to extend the definition of prescribers to include nurse prescribers, allowing dental practices to delegate the taking of X-rays and allowing exceptions to the rule that the radiographers must be in attendance during medical radiological procedures.

ROAD TRANSPORT

Carriage of dangerous goods by road The Carriage of Dangerous Goods by Road Act 1998 implemented in general terms the United Nations ADR Agreement on the Carriage of Dangerous Goods. The Carriage of Dangerous Goods by Road Regulations 2007 (S.I. No. 288 of 2007) (the CDGR Regulations), which were made under the 1998 Act (and as supplemented by the European Communities (Carriage of Dangerous Goods by Road) (ADR Miscellaneous Provisions) Regulations 2007 (S.I. No. 289 of 2007)), set down detailed requirements for the vehicles, tanks, tank containers, receptacles and packages containing dangerous goods, including petrol products, as defined in the ADR Agreement. The 1998 Act implemented the general principles of the ADR Agreement, while the 2007 Regulations implement its detailed requirements. The 2007 Regulations also implemented Directive 94/55/EC on the Transport of Dangerous Goods by Road, as amended. The 2007 Regulations require, for example, that the drivers and others, such as the consignor, involved in the carriage of the dangerous goods by road (including their packing, loading, filling, transport and unloading) be adequately trained and, in the case of drivers, hold certificates of such training. The 2007 Regulations also contain provisions on an EC harmonised approach to the road checks aspect of their enforcement. The 2007 Regulations replaced the Carriage of Dangerous Goods by Road Regulations 2006 (*Annual Review of Irish Law 2006*, p.521).

Social Welfare Law

GERARD WHYTE Lecturer in Law, Trinity College, Dublin

PRIMARY LEGISLATION

Two pieces of social welfare legislation were enacted during 2007, the Social Welfare and Pensions Act 2007 and the Social Welfare Act 2007.

The Social Welfare and Pensions Act 2007 provides for a number of measures announced in the 2007 Budget. Section 3 amends the definition of "volunteer development worker" while s.4 provides for an increase in child benefit rates. Section 5 (commenced by S.I. No.210 of 2007) provides that where a person who has been in receipt of illness benefit for a period of at least two years returns to work but, within a period of 26 weeks, finds that s/he is unable to continue, s/he will be entitled to resume claiming Illness Benefit at a rate not lower than that previously received by him/her and without having to serve three waiting days. Similar provision is made for a claimant of Illness Benefit who transfers to Carer's Benefit or Carer's Allowance but who finds that s/he has to resume claiming Illness Benefit. This section also provides for a technical amendment in relation to those transferring from Injury Benefit to Illness Benefit, removes an obsolete reference to the term "rules of behaviour" in s.46 of the Social Welfare (Consolidation) Act 2005 and provides that a person shall not be disqualified for receipt of Illness Benefit while engaged in such type of employment or training as may be prescribed. Section 6 effects certain improvements to the Maternity Benefit scheme, including entitling the father of a newborn child whose mother has died to claim this benefit without having to satisfy the contribution conditions in his own right and providing for the payment of not less than six weeks benefit following the death of the mother. Section 6 also clarifies that Maternity Benefit will not be payable where the mother engages in any form of insurable employment or self-employment or where she fails to attend for medical examination without good reason. Similar changes are made, mutatis mutandis, to Adoptive Benefit by s.7. Section 8 (commenced by S.I. No. 219 of 2007) improves entitlement to Jobseeker's Benefit by providing that where a claimant of this benefit transfers to Carer's Benefit or Allowance and subsequently transfers back to Jobseeker's Benefit, the latter benefit will be paid at the rate received by the claimant before s/he transferred to the carer's payment. Section 9 (commenced in part by S.I. No. 702 of 2007) amends the means test for Jobseeker's Allowance, Pre-Retirement Allowance, Farm Assist and Disability Allowance by providing that the means of a couple will be halved where the claimant's spouse or partner is in receipt of a social welfare payment in his/her own right or is participating in certain approved courses. Section 10 effects a number of changes to the provisions relating to the cost of medical care under the Occupational Injuries Code. These include the deletion of obsolete provisions relating to notification of medical care and prescribing 12 months as the period within which a claim for medical care must be lodged. Section 11 provides for the deletion of an obsolete reference to "rules of behaviour" in relation to disqualification for the purpose of the Injury Benefit and Disablement Benefit schemes and further provides that a person shall not be disqualified for receipt of either such benefit while engaged in such employment or training as may be prescribed. Section 12 provides for the inclusion of education and training among the activities in which a claimant of Carer's Benefit may engage without disqualifying him/ herself for receipt of this payment, while s.13 clarifies the date of entry into insurance for the purpose of State Pension (Contributory). Section 14 (commenced by S.I. No. 749 of 2007) provides that Qualified Adult Allowance may be paid directly to the qualified adult under the State Pension (Contributory), State Pension (Transitional) and State Pension (Non-Contributory) schemes. Pursuant to s.15, a claimant of Invalidity Pension who subsequently qualifies for State Pension (Contributory) or a pension payable, under reciprocal arrangements, by another state shall be entitled to receive whichever payment is the more beneficial. Section 16 provides for the deletion of an obsolete reference to "rules of behaviour" in relation to disqualification for the purpose of the Invalidity Pension and further provides that a person shall not be disqualified for receipt of such pension while engaged in such employment or training as may be prescribed. Section 17 provides that Guardian's Payment (Contributory) and Guardian's Payment (Non-Contributory) shall not be payable simultaneously with a payment under Pt VI of the Child Care Act 1991, while s.18 (commenced by S.I. No. 256 of 2007) extends the Bereavement Grant to apply to the death of a person between the age of 16 and 22 who is in receipt of Disability Allowance. Section 19 clarifies that the Widowed Parent Grant is payable to claimants of Widow's (Contributory) Pension and Widower's (Contributory) Pension, while s.20 (commenced by S.I. No. 256 of 2007) provides that where a claimant of Widow's (Non-Contributory) Pension or Widower's (Non-Contributory) Pension ceases to be a widow or widower and subsequently qualifies for Jobseeker's Allowance, s/he will not have to wait the usual three-day waiting period before claiming the Allowance. Section 15 of the Social Welfare Law Reform and Pensions Act 2006 provided for the phasing out of Pre-Retirement Allowance, but s.21 of the 2007 Act (commenced by S.I. No. 699 of 2007) provides that this allowance will remain payable to a person who ceases to be entitled to Carer's Allowance by virtue of no longer being regarded as a carer where that person had been in receipt of Pre-Retirement Allowance immediately prior to qualifying for Carer's Allowance. Section 22 increases the upper income limit for eligibility for One-Parent Family Allowance, while s.23 empowers the Minister to provide for a transitional reduced rate payment for women who cease to be entitled to Deserted Wife's Benefit because their earnings exceed the prescribed upper limit. Both of these provisions are commenced by S.I. No. 219 of 2007. Generally speaking, a social welfare claimant cannot claim two or more welfare payments simultaneously. However, s.24 (commenced by S.I. No. 699 of 2007) now provides for the introduction of a new means-tested payment of up to half the Carer's Allowance rate which will be payable to carers who are simultaneously in receipt of another social welfare payment. Section 25 (commenced by S.I. No. 256 of 2007) entitles a person returning to full-time employment who has been without such employment during the previous 12 months to continue to receive Rent Supplement provided s/he is on a waiting list for accommodation operated by the Department of the Environment, Heritage and Local Government. This provision also applies to participants in Area Allowance Enterprise Schemes, Community Employment and Back to Work Allowance Schemes who are also on a departmental waiting list for accommodation. The section further provides for powers to preclude payment of Rent Supplement where rental accommodation does not meet the standards set down by the Department of the Environment, Heritage and Local Government or where the claimant resides in a designated area of regeneration and also effects a series of amendments to provisions governing the payment and administration of the Supplementary Welfare Allowance scheme in order to facilitate the transfer of those functions from the HSE to the Department of Social and Family Affairs. Section 26 provides for the deletion of an obsolete reference in the rules of behaviour in the 2005 Act in so far as those rules apply to Disability Allowance, while s.27 repeals s.220(2)(b) of the 2005 Act which had provided that, for the purposes of Child Benefit, a qualified child could not be regarded as normally residing with more than one person. Section 28 (commenced by S.I. No. 219 of 2007) increases the amount of the annual Respite Care Grant and further provides that it may be claimed, subject to prescribed conditions, by persons engaged in training and education. Section 29 clarifies the obligation of a claimant to provide information and evidence in support of a claim for benefit and to inform the Department of any relevant change of circumstances while claiming welfare. Section 30 prescribes the criteria to be taken into account in determining whether a claimant is habitually resident in Ireland, while s.31 provides for the disclosure of relevant employment information between the Minister for Social and Family Affairs and the Minister for Enterprise, Trade and Employment in order to facilitate the operation of a new agency established to ensure compliance with employment rights. Section 32 provides for a number of measures to tackle social welfare fraud, while s.33 expands the Household Budgeting Scheme to encompass any telecommunications provider registered with the Commission for Communications Regulation. Section 34 (commenced by S.I. No. 268 of 2007) provides that managers of social welfare branches and their staff may decide claims for certain social welfare payments while ss.35 (commenced by

S.I. Nos 146 and 256 of 2007) and 36 (commenced by S.I. No. 256 of 2007) effect a number of amendments to the means tests governing social assistance payments.

Finally, Pt 3 of the Act provides for various amendments to the Pensions Act 1990 while Pt 4 effects certain amendments to the Taxes Consolidation Act 1997, the Combat Poverty Agency Act 1986 and the Family Support Agency Act 2001.

The Social Welfare Act 2007 provides for new rates of social welfare payments and also amends the income limits above and below which PRSI is not payable by employed contributors—ss.2–5. Section 6 increases the income limit above which PRSI is not payable by optional contributors, while s.7 provides for an increase in the amount of the Widowed Parent Grant. Finally, s.8 effects some changes in respect of health contributions.

SECONDARY LEGISLATION

During 2007, the Minister for Social and Family Affairs promulgated 29 statutory instruments relating to the social welfare code. They are as follows:

Social Welfare (Consolidated Payments Provisions) (Amendment) (Jobseeker's Benefit) (Redundancy—Exemption from Disqualification) Regulations 2007 (S.I. No. 43 of 2007)   Section 68 of the Social Welfare Consolidation Act 2005 provides that a person under the age of 55 who receives monies in respect of redundancy in excess of a prescribed amount may be disqualified for receiving Jobseeker's Benefit for a period of up to nine weeks. These regulations increase the amount prescribed for the purpose of this disqualification to €50,000.

Social Welfare (Consolidated Supplementary Welfare Allowance) (Amendment) (Diet Supplement and Maximum Rents) Regulations 2007 (S.I. No. 44 of 2007)   These Regulations provide for revised rates of diet supplement under the Supplementary Welfare Allowance Scheme and also provide for the continuation until 30 June 2008 of the levels of maximum rent in respect of which rent supplement is paid.

Social Welfare (Consolidated Occupational Injuries) Regulations 2007 (S.I. No. 102 of 2007)   These regulations consolidate the regulatory provisions governing Occupational Injuries Benefits, relating to:

• occupational injuries;

• prescribed diseases; and

• general provisions for claims and payments.

Social Welfare (Consolidated Payments Provisions) (Amendment) (No. 1) (Maternity Benefit and Miscellaneous Provisions) Regulations 2007 (S.I. No. 128 of 2007) These regulations provide for the extension of the duration of payment of Maternity Benefit by four weeks, consequential on the extension of paid Maternity Leave. In addition, the regulations provide for a technical amendment by inserting at art 88E a means disregard of €1,270, in relation to the harvesting of seaweed, for the Jobseeker's Allowance and Pre-Retirement Allowance schemes.

Social Welfare (Consolidated Claims, Payments and Control) Regulations 2007 (S.I. No. 142 of 2007) For the past number of years, the Department of Social and Family Affairs has consolidated regulations relating to various parts of the social welfare code. These regulations represent a major advance in this regard as they consolidate the regulatory provisions relating to:

• All of the social insurance payments other than Occupational Injuries Benefits (Pt 2).

• All of the social assistance payments, other than supplementary welfare allowance (Pt 3).

• Child Benefit (Pt 4).

• Respite Care Grant (Pt 5).

• Family Income Supplement (Pt 6).

• Related provisions governing the making of claims and payments (Pt 7) including:
    • loss of purchasing power;
    • absence from state and imprisonment;
    • overlapping payments—provisions which set out the circumstances in which a person may receive more than one social welfare payment at the same time;
    • island allowance.

• Control provisions (Pt 8).

• Overpayments (Pt 9).

• Liable Relatives (Pt 10).

Social Welfare and Pensions Act 2007 (Section 35) (Commencement) Order 2007 (Consolidated Occupational Injuries) Regulations 2007 (S.I. No. 146 of 2007) This Order provides for the commencement, with effect from the first week in April 2007, of ss.35(a)(ii), 35(a)(iii), 35(b)(ii), 35(c)(ii) and 35(c)(iii) of the Social Welfare and Pensions Act 2007.

Social Welfare (Consolidated Claims, Payments and Control) (Amendment) (Carer's Income Disregard and Family Income Supplement) Regulations 2007 (S.I. No. 148 of 2007) Article 4 of these Regulations increases the weekly income that a claimant of Carer's Benefit may legitimately earn through employment or self-employment to €320 per week, effective from 5th April 2007. The regulations further provide for an increase in the income disregarded for the purposes of Carer's Allowance. In addition, these regulations also provide for the assessment of rental income in determining the income of a family for the purposes of Family Income Supplement.

Social Welfare (Consolidated Claims, Payments and Control) (Amendment) (No.1) (Miscellaneous Provisions) Regulations 2007 (S.I. No. 176 of 2007) These Regulations correct a printing error in the citation of the Social Welfare (Consolidated Claims, Payments and Control) Regulations and the Social Welfare (Consolidated Claims, Payments and Control) (Amendment) (Carer's Income Disregard and Family Income Supplement) Regulations 2007.

Social Welfare and Pensions Act 2007 (Sections 5, 8, 22, 23 and 28) (Commencement) Order 2007 (Consolidated Occupational Injuries) Regulations 2007 (S.I. No. 219 of 2007) This Order provides for the commencement of ss.5, 8, 22, 23 and 28 of the Social Welfare and Pensions Act 2007.

Social Welfare (Consolidated Supplementary Welfare Allowance) Regulations 2007 (S.I. No. 221 of 2007) These Regulations provide for an increase in the maximum amount of Rent Supplement payable to tenants in voluntary housing developments funded through the local authority Capital Assistance Scheme.

Social Welfare (Consolidated Claims, Payments and Control) (Amendment) (No. 2) (Illness, Jobseeker's, Maternity, Adoptive and Deserted Wife's Benefit) Regulations 2007 (S.I. No. 222 of 2007) Article 4 of these Regulations provides for an improvement in the conditions for receipt of Illness Benefit and Jobseeker's Benefit for a person who was initially in receipt of either benefit payment, but who subsequently transferred to Carer's Benefit or Carer's Allowance and then transfers back to either Illness Benefit or Jobseeker's Benefit. Where it is more beneficial to the person, the rate of Illness Benefit or Jobseeker's Benefit will be restored to the level which was in payment prior to the period during which he or she was in receipt of Carer's Benefit or Carer's Allowance.

Article 5 of these Regulations clarifies the position in relation to disqualification for receipt of Maternity Benefit and Adoptive Benefit by providing that such benefit will not be payable where a person engages in any form of insurable employment or self-employment.

Social welfare legislation currently provides that a woman in receipt of Deserted Wife's Benefit may engage in employment or self-employment, subject to satisfying certain conditions, including income-related conditions. Articles 6 and 7 provide for the replacement of existing income thresholds with a single annual income limit of €20,000. These Regulations further provide that where a claimant of Deserted Wife's Benefit exceeds the annual income limit of €20,000, she may receive a transitional payment, equivalent to half the former rate of Deserted Wife's Benefit payable, for a further six months.

Social Welfare (Consolidated Claims, Payments and Control) (Amendment) (No. 3) (Pre-Retirement Allowance) Regulations 2007 (S.I. No. 223 of 2007) These Regulations provide for the phasing out of Pre-Retirement Allowance with effect from July 4, 2007. From that date new applicants will not be admitted to the scheme. However, those in receipt of the allowance on that date will continue to be paid for the duration of their continuous period of retirement.

Social Welfare and Pensions Act 2007 (Sections 18, 20, 25(1), 35 and 36) (Commencement) Order 2007 (Consolidated Occupational Injuries) Regulations 2007 (S.I. No. 256 of 2007) This Order provides for the commencement of ss.18, 20, 25(1), 35(b)(i), 35(c)(i), 35(d) and 36 of the Social Welfare and Pensions Act 2007.

Social Welfare (Consolidated Supplementary Welfare Allowance) (Amendment) (No. 3) Regulations 2007 (S.I. No. 267 of 2007) These Regulations provide for the removal of the Family Income Supplement disregard in the assessment of means for rent supplement purposes. These Regulations also provide for a number of miscellaneous amendments to the Regulations governing Supplementary Welfare Allowance, in advance of the promulgation of new consolidated regulations for the scheme.

Social Welfare and Pensions Act 2007 (Section 34) (Commencement) Order 2007 (S.I. No. 268 of 2007) This Order provides for the commencement of s.34 of the Social Welfare and Pensions Act 2007.

Social Welfare (Consolidated Contributions and Insurability) (Amendment) (Modified Social Insurance) Regulations 2007 (S.I. No. 298 of 2007) These Regulations provide for the continuation of a modified rate of social insurance payable by certain public sector employees for persons who, on April 5, 1995 were employed by eircom plc and who, immediately on ceasing to be employed by eircom plc, become employed by Eircell 2000 plc and subsequently by Vodafone Group Services Ireland Ltd under terms and conditions which provide that such persons continue to be employed in a permanent and pensionable capacity and for payment during illness on a basis considered adequate by the Minister.

Social Welfare (Consolidated Supplementary Welfare Allowance) Regulations 2007 (S.I. No. 412 of 2007) These Regulations consolidate the regulatory provisions governing Supplementary Welfare Allowance.

Social Welfare (Consolidated Claims, Payments and Control) (Amendment No. 4) (Bereavement Grant and Payments after Death) Regulations 2007 (S.I. No. 536 of 2007) These Regulations outline the circumstances under which an award of Bereavement Grant and six weeks after-death payments may be made without the need for formal application or referral to a Deciding Officer for decision.

Social Welfare and Pensions Act 2007 (Sections 21 and 24) (Commencement) Order 2007 (S.I. No. 699 of 2007) This Order provides for the commencement of ss.21(b), 21(c) and 24 of the Social Welfare and Pensions Act 2007.

Social Welfare (Consolidated Claims, Payments and Control) (Amendment No.5) (Assessment of Earnings) Regulations 2007 (S.I. No. 700 of 2007) These Regulations amend provisions governing the means test for the purposes of Jobseeker's Allowance, Pre-Retirement Allowance, Disability Allowance and Farm Assist by removing the current provision whereby a recipient of Jobseeker's Allowance, Pre-Retirement Allowance, Farm Assist and Disability Allowance shall only be regarded as wholly or mainly maintaining his or her spouse where the spouse's weekly income does not exceed €100 per week. These Regulations also provide for the retention, in certain circumstances, of the current provisions of these schemes in relation to wholly or mainly maintaining a spouse.

The Regulations introduce an earnings disregard of €20 per day where a recipient of Jobseeker's Allowance or Farm Assist engages in insurable employment and is also in receipt of an increase in relation to a qualified child. The current disregard of €12.70 per day where a recipient of these schemes is engaged in insurable employment and is not in receipt of an increase in respect of a qualified child is increased to €20 per week

These Regulations also provide for the disregard of superannuation contributions, social insurance contributions, health contributions and trade union contributions from the assessment of weekly earnings from employment or self-employment of a rehabilitative nature for the purposes of Disability Allowance.

The Regulations provide for the introduction of an earnings disregard of €20 per day, subject to a maximum of €60 per week, where the spouse of a recipient of Jobseeker's Allowance, Pre-Retirement Allowance, Farm Assist and Disability Allowance engages in insurable employment. They further provide that 60 per cent of earnings in excess of the amount disregarded are assessed and also provide for the retention of the current assessment provisions in relation to the insurable earnings of a spouse subject to certain conditions.

These Regulations allow for carers in receipt of a payment under s.186A of the Principal Act to satisfy the definition of qualified adult and ensure that a payment received under s.186A is disregarded in calculating the income limit for qualified adults.

They also provide for technical amendments to the Principal Regulations.

Social Welfare (Bilateral Agreement with the United Kingdom on Social Security) Order 2007 (S.I. No. 701 of 2007) This Order gives effect to the Bilateral Agreement on social security made between Ireland and the United Kingdom which comes into effect from October 1, 2007. The Order provides that the Social Welfare Acts and relevant Regulations will be modified to take account of the provisions of the Agreement. *Quaere,* however, whether this Order can modify provisions of the Social Welfare Acts, having regard to Art.15.2.1 of the Constitution.

Social Welfare and Pensions Act 2007 (Section 9) (Commencement) Order 2007 (S.I. No. 702 of 2007) This Order provides for the commencement of s.9 (other than paragraphs (b), (e)(i), (g)(i) and (i) of that section) of the Social Welfare and Pensions Act 2007.

Social Welfare (Temporary Provisions) Regulations 2007 (S.I. No. 748 of 2007) These Regulations provide for the payment of a Christmas Bonus to long-term social welfare claimants.

Social Welfare and Pensions Act 2007 (Section 14) (Commencement) Order 2007 (S.I. No. 749 of 2007) This Order provides for the commencement of s.14 of the 2007 Act.

Social Welfare (Consolidated Claims, Payments and Control) (Amendment) (No.7) (Child Benefit) Regulations 2007 (S.I. No. 859 of 2007) These Regulations provide for amendment to the rules used to determine the person with whom the qualified child resides for the purposes of child benefit and as a consequence for the early childcare supplement. It also provides for the extension of child benefit to children over the age of 16 who are receiving home schooling.

Social Welfare (Consolidated Claims, Payments and Control) (Amendment No. 6) (Entitlement to Pro-Rata State Pension) Regulations 2007 (S.I. No. 860 of 2007) These Regulations provide for the amendment of the provisions governing the entitlement to pro-rata State pension (contributory) and State pension (transition) by bringing the regulations into line with the contribution conditions set out in the Social Welfare Consolidation Act 2005.

Social Welfare (Consolidated Claims, Payments and Control) (Amendment) (No. 8) (Increase in Rates) Regulations 2007 (S.I. No. 862 of 2007) These Regulations provide for increases in the reduced rates of Illness Benefit, Jobseeker's Benefit, Health and Safety Benefit, State Pension (Contributory), State Pension (Transition), Widow's and Widower's (Contributory) Pension and Deserted Wife's Benefit, and also provide for increases in the rates of tapered increases in respect of Qualified Adults. They also provide for increases in the minimum weekly rate of Maternity Benefit and Adoptive Benefit and for the disregard of social insurance contributions, health contributions, superannuation contributions and trade union subscriptions when calculating means from employment of a rehabilitative nature for the purposes of the Blind Pension.

Social Welfare (Rent Allowance) (Amendment) Regulations 2007 (S.I. No. 863 of 2007) These Regulations provide for increases in the amount of means disregarded for people affected by the decontrol of rents and the minimum rent for the purposes of the Rent Allowance scheme with effect from January 2008.

Social Welfare (Occupational Injuries) Regulations 2007 (S.I. No. 864 of 2007) These Regulations provide for increases in the reduced rates of disablement gratuities appropriate to degrees of disablement assessed at 19 per cent or less, Disablement Pension payable in lieu of such gratuities and Injury Benefit.

Case law   During 2007, there would appear to have been only one judgment of the Superior Courts dealing with social welfare law. In *Iarnród Éireann v Social Welfare Tribunal* [2007] I.E.H.C. 406; High Court, November 30, 2007, the applicant company sought to challenge a decision of the tribunal awarding unemployment benefit and unemployment assistance to a number of the company's employees who had been out of work for a number of weeks during 2000 as a result of a trade dispute. Section 47(1) of the Social Welfare (Consolidation) Act 1993 (see now s.68 of the Social Welfare (Consolidation) Act 2005) provided:

> "A person who has lost employment by reason of a stoppage of work which was due to a trade dispute at the factory, workshop, farm or other premises or place at which he was employed shall be disqualified for receiving unemployment benefit as long as the stoppage of the work continues, except in a case where he has, during the stoppage of work, become *'bona fide'* employed elsewhere in the occupation which he usually follows or has become regularly engaged in some other occupation:
>
> > Provided that the foregoing provisions of this subsection shall not apply to a person who is not participating in or directly interested in the trade dispute which caused the stoppage of work."

Section 125(3) of the 1993 Act made similar provision, mutatis mutandis, in respect of unemployment assistance and this provision is now contained in s.147(2) of the 2005 Act.

By virtue of ss.274–5 of the 1993 Act (see now ss.331–332 of the 2005 Act) a person disqualified for receipt of, inter alia, unemployment benefit or unemployment assistance, could apply to the Social Welfare Tribunal for a ruling that s/he was unreasonably deprived of employment during the dispute, in which case the tribunal could order that unemployment benefit or assistance be paid to the claimant.

Section 275(c) of the 1993 Act further provided for an appeal on questions of law against a decision of the tribunal to the High Court. It also provided that an interested party could apply to the tribunal to review its decision where:

> "... a material change has occurred in the circumstances of the stoppage of work or of the trade dispute which caused the stoppage of work, or ... there is new evidence or new facts which in the opinion of the Tribunal could have affected its decision."

In the instant case, the tribunal had originally held that the company's employees had been unreasonably deprived of employment and had ruled that they were entitled to unemployment payments. The company requested the tribunal to review this decision but the review upheld the original decision on the ground that no new facts had been brought to the attention of the tribunal of which it was previously unaware and the company now sought to challenge this second decision by way of judicial review.

The company contended that, contrary to the ruling of the tribunal on the review, it had submitted new evidence on the occasion of the review. While accepting that the employer was an interested party for the purpose of s.275(c), Murphy J. ruled, citing *Smyth v Tunney* [1996] 1 I.L.R.M. 219, that the reference to "new evidence" in the same provision meant evidence "which is not merely additional to that adduced on the former occasion but could not reasonably have been expected to be produced then". Moreover, the burden of proof rested on the applicant and the High Court would not set aside findings of primary facts unless there was no evidence whatsoever to support them. In the instant case, the tribunal had made a finding that there were no new facts before it at the review hearing that were not already before it at the adjudication hearing. Murphy J. further ruled that no point of law arose in the case and so concluded that the applicant company was not entitled to the reliefs sought.

Sports Law

DR NEVILLE COX, Lecturer in Law, Trinity College, Dublin

ADMINISTRATIVE LAW AND JUDICIAL REVIEW

A major statement as to the proper role of the law in regulating disputes between athletes and governing bodies was given in the High Court in *Gould v McSweeney* [2007] I.E.H.C. 5. Together with the decision of Clarke J. in *J R M Sports Ltd t/a Limerick Football Club v Football Association of Ireland* [2007] I.E.H.C. 67, which we considered in last year's *Annual Review*, this decision would appear to represent the law in this area and is indicative, and strongly so, of the enormous discretion afforded to sports governing bodies in terms of how they apply their rules and indeed how they conduct their disciplinary procedures.

The facts of the case are somewhat unusual, not least because it involves the sport of road bowling. The plaintiff was a member of Ból Chumann na hÉireann, the governing body for the sport, and was very successful at the sport having represented Ireland on occasion. In May 2006 he was due to compete in the quarter final of the Cork County road bowling championships, a game which he won. There was a large attendance at the game (some 3000) people, and some €9,000 raised in bets.

However, the plaintiff's victory was marred by certain events prior to the game, where, in practising for the competition, he rolled several balls in the direction of a lay-by where they hit parked cars and on another occasion, rolled a ball which narrowly missed a man in a wheelchair. He and his opponent were asked by a steward (who was also secretary of the association) to move further down the road in order to avoid further risk to passers-by but, whereas the opponent did what he was told, it would appear that the plaintiff refused to do so, and instead verbally abused the steward in question. Evidence was also given by the chairman of the referees' association that the referee could, at this point, have simply disqualified the plaintiff for his dangerous behaviour, but in light of the crowds that were present, it was decided not to do so (a course of action approved of by the judge). However, a full report of the events was made by the referee to the association.

Prior to a meeting of the association, who investigated the matter and determined that the plaintiff should be suspended for two years (which investigation and determination were fundamentally at issue in the case), the plaintiff wrote a letter of apology both for his behaviour and for any offence that it caused to the steward in question (Mr Brendan Hayes). Following this meeting of the association (at which the plaintiff was present), it was decided to suspend him from all road bowling under the auspices of the association for two years.

The plaintiff successfully obtained an interlocutory injunction prohibiting the imposition of such a suspension and, in the present case, sought a declaration that the decision was in breach of natural and constitutional justice and in particular of the maxims *audi alterem partem* and *nemo iudex in causa sua*. The essence of the plaintiff's claim was first that he was insufficiently able to present his case because:

(1) he was not given sight of the relevant referee's report prior to the meeting;

(2) whereas he was represented by a member of the association he was denied access to a lawyer, even though the association's legal representative was present; and

(3) he was not allowed to cross-examine witnesses.

Secondly, he claimed that there was both apparent and objective bias in the way in which the process operated in that Mr Brendan Hayes, who was essentially one of the complainants against him, was allowed to be present at the meeting as secretary to the executive and was thus involved in the process by which the decision to suspend the plaintiff was reached. On the other hand, he does not appear to have linked such claims to the degree of sanction imposed on him—a matter to which reference will be made later.

Smyth J. rejected the plaintiff's claim. He noted that this was an amateur sports organisation and one whose ties with its members was based on the law of contract. He pointed out that, whereas there might be certain concerns at the manner in which the disciplinary process operated, nonetheless there was no evidence that the plaintiff had suffered prejudice as a result. Thus, whereas the plaintiff was not given sight of the referee's report, he was, however, given full notice of the charge against him and knew the case he had to meet. Furthermore, whereas he was not permitted to have legal representation, equally he did not inform the meeting that his solicitor was present and, indeed, the court was of the view that the questions which were asked by his representative had been drafted with the benefit of legal advice. Moreover, the court was of the view that the relevant points of controversy were matters of fact and not law. Finally, the court accepted that whereas the plaintiff was not allowed to cross-examine witnesses, equally he did not raise this as a matter of concern when the hearing was actually going on.

The court also rejected the claim that the presence of Mr Brendan Hayes at the meeting raised concerns of bias. Smyth J. suggested that "as a counsel of perfection" it might have been preferable if Mr Hayes had not been present; on the other hand, the judge concluded that he did not (as was alleged) run the meeting, nor did he vote at it. In other words, he was only present as secretary of the association, (which was something he was entitled to do) and he did not influence the process. Pivotally, however, there was no suggestion that anyone who would actually make the decision against the plaintiff was biased against him.

Finally, the court rejected the suggestion that there was an inequality of arms as regards the parties at the hearing in light of the fact that the association's legal adviser was present. Smyth J. concluded that the role of that adviser was that of an impartial assistant; he did not vote or in any other way influence the meeting. Thus, on the evidence the court concluded that, in reality, neither party was advised (in terms of tactics) by a lawyer and hence that no such inequality of arms existed.

On this basis the court found that there was no breach of the rules of natural and constitutional justice, and that if there were any irregularities in the procedures adopted, these were not such as to prejudice the plaintiff. As has been mentioned above, it does not appear from the case that a complaint was made as to the disproportionate nature of the penalty in question, and certainly there was no consideration of such an issue by the court.

What is particularly significant about the decision (in terms of the long-term development of this area of law) is the enormous level of discretion which is afforded to the governing body in this case. There is some suggestion that the court did have some concerns that the procedures adopted were inappropriate in certain ways (thus Smyth J. accepted that "[l]awyers may well be critical of the order or the want of order with which the meeting was conducted") but nonetheless and despite such concerns it was prepared to uphold the legality of the process and the result which was reached. Effectively the conclusion of the court appears to have been that this was an amateur body which should (as we shall see below) be afforded a discretion as to how it wished to conduct itself, and thus whereas there were discrepancies n the procedures it adopted, these were not fatal as far as its decision was concerned, not least because the plaintiff suffered no discernible prejudice as a result.

In light, however, of the degree of penalty imposed on the plaintiff, it is arguable that the concerns of the plaintiff were treated rather lightly. After all, he was suspended from all competitive road bowling for two years, which is precisely the penalty he would have received had he been, for example, a swimmer who was accused of using steroids. Yet, in the latter case, the athlete would be entitled (under the World Anti-Doping Code or, domestically, the Irish Anti-Doping Rules) to legal representation (irrespective of whether or not the issues at stake were primarily ones of fact); to full copies of all relevant documentary evidence against him or otherwise connected with his case; to cross-examine witnesses and so on, such that the level of procedures required would have been nearly as high as those expected in a criminal court. Moreover, there would be absolutely no possibility in a doping hearing that anyone who was involved in the case in the role of a complainant could also be involved, however, remotely, in the process by which judgment was reached.

What is unclear is why, given that in the doping context such very significant procedural safeguards apply, a similar approach should not have been taken in the present case *given that the sanction imposed on the plaintiff was comparable to the sanction imposed on someone found to have committed a doping offence.* Smyth J. distinguished the case of *Quirke v BLE* [1988] I.R. 83 from the present case on the basis that that case involved an allegation that the applicant had cheated in a competitive situation. Quite apart from the fact that the doping safeguards will apply even in cases where there is no moral allegation of cheating being raised (as where an athlete is alleged, unintentionally, to have a banned substance in his or her system), the point is that the fact that the athlete was accused of cheating was simply not the dominant issue in *Quirke v BLE*. Rather, in that case the reason why particularly high standards were expected of the relevant governing body was precisely because of the very serious penalty being imposed on the applicant. It is perhaps notable that, in assessing whether the procedures followed in the present case were fair, Smyth J. does not take the standard approach of Irish law of linking the fairness of such procedures to the degree of seriousness of the matter and of linking the seriousness of the matter to the level of penalty being imposed following the disciplinary process.

What emerges by inference from the judgment is a clear view that because this was an amateur sports body (albeit the court expressly declined to lay emphasis on the fact that this was not an issue with any financial implications for the applicant) it would be simply inappropriate for the court to interfere with its own discretion as to how it should conduct its business. Thus Smyth J. concluded that:

> "Sports organisations do best to resolve differences under their own governing codes rather than resort to courts of law. Issues of natural justice are important but the substance of matters rather than their form are important in seeking to resolve internal disputes in such organisation and recourse to the courts should be a last resort and that only in the rarest of cases".

This is a statement that will be welcomed with open arms by sports governing bodies, for of course it is absolutely correct. Sports organisations *do* undoubtedly benefit from resolving their disputes internally (and almost universally the rules of governing bodies both domestic and international are drafted with the intention of keeping the law and the courts away from sport). The problem, however, is that members of sports organisations with whom they are in conflict will inevitably do badly if their dispute with the organisation is to be decided exclusively in accordance with rules created by the organisation and decided by a body that essentially represents the organisation. Legally such a situation becomes problematic where issues of natural justice arise, and in such circumstances and in defence of the applicant's constitutional rights, it is appropriate for the courts to intervene, and arguably with greater alacrity than is the case at Irish law following the decision in *Gould v McSweeney*

In December 2007, the long-running dispute between the Thomas Davis GAA club and South Dublin County Council concerning the types of sport that could be played at the proposed new 6,000-seat stadium (which had been the beneficiary of significant government funding) at Whitestown Way in Tallaght was brought to a conclusion with the decision of the High Court in *Cumann Tomás Daibhís v South Dublin County Council* [2007] I.E.H.C. 426 (December 14, 2007). This decision is more a matter of planning law than sports law, but because of the subject-matter of the case it merits some brief consideration in this chapter.

The background to the case is as follows. In 2005, the defendant council had proposed that the stadium in question (which would be home to the Shamrock Rovers Football Club) would be used only for soccer. Following a public consultation process and a recommendation by the Tallaght Area Committee in 2005, however, the members of the council unanimously adopted a resolution in favour of permitting the stadium to be used for a multiplicity of sports which would involve developing a larger-sized pitch suitable for Gaelic games. Following communication with the then Minister for Arts, Sport and Tourism, Mr John O'Donoghue, in which he said that government funding for the stadium would only proceed if the stadium was to be a "soccer only" one, the council passed a subsequent resolution (in February 2006) reverting to its earlier proposal for a soccer stadium.

The applicants sought a judicial review of this decision (having obtained leave to bring such a claim in April 2007), alleging that under the terms of s.179(4) of the Planning and Development Act 2000, the Council did not have legal authority to override the decision taken by the members of the council in December 2005 to vary or modify the development for which planning permission had originally been sought, which decision had been made following consideration of submissions and observations made by the public and consideration of the proper planning and sustainable development of the area. Moreover, it was further claimed that the resolution of February 2006 was invalid, being outside the six-month time limit provided by the legislation for a resolution to be passed authorising a development otherwise than in the terms of the report of the county manager. On the other hand the notice party (Shamrock Rovers) claimed that there had been substantial compliance with s.179 and that the net effect of the relief sought by the applicant would be to frustrate the development of the stadium in that the Government would only fund it if it was a soccer only one.

In his judgment, Murphy J. found for the defendants and refused the reliefs sought. He concluded that whereas there might have been some defect in form in the manner in which the defendant council conducted its business, equally there was no defect in substance, in that the general requirements of public consultation under the terms of the Act had been fulfilled. Moreover, the court further found that, as a matter of discretion, it was an appropriate step for the council to refuse to commit itself to unbudgeted expenditure, as it would inevitably be doing if it proceeded with the idea for a multi-sport stadium in a situation where the necessary funding was conditional on it being reserved for soccer.

In October 2007, a new body was set up with the aim of attempting to ensure that "sporting disputes" would not end up in the courts but would rather be dealt with through a non-litigious disputes resolution process, "Just Sport Ireland", a creation of its administrating body, the Federation of Irish Sports, details of which are available at *www.justsport.ie*. The FIS was founded in 2002 and now has 62 governing bodies affiliated to it, including the GAA, IRFU and FAI and it is supported by the Irish Sports Council and the Bar Council.

Just Sport Ireland is intended to deal with a wide range of issues that may arise in the course of the relationship between an athlete and a governing body, but two of the most important such issues, namely doping and employment law issues are excluded from its remit. Disputes are to be resolved by way either of mediation or arbitration and it is hoped that the net effect of the body will be to ensure that such disputes are resolved in an inexpensive and expeditious manner.

What remains uncertain is whether there will be any interplay between this body and the disputes resolution authority (DRA) of the GAA. In this light it is worth pointing out that the work of the DRA continues to increase. This is despite some criticism within the GAA to the effect that, whereas the existence of the DRA has ensured that challenges to decisions of regulatory bodies have not ended up in court, nonetheless there is a perception that it is merely one more rung on the ladder as far as the internal appeal system of the organisation is concerned. Indeed it remains a criticism of some of the cases that have come before the DRA (and there were 22 reported decisions of the DRA in 2007, many of which dealt with genuinely high-profile events) that they do not genuinely involve a challenge as to the legality of an impugned decision of the association, but rather represent an attempt to seek yet one more appeal of such decision. It is critical if the DRA is to continue to grow in importance that this distinction be preserved, possibly by providing and relying on a procedure whereby cases can be stuck out on a preliminary basis for not disclosing a cause of action on their face.

CRIMINAL LAW

Whereas there were no recorded convictions for "on-field violence" in 2007, there were two significant cases in which acquittals of persons accused of "on-field violence" were recorded. In *DPP v Mullins* (Dublin Circuit Criminal Court, January 19, 2007) the defendant was accused of assaulting an opposing team member during an intermediate football league game. In 2005, a jury had failed to reach a verdict in an earlier trial of the matter, but in January 2007, in a second trial before Dublin Circuit Criminal Court, he was eventually acquitted. Perhaps significantly, however, the defendant was denied his costs of the earlier trial in which the jury had failed to reach a verdict.

In *DPP v O'Connor* (Tralee Circuit Criminal Court, November 1, 2007) the defendant was accused of striking an opponent during a challenge GAA football match on Valentia Island, leaving him with a fractured jaw and four dislocated teeth. He accepted that he had punched the victim, but said that it was a pure act of self-defence after he himself had been punched. Perhaps notably, the referee at the game made no statement to the Gardaí but, in any event, the jury took only 12 minutes to return a verdict of not guilty in the case.

In perhaps a slightly less usual situation of prosecution connected with engaging in a sporting activity, in July 2007 an angler lost his appeal against his conviction for illegally fishing, on the basis that he was not a member of a club that was authorised to fish at a particular point in the river Blackwater in Cappoquin. The prosecution was brought by the Cappoquin Salmon and Trout anglers Association (CSTAA) which had sole rights to the fishery in accordance with an agreement with the Duke of Devonshire's company Lismore Estates which had fishing rights over that stretch of water. The defendant, Michael O'Shea, had been fined €50 in Cappoquin District Court on July 5 2003, and had claimed that he had permission to fish on the river from the relevant landowners, but was unable to prove that the landowners in question also owned the relevant fishery. Buttimer J. in the Waterford Circuit Court upheld the conviction but made no order as to costs.

DOPING CASES

The work of the Irish Sports Council anti-doping unit continued in 2007 with some 1,135 tests being carried out on athletes both in Ireland and abroad and across 37 sports. This record number of tests were conducted on an in-competition and out-of-competition basis and there were three positive tests.

In addition, in 2007 the Sports Council finally reached an agreement with Gareth Turnbull (an athlete who had been accused of doping but who demonstrated at his hearing that his positive test for testosterone was the result of natural factors coupled with the consumption of alcohol on the night before the test) as to the discharge of a significant percentage of the costs he incurred in his defence. Mr Turnbull's case is analysed in the *Annual Review of Irish Law 2006*.

Torts

OCCUPIERS' LIABILITY

Duty to trespassers The decision of Peart J. in *Ryan v Golden Vale Co-operative Mart Ltd* [2007] I.E.H.C. 159 may not seem to be hugely important: a trespassing child injured by a gate probably caused to swing in his direction by one of his juvenile colleagues failed in his claim for negligence against the occupier. Yet the manner in which Peart J. analysed the claim is of general interest.

The plaintiff was aged 10 at the time of the accident. He was taking a shortcut through the defendant's premises, with three companions. The gate was made of tubular steel, with two halves, having a combined span of 24 feet. The plaintiff claimed that the gate was open and that one of his companions swung the gate inwards in his direction as he was passing through. The basis of the claim for negligence was that the defendant ought to have known that the gate was an allurement for boys such as the plaintiff and his companions and should have ensured that the gate was locked.

Peart J., with some reluctance, concluded that the facts were as alleged. He stated:

> "The plaintiff must establish that the defendants owed a duty of care to the plaintiff, that there was a breach of that duty towards him, and that as a result of that breach injury was suffered. The ultimate question will be did the duty of care owed to the plaintiff extend to ensuring that the gate was locked. The questions of the extent of the duty of care owed and of the foreseeability of injury to the plaintiff must be considered.
>
> In his judgment in the Supreme Court in *Breslin v Corcoran*, unreported, March 23, 2003, Mr Justice Fennelly states as follows, having first considered the well-known English authorities in the area of foreseeability of damage arising from an intervening event in *Dorset Yacht Co Ltd v Home Office* [1970] A.C. 104 and *Smith v Littlewoods Organisation Ltd* [1987] A.C. 241:
>
> > 'From all these cases I draw the following conclusion. A person is not normally liable if he has committed an act of carelessness, where the damage has been directly caused by the intervening independent act of another person, for whom he is not otherwise vicariously liable. Such liability may exist, where the damage

> caused by that other person was the very kind of thing which he was bound to expect and guard against and the resulting damage was likely to happen, if he did not.'

I should follow the same reasoning in the present case in relation to the foreseeability of injury to this plaintiff.

I am satisfied that the plaintiff is within the category of person to whom a duty of care was owed, albeit that he was on the defendant's premises without permission. He was a trespasser. In those circumstances, the defendants are under a duty to ensure that while on the premises he was not exposed to a danger, which it could be reasonably foreseen might cause him an injury. If for example there was something on the defendant's premises, which was inherently dangerous, and it was reasonably foreseeable that a child might be allured to it, then if injury results to such a child the defendants could be held liable. In such circumstances it would be incumbent on the defendants to ensure that access to their premises or at least to the dangerous object upon it was not possible.

In the present case this injury to the plaintiff did not result from contact with an object, which was a trap in the usual sense. It is not a case where, for example, a dangerous and unprotected slurry pit was present and into which the plaintiff fell. It is not a case in which the plaintiff climbs up onto some inherently dangerous structure or piece of machinery, and which the defendants ought to have prevented by suitable protection of same.

In this case there was a gate, which provides access into and out of the defendant's premises. In my view there is nothing intrinsically alluring about such a gate. There is no evidence that it was in any way defective and that such a defect caused injury to the plaintiff. It did not for example fall upon him causing him this injury. It was simply a gate. I cannot regard that gate as an allurement to the plaintiff in the sense that it obliged the defendant to ensure that it was fastened with a lock at all times. As I have said, I am assuming for the purpose of this case that it was unlocked, and I am giving the plaintiff the benefit of the doubt, which I have about that fact.

To find that it was foreseeable that a child would be injured in circumstances where another child or children either opened this unlocked gate or found it open and then proceeded to swing it back in the direction of the plaintiff would be to cast an unfair and unreasonable burden of foreseeability on the defendants and would mean that it was a requirement that at all times all gates into premises throughout the country would have to be locked at all times to ensure that no child could open it, in order to ensure that nobody was injured by this sort of action by another child.

In my view it would be unfair and unreasonable for a duty of care to

be extended so wide. It was not reasonably foreseeable by the defendants
that this gate, even if left closed but unlocked or even left slightly ajar,
was a trap or potential danger to someone such as the plaintiff, or an
allurement as alleged. It was an inherently safe gate without defect,
and was there to enable access and egress to and from the premises in
the normal way.

The injury, which the plaintiff sustained, was serious and has left
him with a permanent physical deficit. But the plaintiff must realise that
simply because he receives an injury in this way does not mean that
the defendants are to be blamed for it. In my view even if the gate was
unlocked it did not present any inherent danger to the plaintiff, which the
defendant was under a duty to prevent. Things may have been different
if, while on the premises having entered through an unlocked gate, he
had been injured by something inherently dangerous and a trap for the
plaintiff, but that is not the case here."

The language of "allurements" and "traps" reminds us strongly of the pre-1995
Act position. The concept of an "allurement" had a long tradition, converting
many a trespassing child into an implied licensee. The concept of a "trap"
was associated with the duty owed by the occupier to the licensee to warn of
hidden dangers of which the occupier was aware or to avoid setting a trap for
the licensee.

One might be forgiven for having assumed that the 1995 Act swept all of
this terminology into history. It is a little curious that no mention is made in
the judgment of the 1995 Act and that Peart J. appears to proceed on the basis
that a claim for common law negligence taken by a trespasser in respect of
a danger due to the state of the premises is capable in principle of yielding
a verdict in favour of the trespasser. Nonetheless, the judgment forces us to
examine how the 1995 Act should deal with factual circumstances which under
the former law would have constituted an "allurement". When one scrutinises
the definition of "visitor" in s.1(1), one finds that it extends to an entrant, other
than a recreational user, who is present on the premises "at the invitation, or
with the permission, of the occupier..." Neither invitation nor permission need
be express. (It is worth noting that the legislation is sensitive to the distinction
between express and non-express invitations: see the definition in s.1(1) of
"recreational use".) If we take as an example some situation which in former
law would undoubtedly have been characterised as an "allurement", in attracting
young people onto the property without the express invitation or permission of
the occupier, could it be argued that it should be considered to involve implied
invitation or permission for the purposes of s.1(1) and that the allured child is
thus a "visitor" to whom the common duty of care is owed?

If the answer to this question is in the affirmative, this will no doubt come
as a surprise to many people. Yet this conclusion surely follows unless one is

to exclude, a priori, the concept of implied invitation or permission. Manifestly, implied permission is envisaged by the Act, otherwise a range of entirely innocent and legitimate entrants would have to be characterised as trespassers. The neighbouring child who, without express permission from the occupier, retrieves his football from a garden unbounded by any hedge or wall is clearly not a trespasser. What about a child who is attracted onto premises where an abandoned ice-cream van is playing music?

Brief mention may be made of the ex tempore Supreme Court decision in *Raleigh v Iarnród Éireann* on November 30, 2006, *Irish Times*, December 1, 2006, because the High Court judgment, of O'Donovan J., on December 19, 2003, was so clearly unacceptable. A heavily intoxicated young man who was struck by a train after he had fallen asleep on the railway line succeeded at trial because the defendant was regarded as negligent in failing to take appropriate steps to prevent youths from congregating on the railway line at this point. His damages were reduced by 85 per cent to take account of his contributory negligence. The Supreme Court reversed this. Murray C.J. is reported as having observed that the plaintiff had been the "author of his own misfortune". Iarnród Éireann could not have been expected to foresee such acts of "folly" or "stupidity" by adults who came onto the property. Iarnród Éireann had not been under an obligation to erect a palisade fence at the point where the plaintiff and others entered onto the embankment. For insightful analysis of *Raleigh,* see Ray and Des Ryan, "Claims by Trespassers and Recreational Users under the Occupiers' Liability Act 1995: Recent Developments" 2 *Quarterly Review of Tort Law* No 1, 15–16. ·

Pavement injury In *McCluskey v Dublin City Council* [2007] I.E.H.C. 4, the plaintiff fell on a pavement in a Dublin suburb at a place where there had been an irregular subsidence below the level of the adjoining pavement. He sued Dublin City Council and four other institutional defendants who, he alleged, had been involved at some relevant time in excavating the pavement. The evidential challenge for de Valera J. was to determine which of the defendants was, or were responsible.

De Valera had no hesitation in dismissing the claim against Dublin City Council. At most, its involvement could only constitute nonfeasance. The evidence reduced itself to a contest between An Bord Gáis and NTL (and its predecessors). The balance of probabilities tilted barely towards imposing liability on NTL as the last entity to work on the excavation. The reinstatement work had clearly been carried out in an inadequate way.

The accident happened around 9.30 p.m. in the middle of July. De Valera J. reduced the award by 30 per cent to take account of the plaintiff's contributory negligence, stating:

"The plaintiff knew the area well; at the time of his fall it was still

> bright…and he cannot have been keeping a sufficiently careful lookout.
> It is inevitable from the condition of the path at the time of his fall that
> the surface had been defective for come considerable time."

The suggestion here is that the plaintiff, on the basis of his extensive knowledge
of the footpath, should have that dimension factored into the assessment of
the questions of contributory negligence and its quantum. The idea that a
differential standard should be applied, based on prior knowledge or experience
of the damages, raises theoretical questions as to whether this offends against
the objectivity of the standard of care when determining negligence and
contributory negligence.

NEGLIGENTLY INDUCED PSYCHIATRIC INJURY

A and W v C and D [2007] I.E.H.C. 120 involved the imposition of liability
for negligently induced psychiatric injury in somewhat unusual circumstances.
Since 1983 A, the son of a wealthy testator, and W, the son's wife, had been
living on a farm owned by the testator. They had a child born in 1998. The son
had been working on the farm for his father for many years, even pre-dating the
marriage. The father died in 1998. His will had the effect of ending his son's
entitlement to stay on the farm. On April 9, 2000, A, who was still residing at
the farm, constructed a wall in the yard, to which C and D, A's brothers who
were personal representatives of their father's will, took exception on the basis
that they had not given their prior consent and that it restricted access to certain
premises. This was conveyed to A and W in a letter from C and D's solicitor,
which called on them to remove the wall and threatened legal proceedings if
they did not. After further correspondence between the parties' solicitors, in
which A and W asserted that there had been prior consultation, on May 10,
2000, at 6 a.m., a loading shovel, driven by B (another brother) was used to
demolish the wall. A had already got up and was already at work. W was still
in bed. When she heard and saw what was happening she became hysterical.
She attempted unsuccessfully to stop the demolition with a jeep. She had in the
past suffered psychiatric problems and had twicd received treatment in mental
hospitals. She expressed concern that the demolition of her wall exposed her
son to danger from the open slurry pits and working machinery.

The defendants admitted to cutting off the electricity supply while the wall
was demolished. Laffoy J. said that she had:

> "… absolutely no doubt … that the defendants acted in a highly
> irresponsible and an extremely provocative manner in demolishing
> the wall. The reason giving by C for not awaiting the outcome of the

correspondence between the solicitors was that he and his co-executor were frustrated at the pace at which the matter was moving. When he was asked in cross-examination whether he considered the risk of a serious incident if A was at home, his response was that he kind of expected that, but added that the wall was demolished in less than two minutes. C likened A to a child who is told he cannot have a sweet or a bully in the school yard when one tries to stand up to him. He said he, C, felt no responsibility for what happened and he had no regrets in relation to the manner in which the wall was removed. The quickest and least stressful method had been used from his perspective."

Laffoy J. held that the defendants were not liable for trespass or under the rule in W*ilkinson v Downton* [1897] 2 Q.B. 57. The former claim failed because of Laffoy J.'s conclusion that A had not established title by adverse possession to the farm. The latter claim could not get off the ground because it had not been pleaded. The claim of negligence, however, succeeded. Laffoy J., inspired by a passage from Geoghegan J.'s judgment in *Fletcher v Commissioners of Public Works* [2003] I.R. 465 at 491, was of the view that the instant case did:

"… not warrant the type of analysis which courts have had to embark on in the so-called 'nervous shock' cases, such as *Kelly v. Hennessy* [1995] 3 IR 253, or the so-called 'fear of disease' cases, such as *Fletcher v. The Commissioners of Public Works*. It seems to me that this case is more akin to the ordinary motor accident or workplace injury case than to the nervous shock case. If an adjoining landowner, at 6 a.m., demolishes a contentious wall at the back of a house in which a family reside, which is within earshot and sight of the house, a person in the house whom it may reasonably be foreseen may be traumatised by the manner in which the demolition is carried out must come within the 'neighbour' principle."

Laffoy J. considered that, if she was wrong in that conclusion, then the criteria set out by Hamilton C.J. in *Kelly v Hennessy* for recovery of damages for nervous shock were applicable.

She had suffered "nervous shock" in that she had suffered a recognisable psychiatric illness caused as a result of the defendant's act. It had been sustained by reason of an apprehended physical injury to a person other than herself—her infant son. The defendants had owed her a duty of care not to cause her a reasonably foreseeable injury in the form of nervous shock. The defendants had been apprised in the correspondence of the concerns that A and W had in relation to their 18-month-old son.

Laffoy J. was satisfied that the evidence established a requirement that a plaintiff apprehend physical injury to self or another:

"While it would appear that [W.] did not apprehend any physical injury to herself on the occasion, it is absolutely clear that the whole focus of her distress, stress and anxiety related to her perception that, because of the demolition of the wall, [her son] was in imminent danger of serious physical injury. [One psychiatrist] in his report expressed the opinion that it is reasonable to suggest that she was very concerned about [her son]'s safety and became obsessed about that aspect. [Another psychiatrist] …. said she was 'obsessed' about the wall and that its demolition had a devastating effect on her mental health. When he first saw her after the demolition of the wall, which was on 11th November, 2000, she was very distressed and referred constantly to the demolition of the wall and her fears in relation to [her son]."

Laffoy J. had no doubt that the defendants had owed a duty of care to W and that injury in the form of nervous shock to her was reasonably foreseeable. Because of the similarity to a motor accident or a workplace injury case, any deeper analysis could be dispensed with, in Laffoy J.'s view. However, viewing the factual circumstances objectively, she considered that a reasonable person would have foreseen that the actions which the defendants intended to embark on were likely to have serious psychological consequences for W.

Accordingly, Laffoy J. was satisfied that the defendants were liable in damages for the psychiatric injury which their actions in demolishing the wall caused W. W had a history of psychiatric illness which extended back to 1983, when she had been admitted to a psychiatric hospital for two weeks, suffering from stress and depression. She was admitted again for six weeks in April 1999, with the same condition, six months after the birth of her son. After the demolition of the wall in May 2000, W had eight periods of hospitalisation in psychiatric institutions, from November 2000 to February 2004. One psychiatrist testified that, in his opinion, the constant distress she had suffered in relation to the wall's demolition and the fact that her son might fall into a drain or slurry pit had exacerbated and prolonged her clinical state. Another psychiatrist gave evidence that, when he had examined W in June 1996, there was no evidence of depression. She had maintained that she had remained well largely because her son was now seven-and-a-half years of age and that many of the fears she had originally had receded by then. Laffoy J. awarded general damages of €40,000 for pain and suffering to the time of trial and a further €10,000 for future pain and suffering.

The decision merits a few observations. First, the act of demolishing the wall, not in itself a violation of the property rights of A or W, became tortious because it caused foreseeable serious distress and (it seems from the judgment) foreseeable psychiatric injury to an "egg shell skull" plaintiff. As a general principle, a defendant is liable to an "egg shell skull" plaintiff only where the conduct, independently of the plaintiff's particular vulnerability, constitutes negligence. It seems that Laffoy J. regarded the demolition at 6 a.m. as foreseeably capable of causing traumatisation, even to a person of ordinary fortitude. Whether such an outcome would constitute actionable negligence is perhaps debatable: trauma falls well short of the foreseeable psychiatric injury required by the Supreme Court in *Kelly v Hennessy*.

Secondly, Laffoy J. evinced obvious enthusiasm for Geoghegan J.'s view, in *Fletcher*, that questions of foreseeability and duty of care merged in an "ordinary motor accident or factories injury" claim. If this robust approach were to be applied in the context of psychiatric injury, it might simplify the judicial task in cases such as *Page v Smith* [1996] A.C. 155, where the plaintiff, in a minor traffic accident, did not suffer foreseeable physical injury but did suffer an unforeseeable psychiatric injury.

Devlin v National Maternity Hospital [2007] I.E.S.C. 50 is an important, and disappointing, decision on the limits of liability for negligently caused psychiatric injury. It involved a three-member Bench of the Supreme Court— Murray C.J., Denham and Finnegan JJ. It is to be hoped that, when the matter is revisited by a full Bench, a more extensive analysis will be given to this crucially important issue.

The facts of the case were sad. The plaintiff had given birth to a stillborn infant in 1988. Without her knowledge, the hospital had performed a post-mortem and retained the deceased infant's organs. When she learned of the position many years later, the plaintiff suffered a post-traumatic stress disorder. The trial judge dismissed the plaintiff's claim for negligence (and other claims). The Supreme Court dismissed the appeal on the claim for negligence.

Denham J. delivered a judgment with which Murray C.J. and Finnegan J. concurred. She reasoned as follows. Post-traumatic stress disorder is a psychiatric illness. The Supreme Court decision in *Kelly v Hennessy* [1995] 3 I.R. 253 had set out five conditions for the recovery of damages for nervous shock, the fourth of which was that the shock be sustained "by reason of actual or apprehended physical injury to the plaintiff or a person other than the plaintiff". Keane C.J. in *Fletcher v Commissioners of Public Works* [2003] 2 I.L.R.M. 94 had endorsed the conditions set out in *Kelly v Hennessy*. In the instant case, the fourth condition had not been fulfilled. Therefore the claim had rightly been rejected. To extend the current law "could have serious repercussions". Any development to embrace circumstances such as arose in the instant case "would give rise to uncertainty in the law of liability generally and to potentially unforeseeable repercussions".

It is unfortunate that the bold and insightful approach to liability for negligently induced psychiatric injury which characterised the Irish courts over a century ago should today find no echo. Whereas Denham J. had displayed a willingness in the High Court decision of *Mullally v Bus Eireann* [1992] I.L.R.M. 722 to take a broad and generous approach to the subject, a shallow and derivative formalism descended on the Supreme Court in *Kelly v Hennessy* in which the harshest phrases from House of Lords' judgments were parroted with no supporting principled analysis. In *Devlin v National Maternity Hospital*, there is only the most basic attempt to address policy issues and no attempt at all to consider issues of principle.

Why should cases involving negligently induced foreseeable psychiatric injury be problematic? In *Fletcher v Commissioners of Public Works*, Keane C.J. made an attempt to identify the policy factors. The first was that the law did not permit the recovery of damages for mental anguish or grief resulting from bereavement or injury to a member of one's family caused by another's wrong. The second was that it was "an inescapable fact that, because psychiatric illness is frequently less susceptible to precise diagnosis, the courts may have to adopt a more circumspect approach to such cases." The third was that:

> "[t]he phenomenon, familiar to all judges and practitioners who have been concerned in personal injury cases, that the prospect of compensation at a subtle and subconscious level does nothing to assist a plaintiff's recovery from physical injury and may positively impede it, can arise even more acutely in cases of alleged psychiatric illness.'

Finally, the abolition or relaxation of the special rules governing the recovery of damages for psychiatric harm "would greatly increase the class of person who can recover damages in tort and may result in a burden of liability on defendants disproportionate to the wrongful conduct involved." An example would be traffic accidents, which might involve a momentary lapse of concentration.

It must be acknowledged that these policy objections are less than fully convincing. One can see why courts might hesitate about compensating grief resulting from bereavement or from another's injury but where this grief generates a foreseeable psychiatric injury the basis for hesitation is displaced. As to the lack of susceptibility of psychiatric injury to precise diagnosis, this has echoes of the scepticism of British courts in the 19th century—notably the Privy Council in *Victorian Railway Commissioners v Coultas* 13 App. Cas. 222 (1888) —about the objective basis for psychiatric injury. The idea that denying those who have suffered a foreseeable psychiatric injury will assist their recovery is debatable. The final policy concern, about potentially disproportionate liability, has some merit and best explains the judicial contortions in Britain about primary and secondary victims—which classification, incidentally, it is notable that Irish judges have, with rare exception, shown a healthy reluctance to adopt.

PROFESSIONAL NEGLIGENCE

Failed tubal ligation   In *Byrne v Ryan* [2007] I.E.H.C. 207, Kelly J. awarded compensation to the plaintiff where she gave birth to two children after a failed tubal ligation. Rather than clip one of the plaintiff's fallopian tubes, the surgeon had in fact attached the clip to tissue beside it. Applying the *Dunne* test, Kelly J. held that this constituted negligence.

The plaintiff had signed a consent form in which she had consented to undergo the procedure and acknowledged that there was a possibility that she might "not become or remain sterile". The defendant contended that, in executing this document, the plaintiff had consented to the risk of a failed sterilisation. Kelly J. did not accept this argument:

> "First, the document in its terms is a consent to the operation being carried out and the administration of an anaesthetic. It is not a consent to the carrying out of a failure; still less is it a consent to the carrying out of the operation in a negligent fashion. It merely records the plaintiff's understanding that there is a possibility of failure. It might be possible to draft a form of consent which would exclude liability on the part of a doctor for negligent treatment but there is no attempt to do so here. In my view the consent executed by the plaintiff cannot be regarded as one which exonerates Dr. Murray in respect of his failure to effectively clip both fallopian tubes."

At no stage during her pregnancy or after delivery was the plaintiff clearly informed by any doctor, nurse or other hospital personnel that her tubal ligation had failed. An expert witness described the position as follows:

> "This is a case of the 'emperor's clothes' here. Everybody was not facing up to the obvious that this woman had had a failed tubal ligation and that plan B should come into play and that her tubes should be checked or she should be offered sterilisation again. Everybody was hedging around the main issue that there had been a problem".

Kelly J. concluded that this also constituted a breach of the defendant's duty of care to the plaintiff. Since she had not been properly advised of the position, she was exposed to the risk of becoming pregnant again, an event which transpired.

Kelly J. went on to award €90,000 damages to the plaintiff for having to undergo a second tubal litigation and (as conceded by the defendant) for the pain, suffering and inconvenience of pregnancy and childbirth. He dismissed, however, the plaintiff's claim for damages of €381,678 for the upbringing of the two children. This latter issue raises vast questions of a philosophical, normative and policy character. Courts around the world have tended to resist making awards in these circumstances but the position is far from unanimous. The House of Lords and the High Court of Australia are in disagreement and each court is itself divided on the issue: see *McFarlane v Tayside Health Board* [2000] 2 A.C. 59; *Rees v Darlington Memorial Hospital NHS Trust* [2004] 1 A.C. 309; *Cattanach v Melchior* 215 C.L.R. 1 (2003). It is hard to disagree with the observation of Evelyn Ellis and Brenda McGivern, "The Wrongfulness or Rightfulness of Actions for Wrongful Life" (2007) 15 Tort L. Rev 135 at 143 that the recent tranche of cases in the Court of Appeal and House of Lords "leaves English law in a state of considerable disarray".

In *Byrne v Ryan*, Kelly J., invoking the *Glencar test* for determining whether a duty of care should be imposed, concluded that "it would not be fair or reasonable to visit a doctor who negligently performs a sterilisation procedure with the cost of rearing a healthy child that is conceived and born subsequently to the failure of such procedure." A decision in favour of the claim "would open the door to a limitless range of claims related to every aspect of family life." He went on to say that he obtained:

> "... some comfort that, in arriving at this decision, the court is in harmony with the majority of decisions in the common law world. The vast majority of state courts in the United States, the courts of England and Wales, Scotland and a number of civil law courts are of like mind.
> I am also of opinion that the conclusion which I have arrived at blends more harmoniously with the constitutional order which obtains in this jurisdiction than would a decision to the contrary. The value which the Constitution places upon the family, the dignity and protection which it affords to human life are matters which are, in my view, better served by a decision to deny rather than allow damages of the type claimed."

Whether the international position is as clear as Kelly J. suggests may perhaps be debated. There are, however, constitutional considerations, as Kelly J. noted, which distinguish Irish law from the legal dispensation in other common law jurisdictions.

Negligent health care   In *Myles v McQuillan* [2007] I.E.H.C. 333, the plaintiff, who had ulcerative colitis, suffered a perforation of the colon with serious sequelae. She had been seeking medical treatment at a hospital which had been less than satisfactory. A consultant charged with her care had been guilty of "a serious failure in communication and consultations with her" and the hospital itself had repeatedly failed in a similar obligation to her. She had been placed on a drug which was inappropriate to her condition as it was linked to ulceration of the colon. After treatment in the hospital, she was released without her family being advised to bring her back if her symptoms deteriorated. When this occurred and her mother had telephoned the hospital late at night the hospital had not advised that she should be admitted immediately or taken to a general practitioner for immediate treatment but instead told her that she should be given two Paracetamol tablets and taken to a general practitioner the following morning. This latter failure constituted "clear and serious negligence by the hospital", in Quirke J.'s view.

Quirke J. was satisfied that the defendant's negligence had caused the perforation. He apportioned fault by ascribing 35 per cent to the consultant and 65 per cent to the hospital.

Informed consent   The decision of the Supreme Court in *Fitzpatrick v White* [2007] I.E.S.C. 51 has contributed greatly to the clarification of the law on informed consent, which had been in an uncertain state. In *Walsh v Family Planning Services Ltd* [1992] 1 I.R. 505 the Supreme Court was divided as to the test for disclosure. Finlay C.J. and McCarthy J. appeared to favour a requirement that protected the doctor who had complied with a customary practice of disclosure save in cases where disclosure was obviously necessary. This, in essence, is the extension to disclosure of the test in relation to treatment set out in *Dunne v National Maternity Hospital* [1989] I.R. 91. O'Flaherty J. rejected the application of the *Dunne* test in the context of disclosure and Hederman J. concurred with him. O'Flaherty J. preferred a test, expressed in terms of "the established principles of negligence", requiring disclosure of material risks.

In *Walsh*, the plaintiff had undergone a vasectomy, carried out with due care, which resulted in very serious consequences, including impotence and severe pain. The risk of these consequences, inherent in the treatment, was very small indeed. The majority of the Supreme Court held that the warning that had been given was adequate in the circumstances.

Reading *Walsh* from a distance of more than 15 years, one can discern a judicial tension on the issue of disclosure of risk. McCarthy J. considered that, "in a case such as the present", the two tests, of customary practices of disclosure subject to override in cases where disclosure was obviously necessary and of disclosure of all material risks incident to the proposed treatment, respectively, were "essentially the same". McCarthy J. went on to observe:

> "In determining whether or not to have an operation in which sexual capacity is concerned, it seem to me that to supply the patient with the material facts is so obviously necessary to all informed choice on the part of the patient that no reasonably prudent medical doctor would fail to make it. What then is material? Apart from the success ratio of the operation, what could be more material than sexual capacity after the operation and its immediate sequelae. Whatever about temporary or protracted pain or discomfort, the only information given to the plaintiff and his wife on the scope of sexual capacity, upon which they placed so much emphasis, was that contained in the brief paragraph headed 'Does it affect your sex life? No.' This is not a question of merely determining that a particular outcome is so rare as not to warrant such disclosure

that might upset a patient but, rather, that those concerned, and this includes the authors of the information sheet, if they knew of such a risk, however remote, had a duty to inform those so critically concerned with that risk. Remote percentages of risk lose their significance to those unfortunate enough to be 100% involved. In my view it is inescapable that the defendants, possessed as they were of this knowledge, were in breach of their duty to the plaintiff, and to his wife, for failing to identify the risk of impotence, whether it be functional due to pain and discomfort, or mechanical due to some other cause."

O'Flaherty J.'s observations on this theme are also worth recording:

"I have no hesitation in saying that where there is a question of elective surgery which is not essential to health or bodily well-being, if there is a risk—however exceptional or remote—of grave consequences involving severe pain stretching for an appreciable time into the future and involving the possibility of further operative procedures, the exercise of the duty of care owed by the defendants requires that such possible consequences should be explained in the clearest language to the plaintiff."

Since Finlay C.J.'s judgment is generally understood as involving the most restrictive elaboration of the duty of disclosure, it may be useful to record here the language he used when holding that there had been no breach of that duty:

"The ... issue arises ... as to whether, having regard to the evidence as to what occurred to the plaintiff in addition to the ongoing pain... consisting of various surgical interventions, the removal of one testicle and, apparently, a loss of potency as distinct from or in addition to a loss of sexual capacity due to pain were matters which were, on a standard of reasonable care, a possible consequence he should have been warned about. I am satisfied that the evidence did not establish that these consequences were a known complication of a carefully carried out operation of vasectomy, and that the furthest the evidence went was ... the existence of an ongoing indefinite pain, arising from orchialgia, in a very limited number of cases, indeed, expressed in single numbers amongst multiple thousands. For this reason, I conclude that ... the warning ... was sufficient, on the facts, to discharge [the doctor's] responsibility to exercise reasonable care".

What is interesting about these quoted passages is that they set the requirement for disclosure, at all events in respect of elective treatments, at a very high level. Even applying the *Dunne* test, disclosure of "a known complication", however infrequent its incidence, may be necessary. It was the lack of prior knowledge of the particular risk, that eventuated, rather than its unlikelihood, which excused its non-disclosure. As O'Flaherty J. observed, "[t]he catalogue of misfortunes of this plaintiff, it must be said, went beyond anything previously known; his situation appears unique".

In the High Court decision of *Geoghegan v Harris* [2000] 3 I.R. 536, Kearns J. laid great emphasis on the fact that the risk of chronic neuropathic pain, albeit a very low one, had been a known complication of a dental implant operation rendering its disclosure imperative. For analysis of Kearns J.'s judgment, see *The Annual Review of Irish Law 2000*, (pp.434–441). Kearns J.'s approach is of particular interest in favouring the view that elective and non-elective treatment should involve the same obligation of disclosure and in applying ultimately a subjective test for causation, guided, where helpful, by reference to how a reasonable person in the plaintiff's position would have acted.

In *Fitzpatrick v White* [2007] I.E.S.C. 51, a Supreme Court comprising of Kearns, Macken and Finnegan JJ. revisited the issue. The plaintiff, who had a squint in his left eye, underwent surgery which, with no negligence on the part of the surgeon, had an unhappy outcome involving double vision, headaches and a poor cosmetic result. A rare complication involving the loss or slippage of the medial rectus muscle occurred. The risk of this happening had been mentioned by the surgeon before the operation.

At trial the plaintiff alleged that a proper warning of the risk had not been given. White J. held on the evidence that such a warning had in fact been given. On appeal, the concentration of the plaintiff's argument was that the warning, which had been given at a time when he already committed himself to the operation and was within 30 minutes of being taken to theatre, was simply too late to enable him to provide an effective informed consent.

Kearns J.'s judgment in the Supreme Court met with the concurrence of his two colleagues. He sought to draw from the differing approaches in *Walsh* the common conclusion on "two critical questions", namely:

"(a) The requirement on a medical practitioner to give a warning of any material risk which is a 'known complication' of an operative procedure properly carried out

(b) The test of materiality in elective surgery is to enquire only if there is any risk, however exceptional or remote, of grave consequences involving severe pain stretching for an appreciable time into the future."

Kearns J. proceeded to analyse developments in other common law jurisdictions. He interpreted passages from a number of speeches in the House of Lords decision of *Chester v Afshar* [2005] 1 A.C. 134 as supportive of a patient-centred approach requiring disclosure of a significant risk which would affect the judgment of a reasonable patient. (Lord Woolf M.R. had set out this test in *Pearce v United Bristol Healthcare NHS Trust* [1999] 48 B.M.L.R. 118.)

Kearns J. noted that the patient-centred approach had been adopted in virtually every major common law jurisdiction, including Australia (*Rogers v Whitaker* (1992)175 C.L.R. 479; *Rosenberg v Percival* [2001] H.C.A. 18), Canada (*Reibl v Hughes* [1980] 2 S.C.R. 880) and the United States of America *(Canterbury v Spence* (1972) 464 F. 2d 772). In *Rosenburg,* Kirby J. had set out arguments for and against confining the patient-centred rule, which Kearns J. extrapolated in his judgment. In favour of confining the rule, the following arguments were adumbrated:

> "a) That some patients would not wish to be unsettled by unnecessary disclosures by professional experts whom they trust, or about risks or concerns that, in any case, they would only understand imperfectly;
>
> b) That it is impossible, within sensible time constraints, for a professional person to communicate the detail of every tiny complication that may accompany medical procedures;
>
> c) That the efficacy of warnings against slight risks had not been objectively established;
>
> d) That belief in the efficacy of warnings is a lawyer's fancy which other lawyers then seek to circumvent by drafting substantial consent and waiver forms."

The arguments in favour of leaving the patient-centred rule unscathed were as follows:

> "a) The rule recognises individual autonomy which should be viewed in the wider context of an emerging appreciation of basic human rights and human dignity which requires informed agreement to invasive treatment, save for that which might be required in an emergency or otherwise out of necessity;
>
> b) Reality demands a recognition of the fact that, sometimes, defects of communication will justify the imposition of minimum legal obligations so that even medical practitioners who are in a hurry, or who may have comparatively less skill or inclination for communication, are obliged to pause and provide warnings of the kind mandated by *Rogers*;
>
> c) Such obligations redress, to some small degree, the risks of conflicts between interest and duty which a medical practitioner may sometimes face in favouring one healthcare procedure over another;

    e)   The legal obligation to provide warnings may sometimes help to redress the inherent inequality and power between a medical practitioner and a vulnerable patient;

    f)   That provision of detailed warnings will enable the ultimate choice to undertake or refuse an invasive procedure to not only rest, but also be seen to rest, on the patient rather than the healthcare provider thereby reducing the likelihood for recriminations and litigation following the disappointment that sometimes ensues in the aftermath of treatment."

In a crucial passage in his judgment, Kearns J. stated:

> "The analysis undertaken by both Kirby J and the other members of the High Court of Australia in *Rosenberg v Percival* supports the argument that the giving of an adequate warning, far from being a source of nuisance for doctors, should be seen as an opportunity to ensure they are protected from subsequent litigation at the suit of disappointed patients. I am thus fortified to express in rather more vigorous terms than I did in *Geoghegan v. Harris* my view that the patient centred test is preferable, and ultimately more satisfactory from the point of view of both doctor and patient alike, than any 'doctor centred' approach favoured by part of this Court in *Walsh v. Family Planning Services.*"

As regards the content of the warning, Kearns J. did not consider that a Bench composed of three members was free to depart from the views expressed by a court of five members in *Walsh* to the effect that a warning must in every case be given of a risk, however remote, of grave consequences involving severe pain continuing into the future and involving further operative intervention. In respect of cases not involving such a specific risk, however, Kearns J. considered himself entitled to distinguish *Walsh* by offering "a somewhat less extreme view of the scope of the duty" of disclosure. In another crucial passage of his judgment, Kearns J. observed:

> "I would see as more reasonable for those cases the test outlined by Lord Woolf, namely, that if there is a significant risk which would affect the judgment of a reasonable patient, then in the normal course it is the responsibility of a doctor to inform the patient of that significant risk. This is still an onerous test and not dissimilar from the requirement enunciated in *Rogers v Whitaker*, and in this context I would regard the words 'significant risk' and 'material risk' as interchangeable. In *Geoghegan v. Harris* I suggested that any consideration of 'materiality' would involve consideration of both (a) the severity of the consequences and (b) the statistical frequency of the risk. Putting it another way, a

risk may be seen as material if, in the circumstances of the particular case, a reasonable person in the patient's position, if warned of the risk, would be likely to attach significance to it. I am leaving to one side here considerations of those cases where the medical practitioner may be aware that the particular patient, if warned of the risk, would be likely to attach significance to it where another patient might not."

Turning to the question of the late timing of the warning, Kearns J. noted that, although a number of experts had given evidence to the effect that it had certain advantages for day patients, it seemed to him that the disadvantages were far greater:

"... including the possibility of an embittered patient later asserting that he was too stressed or in too much pain to understand what was said or to make a free decision and that he was thus effectively deprived of any choice."

In the instant case, however, the plaintiff had given no evidence of being unduly stressed or anxious on the day of his operation; he had not been in pain and had not been sedated prior to his operation:

"He was facing into what could fairly be described as a minor operation only. His evidence suggested he was in a clear and lucid mental state on the day of the operation and well capable of making a decision. He described how his conversation with Mr. Goggin was both cordial and relaxed. While the plaintiff said he would have 'walked straight out of the hospital' had he been warned on the day, he did not say he could not deal with a warning given at that point in time. In fact he said the opposite. In the absence of clear evidence that the plaintiff was actually disadvantaged in some material way by the lateness of the warning, I would not, on the facts of this case and without more, declare or find the warning given to be invalid because it was given at a late stage. There is nothing in the evidence to suggest the plaintiff could not assimilate or properly understand what he was being told. I would make the point strongly however that in other cases where a warning is given late in the day, particularly where the surgery is elective surgery, the outcome might well be different."

With respect, this analysis appears to address what is really a causation issue rather than that of whether the lateness of the disclosure constituted a breach of duty. In any event, Kearns J. went on to address the causation issue expressly, upholding White J.'s finding. Kearns J. stated:

"For the sake of completeness ... I think I should say that, even had I concluded that the warning given on the day of the operation in this case was void or ineffective, I would not consider the trial judge's finding on causation to have been mistaken. If it were necessary to apply an objective test as to what a reasonable patient would have done if warned days or weeks in advance of his operation in an outpatient setting of the particular risk which later arose in this case, I am satisfied that such a patient, anxious to achieve a cosmetic improvement to his eyes, would, having placed the benefits of the proposed surgery in balance with the statistically remote risk of muscle slippage causing diplopia, have nonetheless opted to proceed with the surgery."

Some observations about the decision in *Fitzpatrick v White* seem appropriate. First, any idea that the *Dunne* test should apply to disclosure of risk is rejected, in spite of the apparent, albeit somewhat ambiguous, support it received in the judgments of Finlay C.J. and McCarthy J. in *Walsh*. Secondly, it is perhaps unfortunate that Kearns J. chose to give special favour to Lord Woolf's test in *Pearse* since there is a potential difference between the concept of a significant risk and a material risk. Kearns J. emphasised that he regarded them as interchangeable but this is not necessarily so. A risk may be significant in the sense that a person would be *likely to attach significance to it* (whether that person is the hypothetical reasonable patient or the particular patient in the case). A risk may also be significant in the statistical sense, dislocated from the context of the patient, his or her circumstances and his or her values. Thus a court might be disposed to hold as significant a risk of a particular percentage. It is interesting that, in *Chester v Afshar*, on which Kearns J. sought to place some reliance, Lord Steyn referred to a surgeon's duty to warn a patient of "a serious risk of injury" and, having quoted from Lord Woolf's judgment in *Pearce* with apparent approval, went on to observe:

"A surgeon owes a legal duty to a patient to warn him or her in general terms of possible serious risks involved in the procedure ..."

Later in his speech, Lord Steyn referred to the surgeon's negligent failure to warn the patient of the "small risk of serious injury". It seems that significance of risk is here being determined by the twin factors of likelihood of occurrence and potential gravity of injury should an untoward event occur. Of course both of these factors are relevant to materiality of risk but they are not identical to it.

It is worth bearing in mind that, in *Chester v Afshar*, the trial judge had applied a test for disclosure that was quite traditional and far removed from a materiality test. The defendant, by common consent, had failed that test. It is therefore perhaps unwise to interpret remarks by Lords Hoffman and Hope as providing any substantive support for the materiality test, though it would scarcely be surprising if the House of Lords does endorse this test when the issue squarely arises.

Auctioneers　*Walsh v Jones Lang Lasalle Ltd* [2007] I.E.H.C. 28 is an important case on the issue of auctioneers' negligence and, more broadly, on negligent misstatement. The plaintiff purchased a property in Upper Gardiner Street in Dublin which had been described in the defendant auctioneer's brochure as having a total floor area of 23,057 square feet when the correct figure was 21,248 square feet. The brochure contained a clause in small print at the bottom of the front page which stated:

> "Whilst every care has been taken in the preparation of these particulars, and they are believed to be correct, they are not warranted and intending purchasers/lessees should satisfy themselves as to the correctness of the information given."

The plaintiff had made no attempt to measure the floor area. He said in evidence that he had never done so when purchasing properties and had depended "on the reputation, credibility and integrity of the person advertising…"

Quirke J. imposed liability. The defendant was a large firm with an excellent reputation for competence, probity and integrity in its business dealings. It relied on its reputation for excellence in order to encourage prospective customers to avail themselves of its services. The brochure was an integral part of a tendering process designed to maximise the price which potential purchasers would pay for the property. It was to be expected that the potential purchasers would rely upon the information contained within the brochure when deciding whether to offer to purchase. Prima facie, therefore, the relationship between the plaintiff and the defendant was sufficiently proximate to give rise to a "special relationship" of the kind identified by the Supreme Court (Geoghegan and Kearns JJ.) in *Wildgust v Bank of Ireland* [2006] I.E.S.C. 19.

Quirke J. accepted evidence that it was not the practice for prospective purchasers of commercial property in Dublin to measure the floor areas of properties before offering to purchase. Whilst he also accepted evidence that prudent purchasers should, where possible, measure floor areas and carry out detailed inspections before purchasing properties, Quirke J. was satisfied on the evidence that, where detailed and precise measurements of commercial properties were provided within the brochures of experienced and reputable auctioneers, it was the practice for prospective purchasers to rely upon the accuracy of those measurements, subject to potential minor miscalculations.

Turning to the language contained in the brochure, Quirke J. observed:

> "It is difficult to accept that 'every care has been taken in the preparation of these particulars' because the floor area, (perhaps the most important particular found within the brochure), was overstated to a degree which was seriously misleading to prospective purchasers. The area of the first

floor, (which had a rental value in the region of IR £20.00 per square foot), was overstated by more than 1800 square feet.

Undeniably the defendant published grossly inaccurate measurements of the floor area of the property within its sales brochure. It knew or ought to have known that the plaintiff and the other prospective purchasers, to whom the brochure was directed, would rely upon and be influenced by measurements of such apparent precision.

The defendant, nonetheless, argued that it is not liable for any absence of care on its part because the 'waiver' provided that the particulars '... are not warranted and intending purchasers/lessees should satisfy themselves as to the correctness of the information given.' I do not accept that this provision is sufficient to relieve the defendant of liability in the circumstances of this case...

If the defendant wished to reserve to itself the right, (a) to publish within its sales brochure, precise measurements which were in fact grossly inaccurate and, (b) to relieve itself of liability to the category of persons to whom the brochure and its contents were directed, then there was an obligation upon the defendant to draw to the attention of the plaintiff and other prospective purchasers the fact that the seemingly precise measurements published were likely to be wholly unreliable and should not be relied upon in any circumstances.

By including within its brochure an enigmatic sentence in small print claiming to have taken particular care in the preparation of all of the particulars within the brochure but advising prospective purchasers to 'satisfy themselves as to the correctness of the information given' the defendant failed to discharge that obligation."

Quirke J. emphasised that the defendant knew, or ought to have known, that the plaintiff, and the other perspective purchasers of a property, would estimate the value of the property with particular reference to the rental income recoverable from the property. The rental income, in turn, was dependent upon a precise measurement of the floor area available for letting. It was that precise measurement which the defendant had purported to provide within its brochure. It was clearly foreseeable by the defendant that an overstatement of the floor area of the property would give rise to an inflated estimate of the rental income recoverable from the property and a corresponding inflation in the estimated value of the property.

Quirke J. stated:

"It follows that loss and damage to the plaintiff in this case was reasonably foreseeable by the defendant. Having found, as I have, that, (a) the relationship between the plaintiff and the defendant was sufficiently proximate to give rise to a 'special relationship' of the kind

> identified in *Wildgust* and, (b) that the loss allegedly sustained by the plaintiff was reasonably foreseeable in the circumstances and, (c) that the imposition upon the defendant of such a duty is, in the circumstances not unfair, unjust or unreasonable, it follows that I am satisfied on the facts of this case that the defendant owed a duty of care to the plaintiff to ensure that the calculation of the floor area of the property in which the defendant published in its sales brochure was accurate."

Quirke J. went on to hold that the plaintiff had not been guilty of contributory negligence in failing to carry out a survey of the premises prior to his entry into the contract before the purchase of the property:

> "No evidence was adduced in these proceedings suggesting that it is, or was, or has been a practice for prospective purchasers to measure the floor areas of properties after entering into the contract for purchase and before the completion of the contract.
>
> Mr. Peter Rowan and Mr. Healy stated that in their opinions that prudent prospective purchasers should measure floor areas and carry out detailed inspections before offering to purchase commercial property in Dublin however, I did not understand any expert witness to suggest that, where, as in this case, a prospective purchaser relied upon the precise measurements contained within the selling agents sales brochure when offering to purchase, it would be desirable for those measurements to be confirmed by way of a detailed inspection and survey between the date when the contract for sale is executed and the date when the purchase is completed.
>
> It might well be that if such an inspection and survey had been carried out on behalf of the plaintiff then the miscalculation would have been discovered. However, no evidence has been adduced in these proceedings to support the contention that such an inspection or survey should have been carried out in order to confirm the precise measurements contained within the brochure.
>
> In the circumstances then I am not satisfied that any contributing negligence on the part of the plaintiff has been established by way of evidence in these proceedings."

It has to be said that the failure to find the plaintiff guilty of any contributory negligence is surprising. Purchasers of property surely have some responsibility for looking after their own interests rather than leaving it all to the vendor's auctioneer, especially where the purported waiver in the brochure, even if ineffective in exempting the defendant from a duty of care or for liability for the representation, at least reminded prospective purchasers of the need for prudence.

BREACH OF STATUTORY DUTY

In *Doherty v South Dublin County Council* [2007] I.E.H.C. 4, Charleton J. rejected the argument that the breach of the Equal Status Acts 2000–2004 could generate an entitlement to compensation outside the scope of the machinery for redress that this legislation specifically prescribed. The applicants for judicial review were elderly Travellers in necessitous circumstances who sought accommodation in a caravan, whereas the Council insisted that the only accommodation it would provide was a house. The applicants argued that the Council was discriminating against them as members of the Traveller Community by failing to respect their nomadic culture.

Charleton J. provided an elaborate analysis of the circumstances in which a remedy for breach of a legislative obligation might be available outside the confines of the framework of compliance established by legislation. In his view, the equal status legislation had not created new legal norms justiciable outside its framework. He drew analogies with the planning legislation and legislation for unfair dismissals. He observed:

> "Many of the rights and obligations created by modern statute were never justiciable until they were created by the passage of legislation… Where … an Act creates an entirely new legal norm and provides for a new mechanism for enforcement under its provisions, its purpose is not to oust to the jurisdiction of the High Court but, instead, to establish new means for the disposal of controversies connected with those legal norms. In such an instance, administrative norms, and not judicial ones are set: the means of disposal is also administrative and not within the judicial sphere unless it is invoked under the legislative scheme. In the case of the Planning Acts, in employment rights matters and, I would hold, under the Equal Status Acts, 2000–2004, these new legal norms and a new means of disposal through tribunal are created. This expressly bypasses the courts in dealing with these matters …
>
> In my judgment it is no function of the High Court, at first instance, to adjudicate on planning matters, to assess income tax, to decide on unfair dismissal or to decide whether there has been unequal treatment."

Charleton J. acknowledged that that there was a category of legislation which created specific rights under statute, breaches of which could be pleaded as tortious liability as breaches of statutory duty. An example of this was the Safety and Industry legislative code. This created conditions whereby workers might be safely employed, breaches of which were criminal offences. A failure to comply with these was not simply a crime triable before the court given jurisdiction in that regard, but also as a breach of the worker's rights which could give rise to damages.

The general test developed in the law of tort had been stated by Lord Diplock in *Lonrho Limited v Shell Petroleum Co Limited* [1982] A.C. 173 where he indicated that the existence of a statutory provision could give rise to a right in damages:

"1. Where the provision is designed for the protection or benefit of a particular class of persons and a member of that class is injured as a result of the breach; or

2. Where the provision creates a public right, but the plaintiff has suffered particular injury over and above the type of harm suffered by the public generally."

Charleton J. observed:

"The ultimate test, however, is a matter of statutory interpretation. The issue is whether the legislature intended that private law rights of action should be conferred upon individuals where breaches of statutory duty are shown to have occurred. Of itself, the fact that a particular provision was intended to protect certain individuals, such as member of the Irish Traveller community, is not sufficient to confer a right of action before a court. Legislation creates obligations. All of the case law concerned with private law rights centres around categories of legislation where the right of enforcement is not specifically stated to be in the context of a civil claim. Often, the breach is triable before a criminal court. In addition, rights of action in private law may be created where the breach of the protection has caused an injury to the persons in respect of whom it was designed to provide protection and where the legislation creates a public right where the plaintiff has suffered a particular injury as a result of the breach. The fundamental rule of statutory interpretation remains, however, that stated by Tenterden C.J. in *Doe d, Bishop of Rochester v. Bridges* [1824–34] All E.R. Rep. 167 at p. 170:

'Where an act creates an obligation, and enforces the performance in a specified manner, we take it to be a general rule that performance cannot be enforced in any other manner.'

The rules as to determining tort liability arise by virtue of an exception to that rule."

Charleton J. noted that, in amending s.21 of the Equal Status Act 2000, s.54 of the Equality Act 2004 substituted for the words "to seek redress under this Act", with "to seek redress by referring the case to the Director". Here, a specific legal obligation had been created for the first time by statute, a mode of enforcement had been set up through an agency which was thereby created and limited rights of access to the courts had been created. In Charleton J.'s judgment, this amounted to the creation of a separate legislative and administrative scheme which did not create a series of private rights which were "either enforceable in damages, or outside the context of that scheme".

Charleton J.'s analysis contains some formidable arguments in favour of the conclusion he reaches. There are, however, some wider questions that may be worth reflecting upon.

The applicants were arguing that they were the victims of discrimination. If a person is the victim of unconstitutional discrimination, then, apart altogether from any remedy that the equality legislation may prescribe, he or she is entitled to compensation in damages (or, in appropriate cases, by way of injunction) under the principle enunciated in *Meskell v Coras Iompair Eireann* [1973] I.R. 121. According to *Hanrahan v Merck Sharp & Dohme (Ireland) Ltd* [1988] I.L.R.M. 629, the system of tort law is presumptively the avenue of compensation for victims of breaches of constitutional rights; only if the particular tort is "basically ineffective" in protecting the constitutional right in question will it be necessary for a court to fashion a remedy based expressly on the Constitution.

Irish courts have not yet been called on to address the question of discrimination under the rubric of a common law tort. In Canada over a quarter of a century ago, the Ontario Court of Appeal recognised such a tort flowing from a breach of the Ontario Human Rights Code—a legislative measure quite similar to the Irish Equality Acts 2000–2004—but the Supreme Court reversed this: *Seneca College v Bhadauria* [1981] 2 S.C.R. 181. Laskin C.J., delivering the judgment of the court, stated:

> "It is one thing to apply a common law duty of care to standards of behaviour under a statute; that is simply to apply the law of negligence in the recognition of so-called statutory torts. It is quite a different thing to create by judicial fiat an obligation—one in no sense analogous to a duty of care in the law of negligence—to confer an economic benefit upon certain persons, with whom the alleged obligor has no connection, and solely on the basis of a breach of a statute which itself provides comprehensively for remedies for its breach."

Laskin C.J. noted that none of the earlier cases related to a refusal to recruit or to employ. They exhibited "a strict *laisser faire* policy, even where the business or service whose facilities were denied on the grounds of colour or race or ancestry was under government licence …" The only cases where the victim of discrimination based on race or colour had been succeeded were those based on innkeepers' liability; innkeepers historically had an obligation to receive travellers irrespective of race, colour or other arbitrary disqualification. Adopting an approach which anticipates that of Charleton J. in *Doherty*, Laskin C.J. invoked the plenitude of the remedial procedures under the Code as a reason for not supplementing them with a remedy in tort:

"[T]he enforcement scheme under The Ontario Human Rights Code ranges from administrative enforcement through complaint and settlement procedures to adjudicative or quasi-adjudicative enforcement by boards of inquiry. The boards are invested with a wide range of remedial authority including the award of compensation (damages in effect), and to full curial enforcement by wide rights of appeal which, potentially, could bring cases under the Code to this Court...

The view taken by the Ontario Court of Appeal is a bold one and may be commended as an attempt to advance the common law. In my opinion, however, this is foreclosed by the legislative initiative which overtook the existing common law in Ontario and established a different regime which does not exclude the courts but rather makes them part of the enforcement machinery under the Code."

In Canada there was no Constitution containing justiciable fundamental rights protection and vindication by way of compensation against infringements by the State or non-state actors. In Ireland, by way of contrast, such a system is well established. Moreover, there is common law authority to the effect that a right should have the means for its enforcement. In *Ashby v White*, 2 Ld. Raym. 939 (1703) Holt C.J., dealing with a denial of a right to vote, said:

"If the plaintiff has a right, he must of necessity have a means to vindicate and maintain it, and a remedy if he is injured in the exercise or enjoyment of it; and indeed it is a vain thing to imagine a right without a remedy; for want of right and want of remedy are reciprocal."

This is close to the language of *Meskell*. One should also recall that, in *Cosgrove v Ireland* [1982] I.L.R.M. 48, McWilliam J. awarded compensation for infringement of a statutory right—of a parent to guardianship of his children—which gave substance to a right grounded in Arts 41 and 42 of the Constitution.

One must acknowledge that the proposition that Art.40.1 translates easily into litigation against non-state actors under the *Meskell* principle is far from self-evident. A debate has taken place as to whether other constitutionally protected rights, such as those of association, privacy and autonomy, restrict the full force of a claim for unconstitutional discrimination. It is also a matter of debate whether the equality legislation constitutes a complete system of legal redress for vindicating a person's rights under Article 40.0. There is no *a priori* reason for holding that only the system can have such a function.

CAUSATION

Hayes v Minister for Finance [2007] I.E.S.C. 8 is in one sense a simple case. The plaintiff, a pillion passenger on a 500 cc motorcycle driven by her boyfriend, Lynch, was injured when Lynch, driving at speed, crashed into another vehicle. Twenty-three miles earlier in the journey, Lynch, travelling at 80 miles per hour, had encountered a speed trap but failed to stop. The Gardaí had given chase, initially at speeds in excess of 100 mph but, for 10 miles before the accident occurred, at no more than 50 mph since the quality of the road had disimproved. The Garda vehicle that was coming behind the motorcycle did not reach the scene of the accident for a minute and a half. The plaintiff had sued the defendant on the basis that the Gardaí had negligently occasioned the accident by a needless pursuit at high speed of a person guilty of only a motoring offence. This claim succeeded before Finlay Geoghegan J. but the Supreme Court reversed that decision.

The asserted belief of the Gardaí who initiated the pursuit that Lynch must have been engaged in more serious criminality since otherwise he would have stopped at the speed trap was accepted as "both objectively reasonable and held bona fide" by Kearns J. (Hardiman and Finnegan JJ. concurring). Both parties accepted that the driver of a police vehicle pursuing another vehicle owed a duty of care to other road users, including the driver of the other vehicle who might be guilty of some sort of criminal behaviour. There was no real dispute that the standard of care might vary. Lord Reed had put it well in the Court of Session decision of *Gilfillan v Barbour* [2004] S.C.L.R. 92:

> "The only question, as it seems to me, is whether it is reasonable for him in the particular circumstances to drive at a given speed, notwithstanding the risk of possibly injuring another road user. The answer to that question must depend on the circumstances, in particular those circumstances relevant to the urgency of the police business on which he is engaged, and those circumstances relevant to the degree of risk which he is taking. For example, in deciding whether it was reasonable for a police driver to drive at a given speed, and to take the concomitant risks as regards other road users, it might be relevant to know whether he was in pursuit of an escaping murderer or in pursuit of a motorist with defective lights; whether he was trying to get an injured man to hospital in time to save his life, or trying to catch a car thief. There will of course be circumstances where the risk to other road users is so high that it would not be reasonable to take that risk, however urgent the police business might be."

One might have thought that the case could have been disposed of by a fairly simple process of analysis: the decision to pursue was reasonable in the circumstances; the speed may for some period have been faster than was reasonable but clearly had come down to a reasonable level long before the accident occurred. Any negligence of which the pursuing Gardaí may in the early stage have been guilty simply had no causal relevance to the accident. Instead Kearns J.'s judgment ranged widely over the troublesome concept of *novus actus interveniens*. He quoted two passages from McMahon and Binchy's *Law of Torts*, 3rd edn (Dublin: Tottel Publishing, 2000), the latter of which concludes that:

> "... the courts are less likely to find that a *novus actus* is the sole cause of the plaintiff's injury nowadays. It is only in very extreme cases that the nature of the third party's act will break the chain completely between the defendant's original conduct and the plaintiff's damage."

Kearns J. observed:

> "In my view this is an extreme case. It is true to say that the motorcyclist asserted a belief that he was still being pursued by the garda vehicle [at a point ten miles before the accident occurred]. Even if that was his initial belief, he must have known that the garda vehicle, which had been caught up behind the articulated truck which presumably he himself had overtaken, was nowhere near him as he came to [close to the place where the accident occurred]. He was not being driven at, intimidated or menaced by the garda vehicle in any way whatsoever. Indeed after a pursuit distance of 28 miles it would be difficult to surmise that Mr Lynch could have been in a 'panicked' condition, if indeed he ever was in the first place. As we know the garda vehicle was behind by perhaps more than a mile at the stage when the accident occurred. Did the garda vehicle in those circumstances cause or make any real contribution to what happened at the bend in the roadway? It seems to me that any sensible application of the principles laid down in *Conole v. Redbank Oyster Company* [1976] I.R. 191 must lead to the conclusion that the effective negligence leading to the accident was that of the motorcyclist."

Kearns J. went on to express the legal position in simpler terms:

> "[I]f there had been some want of care in the present case in continuing to follow the motor bike... I am nonetheless firmly of the view that it was not causative of the plaintiff's injuries, nor did it contribute to them in any material way. Putting it another way, the driving of the garda vehicle may have been a causa *sine qua non* but the *causa causans* of the plaintiff's injuries was Mr Lynch's driving at the bend at [where the accident occurred]".

The following passage from Kearns J.'s judgment is of particular interest:

> "[G]iven that the plaintiff in this case may well have been completely blameless (despite allegations of contributory negligence raised against her), it is worth considering whether policy considerations should encourage this Court to relax the requirements of establishing causation for that reason. In the instant case that would mean that the Court would have to infer that the mere fact of the garda pursuit is of itself and without more to be regarded as having made a material contribution to the plaintiff's injuries. However, I think that would be a hazardous and dangerous course to adopt not least because there are in this case policy considerations of an even more compelling nature which require that the gardaí be permitted to carry out their discretionary powers in upholding the law without undue fear or apprehension of sanctions for so doing. A high premium is placed on road safety in modern Ireland where there is an unacceptable level of road deaths many of which are caused by speeding. To hinder the gardaí in their efforts to prevent such offences by unduly relaxing the requirement to establish causation would offend those "just and reasonable" considerations to which Keane CJ adverted when considering the duty of care in *Glencar Explorations p.l.c. v Mayo County Council (No 2)* [2003] 1 I.R.84."

This passage suggests a willingness to open the Pandora's box of causation rules which do not have to obey the "but for" test. The House of Lords has succumbed to this temptation in *Fairchild v Glenhaven Funeral Services Ltd* [2003] 1 A.C. 32 and *Chester v Afshar* [2005] 1 A.C. 134 but in *Quinn v Mid Western Health Board* [2005] I.E.S.C. 19 Kearns J. held firm. See our discussion in the *Annual Review of Irish Law 2005*, pp.714-718.

RESCUERS

In *O'Neill v Dunnes Stores* [2007] I.E.H.C. 33, the plaintiff went to the assistance of a security officer working alone during the evening in the defendant's store in a shopping centre in Thurles, who was attempting to apprehend one of two young men suspected of stealing bottles from the off-licence. A member of the Garda Siochána arrived on the scene. The second shoplifter, who had gone away briefly, returned brandishing a motorcycle chain which he used to attack the plaintiff on the face.

Normally three security personnel would be on duty at the store, which consisted of a drapery, grocery and off-licence. On the particular evening, neither the security manager nor a part-time security officer was on duty. The protocol was that, if outnumbered, security officer should get help rather than attempt an arrest. The security officer was not carrying his two-way radio at the time of the incident.

Kelly J. imposed liability on the basis that the defendant store had through its negligence induced the rescue attempt by the plaintiff. The plaintiff had responded to a call for help by a member of staff on the directions of the security officer, who was "certainly in need of help". The security officer was dealing with a violent and aggressive person armed with at least one bottle who was attempting to use it on him. That person was engaged in a joint endeavour with the other shoplifter" and although the latter was not present "he was likely to arrive there very quickly and indeed did so." Kelly J. identified three grounds of negligence. The employment of a single security officer to cover the entire of the premises at that time of day was inadequate. The lack of a two-way radio slowed down communications seeking help. The security officer, while conscientiously attempting to do his duty, would have been more sensible to have adopted a different approach. "When confronted with two drunken louts, both with bottles in their jacket pockets, it would have been safer to have contacted the police before endeavouring a citizen's arrest..." The police station was next door and closed circuit television was in operation in the store. Kelly J. was satisfied that his holding would not mean, as defence counsel had indicated, that he was writing a shoplifters' charter by deterring security officers from attempting to detain suspected shoplifters:

> "There would have been little difficulty in bringing the situation under control if the defendant had a sufficient number of security personnel with the appropriate two-way radio equipment in operation on the evening in question. Alternatively the protocol could have been observed, the police called, the suspects observed and arrested afterwards."

NUISANCE

An important issue, yet to be fully explored by our courts, is whether the tort of private nuisance has a role in responding to harassment or molestation. In England, in *Khorasandjian v Bush* [1993] 2 F.L.R. 66, the Court of Appeal held that persistent phone calls could constitute nuisance but in *Hunter v Canary Wharf Ltd* [1997] A.C. 655, which emphasised the characteristics of nuisance as a tort protecting propriety interests, *Khorasandjian* was regarded as a closet introduction of a tort of harassment.

In *Domican v AXA Insurance Ltd* [2007] I.E.H.C. 14, Clarke J. left the question unresolved as the evidence had not, in his view, established that the actions of the defendant insurance company, in insisting on copying the plaintiff all its correspondence with the plaintiff's solicitor in respect of a tort claim, contrary to his express instructions, "could not amount to a private nuisance or to harassment or molestation". Clarke J. noted that "[c]ertainly *Khorasandjian v Bush* suggest[ed the] possibility" that excessive communication by letter, fax, telephone or any other medium might amount to a private nuisance or to harassment sufficient to give rise to a civil wrong. If such a course of action were found to exist it seemed to Clarke J. that it could arise only where the extent of the communication "was such as might interfere, to a material extent, with the reasonable enjoyment by a person of their home, place of business, or life".

RULE IN *RYLANDS V FLETCHER*

In *Udarás na Gaeltachta v Uisce Glan Teoranta* [2007] I.E.H.C. 95, O'Neill J. dismissed a claim made under the rule in *Rylands v Fletcher* where a "ground heave"—the reverse of subsidence—occurred on factory premises which the plaintiff had leased to the defendant. The defendant was engaged in the business of manufacturing aluminum sulfate (alum), which was used for the purification of water. Large quantities of sulphuric acid were used in the process. The plaintiff claimed that the defendant had let sulphuric acid escape into the ground underneath the factory and that this had caused the ground heave. O'Neill J. concluded on the evidence that it was highly unlikely that any significant discharge had occurred, although he did not accept the heave could be explained by water pressure resulting from a very high water table combined with very wet weather and other factors. O'Neill dismissed the claim under the rule in *Rylands v Fletcher* for two reasons. The defendant had not caused or permitted the escape of a dangerous substance and there had been no escape beyond the boundaries of the leased premises. For the same reason, O'Neill J. also dismissed a claim based on nuisance.

RIGHT TO PRIVACY

In *Domican v AXA Insurance Ltd* [2007] I.E.H.C. 14, Clarke J. held that the plaintiff litigant's right to privacy had not been violated where the defendant, who was insurer of a person whom he had sued in a personal injuries action, persisted, contrary to his express instructions, in copying communications between it and the plaintiff's solicitor. Clarke J. considered that the plaintiff's "undoubted" right to privacy had to be understood in the context of the defendant's "undoubted constitutional right to communicate", which had been identified in cases such as *Attorney-General v Paperlink* [1984] I.L.R.M. 373 and *Murphy v Independent Radio and Television Commission* [1999] I.R. 12. The background to the relationship between the parties was that they were "inevitably involved with each other". They were bound by the litigation nexus and were not, therefore, total strangers. It was, in Clarke J.'s view necessary that there be some communication between them "with appropriate respect for both parties' rights". Clarke J. was not satisfied that the plaintiff's right to privacy extended to "the narrow question" of the manner in which communication with him was to be conducted. Clarke J. added: "Indeed most of the decided cases involve obtaining and disclosing information rather than communicating information". Clearly if the manner of such communication were oppressive different considerations might apply. It could, however:

> "... hardly be said that the simple receipt of information by being copied directly with it in circumstances where the person concerned will, necessarily, have to receive the same information indirectly through his solicitors could in any event amount to a breach of the constitutional right to privacy."

In a similar vein it did not seem to Clarke J. that the actions of AXA could be said to be in breach of the right to privacy guaranteed by the European Convention on Human Rights as applied in Ireland by the European Convention on Human Rights Act 2003.

The holding in this case will be regarded by many as commonsense and justified. People should not be permitted to place undue boundaries around themselves when engaging in the commercial and other relationships that characterise daily life. As against this, one should perhaps have some regard for the background to this litigation. The Personal Injuries Assessment Board Act 2003 had, controversially, sought to transform the process of personal injury litigation by forcing plaintiffs, as a precondition of litigation, to undergo a system of scrutiny and putative assessment of the extent and monetary value of their injuries before proceeding further with their claim in court. The justification offered for the legislation was that it would reduce costs by encouraging plaintiffs to settle their claims without going to court. There is, however, a price to be paid for this policy. In making it, in practice, harder for lawyers to be involved, the Act creates the risk that injured people, without the benefit of full professional advice and services, may settle their claims in innocence of the fact that, with that advice and those services, they would have received more compensation. There are less obvious, but no less real, dangers. The more the insurance companies communicate directly with plaintiffs, the greater is the risk that some plaintiffs may be tempted to settle, too soon or for less than the claim is worth. It takes professional skill and experience to interpret letters from insurance companies. A plaintiff might well consider it desirable not to run the risk and to leave matters fully in the hands of the professionals he or she has recruited to do this job. Such a decision to stay out of the loop of communication, therefore, would be prudent rather than quixotic.

Where the desire of a litigant not to be distributed by communication addressed by an insurance company to his or her solicitor has a rational basis and where an insurance company breaches an express instruction to that effect, not only in his or her case but as a "standard practice", there is a reasonable case that courts should extend protection to the right to privacy in such circumstances. An insurance company would be prejudiced not one whit by adhering to the instruction, whereas, in frequently breaching it, an insurance company might in some cases derive an illegitimate strategic advantage over some plaintiffs who understandably lack the experience to interpret communications in the light of professional experience and expertise.

In *Gray v Minister for Justice, Equality and Law Reform* [2007] I.E.H.C. 52, Quirke J. awarded damages to members of a family who had given temporary accommodation to a relative just released from prison having served 12 years for a rape offence where the local newspaper published a graphic story revealing his presence there, which resulted in such hostility to the family that they were obliged to leave their home and return to Dublin. A journalist had obtained information and verification from a member or members of An Garda Síochána. Quirke J., applying the "two-step" test for the duty of care set out in *Ward v McMaster* [1998] I.R. 337 rather than the "three-step" test prescribed in *Glencar Exploration plc v Mayo County Council* [2003] 1 I.R. 84 and, invoking the relevant precedent of *Hanahoe v Hussey* [1998] 2 I.R. 69, held that a duty of care arose in the circumstances:

> "The proximate relationship between the State and those of its citizens who may be affected by the State's procurement of sensitive and confidential information is undeniable. That relationship can give rise to a duty of care owed by the State to persons who may be adversely affected by the disclosure or publication of such information. The negligent disclosure of sensitive and confidential information by Gardaí to journalists or other members of the media will give rise to a cause of action for damages for negligence if the disclosure results in reasonably foreseeable loss, damage or injury to a person affected by the disclosure."

Quirke J. was "acutely conscious" of the dilemma facing members of An Garda Síochána where a dangerous convicted rapist was present in the community. It was reasonable for them to take appropriate steps to ensure that he did not pose a risk to the public and in particular to children. The Garda policy was not to notify neighbouring residents as this, in the words of the Superintendent who gave evidence, might result in "a bigger crime on your hands than what you were trying to prevent". Instead the policy was to monitor the person's behaviour and whereabouts and keep him under surveillance. In the instant case, however, there had been a clear breach of the Garda Síochána (Discipline) Regulations 1989 and this constituted actionable negligence. Quirke J. also held that there had been a violation of the plaintiffs' constitutional right to privacy; the disclosure to the newspaper could not be justified on the basis of a need to vindicate the constitutional rights of others and by the requirements of the common good.

THE RULE IN *WILKINSON V DOWNTON*

In *M O'C v The KLH* [2006] I.E.H.C. 1999, Dunne J. addressed for the first time in an Irish court the proper characterisation of the rule in *Wilkinson v Downton* [1897] 2 Q.B. 57. In that case the plaintiff had suffered a violent shock when the defendant, as a practical joke, told her falsely that her husband had been seriously injured in a traffic accident. The Privy Council, in *Victorian Railway Commissioners v Coultas*, 13 App. Cas. 222 (1888), less than a decade previously, had held that there should be no compensation for negligently induced "nervous shock". In *Wilkinson v Downton*, Wright J., although of the view that the foolish defendant had not intended to cause the injury that the plaintiff had sustained, held that he should nonetheless be liable as he had:

> "... wilfully done an act calculated to cause physical harm to the plaintiff, that is to say, to infringe her legal right to personal safety, and ... in fact thereby caused physical harm to her. That proposition without more appears to me to state a good cause of action, there being no justification alleged for the act. The wilful *injuria* is in law malicious, although no malicious purpose to cause the harm which was caused nor any motive of spite is imputed to the defendant."

In Britain, the decision has not thriven in recent years. In the House of Lords decision in *Wainright v Home Office* [2004] 2 A.C. 406, Lord Hoffman considered that:

> "[t]he policy considerations which limit the heads of recoverable damages in negligence do not apply equally to torts of intention. If someone actually intends to cause harm by a wrongful act and does so, there is ordinarily no reason why he should not have to pay compensation. But I think that if you adopt such a principle, you have to be very careful about what you mean by intend. In *Wilkinson v. Downton,* Wright J. wanted to water down the concept of intention as much as possible. He clearly thought... that the plaintiff should succeed whether the conduct of the defendant was intentional or negligent. But the *Victorian Railway Commissioners* case prevented him from saying so. So he devised a concept of imputed intention which sailed as close to negligence as he felt he could go. If on the other hand one is going to draw a principled distinction which justifies abandoning the rule that damages from mere distress are not recoverable, imputed intention will not do. The defendant must actually have acted in a way which he knew

to be unjustifiable and intended to cause harm or at least acted without caring whether he caused harm or not. ... *Wilkinson v. Downton* ... does not provide a remedy for distress which does not amount to recognised psychiatric injury and so far as there may be a tort of intention under which such damage is recoverable, the necessary intention was not established. I am also in complete agreement with Buxton LJ [2002] QB 1334, 1355 to 1356, paras. 67–72, that *Wilkinson v. Downton* had nothing to do with trespass to the person."

In the instant case, the plaintiff, an employee, sued her employer for a range of claims, including breach of contract and negligence. She claimed that the second named defendant, a co-worker, had sexually assaulted her, and that her employer had failed to take appropriate action in response. She also claimed that her employer had subjected her to ongoing harassment, victimisation, intimidation and isolation. The case was set down for trial by judge and jury. The first defendant sought to have this order set aside on the basis that the case came within the scope of s.1(1) of the Courts Act 1988 and was not saved for jury trial by s.1(3), since the range of claims were beyond what was envisaged by that subsection, which preserves the right for jury trial for:

> "(a) an action where the damage is claimed consist only of damages for false imprisonment or intention of trespass to the person or both,
> (b) an action where the damages claimed consist of damages for false imprisonment or intentional trespass to the person or both and damages (where claimed in addition, or as an alternative,
> to the other damages claimed) for another cause of action in respect of the same act or omission, unless it appears to the court on the application of any party, made not later than seven days after the giving notice of trial or at such later time as the court shall allow, or on its own motion at the trial, that, having regard to the evidence likely to be given at the trial in support of the claim, it is not reasonable to claim damages for false imprisonment or intentional trespass to the person or both as the case may be, in respect of that act or omission ..."

Dunne J. agreed with the first named defendant and set aside the order for jury trial. She distinguished *Sheridan v Kelly and McDonnell*, Supreme Court, April 6, 2006 (noted in the *Annual Review of Irish Law 2006*, pp.481–482) on the basis that in the instant case the claims went far beyond those in *Sheridan*. There were "a number of separate causes of action in respect of separate incidents and an ongoing pattern of behaviour". The argument by counsel for the plaintiff that the matters described as victimisation, isolation and harassment could come within the definition of intentional trespass to the person had no authority to support it and was premised on "the slim foundation" provided by *Wilkinson v Downton*. Dunne J. regarded Lord Hoffman's comments to the effect that *Wilkinson v Downton* had nothing to do with trespass as "a persuasive authority". Dunne J. considered it impossible to reach the conclusion that the matters complained of by the plaintiff as amounting to intimidation, harassment and victimisation could come within a definition of intentional trespass to the person. She was "not of the view that on their own or considered together perhaps under the heading of harassment, they could be considered as a tort as opposed to a heading of damages in negligence or breach of contract" though she acknowledged that it was not necessary to come to a final view on this issue.

The case is of interest, of course, on the issue of entitlement to jury trial but it is also of significance in the respect Dunne J. gave to the evisceration of *Wilkinson v Downton* by Lord Hoffman.

VICARIOUS LIABILITY

Health care providers Kelly J. in *Byrne v Ryan* [2007] I.E.H.C. 2007 came to clearer conclusions on vicarious liability and primary liability than in any previous Irish decision relating to the provision of medical care in an institutional context. The facts of the case are set out above, p.540. For the past half-century, in the shadow of a national health service, British courts have extended the principle of vicarious liability well beyond the traditional control-based test. Up to now, many commentators had assumed that the same rule should apply in Ireland, but express judicial authority was lacking. Kelly J. has provided this authority. He referred to the decisions of *Cassidy v Ministry of Health* [1951] 2 K.B. 343 and *Roe v Minister of Health* [1954] 2 Q.B. 66 and observed:

> "The views of the members of the Court of Appeal in these two cases, expressed as they were over 50 years ago, appear to be correct to this day and of application in the instant case.
>
> The plaintiff was referred not to a particular surgeon but to the Coombe Hospital. She had no say in the choice of who would carry out her sterilisation. It was done by Dr. Murray. He was part of the 'organisation' or permanent staff of the hospital. The performance of the operation was part of a service provided by the hospital to the plaintiff. Dr. Murray was the person in the hospital's organisation via whom that service was provided.
>
> In these circumstances it matters not whether Dr. Murray was employed under a contract of service or a contract for services. In my view having regard to the principles enunciated in both *Cassidy* and *Roe's* case the hospital here is liable for any want of care on the part of Dr. Murray."

Kelly J. was in fact willing to go further and accept the idea that a hospital may have a *primary*, as well as vicarious, liability towards its patients. He relied on a passage from the 19th edition of *Clerk & Lindsell on Torts*, which included a quotation from Browne Wilkinson V.C.'s judgment in *Wilsher v Essex Area Health Authority* [1987] 1 Q.B. 730 to the effect that:

> "[a] health authority which so conducts its hospital that it fails to provide doctors of sufficient skill and experience to give the treatment offered at the hospital may be directly liable in negligence to the patient".

Kelly J. commented:

> "This quotation is cited as being illustrative of cases where a hospital may be found to have been in breach of its own primary duty of care to its patients. It is suggested that on the evidence in the present case no issue arises as to any alleged breach by the hospital of its primary responsibility to its patient and the only possible basis for a finding of liability against it is on the basis of vicarious liability in respect of the performance of the sterilisation. This is not correct. There was in my view a breach of the hospital's primary duty to inform the plaintiff of the failure of the sterilisation so the question of vicarious liability does not arise on that issue. On the question of the failed sterilisation there was also in my view a breach of primary duty given the fact that the plaintiff was a public patient referred to the hospital and not to an individual consultant. Fortification for this view can also be had by reference to those parts of Dr. Murray's contract which I have emphasised and in particular clause 5.3, 6.4.2 and 6.4.3 of the memorandum of agreement. Lest however I am wrong in this view I will deal with the question of vicarious responsibility for the failed operation."

Questions will inevitably arise as to the implications of Kelly J.'s analysis for the provision of healthcare to private patients. In *Gray v Minister for Justice, Equality and Law Reform* [2007] I.E.H.C. 52, Quirke J. imposed liability in negligence and for infringement of the plaintiffs' constitutional right to privacy where a member or members of the Garda Síochána had enabled a journalist to obtain information and verification of a story that a dangerous convicted rapist was living with the plaintiffs after he had been released from prison. This had resulted in the family being effectively driven from town.

As regards vicarious liability, the defendants argued that the State should not be liable for the negligent or unlawful acts or omissions of members of An Garda Síochána in the circumstances. Quirke J. rejected that argument as follows:

> "The liability of the State for the tortious acts and omissions of its servants and agents is well settled. Liability can be avoided where a

servant or agent is acting outside the scope of his or her employment. However, the civil wrong which has been established in this case was a wrong committed by a servant and agent of the State. The wrong was the unlawful disclosure of confidential and sensitive information procured by the State. The duty to keep that information confidential rested with the State.

The State is vicariously liable in such circumstances for the negligence of its servants and agents and for any breach by its servants and agents of the constitutionally protected rights of its citizens arising out of that negligence."

The suggestion here, it seems, is that the State should be vicariously liable in all circumstances where a servant or agent breaches a constitutionally protected right. That is a bold proposition, since it is possible to conceive of many circumstances in which the servant or agent will be acting completely outside the scope of his or her authority. In the instant case, there was no evidential clarity as to who had made the improper disclosure or as to what his or her motivation might have been. Speaking generally, and not in the context of the instant case, there is an important difference between a misconceived attempt to serve the common good by an unattributed disclosure and a crass desire to make money, for example. Of course, from the point of view of a victim of a breach of privacy it makes no difference what the motivation was, but from the standpoint of legal principle it may be crucial.

DAMAGES

General damages   In *Myles v McQuillan* [2007] I.E.H.C. 333, Quirke J. awarded €300,000 damages for pain and suffering to a young woman for devastating injuries she suffered when her colon perforated as a result of negligence in her medical care. He described the injuries as "catastrophic". They included pain, surgery, infection, disease, constant admissions to hospital and psychological damage.

In *Kelly v Lacey* [2007] 1 I.E.H.C. 265, McGovern J. awarded €150,000 for pain and suffering to the time of trial and a further €150,000 for future pain and suffering to a teenage girl, born in 1991, who was seriously injured when struck by a car in 2004. She was pinned under the car for some time after the accident and received burns to her leg, probably from the exhaust. She also suffered severe and disfiguring injuries to her abdomen, arms, face and leg. These were likely to remain permanent. McGovern J. observed that the leg injury was "grossly disfiguring, involving a substantial portion of her skin with a huge indentation". This, he said, ruled out many forms of normal clothing for the rest of her life. She had a scar on her collar bone which was "quite obvious and disfiguring" and which significantly limited her choice of clothing, causing her great upset. The plaintiff did not want to go swimming any more and was no longer able to take part in contact sports as a bump on a scar could lead to ulceration. When assessing the general damages, McGovern J. balanced all of these very serious aspects with the fact that the plaintiff was "not suffering any significant physical disability in terms of her general mobility" and that, when dressed in a way that covered the scars on her legs and abdomen, she presented "as an attractive and normal looking 16 year old girl" because the facial scarring was quite pale and not noticeably disfiguring.

In *McCluskey v Dublin City Council* [2007] I.E.H.C. 4, the plaintiff, a window fitter, injured his right wrist and left hand when he fell on a defective pavement. He was unable for 11 months to work to his pre-accident standard. De Valera J. was satisfied, however, that thereafter:

> "... he was able to undertake all work to his pre-accident standard, and... even if he did not want to return to his pre-accident work as a window fitter (and I don't accept this would have been physically beyond his powers) he is capable of many other forms of endeavour which would remunerate him to the same or to a greater extent than before and in today's economic conditions I find it impossible to accept that such jobs are not obtainable by [him]."

De Valera J. awarded the plaintiff general damages of €35,000 to trial and €15,000 for future pain and suffering, as well as compensation for the reduced earning capacity during the eleven months. (Damages were reduced by 30 per cent to take account of the plaintiff's contributory negligence in failing to keep a proper lookout).

In *O'Neill v Dunnes Stores* [2007] I.E.H.C. 33, the plaintiff was struck in the face with a motorcycle chain by one shoplifter when he went to the assistance of a security officer who was attempting to effect the arrest of another. The plaintiff "had a horrible experience which gave rise to substantial injuries to his jaw, nose and neck". He had to have two operations on his jaw and at the time of trial, nearly five years later, was still having ongoing treatment for the neck injuries. His ability to participate in sport, which he had enjoyed greatly, was much diminished. Kelly J. awarded the plaintiff €40,000 for pain and suffering to date and €10,000 for future pain and suffering.

Aggravated and exemplary damages   The Supreme Court decision in *Shortt v An Garda Síochána* [2007] I.E.S.C. 9 represents the most thorough analysis of the law on aggravated and exemplary damages that the Court has made for many years. The judgments of Murray C.J. and Hardiman J. cover a range of issues and offer guidance for future trial judges. They do, however, leave some questions still unresolved and the answers they provide for some other questions are not always entirely satisfactory.

In *Shortt*, the Supreme Court addressed the subject of aggravated damages in a manner that, from one point of view, may be regarded as helpful in clarifying practical aspects of awards for aggravated damages but, from another point of view, may be considered retrograde. The court missed a perfect opportunity to reassess the entire conceptual basis for such awards. That the theoretical basis of awards of aggravated damages is in serious need of such reassessment can scarcely be denied. There are pressing arguments that the entire edifice should be taken down and reassembled more convincingly within an unambiguous compensatory framework.

Let us remind ourselves of the historical background. Prior to *Rookes v Barnard* [1964] A.C. 1129, aggravated damages were not treated as a distinctive sub-category of compensatory damages. On the contrary, judges, when awarding exemplary damages, on occasion were happy to characterise them as "aggravated": see, e.g. *Lavender v Betts* [1942] 2 All E.R. 72 at 74. In *Rookes v Barnard*, Lord Devlin for the first time clearly identified aggravated damages as a particular species of compensatory damages.

In Ireland, the *locus classicus* is the passage from Finlay C.J.'s judgment in *Conway v INTO* [1991] 2 I.R. 305 at 317:

> "Aggravated damages [are] compensatory damages increased by reason of:
> (a) The manner in which the wrong was committed, involving such elements as oppressiveness, arrogance or outrage, or
> (b) the conduct of the wrongdoer after the commission of the wrong, such as a refusal to apologise or to ameliorate the harm done or the making of threats to repeat the wrong, or
> (c) conduct of the wrongdoer and/or his representatives in the defence of the claim of the wronged plaintiff, up to and including the trial of the action.
>
> Such a list of the circumstances which may aggravate compensatory damages until they can properly be classified as aggravated damages is not intended to be in anyway finite or complete. Furthermore, the circumstances which may properly form an aggravating feature in the measurement of compensatory damages must, in many instances, be in part a recognition of the added hurt or insult to a plaintiff who is being wronged, and in part also a recognition of the cavalier or outrageous conduct of the defendant."

Two questions arise about the notion of aggravated damages, as described by Lord Devlin in *Rookes v Bernard* and by Finlay C.J. in *Conway v INTO*. If they truly constitute a sub-category of compensatory damages, why should the outrageousness of the defendant's conduct be a factor for enhancing the amount of compensation in the absence of added hurt or insult to the plaintiff?

And why should it matter which tort the defendant committed, once it can be shown to have involved outrageous conduct or added hurt or insult?

The truth of the matter is that aggravated damages were conceived by Lord Devlin as serving the pragmatic purpose of taming exemplary damages. If, as *Rookes v Barnard* prescribed, exemplary damages could in future be awarded in only three specific types of case, it was necessary to have some way of dealing with egregious misconduct falling outside these three cases. Aggravated damages are the poor relation of exemplary damages, ostensibly compensatory in their rationale but in truth reflective of an intuition that outrageous delictual behaviour should merit a premium, not necessarily dependent upon the subjective response of the victim.

Over the years prior to the *Shortt* decision, the Irish courts struggled with the consequences that flow from the somewhat primitive conceptual origins of the doctrine of aggravated damages. On the question of whether aggravated damages should be capable of being awarded in claims for negligence, the Supreme Court, in *Swaine v Commission for Public Works in Ireland* [2003] I.E.S.C. 30, while not taking a definitive position, evinced clear hostility to recognising such a possibility.

It now seems clear that the approach taken in *Swaine* no longer commands judicial support. In *Philp v Ryan* [2004] I.E.S.C. 105, the Supreme Court awarded €55,000 aggravated damages in a professional negligence claim where the first defendant had altered his clinical notes on a key issue, misleading his own legal advisers and expert witness. This had made his defence seem much stronger than it really was. What McCracken J. described as "[t]he truly appalling feature in th[e] case" was that the defendants' advisers had been told of the alteration by the first defendant over a week before the commencement of the action. They had not informed the plaintiff's solicitors of the true facts. Moreover they had not sought to have their own client prove the notes until they were called for by the trial judge. McCracken J. stated:

> "In reviewing the law at the beginning of this judgment I pointed out that some doubt had been expressed as to whether aggravated damages should be awarded in negligence claims. I have no doubt that this is a classic example of a case where such damages can and should be awarded."

Let us now consider how the question of aggravated damages was addressed in *Shortt*. In the High Court, Finnegan P. declined to award aggravated damages. He stated:

> "It can be said that ... aggravated ... damages are awarded in respect of the external circumstances accompanying the cause of action. The former are measured on the basis of compensation. They represent additional compensation to a plaintiff where his sense of injury is

heightened by the manner in which or the motive for which the act giving rise to the claim was committed. Such damages represent a recognition of the added hurt or insult to the plaintiff who has been wronged and a recognition of the cavalier or outrageous conduct of the defendant. They can extend to conduct subsequent to the conduct which gives rise to the claim. See *Conway v. INTO* [1991] 2 IR 305. Having regard to the evidence adduced on the application for a certificate pursuant to the Criminal Procedure Act, 1993, s.9(1) it is fair to say that the plaintiff was sacrificed in order to assist the career and ambitions of a number of members of the Garda Síochána. However the Court must be diligent to ensure that there is no element of double compensation. The award of damages by analogy to the Common Law in relation to those causes of action which the defendant's conduct would constitute is intended to take account of injury to feelings, loss of dignity, humiliation, frustration, helplessness and despair including in the case of a claim under the 1993 Act despair at the failure of the criminal justice system. In these circumstances I do not think it appropriate to make an award under this heading".

On appeal, the Supreme Court took a different view. It considered that a global award should be made which included "ordinary general damages" and aggravated damages. It may be useful first to examine what Murray C.J. had to say on the subject:

"As Finlay C.J. pointed out in [*Conway*], general damages, or ordinary compensatory damages are sums calculated to recompense a wronged plaintiff for physical injury, mental distress, anxiety, deprivation of convenience, or other harmful effects of a wrongful act. There may indeed be particular aspects of a wrong reflected in the level of ordinary compensatory damages which are closely connected or interwoven with other factors which could give rise to aggravated damages. It could be difficult for a jury or a trial Judge in awarding ordinary compensatory damages not to have regard to the fact that, for example, a deprivation of liberty had been carried out by Garda officers in abuse of the law or in a male fide manipulation of the due process of the law.

However, as the principles referred to make clear, ordinary compensation is designed to compensate the direct effects of the wrong on the person who suffered it.

On the other hand aggravated damages represent an augmentation of the ordinary compensatory damages by reason of the manner in which the wrong was committed, the conduct of the wrongdoer at the time and subsequent to the commission of the wrong or wrongs involved. Aggravated damages have also been described as constituting '... additional compensation for the injured feelings of the plaintiff where his sense of injury resulting from the tort is justifiably heightened by the manner in which or the motive for which the defendant did it.'" (White, *Irish Law of Damages*, p.7; Butterworth (Ireland) Ltd. 1989).

In my view where there are clearly identifiable circumstances in a case of this nature which comprise the substantial aggravating factors referred to in the principles in Conway, allowing for the fact that the factors outlined there were not intended to be definitive, then compensation by way of aggravated damages must be included in the award.

A global figure for compensatory damages may well be appropriate where the circumstances of the case indicate that the factors giving rise to aggravated damages are relatively marginal to the substantive wrongs which entitle a plaintiff to ordinary compensatory damages.

Furthermore, in cases which warrant the award of aggravated damages and where the circumstances attenuant to the commission of the wrongs in cause are closely interwoven with the factors which give rise to such damages it may be appropriate to award a global figure for compensatory damages provided the award is expressly stated to include both ordinary and aggravated damages. In a court of trial at first instance it may well be preferable, in the circumstances of the case and in the discretion of the trial Judge, that the awards of ordinary compensatory damages and aggravated damages be separately identified under their respective heads. This would facilitate the review of such awards on appeal.

I think one must accept that in making these awards the distinction between serious elements of the wrong committed and aggravating factors may at times be a very fine one or indeed there may be an overlap. Thus, although ordinary compensatory damages and aggravated compensatory damages may be conceptually distinct it will often be difficult in practice to exclude overlapping elements in the assessment of ordinary compensatory damages to be paid to a plaintiff. The primary compensatory damages are the ordinary damages which may be increased by reason of the aggravating circumstances. For these reasons, and indeed as a matter of general principle, I agree with the submission by counsel for the State that where distinct amounts of damages are being awarded on the basis of both ordinary and aggravated damages the totality of any amounts attributed under these two headings should be considered with a view to ascertaining whether the total sum awarded represents fair compensation for the totality of the injury and loss suffered by the plaintiff. In *Reddy v Bates* [1984] ILRM 197 at 202, in a claim for personal injuries, loss and damage, this Court stated:

'... [I]n a case such as this, where damages are to be assessed under several headings, where the jury has added the various sums awarded and arrived at a total of damages, they should then

consider this total sum, as should this Court and any appeal, for
the purpose of ascertaining whether the total sum awarded is, in
the circumstances of the case, fair compensation for the plaintiff
for the injuries suffered, or whether it is out of all proportion to
such circumstances.'

Such an approach, by way of analogy, in cases of this nature should
obviate the risk of double compensation without undermining the
entitlement of a plaintiff to damages under both headings."

What is one to make of this analysis? Murray C.J. makes a distinction
between compensatory and aggravated damages on the basis that "ordinary
compensation is designed to compensate the direct effects of the wrong on
the person who suffered it", whereas aggravated damages "represent an
augmentation of the ordinary compensation by reason of the manner in which
the wrong was committed [and] the conduct of the wrongdoer at the time and
subsequent to the compensation of the wrong or wrongs involved." This is a
reasonably faithful reiteration of Finlay C.J.'s statement in *Conway*, though
the notion of compensation for "direct effects of the wrong" on the victim
may raise unnecessary concerns about a revival of the *Polemis* test. It will be
recalled that in *Re Polemis* [1921] 3 K.B. 560, the English Court of Appeal
held that liability should extend to the direct consequences of the negligent
conduct, even where those consequences were not reasonably foreseeable.
The converse of this was that foreseeable but indirect consequences were
not to be compensated. In the Privy Council decision of *The Wagon Mound
(No. 1)* [1961] A.C. 388, the directness test was rejected in favour of that of
reasonable foreseeability and this latter test is, of course, the one that Irish
courts favour. A plaintiff who sustains reasonably foreseeable, though indirect,
injury is fully entitled to be compensated for the injury. Nothing that Murray
C.J. says regarding the "direct" effects on the plaintiff should be considered
to roll back on this entitlement.

The Chief Justice's other observations on the distinction between
compensatory and aggravated damages and the manner in which trial judges
should determine whether to make a global award are of particular interest.
They represent a valiant attempt to make the distinction work well in
practice, clarifying the position both for trial judges and the Supreme Court
on appeal.

What emerges from his analysis is the artificial and uncovering character
of the distinction in the first place. If a global award is desirable in cases
where the factors giving rise to aggravated damages are relatively marginal
to the substantive wrongs which entitle a plaintiff to ordinary compensatory
damages and in cases where "the circumstances attenuant to the commission
of the wrongs in cause are closely interwoven with the factors which give rise
to such damages", would it not be simpler for there to be no such distinction at
all? For the so-called "global figure" in these circumstances is surely no more

than what a court would have awarded under the compensatory rubric had the concept of aggravated damages never been imposed on the law.

This suspicion derives further support from Murray C.J.'s acknowledgement that the distinction "may at times be a very fine one or indeed there may be an overlap". The full truth is simpler and starker: the "distinction" is one without a difference.

Murray C.J.'s resort to *Reddy v Bates* here is unfortunate. The idea floated in *Reddy v Bates* was that, both at trial and on appeal, the total sum awarded should be reassessed to ascertain whether it is too high. This makes some sense as a check against unintended duplication of compensation where several heads of compensation are involved. In the case of "ordinary" compensatory and aggravated damages, however, there is an *inherent* danger of overcompensation since there is no conceptually defensible way of distinguishing between compensation for the manner in which a wrong was committed and compensation to the plaintiff for his or her experience as the victim of it.

Let us now consider Hardiman J.'s approach to awards for aggravated damages. He took issue with Finnegan P.'s reference to the fact that ordinary principles of compensation would take account of the injury to the plaintiff's feelings, his loss of dignity, his humiliation, frustration, helplessness and despair at the failure of the justice system and Finnegan P.'s conclusion that, when this fact was taken into account, a further award for aggravated damages would not be appropriate. Hardiman J. stated:

> "All of the factors just listed relate to feelings and perceptions of the plaintiff. It is quite true to say that such consequential injury to feelings, which may be extreme, are included in the things which an award of 'ordinary compensatory damages' are to redress. In the extract from the judgment of Finlay C.J. in *Conway*, … he refers under the heading of ordinary compensatory damages to 'mental distress, anxiety, deprivation of convenience or other harmful effects…'
>
> Aggravated damages, on the other hand, focus, not on the feelings of the plaintiff, but on the actions and demeanour of the defendant. This emerges clearly from a consideration of the indicative list of three criteria on the basis of any one of which aggravated damages may be awarded. This is contained in the judgment of Finlay C.J. at p.317. Whether the commission of the tort occurred in a manner involving 'oppressiveness, arrogance or outrage', whether the wrongdoer's conduct after the tort 'such as a refusal to apologise or ameliorate the harm done or the making of threats to repeat the wrong' exacerbate the wrong; whether the conduct of the wrongdoer 'in the defence of the claim of the wronged plaintiff' will aggravate the damages—all feature on the conduct of the defendant, their servants or agents and not on the plaintiff. Aggravated damages are compensatory damages increased by

the presence or absence of the factors mentioned by Finlay C.J. or others. It is, therefore, wrong in principle to say that an award of compensatory damages which takes account of the plaintiff's emotional distress (here, an extremely important factor: the man was driven to despair) exhausts the capacity for an award of aggravated damages.

But that is not the end of the issue on aggravated damages because [counsel for An Garda Síochána] contends, in the alternative, that all of the factors which might otherwise ground an award of aggravated damages were, in the particular circumstances of the present case, 'inherent in the claim'. If this submission means that because Mr. Shortt's claim was for damage caused by a conspiracy by gardaí, he is debarred from an award of aggravated damages because the wrongdoers' status as gardaí was essential to enable them to act as they did, I cannot accept it. It is quite possible to be damnified by perjury on the part of a person who is not a member of An Garda Síochána or the holder of any official position. Equally, it is quite possible to be deprived of one's liberty, perhaps for years, (by, for example, terrorists as in the case of Mr. Terry Waite), without any ostensible process of law. Even apart from the status of the immediate wrongdoers, there are in my view many features of 'oppressiveness arrogance or outrage' about the conduct of the 'paying parties' in the present case. A series of false charges were preferred against an innocent man in the cynical expectation that he would, and would be advised to, plead guilty to at least one of them as part of a 'semi-deal'. As a result of his refusal to do this he was sent forward to a higher court without sufficient evidence and eventually received a three year sentence. This caused some drunken distress to one of the wrongdoers but he absolutely refused 'to apologise or to ameliorate the harm done', as did his superior. Moreover, it appears to me, the offer to get him early release if he withdrew his appeal, thereby acknowledging his guilt, clearly and necessarily implied that if he did not do so he would be left to rot in jail which is clearly in my view a 'threat to repeat the wrong', or at least to continue it. Furthermore, the conduct of the wrongdoers after Mr. Shortt's release was equally scandalous: his attempt to obtain the redress of having his conviction declared a miscarriage of justice was met with deliberate cynical and continuous perjury during the long hearing in the Court of Criminal Appeal.

From the foregoing it will be clear that I accept the submission of [counsel for the plaintiff] that Mr. Shortt 'ticked all the boxes' for an award of aggravated damages. It would be sufficient if he ticked one. Furthermore, it seems to me that many of the features just mentioned are separate and apart from the initial conspiracy, even though they would not have occurred but for that seminal event. It was not necessary to the conspiracy, for example, that the plaintiff be denied temporary release, that an attempt was made to get him to acknowledge his guilt as the price of early release, or that perjured evidence was deployed in answer to his claim for redress.

Not only this is a case where aggravated damages, in addition to ordinary compensatory damages are available; I believe it is case where it is imperatively necessary in justice that they be awarded."

Hardiman J.'s observations merit a couple of observations. His first point, that it would be wrong deny aggravated damages by reason of the fact that a compensatory award took full account of the injury to the plaintiff's feelings, is formally correct but does not fully address the substance of Finnegan P.'s approach. Finnegan P. was not presenting a syllogism with a false conclusion: he was making the perfectly valid point that the facts of a case may be such that compensation for injury to a plaintiff's feelings may fully capture the egregious dimension of the defendant's wrongdoing. If, for example, a teacher humiliates a pupil by requiring him to wear a dunce's cap in front of the class, an award which takes account of the injury to the pupil's feelings must necessarily be affected by the depth of wrongfulness of the humiliating act. There will be some rare cases in which the victim has such severe learning difficulty as to be complexly unaware of the humiliating dimension to the event. In such circumstances, a substantial award of compensation should nonetheless be made, apart together from any consideration of aggravated or exemplary damages. A serious wrong has been committed. It does not cease to be a wrong by reason of the fact that the victim is unaware of its wrongfulness. The tort of battery may be committed on a victim who will never be aware of its having occurred and the damages will not necessarily be insignificant on that account. Even if traditional principles of tort law denied substantial compensation in cases such as this—and they do not—the Constitution surely requires vindication of rights, including the right to dignity, entirely independently of the victim's consciousness of violation. Aggravated damages are not necessary to afford such compensation.

As to Hardiman J.'s second point, it may respectfully be suggested that it involves a debatable process of analysis. Hardiman J. appears to see some injustice in denying aggravated damages where, under ordinary compensatory principles, substantial compensation for the egregiousness of the conduct is inherent in the claim. His argument apparently can be reduced to the idea that denying aggravated damages in claims against Gardaí by virtue of their status would constitute some type of discrimination. This analysis may be contested. An award of aggravated damages may be considered inappropriate simply because the egregious nature of the wrongdoing has already been fully reflected in the award under ordinary compensatory principles: in cases where the wrongdoing is by members of the Garda Síochána, the egregiousness is manifest in a way that may not be so in the case of wrongdoing by others, but in such latter case, if the wrongdoing is equally manifest and already fully compensated under ordinary compensatory principles, aggravated damages would equally be inappropriate. No discrimination is here involved.

Let us turn now to the Supreme Court's analysis of the question of exemplary damages in *Shortt*. It is a source of wonder that nearly half a century after it was decided, no one can say with certainly whether the House of Lords decision in *Rookes v Barnard* [1964] A.C. 1129 represents the law in Ireland on exemplary damages. Before *Shortt*, the balance of judicial authority was tilting against endorsement of the *Rookes v Barnard* limitations; after *Shortt* that balance is tilting even more strongly against endorsement but a golden opportunity to put the matter beyond any doubt was missed by the court.

It may be recalled that, in *Rookes v Barnard*, the House of Lords held that, in future, exemplary damages might be awarded in only three categories of cases:

(1) The "oppressive arbitrary or unconstitutional action by the servants of government".
(2) Where "the defendant's conduct has been calculated by him to make a profit for himself which may well exceed the compensation payable to the plaintiff".
(3) Where exemplary damages were "expressly authorised" by statute.

Moreover, three considerations applied to an award of exemplary damages:

(1) A plaintiff should not be able to recover exemplary damages unless he had been the victim of the punishable behaviour. No one should be permitted to obtain "a windfall" in consequence of oppressive conduct towards another which did not affect him, although it constituted a tort in respect of him.
(2) Since the power to award exemplary damages constituted a weapon that could be used against liberty as well as in defence of liberty, it should be "used with restraint".
(3) The means of the parties, which are irrelevant in assessing damages under the compensatory criterion, should be material in the assessment of exemplary damages, since "[e]verything which aggravates or mitigates the defendant's conduct is relevant".

Over the years, the Supreme Court vacillated on whether to endorse *Rookes v Barnard*. Judges showed some reluctance to commit themselves on the question. On a number of occasions they noted that the facts of the case fell within one of the *Rookes v Barnard* categories (usually the first); they did not go on in such instances to clarify whether that conjunction explained an award of exemplary damages which otherwise would not have been capable of being made.

The decisions are analysed in detail in McMahon & Binchy's *Law of Torts*, 3rd edn (Dublin: Tottel Publishing, 2000), paras 44.16–44.54. Here we need only note the sharp division of judicial opinion on the question in *McIntyre v Lewis* [1991] 1 I.R. 121 and the strong tilt towards rejection of the *Rookes v Barnard* categories in *Conway v Irish National Teachers Organisation* [1991] 2 I.R. 305.

In *Conway*, Finlay C.J. set out the relevant principles for awarding exemplary damages in actions for tort or for breach of a constitutional right, in a passage that has received judicial endorsement in several later decisions. Exemplary damages, he said, were:

> "... damages arising from the nature of the wrong which has been committed and/or the manner of its commission which are intended to mark the court's particular disapproval of the defendant's conduct in all the circumstances of the case and its decision that it should publicly be seen to have punished in the defendant for such conduct by awarding such damages, quite apart from its obligation, where it may exist in the same case, to compensate the plaintiff for the damage which he or she has suffered."

In *Shortt*, Murray C.J. said that he was "quite satisfied" that the principles relating to damages awards set out by Finlay C.J. in *Conway* applied in the instant case. He went on to make the following observation later in his judgment:

> "Although I agree with the views of McCarthy J. in *McIntyre -v- Lewis*, that the restriction of exemplary damages to certain categories of cases as stated by Lord Devlin in *Rookes –v- Barnard* [1964] A.C. 1129 has no application in our law, that question does not need to be addressed in this case, if it needs to be further addressed at all."

Hardiman J. made no reference to the question in his judgment but it seems reasonable to interpret it as being consistent only with the rejection of the *Rookes v Barnard* limitations. It is a pity that the issue was not finally disposed of. The case law as a whole appears strongly to point towards rejection but, formally at least and perhaps even substantively, the point is still open to debate.

The court's analysis in *Shortt* of the goals of punishment and deterrence in making awards for exemplary damages raises more questions than it resolves. In sentencing in criminal cases, the goals of punishment (or retribution) and deterrence, together with rehabilitation and containment, all must be considered. This can lead to pulls in opposing directions, where, for example, retribution and rehabilitation seem to suggest radically different sentences. In tort actions, the judicial role when awarding exemplary damages is—or should be—less complex. The essential goal is punitive, in the sense of providing a public sanction (albeit to the benefit of the plaintiff) for egregious wrongdoing. Of course a deterrent element cannot be discounted, especially where the State or other public body is a defendant, but it sometimes will be completely lacking. Perhaps the concept of "punishment" in this civil context should be seen as having a distinctive meaning. Although it results in a sanction, the object is not reducible to that. An award of exemplary damages represents the public record by the court of the egregiousness of the defendant's conduct: letting the light shine on such wrongdoing is considered a fitting response and the award of exemplary damages calls public attention to the wrong.

In *Shortt*, both Murray C.J. and Hardiman J. concluded that the punitive element was not central in the circumstances of the case, where a state institution was the defendant. Murray C.J. stated:

> "Exemplary damages are not compensatory. They are, in a sense, a windfall for the plaintiff. Exemplary damages serve several potential purposes including to mark the Court's disapproval of outrageous conduct on the part of a defendant. In the case of a jury they may reflect the indignation of ordinary law abiding citizens at such conduct.
>
> They are also punitive... They may financially punish a defendant as a deterrent to that defendant as well as a deterrent generally to the arrogant use or abuse of power. In their purely punitive dimension the means of a defendant may be relevant in order to ensure that the punishment is proportionate. However the purely punitive element of these damages is hardly relevant where the State is the defendant since no individual, let alone those persons who have actually committed the wrong, will bear responsibilty for paying any of the damages. The liability of the State to pay arises from its vicarious responsibility for its servants or agents and the payment of damages is made out of public funds.
>
> This of course does not relieve the State from its liability for such damages (see for example *McIntyre v Lewis* ...). The award of exemplary damages is, in the words of Finlay C.J. in *Conway*, 'one of the most effective deterrent powers which a civil court has: the award of exemplary or punitive damages.' It is a power which must be available to the Court where there is serious abuse of power by or on behalf of the State. Such an award against the State, in appropriate cases, marks the Court's public disapproval of abuse of power so as to demonstrate that such wrongdoing will not be tolerated. Although in the form of a financial penalty it is in substance also a moral sanction, a mirror to 'the proper indignation of the public'. Such damages remind the other organs of State that there is not only a duty to compensate a wronged

citizen by way of monetary damages but to take all steps necessary designed to ensure, as far as practicable, that such deliberate abuse of power is not repeated but is prevented.

In awarding exemplary or punitive damages a Court is at large as to the amount which it considers appropriate to express its disapproval and therefore it must exercise any such power with restraint. The amount awarded should be no more than is necessitated to convey in this case, to the State, and the public at large, the level of its disapproval in the light of the gravity of the State's conduct. In my view this can only be achieved in this case by making a separate and distinct award for exemplary damages."

Hardiman J. stated:

"As is pointed out in the judgments in *Conway* the term 'exemplary' is sometimes used interchangeably with 'punitive'. The learned judges in that case explained the reason for their preferring the former term. On the facts of the present case, I would share that preference. Even if this plaintiff were awarded a truly enormous sum under this heading, I doubt if it could be described in any real sense as 'punitive'. The money would not come from the pocket of any individual or even from any individual company or other business entity. It would in the end be levied on the tax payer and neither the gardaí who committed the tort, or any individual member of the force, would be one cent the worse for the award. Such an award cannot truly be described as punitive. On the other hand it seems quite possible to make an award which will 'make an example of' the wrongdoers here and the legal entities responsible for them by marking in terms that everyone can understand the sheer evil of what was done and the detestation which the Courts, speaking for civil society in general, must feel and express for it."

Later in his judgment, Hardiman J. observed:

"I have already said that I prefer, at least in the context of a case such as this where the defendants are State Authorities, to regard the sort of damages now under discussion as exemplary rather than punitive, for the reasons given above. The State itself, or a State Authority, is simply not capable of registering personally the punitive aspects of such an award, as a private individual or company is. The classic modes of legal punishment are deprivation of liberty by imprisonment or of property by way of fine: these cannot meaningfully be imposed on a State authority. In the calculation of exemplary damages against a private entity, the means of the wrongdoer are to be taken into account: the reason for this is to graduate the penal element in accordance with the means of the offender. But no individual wrongdoer will lose anything by reason of the award in this case. It would be ludicrous, and plainly contrary to the public interest, to make an award against a public authority such as the Commissioner of An Garda Síochána so large as to reduce the capacity of An Garda Síochána to perform its statutory functions.

Accordingly, I am of the opinion that in a case such as the present where the defendants are public authorities, the principal consideration in calculating the amount of an award of exemplary damages must be the amount necessary '… truly to make an example of the wrongdoer so as to show others that such wrong will not be tolerated and more to the point will not be relieved on the payment of merely compensatory damages'.

But I wish to emphasise that, in an appropriate case, both the punitive and the exemplary heads of damage are available to a Court addressing a case on its individual facts."

The point made by both Murray C.J. and Hardiman J. about the futility of trying to punish the State is at one level a good one; it would, however, become a bad one if it were to lead future courts into making sharp distinctions between punitive and deterrent goals based on the particular impact a punitive rationale might have on the defendant in question. One would not wish to have a situation where, of two defendants guilty of identical egregious conduct, the award of exemplary damages against one was less than against the other because of the futility from one perspective of trying to punish that defendant. Probing too deeply the rationale (or rationales) for making awards of exemplary damages could lead to an unduly technical approach which could involve discrimination between defendants (and, indirectly) plaintiffs. Of course the circumstances of the particular defendant are broadly relevant: some may consider that to be beaten up by a garda or prison officer is worse than by a private person (though even here it may depend on who that person is).

The whole question of the relevance of the means of the defendant is hugely controversial. Here we merely note that it can raise constitutional concerns unless handled with the greatest of sensitivity.

Finnegan P. in the High Court had awarded only £50,000 exemplary damages as he felt he had to be "conscious of the risk of double compensation". This statement did not meet with the approval of the Supreme Court. Murray C.J. observed that:

"… in certain circumstances the substantial level of compensatory damages may be a factor to be taken into account when the Court is exercising its discretion as to the exemplary damages necessitated by the need to mark its disapproval of the defendants conduct but the notion of double compensation has nothing to do with that."

On the question whether an award of exemplary damages should be a fraction rather than a multiple of the amount awarded by way of compensatory (including aggravated) damages, as had been suggested by O'Flaherty J. in *McIntyre v Lewis*, Murray C.J. considered that O'Flaherty J.'s suggestion had been:

"…made in the context of a cautionary approach which he correctly felt the Courts should follow with regard to the award of exemplary damages. However I do not agree that the discretion of the Court in awarding exemplary damages in a case where it otherwise feels it proper to do so should invariably be constrained by a rule that they be a fraction of the compensatory, including aggravated, damages awarded. The discretion of a Court to award exemplary damages in the vindication of rights and as a mark of its disapproval of the conduct of a defendant, should not be constrained in that manner but exercised according to the circumstances of each case even if in many cases the appropriate award of exemplary damages might well be a fraction of the overall compensatory damages."

Hardiman J. was equally dismissive of O'Flaherty J.'s approach. He stated:

"I wish to say that I cannot agree with this statement. It is inconsistent with the actual result in *McIntyre v. Lewis*. But, more importantly, it is contrary to what I am satisfied is the true principle of aggravated damages in an action against State Authorities: that it be sufficient 'truly to make an example' of the wrongdoers and that it be effective to deter a repetition."

Having discussed the *Shortt* decision in great detail, let us look briefly at a few other decisions in 2007 in which the issue of aggravated or exemplary damages fell for consideration.

Section 128(1) of the Copyright and Related Rights Act 2000 is unusual in permitting a court, either in addition, or as an alternative, to compensating the victim of an infringement of copyright for financial loss, to award aggravated or exemplary damages or both aggravated and exemplary damages. In *Retail Systems Technology Ltd v McGuire* [2007] I.E.H.C. 13, Kelly J. awarded aggravated damages of €10,000 (in addition to €204,000 by way of compensatory damages) to take account of the way the defendants had conducted the litigation. Kelly J. had no doubt but that their behaviour throughout had been less than satisfactory. They had "procrastinated and delayed" on many occasions; information had been obtained, both by discovery and particulars, only after numerous applications to court. In Kelly J.'s view, an award of aggravated but not exemplary, damages was appropriate to demonstrate the court's disapproval of the defendants' behaviour.

Ahmed v Health Service Executive [2007] I.E.H.C. 312 contains an interesting, albeit brief, discussion of the question whether aggravated or exemplary damages may be awarded for breach of contract. The plaintiff had been employed by the defendant as a consultant surgeon as a contract of indefinite duration. The defendant breached that contract in failing to permit him engage in work of a particular category. Laffoy J., in earlier proceedings ([2006] I.E.H.C. 245), imposed liability. In the initial proceedings she addressed the question of damages. She awarded €300,000 damages for breach of contract. Although she accepted that the plaintiff had suffered "shock, upset, anxiety, stress, general unhappiness and general inconvenience", she saw no basis in the instant case for awarding general damages. Referring to *Carroll v Bus Atha Cliath* [2005] 4 I.R. 184, Laffoy J. expressed the view that the primary consideration which had led Clarke J. to refuse to award damages in *Carroll* applied equally to the facts in the instant case. There had been no evidence that the plaintiff had suffered "any clinical medical condition" because of the defendant's breach of contract.

Counsel for the plaintiff, having referred to *Conway v Irish National Teachers' Organisation* [1991] 2 I.R. 305 and *Shortt v Commissioner of An Garda Siochána* [2007] I.E.S.C. 9, had submitted that the same principle for awarding damages as applied to breach of a constitutional right should apply to an award of damages for breach of contract. Laffoy J. did not agree. She could:

> "… not see, in point of principle, how aggravated or exemplary damages could be awarded for breach of a term of a contract of employment where there is no entitlement to general damages and where the relationship of employer and employee is ongoing".

In any event, although the defendant's treatment of the plaintiff had been shoddy, if the plaintiff's cause of action was one which entitled the court to consider awarding aggravated damages, the conduct of the defendant when considered in its totality, including apologising to the plaintiff, had not been of the type which Finlay C.J. in *Conway* had identified as giving rise to an entitlement to aggravated damages. Nor would there be any basis for awarding exemplary damages.

This analysis provokes reflection. The relationship between constitutional law and civil law needs further probing in a jurisdiction which recognises the principle of horizontality of rights protection. In *Hanrahan v Merck Sharpe & Dohme (Ireland) Ltd* [1988] I.L.R.M. 629 the Supreme Court sought to utilise the corpus of tort law as the presumptive machinery for compensating victims of infringements of constitutional rights. Only if the particular tort was "basically ineffective" in compensating the victim should a court have to resort to a free-standing remedy independent of the tort system. Yet it is not just the tort system that serves to protect constitutional rights from infringement: the law of contract has just as important a function in protecting people from infringements of their right to property, livelihood and physical and psychological integrity.

When the Supreme Court in *Conway* and *Shortt* was addressing the question of the relationship between protection of constitutional rights and the civil law system, it was doing so in contexts which were manifestly tortious in character and had not a trace of a contractual dimension. It would seem mistaken to imagine that the Court was seeking to assert that the only way that the civil law can protect constitutional rights is through the medium of tort law. Clearly, the law of contract, property and equitable remedies, for example, can provide further important protection.

Whistleblower Protection

ESTELLE FELDMAN, Research Associate, Trinity College, Dublin

INTRODUCTION

The objective of whistleblower protection legislation is to encourage the disclosure of wrongdoing. Generally there is preference for disclosure within organisations so that the situation at issue can be corrected whilst minimising the damage that the organisation would inevitably suffer with more public disclosure; however, where there are statutory regulators, allowances are made for disclosure of error and malpractice outside the organisation. The theory is that if bona fide whistleblowers are encouraged by, rather than fearful of, organisational procedures that facilitate dealing with misconduct, greater transparency and accountability will result. As a consequence, the incidence of corrupt practices will diminish. It may be noted, first, that fundamental to this reasoning is a recognition that inherent within all human endeavour is a propensity to be corrupt and that secrecy is a significant factor in allowing corruption to flourish. Secondly, as the title of this chapter indicates, there is recognition that a whistleblower may suffer detriment as a consequence of disclosing; hence, legislation dealing with disclosure of misconduct needs to provide protection for the discloser against any harm or loss that may result. These two points seem to underlie the terminology used in legislation where language affirms the act of disclosure, namely "public interest disclosure" and "protected disclosure". For purposes of simplicity the person making a disclosure of alleged wrongdoing to a regulator is referred to in this chapter as a whistleblower, although this is not always desirable terminology.

In Ireland in recent years we have witnessed the first tentative moves towards whistleblower protection, with the acknowledgment that in some critical spheres of activity the bona fide informant is to be encouraged. Calls for general whistleblower protection are not uncommon, but the statutory provisions now in place, e.g. Protections for Persons Reporting Child Abuse Act 1998; Pt 14 of the Health Act 2007; and Protection of Disclosures of Information and Garda Síochána (Confidential Reporting of Corruption or Malpractice) Regulations 2007 demonstrate not only a lack of a coherent approach by the Oireachtas, but fundamental misunderstanding of what is and what is not achievable in terms of protecting whistleblowers.

THE WHISTLEBLOWING PROCESS

For the purposes of this introductory chapter for the *Annual Review*, the definition of a whistleblower is confined to describing a good faith whistleblower, since much of the legislation requires good faith if a disclosure is to attract protection. The good faith whistleblower is someone who is motivated by a belief that something that is perceived to be wrong ought to be rectified. At its most basic, if something is not as it should be in an organisation and a member of that organisation is concerned about it, the natural thing to do ought to be to report what is wrong to the next person up the line. In the case of something very serious, perhaps the report ought to be directly to the most senior people. It is when this report is ignored or denied, yet the individual persists in insisting that something is wrong, that that individual could well be described as a whistleblower.

In a complex organisation the next action may involve reporting to another section or division; in all organisations, if it involves going to outside agencies, whether they be designated statutory protection and enforcement bodies and/or the media, the person is most definitely categorised as a whistleblower. This is not an inevitable progression but generally results from a situation where the complainant becomes so disaffected and alienated by the failure of the organisation's internal mechanisms to rectify what is perceived as something wrong that the fault is revealed to an outsider. Thus, the two inevitable stages in the process of whistleblowing are 'causation' and 'disclosure'. As noted, the first stage is when a person perceives an activity as mistaken, illegal, unethical, or immoral. The whistleblower can choose to ignore this perception, to acquiesce in the conduct of the activity, to participate, to object or to walk away. Over time these five choices are not mutually exclusive as an individual's mind may change as to how to behave at any given time. Irrespective of personal conduct, there may be no option but to proceed to disclosure, the second stage.

In situations of disclosure, the response of some management structures is to get rid of the problem, not by sorting out the revealed wrong, but by sorting out the whistleblower. Thus, stage three of the whistleblowing process is 'retaliation'. If silence is not forthcoming, then management endeavours to discredit the whistleblower so that the reports can be dismissed and denigrated as unreliable and/or embittered ramblings from an incompetent and untrustworthy source. Of course, there are circumstances where statutory provisions require disclosure to regulators but very often this has not precluded and does not prevent discriminatory retaliation.

Employee vulnerability   Not all whistleblowers are victims of sustained campaigns to discredit but the phenomenon transcends cultures and societies as the numerous cases publicised in the media show. For all whistleblowers who are subjected to campaigns to discredit, the personal consequences are devastating. The true stories of the ordinary people who find themselves thrust into this role match the substance of blockbuster fictional thrillers. Over the years some of the more publicly known whistleblowing stories have been immortalised by Hollywood. Well-documented examples are *Serpico* and *Silkwood*, whistleblowers whose normal work in the New York police force and the nuclear industry respectively could involve life-threatening activities so that "accidents" were very difficult to lay at the door of management as part of a deliberate policy to silence. *The Insider* immortalised Geoffrey Wigand, who blew the whistle on the tobacco industry. As depicted on screen, without extraordinary vigilance approaching paranoia, this whistleblower could also have met with a grave accident.

A European *cause célèbre* is Stanley Adams and the Hoffman LaRoche case, not a Hollywood movie but portrayed many years ago in a Channel 4 TV documentary drama. The law enforcement agencies of the Swiss Government, acting on information provided by the European Commission, supported the vindictive management campaign against Adams resulting in malicious imprisonment of the whistleblower, his wife's suicide, his conviction for treason and his subsequent temporary exile from Switzerland (Adams, *Roche versus Adams* (London: Jonathan Cape, 1984)); *Donnez Report*, March 31, 1980, Legal Affairs Committee of the European Parliament, European Parliament Working Documents 1980–1981 (1-44/80)). The European Commission behaved disgracefully once again when in 1998, Paul van Buitenen, a Dutch national employed as an internal auditor, revealed massive persistent corruption at the most senior level (van Buitenen, *Blowing the Whistle: One man's fight against fraud in the European Commission* (London: Politicos Pub, 2000)). At the end of the day, although the Commission as a consequence resigned en block, van Buitenen suffered suspension and was no longer permitted to work in the internal audit function.

The individual versus the institution can be "legitimately" bullied, harassed and harried. Clearly, it is not a difficult thing for management to do. Fortunately, there are only a limited number of professions where management can hope to get away with shooting (Frank Serpico), poisoning (Karen Silkwood), imprisoning or exiling (Stanley Adams) whistleblowers. However, all can engage in the subtle withholding or twisting of information so that the individual is set up to fail. This is almost impossible to prove, no matter how blatant and transparent to the victim. Perhaps this is the ultimate paradox for the whistleblower to deal with: condemned on the one hand for highlighting an error that the organisation will not admit to, and condemned on the other for committing far less serious errors forced by the consequences of this self-same condemnation. The impact of a sustained campaign to discredit is an ever-recurring nightmare and torment for the whistleblower.

Statutory remedy Without a true understanding of the unique character of the whistleblowing process as it proceeds through its stages of causation, disclosure and retaliation, the statutory remedy envisaged is likely to be inadequate. For example, in preparing its whistleblower protection legislation the UK Government's preferred remedy for compensation on whistleblower dismissal was to adopt the existing statutory whistleblowing provisions for the dismissal of health and safety representatives and pension fund trustees. Such an approach is inadequate for two reasons. The first is that, whereas there may be some similarities in the actions of all whistleblowers, in the cases of pension fund trustees and health and safety representatives, these are persons with a designated function of a regulatory nature specified in law. Additionally, they have the foundation and umbrella of specified rules and regulations within which to act. Generally a whistleblower does not have this kind of security. To blow the whistle outside a strict regulatory framework is very much a leap in the dark and very much an act of faith. The personal risk undertaken is, therefore, far greater. Secondly, the possibility for alternative employment, albeit having been found to have been wrongfully dismissed, is negligible. To be dismissed for blowing the whistle could well be the termination of any opportunity of future gainful employment.

Following representations from key interests, the UK authorities introduced a much broader compensatory scheme. It was noted at the time in the UK *Current Law Statutes* that these proposals were criticised by:

> "[a]n unprecedented consensus among business, unions and professional interests [which] shared the view of 85 per cent of consultees and favoured full compensation for whistleblowers. The Institute of Directors felt the precedent of health and safety representatives was 'wholly inappropriate', while the Confederation of British Industry expressed reservations about the high minimum and low maximum awards in it. It should be added that both bodies emphasised that they saw this Act primarily as a governance measure, rather than as a traditional employment matter." *Public Interest Disclosure Act 1998 (Chapter 23), Current Law Statutes, Sweet & Maxwell, Explanatory note to s.8(4).*

WHISTLEBLOWER PROTECTION IN THE UNITED STATES

It is a widely held view that the United States has effective whistleblower protection legislation. The facts give lie to that opinion irrespective of whether one is a non-federal employee or a federal employee. In the United States there is a difference in the legislative treatment of each sector.

Non-federal employees   In the non-federal sector the "employment-at-will" doctrine leaves the whistleblower employee particularly vulnerable. Absent specific statutory protection, it is only when a disclosure can be classified as a "public policy exception" to the common law doctrine that an employee may be protected in law. Unfortunately, these exceptions vary from state to state and their application is quite inconsistent. The uneven impact of statutory as well as common law protection in the United States is well documented in the academic literature, e.g. Dworkin and Callahan, "Internal Whistleblowing: Protecting the Interests of the Employee, the Organization, and Society" (1991) 29 *American Business Law Journal* 267–308.

The progress of a Colorado case outlines how difficult it can be for a good faith whistleblower to pursue a legal remedy. A supervisory employee with an advanced degree in mechanical engineering engaged in research projects for the space shuttle programme was fired in 1975, allegedly for repeatedly reporting to his own superiors substandard workmanship, overstated performance claims, misappropriation of materials and budgeting discrepancies which constituted fraud by his employers against the National Aeronautics Space Administration (NASA) and, hence, the US Government. A claim in tort for wrongful discharge was filed in 1981; the trial court entered a directed verdict against the plaintiff ruling that Colorado did not recognise a claim for wrongful discharge and that the claim was time-barred. On appeal, the Court of Appeals reversed the verdict and remanded the case for new trial (*Lorenz v Martin Marietta Corp Inc* (802 P.2d 1146 (Colo. App. 1990)). In 1992 the Colorado Supreme Court upheld the decision of the appeal court permitting the retroactive application of a judicial decision because it involved conduct that was clearly prohibited by federal law, because retroactive application would further the purpose and effect of the public-policy exception to the at-will employment doctrine, and because the equities favoured retroactive application in order to avoid penalising [the plaintiff] for his responsible actions and releasing [the defendant company] from any liability for its alleged tortious conduct (*Martin Marietta Corp v Lorenz*, 823 P.2d 100 (Colo. 1992)).

As regards the merit of this particular whistleblower, the court held that the at-will employee had established a prima facia case of wrongful discharge under the public policy exception. There does not appear to be a report of a retrial so it might be assumed that 17 years after his wrongful discharge the whistleblower and his erstwhile employers settled his action. It may be noted that it was in 1986 that the space shuttle *Challenger* exploded shortly after launch killing all occupants, a tragedy of immense significance to the NASA projects. This catastrophic event appears to have had no effect on the ability of the wronged sub-contracted employee to gain redress despite being fired for highlighting faults in the NASA contracts.

Federal employees   With regard to federal employees, the protection of whistleblowers has long been a serious problem. The Civil Service Reform

Act of 1978 was expected to provide relief against reprisal for blowing the whistle on mismanagement, waste, fraud and abuse in the federal Government. Unfortunately, the 1978 Act was insufficient to protect employees and in 1989 Congress passed the Whistleblower Protection Act to further strengthen and improve the protections for whistleblowers in the federal Government. Stated very briefly, the Office of Special Counsel (OSC) was established to aid a whistleblower in having his or her disclosure investigated; in preserving anonymity in so far as is possible; and in preventing retaliatory action against the whistleblower. In cases of retaliation the Office of Special Counsel is supposed to aid in proceedings and ensure appropriate remedies and penalties. It may be noted that the history of the Office is a recital of failure to fulfil these ends. The first incumbent, Alex Kozinski, using the Office of Special Counsel (OSC)'s own manual as a guide, taught a course for federal managers on how to fire employees without OSC interference. In the 1990s, evidence at Senate oversight hearings on whistleblower protection presented a well-substantiated litany of complaints of, inter alia, breaches of anonymity, unauthorised leaks of confidential information and lack of explanation of findings against the whistleblower.

With regard to the OSC nothing has improved. The current incumbent, Scott J. Bloch, appointed in 2004 by President Bush, has repeatedly been accused of using his office to promote conservative social causes. The Inspector-General of the Office of Personal Management began investigating Mr Bloch in 2005 arising from complaints filed by employees of the OSC including the most senior investigators. The Special Counsel has been accused of failing to protect federal workers from discrimination based on their sexual orientation and of retaliating, through intimidation and involuntary transfers, against employees who complained. During this investigation the Special Counsel hired the technology service "Geeks on Call" to erase his computer hard drive and those of two aides, giving rise to new allegations that he was obstructing justice. In May 2007, at the time of writing, a task force of the FBI almost two dozen strong raided the offices of Special Counsel to seize hard drives and files related to the latest accusations (additional sources: *The Washington Post*, *The New York Times*).

By contrast to the heads of other federal agencies, the head of the OSC can only be removed by the President for a cause such as inefficiency or abuse of power. These protections were designed to insulate the OSC from political pressure by officials it investigates.

An organisation which has consistently given evidence to oversight hearings of the inadequacy and dishonesty of the OSC is the Government Accountability Project (GAP), a non-profit organisation created in 1977 to protect the public interest and promote government and corporate accountability by advancing occupational free speech, defending whistleblowers and empowering citizen activists. GAP represents wronged whistleblowers in federal court where the standard of proof required of the complainant to establish that retaliation has taken place was judicially established in the initial case as irrefragable, a previously unheard-of standard higher than that required for criminal trials; hence, GAP must be very selective in representing only whistleblowers who can present evidence that their federal employer cannot dispute or disprove (source: private conversation with Deputy Legal Director of GAP).

Whistleblowing for reward or Qui tam   By comparison to the unimaginable difficulties faced by good faith whistleblowers, there is a very effective system in place to reward those who blow the whistle on fraud against the federal Government. This is known as *Qui Tam*. The Federal False Claims (Amendment) Act 1986, sometimes known as the Lincoln Law, first came into force during the Civil War and was directed primarily at war profiteers. Historically the *qui tam* lawsuit originated in the 13th century when private citizens sought to protect the King's interest, "*Qui tam pro domino rege quam pro se ipso in hac parte sequitur ...*" *(who sues on behalf of the King as well as for himself)*. It was resurrected in the 19th century in the False Claims Act of 1863 by federal lawmakers, primarily to combat the supply to the Union Army of arms crates filled with sawdust rather than muskets, and the delivery of allegedly fit mules which were diseased, blind, overpriced or had already been purchased (several times). In the absence of developed systems of federal law enforcement machinery, the lawmakers sought to enlist the help of private citizens to police and prevent such fraudulent activity.

In the mid-1980s, following some high-profile cases of fraud against the federal Government, the laws were reintroduced. According to the latest statistics from the United States Department of Justice, well in excess of $1billion per year is recovered by the Government through *qui tam* civil suits. The two primary areas for recovery are defence procurement and health care.

The *qui tam*, or whistleblower provisions of the False Claims Act, allow private individuals or corporations with knowledge of fraud against the Federal Government to bring an action on behalf of the United States and to receive, if successful, a percentage of the recovery. There is no requirement that the plaintiff be directly involved as a victim of the fraud and tax fraud is excluded. If the Government takes the suit, the relator may be entitled to recover between 15 and 20 per cent of the proceeds of the award or settlement. If the Federal Government declines the action and does not participate, the relator may take the action alone and, if successful, is entitled to receive between 25 and 30 per cent of the proceeds. A successful plaintiff may also be awarded costs. The Act penalises the fraudulent body with monetary damages equalling three times the amount of damages sustained by the Federal Government as well as fines of up to $10,000 for each false claim. In order to be recognised as such, the relator must be an independent "original source" of the information, and must be able to show that this information could not have been derived arising from prior public disclosure.

The general view is that the *qui tam* bounty provides the financial wherewithal by which fraud can be brought to light. It offers the likelihood of compensation to people who could not afford the risks to their careers and livelihood that becoming a whistleblower frequently entails. Corporations and business people can also be compensated by *qui tam* actions where market share has suffered as a result of fraudulent, anti-competitive and abusive practices in their industry. The first reported *qui tam* action taken by a non-US citizen for activities taking place outside the US involved a United Kingdom company supplying parts to the United States airforce; the case was reported in July 1998 with settlement in excess of £7 million ("TI settles US 'whistleblower' action for £7m" *Financial Times*, July 28, 1998; "Whistleblower reward as British firm settles", *The Guardian*, July 31, 1998).

WHISTLEBLOWER PROTECTION IN THE UNITED KINGDOM

The Public Interest Disclosure Act 1998 has bolstered protection for whistleblowers who are in a position to avail of it. The necessity to act in good faith and with reasonableness by the employee are positive critical aspects of the legislation. Disclosures should be confined within the organisation whenever possible. The legislation renders void the duty of confidentiality that an employee is deemed to owe an employer, or any other "gagging" clause express or implied that may be in a contract of employment. Thus, an employer against whom a protected disclosure is made may not use the traditional weapon against the employee of suing for breach of contract. Secondly, the Act protects disclosure of extraterritorial issues. Finally, it establishes an employee's right not to be subject to detriment for making a protected disclosure. This is the sine qua non of such legislation. Unlike the United States, a disclosure is not protected if personal gain is involved. Further, a disclosure is not protected if the person commits an offence by making it. A major flaw in the UK Act is that no statutory protection is provided in relation to breaches of the Official Secrets Act.

A key objective of the introduction of the Public Interest Disclosure Act is to move away from a culture of "blame" to a culture of "support". Organisations are encouraged to introduce whistleblowing procedures and policies so as to exclude the possibility of "protected disclosures". At the forefront of advocating this culture change so that there will be no need for external disclosure is a registered charity established in 1993 called Public Concern At Work (PCAW), the UK equivalent of GAP in the US. Its objective is to promote good practice and compliance with the law across the public, private and voluntary sectors by focusing on the accountability of those in charge and the responsibility of those who work. PCAW is wholly independent of Government and is recognised as a legal advice centre by the Bar Council.

Prior to the new legislation coming into effect, the leading whistleblowing authority was *Gartside v Outram* (1856) 26 L.J. Ch. 113, in which the following was held:

> "The true doctrine is, that there is no confidence as to the disclosure of iniquity. You cannot make me the confidant of a crime or a fraud, and be entitled to close up my lips upon any secret which you have the audacity to disclose to me relating to any fraudulent intentions on your part: such a confidence cannot exist" ((1856) 26 L.J.Ch. 113 at 114).

WHISTLEBLOWER PROTECTION IN IRELAND

Informer or informant   In looking at whistleblowing in Ireland there is some insight into the Irish antipathy to any notion of the "informer" in *Berry v Irish Times* [1973] I.R. 368, a Supreme Court defamation judgment. McLoughlin J., dissenting on the substantive issue, was rather vehement on the Irish opinion of informers:

> "[T]he suggestion is that this Irishman, the plaintiff, had acted as a spy and informer for the British police concerning republicans in England, thus putting the plaintiff into the same category as the spies and informers of earlier centuries who were regarded with loathing and abomination by all decent people" ([1973] I.R. 368 at 379).

On the other hand, O'Dalaigh C.J. (Walsh and Budd JJ. concurring), during the course of presenting the majority verdict, gave some support to the activity that we would nowadays refer to as whistleblowing:

> "[F]or historical reasons it is to be assumed that the word 'informer' has a special and defamatory meaning and is, because of such special meaning to be distinguished from the word 'informant' which itself certainly is not defamatory in its ordinary meaning" ([1973] I.R. 368 at 378).

Applying *Gartside v Outram*   The first modern whistleblowing case dealt with by the Irish superior courts was *National Irish Bank Ltd v RTÉ* [1998] 2 I.L.R.M. 196, a case regarding whistleblowing to the media. Consideration was given, inter alia, to the public disclosure by RTÉ of confidential information relating to certain of NIB's dealings with its customers which would tend to identify customers, or accounts, or transactions on any account relating to a particular scheme of insurance policies with Clerical Medical International (CMI), an offshore company. This information had come into RTÉ's possession from some customers as well as former bank employees. In holding that there exists a duty and right of confidentiality in certain relationships such as banker and customer, Lynch J. (O'Flaherty and Barrington JJ. concurring) nevertheless held that this was outweighed by the public interest in defeating wrongdoing by publication of information relating to allegations of serious tax evasion, "a matter of genuine interest and importance to the general public and especially the vast majority who are law abiding tax payers". However, RTÉ was warned that "it should be very sure and should take all necessary steps to ensure that it does not publish the names of innocent investors" ([1998] 2 I.L.R.M. 196 at 205). Albeit dissenting, Keane J. affirmed the common law dictum from *Gartside v Outram* that "there is no confidence in iniquity".

Consequent on RTÉ's disclosures of wrongdoing in NIB, allegedly by management direction, disclosures which did not require identifying specific customers, a number of investigations were instituted into the bank's affairs by different regulators, internal and external. The external inquiries included the appointment of inspectors under the Companies Act 1990. Litigation in relation to this investigation resulted in the second of the Supreme Court judgments of consequence to potential whistleblowers and their employers, *Re National Irish Bank (No. 1)* [1999] 3 I.R. 145. The right to silence and the right not to self-incriminate were considered in relation to statutory requirements to disclose to the inspectors. This case is comprehensively discussed in previous *Annual Reviews* especially in relation to the judgment of Kearns J. in *Dunnes Stores v Ryan* [2002] 2 I.R. 60, e.g. *Annual Review of Irish Law 2002*, p.118 and *Annual Review of Irish Law 2003*, pp.331 *et seq*.

Statutory whistleblower provisions *Protections for Persons Reporting Child Abuse Act 1998,* sui generis   This statute does not appear to have been applied in any action to date. It was analysed in *Annual Review of Irish Law 1998*, pp.653-654 and in Feldman, 'Whistleblower Protection: Comparative Legal Developments' (1999) 17 *I.L.T.* 264. However, despite its inadequacies it does appear to be taken as a basis for subsequent provisions purporting to protect whistleblowers. What seems to have escaped notice is that this Act serves a very specific purpose for the community at large and children in particular and it should, therefore, be treated sui generis and not as a model for any other whistleblower protection provisions. On the one hand, there is a huge public interest to be served in reporting child abuse, a heinous activity, and a proportionate and consequent public interest in ensuring that those who so report, reasonably and in good faith, are protected from detriment. On the other hand, there is an equally huge public interest to be served in ensuring that nobody is falsely accused of child abuse, the punishment for which false accusation, if wilful, should indeed be treated as a serious criminal matter carrying a penalty of fine or imprisonment. However, later statutory provisions also include criminal penalty for a person who makes a disclosure which they "reasonably ought to know to be false". This is quite a different standard than the "reasonably and in good faith" standard of the Protections for Persons Reporting Child Abuse Act.

Criminalising whistleblowers in the health sector   *Part 14 of the Health Act 2007, Protection of Disclosures of Information*   In an appalling development, these words "reasonably ought to know to be false" are included in a provision of the health service protected disclosures legislation which states as follows in the Health Act 2007, Pt 14 amending the Health Act 2004:

> "55S.—(1) A person who makes a disclosure which the person knows or reasonably ought to know to be false is guilty of an offence.
>   (2) A person guilty of an offence under this section is liable—
>   (a) on summary conviction, to a fine not exceeding €5,000 or to imprisonment for a term not exceeding 12 months or to both,
>   (b) on conviction on indictment, to a fine not exceeding €50,000 or to imprisonment for a term not exceeding 3 years or to both.
> (3) Notwithstanding section 10(4) of the Petty Sessions (Ireland) Act 1851, summary proceedings for an offence under this Act may be instituted within 2 years from the date on which the offence was committed or, if later, 2 years from the date on which evidence that, in the opinion of a member of the Garda Síochána, is sufficient to justify the bringing of the proceedings.
>   (4) For the purposes of subsection (3) of this section, a certificate signed by a Superintendent of the Garda Síochána as to the date on which the evidence referred to in that subsection relating to the offence concerned came to his or her knowledge is prima facie evidence thereof and in any legal proceedings a document purporting to be a certificate issued for the purpose of this subsection and to be so signed is deemed to be so signed and shall be admitted as evidence without proof of the signature of the Superintendent purporting to sign the certificate."

Who could have any confidence in a system that without any clarity as to who will decide that a person "reasonably ought to know" imposes such draconian punishment for not knowing? So much for acknowledging international expert opinion, e.g. the "Bristol Babies Inquiry", that the imperative in the health service in order to encourage more openness is to move away from a culture of blame.

Provisions a mere tag on   There are undoubtedly some very positive aspects to the provisions regarding protected disclosures for those providing healthcare. Unfortunately, the manner in which the Oireachtas has passed this most important legislation shows almost utter indifference to the basic premise of providing whistleblower protection, namely promotion of openness and accountability. The provisions have clearly been tagged onto a Health Act that was about something else entirely. This is illustrated by the Long Title:

> "An Act to establish a body to be known as an tÚdarás um Fhaisnéis agus Cáilocht Sláinte or, in the English language, as the Health Information and Quality Authority and Oifig an Phríomh-chigire Seirbhísí Sóisialacha or, in the English language, the Office of the Chief Inspector of Social Services and to provide for the dissolution of certain bodies; to provide for the transfer of the functions of the dissolved bodies and their employees to the Health Information and Quality Authority; to provide for a scheme of registration and inspection of residential services for older people, persons with disabilities and children in need of care and protection; to provide for the repeal and amendment of certain other acts; and to provide for related matters."

The rush to ensure that good faith whistleblowers in the Health Services should be encouraged and protected primarily arose out of two significant whistleblowing events. In the first, courageous whistleblowers exposed the tragic circumstances of numerous unnecessary major gynaecological procedures performed by Dr Michael Neary, subsequently struck off the Medical Register. Secondly, revelations regarding elder abuse in residential nursing homes were brought to a horrified public's attention by a covert RTÉ reporter in Leas Cross Nursing Home, which was consequently closed down. Hence, an obvious question is to ask who is responsible for downgrading the extraordinary importance of these statutory provisions to a "related matter": was it someone in the Department of Health and Children, was it the Health Service Executive, or was it just the inability of the members of the Oireachtas to understand that whistleblower protection should preferably be a stand-alone statute in plain English and failing that a clearly signposted set of provisions? These provisions were included as an amendment to the Health Act 2004 which established the Health Service Executive.

No reassurance for whistleblower   Moreover, a member of the health professions considering making a disclosure could obtain no comfort whatsoever from the indigestible appearance, confusing language and slipshod fashion in which these important provisions have been placed on the statute book. The provisions to amend the Health Act 2004 commence at s.103 of the 2007 Act, and continue for approximately 14 pages referencing ss.55A to 55T, 20 sections of the Health Act 2004 as amended. In that space there are 86 cross-references either to sections or subsections of the Health Act 2007 or to sections of 14 other Acts. One of these latter references is to s.45 of the Medical Practitioners Act 1978 which was repealed in its entirety by the

Medical Practitioners Act 2007 which came into law less than three weeks after the Health Act 2007. Not only would a health professional have difficulty making sense of this, it would require a legal professional of extraordinary stamina as well as ability.

Garda Síochána (Confidential Reporting of Corruption or Malpractice) Regulations 2007   By contrast to the health provisions, the disclosure provisions for the Garda Síochána can be viewed in a much more positive light. Much is said regarding preserving confidential the identity of a "confidential reporter" (s.9). Unfortunately, the fault lines in these Regulations are so fundamental that these provisions, too, fail the test as suitable statutory protection for organisational whistleblowers. One of the key objectives of such provisions must be to engender such confidence in the ordinary member of the organisation that corruption will be disclosed without any substantial fear of reprisal. One way to do that is to have an independent mechanism for receipt of the disclosure: independent from the authority of the organisation, as well as independent and authoritative in performance of the function of confidential recipient. Mr Brian McCarthy, recently retired Secretary-General to the President, was appointed first confidential recipient in March 2007. That very praiseworthy element of these Regulations, namely the appointment of a confidential recipient (s.6), is marred by the strictures placed on that position, the performance of which allows for no exercise of discretion.

"Each confidential report" or disclosure received "shall" be transmitted to the Commissioner (s.7), who has the authority without having to involve the confidential recipient in the decision process, to decide whether a disclosure is false, frivolous or vexatious (s.8). In essence, despite the eminence and ability of the appointee, the confidential recipient is reduced to little more than a glorified post-box. Further, the Commissioner may also appoint a "member or civilian [member of civilian staff of Garda Síochána]" as a confidential recipient, which says little for the independence of the position.

The legislative purpose of these Regulations is for the establishment of a Charter (s.4), which at the time of writing has not yet been published. With regard to the possibility that the balance of these Regulations may be unconstitutional, see the Constitutional Law chapter in this *Annual Review*.

Whistleblower Protection Bill 1999   The Whistleblower Protection Bill 1999, published by the Labour Party, reflected the principles of disclosure incorporated in the Protections for Persons Reporting Child Abuse Act 1998. It is analysed in this chapter as there is still a mistaken belief among politicians and the public that this would have been a satisfactory statute. What was referred to as a "communication" in the Act is the equivalent of a "protected disclosure" in the Bill. The Bill also clearly drew on the UK Public Interest Disclosure Act 1998. Section 2 of the Bill defined a "protected disclosure" almost word for word in the terms of that Act. It means any disclosure of information which, in the reasonable belief of the employee making the disclosure, tends to show the commission of a criminal offence, breach of legal obligation, miscarriage of justice, endangering of the health and safety of any individual, damaging of the environment and the deliberate concealment of any information relating to these. To qualify as a protected disclosure it must be made in accordance with s.3, which dealt with the persons to whom a protected disclosure is to be made and in what circumstances.

Section 4 dealt with protection against liability in damages and s.5 prohibited penalisation of an employee for making a protected disclosure and the procedures to be followed for breach of this section. This more or less follows the process outlined in the Protections for Persons Reporting Child Abuse Act 1998 and was very much in the mode of the standard industrial relations process by reference to a rights commissioner or the Employment Appeals Tribunal. In these fora, the Bill prescribes a cap of 104 weeks' remuneration for whatever penalisation the whistleblower has experienced. It appears as if problems experienced over years by employees who dared to be whistleblowers had not been given serious consideration here. The failure in s.5 to take any account of the peculiar difficulties faced by whistleblowers demonstrated a certain lack of legislative imagination.

There were a number of omissions in the Bill. There appeared to be no onus on the person to whom the disclosure is made to act even to investigate what is complained of. There was no provision for a protected disclosure to a professional body. Thus, an accountant was not protected who seeks advice from his or her professional institute on matters such as money laundering where there are legal obligations to disclose. Similarly, a doctor or nurse was not protected who might seek advice from their professional bodies on issues relating to conflicting interests of, say, patient confidentiality versus disclosure.

There was no comprehensive disposition of the legality and efficacy of confidentiality clauses in contracts in the light of the Bill's provisions. Section 4(1) prevented the employer from suing for damages in respect of a protected disclosure. Presumably this included an action for damages for breach of contract in respect of a confidentiality clause. Injunctions in relation to confidentiality clauses were not expressly dealt with in the Bill. There was no reference to penalties for knowingly making a false disclosure. Surprisingly, there was no reference whatsoever to the Official Secrets Act 1963, which the Oireachtas Select Committee on Legislation and Security, some two years earlier in 1997, recommended should be repealed.

Despite these criticisms the Bill was welcomed as it was anticipated that it would provide the first real stepping stone in the process of debate that would eventually result in statutory protection for good faith whistleblowers. Unfortunately, in the intervening years an informed debate has not taken place. Instead, as has been described above, there have been a number of inappropriate and inadequate statutory provisions passed by the Oireachtas.

Pyrrhic victory   Employees contemplating the actions that the new Irish statutory provisions wish to encourage need to be aware that winning actions for wrongful dismissal can rank all too often as a pyrrhic victory. As has been noted, the Protections for Persons Reporting Child Abuse Act confers a right on employees not to be subjected to any detriment for making a protected disclosure. It ought to be a serious offence for anyone to interfere wilfully with an individual's right conferred by law. This is particularly so in a dominant power relationship. Further, there is a reasonable implication that an employer who victimises a bona fide whistleblower under the terms of the Act is doing so to cover up whatever offence has been disclosed. Therefore, over and above any remedy available to a victimised employee, the appropriate regulator ought to exact some penalty from whoever is guilty of such conduct. Such sanction should be independent of any action taken by the victimised employee. The absence of such provisions may prove a serious weakness in the body of legislation.

Oireachtas's responsibility   Experience shows that unless the person making the disclosure has amazing tenacity and perseverance they are likely to suffer tremendous personal harm and nothing will have been achieved to stop the wrongdoing. The responsibility is on the Oireachtas to ensure that whistleblower protection provisions are simple to understand and clear enough to encourage a person to make the disclosure in anticipation of powerful and sustained protection.

RECOMMENDATIONS

The following are recommendations regarding the role of regulators in relation to whistleblowers:

1. Regulators should be under a statutory obligation to investigate ALL reports of wrongdoing appropriate to the specific office except anonymous disclosures.

2. Regulators may exercise discretion in investigating anonymous disclosures.

3. In case of disclosures which are not appropriate to the specific function of a regulator, advice must be given to a whistleblower as to the appropriate regulator(s) with whom to communicate.

4. Regulators should be under a statutory obligation to preserve the confidentiality of whistleblowers as a matter of course.

5. Regulators should be under a statutory obligation to keep the whistleblower advised in so far as is possible of the progress of an investigation. Regulators are not obliged to reveal details of such an investigation, but must keep in touch with a whistleblower.

6. In circumstances of an investigation during which it is desirable or necessary to reveal the identity of a whistleblower due to either the identifiable nature of the disclosure or to ensure the comprehensiveness of the investigation, the regulator should be under a statutory obligation to inform the whistleblower in advance. Furthermore, the regulator should be under a statutory obligation to discuss the reasons for disclosure of identity with the whistleblower and to indicate in what manner the regulator intends to protect the whistleblower from detriment.

7. Regulators should be under a statutory obligation to inform person(s) and organisation(s) which are the subject of such an investigation that the whistleblower is under the protection of the regulator.

8. It should be an offence for person(s) and organisation(s) which are the subject of an investigation to take, acquiesce in, or turn a blind eye to behaviour that is likely to cause the whistleblower detriment.

9. A statutory function of regulators should be to institute court proceedings in relation to offences under 8.

10. Where alleged detriment does occur to a whistleblower, and that whistleblower chooses to take an unfair dismissal action and/or a civil action for damages in this regard, regulators should be under a statutory obligation to make available documentary and/or other appropriate evidence to such a whistleblower save where such evidence may jeopardise an investigation or the work of the regulator's office. In such a case, the regulator should apply to the High Court to be excused of this obligation until such time as the possible jeopardy is no longer a concern.

Brief explanatory notes on recommendations

1. The primary aim of a bona fide whistleblower is that the alleged wrongdoing is rectified. An obligation to investigate is, therefore, essential. If safeguards are in place to preserve confidentiality, there is little reason why a whistleblower should wish to be anonymous. This will not preclude the malicious whistleblower but it will ensure that a regulator will examine and confront the evidence proffered directly, action which should limit the scope for vexatious and malicious complaints.

2. An anonymous disclosure may well voice legitimate concerns. Regulators need the scope to act if deemed appropriate.

3. A whistleblower is not always aware of the appropriate channels by which to report wrongdoing.

4. In situations of disclosure, the response is often to get rid of the problem, not by sorting out the revealed wrong, but by sorting out the whistleblower. Consequently, identification of the whistleblower is a matter of extreme importance to the "wrongdoer", and preserving anonymity is perhaps of greater importance to the whistleblower.

5. It is important to reflect on the impact of even the mere threat of retaliation and victimisation on a person who, in good faith, is thrust into the role of whistleblower. Whistleblowers need constant reassurance.

6. In addition to the above there is already a statutory precedent in relation to third party disclosures under, e.g. the Freedom of Information Act 1997, s.27(2)(a).

7. A warning of this nature may be sufficient to nip any thought of retaliation against the whistleblower in the bud.

8. Where a person, in this case a whistleblower, is afforded a statutory right of protection, it ought to be a serious offence for anyone to interfere wilfully with such a right. This is particularly so in a dominant power relationship. Further, there is a reasonable implication that an employer who victimises a bona fide whistleblower is doing so to cover up whatever offence has been disclosed. As to the "catch-all" nature of the recommendation, statutory precedents are long established, e.g. Sale of Goods and Supply of Services Act 1980, s.6(2).

9. The Director of Consumer Affairs was given statutory authority to prosecute offences under s.7 of that Act.

10. Civil remedies must be available to a victimised whistleblower. There is statutory precedent, albeit inadequate to victimised employees, under s.4 of the Protections for Persons Reporting Child Abuse Act 1998. As a matter of reinforcement of an offence and of fairness to the whistleblower, the protection by regulators must include co-operation within the law with the whistleblower. The fact that a refusal to co-operate would require High Court sanction should inhibit vexatious and frivolous civil actions.

What about a whistleblower who discloses for malice or reasons of self-interest? Recommendations 1 and 2 ensure that anonymous disclosures are not given the same weight as those by a named informant. This will not preclude the malicious whistleblower nor is it intended to suggest that because a whistleblower's motives are not of the purest, the disclosure should be disregarded. This matter has been dealt with by the English courts in *Re a Company's Application* [1989] Ch. 477; [1989] 3 W.L.R. 265 Ch. D. In this case the defendant was employed in a fairly senior post, including holding the position of compliance officer, by a company involved in the supply of financial advice and in the financial management of clients' investment portfolios. The company's activities were regulated by the Financial Investment Management and Brokers' Regulatory authority (FIMBRA) pursuant to the provisions of the Financial Services Act 1986. The company alleged malice on the part of the informant. Scott J. considered the question of malice:

> "It may be the case that the information proposed to be given, the allegations proposed to be made by the defendant to F.I.M.B.R.A., and for that matter by the defendant to the Inland Revenue, are allegations made out of malice and based upon fiction or invention. But if that is so, then I ask myself what harm will be done. F.I.M.B.R.A. may decide that the allegations are not worth investigating. In that case, no harm will have been done. Or F.I.M.B.R.A. may decide that an investigation is necessary. In that case, if the allegations turn out to be baseless, nothing will follow the investigation. and if harm is caused by the investigation itself, it is harm which is implicit in the regulatory role of F.I.M.B.R.A. It may be that what is put before F.I.M.B.R.A. includes some confidential information. But that information would, as it seems to me, be information which F.I.M.B.R.A. could at any time obtain by the spot checks that it is entitled to carry out. I doubt whether an employee of a financial services company such as the plaintiff owes a duty of confidence which extends to an obligation not to disclose information to the regulatory authority F.I.M.B.R.A." ([1989] Ch. 477 at 479).

Subject Index